THE AMERICAN REVOLUTION AND
THE HABSBURG MONARCHY

THE REVOLUTIONARY AGE

Francis D. Cogliano and Patrick Griffin, Editors

The American Revolution and the Habsburg Monarchy

Jonathan Singerton

UNIVERSITY OF VIRGINIA PRESS

Charlottesville and London

University of Virginia Press
© 2022 by the Rector and Visitors of the University of Virginia
First published 2022
ISBN 978-0-8139-4821-8 (hardcover)
ISBN 978-0-8139-4822-5 (paper)
ISBN 978-0-8139-4823-2 (ebook)

1 3 5 7 9 8 6 4 2

Library of Congress Cataloging-in-Publication Data is available for this title.

Cover art:
Benjamin Franklin, by Joseph S. Duplessis, ca. 1785 (© National Portrait Gallery,
Smithsonian Institution; gift of the Morris and Gwendolyn Cafritz Foundation);
Maria Theresa, by Martin van Meytens the Younger, ca. 1759 (© Gemäldegalerie der
Akademie der Bildenden Künste Wien / Paintings Gallery at the Academy of Fine
Arts, Vienna. No. AKG349014)

To my parents, Julia and Kevin,

and

to historian William O'Reilly

S|H   **The Sustainable History Monograph Pilot**
M|P   Opening Up the Past, Publishing for the Future

This book is published as part of the Sustainable History
Monograph Pilot. With the generous support of the
Andrew W. Mellon Foundation, the Pilot uses cutting-edge
publishing technology to produce open access digital editions
of high-quality, peer-reviewed monographs from leading
university presses. Free digital editions can be downloaded
from: Books at JSTOR, EBSCO, Internet Archive, OAPEN,
Project MUSE, ScienceOpen, and many other open
repositories.

When you cite the book, please\ include the following
URL for its Digital Object Identifier (DOI):
https://doi.org/10.52156/m.5768

We are eager to learn more about how you discovered this
title and how you are using it. We hope you will spend a few
minutes answering a couple of questions at this URL:
https://www.longleafservices.org/shmp-survey/

More information about the Sustainable History Monograph
Pilot can be found at https://www.longleafservices.org.

CONTENTS

ILLUSTRATIONS

ACKNOWLEDGMENTS

This book began life in the mind of a curious undergraduate and grew into the present work contained between these covers. Along the way, I have been aided by scores of generous academics, individuals, and institutions. In the process of completing this book, I have used material from nearly fifty archives and repositories in North America and Europe. Achieving this would not have been possible without generous support from the Dietrich W. Botstiber Institute for Austrian-American Studies (BIAAS), the Austrian Federal Ministry for Education, Science, and Research (BMBWF), the Robert H. Smith International Center for Jefferson Studies at Monticello (ICJS), the British Association of American Studies (BAAS), the Anglo-Austrian Society in London, and the School of History at the University of Edinburgh. Likewise, my research would not have been possible had it not been for the countless dedicated archivists at work in Austria, Belgium, Croatia, Czechia, Denmark, France, Germany, Hungary, Italy, Slovakia, Sweden, the United Kingdom, and the United States of America as well as the librarians at the Universities of Edinburgh, Cambridge, Vienna, and Innsbruck. My special thanks to Bayard Miller (Library of the American Philosophical Society), Bruce Kirby (Library of Congress), Judy S. Hynson (Jessie Ball duPont Memorial Library at Stratford Hall), Tomáš Ondrejšík (Verejná knižnica Jána Bocatia), and, most of all, to Zdisi Röhsner (Haus-, Hof- und Staatsarchiv). I thank also Count Bartolomäus Khevenhüller and Dr. Markus Trauttmansdorff for allowing me to view their respective family archives.

There have been several intellectual homes where I wrote this book and gladly found myself part of an academic community. At Edinburgh, then and now, I have gained so much from an array of scholars, both students and staff alike. I owe a particular indebtedness to my former supervisory team at the University of Edinburgh, particularly to Francis D. Cogliano who served (and continues to serve) as a benevolent mentor to whom I owe my greatest academic respect for his unfailing support and good-natured humour. Similarly, David Kaufman has proven to be an unflagging advisor regardless of the demands on his own time. I would also like to thank Thomas Ahnert and Fabian Hilfrich, two stellar historians who never allowed their German heritage to hinder the study of Austrian or Habsburg history. I count myself fortunate to be numbered one of "la familia" and would like to thank some other commendable members, especially Krysten Blackstone, Victor Cazares-Lira, Matthew P. Dziennik, Devin C. Grier, Michael S. Griggs, Alley M. Jordan, Jane C. Judge, Ryan D. McGuinness, and Gaye S. Wilson as well as the many friends, particularly Malcolm C. Craig, Roseanna Doughty, Anita Klingler, and Fraser Raeburn among others, who made Scotland's capital city such a wonderful place to inhabit.

In Austria, I consider myself incredibly lucky to have worked among some of the finest scholars of the Habsburg Monarchy. At the Austrian Academy of Science's Institut für die Erforschung der Habsburgermonarchie und des Balkanraumes (formerly the Institut für Neuzeit- und Zeitgeschichtsforschung), I encountered a host of generous and learned people, many of whom are now good friends. Among current and past IHB members, I would like to thank: Ilya Berkovich, Wladimir Fischer-Nebmaier, Michael Gehler, William D. Godsey, Doris Gruber, Barbara Haider-Wilson, Ulrike Harmat, Hans Peter Hye, Veronika Hyden-Hanscho, Maximilian Kaiser, Katrin Keller, Sarah Knoll, Stephan Kurz, Börries Kuzmany, Vera Machat, Petr Maťa, Michael Portmann, Marion Romberg, Karin Schneider, and David Schriffl. In Vienna generally, I am grateful to Matti Bunzl, Franz Leander Fillafer, Klemens Kaps, Vic Huber, Thomas Stöckinger, Karl Vocelka, and "il Presidente" Thomas Wallnig. At the University of Innsbruck, new colleagues have been supportive and welcoming. I thank especially Gunda Barth-Scalmani, Petra Büttinger, Anne-Sophie Dénoue, Stefan Ehrenpreis, Mona Garloff, Giovanni Merola, Alexander Piff, Caroline Posch, Martin Rohde, Kurt Scharr, Lukas Stelzhammer, Claudius Ströhle, and Judith Walder. Ellinor Forster has been a superb mentor and inspiration to me. Walter Leibhart, also of this parish, kindly produced the excellent maps for this monograph.

In the United States, I have come to know many brilliant individuals. For their unfaltering assistance and friendship, I thank Günter J. Bischof, Samuel K. Fisher, Patrick Griffin, J. Kent McGaughy, John Nelson, Kate Ohno, Ronald B. Schechter, Andrew J. O'Shaughnessy, Nicole M. Phelps, Kristina E. Poznan, Trent Taylor, Anna Vincenzi, Elliot Visconsi, and, especially, Gaye and Jim Wilson. Strewn in between these places are a number of indelible supporters, whom I also take great pleasure in acknowledging their largesse and encouragement: Derek E. D. Beales, Tom Cutterham, David Do Paço, Klaas van Gelder, Jonathan E. Gumz, Marion Huibrechts, Pieter M. Judson, Grete Klingenstein, László Kontler, Christine Lebeau, Csaba Lévai, David Motadel, Stephen Mullen, Simon P. Newman, Colin Nicolson, William O'Reilly, Munro Price, Hamish

M. Scott, Edwin Sheffield, Adam Storring, and György Toth. I have benefitted also from knowing the descendants of the Beelen-Bertholff family in Europe and North America, namely Anne de Beelen Hart Martin, Benoit Villeneuve de Janti, and Charles Villeneuve de Janti. Additionally, I am grateful to the many personal friends and their families who have hosted me on my various travels: Zsófi Berkes, Sebastian Fuchs, Steffi Kothbauer, Peter Petrus, Anna Staudigl, Emma Stewart, Andreas Ullmann, and Eva Wachter. Herzlichen Dank.

Several individuals deserve a special note of thanks. Frank Cogliano and Patrick Griffin kindly invited me to make this book part of their exceptional series on the Age of Revolutions. I thank them for this opportunity and congratulate them on their continued successes in revitalising the most crucial period in American history. Both Jonathan Gumz and David Motadel have been outstanding champions and merit my unreserved gratitude. Treating me as an equal, long before I felt qualified to be one, has been one of the many in ways which these two remarkable scholars have helped to create this work. Csaba Lévai warrants an equivalent recognition for his dedication and kindness shown to me throughout many years. I thank him for his continual charity and friendship. Likewise, I am indebted to the supreme amiability of Barbara Haider-Wilson and William D. Godsey, both of whom have been model historians, ideal colleagues, and the kindest of friends over the years. Finally, it would be remiss of me not to express my profound gratitude to William O'Reilly, a man of great acuity who possesses such a similar vision for the history of the Habsburg Monarchy that he once told me I had written a book he had wished to write. I take that to be one of the highest compliments achievable. It is for this reason, and in recognition of his stalwart compassion, that he shares the dedication of this book.

In the final stages of preparation, I benefited from close readings by friends and experts. I thank in particular for their generosity Ivo Cerman, Luca Codignola, Markus Debertol, Matthew P. Dziennik, Ellinor Forster, Charles Ingrao, Csaba Lévai, Heinz Noflatscher, William O'Reilly, Marion Romberg, Bálint Varga, and Gaye Wilson. At earlier stages, I received invaluable feedback from Jonathan R. Dull, William D. Godsey, Klemens Kaps, Silvia Marzagalli, Kate Ohno, Janet Polasky, and Munro Price in particular. I owe an immense gratitude for all their time and advice given but, naturally, any remaining inaccuracies are mine and mine alone. On this note, I thank my copyeditor, Annie Boisvert, for her perfection of the manuscript. I am sincerely grateful to Nadine Zimmerli as an editor for her steadfast support and meticulous eye. Although an expert in her own right on German-American history, she exercised no prejudice against the Habsburgs taking centre stage. I am humbled to learn that I had some of the best peers qualified to review the manuscript on behalf of the University of Virginia Press, namely: Franz Leander Fillafer, Eliga H. Gould, and Nicole M. Phelps. Franz, Lige, and Nicole expended considerable enthusiasm towards making this a better book and I have certainly benefited from their combined wisdom. I hope I have made all of them, as well as those listed above, proud of the resulting work.

Most of all, I am deeply thankful to my family: my parents Julia and Kevin, my wife, and my grandfather who collectively formed the backbone of my ability to pursue this work through their ceaseless commitment and unwavering readiness to be my most trusted advisors, truest companions, and most loving advocates possible. Without their devotion, there would be no book and although the past year went by without seeing three out of the four of them, I still felt assured of their resolve. My words can only reflect the smallest fraction of my appreciation and gratitude.

Innsbruck, July 2021

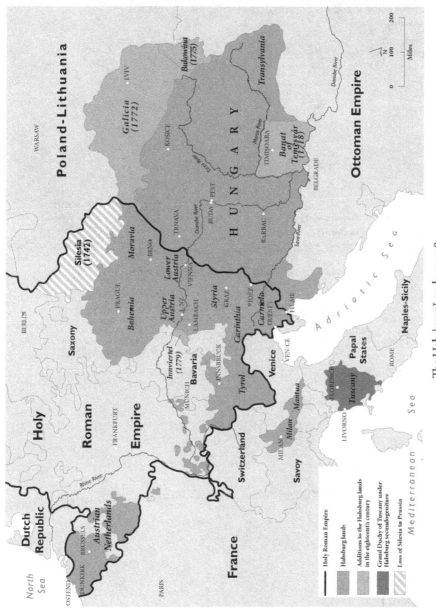

The Habsburg Lands ca. 1783

Legend:
- Holy Roman Empire
- Habsburg lands
- Additions to the Habsburg lands in the eighteenth century
- Grand Duchy of Tuscany under Habsburg secundogeniture
- Loss of Silesia to Prussia

Labels on map:

North Sea

Dutch Republic

Poland-Lithuania

WARSAW

Holy Roman Empire

BERLIN

Saxony

Silesia (1742)

Galicia (1772)

LVIV

Bukowina (1775)

Transylvania

Moravia

BRNO

KOŠICE

Tisza River

H U N G A R Y

Banat of Temesvár (1718)

TIMIŞOARA

BELGRADE

Ottoman Empire

Danube River

PRAGUE

Bohemia

TRNAVA

Danube River

BUDA

PEST

Marcs River

Upper Austria

Lower Austria

LINZ

VIENNA

BÁCBAC

Sava River

Styria

GRAZ

LAMBACH

FRANKFURT

Innviertel (1779)

Bavaria

INNSBRUCK

Tyrol

MUNICH

Carinthia

Carniola

VIDEZ

TRENT

FIUME

A d r i a t i c   S e a

Switzerland

Venice

VENICE

Savoy

MILAN

Milan

Mantua

Papal States

FLORENCE

Tuscany

LIVORNO

ROME

Naples-Sicily

France

PARIS

OSTEND

DUNKIRK

BRUSSELS

Austrian Netherlands

Rhine River

Mediterranean Sea

N

0   100   200
Miles

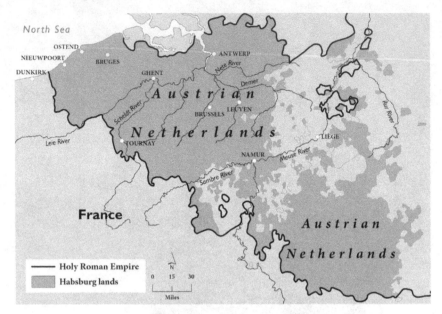

The Austrian Netherlands ca. 1783

Proclamation Line of 1763 (original extent of the thirteen colonies)

US territory defined by the Treaty of Paris (1783)

British territory

Spanish territory

Disputed territory

Mohawk **Native American nations**

Lake Superior

British North America

Chippewa

St. Lawrence River

Lake Huron

Mohawk

Ottawa

Lake Ontario

Oneida

Lake Michigan

Cohnawaghans

SCHENECTADY

Mississippi River

FORT DETROIT

Lake Erie

ALBANY

BOSTON

Wyandotte

Northwest Territory

Delaware

PITTSBURGH

NEW LONDON

NEW YORK

Missouri River

Great River

CONEWAGO

YORK

PHILADELPHIA

BALTIMORE

Spanish Louisiana

United States

NORFOLK

Arkansas River

Muscogee Creeks

CHARLESTON

ATLANTIC OCEAN

SAVANNAH

Sp. West Florida

NEW ORLEANS

Sp. East Florida

Gulf of Mexico

Br. Bahamas

N

0   250   500

Miles

The United States of America ca. 1783

Introduction

BENJAMIN SILAS ARTHUR SCHUSTER.

It sounds a peculiar yet familiar name, right?

The same unplaceable strangeness struck the Viennese onlookers and well-wishers gathered at St. Stephan's Cathedral in 1778. They had assembled for the baptism of baby Benjamin, whose parents, Johann and Maria Schuster, had decided to name him in honour of the three American representatives in Paris: Benjamin Franklin, Silas Deane, and Arthur Lee. So great was their admiration for the revolutionary trio that the baptism entry recorded the American representatives as godfathers in absentia.[1] Buoyed by ineffable feelings of fatherhood, Johann Schuster wrote to his new-born son's first namesake within a week. He informed Franklin of his pride in their "little American" (*notre petit Américain*) who served as a daily reminder of the "illustrious and dear people" who strove for liberty half a world away.[2] Five years later, at the close of the War of American Independence, Schuster wrote again. He congratulated Franklin on the successful independence of the United States, a cause "engraved upon [his] heart" and for which he had earnestly prayed. In the meantime, however, his wife Maria had died. "She took with her to the grave, a consideration equal to mine for you and all your comrades," he found some comfort in confiding to Franklin.[3] The Schusters' enthusiasm for the revolutionary cause lasted throughout the American Revolution and beyond. History does not record what happened further to the Schuster family or how Benjamin S. A. Schuster felt growing up as Vienna's embodiment of revolutionary heroes from across the Atlantic.[4] They are a family with little trace except for their unbridled dedication to an America which they never visited apart from in their minds and hearts. They are a family whose reaction, enthusiasm, and voice in the story of the American Revolution has been almost forgotten.

The Schusters were by no means alone. Across the entirety of the Habsburg lands, which stretched from the Austrian Netherlands (present-day Belgium) in the West to the furthest reaches of the Transylvanian hills in the East, the American Revolution influenced the lives of Habsburg inhabitants. The Revolution was a diplomatic conundrum for Habsburg rulers, a commercial opportunity for some, and a cultural phenomenon for everyone. The Revolution altered the economic

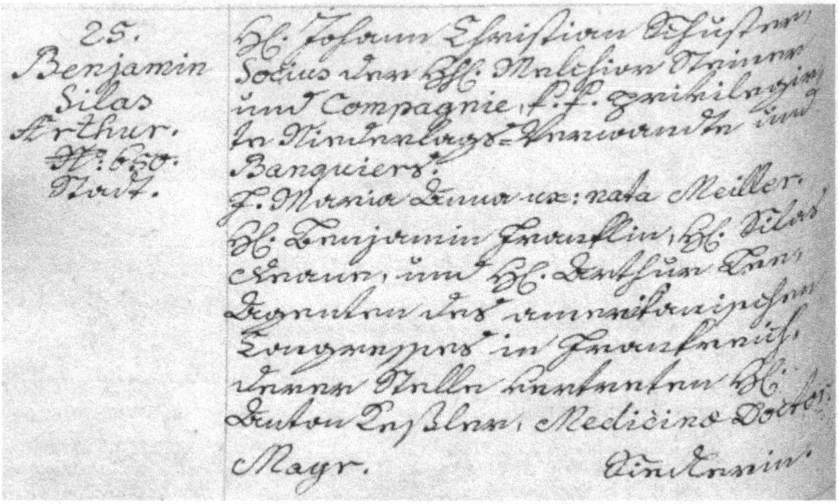

FIGURE I. Baptismal entry of Benjamin Silas Arthur
Schuster in St. Stephen's Cathedral, Vienna

fortunes of Habsburg merchants. John Adams noted how the towns of Bruges and Ostend in the Austrian Netherlands had "grown out of the American Revolution," at the same time as Hungarians rejoiced over the devastation of Virginian tobacco crops which "now [allowed] the Hungarians a share of their one-time profits." A group of Bohemian glassmakers, meanwhile, assembled in the town of Nový Bor (Hajda/Haida) for a great feast to celebrate the end of the war which had sapped their trade and disrupted exports.[5]

Unravelling the meaning of the American Revolution in the lands of the Habsburg Monarchy forms the core of this book. It is admittedly an unfamiliar territory for viewing the effects of one of the most consequential political moments in history. Yet, when viewed from this vantage point, the familiar American Revolution looks rather different. Developing a political consciousness centred on individual rights and protection of liberty against tyranny was a key component in the American Revolution and, to be sure, there were some figures in the Habsburg lands—as there were elsewhere—who recognised the potency and danger of this emergent ideology. Fundamentally, the Revolution represented the struggle for the birth of a new nation. Yet this was not the only understanding of the American Revolution. We might assume the Habsburgs would be unwelcoming to such an event, but the chaos of war bred challenges as well as opportunities in equal measure. To the Habsburg monarchs and their subjects, the American Revolution contained great commercial opportunity and not just potential threats to their security. In this first instance of democratic revolution, individuals in power in the Habsburg lands were not the reactionary and repressive bogeymen we tend to think about from the nineteenth century, but rather, they formulated a cautiously interested, and, in many cases, enthused response to the creation of the United States of America.

Mental landscapes and worldscapes changed fundamentally for many Habsburg inhabitants. For centuries, 'America' had been filtered through various lenses, from the religious frescoes adorning village churches to the doubtful propaganda peddled by recruiters who sought to lure prospective emigrants.[6] But the Revolution made America an event for the first time, a point of fixation and fascination about which conversations formed and about whose future debates raged. Habsburg authors devoted books to the topic; some to ride the wave of fascination over America and others to praise its virtuous revolutionary leaders. In Viennese salons and palaces, the incessant chatter over the Americans enraged the British ambassador, who warned his superiors that "everyone here talks wildly about liberty."[7] This obsession existed beyond the aristocracy. The "shot heard 'round the world" reached keen and supportive ears across the Habsburg Monarchy.[8] The American Revolution advanced the concept of "revolution" in Habsburg minds to mean a more sudden political change rather than the literal revolving around a fixed point such as the Copernican orbit of planets.[9] Reflecting on the transformation in public awareness of American revolutionary events, the Hungarian author Ferenc Kazinczy asked rhetorically, "What be our gatherings in villages until now than mere discussion of which hound is more worthy, the tan or the black, and what number among us knew whether the Atlantic Ocean lies East or West of us?"[10] The American Revolution widened the intellectual horizons of many in the Habsburg Monarchy and, in doing so, left an indelible legacy which lasted into the next century.

This book is about the meaning of the American Revolution for the Habsburg Monarchy and, at the same time, the Habsburg moment in the American Revolution. It is a story about how one of Europe's most important dynasties managed the first opening salvo in what would become a succession of revolutionary crises stretching into the mid-nineteenth century. This was both a moment of challenge and opportunity for the people living in the Habsburg realms. Some like Schuster and his family welcomed the dawn of this new age; others, like the Habsburg monarch Maria Theresa and her State Chancellor Prince Wenzel Anton von Kaunitz greeted these developments with more scepticism. Opportunity lay in the chance to engage with the wider world through commercial channels created in the wake of the American Revolution. It also represented a potential realisation of long-held dynastic designs for imperial projects beyond the European mainland in emulation of rival powers.[11] Pursuing this potential extended the Habsburg influence in the western hemisphere. The first Habsburg representative beyond Europe arrived in Philadelphia as a result shortly after the conclusion of the war.

Difficulty accompanied opportunity. The upheavals of the War of American Independence presented individuals in the Habsburg Monarchy with new challenges. At several points, the American Revolution threatened the international position of the Habsburg Monarchy, and its rulers' struggle to remain a neutral power continued throughout the war. For all neutral powers, assuming impartiality was a difficult process often fraught and marred by international controversy. In the Habsburg case, neutrality pitted the Monarchy against belligerents who sought to either erode or entrench their neutral status. Crucially, the Habsburg position vis-à-vis the war was at one point or another a concern for all belligerents, including the American patriots. Later, as the war progressed and American independence from Britain became an increasingly likely reality, the struggle for neutrality gradually became the struggle for a relationship with the sovereign United States of America. Habsburg ministers believed in the potential advantages of American trade and took great steps to secure it. Through the American Revolution, the Habsburgs imagined a transatlantic expansion of imperial and commercial power. Yet pursuing such dreams came at a cost. The Habsburg Monarchy was not immune to the effects of revolutionary fervour. The American Revolution exemplified the best achievement of humanity to many in the Habsburg lands who later called for similar reforms, imparting a legacy which instigated conspiracy, reformism, and revolt.[12] The American Revolution had a deep-rooted impact in the Habsburg lands which ultimately lasted through to the nineteenth century.

The "Habsburg moment" in the American Revolution unites several instances when the Habsburg Monarchy became a focal point in the War of American Independence and exerted an influence on the war's outcome. Few historians today realise the role played by the Habsburg Monarchy in shaping the American Revolution economically and politically. Yet the Monarchy was a factor in the American Revolution despite how unlikely and unexpected this may seem to readers today. The Habsburg Monarchy was one of the great neutral powers in the War of American Independence as one of the largest states in eighteenth-century Europe with extensive territories, military capacity, and dynastic influence over the Holy Roman Empire—the source of tens of thousands of Hessian recruits for the British. The Habsburg territories encompassed a population of roughly

25 million and employed one of the largest European armies.[13] In addition, from the early 1770s onwards, vital munitions manufactured in Liège passed through Habsburg lands in the Austrian Netherlands in order to supply the patriots in the American Revolution.[14] Moreover, the Austrian Netherlands served over thirty prominent Americans throughout the war as a base of operations and from 1780, the port of Ostend became the emporium of all belligerents seeking to transport goods safely into the Atlantic under neutral colours.[15]

Most importantly, Vienna became a fulcrum around which the war would have turned if the Monarchy had joined one side or another. This was especially true following the Franco-American alliance of 1778 when efforts to cajole the Habsburgs into the War of American Independence reached an early crescendo. Winning over the Habsburgs became a frequent aim of the British who increasingly saw them as their last hope in Europe for deliverance from the war. Competition over the fate of the Habsburgs placed them unexpectedly at the forefront of the first serious attempts for peaceful mediation to the conflict which, if it had been successful, would have resulted in the Peace of Vienna in 1781 rather than the Peace of Paris in 1783. These moments in the American Revolution have been overlooked but recognising the importance of this wider international context to the American founding is necessary if we are to fully appreciate the complexity and globality of the American Revolution.

Including the Habsburg Monarchy in the history of the American Revolution, therefore, serves to broaden the international horizon and redefine the spatial context of American independence. The foundation of the United States was as deeply enmeshed within a European framework of shifting alliances and preconceptions as it was in North America.[16] The War of American Independence all too often appears as a war which occurred within a North American context but from 1778 onwards, the war's ultimate determination, and with it American sovereignty, rested increasingly within Europe.[17] Even American independence and the post-sovereign self-fashioning of the new republic transpired with a view towards finding a place in the pre-existing international order dictated by European states.[18]

Uncovering the continental European dimension within the American Revolution requires situating the Revolution within different European national contexts. Whilst promising advances are being made for western Europe—especially Ireland and Spain, to only name two cases—there are still multiple *terrae incognitae* ripe for the historians of eighteenth-century America. It seems the further east one moves, the less aware we are—despite the existence of many illuminating works.[19] In the public and general academic imagination, regions such as central and eastern Europe or Scandinavia have boiled down to those made famous by their participation in the American Revolution such as the Hessians or Tadeusz Kościuszko or perhaps Axel von Fersen, the possible Swedish lover of Marie Antoinette.[20] The reduction to these figures, important though they were, often obscures the deeper level of the Revolution's connection to and impact on these regions. In the case of the Habsburg Monarchy, the situation is worse still, with no comparable character firmly in the public mind as a tangible connection between these lands and the American Revolution. There is no reason for this obscurity; as the pages that follow will reveal, there was a host of influential individuals who considered themselves part of the American Revolution in the Habsburg Monarchy.

In expanding the international dimensions of the American Revolution, this book speaks directly to the field of Atlantic history, which, until recently, has been the prevailing historiographical framework for histories of the American Revolution abroad. Proponents of Atlantic history posit the transit of peoples, ideas, and commodities around the Atlantic basin as responsible for creating a single connective space during the seventeenth and eighteenth centuries.[21] Atlantic history has brokered fruitful connections between historical foci, bringing historians of different periods and spaces into a common dialogue. Attempts to form a consensual definition have proven difficult with the boundaries of the Atlantic itself functioning as the most commonly accepted parameter.[22]

Despite several decades of innovative histories, however, Atlantic history might be drying up. Atlantic fatigue has set in, especially among historians of the American Revolution, who have shifted towards newer geographic locales for fresh perspectives.[23] In the last decade, histories of the American Revolution have increasingly taken place within a continental or hemispheric space. Built upon a rising cognisance of Spanish-American and Native American presence in the Age of Revolutions, the continental and hemispheric viewpoints implicitly re-orientate attention away from the East of the thirteen colonies (the Atlantic) and present the Revolution as either inextricable from the West or as the first in a vertical wave of revolutionary movement from the North to the South.[24] This embrace of multidirectional approaches to the Revolution does not prejudice the Atlantic, but rather reframes the Atlantic world within a larger spatial dimension.[25] Some have taken to calling this new convergence "vast early America" as a signifier for viewing the wider entanglement of early American history from multiple geographies and imperial vantage points.[26] Such repositioning of our conceptions, both of Atlantic history and of early American history, can be instructive when also applied in the other direction; from further east as well as further west. In this reformulation the Habsburg Monarchy can be seen as a continuation of current trends to discern the various polarities of early America.

Atlantic history has long seemed distinct from, or even antithetical to, the Central European "hinterland" but the Habsburg experience in the American Revolution demonstrates this fallacy. Admittedly, the Habsburg lands did not stretch into the Atlantic. There were no new-world outposts under the rule of the Austrian branch of the House of Habsburg—although ministers in Vienna and Brussels seriously considered acquiring such territory during the Revolution and one of their colonial missions ostensibly laid claim to the southern-Atlantic islands of Tristan da Cunha in 1777.[27] The commercial entrepôts of Ostend on the North Sea and Trieste in the Adriatic functioned instead as the connective nodes to the Atlantic nexus initially indirectly and, as a result of the Revolution, directly in the 1780s. Despite connection through the transfer of people and trade, it would seem inaccurate to demarcate these spaces as the Atlantic, however.[28] Yet for the Habsburgs faced with the upheavals of the American Revolution, what happened on one side of the Straits of Gibraltar mattered for the other. It was for this reason that Habsburg ministers tasked the secretary to the Habsburg legation in Madrid with planning contingencies for Habsburg commerce in the Atlantic and Mediterranean following the Spanish entry into the war.[29] The maritime consequences of the American Revolution reverberated in the Habsburg lands despite their distance from the Atlantic Ocean.

Recently, scholars have paid ever-greater attention to the role of the oceans in the shaping of terrestrial human history on a global scale. The ubiquity of waterways and waterbodies lends itself easily to this frame of reference where continents and coastlines became subsumed within a globally interconnected and interdependent "world ocean" system.[30] Island outposts and port cities, in particular, commanded a prominent role in facilitating connection across maritime spaces—as have ecological, geological, and meteorological attributes of the seas themselves.[31] The Habsburg Monarchy presents an interesting lacuna within this emerging historical perspective, for two reasons. First, the Habsburg Monarchy is perceived conventionally as composed of "landlocked" entities with little or no maritime interests—this is in spite of an extensive existing literature proving otherwise.[32] Yet this "inland" nature does not deny the Austrian Habsburgs an oceanic past. Indirect connections through rivers and overland routes connected much of Central Europe to the seas.[33] Secondly, the intrepid maritime imperialism of the Austrian Habsburgs in the eighteenth and nineteenth centuries through exploration, commerce, and transoceanic colonisation represented a concerted effort to transcend the terrestrial and maritime understandings of empire.[34] The American Revolution was by no means the first or the only oceanic episode in Austrian Habsburg history but its effects, at sea and on land, influenced the development of Habsburg overseas ventures and fortunes in ways that have not been previously acknowledged.

In many ways, this book serves as a maritime history of the Habsburg Monarchy. Current accounts of the overseas activities of the Austrian Habsburgs tend to centre on the attempts to colonise and trade in Asia during the early and late eighteenth century. The *Generale Keijzerlijcke Indische Compagnie* (General Imperial India Company) of the 1720s in Ostend and William Bolts's expeditions to India and China in the 1770s and 1780s are well known.[35] Both of these initiatives ended in abject failure with short-lived commercial factories founded in Canton, China and along the Coromandel Coast at Covelong (Kovalam) and at Bankibazar (Ichapur) in India. The American Revolution, however, offers a counterpoint to this Habsburg maritime experience. It enabled new commercial opportunities for the Austrian Habsburgs after the established imperial Atlantic systems suffered disruption. Established trading routes relied upon Habsburg neutrality to maintain the flow of goods, communications, and people. As mentioned above, American revolutionaries and other belligerents sourced munitions from Liège which had to be procured through the canals, rivers, and roads of the Austrian Netherlands.[36] The Revolution similarly shaped economic fortunes in Austria, Bohemia, Moravia, and the Hungarian lands both during and after the war. As Matyas Rát, editor of the Hungarian newspaper *Magyar Hírmondó*, asked his readers, "Who would think that the riots taking place there [the American colonies] could have been of benefit to our country?"[37] The American Revolution, in other words, furthered the oceanic entanglement of the Habsburg Monarchy in the late eighteenth century through the lure of profit and improvement.

In general, examining the effects of the American Revolution upon the Habsburg Monarchy further globalises its history. Few overviews of Habsburg history today recognise the global contexts of the eighteenth-century Monarchy.[38] The global backdrop appears either absent for a Monarchy usually perceived (and presented) as a landlocked Central European power or takes the form of studies of isolated facets of Habsburg global connections. We have a growing understanding of the Habsburg ambition to form global linkages through the development of extra-European commerce, the sponsorship of scientific missions throughout the eighteenth and nineteenth centuries, and the creation of institutions designed to enable transcultural contact.[39] The ability of the Habsburgs to attract and cultivate individuals who broadly functioned as global facilitators is similarly growing in acknowledgement across different disciplines.[40] Yet we still lack a unified vision synthesising these threads into the reality which was the eighteenth-century Habsburg Monarchy. Integrating the transoceanic experience of the Habsburg Monarchy and its struggles to acquire trading privileges and geographical information about non-European territories—as was the case with the new United States—therefore puts the eighteenth-century Habsburg experience in a more appropriate framework.[41]

The American Revolution was the Habsburg Monarchy's first encounter with what is commonly termed the Age of Revolutions, a period characterised by the intense political struggles that took place in Europe, Asia, and the Americas.[42] In geographic terms, historians traditionally designated the Atlantic as a central emanating point for the Age of Revolutions with America and France as sibling instigators.[43] Yet much like Atlantic history, the Age of Revolutions has undergone continual refinement and alteration. Modifiers such as *democratic, imperial,* and *global* prefixed to Revolution reflect the various reframings of a turbulent age generally stretching from the American Revolution up to the Revolutions of 1848.[44] The recent transnational and global turns have shifted attention to the mobility of revolutionary advocates and the smaller spaces experiencing revolutionary change—but most of these efforts remain concentrated within the Atlantic world.[45] In her transnational history of the revolutionary age from Haiti to the Low Countries, historian Janet Polasky articulated the permeability of the European mainland in the transmission of revolutionary ideas.[46] Polasky's vision makes good on the original expansive Age of Revolutions present in Robert R. Palmer's works. Palmer was one of the few historians who connected the totality of the European space within the period of the American Revolution.[47] Yet even Palmer did not fully realise the impact of the American Revolution upon the Habsburg Monarchy. In Palmer's works, the 1787 revolt in the Austrian Netherlands and the 1794 conspiracies in Vienna and Hungary were the only substantive responses to the Revolution.[48] But the taking up of arms is not the only legitimate response to revolutionary movements; some, like the Schusters, were inspired in other ways and made their response known peacefully.

Palmer only became convinced "that an 'American dream' existed in Germany as much as in France" some years later following the work of Horst Dippel who meticulously traced the reaction of German-speaking people to the Revolution.[49] Dippel's richly researched account deftly articulated the meaning of the Revolution for the German-speaking Habsburg populace but in severing them from the rest of the Monarchy, we are left with an incomplete understanding of the Revolution's impact in the Habsburg lands. Moreover, Dippel's in-depth analysis along with his bibliographic compilation of contemporary German-language works on the Revolution have been rather underutilised by historians of the American Revolution.[50] As a result, the Habsburg Monarchy appears as a latecomer to the party—a guest who did not quite receive the invitation first time around and first showed up either in the 1790s brimming with Jacobins or the late 1840s accompanied by nationalists and secessionists.[51] The Habsburgs only became symptomatic with revolutionary fervour, so the current narrative goes, when inhabitants became piqued by the Josephine reforms of the 1780s and had witnessed the example of the French Revolution.[52] By tracing the antecedents in the Habsburg response to the American Revolution, this book effectively contextualises the Habsburg responses to later revolutionary currents.

Contrary to conventional expectations, the Habsburg Monarchy was not a reactionary power at the beginning of the Age of Revolution, as this book will show. To be sure, there were individuals in the Habsburg Monarchy who were more guarded towards or even criticised the American Revolution, but many looked positively on the American cause. Ministers and merchants across the Habsburgs lands were attentive to the changing fortunes of their neighbours and sought to harness the disruption caused by the revolutionary turmoil in North America. After 1783, moreover, preserving the economic benefit created through American independence outweighed the ideological gulf between monarchy and republic. The danger lay, however, in the cultural effects of the American Revolution, in its example of righteous self-preservation against tyranny. What America came to represent posed the real challenge. As time went on and the flame of revolutionary spirit spread to Europe, stakeholders in the Habsburg regime sought to dampen the embers of dissent in their own lands. Yet it was only in the wake of another revolution, which begun in France in 1789, that American influence, ideals, and discussion became intolerable as the instigator of a turbulent, destructive era.

Divergence between the United States of America and the Habsburg Monarchy became a distinctive hallmark from the 1790s onwards. The figure of Emperor Joseph II, who reigned jointly with his mother Maria Theresa during the outbreak of the American Revolution, best demonstrates the generational schism that emerged over the Habsburg Monarchy. John Adams once referred to him in 1783 as "one of the greatest men of the present age," whereas the American poet Joel Barlow denounced the Habsburg monarch ten years later as "The ape of wisdom and the slave of gold, Theresa's son, who, with a feeble grace, just mimics all the vices of his race."[53] In time, the United States and the Habsburg Monarchy became the archetype for progressive and conservative standard-bearers and became increasingly uncomfortable in their connections to one another. The revolutionary year of 1848 proved a litmus test for such disparity, with American support of Hungarians against the "un-democratic" Habsburg regime almost bringing the two states to declaring war in the decade afterwards.[54] Prince Klemens von Metternich's sense that America represented a sleeping giant which "in five years gets to where it otherwise would have taken two centuries" still dominates our perception of the two countries; one as sclerotic and a declining power in the late-nineteenth century versus the rise of a dynamic society and international heavyweight.[55] It has led to our perception of the two powers as having little or no connection. In the early twentieth century, Harvard historian and direct descendant of Thomas Jefferson, Archibald Cary Coolidge wrote "with Austria-Hungary the United States has never had much to do" and almost a century later, historian Thomas A. Schwartz declared that, "If you teach a survey course on the history of American foreign relations, chances are that you don't spend very much time on the Austrian-Hungarian Empire."[56] This malaise originating from the reactionary 1790s should not obscure the actual time of connection between the Habsburg Monarchy and the United States, when, for almost two decades, these two powers were not adversaries, not antagonistic, nor dichotomies but rather mutually interested, inquisitive, and enterprising with one another.

The American Revolution is, therefore, the proper starting point for historicising bilateral relations between the United States and the Habsburg Monarchy and its successor states. Although diplomatic recognition proved elusive until the first bilateral treaties of the 1820s and the first mutual exchange of representatives in 1838, the 1770s and 1780s witnessed the first concerted efforts to forge US-Habsburg relations.[57] Political histories of this relationship have often sidelined this crucial period, if acknowledged at all, as an era of "benign neglect" with little perceived interaction.[58] This misconception explains why transatlantic histories of Austria-Hungary and its successor states predominantly tend to focus on the extensive migrations of the late nineteenth and early twentieth centuries.[59] American financial support provided to Austria in the post–World War II period sparked a rise in the field of American Studies (*Amerikanistik*) which centred on the more immediate relationship between the United States and the Austrian Republic.[60] A similar situation developed in Czechia, Hungary, and Slovakia following the collapse of the Communist system in the 1990s.[61] These circumstances have undoubtedly fostered a nuanced awareness of Central European ties with North America. Yet these separate historiographies have also inadvertently demoted eighteenth-century connections between these lands. The period of the American Revolution and the republic's founding remains a bountiful era of informal relations as a result.

Of course, this is not to say that no histories of the American Revolution and the Habsburg Monarchy exist. It is to say only that those available have been written from a disaggregated viewpoint. Rather than treating the Habsburg Monarchy as a whole, as this book does, these histories present the Habsburg reception and reaction to the American Revolution through anachronistic regional or nation-state perspectives. Austrian, Belgian, and Hungarian historians—to name but a few—have written individual histories of "Austria and the American Revolution," "Belgium and the American Revolution," and "Hungary and the American Revolution."[62] Nation-state perspectives arguably have merit as they allow for a focus on the specific modalities of each constituent region of the composite Habsburg Monarchy. The same can be said of the anachronistic regional perspectives where portions of the Habsburg Monarchy have been repurposed as part of a wider "German" or "East-Central European" response to the Revolution.[63] These reorientations can create meaningful comparisons with other eighteenth-century polities such as Prussia or the Polish-Lithuanian Commonwealth. Yet these nation-state perspectives run the risk of promoting perceived exceptionalism within the Habsburg Monarchy. When we only have articles written on the Hungarian military officers who went to fight for the American cause, it overshadows the reality that men from across the Habsburg lands went to fight for the Revolution in relatively equal numbers.[64] Moreover, this perspective downplays the significant interplay of regional interests within composite states. The Habsburg Monarchy of the eighteenth century was a composite state consisting of several distinct territories under the rule of a sovereign dynasty.[65] Responses to the American Revolution in the Austrian Netherlands ultimately affected the decision-making process in Vienna and vice versa. Moreover, one region's actions could set the tone for the external perception of the entire Monarchy as a neutral power during the War of American Independence. Thus the decisions of local magistrates, committees, and governors, such as those in the Austrian Netherlands, for example, coloured the British impression of the Habsburgs. The same was especially true for Habsburg diplomats at foreign courts as well as those in service to other members of the House of Habsburg, but who were not representatives of the Habsburg Monarchy. It is for this reason that the Grand Duchy of Tuscany, ruled under secundogeniture terms by the Habsburg dynasty, is paramount to understanding the complex interrelationship between the Habsburg Monarchy and the American Revolution. American patriots and British envoys, for instance, both interpreted the independent policies of the emperor's younger brother in Tuscany as commensurate with the wider policy of the Habsburg Monarchy. Tuscany's inclusion in this narrative is therefore crucial. Analysing various regional influences, as this book does, is a fundamental step in chronicling and understanding the Habsburg response to the American Revolution as a whole.

The importance of multi-archival and multilingual research in crafting new histories of both the Habsburg Monarchy and the American Revolution should become self-evident throughout this book. Austrian archivist-historian Hans Schlitter exercised this mantra in the 1880s when he completed the only other monograph on this topic. His *Die Beziehungen Österreichs zu den Vereinigten Staaten 1778-1787* (Austria's relations with the United States, 1778–1787) utilised sources at the Austrian State Archives (where he served later as one of the archival directors) and from a field trip to Washington, DC, sponsored both by his father and the education ministry.[66] Schlitter's combination of sources made him realise the interconnected goals shared by American citizens and Habsburg subjects and allowed him to write one of the best international histories of the Habsburg Monarchy of his time. Although Schlitter's work was pioneering for its time, it is still a work very much *of* its time as a study of the few great individuals of the Revolution and analysis limited largely to state-level diplomacy between the two states. In Schlitter's rendering, the ideas of the Revolution were largely absent. The economic lure of a sovereign United States, which tempted the Monarchy's mercantile classes and attracted foreign merchants to its ports, counted for little.[67] Now, this present book considers all three elements together. The American Revolution was not solely a diplomatic problem for the Habsburg Monarchy but also a commercial opportunity and a cultural obsession. One factor did not operate without affecting the other. Analysing these elements in tandem reveals the whole and showcases the breadth of the Habsburg engagement with the Revolution and the independent American republic.

What follows is a chronological analysis of the effects of the American Revolution in the Habsburg lands and the Habsburg response to American independence before the time of the French Revolution. The United States did not appear out of a vacuum in the 1770s, but rather its colonial ancestry formed an important part in the European reception and recognition of the new American republic announced in 1776. In charting this dynamic episode in American and Central European history, it is crucial, therefore, to be aware of how the United States fitted into a continuum of Habsburg perceptions of the Americas since the discovery of the New World. Once disquietude among the thirteen colonies erupted into open conflict, the American Revolution was an unavoidable political event to inhabitants across the Habsburg lands. The outbreak of war posed many initial challenges for the Habsburg Monarchy, which culminated in the dramatic first diplomatic mission of an American representative to the Habsburg court in 1778. Yet by the final years of the war, Habsburg officials had recognised the potential gains in the revolutionary turmoil and sought to profit, both economically and politically, from the conflagration engulfing the Atlantic world. In surmounting these diplomatic challenges, the economic significance of the American Revolution for the Habsburgs became clear and the efforts to secure this commercial opportunity formed an ill-fated priority of the postwar agenda. Though the attraction of American commerce proved great and brought the Habsburgs into greater contact with the peoples of North America, the fatal influence of one prominent American revolutionary protected these designs for decades to come. This book concludes by chronicling the lingering American dream in the Habsburg lands which lasted for generations beyond the Revolution itself. Throughout this book, a whole host of figures emerge. Some will be familiar to many; some will be unknown to most; and some may be surprising inclusions, but all were in their own ways central in constructing the meaning of the American Revolution in the Habsburg lands. If it were not for people like Johann and Maria Schuster after all, we would be unaware of the immense impact of the American Revolution on the Habsburg Monarchy.

CHAPTER ONE

"England Is the Motherland and America the Daughter?"

Colonial and Revolutionary America in the Habsburg Mind

P EOPLE IN THE HABSBURG lands had formed a deep connection with America long before the American Revolution. For centuries prior to the outbreak of war in the 1770s, knowledge of an "America" and then many "Americas" had come through several mediums. Dynastic servants, Jesuits missionaries, merchant traders, newspaper editors, and artists came together to weave different strands into the tapestry of the Habsburg outlook on the New World; they influenced the wider perception of America and helped to shape the mental worlds of their contemporaries. This process began with the voyage of Christopher Columbus and was still underway by the time of the Declaration of American Independence and the Siege of Yorktown. It was a muddy process, one shaped as much by events in the Americas as it was by events in Europe. In the Habsburg case, it was also a process shaped by geographical proximities and cultural legacies: the abjugation from Habsburg Spain and the abrasion against the Ottomans. Negatives—depopulation, censorship, sickness and disease—also played a role. By the eighteenth century, however, a singular Habsburg preconception of America came to exist, one based on a blend of pseudo-scientific observations largely from Catholic missionaries and coloured by late-Baroque rationalism. As revolution approached in the 1760s, attention shifted northwards towards the British North American colonies. New commentators focused on the potentiality of America, its bountiful landscape, and the harmonising nature of its commerce in more universal tones rather than a foreign land of oddities.

In charting this rise of colonial and revolutionary America in the Habsburg mind, one fact becomes clear: the Habsburg Monarchy was not a detached entity from the Atlantic maritime world. On the contrary, Habsburg inhabitants learned about America with relatively equal pace as much of western Europe.

Many Habsburg subjects, moreover, contributed to the discourse around the Americas from the Hungarian István Budai Permanius, whose poems waxed lyrical about Newfoundland, to the Brno-based tax collector and publicist Heinrich Georg Hoff, who counted George Washington as among one of the most remarkable and famous people in the world.[1] Entwined within the richly interwoven European narratives on America was a continuous Habsburg thread. Unpicking this thread not only contextualises the meaning of the American Revolution in the Habsburg world but also better contextualises that same Habsburg world, one which encompassed a broad, global outlook as well as a European one.[2]

Post-Columbian America and the Habsburg Monarchy

The voyages of discovery from Christopher Columbus's arrival in 1492 to the confirmation of a separate hemisphere in the voyage of Amerigo Vespucci implanted a new spatial order in European minds. The Habsburg Monarchy of the eighteenth century did not yet exist at that time. Bohemia and Hungary were independent kingdoms. The Austrian dominions were fragmented as several duchies and, up until a few years before Columbus's landing in the Bahamas, had been partly conquered by the Hungarian King Matthias Corvinus. Emperor Maximilian I's reconquest of the Austrian territories throughout the 1480s consolidated his reputation. Maximilian sought to commemorate his achievements in imperial propaganda. He ordered the completion of the *Triumphal Procession*, a series of woodblock prints, spanning 54 metres in length. Conceived by Maximilian and an Austrian cartographer before being worked on by several artists including Albrecht Dürer and Hans Burgkmair, the series depicted a fantastical allegorical train of carriages containing the emperor's subjects to proclaim his glory. One such group was the warriors of Calicut, a malleable sixteenth-century term denoting people beyond the seas, including Americans.[3] Half-dressed in feather skirts and headdresses, erroneously clutching European bladed spears, the ensemble reflected the new cognizance of America in the Habsburg mind. On another plate, the people of Calicut appear as bare-breasted women carrying bountiful produce, tending to oxen and rams while one features a monkey combing her hair and headdress. In this case, the plates served Maximilian's desire to display his worldly omnipotence.[4] To erase any shadow of a doubt, Maximilian sanctioned an accompanying verse to reinforce his ties to the Calicut and connection to the New World: "The Emperor in his warlike pride, conquering nations far and wide, has brought beneath our Empire's yoke the far-off Calicuttish folk."[5]

It was a Habsburg device deployed again in the real-life procession held in Brussels in 1517 to mark the accession of Maximilian's grandson (and future heir) Charles of Ghent to the Spanish throne as Carlos I (known more famously as Charles V). A group of Amerindians preceded a final float which carried a giant golden globe as if to fulfil Maximilian's earlier vision.[6] For the Habsburg rulers contemporary to the discovery of the New World, inclusion of the Amerindian float in their displays of power meant projecting their interests upon it. As rulers of the Holy Roman Empire, an edifice commonly understood to be universalist in scope, Maximilian saw new extra-European territory as falling under his patrimony as a universal emperor.[7] But staking a theoretical claim was not the only result. By incorporating America, the Habsburgs also served to revitalise their image as modern rulers, bringing the new, wondrous, and exotic to the people in such public processions and prints. Maximilian planned for the *Triumph* series to be hung in all major halls throughout the Holy Roman Empire and had various copies made of the panels. In a later version by a Tyrolean artist, the Calcuttish warriors appear even further defined by the Habsburg psyche; possessing beards, wearing sandals, carrying rounded shields, and brandishing bows more akin to an Arabian style than anything related to the New World.[8] Maximilian alluded to further claims in his written plans for the *Triumphal Arch*, which included the "1,500 islands"—a reference to Columbus's letter about 1,400 sighted islands—as one of his patrimonial crests adorning the monument.[9] It was only fitting that the first Latin publications of Amerigo Vespucci's voyages, which capitulated his prominence and helped enshrine the name America for the new continent, bore dedications to Maximilian.[10]

Amassing new-world objects for semi-private display was another route to utilise America for personal enhancement. Habsburg elites were no different from their European contemporaries who sought to acquire American objects for their collections. Emperors Maximilian I through to Rudolf II all collected new-world curiosities for their wonder cabinets (*Wunderkammern*).[11] Maximilian's daughter, Margaret of Austria, was one of the earliest collectors owing to her brief second marriage to Don Juan, son of Ferdinand and Isabella of Spain in the 1490s. She saw herself as a future ruler of the newfound dominions over which the Spanish monarchs had claimed sovereignty for themselves. By 1524, she had acquired nearly two hundred American artefacts.[12] In general, the Habsburg obsession with the Spanish throne and its territories in the New World fostered an American prominence in the dynastic lands of Central Europe. Emperor Ferdinand I, who was born and raised in Spain, prized his collection of Americana.[13] He retained personal connections with numerous

Spanish courtiers who informed him of the latest American discoveries.[14] His son and heir, Maximilian II, followed much the same interest, instructing his ambassador in Madrid to collect the rarest and most spectacular new-world objects.[15] Ferdinand I's other son, Ferdinand, who ruled as a sovereign in the secundogeniture of the Tyrol and Further Austria, also placed great value on obtaining and exhibiting Americana. His most notable possessions included Aztec feather garments, headdresses, and shields such as those worn by the Aztec figures featured in *Esther und Avasver*, a painting which he displayed prominently at Schloss Ambras near Innsbruck.[16]

Dreams of owning the New World and of reconnecting with Spain persisted throughout the dynastic line of the Austrian Habsburgs. The father of Maria Theresa, Emperor Charles VI, yearned to recreate a Spanish-Austrian world empire centred on the colonial conquests in the New World.[17] After his forced relocation from Barcelona to Vienna upon the death of his brother, Charles contorted the Central European space he found around him towards such a vision. He filled the court with Spanish personnel and reformed institutions to be more like Spanish colonial enterprises. The Karlskirche in Vienna became perhaps the most tangible manifestation of his imperialist aims with its dual columns representing the Pillars of Hercules at the Straits of Gibraltar opening out to the Atlantic.[18] This Spanish-New World influence was still alive and well in the generation of the American Revolution. Maria Theresa's court processions as well as portraits of her and her husband Francis Stephan boldly showed off Spanish-styled clothes and fashions.[19]

Illusions of the rulers often affected the allusions of the ruled. Habsburg elites emulated the incorporation of America through collecting and self-fashioning. Prince Pál Esterházy, for example, acquired engravings of Amerindians after observing the collections of Rudolf II in Vienna.[20] In mimicking the tastes of the Habsburg monarchs, courtiers and nobles precipitated a wider craze for Americana. Fetishising parrots became one symptom of this trickle-down mania. The quest for these new-world birds, mainly from the "land of parrots" (Brazil), was a longstanding obsession of the Habsburg rulers from Rudolf II to Francis Stephan.[21] Such imperial projects provoked a cultural fascination around the colourful avians. The Archduke Sigismund Francis of Tyrol and Further Austria purchased an ornate parrot clock, and in Bohemia, a surviving inventory of ball costumes features a courtly couple bedecked in parrot feathers.[22] Donning new-world dress became a fashionable exercise among Habsburg nobles as proud portraits of the Netolicky and Schwarzenberg families can attest.[23] In Prague, the imperial feather-worker Jan Fuchs established a shop to cater for city elites and their fascination for colourful plumes.[24] Aristocrats consciously sought out and absorbed Americana through friendships, family networks, grand tours, and diplomatic offices.[25] As time wore on, these elites developed more consumer-orientated tastes for Americana. The exotic gave way to the luxurious. Consumables and commodities such as sugar, coffee, and beaver hats became *en vogue* and with them the first indirect commercial pathways to the Americas emerged.[26] In turn, America became less a curious land and more a source of produce, industry, and exploitation for Habsburg inhabitants.[27]

Allegorical art was one medium in which the colonial image of America remained constant. From the late Renaissance to the early nineteenth century, artists developed a visual metaphor for America. Continental allegories depicting the four continents of the earth—Africa, America, Asia, and Europe—became an artistic shorthand throughout the southern lands of the Holy Roman Empire.[28] No less than ninety American allegories appeared on the ceilings and walls of parish churches, manorial houses, monastic libraries, and grand palaces across the Austrian lands between 1645 and 1832.[29] In these frescoes, the personification of America often took the form of a woman (or cherub) half-dressed and crowned with a feather headdress. Commonly associated animals, including the much-adored parrots, featured alongside alligators and armadillos. Inferences oscillated between representations of a noble savage and princely figure, but a sense of inferiority was always apparent, reinforced by the position of America as subordinate to Europe and Asia and a counterpart to Africa. The locations of these allegories reflected the further trickling-down of American interest within Habsburg society. Prior to 1710, the majority abounded in the palaces of Lower Austria and Styria such as Schloss Eggenberg near Graz and the Lower Belvedere near Vienna. Later, American allegories appeared predominantly in abbeys and monasteries before reaching parish churches in the mid-eighteenth century. These images introduced the concept of America to ordinary people who came to these everyday places of worship. Consciously and unconsciously, such iconography shaped the mental worldview of Catholic churchgoers across the Austrian lands.[30] Despite this localised influence, parish reliefs did not hold a monopoly on the religious vision of the Americas in Central Europe.

The Society of Jesus was responsible for the most popular religious lens on the Americas in the Habsburg lands. Whereas fashion and art had solidified forms of the exotic, Jesuit missionaries from the Austrian Habsburg lands created a more nuanced picture of the Americas. Officially formed in 1540, the Society of Jesus grew steadily in the Habsburg lands. Of the 5,340 Jesuits of the German assistancy in 1750, over half originated from the Austrian and Bohemian provinces.[31] Jesuits from the Habsburg lands enthusiastically participated in the missionising efforts of the order in the Americas. At least 737 Jesuits travelled westward for this purpose from the German assistancy; around forty percent came from the Austrian, Bohemian and Tyrolean provinces.[32] A similar enthusiasm existed in Hungary.[33] Completing this mission brought Jesuits into close contact with inhabitants from Brazil to the plains of North America.[34] From these intense and sustained encounters, often lasting years, Jesuits from the Habsburg lands formulated pejorative views of their hosts and neighbours. Indigenous societies seemed "primitive" even "uncivilised" rather than conforming to the idyllic representations of the "noble savage" or "children of nature" tropes.[35] Missionaries played an important role in brokering this new view to people in their native lands by writing reports to their peers in provincial seminaries and to their families.[36]

   Central European Jesuits also aimed to publish their letters in specialised journals in their native lands. In the Habsburg lands, two Jesuit journals stand out as influential in shaping the Central European perception of America. In the first instance, Jesuits at the University of Trnava (Nagyszombat) began publication of an annual almanac in 1676. Reports from missionaries in the New World featured throughout. Typical entries focused on the savagery and dissimilarity of the Native peoples.[37] The 1709 issue, for example, featured news of the "Indos" who had dog's teeth and barked.[38] The Bohemian Jesuit Joseph Neumann, for instance, published in Prague a bloody memoir in Latin of his mission during the Tarahumara revolts against the Spanish and Jesuit presence in New Spain in the 1690s.[39] Another Bohemian Jesuit, Adam Gilg, formulated his American reality with harsher words in a letter home. America, in his opinion, was "a garden full of spines deprived of all human consolation." [40] Such information appeared as evidence in treatises written by Jesuit fathers at Trnava who strove to comprehend mankind in all its unusual forms from the "harmonious" to the "imperfect."[41] Their treatises on geography, avians, botany, and dendrology all cited examples from New World observations. From the men who outran deer in Florida to fantastical golden trees in the Caribbean to the worshiped *Quetzaltototl* birds of the Aztecs, such information supplemented the growing global outlook of Central European Jesuits who sought to conform new discoveries into a rationalised knowledge system.[42] Information contained in the Trnava almanac reached large audiences. The main editor of the almanac, the polymath professor Márton Szentiványi, repurposed this information for further publications which were translated into German and French.[43] Szentiványi's refashioning of new-world knowledge also reached other Jesuit centres of the Hungarian lands long after his death in 1708. In Košice, for example, parts of his treatises were printed in the *Calendarium* of the Jesuit university in 1754.[44] The Jesuit father Pál Bertalanffi reworked much of the Hungarian Jesuit knowledge into his 1757 geography of the Americas.[45] The endless cycles of circulation and recirculation through multiple authors, from Jesuits present in the Americas to the editors of almanacs in Hungary to their translators and readers, ensured the constant diffusion of Jesuit knowledge about the New World in the Habsburg lands up to the time of the American Revolution.

If Hungarian Jesuits had Trnava as their epicentre of world-knowledge generation, then the Jesuits of the Austrian province had the city of Graz. For thirty-five years between 1726 and 1761, Jesuits in the city produced *Der Neue Welt-Bott* (The New World Messenger), founded by Joseph Stöcklein.[46] Stöcklein's initiative was a similar undertaking to Szentiványi's almanac in Trnava and followed examples of French Jesuit journals about the New World, which reproduced translated accounts and transcribed oral testimonies of missionaries.[47] By presenting actual assertions of missionaries, albeit somewhat edited, Stöcklein directly transported his readers to an eyewitness position. Furthermore, accounts published in *Der Neue Welt-Bott* appeared in the vernacular German rather than Latin, reflecting Stöcklein's broader aims for dissemination beyond the clergy.[48] In producing such rich content, around 812 reports in total, Stöcklein's endeavour paid off as *Der Neue Welt-Bott* became one of the most influential sources of new-world information in the German-speaking lands.[49] Although the journal featured reports from Jesuits across the world, fully one quarter (203 reports) featured the Americas.[50] *Der Neue Welt-Bott* presented a wondrous vision across the Atlantic. It was a land filled with mysterious animals and peoples in need of converting by a "civilised," learned preacher.[51] Aiming to serve German-speaking readers, Stöcklein selected letters showing non-German missionaries (except for the Bohemians and Hungarians) as "vainglorious and boastful" or "cruel and greedy."[52] Combined with extensive imagery, *Der Neue Welt-Bott* served to create vindication and enthusiasm for the Germanic—and in this case, Habsburg—presence in the Americas.[53] Stöcklein's mission to not only to feed the "German" "appetite for knowledge" but also to elevate the endeavours of his fellow countrymen that increased the Habsburg sense of purpose in the New World and, at the same time, made it less alien.[54] It was no surprise that young Jesuits from the Habsburg Monarchy who ventured to the New World after reading Stöcklein's journal specifically wrote accounts intended for publication in subsequent editions.[55]

First-hand accounts of America in the Habsburg lands rose after the sudden prosecution of the Jesuit order in the Spanish empire in 1767. Following the decree banning all Jesuit activity in Asia and America, around three hundred Central European Jesuits attempted to return home.[56] A return to normalcy became increasingly difficult following the general suppression of the Jesuit order in 1773.[57] Many ex-missionaries turned to printing their memoirs in order to supplement their position, resulting in a literature boom which often portrayed the colonial Americas in a nostalgic fashion.[58] The fantastical series of fourty-seven watercolours depicting mission life in Baja California with German and Spanish subtitles by the exiled Ignaz Tirsch in Znojmo best represent a Habsburg Jesuit's case of longing for former life in the New World.[59] Jesuits in the Habsburg lands enjoyed relative freedom under the more pious and tolerant reigns of Maria Theresa and Joseph II.[60] Martin Dobrizhoffer, a Jesuit who missionised among the Guraní and Abipone peoples of Paraguay from 1749, settled in Vienna after the suppression, where, through the patronage of Maria Theresa, he worked as one of her more favoured court preachers.[61] In fact, she often sent for Dobrizhoffer to preach to her personally so that she "might hear his adventures from his own lips."[62] The publication of his monumental three-volume *Historia de Abiponibus; equestri, bellicosaque Paraquarieae natione* (A History of the Abipones, an Equestrian Warrior Nation of Paraguay) in Vienna in 1784 was due to his royal patronage and an immediate German translation followed.[63] In the preface to his work, Dobrizhoffer explained his rationale for writing his account, which does much to illuminate the widespread interest in Americana in the Habsburg Monarchy by the late eighteenth century. Whereas in America Dobrizhoffer had been continually interrogated about Europe, in Austria he was "frequently questioned concerning America" and sought to alleviate himself of this trouble but writing "this little history" on the advice of "some person of distinction," referring to Maria Theresa.[64] The thirst for first-hand accounts of the Americas from returning Jesuits peaked in the years of the American Revolution. It was not only Dobrizhoffer and Tirsch who contributed to the blossoming field of ex-Jesuit studies on America. American works continued to appear by Jesuits who had sought refuge in the Habsburg lands such as Bernhard Havestadt–, Franz Xaver Veigl, and Florian Paucke who settled in Vienna, Klagenfurt, and the Cistercian abbey of Zwettl, respectively.[65] Such works by returning Jesuits and their predecessors embedded a deeper understanding of the Americas in the Habsburg web of knowledge.[66] Yet given the geography of the Spanish empire and the preponderance of Jesuit missions in central and southern America, these

Jesuit accounts transfixed the Habsburg gaze towards these regions rather than North America. It was only as news of the domestic grievances in the British colonies filtered through in the 1760s that the orientation shifted northwards and a new American arena became the focus of attention.

The Dawn of North America

The mid-eighteenth century witnessed a marked decline of hispano-centric Americanism within Habsburg audiences whilst British North America captured an increasing share of the attention. Discussions over southern and central America continued but observers in the mid-eighteenth-century Habsburg lands began to recognise a prosperous, yet precarious situation developing in the British colonies. Prognostications swirled over the future of the colonies and the nature of the colonists living there as new information came to light. Economists, scientists, librettists, and newspaper editors contributed to these emerging debates. The ideas put forward by these individuals owed a debt to the previous centuries of knowledge about the Americas but advanced conversations around the thirteen colonies that would later become the United States of America. Engagement with the complexity of America was not uniform across the Habsburg lands on the eve of the Revolution. Each region—Habsburg Milan, Tuscany, the Austrian Netherlands, Austria-Bohemia, and the Hungarian lands—ascribed their own importance to events and ideas circulating about North America. As the American Revolution dawned, however, the tumult occurring across the Atlantic interested peoples of all areas of the Habsburg Monarchy.

The genre of emigration literature first saw a shift towards North America. Over the course of the eighteenth century, one in three inhabitants of the Holy Roman Empire relocated to territories outside its imperial borders.[67] Around 100,000 German-speaking migrants sailed to British North America prior to 1776.[68] Transatlantic migration from provinces bordering the Habsburg lands formed part of this movement, with the most notable cases involving victims of religious persecution such as the Salzburgers, who arrived in Georgia in 1734, and the Moravian Herrnhuters, who followed Count Nikolaus Ludwig von Zinzendorf and David Nitschmann to Pennsylvania in 1741.[69] Total emigration from the Habsburg lands proper to North America only reached several thousands at most, however.[70] Another substantial block of German speakers, totalling around 500,000 people, travelled eastwards following resettlement schemes to populate the Hungarian lands and the newly reconquered Banat of Temesvar from the Ottomans in 1717.[71] The resulting demand for colonists pitted migrant recruiters against one another over the supply of human capital.[72] Popular conceptions of emigration destinations in North America and the eastern lands became increasingly distorted by the advertising of these recruitment drives. Recruiters frequently depicted North America as a land of proverbial milk and honey.[73] Land was cheap there; work was plentiful; religious persecution did not exist, and so on. Even hunting was easier, as the bison, to take one recruiter's word, wandered into your house almost begging to be shot and slaughtered.[74] The ideal of American life appeared so strongly to prospective German migrants that recruiters for the eastern part of the Habsburg lands chose to imitate the claims. The Banat of Temesvar became known as "Europe's America" in an effort to ascribe positive connotations with North America to the Hungarian interior.[75] Letters sent back from emigrants to their home communities established a better sense of the harsher realities, but these did little to deter future migrants who relied upon manuals when crossing the Atlantic.[76] It was possible to walk through the eighteenth-century Habsburg lands and hear the buzz of excitement about America. Towards the close of the century, one writer arrived at a tavern in lower Styria and heard tales of the innkeeper's grandfather and his adventures in America. The writer subsequently published his diary, calling him the "Styrian Robinson Crusoe."[77]

Positive depictions of life in North America created defenders and detractors in Europe. A naturalist, Georges-Louis Leclerc, comte de Buffon led the charge in admonishing American qualities. Buffon contended that the presence of smaller creatures in the New World along with the less populous Native peoples pointed to a general American inferiority compared to the inhabitants and nature in Eurasia. Buffon's theory of "American degeneracy," as it came to be known, ignited and fascinated readers in the Habsburg lands as it did elsewhere in Europe. Yet to some, these theories seemed incompatible with the economic vitality of British American colonists. Intellectuals challenged Buffon's ideas, especially in the Habsburg provinces in the Italian peninsula. The Milanese mathematics professor Paolo Frisi attacked the leading works of Buffon and his supporter Cornelius de Pauw.[78] Frisi argued America was a fertile land populated by intelligent people.[79] The ultimate proof, Frisi concluded, lay in the example of North America, especially "in Philadelphia where all the other glories of Europe have already been emulated." British colonists, Frisi noted, had engaged in a series of pioneering scientific studies, leading them to "controlling the fire of heaven and calculating the quantity of matter in comets."[80] His examples alluded to Benjamin Franklin's electrical experiments and John Winthrop's studies on comets. In exemplifying North America, Frisi shifted focus away from South America. For Frisi, the British colonies in North America served as a repudiation of degeneracy and offered a convincing model for American prosperity and contribution to European life.

Frisi was not alone in his rebuttal of degeneracy and promotion of British North America as the paragon of colonial virtue and enterprise. The Milanese nobleman Gian Rinaldo Carli published his own polemic refuting degeneracy ideas. Written during the course of the American Revolution, Carli's *Lettere Americane* drew more heavily on the North American example and contained far more vitriol for De Pauw personally. "He thinks everything outside of Breslau and Berlin as barbaric and savage," Carli decried before he claimed De Pauw was an alcoholic who "is drinking beer at this very moment as I write."[81] Carli likewise extolled British colonial examples and won the greater share of acclaim for his *ad hominem* treatise with subsequent translations in French and German.[82] Franklin, to whom the *Lettere Americane* was dedicated, wrote personally to Carli's publisher to extend his thanks for Carli's "witty defens [*sic*] against the attacks of that misinformed and malignant Writer."[83] Indeed, Carli had done much to propagate Franklin's reputation among the Milanese. An anonymous reviewer of the *Lettere Americane* praised Carli in 1782 for confirming that "the immortal American Mr. Franklin demonstrates the health and greatness of that new American nation."[84]

Friedrich Wilhelm Taube became one of the most knowledgeable commentators of his day on North American matters. Born in London as the son of Queen Charlotte's personal physician, Taube spent his youth in the British capital before the queen's death in 1737 provoked his family's relocation to Hannover where the young Taube studied law at the University of Göttingen. Taube later worked as a lawyer but spent many years travelling, which reportedly included a trip to North America.[85] Upon his return to Europe, Taube eventually became the legation secretary in the Habsburg embassy in London, utilising his German and English fluency and quickly establishing himself as an expert on the British economy, with a particular interest in Britain's emerging struggles to tax North Americans. In 1766, he published his first work on the issue titled *Thoughts on the Present State of our Colonies in North America*, but no known copy survives today.[86] One description of this work, however, attests that Taube collected the evidence for it from "his friends in North America."[87] The work was well received and Maria Theresa honoured him with a golden medallion. Later that year, Taube unfortunately penned a critical report on the British government's handling of the situation, which prompted his recall back to Vienna. Still of use and recognised for his talents, he joined the Council of Commerce (*Commerzrat*) as a counsellor (*Hofskretär*) in compensation.[88]

Subsequently, Taube published his magnum opus in Vienna in 1774, his *Historische und politische Abschilderung der Engländischen Manufacturen* (Historical and political depictions of English manufacturers).[89] In this work, he detailed the nature of the British economy, ranging from the goods produced to the scale and health of Britain's international trade across the world. The book's comprehensiveness made it a popular success, and this work included plenty of reference to the situation of the British colonies in North America. He highlighted for his readers the future prosperity of North America based on its economic vibrancy, growing population, and abundance of land. "That the land in America is so plentiful and inexpensive," he explained, "even the workers, servants, and day-labourers who know something of farming, can in a short time save so much money."[90] Such attractive economic vitality clarified, in Taube's view, why the population grew so rapidly since young men could easily provide for their families, therefore allowing American couples to marry earlier and have an average of eight children.[91] Although much less explicitly than Frisi and Carli, Taube's convictions also flatly contradicted the ideas of American degeneracy. He argued, moreover, that the colonists were united by shared values of freedom of commerce and equal rights before the law.[92] This common principle stood in contrast to the evermore restrictive policies imposed on them by their government in London. Taube made a forthright prediction that open conflict would come between the Americans and the British. Already in 1774, he wrote of the inevitability of American independence, which he believed would arise when Americans became "weary enough of English supremacy" and he was made all the more certain by the recent protests for which the colonists went without any chastisement for their disobedience.[93] "So it seems doubtful," Taube concluded, "to say whether England has more cause to fear or to hope from its colonies."[94]

As the tensions led to bloodshed in the colonies, Taube wrote more works outlining his views. In 1776, he published his *Geschichte der Engländischen Handelschaft, Manufacturen, Colonien und Schiffahrt* (A history of English commerce, manufacturing, colonies and shipping). In an appended essay on the "true causes of the current war in North America," Taube squarely blamed the excessive taxation of the American colonists by the British, which itself lay in the historical development of the British economy.[95] From Taube's *longue durée* perspective, quite uncommon among German commentators at the time, the

American Revolution was an entirely foreseeable event. "Soon after the Treaty of Paris in 1763," he explained in the introduction, "there began a longing for free trade in the hearts of the Americans."[96] The Tea and Stamp Acts had denied them this natural desire and so the British were at fault for not listening to their unrepresented colonists. A strikingly sympathetic argument, Taube touched upon this theme again in his revised second edition of the *Historische und politische Abschilderung der Engländischen Manufacturen*, which he expanded into two volumes in 1777 and 1778.[97] In the second volume, Taube took great pains to reiterate the "tremendous changes" and damage done to the British economy by their disastrous war in North America.[98] Yet Taube planned to publish his best material on that topic in a new third volume focused solely on the American Revolution.[99] What laudatory views of America and further criticisms of the British position this work would have contained we cannot know since Taube died suddenly in June 1778. In spite of his premature death, Taube's works helped to pivot attention towards the peril and potential of the American colonists in North America. His works reached a large audience even in England, where the 1774 German edition appeared on the shelves of the Foreign Circulating Library in Leeds.[100] Not all reception was positive, however. The free-market advocate and court economist Count Karl von Zinzendorf read Taube's volumes in December 1778 with great disgust. As a man who had studied the British economy and American colonial situation, Zinzendorf disagreed with Taube's praise for the American boycott of British goods.[101] "It is a compilation containing some curious facts interspersed with false or superficial reasoning," he noted in his diary.[102] Superficial or not, Taube had sown the seeds of discussion among the inhabitants of the Habsburg Monarchy. Years later, even Zinzendorf was still reading Taube's texts.[103]

One man in Vienna undoubtedly aware of Taube's texts was Jacques Accarias de Sérionne. Like Taube, Sérionne was not a native of the Habsburg Monarchy. Born in Châtillon-en-Diois in southeastern France, Sérionne rose through the French administrative ranks before several risky investments forced him to flee Paris in the late 1750s. He settled in Brussels where he advised regional authorities on economic matters for almost a decade. In 1768, he relocated to Vienna as an advisor in the State Chancellery (*Staatskanzlei*) before moving to Hungary as an agent for the Batthyány family.[104] It was during these wandering years that Sérionne became one of Europe's most popular economic essayists, publishing a variety of influential texts.[105] In Brussels, he founded the *Journal de Commerce* which ran for forty-eight issues with state support.[106] From his experience in France and as editor of the *Journal*, Sérionne became acutely aware of colonial economic policies. In nine issues of the *Journal*, Sérionne penned essays on the colonial economies of Portugal and Spain.[107] Sérionne took a harsh line towards the effects of colonial enterprise. He looked backwards rather than forwards and saw in the previous decadence of the Spanish empire how corrosively the colonial market could undermine the metropole. In 1761 he published his *Les intérêts des nations* (The interests of nations) followed by his *La richesse de l'Angleterre* (The riches of England) in Vienna in 1771.[108]

In *La richesse*, Sérionne took aim squarely at the American colonies, which he felt had sapped the English commercial system. From Sérionne's perspective a country could only count on its material wealth for economic strength. England, with its vast resources in timber and minerals, enjoyed a stable footing but the establishment of colonial projects had turned this economic system towards venture capitalism. Public credit served no one and private enterprise sequestered away the resources of the state. He noted how the American colonies had all been founded by private companies and had become their "richest branches of trade."[109] In agreement with authors like Taube, Sérionne echoed the vitality of these American colonies but rather than praise their might, he predicted inevitable conflict. "It is astonishing," he wrote in *La richesse*, "that a nation as enlightened as the English, has not foreseen in the projects of its plantations of North America, that those colonies which gather the same fruits and which have exactly the same industry as their metropolis, must necessarily become its rivals and therefore infinitely harmful."[110] Sérionne went further with added prescience. He awaited the eventual independence of the American colonies. Written during his Hungarian employment in 1771, Sérionne lamented how it was too late for the British. The Americans had already been allowed to become too powerful for them to be subjugated indefinitely.[111] "The Englishmen of America are as good as the Englishmen of Europe," he warned, "and three or four thousand troops, which are about all that a European nation can transport to America, would not be enough of an army for them."[112] True, he acknowledged, the path to American independence had begun with the Stamp Act crisis, but it was fuelled by the "unceasing" rivalry of trade between the two sides. It would be completed only when the "embarrassment of such division" would interest all the "other industrious nations of Europe."[113] In other words, not one but two commentators under the Habsburg Monarchy expounded the strengths of the American colonies and predicted the course of the War of American Independence several years before its outbreak.

The economic aspects of the American Revolution became one of the most intriguing details for Habsburg observers as attention shifted towards North

FIGURE 2. Portrait of Father Maurus Lindemayr of the
Benedictine Abbey in Lambach, Upper Austria

America. In Lambach Abbey in Upper Austria, one Benedictine monk wrote
a play about the Revolution's commercial fallout. Written in heavy Austrian
dialect in 1780, Father Maurus Lindemayr's three-act drama *Der engländische
Patriotismus* (English patriotism) featured two English merchants coping with
wartime turmoil.[114] The first, Hickshot, denounces the American "rebels" he
reads so much about in the newspapers and yearns for peace.[115] "I toss and turn
at night; you'd have to scorch Philadelphia for me and blow Boston to smith-
ereens," he recalls in one aria.[116] A proud Londoner and Tory, Hickshot defines
his Englishness upon anti-American lines. "Good" Englishmen should, in Hickshot's view, "curse the colonists [and], like the Antichrist, strike thunder into
the rebel! To pray for that is to be a Brit."[117] Hickshot's staunch sentiment is
counterbalanced by a Bristol merchant named Smedley who trades freely with
the Americans. Lindemayr's play was not anti-American, however. Debate over
the colonies is complicated by additional characters, such as Hickshot's lackey
John who acts confused by events. He asks at one point whether England is the
motherland and America the daughter (*"England ist ja das Mutterreich, und
Amerika ist die Tochter?"*).[118] In a one-sided conversation between John and
another, more cognisant Hickshot lackey, the clearest distillation of the new

definition of America appears. Hagel, in response to John's incessant misunderstanding of the impact of the Revolution, proclaims "for me America may be a part of the world but it is no longer a continent (*Weltheil*)."[119] Before this, Hagel spells out for John how North America is in fact many component pieces including New France, "*Neubritannien*," Acadia, New England, New Holland, New Denmark, New Spain, Virginia, Florida, and the lands of the Huron and Iroquois.[120] In Lindemayr's theatrical depiction, America was no longer a single entity but rather a fractured land reflecting the disaggregation unfolding across the Atlantic. Lindemayr's vision of America reached audiences beyond his monastery at Lambach. Augustinians frequently performed his plays in nearby Sankt Florian and Linz and in the neighbouring Archbishopric of Salzburg, Michael Haydn—Joseph Haydn's less famous younger brother—set the play to music.[121] Through song and drama, they articulated the new political constellation unfolding across the Atlantic.

Taube, Sérionne, and Lindemayr were not alone in their reorientation towards North America. On the stages and in the palatial concert halls of the Habsburg lands, theatrical and instrumental works also guided outlooks northwards. Joseph Marius Babo's 1778 play *Das Winterquartier in Amerika* (The winter quarter in America) centred on Hessian mercenaries and the quartering of soldiers among the colonists, for instance.[122] This trend had begun already in the 1750s. One of the most popular and controversial dramatists in Vienna at that time, Joseph Felix von Kurz staged a pantomime called *Arlequin, der neue Abgott Ram in Amerika* (Harlequin, the new idol Ram in America).[123] The titular character Arelquin finds himself shipwrecked on the fictive American island of Tschaladey where, through comical altercations with a magician, he becomes mistakenly transformed into the deity Ram for the native "Indian" islanders. Kurz invoked standard stereotypes of American savagery typical of the prejudicial colonial lens, but the pantomime's end implied the existence of a more sophisticated North America as Arlequin is rescued by Dutch traders heading to the West Indies or New Netherlands.[124] Kurz's drama was also popular in Prague and Bratislava.[125] The piece was revived in Vienna in 1766 and appeared again in the 1770s under the name *Die Insul der Wilden* (The island of the savages).[126] This time the elder Haydn, Joseph, wrote music for the pantomime's arias.[127] And it was not the only piece by him to deal with an American theme.

Joseph Haydn's cosmos was filled with American imagery. His patron, Prince Nikolaus Esterházy, employed a servant from the West Indies whom Haydn knew well and whose mixed-race son he tutored.[128] At the Esterháza court in Hungary, where Haydn lived and worked for most of his life, depictions of South

American characters became commonplace through adaptations of works such as Voltaire's *Alzire, ou les Américains* (Alzire, or the Americans) (1736) and Graun's *Montezuma* (1755).[129] Haydn followed this trend by composing his own works to American themes, but he primarily composed around North American tropes. His symphonies, no. 34 in D minor (1765) and no. 49 in F minor (1768), made allusions to the Quakers in the popular comedy *La jeune Indienne* (The young Indian girl) (1764) by Nicholas Chamfort, a popular fixture throughout the 1760s and 1770s in Vienna as *Die junge Indianerin* (The young Indian girl). In 1779, Haydn set a libretto of *L'isola disabitata* (The deserted island) to music by the Viennese court poet Pietro Mestastasio. The performance referred to a Caribbean moral tale of an English salve-owner whose life is saved by a West Indian girl, who he eventually sells into slavery for social advancement.[130] Within the walls of Esterháza, Haydn learned about America from his careful reading of William Robertson's *A History of America* before his journey to London in the 1790s brought him into personal contact with West Indian merchants and exiled American loyalists.[131]

Beyond Esterháza, Habsburg audiences (mainly the nobility) digested an influx of new American imagery through operas.[132] Popular works in Vienna often revolved around new-world themes but in the 1760s and 1770s, the figure of the Quaker loomed large over this cultural space. Viennese conceptions of the Quakers were imported from abroad, in works such as Chamfort's *La Jeune Indienne* (The young Indian girl) and Guglielmi's *La Quakera Spiritosa* (The spiritual quakeress).[133] The Tuscan-born librettist Ranieri de Calzabigi was one of the most influential dramatists living in Vienna; he popularised Quaker characters and a more favourable vision of North America.[134] His operatic libretto *Amiti e Ontario* (1772/1774) takes place in Pennsylvania where two Native Americans, a female Amiti and a male Ontario, are owned by a Quaker, Mr. Dull, who falls in love with Amiti, whilst his relative Mrs. Bubble falls for Ontario. Dull plans to free both of the enslaved in order to go ahead with the marriages but Amiti and Ontario have concealed their own love for each other from him. When this is revealed, Dull, inspired by their true love, responds leniently and honours their freedom despite his own feelings of affection and his power over them.[135] Although the main Quaker character, Dull, is represented as a slave owner, his benevolence and self-sacrifice shines through, even towards Native Americans. Calzabigi's choice of Mr. Dull as a name seemed loaded with intent as it conjured up connotations with the German *duldsam* (meaning tolerant or indulgent) to further reinforce the positive attributes of the character and his actions at the end of the opera.[136]

As fictive as the characters' names sounded, Calzabigi played on the realistic antagonism between Great Britain and the North American colonies.
Mr. Dull's relative, Mrs. Bubble, is made out to be an Anglican who decries
Dull's plans for freedom for Amiti and Ontario and offers to buy one of them
herself—her preference is, of course, for her beloved Ontario. Her interjection
provokes an abolitionist declaration from Dull, which not only underscores
the moral superiority of the Pennsylvanian but, in the context of the emerging
transatlantic split, serves to undermine the British stance vis-à-vis slavery.[137] In
creating a character like Mr. Dull, Calzabigi was not only demonstrating how
North America offered a more enlightened example to the world but he was
also echoing the thoughts of other intellectuals in the Habsburg lands. It was
as if Calzabigi had read and dramatised the reports of the *Gazzetta di Milano*
which announced how Quakers in Pennsylvania "gave an unusual proof of love
for humanity [as] the majority of the residents of that colony agreed to free all
their black Slaves."[138] Despite the reflections in Calzabigi's opera, discussions on
slavery and the abolition of the slave trade in Central Europe remained muted
until the early nineteenth century.[139] Yet Calzabigi's rendering of Pennsylvanian
Quakers in *Amiti e Ontario* endured throughout the age of the American Revolution and throughout the Habsburg lands. Giuseppe Scarlatti composed music
for its premiere at the Burgtheater in Vienna and for a private performance at the
Auersperg family residence.[140] The work was subsequently adapted by Neapolitan librettists and composers into *Le gare generose* (The contests in generosity) in
1786, which saw Mr. Dull relocated to Boston and devoid of any Quakerism.[141]
The new version arrived back in Vienna the following year with additional revisions by Lorenzo da Ponte and Carl Ditters von Dittersdorf whose changes retained the core of Calzabigi's vision of virtuous North American inhabitants.[142]
As the musicologist Pierpaolo Polzonetti points out, America in these operatic
performances "was not represented as an exotic, primitivistic land" but rather
as "modern, business-orientated, and politically and socially more advanced."[143]
By the 1780s, North America had firmly entered the cultural zeitgeist of the
Habsburg lands through drama and print to create a rising awareness of the different character of the British colonies and their increasingly uncertain future.

Conclusion

The notion of America fascinated the inhabitants of the Habsburg lands long
before the American Revolution, and various views of the New World circulated via several mediums in Central Europe. America functioned as a symbol

for Habsburg rulers and elites seeking to display their worldly wealth, and it appealed to aristocratic sensibilities for the latest fashions and curiosity for new-world artefacts. Religious lenses often depicted the New World as primitive and inferior, but information from first-hand reports became the bedrock for new global epistemologies. Jesuit authors in Trnava and Graz contributed to the proliferation of American knowledge. Returning Jesuits kept alive the curiosity and captivation with the Americas; even Maria Theresa was susceptible to the opportunities to learn indirectly about American encounters. As the first murmurings of the American Revolution began in the mid-eighteenth century, Habsburg inhabitants became increasingly aware of the situation in British North America, and Habsburg intellectuals developed distinct responses to these disturbances. Taube and Sérionne correctly articulated the colonial challenge to Great Britain and believed in the inevitability of American independence. In Habsburg Lombardy, Frisi and Carli refuted ideas of American degeneracy using examples of progress from the British colonies. The shift towards a progressive, industrious view of North America occurred simultaneously in drama and music. Colonists in the thirteen British colonies represented a tolerant and prosperous people on stage and in sound, and theatrical performances, especially, reinforced understandings of the colonial contest erupting in North America. England was the motherland and America was the daughter, but the question in Habsburg minds became: for how long?

CHAPTER TWO

"Some Here Are Warm for the Part of America"

The American Revolution and the Imperial Court at Vienna, 1776–1783

"**E**VERY IDLE FELLOW TALKS of America," complained the British ambassador Sir Robert Murray Keith about his Viennese neighbours to his friends in London.[1] He first sounded that alarm in 1774. As time rumbled on, the rumours of discontent between Great Britain and her thirteen colonies became an unavoidable fact, much to the fascination of the "idle" onlookers in Vienna. When war broke out a year later and the unilateral announcement of independence followed another year after, Viennese courtiers became fully aware and engrossed by events transpiring across the Atlantic. They were not merely passive observers, however. American news fuelled sympathies as well as speculation. There were those who felt content to follow events closely and those who could not do so without expressing their support. There were, of course, those who disagreed with the American crusade, but they were in a minority. The imperial court at Vienna was a largely pro-American scene. When the first official American representative, William Lee, arrived in Vienna in 1778, he could write home with pride about how "Some here are Warm for the part of America."[2]

Identifying who these "warm" supporters of the American Revolution were within the Viennese court reveals the widespread interest in American affairs within Habsburg government circles. This includes individuals who worked and attended court in Vienna, from the clerks to the socialites to the highest echelons of political circles, including the imperial family themself. The rather pro-American stance to be found across this hierarchy might seem surprising at first but it speaks to the cultural and intellectual power of the American Revolution. Discussing the attitudes of imperial courtiers in Vienna is a necessary step in understanding the American Revolution's impact upon the Habsburg Monarchy, especially since courtiers' knowledge and opinions shaped the policies of the Habsburg dynasty and the policy of the Holy Roman Empire.[3]

The nobility, moreover, were social shapers, signifying contemporary intellectual and cultural currents.[4] Whilst French and British influences were undeniable in their socio-cultural cosmos, a distinct American line entered the highest Habsburg circles as a result of the fascination surrounding the Revolution as a political event. Absorption of the American Revolution at the Viennese court produced discernible effects; it shaped the monarchs' responses to the Revolution as well as the first American envoy's chances of success. As a continual site of cultural exchange, political patronage, and social visibility, the imperial court at Vienna also determined, in part, the cultural tone for the rest of the Habsburg lands. Fascination with the American Revolution, once signalled there, became an obsession across the whole of the Monarchy. In doing so, courtiers not only defined their own cultural cosmos but also the wider reception of America throughout the Habsburg Monarchy.

Imperial Courtiers and the American Revolution

Individuals rarely commit to paper with their own name something which they do not believe to be true. In this sense, letters written to Benjamin Franklin, arguably the most famous celebrity of the revolutionary cause in Europe, provide one of the most insightful windows into the effects of the American Revolution and its widespread popularity within the Habsburg Monarchy. It is, admittedly, an imperfect window; one which marginalises those who felt disgruntled by the American revolutionary influence, or those whose letters have failed to be preserved. But the outpouring of sentiment manifested in the surviving letters from the Viennese elites does offer an illuminating perspective as to how the American cause was received among imperial courtiers. Three officials contacted Franklin from inside the walls of the Hofburg, the main residence of the Habsburgs in Vienna. The earliest message came from Joseph Bek, a comptroller (*Raitrat*) in the accounting department of the war ministry (the *Hofkriegsbuchhalterei*). Bek's letter gushed with his enthusiasm for the United States. He hoped to emigrate and serve through Franklin's sponsorship. His desire to "sacrifice" himself for the American cause came from his reading of "The History of America," which likely referred to William Robertson's volumes of the same name.[5] Bek possibly received these tomes through his friendship with the Zinzendorfs; Count Karl von Zinzendorf, the governor of Trieste, who knew Robertson personally from his visit to Scotland and read his works, and his half-brother Count Ludwig von Zinzendorf who, as president of the former Court Accounting Chamber (*Hofrechnungskammer*), wrote a recommendation for Bek to Franklin.[6]

Whereas Bek requested Franklin's assistance—an example that many others in the Habsburg Monarchy would emulate—two other courtiers sought to offer gifts to Franklin. Paul Strattmann worked in the Court Library (*Hofbibliothek*) as a court censor when he wrote to Franklin offering a catalogue of French books.[7] His gift to Franklin was a token of esteem but also as an offer of service should Franklin need a librarian.[8] In 1786, Johann Melchior von Birkenstock, another member of the censorship committee and court councillor (*Hofrat*), gifted Franklin a copy of his work commemorating Frederick II of Prussia, which Franklin deemed worthy enough to acknowledge.[9] Importantly, Birkenstock shared with Franklin a deeply held sentiment for the United States. "I pray to God," Birkenstock informed Franklin, "that he will preserve for you for the glory of your country, for the consolation of all good people, a long succession of years, and that he will fill you with blessings reserved for the most worthy mortals." These were hardly empty words since Birkenstock asked Franklin to "accept these vows, Sir, as true and sincere."[10] Vowing to pray for the prosperity of the United States was a remarkable promise for a Viennese courtier to make, especially one who sat on the censorship committee within a monarchical state.

Such sentiments espoused by Birkenstock and Strattmann help explain the relatively lax censorship of Americana in the Habsburg lands during this period.[11] From mid-century onwards, censorship in the Habsburg Monarchy fell under the purview of a central committee consisting of religious officials, university elders, and several courtiers.[12] After Maria Theresa's death in 1780, her son Joseph II relaxed many of these efforts and allowed a flood of new domestic works to enter market.[13] From 1754 until the thaw of the 1780s, the committee maintained a running list of banned works in the *Catalogus librorum prohibitorum* (The catalogue of prohibited books), which mainly consisted of works critiquing the clergy, philosophical and literary works deemed too "radical," and, of course, pornography. In all, the committee banned 5,000 works in the period before Joseph II's sole accession and only a few hundred thereafter.[14] The vast majority were French and German works; English texts numbered just over a hundred by 1791.[15] During the Revolution, only seven works relating to America appeared on the censors' lists.[16] In 1776, three books received the "*damnatur*" (rejected) grade as retroactive bans on works of fiction which portrayed America in an adventurous light. Apart from a German translation of William Russel's *History of America*, the remaining texts pertained directly to the Revolution and included a German rendition of one of Samuel Adams's speeches.[17] No other revolutionary tract or American figure's works were banned in the Habsburg Monarchy until the 1790s. The reaction was the same in other regions such as the Austrian Netherlands and Habsburg Lombardy where censorship rates were lower and the Catholic Church determined efforts towards more religious and moral matters rather than political tracts.[18] The relatively lenient attitude of censorship officials towards Americana, combined with the fact most nobles could obtain outlawed works through various means, effectively rendered the imperial court and the Habsburg Monarchy completely permeable to the expansive literature surrounding the Revolution.[19]

Newspapers in the Habsburg Monarchy reported on American matters rather freely but when editors did fall foul to censorship due to the Revolution, they received support from the court nobility. The state-sponsored *Wienerisches Diarium* produced the highest amount of Americana in the Habsburg Monarchy out of twenty-four other newspapers and periodicals which discussed the Revolution.[20] From tumultuous Boston in 1774 to surrender at Yorktown in 1781, around 3,500 pages described revolutionary events in the *Diarium*.[21] In April 1779, its editors created a separate "American News" section.[22] Texts by American revolutionaries frequently appeared in German translation without any difficulty from censors. In fact, Thomas Jefferson's *Summary View of the Rights of British America* became the first such published text in late 1774.[23] There were some signs of self-censorship, however. Prior to 1776, for example, emigration to North America was a reoccurring theme in the *Diarium* but this topic halted abruptly from then until the end of the war.[24] When the Declaration of American Independence became known in Europe, most Habsburg newspapers exercised caution—with the exception of those in Lombardy and Tuscany—by omitting the charges against King George III and printing only the preamble and conclusion.[25] Other newspapers in the Habsburg lands showed clear signs of tampering. In one Hungarian newspaper, the editor apologised to his readers for the blank spaces about the Revolution in previous issues due to what he called the "High Authority."[26]

In December 1777, the *Wienerisches Diarium* incurred the same scrutiny after publishing an article that would become known in Vienna as the "American Catechism." The article outlined the radical devotion of the Revolution's adherents through a fictional interview with a mob of rebellious patriots in the form of a series of fictive questions and answers. The final exchange provided the most alarming refrain: "What shall pass if you should be defeated? Answer: We would set everything ablaze and kill ourselves, our women and children."[27] When Maria Theresa learned of this publication, she was incensed that such an article had been published and sought retribution against the editors.[28] However, one nobleman intervened to protect them from punishment. Count August von Seilern had been the Habsburg ambassador in London during the 1760s where he reported sympathetically about the colonists during the early disturbances with the British in North America.[29] By 1777 he had returned from London and was the Governor of Lower Austria (*Statthalter des Erzherzogtums Österreich unter der Enns*). He interceded in the case over the "American Cathecism" by insisting that the newspapers had not impinged upon monarchical supremacy by printing the text, but rather had merely sought to show the "fanaticism" in North America.[30] Seilern's reluctance to prosecute the editors reflected the general tolerance shown by courtiers towards the flood of Americana during the Revolution.

Across the Habsburg Monarchy, administrators shared similar sentiments. The head of the regional government in Lombardy, Count Johann Josef von Wilczek, convinced Franklin's Milanese friends to confer his "highest esteem" and sought to obtain an original English copy of the constitutions of the United States—this was after one of them had lent him a copy in French.[31] In the Austrian Netherlands, Count Joseph Nicolas Windischgrätz declared Franklin to be a worldwide inspiration.[32] He extolled Franklin's wartime actions, claiming he had done "so much good for [his] country [. . .] and for humanity."[33] In a giddier second letter, written in response to Franklin's simple receipt of the fifty copies of Windischgrätz's latest essay, he confessed his wish to meet Franklin, willing as he was to travel from Brussels to Paris in order to become the "happiest man" in the world if Franklin accepted.[34] Buoyed after their meeting in late April 1785, Windischgrätz wrote once more to reiterate his "eagerness" to fulfil any of Franklin's future "orders" either in the Austrian Netherlands or the Holy Roman Empire.[35]

Windischgrätz was the sort of aristocratic who enjoyed contact with famous minds like Franklin.[36] However, his interactions with Franklin were also somewhat more sincere than his interactions with other famous scholars. In addition to flattering words, Windischgrätz actively supported American activities by acting as a courier for American newspapers, which Franklin sent to Vienna.[37] But Windischgrätz was an erratic intellectual whose progressive views jarred with his contemporaries who thought him to be wild, vain, and an overly utopian thinker.[38] In a series of pamphlets published in the mid-to late 1780s, Windischgrätz dabbled in philosophical and political matters in sometimes meandering tracts. In one treatise, his *De l'âme, de l'intelligence et de la liberté de la volonté* (Of the soul, of intelligence, and of freedom of will), he merged his philosophical studies with Franklin's electrical theories, asserting that human intelligence was defined by an internal electricity.[39] By 1787, his mind had hardened towards the belief that government should not transgress natural rights of subjects.[40] Amid the revolutionary unrest in the Austrian Netherlands in the late 1780s, Windischgrätz advocated constitutional rights and defended these in radical pamphlets that "turned heads" and drew the ire of his friend, Emperor Joseph II.[41] The American Revolution was therefore a natural attraction for Windischgrätz given his intellectual leaning and his admiration of Franklin.

When in Vienna, Windischgrätz was part of a close coterie of influential courtiers thanks to his first wife, the Countess Maria Josepha Windischgrätz (née Erdödy) and her friends. The "society of the five dames" brought together prominent members of the court's aristocracy for almost daily informal gatherings starting in 1767.[42] As a close friend of the Windischgrätzes and fixed member of the group, Count Johann Philipp von Cobenzl noted how the meetings in the Viennese townhouses and country palaces revolved around sipping tea and chatting as "one of us read from an interesting work of some sort."[43] Discussions of the American Revolution featured in these chatty moments. Karl von Zinzendorf noted the oration of an American revolutionary text during one dinner party in 1785 with several of the dames in attendance.[44]

Yet despite the collective being composed of "political and religious radicals," it is doubtful that this coterie harboured much American support beyond perhaps those of the Windischgrätzes.[45] Although Princess Eleonore von Liechtenstein (née Oettingen-Spielberg) delighted in reading Voltaire and became an epitome of an enlightened woman at court, she mistrusted revolutionary movements.[46] For her, the American Revolution was simply a step too far as reflected in her distaste for the upheaval caused by the Revolution. During one meeting, Liechtenstein derided the official "sixth member" of the group whose idleness in trying to end the American Revolution caused her great frustration.[47] The "sixth member" was the emperor, who joined the group from 1769 onwards. At another point, Joseph's visit to the Dutch Republic in 1781 annoyed her further since she felt the visit was mistimed and could damage relations with the British who had just gone to war with the Dutch.[48]

Her preference for ending the American war came from her sister-in-law, another one of the dames, Princess Leopoldine von Liechtenstein (née von Sternberg), who was friends with Lady Juliana Penn, the daughter-in-law of Pennsylvania's founder William Penn. In a letter to Leopoldine, Lady Penn had explained the dire situation of the loyalist dynasty whose family estates had been confiscated by the patriots without compensation. Almost destitute, she appealed to the Liechtensteins for Joseph's intervention, and the duo tried to help. Given the criticism of the emperor's actions, Eleonore and Leopoldine likely knew that Joseph would be unable or unwilling to offer any assistance and so they hesitated until the end of the conflict when they asked an intermediary "in the most pressing way" for Franklin's intercession on behalf of the Penns.[49] Franklin of course ignored the request as he had Lady Penn's earlier direct appeal to him.[50] Though Lady Penn was not successful, her appeal increased the negative views of the American Revolution held by both Eleonore and Leopoldine Liechtenstein. Others within the group also disliked the American cause. At the prominent Burghausen salon, Countess Leopoldine von Kaunitz (née Oettingen-Spielberg) erupted into "a grand tirade against the Americans" when the emperor raised the subject.[51] Such an outburst greased the millwheels of gossip at court.

Apart from the dames, there were several prominent Anglophile salons in Vienna which harboured those more unsympathetic to the American cause. The houses of the Pergen and Thun families constituted this bulwark. Both households shared close ties to the British ambassadors serving in Vienna. Countess Philippine Gabriele von Pergen (née Groschlag) and Count Johann Anton von Pergen considered themselves intimate friends of Sir Robert Murray Keith. Count Pergen command excellent English and wrote extensively to Keith on personal matters when out of town.[52] The previous ambassador David Murry, then Viscount Stormont, occupied the same house as the Thun family on Minoritenplatz and fraternisations were so close that guests suspected an affair between Stormont and Countess Wilhelmine von Thun (née Uhlfeld). Years later, Keith relocated to the same residence.[53] Both households became renowned among British travellers for their hospitality and friendly dispositions towards Britain. The famed travel writer of his age Nathanial Wraxall waxed lyrical on their importance for such visitors to Vienna. "The houses of both [...] form the best resource for the English during their stay in this capital," he wrote.[54]

Count Karl von Zinzendorf, a frequent guest at the Pergen's whenever he was in town, noted the continual presence of English guests.[55] On one occasion, he happened to overhear Countess Pergen reassuring her visitors that there were "ten royalists for every one American" in Vienna.[56] At first, Countess Thun was broadly sympathetic to the Americans. "I am a Bostonian at heart," she wrote to one of her British friends in 1775, but bloodshed dampened her enthusiasm.[57] Both countesses played host to the centre of British life among Viennese courtiers.

There is no evidence of any anti-American sentiments among the wider court nobility apart from pro-British salons and the dames. The first explicitly anti-American propaganda in the Habsburg Monarchy circulated privately after the Napoleonic Wars when most aristocrats viewed all revolution negatively.[58] In fact, courtiers contested the condemnation of the American Revolution by the dames. In 1781, Zinzendorf noted a "dispute about the Americans" over a dinner hosted by the Liechtensteins.[59] He did not describe the argument in any great detail nor the positions of the attendees, leaving us to surmise that the likely pro-American guests were Gottfried van Swieten—Strattmann's boss at the Court Library—and Count Joseph Johann von Seilern, the son of Count Seilern who had defended the publication of the Declaration of American Independence.[60] Likely opposing them were the conservative-minded Bishop of Wiener Neustadt, Johann Heinrich von Kerens and the elderly Prince Heinrich von Auersperg, then aged eighty-four, who were close friends of the Liechtensteins and the British ambassador. In any case, the divides over America between the dames and their guests was enough to merit Zinzendorf's record.

Zinzendorf himself was certainly one of the most learned men in the Habsburg Monarchy about the American Revolution. A Saxon by birth but scion of an ancient Austrian family, Zinzendorf was the nephew of the Protestant evangelist, Count Nikolaus von Zinzendorf who had led the Moravian Herrnhuter to North America in the 1740s.[61] After studying in Jena and moving to Vienna, Karl von Zinzendorf embarked upon a series of state-sponsored commercial tours as a means to gather intelligence on the latest economic and administrative ideas.[62] Great Britain, as part of his tour, was where he gained his intimate knowledge of America. He met Benjamin Franklin in London, walked with William Robertson in Edinburgh, travelled the Highlands with Johan Murray, the fourth earl of Dunmore—before he became the royal governor of Virginia—and dined with Glasgow's infamous tobacco barons.[63] In a report prepared for the Viennese court, simply entitled his *Observations*, Zinzendorf devoted an entire section to the economic and legal arrangements of British North America.[64] Spanning nearly one hundred pages, Zinzendorf described how the colonial government operated in all twenty-six British-American colonies. He listed their major manufactured goods, detailed various colonial currencies, explained property rights, calculated the populations of each colony and their tax incomes, and provided a history of major cities from Boston to Charleston. As a result of his British soujourn, Zinzendorf became an unquestionable authority on the American colonies in the Habsburg Monarchy at the beginning of the Revolution.

Zinzendorf spent most of the American revolutionary years in Trieste where he served as governor between 1776 and 1782. He used his position to procure Americana in Trieste, where traders smuggled anything for a price. He developed a huge appetite for such literature, reading all he could about the Revolution. In 1778, for instance, he read Thomas Paine's *Common Sense*, John Dickinson's *Letters from a Farmer in Pennsylvania*, and the British radical Richard Price's *Observations on the Nature of Civil Liberty*.[65] Zinzendorf's interest persisted long after the war. In the 1790s, he read histories of the Revolution by Americans David Ramsay and Charles Stedman.[66] His personal contacts fleshed out the rest. In 1780, Zinzendorf heard first-hand accounts of the Ticonderoga campaign from English guests over a game of whist.[67] On another occasion, he met with a British veteran of the war.[68] Consuls and merchants became Zinzendorf's avid inform-ers of revolutionary news throughout the period.[69] During his frequent visits to the Vienna, Zinzendorf went out of his way to learn from others about the Revolution.[70] He sought out those more knowledgeable and exchanged texts on American topics.[71] As an inquisitive person, the American Revolution fascinated Zinzendorf throughout this period.

Imperial courtiers were well-informed about the Revolution and animated by its cause. In an age when courtly life and the governance of a nation were so closely linked, the personal opinions of administrators mattered a great deal. Positive reception of the American struggle enabled transparent encouragement among officials for Franklin and his Revolution. In terms of the censorship, the deeply held views of two committee members accounts to some degree for the negligible efforts to curb the flow of Americana during the Revolution. Count Seilern's defence of the *Wienerisches Diarium* reflected his more favourable dis-position towards the American colonies resulting from his earlier time as ambas-sador in London and his advocacy was strong enough to question his monarch's intentions. Zinzendorf's erudition about British North America influenced his later outlook on trade between Trieste and the United States. In short, absorp-tion of the American cause among courtiers influenced tangible aspects of the Habsburg reaction to the Revolution.

Impugning the American Influence at Court

For certain, a curiosity about the American Revolution pervaded the atmosphere at court in Vienna. The nobility was united by an interest in the progress of American affairs. During the revolutionary years, speculations abounded, and news of the latest victories were shared among all ranks of the nobility.[72] This in-cessant obsession of courtiers drove the British ambassador, intent on suppress-ing the issue, to utter despair. The desperation is almost tangible in Sir Robert Murray Keith's personal correspondence with a group of friendly civil servants in London known as "the Gang."[73] "I would give my best suit of gala clothes for the gift of a six months' fore-knowledge of your American affairs," he offered to one friend in the British admiralty.[74] To another he proposed fifty pistols in exchange for any news about the "refractory offspring in America."[75] Keith constantly bemoaned how he was "famished," "parched," "too little informed" about American events and implored his friends to become his "Cicerone in America," or his guide with "their echo to my attentive ear," or his "pilot to guide me into port."[76]

When his friends in London failed him, he often turned to others in the British diplomatic corps but without much success either.[77] The sudden death of his younger brother, Sir Basil Keith, Governor of Jamaica from 1773, left Keith bereft and without another avenue for information.[78] As a member of the Scottish aristocracy, however, Keith often played host to a number of young Scots on their Grand Tours of Europe and came to rely on these informal channels for American news. When the young Scottish aristocrat Henry Hay-Macdougal visited Vienna during the winter of 1776, for example, Keith received letters containing forwarded reports from relatives fighting in North America.[79] Resonant of Keith's desperate situation, Hay-Macdougal informed his father on multiple occasions how "We long much for good American News."[80]

Keith laid bare the reasoning behind his desperation in his personal letters. He sought to combat the "public clamour" for Americana at the Viennese court where, in his opinion, only the voices of "the noisy brawlers for licentious democracy" could be heard.[81] As early as March 1774, Keith bluntly pointed out the precariousness of the situation:

> Everybody here talks wildly about liberty, and electricity, *because they understand neither*; and I am shrewdly suspected to be a friend to monarchy and King George, and therefore to have seen everything that regards America and the Doctor [Franklin] with an eye of partiality. I shall fight, however, a rare battle, under your banner; only give me now and then a few material[s] to dumbfounder my noisy opponents.[82]

Keith clearly felt that an information war was being waged in Vienna between him and those advocating for the Americans. He also wanted to rehabilitate the British standing against "the absurdities with which every paper has been filled" and to "stem with honour the torrent of falsehood and presumption."[83] Following talk of desertions in the British army in North America, Keith was relieved to learn from friends that this was just hearsay and he used this news "to knock half a dozen lies on the head."[84]

Keith sensed, however, that he was fighting a losing battle such was the interest and pro-American feeling among courtiers.[85] Compounding his situation was the increasingly bad turn of events as Britain slowly but surely lost control of the American colonies. Keith could not conceal British defeats from Viennese courtiers. One of Keith's young Scottish visitors commented in a letter to his mother upon learning of the recent naval defeats and of the British surrender after the Siege of Yorktown,

> You can't conceive how our poor country is now despised, even by those who acknowledge the Great Power, Patriotism, and Courage of Great Britain. They ask, have you lost your Senses that you don't procure better commanders, and punish those who behave ill. A Foreigner asks an Englishman [here]: where are all your sailors who distinguished themselves in the last war? Your Hawke, your Boscawen, your Howe, your Keppel, your Gilchrist, your Elliot etc. etc. Those that never sought conquering and who never turned their back to their enemies. The Englishman with silent sorrow shakes his head.[86]

"Silent sorrow" summed up the feeling of shame that clouded Keith's status in Vienna as a result of the war. Such was the bitterness of loss that another of Keith's Scottish guests wrote home to the Highlands towards the end of the war, "I am almost ashamed to wear the English uniform; the taking of Minorca surprises everybody here and I suppose the whole world too."[87] By 1780, the British chances at victory seemed so remote that Keith led his delegation and friends to a chapel in St. Stephen's Cathedral to pray for England.[88]

Among the foreign diplomatic corps at the Viennese court, Keith was most certainly outnumbered by pro-American supporters. He remarked how news of British defeats made it "hard to hold my head as high as I shall ever wish to hold it," especially among the "score of foreign ministers who [...] look upon the faithless Bourbons as the very lords of the ascendant."[89] Indeed, the French delegation acted as a bastion of support for the Americans in Vienna. Prior to 1778 when France openly took part in the conflict, they ensured Franklin had open channels of communication with Vienna.[90] In transporting back and forth letters from his friends, the chief secretary in one instance slipped in his own letter to Franklin, offering him another means of conveyance and supporting the application of the delegation's courier who wished to go fight for the United States.[91] At the same time, another secretary offered to sell Franklin his recipe for improved gunpowder, something which he felt would secure patriot victory.[92] Cardinal Louis de Rohan, the French ambassador from 1772 to 1774, offered one of Franklin's friends in Vienna the use of his palace in Paris should he not have means to visit Franklin.[93] These supportive acts preceded the later hosting and direction of the first American envoy to the court of Vienna by French representatives.

Keith's only hope was the attitude of the State Chancellor (*Staatskanzler*), Prince Wenzel Anton von Kaunitz-Rietberg. As his biographer points out, "no subsequent foreign minister, including Metternich, wielded the kind of domestic influence that Kaunitz did."[94] Kaunitz was the gatekeeper for international affairs. He decided what issues to bring to the monarchs' attention and formulated his own articulations before doing so. It is for this reason that Kaunitz has been touted as a "de facto third head of state."[95] Although Kaunitz was a noted fan of enlightened thinkers and many historians have pointed to his interest in the French philosophes and patronage of the arts, there is no evidence that he held any interest in American ideals.[96] In all his memoranda and discussions on American-related events, Kaunitz adopted an opinion heavily defined by geopolitical considerations and a marked caution towards the upheavals caused by rebellion against British monarchical authority. Containment appears to be the byword for his initial reaction. At no other point was Kaunitz clearer about his fears of democratic revolution than in his remarks on first reading the Declaration of American Independence in the Viennese newspapers. He believed it to contain "extraordinary sections which may cause the spirit of rebellion to spread like a plague."[97] For Kaunitz, the anti-monarchical nature of the Revolution was the seemingly greater danger to ward against.

None of his official or personal writings with the Habsburg monarchs strays from this guarded approach.[98] Much has been made of the terms "insurgents" and "rebels" that Kaunitz used to describe Americans in his despatches to Habsburg diplomats, yet these descriptions do not reveal any great insights into his views on their Revolution since such terms were commonplace among European officials.[99] What is more revealing is that Kaunitz held on to this terminology longer than other officials within the Habsburg administration, perhaps demonstrating that his subtle bias against the Revolution persisted longer than those of his contemporaries.[100] When confronted with the news of Franklin's arrival in Paris amid rumours of an intended alliance, Kaunitz regarded Franklin's intentions as "foolish" if the rumours were true.[101] Kaunitz certainly expressed his belief that any American victory would be "hard to expect" but the effects of one should be prepared for either way.[102] This black-and-white logic surrounding American events is the major characteristic of Kaunitz's reaction to the Revolution.[103] In spite of his dominance over the State Chancellery, Kaunitz's logic was only advisory in nature, as the Habsburg monarchs remained the sole arbiters of executive authority and indeed had rather different ideas.

The Imperial Family and the American Revolution

In considering the position of the foreign monarchs, historians have tended to assume a natural alignment against the Americans since a revolution against the British crown transgressed the rights of rulers. This assumption is only half correct in the Habsburg case. Not all members of the Habsburg dynasty shared a negative outlook on American events. They were equally affected by the same curiosity which intrigued the Viennese court at large.

When the Continental Congress proclaimed independence in 1776, Maria Theresa had ruled the Habsburg Monarchy for just over thirty-five years. Her early reign endured a baptism of fire during the War of Austrian Succession and the failure to reverse territorial losses in the Seven Years' War. She lost all appetite for international conflict and dedicated the remaining years of her reign to securing peace and stability for her realm. It was within this context that the sixty-year-old monarch received the unwelcome news of revolution across the Atlantic. Her initial reaction chimed with Kaunitz: the American Revolution was something to be ended and shielded against in the meantime. When an article known as the "American Catechism"—advancing the American justifications for the war—appeared alongside a translation of the Declaration of American Independence in the *Wienerisches Diarium*, her response centred on stifling public awareness in case it should "breed incivility" within her realms.[104] Maria Theresa was equally fearful about the international fallout of the Revolution. She feared it would lead the whole of Europe to war. "The war in America," she fretted to her daughter Marie Antoinette, queen of France, "may very easily cause a conflagration where I could be driven against my will, especially with our despicable neighbour Prussia."[105] Her fears seemed borne less out of prediction than her memory of the Seven Years' War when conflict in North America had boiled over into a war in continental Europe.

Maria Theresa remained highly vigilant about American events due in part to her paranoia over its consequences. Among the people of the Habsburg court, she may have indeed been the most informed about the actual events of war thanks to her network of informants, which she cultivated up to her death in November 1780. Aside from the steady stream of information from Kaunitz's ministry, she also relied on other court officials for news from America, who supplied to her "reflexions upon the present affaires of the world which she could not so well be informed of by her own ministers."[106] Franklin, by way of his Habsburg correspondents, sensed a way to influence the imperial court. On December 29, 1777, the first of many long reports Franklin penned made its way into the hands of

FIGURE 3. Portrait of Maria Theresa as a widow (ca. 1767)

Maria Theresa's secretary, Baron Karl Joseph von Pichler, which summarised Franklin's views on the current state of the war.[107] Franklin showed a clear determination to influence Maria Theresa towards a more favourable outlook on the Americans. His reports emphasised atrocities committed by the British, the losses suffered by mistreated Hessian recruits, and the significance of American victory at Saratoga. One line spoke directly to her as a sovereign:

> If America without England can become formidable, what would become of England combined again with America? Those who know the natural insolence of the British Nation will think that the common interest of Europe is to keep these two nations separate.[108]

These lines were aimed at coaxing Maria Theresa's support for American independence by reminding her of Britain's propensity for expansion and the dangers of American defeat. Maria Theresa left no written reaction to these texts, but she expressed gratitude to the court officials for supplying her with these informal updates, which demonstrates her curiosity to learn about the Revolution.

When Maria Theresa passed away in late 1780, this dissemination campaign continued with her son Joseph II who from then on ruled as the sole sovereign of the Habsburg Monarchy. He received a French translation of Franklin's views in

1782, which was also read aloud to Joseph's private chamberlain, Count Karl von Hatzfeld—such was the interest at the court.[109] It was not the first time Joseph had received and read such material. In August 1782, a similar set of Franklin's reflections arrived, which the emperor kept personally.[110] Franklin's direct link into the Habsburg court and by extension the royal family was unusual for European courts. In France, American envoys waited on invitations to speak with the king, whereas in Vienna, their desired words could be translated and delivered personally to the Habsburg monarch.

When Joseph II travelled to Paris to visit his sister Marie Antoinette in 1777, two myths regarding him and the American Revolution were born. Only one can be proven. In advance of his journey, Joseph made known the sort of people he wished to meet in the French capital, Franklin included.[111] There was one stumbling block, however. Joseph could not openly invite Franklin to an audience nor could he, as an imperial ruler, pay a visit to a rebellious commoner. Although the meeting between the American revolutionary and the "revolutionary emperor" was intended to be a meeting of enlightened minds, they could not escape the political ramifications if such a meeting were to take place.[112] Yet Joseph seemed determined to meet with Franklin. Intent on finding a solution, Habsburg ministers arranged for an intermediary to host the meeting in an unofficial capacity. They chose Raimondo Niccoli, the head of the Tuscan delegation in Paris and a supportive figure to the Americans, since his service to the emperor's brother and his affinity with Franklin would endear him to both sides.[113]

On Monday, May 26, 1777, Franklin received an invitation to drink hot chocolate at the Hotel de Mirabeau two days later with Niccoli, a Count Falkenstein—Joseph's customary travelling alias—and two Frenchmen.[114] Franklin had all the reason to accept. It was a great opportunity to press the claims of the Americans directly to one of Europe's great powers and to the head of the Holy Roman Empire, the source of German mercenaries for the British. Moreover, the personal admiration between these two men went both ways. Franklin had noted the arrival of the "very industrious" emperor a few weeks earlier.[115] He also later commented that "I respect very much the Character of that Monarch, and think that if I were one of his Subjects he would find me a good One."[116] Franklin and Joseph were to be disappointed, however. Franklin recollected the event on the back of his invitation immediately after the arranged meeting: "The Emperor did not appear, and the Abbé [Niccoli] since tells me that the Number of other persons who occasionally visited him that morning [. . .] prevented his coming [. . . though] at twelve he came but I was gone."[117] As a result Franklin and Joseph never actually met in person and one of the greatest encounters of the enlightenment, perhaps on par with the meeting of Johann Sebastian Bach and Frederick II of Prussia, vanished.

Niccoli obscured the truth from Franklin by telling him a "number of other persons" had prevented Joseph's attendance. The "other persons" were in fact the British delegation in Paris. The British ambassador knew about the meeting and worked to thwart it. He and his secretaries descended upon Joseph that morning and stalled him long enough to prevent him meeting with Franklin.[118] In spite of their endeavours, the British did not prevent one of the emperor's subordinates from attending the meeting. Count Johann Philipp von Cobenzl—the same count who had attended meetings with the dames—recorded in his diary how he enjoyed his time at Count Niccoli's and his "appointment with Doctor Franklin."[119] No further contact came between the two parties during the emperor's stay, however. News of the British subterfuge eventually spread and even soon found its way back to Vienna. "I know he [Joseph] wished to have a discourse with you," one courtier later mourned, "and he should be sorry some management for England had prevented him to instruct himself in the company of a philosopher."[120] Joseph's plan to meet Franklin may have been sabotaged, but his high regard for Franklin still became widely known.

Underhand British actions could not prevent the rumours among French courtiers that Franklin had in fact met Joseph. In 1787, the Scottish statistician and architect William Playfair published a pamphlet titled *Joseph and Benjamin – A Conversation*, which he claimed was based upon "a French manuscript."[121] Whether or not such a French manuscript existed is unknown.[122] Playfair's work was a rich fictional dialogue in which the two men discuss human nature, economic theory, and exchange good humour between them. His version of the encounter was an idealised form of enlightened interaction between men renowned for their progressive inclinations. Playfair's publication cemented the ambiguity of the meeting in the public mindset despite the poor reviews it received in London.[123] In the fictional conversation, the character of Joseph is supportive of Franklin's revolutionary efforts and so the first myth was born.

The second myth arose from one of the many dinners during Joseph's stay in Paris. A guest at one reportedly asked him whether he supported the actions of the American patriots. Joseph cryptically replied something along the lines of "I am a royalist by trade." This remark became arguably Joseph's most well-known utterance on the American Revolution. It was included in numerous contemporary publications but without a credible source.[124] Since then this quotation has appeared frequently, most notably in American literature.[125] There is no single verifiable trace of whether Joseph said this or not. It is likely this phrase was invented. As the Habsburg ambassador commented to Maria Theresa a few months after Joseph's departure, "The public continues to be preoccupied with the details of the emperor's journey; they amuse themselves by composing a thousand anecdotes that I do not believe are genuine."[126] Moreover, it was simply not in keeping with the rest of his visit where everything was carefully choreographed and even the meeting with Franklin was conducted under the strictest measures to avoid any signs of partiality. In all likelihood, Joseph kept his opinions on such matters close to his chest.

Joseph expressed his true feelings on the American Revolution with individuals closer to him. In his personal correspondence with his ambassador in London, Count Ludovico Barbiano di Belgiojoso, Joseph revealed an increasing disdain for British actions in the American Revolution. He disagreed with what he perceived to be Belgiojoso's "slight Anglomania" considering the disastrous campaigns in North America. "You cannot deny," he argued to Belgiojoso, "that it would be impossible to make worse all the affairs of England, that is politically and militarily, from the last years."[127] In subsequent letters, Joseph saw the consequences of the Revolution as overwhelmingly negative for Britain. "The fruits of this disorder," he warned, "where there is neither love of country, nor of the state, nor of the sovereign, will be felt for a long time."[128] This sorrow for the effects of the Revolution was the closest Joseph came to condemning it. However, he did not outright denounce the Americans for causing such chaos. They appeared in his letters as a rather more innocent by-product of British misrule than active instigators—his descriptions mimicking a line espoused by Franklin in the reports that made its way to Joseph at court. In a personal letter to his brother, Joseph voiced his belief in British comeuppance after receiving the "happy" news from Belgiojoso that the famous British Admiral Rodney had been roundly defeated by French forces. "I am not as English as they believe," he confided to him, "nor as they want me to be."[129]

In his private correspondence with the Russian Empress Catherine II, Joseph went a step further. He expressed pity for the "poor Americans" who he felt had been beaten, bankrupted and sat "like frightened hens, waiting for someone to shoot them."[130] "Poor Americans" was a phrase he used often to Catherine even as he described their forces as "superior" and noted that British victory was impossible.[131] In the early 1780s, "Americans" was not yet a fully established term within the Habsburg administrative vocabulary. Kaunitz and others still used the pejoratives "rebels" and "insurgents" but Joseph adopted the newer demonym, perhaps revealing a tacit—or willing—acceptance of their political independence.

FIGURE 4. The brothers Emperor Joseph II and Grand Duke
Pietro Leopoldo of Tuscany by Pompeo Batoni

Joseph's view on the Revolution evolved over the course of the war from an initial interest to be informed like his mother, to wishing to meet with Franklin despite the political consequences, to a natural aversion towards it brought on by the discord created in Britain and, finally, to the acceptance that the United States of America would be a sovereign nation. Throughout it all, Joseph, along with his ministers, struggled to maintain a neutral balance. This was the reason why he came under fire from the dames for not acting to end the war just as the British carefully monitored his actions for sympathising with the Americans. Caught in the middle of what he called a "big and furious game," Joseph's true feelings towards the Revolution centred on frustration with an event not of his design and outside of his control. It was the price to pay for being "a royalist by trade."[132]

The same cannot be said for Joseph's younger brother. As the Grand Duke of Tuscany, Pietro Leopoldo occupied an easier position.[133] The Revolution still affected his grand duchy in a number of ways, however. Commercial ties between the Tuscan ports and the New England fisheries had existed for decades and such connections as well as the lure of further wealth forced the Grand Duke to act sooner on the issue than his brother. Hence Pietro Leopoldo developed an intense interest in the American Revolution, its developments, and ideas. He corresponded with the Tuscan schemer Filippo Mazzei in order to find out more and, knowing the Tuscan delegation in Paris had substantial inroads with the American commissioners, sought to gather further information from them.[134] He received translations of American documents and subscribed to the partisan *Affaires d'Angleterre et d'Amérique* (English and American affairs), which Franklin published with French collaborators.[135] When Pietro Leopoldo temporarily relocated to Vienna in 1778 to deputise for his brother and mother during the War of the Bavarian Succession, he continued this subscription and had the American propaganda delivered directly to the imperial residence at the Hofburg.[136]

In March 1779, Pietro Leopoldo left Vienna for Florence in a disgruntled mood. Over the course of his deputyship, he felt horrified at the running of the Monarchy: finances were poor; civil servants waged interdepartmental war, radicals agitated for religious reform, Hungarians decried new taxation, foreign alliances were either weakened or faltering, and, worst of all, the emperor only uttered "frightful, despotic statements."[137] Upon his return to Florence, he set about a new project to redefine the political order between subjects and sovereign in Tuscany. In his *Primo distesto ed idee sopra la formazione degli stati nuova costituzione pubblica* (First draft and ideas on the formation of states and the new public constitution), he planned to relinquish absolute power in favour of popular consent.[138] Such ideas, he argued, were more in line with the modern ideals of French philosophers, whom he deeply admired.[139] Pietro Leopoldo's new constitutional ambitions owed a share of influence to American thinkers, too. In one section, Pietro Leopoldo declared every Tuscan had "an equal right to happiness, well-being, security and property."[140] The familiar-sounding line is unequivocally American. Tuscan newspapers had published complete translations of the Declaration of American Independence years earlier with the immortal phrase, "life, liberty, and the pursuit of happiness."[141] But another American declaration might have been his inspiration; in June 1776, the Virginia Convention adopted George Mason's Declaration of Rights which also proclaimed the rights to "life and liberty, [. . .] property, and pursuing and obtaining happiness and safety."[142]

Pietro Leopoldo's new plans contained many echoes of the Virginian Declaration of Rights yet it was Pennsylvania's constitution of 1776 which provided him with concrete ideas about how best to enact more enlightened government.[143] He studied a French translation of the Pennsylvanian constitution intently, producing a handwritten copy and his own ten-page *Observations*.[144] Pietro Leopoldo's notes were his gut-reactions to the ideas he encountered in the American text, offering a fascinating insight into a Habsburg archduke's first-hand take on the radical democratic experiments unfolding across the Atlantic. His *Observations* opened with a bold declaration of his own admiration for American political ideas: "What I ask is that, in order to make a good [legal] code in all states, even in monarchies, one begins with the principle posed by the Americans, the principle of equality."[145] Pietro Leopoldo saw this core American value as the basis for any good form of government; "political equality," he later noted, "is essential to the democratic order [. . .] there should be no exception for anyone."[146] In his view, the safeguarding of this equality clearly existed in Pennsylvania's constitution through innovations such as limited terms and the rotation of positions, which Pietro Leopoldo felt would eradicate any abuses of power.

For the next three years, the Grand Duke toiled away on his constitutional project, swapping ideas and drafts with his chief minister Francesco Maria Gianni.[147] Concerning the extension of what Pietro Leopoldo termed peoples' "sacrosanct natural rights"—another allusion to "unalienable rights" in the Declaration of American Independence—and Pietro Leopoldo's calls for wider democratic participation, Gianni frequently dissented. Gianni saw the Tuscan people as unfit for democratic duty. The notorious Medici family had ruled Tuscany for the better part of three centuries before the Habsburgs took control in 1737; such a legacy, Gianni claimed, had corrupted the Tuscan people beyond recognition. They could not be entrusted to act for the greater good.[148] Pietro Leopoldo might have agreed with him. In an earlier study of his Tuscan holdings, the Grand Duke acknowledged that his people possessed a "certain shrewdness" or "deception" and were "always divided amongst themselves."[149] In his *Observations*, Pietro Leopoldo had already conceded, "When one understands the human heart, one sees how difficult it is to sustain governments at a certain degree of perfection. It is men who govern and [for perfect government] it would be necessary that the leaders be above man, that they be angels."[150] As much as Pietro Leopoldo endeavoured to endow his subjects with greater rights, his constitutional project stagnated. The bout of intense collaboration with Gianni starting in 1779 gave way to long periods of apathy throughout the 1780s.[151] Despite the immensity of his reform achievements in Tuscany, Pietro Leopoldo's constitutional ideas remained in draft form.[152] Notwithstanding, for a brief time during the American Revolution, a Habsburg ruler seriously contemplated its ideas and sought to implement them in his own lands.

Conclusion

If we are to understand the magnitude of the American Revolution, we must be able to comprehend its totality. The imperial court at Vienna, far removed from the Atlantic coastline, was not impervious to American revolutionary sentiments. Courtiers expressed a large degree of fascination for the goings-on in North America. The ideals they encountered, the gossip it produced, even the disagreements it provoked, set the imperial court abuzz. Much to the despair of the British ambassador in Vienna, there was a positive attitude towards American victories and little by way of counter-revolutionary rhetoric. There is little evidence to show that the Viennese court was a divided society over the Revolution and much to show that it was generally supportive. Noblemen such as Seilern, Wilczek, and Windischgrätz and administrators such as Bek and Birkenstock looked favourably upon the success of the patriots. Zinzendorf, one of the most knowledgeable bureaucrats, devoured whatever information he could come across regarding the Revolution.

Franklin gained unrivalled access to the monarchs unlike anywhere else in Europe. The imperial family were awash with information about the American Revolution: Maria Theresa read tailor-made reports by Franklin whereas Joseph sought to meet the latter for himself whilst his brother Pietro Leopoldo mused upon the Revolution's principles. It can be of no surprise to anyone that when the first American representative arrived in Vienna in May 1778, he exclaimed how "some here are warm for the part of America." The cultural phenomenon of the American Revolution, its spectacle and its influence, forces us to recognise the magnitude of its reach—even in a place we might assume to be too remote and within circles previously assumed to be too anti-revolutionary.

CHAPTER THREE

"Angels of the New Republic"

The American Revolutionary Influence in the Habsburg Lands,
1776–1789

I N THE ARKADENHOF, the central courtyard of the University of Vienna, a gallery of pillared busts entreats the visitor. Along the row of marbled figures and underneath the Tuscan-sloped arches of amaranth pink and almond yellow stands a scientist with a smirk. *"JOH INGEN - HOUSZ 1730 - 1799 ARCHIATER CAESAREVS 1768 - 1799 QVA RATIONE PLANTAE ALANTVR PRIMVS PERSPEXIT"*—"Jan Ingenhousz (1730 1799), Court Physician (1768–1799), Discoverer of Photosynthesis." An ordinary scientist for those who happen to notice his visage as they stroll through the hallowed hallways. Ingenhousz was not a conventional character, however. Neither an alumnus nor ever a full member of the university, nor even an Austrian for that matter, Ingenhousz's inclusion in the Viennese Valhalla came about due to the determination of his first biographer, the botany professor Julius Wiesner. Erected in 1905, the artistic rendering of Ingenhousz arrived in time for Wiesner's organisation of the second International Botanic Conference which took place in Vienna that year.[1] As cognizant as Wiesner and other biographers have been of Ingenhousz's discovery of photosynthesis and of his contemporary celebrity, his role in bringing the American Revolution to Vienna has gone unnoticed. He was Franklin's contact at the imperial court. He was the disseminator of American propaganda to Maria Theresa and Joseph II. He explained the American Revolution to people like Zinzendorf. Ingenhousz was the great partisan of the revolutionary cause in the Habsburg Monarchy. His unfettered access to the court allowed him to be the spokesman for the patriots, the defender of Franklin, and the focal point for others interested in the revolutionary turmoil across the Atlantic. There is still space for such a recognition on the plinth.

FIGURE 5. The memorial bust of the great partisan of the American cause, Dr. Jan Ingenhousz in the central courtyard of the University of Vienna

The American Revolution became a diplomatic conundrum and a commercial opportunity for the Habsburg Monarchy, but it remained throughout its course a cultural phenomenon. Contemporary observers and historians alike have noted the Revolution's intellectual and cultural impact across Europe.[2] Yet their accounts neither acknowledge the immediate impact of the Revolution on the Habsburg lands nor the breadth of its effects. The effects of the Revolution simmered before they burned. The American precedent inspired the United States of Belgium in the Austrian Netherlands in the late 1780s as well as the Revolutions of 1848. Although prominent examples, these instances were not the first symptoms of American revolutionary influence in the Habsburg Monarchy. Instead, individuals in the Habsburg lands reacted positively and vehemently to the unfolding events transpiring across the Atlantic. Observers of the Revolution across the Habsburg lands felt compelled to act; some to promote the revolutionary goals, other sought to enlist for the cause, and many wished for the Revolution to succeed. Events begot emotions which in turn produced actions. We have already seen how one family, the Schusters of Vienna, named their child in honour of patriot revolutionaries. Across the Habsburg Monarchy, individuals responded positively to the struggle against British rule in the thirteen colonies. This positivity signals a need for the wider acknowledgement of the influence and impact of the American Revolution in Europe.

The Franklin Factor

Benjamin Franklin was undoubtedly the popular face of the American Revolution in Europe. For people across the Habsburg this famous scientist-turned-revolutionary embodied the spirit of the American cause. The hundreds of surviving letters from Franklin's correspondents across the length and breadth of the Habsburg Monarchy are testament to the enduring appeal of Franklin and the Revolution he represented in the minds of many Habsburg inhabitants. His correspondence yet again provides a useful barometer for American interest in the Habsburg Monarchy. In the words of one historian, "the number of Franklin correspondents from that area is amazing." "They confirm," he added, "the impression that pro-American sympathies were widespread in this area," especially in Vienna, which he also surmised "was much better informed about American events than the court of the Prussian king."[3] Indeed, the number of existent Franklin correspondents from the Habsburg Monarchy outnumbers Prussian correspondents by almost five to one.[4]

Franklin received at least 258 letters from 97 individuals who either resided in or were natural-born subjects of the Habsburg Monarchy between 1775 and 1789.[5] Notorious for never keeping up with his mail, Franklin sent a total of forty-nine letters back to sixteen individuals. Franklin's letter exchange with Habsburg residents and subjects amounted to almost two percent of his total (incoming and outgoing) correspondence.[6] No other American corresponded with as many individuals from the Habsburg lands during this period, reflecting Franklin's overwhelming centrality in the Habsburg interest for the American Revolution. His correspondents came from all corners of the monarchy and beyond; from Lemberg (nowadays Lviv in the Ukraine) to Linz. At one point or another, Franklin received supportive messages from every province of the Habsburg lands.

Professional interests played a large role in determining who chose to write to Franklin. Intellectuals, scientists, and men of letters were pivotal in crafting the first positive views of Franklin and his later participation in the Revolution. Many had met Franklin personally. Professor František Antonín Steinský was a gifted polymath and professor of auxiliary historical sciences at the Charles University in Prague.[7] He detoured to Paris during his European tour in 1780 to explicitly meet with Franklin, whom he admired and had sign his autograph book. A cordial friendship developed between them that continued after

FIGURE 6. Benjamin Franklin's arrival at Versailles by an
unknown engraver (ca. 1778)

Steinský's return to Prague, where he functioned as Franklin's promoter among
the Bohemian intelligentsia.[8] The two kept each other informed of scientific
developments in North America and Central Europe, exchanged books, and
Steinský gifted Franklin's works to other Habsburg scientists.[9] In 1789, Steinský
became one of the first Habsburg subjects elected to the American Philosophical
Society at Franklin's behest.[10]

In Milan, Marsilio Landriani helped to popularise Franklin's scientific reputation. Landriani endorsed the advantages of Franklin's famed electrical conductors. In his *Dell'utilità dei conduttori elettrici* (On the utility of electrical
conductors) (1784), he praised the "immortal" Franklin's invention and referred
to the lightning rod as the "Franklinian bar."[11] At the same time, the director of
the Oriental Academy in Vienna, Johann von Gott Nekrep, returned from visiting Franklin in Paris and lauded him among colleagues. "Vienna," he informed
Franklin, "is more than ever desirous to see so sage and so able a Statesman, and
so a philosopher."[12]

Franklin's scientific fame had secured him an admiring audience long before 1776, but his perceived support of the Revolution followed by his arrival in
Paris as American ambassador made him the Revolution's tangible contact for
many Europeans. Military personnel consistently approached Franklin, both
in person and in writing, in order to offer their services for the young republic.
In total, twenty-one people from the Habsburg lands offered Franklin military

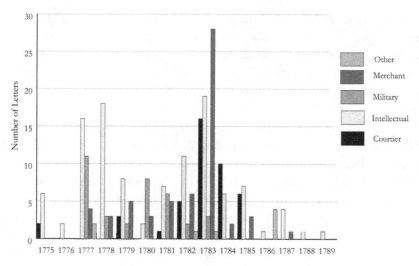

CHART I. Letters received by Franklin from the Habsburg
Monarchy, by background, 1775–1789.

service. Applications came from across Europe, however, not just the Habsburg
Monarchy. Many did so out of desire for employment, especially during periods
of peacetime in Europe. In the chart above, it is possible to see the correlation
between Habsburg military approaches to Franklin and the times of war. When
forces were mobilised for the War of the Bavarian Succession between Prussia and the Habsburgs in 1778, military solicitations to Franklin dropped but
picked up again in the final two years of combat in North America. After hostilities ceased in 1783, nobody with a military connection wrote to him from the
Habsburg lands. A majority of the offers came from officers, but more ordinary
soldiers also wrote to Franklin.[13]

Several soldiers were sincerely inspired by the revolutionary cause. Mihály
Kováts de Fabriczy was a Hungarian nobleman and highly decorated soldier who
found his own way to North America in 1777. In a letter to Franklin, he shared
his motivation for doing so:

I now am here of my own free will, having taken all the horrible and trouble
of this journey, and I am willing to sacrifice myself wholly and faithfully as
is to be expected of an honest soldier facing the hazards and great dangers
of the war, to the detriment of Joseph [II] as well as for the freedom of your
great Congress.[14]

Similar sentiments can be found in other letters to Franklin. Two cavalry officers stationed in Babarc near Mohács in southern Hungary offered to desert for

America. "Born in the Empire," they wrote, "where we still breathe some Freedom, and [are] burning with the Desire to spend our Days in a Country where Freedom will make so many happy." In other words, they applied for service out of ideological concerns.[15] This zeal was widespread among Habsburg officers. Count Franz Leopold Barbo von Waxenstein in Vidéz, Slovenia, described himself as "burning with a noble desire to serve [Franklin's] country and find glory or death" and Captain Hippolytus Verité, commander of the Hungarian engineers stationed at Olomouc, Moravia, so desired "to serve the illustrious Republic" that he planned to quit his Habsburg service after twenty-six years and relocate his family in order to demonstrate his commitment.[16] Verité sensed the wider trend of Habsburg soldiers offering themselves to the Americans and felt the need to distinguish himself among the applicants. "I would ask you not to confuse me with the many Austrian officers," he begged of Franklin, "since it is not the necessity that forces me to seek the services of the United American Colonies [. . .] but only my inclination which makes me seek this change."[17] Throughout the War of American Independence, the desire to fight on behalf of the revolutionary cause was a common sentiment among officers in the Habsburg lands.

Others sought to aid the American cause in different ways. Many felt the need to share their linguistic capabilities. The Viennese physician Dr. Jakob Oberleithner offered his medical talents to Franklin in (somewhat patchy) Latin and asserted his useful proficiency in French and "Slavic Bohemian."[18] The radical author and former court secretary (*Hofsekretär*) to Maria Theresa, Franz Rudolf von Großing, professed his love for America which drove him to seek a secretarial role in America given his "thorough knowledge" of Latin, Italian, French, German, Hungarian, English, Spanish, and "Prussian."[19] Count Friedrich August von Grävenitz was an Aulic Councillor (*Reichshofrat*) in Vienna, who, apparently as one of eighteen children in a large aristocratic family, informed Franklin of his desire to retire to the United States "to acquire a small estate in either Georgia, the Carolinas, or Virginia." With no shred of humility, Grävenitz insisted the United States, as a new country, would need such "accomplished" men.[20]

There were also those who sought to gain from the American Revolution. Merchants were the most obvious collective seeking to exploit revolutionary upheaval to their benefit. Some of them wrote on behalf of their own mercantile houses—like those of *Veuve d'Aubremé &Fils*, *de Vinck & Co.*, and *Salucci & Fils*—whilst some represented consortiums of merchants such as Jean-Guild Wets in Bruges who represented a group of forty Flemish merchants.[21] These mercantile letters to Franklin were often tinged with the sense of uncertainty and their desperate need to obtain more information in order to begin transatlantic trade. Such was the case when Aegidius Dujardin wrote from Ghent in 1778 as one of the first merchants seeking Franklin's help with forging these new transatlantic ties.[22] The majority of Franklin's mercantile correspondents in the Habsburg lands contacted him in 1783 when merchants desired to open and retain trading links to the United States now that peace had been declared. Even though merchants pursued profit more than passion, their interest in the United States as a trading destination greatly affected the overall response of the Habsburgs towards the American Revolution. It will become clear in later chapters just how deep this mercantile vein ran in the formation of Habsburg policy towards the United States.

For now, Franklin's epistolary connections represents the wealth of reactions among various inhabitants across the Habsburg Monarchy. These individuals overwhelmingly looked favourably upon his character and the Revolution he epitomised. For many, the Revolution signified opportunity, progress, or a cause to honour and defend. From Vienna to Vidéz, Brussels to Babarc the American Revolution was not held in contempt but rather praised and supported in the hands and minds of various individuals from a variety of different backgrounds. Their surviving testimony in their letters to Franklin reflects a sympathetic groundswell for the principles of the American Revolution long before the revolutionary turbulence of the 1790s. In the Age of Revolutions, the Habsburg Monarchy was not a land of latecomers but a land of engaged, observant, and even sympathetic inhabitants.

The Making of a Partisan: Jan Ingenhousz

Jan Ingenhousz was Franklin's chief correspondent in the Habsburg Monarchy. He received over half of Franklin's total replies and was Franklin's most prolific correspondent, representing nearly one-quarter of Franklin's Habsburg mail. The two men shared a close friendship which began in London during the 1760s when they met through common scientific interests and their acquaintance Sir John Pringle. In 1768, Ingenhousz left London for Vienna, where he successfully inoculated the imperial family and became the court physician to Maria Theresa. Despite separation, Franklin and Ingenhousz maintained a correspondence lasting from at least 1773 until 1788. Ingenhousz was cognizant of the great value of his connection with Franklin. Throughout the War of American Independence, Ingenhousz took great pains to ensure that this correspondence continued. He sent two copies of his earliest letters to Franklin—one via New York and one via

St. Eustatius—in the hope of reaching him in Philadelphia.[23] He relied upon the Parisian bankers *Tourton & Baur* to safely transmit letters to Franklin following his return to Europe in 1777. Often Ingenhousz concealed his letters in sealed, unaddressed envelopes which the bankers recognised. He reminded Franklin numerous times of the necessity of such clandestine actions and warned him not to trust servants with their mail as they "are too often unfaithful and paid by the police."[24] By 1782, Ingenhousz had secured a more confident route through the Habsburg ambassador in Paris.[25]

The spectre of their correspondence being discovered haunted Ingenhousz throughout the wartime years. For him, the act of communicating to Franklin linked him inextricably to the patriot movement. During his travels across Europe, especially to London in 1777–1778, he acknowledged the risks attached to such a dangerous liaison. Verbal communication through mutual friends was a safer way to correspond, Ingenhousz suggested to Franklin, especially as border guards "could search my pockets and find letters which they could suspect."[26] A few months later, he thought it would be safer to use fictitious names for the letters.[27] Ingenhousz certainly was being overly paranoid. Though he imagined the very real threat of criminality arising from his association with an American revolutionary, there was little actual danger since most elites, even the monarchs themselves, were completely aware of his connection and permitted it. "They know I am known and correspond with a man of such public concern as you are," Ingenhousz demurred. Indeed, for many people in the Habsburg capital, Franklin was the face of the Revolution, but this increased their desire to know more about him and, as we have seen, prompted many to write to him. Nothing ultimately came of Ingenhousz's fears bar a few packages containing American newspapers held hostage in the Viennese post office until after the war had ended.[28] Yet the anxiety Ingenhousz endured from maintaining this correspondence forced an emotional reaction within him: he felt part of the Revolution.

Ingenhousz's initial reaction to the hostilities was shock and dismay. Britain had been his home for many years and had harboured his greatest friendships. Moreover, the American colonies had been a retirement option in his mind, even to the point that he planned to emigrate with his nephew's family[29]—an idea he never completely lost.[30] Since he conceived of the colonies as a refuge for the persecuted and as a harmonious society across the Atlantic, he felt personally affected when conflict broke out in the 1770s. "That country is [*sic*] become the seat of horror and bloodshed, which I took to be the seat of tranquillity and happiness," he exclaimed to Franklin before he lamented on how it could have been "the only seat of undisturbed human felicity."[31] Ingenhousz's early pessimism over the war gradually gave way to the belief that the colonists were the victims and the British ministers the aggressors. The sacking of "defenceless" cities and fermenting of Native Americans against the colonists were in his mind "unwarrantable and imprudent" acts of the British forces in North America.[32]

At the exact same time, however, Ingenhousz chose to share extracts of Franklin's letters with the British ambassador, trading Sir Robert Murray Keith the latest account of his "old and faithful friend" in return for introductions to elites in London.[33] Ingenhousz's transformation took place gradually rather than suddenly. Following a reunion with Franklin in Paris and upon his return to Vienna in 1780, Ingenhousz's resolve towards the patriot side hardened. For one, he never shared letters with Keith again and, moreover, he thought American independence would sufficiently hobble the British who acted so belligerently in his mind that they threatened to destabilise European peace. He spoke no longer of the calamities of the war and instead told Franklin how "necessary it is for the tranquillity of Europe that your Country should remain free" in order to undo the "haughty" British.[34] Within a few years, Ingenhousz had completed his journey from shocked observer to a fervent pro-American supporter.

In his writings on the American Revolution, Ingenhousz's primary motivation was to exonerate Franklin. In 1774, Franklin faced what became known as the "Cockpit Trial" in London: a cross-examination by the Privy Council resulting from Franklin leaking letters to North American publishers which demonstrated the Massachusetts colonial governor had encouraged a crackdown on colonists protesting the new, unpopular taxes. Franklin's actions had provoked a maelstrom of anger and criticism towards the governor, further inflaming an already tense situation. British ministers held Franklin accountable and raked him over the coals during the hearing.[35] Rumours in Vienna (and across Europe) distorted the severity of Franklin's actions, and as a result the prevailing Viennese perception was that Franklin had organised the resistance in North America.

Ingenhousz set out to correct the narrative and dispel the notions of the American Revolution being a "Franklinian plot." In his *Remarques sur les affaires présente de l'Amérique Septentrionale* (Remarks on the current affairs in North America)—written in 1777 ostensibly for Maria Theresa but shared widely among courtiers as well—he repudiated the image of Franklin as a mastermind of rebellion. Ingenhousz instead clarified that the mistreatment of the colonists was the actual "source of discord and of the current insurrection."[36] His explanation carried weight among his peers and superiors given his standing at court and his close connection to Franklin. On more than one occasion Count Karl von Zinzendorf visited Ingenhousz in order to find out more about the American cause which Ingenhousz was all too happy to explain to him.[37]

In his essays written for the Habsburg monarchs that lasted throughout the Revolution, Ingenhousz increasingly defended patriot interests, becoming a reliable mouthpiece for Franklin and the American cause in Vienna. This was arguably his greatest intervention on behalf of the Americans during the war. To be sure, Ingenhousz was feathering his own nest as well. He needed Franklin's information to keep Maria Theresa "in good humour."[38] But Ingenhousz went beyond merely relaying Franklin's reflections. He made translations of Franklin's works and personal letters and accompanied them with short reports of his own about the Revolution.[39] Without doubt, Ingenhousz was the most effective supporter of the American Revolution in the Habsburg Monarchy. He did more than anyone else within the Monarchy to enable the feelings of shared interests with the American cause, to explain their revolutionary goals to a broader audience, and to elucidate sympathy for the American patriots among his circles in Vienna. But he was not alone.

Leaving the Monarchy for America

Joseph Cauffman is a name unknown in the history of the American Revolution.[40] Yet Cauffman represents the profound radicalisation from bystander to fervent patriot that was possible under the ideals of the Revolution, even in a place as seemingly remote as Vienna. Joseph Cauffman was born in Philadelphia in 1755. As the eldest of ten children, he embodied the best hopes of his merchant father Joseph T. Cauffman.[41] Joseph Sr. had arrived in Philadelphia in 1749 from his native Alsace region. A spelling mistake on his Pennsylvanian land deeds forced him to adopt the name "Cauffman" instead of the original "Kauffman," but he lost nothing else of his German-Alsatian heritage.[42] The Cauffman family upheld their Roman Catholic faith, which meant Joseph Sr. found it difficult to obtain a suitable education for his eldest son. Like many well-to-do Catholic families, he decided to send Joseph Jr. to Europe for his education. Thus Joseph Jr. was eleven years old when he left Philadelphia to go, as he put it, "abroad amidst the dangerous rocks of intrigue, wickedness and an insnaring [sic] world."[43]

Cauffman studied first at St. Omer's College in Bruges in the Austrian Netherlands. At Bruges, he could still feel part of his North American roots. Prominent Catholic families, mainly from Maryland, supplied the school with pupils. One of the signers of the Declaration of American Independence, Charles

Carroll of Carrollton had graduated a few years prior and one of his relatives, John Carroll, the future first Archbishop in North America, taught at St. Omer's in Bruges until the eve of the Revolution.[44] Joseph spent five years in Bruges before he enrolled at the University of Vienna. There, he studied medicine, which entailed a two-year course in philosophy before he even saw a cadaver, but which unlocked a prestigious world for him.[45] In the middle-years of his degree, he accompanied various renowned medical practitioners on their rounds of Vienna's poorhouses and clinics such as Dr. Anton de Haen, whom he called his "particular friend" in a boastful letter to his father.[46]

Cauffman was not being arrogant about his situation. In another letter, written in the fateful summer of July 1776, he informed his father that he would sit his exams early, completing his medical degree within three years of specialisation rather than the usual five, a feat "hitherto unknown in this University," he claimed.[47] Emboldened by his first-rate education, Cauffman had mulled over his future career plans for a while. In 1775 he had thought of going to London to work with the famed Dr. John Fothergill. Returning to America was no comparison. He showed little interest in "surpassing our common quacks in Pennsylvania" unless it was as an assistant to the equally famous Dr. John Morgan in Philadelphia.[48] Edinburgh took his fancy in 1776 as he hoped his father could persuade Dr. Benjamin Rush to make some introductions for him there. But by the time he had earned his degree a year later, he had abandoned all such plans.

Cauffman became the University of Vienna's first American-born graduate in 1777.[49] The year became a dramatic turning point in the twenty-two-year-old's life. For many months he had become weary of the rumblings in North America, through the newspapers he read in Vienna.[50] By April 1777, he had become convinced of the need to act, the need to do his part in the Revolution. In a letter he wrote to Franklin, Cauffman outlined his vehement attachment to his homeland, which he made clear was now the United States of America. "I shall always think it the first duty of Man to serve his Country," he proclaimed, and "touched by the present calamities" he wished to honour "one of the most glorious causes."[51] Cauffman felt his excellent medical training made him an ideal candidate to serve in the Continental Army. Gone were the notions of advancing his career in London or Edinburgh. He had expunged these wishful plans from his life's narrative. "I have applied myself with an indefatigable zeal to my studies," he professed to Franklin, "in order to prove one day or another, a worthy citizen of America."[52] Cauffman presented himself as an ardently devout patriot and also offered to spy on Franklin's behalf in Vienna. "No pains shall be thought too great, no stone left unturned, to procure you proper information," he declared.[53]

Cauffman's contact with Franklin came through his friendship with Ingenhousz. Both were members of the medical community in Vienna. They had become friends already by the end of 1776 when Ingenhousz mentioned how he enjoyed "the company of one Mr. Kauffman [sic] from Philadelphia" in a letter to
Franklin.[54] When Ingenhousz departed Vienna for London to present the Baker
lectures at the Royal Society in 1777, it seems Cauffman travelled with him.[55] A
few months later, he served aboard an American frigate, the USS *Randolph*, as
a medic.[56] At the start of 1778, the vessel sailed along with four other American
ships to raid British supply lines in the West Indies. On March 7, spotters faintly
sighted a lone British vessel and over the next few hours the convoy gave chase. In
the dark hours of that evening, the captain of the *Randolph*, Nicholas Biddle, ordered the first shots fired broadside into the British ship they felt was no match.
It was more than a match. The British vessel was in fact a ship of the line and
severely outgunned the plucky frigate. The return volley struck the powder stores
on the *Randolph*, detonating upon impact and blowing the ship apart. Only four
survivors made it to the other vessels as they escaped the disastrous moonlight
engagement. Joseph Cauffman was not among them. Instead, he perished along
with most of the crew and became a martyr to the cause he had become so devoted to after finishing his studies in Vienna. The first American-born student
at the University of Vienna died fighting in the American Revolution.

Joseph Cauffman's story is important because he was not alone. In his letter
to Franklin, Cauffman affixed a note that informed Franklin about the "many
able officers, even of rank," who "begged" him to include mention of their "desire of taking part in the present contest."[57] Whether or not they joined him on
his journey across the Atlantic cannot be ascertained, but there were some who
surely planned to go with him. When news reached Vienna of his death, his
friends were distraught. Dr. Joseph Pelligrini, who had studied alongside him
and worked at a hospital in the Landstrasse district of Vienna, wrote to Franklin
explaining his previous intention to join Cauffman in serving America. Still
undeterred, the unmarried, thirty-something doctor who spoke a smattering of
English offered to fund his own travel if Franklin would help him gain safe passage to Philadelphia. As he confessed to Franklin, he wished to do so out of his
"secret desire for America" because he so revered "the character and morals" of
the new nation.[58] Such motivation stemmed from the zeal of Cauffman's example. Whereas Cauffman had a natural attachment to the place of his birth, Pelligrini's affinity for the American rose from the inspiring actions of his friends.
It was one example of how the "contagion of liberty" permeated even to places
within the Habsburg Monarchy.[59]

Participation, however, worked both ways in the Habsburg Monarchy. As much as there were those who wished to or did go to fight *for* the Revolution, there were also those from the Habsburg lands who went to fight *against* the Revolution. Those who fought against the patriots in the War of American Independence participated as part of the Hessian mercenary forces. Six German principalities supplied the war in North America with around 21,000 men.[60] The Hessian regiments were not just local-born fighters, however. Like many European armies of that time, they were a hotchpotch of nationalities. Some of this patchwork had arisen from voluntary enlistments; foreign men following opportunities for work or signed up by recruiters sent out to fill the ranks. As manpower stocks diminished and demand remained steady, recruiters widened their geographic scope and turned to more illicit practices: bribery, impressment, or coercion.[61] Habsburg ministers denounced such activities as an "evil" because Hessian recruiters interfered with their own recruitment drives for settlement in Eastern Europe.[62] The poaching of military personnel for service in the Hessian regiments in North America became a grave concern to the ministers in the Court War Council (*Hofkriegsrat*) who met several times throughout the war to discuss the problem. At one point, ministers recommended resurrecting an old imperial edict which curtailed unpermitted migration in order to prohibit men from enlisting in the regiments destined for America.[63] Complete prevention proved ultimately futile, however.

Habsburg subjects serving in so-called Hessian regiments were present at almost every major battle of the American Revolution. At least 192 identifiable Habsburgs served in the Hessian forces in North America.[64] There were certainly many more, given the concern of the *Hofkriegsrat*, but archival records cannot indicate the exact scale. Soldiers serving in the Hessian forces originated from across the Habsburg lands. There were men from core regions like Josef von Bosen, a Tyrolean officer from Innsbruck, and Antonin Masorka from Krásny Les in Bohemia. Others came from further afield such as George Frohnhauer from Trieste on the Adriatic and János Messet from Debrecen in Hungary. War was always a deadly business. All four men died during the conflict. In some cases, they never reached North America. Johannes Strosser from Grieskirchen in Upper Austria and Bernard Schäffer from Graz in Styria died at sea crossing the Atlantic. In other cases, some Habsburg subjects survived the war but became displaced after their service. A good number of them may have settled in the Canadian territories, though the majority returned home.[65]

Justus Eggertt was one who returned. He had seen action in almost the entirety of the war. Originally from Leipzig, he had moved to Vienna in 1771 where he suffered a dispute with his employers, the counts of Hoym. In the summer of 1776, he found himself without a job and, perhaps with the help of a local recruiter or perhaps spurred on by the reports in the national newspapers, he decided to enlist in the Hessian service. He joined the Ansbach regiment at Amsterdam and crossed the Atlantic on a British ship, which, as his journal account of the war details, carried more cannons than mattresses for the 250 soldiers aboard.[66] After a gruelling nine-week voyage, they reached Sandy Hook, New Jersey, in mid-August 1776. Days later, Eggertt took part in the largest battle of the entire war, the Battle of Long Island, a British victory that enabled the fall of New York City a few months later, which he survived unharmed. Eggertt fought in several more battles during the New York and New Jersey campaigns. He was stationed in Philadelphia and Baltimore where he quartered with German immigrants, who, he noted with surprise, owned slaves. Eggertt encountered slavery again during his final campaign in the Carolinas, but he only remarked on the higher quantities of slaves working on southern plantations. Landing at Charleston in 1781, Eggertt fought in the "most exceptional heat and severest storms" he had ever experienced. He witnessed many plantations "ruined" by his forces.[67] In his journal, Eggertt estimated that his military life had taken him over "6,000 German miles" before he numbered among the men who surrendered at Yorktown. Eggertt eventually returned to Austria in 1783 where he found work in the military administration in the Trauenviertel region of Upper Austria. He shared stories of his experience of North America up to his death in 1823.[68]

Angels of the New Republic

The military heroes of the American Revolution piqued the interests of many observers across Europe. American military leaders became famous through their depictions in newspapers and periodicals but the yearning for learning more about them was greater still. One man in the Habsburg Monarchy was determined to find out more about these generals and as a result began his own personal journey with the American Revolution. In 1778, Johann (Baptist) Zinner was a historian and prefect at the Imperial and Royal Academy in Buda.[69] He became enraptured by the War of American Independence from descriptions he read in local and regional newspapers. He found that these newspapers often provided competing accounts and contradicting facts, however. Zinner raised this problem in a letter to Franklin that year. The famous turncoat, Benedict Arnold, Zinner complained with some exaggeration, "is sometimes made out to be a German of Mainz, sometimes an American of Connecticut, sometimes a lapsed Capuchin monk, and sometimes a grocer from Norway."[70] How was he to discern the truth? Zinner's dilemma was all the more urgent since he was at work on two books on the American Revolution, and, as a good historian, he needed to separate fact from fiction.

Zinner was deeply motivated about the American Revolution. He travelled from Buda to Vienna in 1778 to meet with the first official American envoy to the Habsburg court, who, he hoped, would be able to provide him with the right information, but he missed the American by a few weeks. He turned to Franklin instead who responded kindly to his request for help. In 1779, Zinner accepted Franklin's invitation to visit him at Passy where he personally received copies of American letters and literature.[71] Equipped with this first-hand material, Zinner headed back to Hungary, where in 1780 he joined the juridical faculty at the Royal Academy at Košice as a professor of statistics and history.[72] At the time, Košice was a provincial metropole where the university had been founded by the local bishop in 1660 as the Universitas Cassovensis and run by the Jesuits until their dissolution. The Royal Academy at Košice was one of five new institutions established under the *Ratio educationis* (Education Law) of 1777.[73] Zinner joined a relatively small scholarly community, where of approximately seventeen staff members taught 372 students in the humanities.[74] Based on his surviving manuscripts, it is clear Zinner shared his American material with his pupils.[75] Zinner, however, was not content with bringing the American Revolution only to Košice; he had bigger plans.

From his academic perch nestled on the eastern side of the Tatra Mountains, far removed from the Atlantic, Zinner worked on several manuscripts chronicling the Revolution. In his letter to Franklin, he noted how he planned two monographs but in fact he completed three in rapid succession. The first book appeared in print in 1782, titled *Merkwürdige Briefe und Schriften der berühmtesten Generäle in Amerika* (Remarkable letters and writings of the most famous generals in America).[76] In 352 pages, Zinner retold various aspects of the revolutionary struggle up to 1780 through 46 indexed letters and thirteen essays, proclamations, and excerpts. Overall, Zinner translated and published either in part or in full over 70 original letters from the leaders of both sides (American and British) of the Revolution. American patriots were the overwhelming focus of his work which included famous names like Franklin, Samuel Adams, Horatio Gates, Charles Lee, and George Washington as well as figures who were less-known to German-speaking audiences such as the politicians Thomas Jefferson and Robert R. Livingston, and generals Israel Putnam, Benjamin Lincoln, and Arthur St. Clair. Most of them received an extensive and accurate biography. Zinner certainly offered the most detailed accounts of these individuals within the German-speaking realm at the time. On the British side, Zinner provided only two much shorter but equally accurate biographies of the British generals John Burgoyne and Thomas Gage.[77] In his introduction to the work, Zinner outlined the need to show both sides of the conflict in order to present a neutral account of the war through the most important writings of the war's leaders.[78] Yet the imbalance within his work already belies his true intentions and partisanship towards the Americans.

Throughout his *Merkwürdige Briefe*, Zinner presented Americans in a kinder light than the British. Burgoyne and Gage, in Zinner's telling, both paled in comparison to the military prowess of the American generals. He noted Burgoyne's failure to defeat the Americans at Saratoga and Gage's Pyrrhic victory at Bunker Hill and subsequent retirement to London as their most noteworthy biographical moments.[79] Both biographies are short compared to any of those of the American leaders. Franklin received the most flattering (and longest) entry which Zinner used as proof that "such a man as Franklin is never to be despised."[80] Combining Franklin's victorious role in the war with his scientific reputation, Zinner rounded out his biography of Franklin with the attribution by Franklin's great admirer, Jean-Baptiste de Beaumont, "*Alterius orbis Vindex, utriusque Lumen*" (Champion of one world, light of both).[81] When Zinner contrasted the unequal treatment of prisoners of war between the Americans and British, he portrayed the British army in an almost barbaric light. He published a letter by the patriot Ethan Allen which described cruel and punitive British captivity.[82] British officers, such as Burgoyne, who turned a blind eye to the mutilation of American prisoners by Native Americans was another point which Zinner dwelled upon and regarded as contemptible.[83] By contrast, Zinner provided a favourable example of humane captivity on the American side with an account by a Hessian soldier.[84] In case the distinction was not clear enough, Zinner remarked that "the Americans meanwhile have observed better the rights of man" than the British who "thought that threats and destruction would lead to victory in this war."[85]

Three texts within Zinner's *Merkwürdige Briefe* aimed at rousing a sympathetic interest towards the American cause. The first was Charles Lee's open letter of June 7, 1775, to Burgoyne, a polemic wherein Lee sought to tie himself to the patriot movement and to place the incoming British general in a tight bind by forcing him to take sides either for or against the nascent patriot movement.[86] Zinner faithfully reproduced Lee's patriotic words in German translation, including Lee's assertion that all Americans "from the first-estate gentlemen, to the lowest planters and farmers" were animated by the same spirit of liberty to "preserve their liberties or perish."[87] Zinner also included Lee's immortal refrain that America was "the last asylum of persecuted liberty."[88] Likewise, Zinner reproduced Samuel Adams's speech on the steps of the Philadelphia statehouse made on August 1, 1776. This was the same speech Habsburg censors had banned in 1780, so it is striking that Zinner dared to republish such material in translation.[89] Zinner's copy of the second edition of *Common Sense*, from which he also provided translated excerpts, would have been equally shocking for the censors.[90] Selected portions of the *Thoughts on the Present State of American Affairs* featured some of the most fiery statements where Zinner paid particular attention to the justifications for the American cause.[91] Zinner echoed the calls to accept the inevitability of the United States as an independent state.[92]

Merkwürdige Briefe was Zinner's first and only published text on the American Revolution. His other two books, which he had mentioned in his letter to Franklin in 1778, were written out by hand but never published.[93] These works were thought lost by historians up until now but have in fact remained in Košice since Zinner's time.[94] Zinner completed the first of these two works in 1783. Titled *Notitia historica de Coloniis Americae Septentrionalis* (Historical notes on the North American colonies), Zinner divided the course of American history into three distinct periods: first, from the discovery of America by Columbus to the end of the Seven Years' War in 1763; second, the colonial disturbances in the 1760s and 1770s and their antecedents in the political history of British America; and third, the alliance with the French and concluding Treaty of Paris in 1783.[95] What purpose Zinner used his *Notitia* for is unclear but given the title and the fact he completed it in the teaching language of the university, it is possible this formed the basis for his courses in universal history at the Royal Academy.[96]

In 1784, Zinner earned a promotion of sorts when he became an ecclesiastical prebendary for the Diocese of Spiš meaning he performed religious duties at the Roman Catholic cathedral of Košice, St. Elisabeth's, in exchange for a stipend.[97] His extra duties in Košice did not distract him from his scholarly output as he completed his largest and final work on the American Revolution that year. In his *Versuch einer Kriegsgeschichte der verbündenen Staaten von Nordamerika* (An attempt towards a military history of the United States of North America), Zinner distilled everything he had learned from studying the American Revolution. It followed a similar pattern to his *Notitia* by outlining the entirety of American history from Columbus to the contemporary state of the postwar United States. Perhaps because Zinner wrote in his native German rather than Latin, he felt able to fully convey his thoughts; accounts of early America, of Columbus's

FIGURE 7. The first page of one of Johann Zinner's histories of
the American Revolution written in eastern Hungary

voyage, and the war itself are expanded and dealt with in greater detail making
the *Notitia* seem like a writing exercise in preparation for the magnum opus. Indeed, the *Versuch einer Kriegsgeschichte* amounted to a gargantuan 106 chapters
over 535 pages. All of this Zinner wrote by hand and attached his own index.[98]

Why did Zinner take such great lengths to write these works? Zinner's motivation to chronicle the American Revolution in some of the most extensive
contemporary accounts stemmed from his deep-seated sympathy for the revolutionary cause. He believed in the American Revolution and its importance in
world history. In a geographically remote part of the Habsburg Monarchy, Zinner composed three monumental works on the Revolution which encompassed
all of American history and provided European audiences with accurate material
on its leaders and their revolutionary views. Zinner laid bare his reason for doing
so in his first letter to Franklin in 1778, when he wrote,

I was born the subject of a great monarch and under a government whose rule is mild [. . .] but I cannot tell you what joy I feel when I hear or read of your progress in America. To speak the truth, I look upon you and all the chiefs of your new republic as angels, sent by heaven to guide and comfort the human race [. . .] and to give public manifestation of this sentiment, I am composing this work.[99]

To "give public manifestation" was Zinner's ultimate aim; such was the conviction and admiration he held for the American revolutionaries. In 1783, he wrote again to Franklin after the completion of his *Merkwürdige Briefe* and informed him that he had dedicated the work to Congress, knowing that it supported "the bravery and courage of your heroes and the dignity of your Congress."[100] In this dedication, written in Latin, Zinner exclaims,

If there was ever a time so worthy of admiration, it is surely that time in which the new Republic rose, [. . .] when through your efforts and through your diligence, you very excellent men, the flag of freedom was raised and defended with the blood of your citizens. In this irreproachable age, some peoples and families fought for the welfare and happiness of the fatherland; others, with exhausted forces, took upon themselves in vain the struggle of the war for the capital with common, good strength, but they were pitifully defeated; the rather hard ones were given into slavery. The Senate and the people of America, on the other hand, happily built the capital in only seven years and founded a new and prosperous republic, which is your glory, in the New World. This is what amazes all peoples and even the far-away peoples. This is what moves me most: that I pass on your young origin, your tireless work for freedom and the memory, that I record the outstanding public announcement of your fame with writings. Onwards, you most excellent men, your name as an example of my fully devoted vigilance, follow the counsel of the just and the good, and you will be held by me with the most glorious praise for those who seek renewal.[101]

Zinner certainly felt part of this Revolution; he felt moved by it, hurt by the bloodshed, and jubilant by the news of American victory. His intellectual determination to chronicle the rise of the new American republic through his position at Košice and his three works reflect the sense of participation and sympathy which he, like many others in the Habsburg Monarchy, experienced. In this case, it meant that some of the most vividly detailed works concerning the American Revolution first saw light at the hand of a Bohemian-born, German-speaking professor at the Royal Academy of Košice in the easternmost corner of the Habsburg lands.

Conclusion

Zinner was not alone. Across the Habsburg lands, people felt moved by the events in North America. Almost one hundred of them felt compelled enough to invest the emotional cost and monetary value in letters to Franklin; some to seek his aid, some to offer praise and advice for his Revolution. Throughout the Habsburg Monarchy, people who felt some level of sympathy with the revolutionary spirit in the thirteen colonies made their opinions known. Vienna, in particular, was home to one of the most ardent and diligent advocates of the American revolutionary cause, Jan Ingenhousz. Circles around Ingenhousz are a case in point. His personal conduit to Franklin through their prior friendship and scientific interests became a tradable commodity among the Viennese. His pro-American feelings were shared by one of his students, the first American-born student at the University of Vienna, Joseph Cauffman who voluntarily left to fight for the American cause. Cauffman in turn spread his revolutionary sentiment among his fellow classmates who enquired after him and sought Franklin's help to enlist.

Individuals like these confirm there was an abundant enthusiasm for the American Revolution in the Habsburg lands. It is against this backdrop that the Habsburg interactions with the new United States took place. Obscured by the negative connotation of revolution after the events transpiring in the French Revolution, these earlier American sentiments in the Habsburg Monarchy have gone largely unnoticed. Such acknowledgement might have been too controversial for academics in the late Habsburg Monarchy of 1905, but it is still possible to add that dedication to Ingenhousz's statute in the Arkadenhof where he should be joined again by his friend, Joseph Cauffman, the university's first American-born student, in remembrance of their support for the American cause.

CHAPTER FOUR

"The Big and Furious Game"

The Difficulty of Habsburg Neutrality in the War of American Independence, 1775–1783

O N JANUARY 19, 1776, three Tuscan sailors awoke to gunpoint. Under the impression they were helping to transport hundreds of smuggled guns across the Mediterranean to the Egyptian port of Alexandria, they probably never thought such weapons would be used on them in the dead of night. But on this occasion, Captain Eastman of the American ship *Betsy* had ordered a clear out. The three Tuscans, as subjects of the Habsburg emperor's brother, were not part of the plan to haul the *Betsy* from Livorno, where they had collected wines and spices along with the smuggled weaponry, to Philadelphia rather than Alexandria. Although they spared them an execution, the crew set the Tuscan trio adrift in a small boat. After several days, they reached the port of Oran on the African coast, exhausted, parched, and barely alive. From there, they managed to cross the straits to Alicante and send word home. News of their forced abandonment travelled back to Livorno and later to Florence and London. From the Habsburg perspective, this was the latest in a series of unfortunate embroilments consequent of the War of American Independence. The three Tuscan sailors, for their part, realised that the American Revolution had a very real impact—with almost fatal consequences—on their lives.[1]

A subject in the Habsburg lands did not have to be directly involved in the American Revolution in order to feel the risks. In the port of Lisbon, a few years later, the family of an imperial ambassador huddled for safety after British ships attempted to capture an American prize in the harbour near their home. They witnessed the terrifying engagement across the bay before cannon balls came screeching through the air seconds later, shattering the walls, destroying the interior but sparing them from an untimely, gruesome death.[2] In the port of Ostend in the Austrian Netherlands, two years after that encounter, residents awoke to the bewildering sight of a capsizing ship lodged upon the shallows of their coastline. Soon British warships descended like hawks to guard the floundered American vessel; it was an unusual sight, which became ever more tinged with tension. Magistrates and merchants fretted over what came next in the courts and in the customs houses.[3]

For those who did share the risks of war—the soldiers, the deserters, the smugglers—their risks became the state's as well. Disputes between merchants over illicit cargoes or the legalities of a deserter who enlisted in a regiment bound for North America marred the delicate diplomatic balancing game which every neutral power strove to maintain during wartime, including the Habsburg realms. Habsburg interests operated in a tangled web of international trade which brought them into disrepute with one or another of the belligerent powers. This is not to say that the Habsburg Monarchy was unique regarding the difficulties associated with neutrality—far from it. Other major European neutrals such as Denmark, Russia, and Sweden were all exposed to the uncertainties of the Revolution. Swedish merchants, for example, prospered from increased trade to the West Indies with exports skyrocketing by a factor of twenty-five between 1777 and 1783.[4] During the same period, however, Swedish merchants endured confiscation and legal disputes with the British admiralty. By 1779, no less than thirty-two Swedish merchant vessels had been tried in the admiralty courts and found guilty of smuggling.[5] The Habsburg experience was by no means exceptional in comparison. It does, however, serve to illustrate the complexity of neutrality in the American Revolution. Habsburg officials and mariners encountered a variety of vicissitudes in attempting to navigate the unsteady world created in the wake of the Revolution.

This chapter brings to light these challenges of neutrality for the Habsburgs. Two sites were of prime contention: the ports of Livorno in Tuscany and Ostend in the Austrian Netherlands. The former, though not a direct appendage of the emperor but instead ruled by his brother, became a litmus test for British officials for the overall temperament of the Habsburg dynasty towards the American revolutionaries. Ostenders, for their part, frequently witnessed the most difficult contestations of neutrality in the Habsburg lands. Both British and American commanders chafed at the neutral principles enacted by regional officials whilst merchants there took full advantage of their lucrative position, much to the chagrin of both sides. Joining these two ports were the hundreds of ships which served as mobile micro-legalities provoking further contestations at sea and in far-flung foreign ports. The Habsburg Monarchy may be underestimated as a maritime power throughout its history, but its mercantile web in the eighteenth century extended well into the Atlantic, Indian, and Pacific oceans. It was this web that expanded and contracted in the turbulent wake of the American Revolution.

Tuscan Terror

Incidents such as the abandonment of the three Tuscans were treated as serious infractions by the British ministry since they viewed the ship, its crew, and captain as British subjects. Thomas Thynne, the third Viscount Weymouth, the British foreign secretary responsible, wasted no time in informing the British Admiralty and ordering a hunt for the *Betsy*.[6] It was his express wish that this "piratical conduct" be curbed and Captain Eastman be brought to justice for such "infamous and wicked proceedings."[7] Sir John Dick, the British consul at Livorno, maintained a vigilant lookout and informed the city's governor to obtain the "piratical master."[8] But the ship proved impossible to track down and with the lag of eighteenth-century communications, any alerts were too late. Fortunately for the British and Habsburgs, a number of the ship's crew mutinied while anchored in Tenerife and piloted the ship back to Cadiz, presumably leaving Captain Eastman to a similar fate as the Tuscans.[9] Once the ship had returned to Livorno a year later, the British ministers decided to reward the sailors and compensate the local Tuscan merchants who had suffered huge losses to their investments. As the British envoy in Florence noted, the whole affair had brought "the honour of the British colours" into question by "an Englishman unworthy of the name," and warned that British trade in the Mediterranean would suffer if generosity to sailors and local merchants was not given.[10] King George agreed and felt the need to apologise personally to the Grand Duke Pietro Leopoldo.[11]

A few months after the *Betsy* incident in 1776, Sir John Dick reported further disturbances in Livorno. He had noticed that a Dutch ship, the *Johanna van Vriesbergh*, had arrived from Rotterdam back in January and loaded up a cargo consisting of 142 cannons, 1,463 cannon balls, 360 barrels of gunpowder, and eighty-four chests of small firearms. What could the Dutch be doing with so many munitions? At the time he did not think much about it. In the intervening months, however, Dick came to realise that the ship's Dutch owners, *Otto Frank & Co.*, were in league with Thomas Morris, a member of the Philadelphia firm *Willing & Morris* and brother of the prominent Pennsylvanian financer Robert Morris. Dick was certain that the weapons were "destined to be reship'd for America."[12] It appeared the *Betsy* had not been an isolated case. And yet the situation deteriorated still further. In the same report, Dick recalled how he had also learned that *Otto Frank & Co.* had ordered an additional 500 barrels of gunpowder via another ship from the Habsburg port of Trieste, where an unfamiliar "Englishman"—implying an American—had procured enough firearms for 17,000 men.[13] The bad news did not stop there. A French ship also embarked from Trieste with equally suspicious cargo and, curiously, transported twenty-six imperial soldiers but with enough military supplies for four regiments.[14] The very next day after he had sent his report, even more alarming news came to him. Another ship, this time Danish, had left Trieste with over 2,100 muskets and other munitions.[15] The whole situation seemed to suggest that the Habsburgs were in cahoots with traders to supply the Americans with munitions. "Yet," Dick wondered aloud in his report, "it is scarce possible to believe that the Emperor [Joseph II] and the Great Duke [Pietro Leopoldo] would have anything to do in such a Business."[16]

Scarce possible, but certainly plausible. Otto Frank himself had met privately with Pietro Leopoldo to talk about these ships during a visit to Livorno, and his nephew had followed up these conversations with another private audience in Florence around the time of the French ship's arrival.[17] Such circumstances suggested Dick's growing concerns were not without some truth to them. The difficulty for the British, however, was that they could not force a halt to these conversations, nor could they direct the trade of an independent state. Dick proffered one solution to his superiors, however: they could procure an edict from Pietro Leopoldo which would limit the export and reshipping of munitions from Tuscan ports so that "*no* Part of them be landed in America."[18] Politicking and intervention in Florence seemed the best solution.

Dick's mind must have been full of conspiratorial musings during his wait for further instructions but before news from London arrived, he had ascertained the simple truth of the matter. The munitions were not destined for the thirteen colonies at all. Rather they formed part of the Habsburg trade mission to Asia.[19] The initiative had started with Willem Bolts, "the Englishman" who was in fact Dutch and had worked for the British East India Company before he had become disillusioned and published inflammatory pamphlets denouncing the British colonial activities in India.[20] His subsequent exile had forced him to seek protection from the Habsburgs and, in return, he ventured the scheme to begin trade between the Habsburg lands and the Far East. The plan had originated two years prior with Bolts's interview with the Habsburg ambassador in London and had been a plan of considerable preoccupation among bureaucrats in Vienna since then.[21] Bolts's project had involved a great number of merchants from all over the Habsburg lands, including Otto Frank and his company.[22]

Habsburg administrators had taken great pains to maintain secrecy around the project—even going as far as having Bolts disguised as a Portuguese trader when travelling from London to Vienna.[23] The level of secrecy was so great that it had successfully dumbfounded Sir John Dick in Livorno and, for a time, the British envoy in Florence, Sir Horace Mann.[24] Unbeknownst to them both, Bolts had also been meeting with the Grand Duke under their noses.[25]

Yet something positive arose out of the scare over Bolts's mission. Mann managed to extract promises from Pietro Leopoldo that "proper security would be given" so that arms and ammunition did not fall into the hands of the Americans.[26] Vindication came in July of 1776 when he received a copy of the octroi explicitly outlawing any handover of weapons to the Americans.[27] Yet British suspicions lingered. Weymouth's next instructions commended Dick's attentiveness and confirmed the intelligence about the East Indies mission, but he also informed Mann of credible links between Americans and Livornese merchants.[28] It was now their task to find out more about these new suspects.

Dick had other plans in mind, though. He spoke frequently of retirement and in July 1776, as the thirteen colonies declared independence, Weymouth granted his wish.[29] The British hunt in Livorno failed before it even began. Before his departure, however, Dick left a parting blow which foreshadowed the difficulties that his successor, Sir John Undy, would face amid rising rumours of Habsburg neutrality being betrayed in Livorno. In May, Dick had read a letter by an Irish captain printed in the *London Chronicle* which reported that he had seen "four large American vessels" fully laden in Livorno's harbour and claimed the Livornese and Americans had "carried on a considerable Trade" for the last ten months.[30] Dick described the account as "a fiction and a downright lye [*sic*]" in a rebuttal addressed to the editors of the *Chronicle*.[31] The spread of disinformation harmed both the British and Habsburgs, whose relations naturally strained as a result of such rumours and hearsay. Undy did not arrive in his new post until November, meaning the British had no certain ways to verify what was exactly occurring in Livorno throughout the summer of 1776.[32]

It was just as well since the British had very little idea indeed about what was happening. In early 1776, Weymouth had informed Mann of rumours that a Livornese merchant by the name of Giuseppe Bettoia was in correspondence with some Americans and tasked him to find out more.[33] By May, Mann had deduced that the person was "an Italian named Mazei [*sic*]" who had transported two ships full of corn and cargo of little consequence from America through Bettoia's trading house in Livorno.[34] Nothing more came of the rumour. The British did not realise the significance of this connection. Filippo Mazzei—often

Philip Mazzei—was a Tuscan by birth but had spent a great period of his life
as a merchant in London where the Habsburg ambassador described him as a
"cunning" but "supremely active man."[35] In London, conversations with Benjamin Franklin convinced Mazzei to carry out a plan to cultivate Tuscan wines in
Virginia.[36] In late 1772, Mazzei shuttered his business in London and returned
briefly to Tuscany where he unsuccessfully tried to obtain official support for his
venture before he set off for Virginia, arriving there in December 1773 on the
suitably named *Triumph*.[37] Mazzei's connection with Bettoia and his father's
firm *Stefano Bettoia e Figlio* began during this period and led to many successful
shipments.[38] The disruptions brought about by the situation in North America
slowly ruined the firm, however, and hampered the return of their latest venture
back to Virginia. Thomas Woodford, captain of the *Norfolk* which carried the
sundry goods for Mazzei and Bettoia, failed to reach the American coastline.[39]
Instead, Bettoia sent him to the safer but less profitable Newfoundland region
and re-registered the ship in Ireland. It was from there in 1776 that Woodford
published his letter in the *London Chronicle* in a likely attempt to drum up
trade—the same article that Dick had refused to believe was true.[40]

Woodford's next American trading venture fell under the direction of a new
company in Livorno, *Antonio Salucci e Figlio*, run by Sebastiano V. Salucci.[41]
It did not end well. Salucci disregarded the original plan laid out by Mazzei
(who knew nothing of the changeover and thought Bettoia to be "a Jesuit thief"
because of his silence) forcing Woodford to travel to Paris in order to obtain
corrected passports from Franklin.[42] All went awry when Woodford's newly
renamed ship, *La Prosperità*, ran into the British blockade off the North American coastline. The ship was captured and taken to New York, where the court
case rumbled on without success for Salucci.[43] It became the first embroilment
between the British legal system and Tuscan traders. Salucci wished to recoup
his losses but did not gain enough support until the end of the war.[44] In 1780,
another Tuscan ship met the same fate and was captured by the British.[45]

The worsening commercial situation in the Atlantic and the Mediterranean
negatively affected British enterprise at Livorno and subsequently undercut the
maritime commerce of Tuscany. After the French entry into the war in March
1778, British ships became prey for French privateers based along the Marseilles
coastline.[46] Whilst war with the French was long expected in London, it took
the British representatives in Florence and Livorno by almost complete surprise.[47] Indeed, the first news they heard of it came from a rumour that Raimondo Niccoli and the Tuscan delegation at Paris had had received advanced
word from the Americans.[48] British merchants in Livorno were left drastically

unprepared as a result. Before long, their businesses dried up as each ship fell foul to French attack, and—as Spain looked to enter the war against the British—prospects of safe passage to British destinations seemed at best precarious as well. "Hardly a day passes without some French Cruiser appearing off this Port, and if some Frigates are not sent to Protect the Trade to and from this Place, no Vessel can escape them," Undy warned in late summer 1778.[49] This dilemma came at a time when British traders were already "greatly alarmed" after months of frequent sightings of American pirates.[50] The situation intensified when the French moved decisively to crush British trade in the Mediterranean in the summer of 1778. The importance of Livorno to British trade was well-known. As Mann reported with great trepidation, if Menorca and Gibraltar were to fall then the British would have "no other Port in the Mediterranean to resort to, but that of Leghorne [Livorno]."[51] The French knew this and demanded British exclusion from trading in Livorno or else a French fleet would "block up" the port. The French ultimatum sent shockwaves through the Florentine court. Pietro Leopoldo expressed "great surprise and indignation" at the startling request.[52]

The Habsburgs faced two major difficulties arising from the War of American Independence. The first was an obvious threat to the economic vitality of their region in Tuscany brought about by disruptions to maritime trade. For decades, Florentine administrators had acknowledged the important commercial contribution of Livorno to the overall economy of Tuscany. The same was the case in Vienna, where "one did not speak of Tuscany except in relation to Livorno."[53] The second difficulty arose out of the new geopolitical question which confronted Pietro Leopoldo and his ministers in Florence: how could they rehabilitate trade without showing partiality? The question came at a particularly inopportune moment as Joseph II requested the Grand Duke's presence in Vienna to aid the War of the Bavarian Succession, and as his sister in Naples, Queen Maria Carolina, had been pushing him to "loan" his most effective naval administrator for Neapolitan service.[54] Any response therefore became rushed, more ad hoc, and relied upon older Tuscan debates over neutrality.

When the Corsican Republic had fallen to French invasion in 1768, the Livornese governor had received instructions to draft neutral contingency measures to prevent loss of trade for Livorno's merchants. Giuseppe Francesco Pierallini, one of the governor's subordinates, compiled the first draft which displeased Florentine ministers. Debates over specific aspects stymied its adoption until the necessity for such legislation diminished following the end of the Corsican crisis. In 1771, the Grand Duke raised the prospect of introducing such a law again before technicalities once more dragged discussion into an inescapable quagmire.[55] Seven years later and faced with the more urgent exigencies of the American Revolution, these theoretical debates were of little importance as the older designs for a neutral policy were literally "dusted off" and quickly implemented.[56] Pietro Leopoldo issued an edict on August 1, 1778, which declared a "strict neutrality" in the port of Livorno.[57] The new edict adhered to the long-standing international precedent of Tuscany observing such neutrality throughout the centuries, but for the first time this principle became law.[58] It demarcated all coastal waters around Tuscany as neutral, disallowed the exchange of fire within its shores, and, to ensure Livornese merchants could thrive, all ships were welcome within the harbour.[59]

Neutrality, however, proved a difficult position to maintain. Aside from the continued skirmishes with rogue privateers and smugglers who shirked the edict, the declaration put the Tuscans at odds with their own commercial aims and with foreign powers. The British were suspect of Article VII within in the edict, which they saw as a total inhibitor to their trade in the port.[60] The article forbade any subjects living in Tuscany to partake in any activity which supported the cause of a foreign war. As Mann pointed out to his superiors, the article's terminology was so loosely defined that it could be construed that this included all foreign subjects living in Tuscany; in effect, prohibiting British merchants from outfitting their ships.[61] Silence from the Tuscan court meant British traders struggled under this cloud of uncertainty for the remainder of the war.

At the same time, strict neutrality was not a convenient situation for Tuscan traders. When Mazzei returned from Virginia in 1779, his audiences with the Grand Duke had to be conducted with the utmost secrecy. Whereas Pietro Leopoldo had openly supported Mazzei and his ideas earlier in the 1770s, amid a European-wide war over American independence, he could not do anything to disturb Tuscan neutrality. The pair exchanged a series of discursive letters,[62] but ultimately Mazzei's arguments found only "deaf ears and a gaping wastebasket" in Florence.[63] Pietro Leopoldo simply could not countenance any official commerce with the Americans—despite the significant advantages such transatlantic trade had to offer—for fear of reprisal from foreign powers. Mazzei became embittered against him for this inactivity and his unrelenting indolence for American prospects.[64]

It was not only Mazzei who Pietro Leopoldo shunned on account of neutrality. In May 1777, Congress designated the South Carolinian planter Ralph Izard as the official envoy to Tuscany. Izard was an ideal candidate. He had already visited Tuscany in 1774.[65] In Paris, Niccoli became his great friend but sought to dissuade him of any notions about venturing to Florence.[66] The ruse worked as

Izard informed Congress of the fruitlessness of such an undertaking. He argued instead that his friendship with Niccoli, "a man of ability and very friendly to our cause," enabled him to "to do my business more effectually than if I had been at Florence."[67] In June 1779, congressional members revoked Izard's commission and ceased any intentions to establish relations with Tuscany. Talk of supporting the transatlantic trade between Livorno and the United States did not occur until after the conclusion of the War of American Independence.[68] Meanwhile, the codification of neutrality during the American Revolution allowed Tuscan legal scholars such as Giovanni Maria Lampredi to develop further the concept for the foundation of future neutral positioning in the French Revolutionary and Napoleonic Wars.[69] In the short term, however, the attempted preservation of the port of Livorno between 1776 and 1783 had come at the cost of postponing Tuscan relations with the United States of America. Moreover, in trying to ensure neutrality between all sides, Tuscans officials had staved off an open attack by the French but at the further cost of British commerce in Livorno. The American Revolution was every bit as much problematic for the Tuscan branch of the Habsburgs as it was for the main dynasty in Vienna.

Disaster at Nieuwpoort

Within the Habsburg family, Pietro Leopoldo was not alone in facing the benefits and predicaments of neutrality in the War of American Independence. By tradition, and since the reincorporation of the Burgundian Inheritance by the Habsburgs following the War of the Spanish Succession in 1714, a member of the imperial family ruled as viceroy over the Austrian Netherlands. In the late eighteenth century, the honour had first fallen to Prince Charles Alexander of Lorraine, the double brother-in-law of Maria Theresa, until his death in 1780 meant Maria Theresa's son-in-law Albert Casimir and daughter Maria Christina, the Duke and Duchess of Teschen, acceded to the position. They exercised nominal power as governors-general of the Austrian Netherlands on behalf of the Habsburgs. Below them existed a minister plenipotentiary who headed a regional government composed of several councillors of state who supervised various administrative councils.[70] On the eve of Revolution, Prince Georg Adam von Starhemberg occupied the post of minister plenipotentiary and along with the Prince of Lorraine, the Teschens, and state bureaucracies in Brussels and Vienna, he too faced the onslaught of difficulties arising from the American Revolution.

The first test of neutrality appeared as soon as April 1776. Captain Gustavus Conyngham was a man with a certain sense of daring about him. He was the first in a string of captains in support of the American cause who blurred the line between naval officer and pirate as they stalked the seas and plundered enemy ships for prizes. Conyngham "terrorised" British commerce in particular, becoming one of the most successful (and notorious) commanders of the Continental Navy—in 1778, he captured twenty-four British vessels alone.[71] Before he began oceanic raiding, Conyngham had focused on supplying the American colonies with war materials. In September 1775, he sailed out of Philadelphia on the *Charming Peggy* at the behest of the Maryland Council of Safety in search of military provisions. His mission led him first to Londonderry where he concealed his ship's true origin before sailing to mainland Europe.

In late December 1775, the *Peggy* arrived at Dunkirk where the usual loading and unloading of goods attracted the scrutiny of the local British consul, Andrew Frazer. The *Peggy* caught his attention when he sensed that barrels of gunpowder had been loaded up in the dead of night—Frazer's keen eyes had noticed how the ship sat lower in the water the next morning.[72] However, Conyngham unexpectedly had the supplies unloaded and the vessel laid up weeks later.[73] Unbeknownst to Frazer, there was a snag. Conyngham had ordered further barrels of gunpowder but the Dutch shipments had not yet arrived.[74] He despatched an agent to Amsterdam to sort out the delay, but weeks passed by until word came back that a consignment from the island of Texel was on its way.[75] Conyngham prepared his ship to sail and Frazer pounced. He had the local commissioner search the ship for "warlike stores" to prevent illegal transport back to America. Instead, they found the *Peggy* was full of various articles but no weaponry save for a few cannons serving as ballast.[76] Frazer was out of luck until three of the crewmen fought with Conyngham about carrying on under his command. As Irish subjects, they applied to Frazer for protection and in doing so handed him proof that the vessel was bound for Philadelphia as well as revealing the true purpose of the voyage.[77] Determined to give Frazer the slip, Conyngham sailed away shortly before midnight on April 2 and brought the Revolution to the doorstep of the Habsburg Monarchy.

Conyngham arrived at the port of Nieuwpoort in the Austrian Netherlands, twenty miles along the coast from Dunkirk, before dawn on April 4. They halted in the main canal just outside the town.[78] The supercargo of the ship, Jonathan Nesbitt, had seen to it that a small Dutch barge, the *Eendragt*, waited for them there with nearly six hundred barrels of gunpowder.[79] Over two days, the vessels transhipped their cargoes, flaxseed for firearms; and on April 6, Conyngham notified the port authorities of the new cargo. The *Eendragt*'s crew raised suspicions for Habsburg officials by requesting that the authorities keep the cargo secret but Louis Loot, the local customs officer, had no problem with the operation since the *Peggy*'s goods were destined for St. Eustatius according to Conyngham's paperwork.[80] All seemed well until another crewman, William Bracken, decided to bolt in the dead of night. He walked the twenty-two miles along the coast back to Dunkirk to tell Frazer of the clandestine activity going on at Nieuwpoort.

The game was up. Frazer immediately informed the British representatives in the Austrian Netherlands and wrote back to London about the confirmation of his suspicions about the *Peggy*. If Conyngham had one saving grace, it was that the British officials in the Austrian Netherlands were not so well organised. The British representative William Gordon was a Jamaican-born Scot who, up to then, had been notably absent from his post. In the years leading up to 1776, Gordon had been away on leave for half of 1774 and, in 1775, he was active in Brussels for only two months.[81] His inactivity turned into complete incapacity following a hunting accident in September 1775 at Enghien, where Gordon had accidentally discharged his rifle and wounded Count Louis Engelbert d'Arenberg. The incident left Gordon traumatised and d'Arenberg blind.[82] For months, Gordon could not fulfil his duties as he shut himself away from court and gradually lost his mind. His secretary took over affairs since Gordon could not even "sett [*sic*] pen to paper" and was confined to bed.[83] Gordon's personal misery combined with a relatively inexperienced British consul in Ostend, John Peter, who had arrived in 1774, meant that any effective action was farfetched.

When Frazer's alarm reached Peter in Ostend, he shared the sense of panic. Peter despatched his deputy, Vice-Consul Patricius Hennessy, to Nieuwpoort to detain the ship if it tried to leave; meanwhile, knowing Gordon's difficulties, Peter personally headed to Brussels at the same time.[84] Gordon, meanwhile, had gotten up the courage to seek out Prince Starhemberg as soon as he had received word on April 9, but the meeting was fruitless. Starhemberg knew nothing of the *Peggy* and defended the actions of the Nieuwpoort authorities; if Conyngham's papers stated St. Eustatius, then who were the Habsburgs to question him. Gordon, Starhemberg insisted, would need to prove otherwise. As much as the meeting proved cordial as it did pointless, Starhemberg thought even less of the man who had disgraced himself at court only a short time ago. In his first report to State Chancellor Prince von Kaunitz on the matter, he explained how Gordon had acted "indecently" by coming to him in such an urgent manner without any discernible issue.[85]

Gordon's subsequent actions further inflamed the situation. The next day, he requested in writing that the Brussels government act to detain the ship since he had proof that Conyngham's ship held munitions destined "for the Rebel subjects of His Majesty."[86] This demand greatly dissatisfied the Habsburg ministers in Brussels. Starhemberg felt insulted and one of his subordinate councillors later described the report as uncalled for and "overly passionate in tone."[87] The Habsburgs resented the presumptive questioning of their local officers and their prejudgements. When no official answer was forthcoming, Gordon decided to force matters along. As Gordon entered his carriage to see Starhemberg once again, John Peter arrived just in time. The two men moved together to press the Habsburg government into action. This meeting went worse than the previous one. Starhemberg described it as "tempestuous" in his account to Count Belgiojoso in London, whom he wished to make a complaint on his behalf to King George about the conduct of the British representatives.[88] The reason for the turbulent atmosphere was Starhemberg's refusal to act since he had received no word from Nieuwpoort and insisted that Gordon and Peter submit a written memorandum to lay out their concerns and evidence. Much to Starhemberg's dismay, Gordon and Peter produced the memorandum a few hours later.[89]

Faced with the pressure to act, officials in Brussels chose to delay yet again. From their perspective, the facts were not so clear-cut. The local magistrate, they decided, would have to ascertain the situation proper and charged him to investigate matters.[90] This decision was also a careful ploy to deflect the situation back to the local authorities and to absolve the regional and imperial governments in Brussels and Vienna of the consequences. Gordon saw through the rouse. He raged to his superiors in London over the government's lethargic response, deriding the "silly, weak, timid, ignorant Minister" in the process.[91] John Peter, again full of distrust, left for Nieuwpoort to ensure the magistrate would act without bias. Frans de Brauwere, the mayor of Nieuwpoort and the magistrate charged with running the investigation, knew the stakes at hand and acted impartially. He ordered interviews of everyone in question and a thorough review of all the ship's papers.[92] The papers saved Conyngham. De Brauwere believed that the *Peggy* had arrived from Londonderry via Dunkirk and was indeed destined only for St. Eustatius. In conclusion, he found no grounds to detain the ship.[93]

However, Peter had already seen to it to have guards quartered aboard during the investigation and now procured a civil writ for the local bailiff to confiscate the vessel in spite of De Brauwere's findings.[94] Effectively detained, and unlawfully in their eyes, Conyngham and Nesbitt staged a breakout in the wee hours of April 15. They imprisoned the guards, threatening to kill them, and made for the open sea under an almost moonless night. Disaster struck—perhaps predictably—when the *Peggy* ran aground on the sandbanks of the Nieuwpoort shallows. She was lodged tight. Conyngham and his remaining crew—by that time consisting of four seamen and two "negroes"—made a desperate dash for the shoreline in rowboats. They escaped with their belongings, a few guns from the hold, and "a small cask of strong liquor" for their nerves. Incredibly, they came full circle, making their way back to Dunkirk and crossing over to New England on the *Industry*, an American vessel with Spanish papers.[95] The flight precipitated an unimaginable diplomatic fallout for Brussels; Conyngham had left a piece of the American Revolution foundering on the doorstep of the Habsburg Monarchy.

The situation deteriorated rapidly. The *Peggy* began to list and started taking on water. The authorities in Nieuwpoort rescued the vessel over the next six days but goods below the waterline suffered irreparable damage from flooding.[96] For John Peter, the escape and dereliction by Conyngham had devastating personal consequences since he held the civil writ for the vessel that now lay semi-submerged offshore. Nesbitt, who had refused to leave the *Peggy* when the others abandoned her, had chosen to stay in order to reclaim the cargo still technically under his purview. He now brought a lawsuit against the British consul.[97] Peter faced financial ruin if the Nieuwpoort magistrates found him guilty of damages. They declared the first hearing in the civil case to begin at the end of April. A few days before the scheduled trial, Gordon intervened at Brussels. He put it to Starhemberg that such a case was invalid as it was between two British subjects. At the same time, he revived the original argument that the *Peggy* had obviously been destined for the colonies given the vast stores of arms in the hold. All to no avail. He found Starhemberg impervious to any reasoning that would release the case to the British judiciary where, in all likelihood, Nesbitt would be the one fined for his actions, not Peter.

Gordon's strained relationship with Starhemberg over this issue exacerbated the diplomatic tensions between the Habsburgs and the British. In his reports to his superiors, Gordon began openly questioning Starhemberg's behaviour and voiced his concern that Starhemberg held sympathies for the Americans. "I wish very sincerely," he confided to Lord Suffolk, "that the Minister who presides so very ably of the affairs of this country was at the American Congress. His conduct on the affairs of America proves him to be their well-wisher."[98] Such critique, though privately held between ambassador and minister, was a damning indictment of the early Habsburg attempt at neutrality.

On the day of the trial between Nesbitt and Peter, Starhemberg received reassurances from Kaunitz in Vienna that his judgement on the matter was well placed. Kaunitz confirmed that it was indeed to be a matter for the local courts

FIGURE 8. The minister plenipotentiary in Brussels during most of the
American Revolution, Prince Georg Adam von Starhemberg

and required no interference or oversight from Brussels. This was a curious but
evidently calculated move by both Kaunitz and Starhemberg, who, despite the
international gravity of the situation, both wished to leave it up to local officials.
This was all the more surprising given Kaunitz's private admission to Starhemberg that Conyngham's actions had clearly demonstrated his allegiance to the
American colonies.[99] Yet they had good reason for their willingness to let matters rumble on below the regional and imperial levels. On the one hand, this
allowed for distance once the foreseeable anti-British outcome had been reached,
but on the other hand it also abjured their direction of foreign policy to the verdict of a local magistrate. If De Brauwere ruled against Peter, then relations with
Great Britain would suffer. In the end, the safeguard of being able to scapegoat a
local official won out in both Kaunitz's and Starhemberg's minds.

Using the deferral to local authorities to shy away from international disputes
would become a hallmark of the Habsburg approach to the dilemmas thrown up
by the War of American Independence, and this strategy was first enacted in the
case over the *Charming Peggy*. For John Peter, the effects of this Habsburg policy

were personally devastating. After another month of protracted legal debates, he lost and received a "compromise deal" whereby he had to shoulder the full costs of the damaged cargo, the costs associated with the rescue of the vessel, and, finally, the costs of the entire lawsuit which amounted to £72,000. He might have been thankful that he was not charged an even higher sum as the "compromise" spared him responsibility for paying the damage to the ship itself.[100] Conyngham, by contrast, went on to begin an illustrious career in the Continental Navy. In his memoirs about the events at Nieuwpoort, he simply mentioned that his detention there had been caused by poor winds and "other difficulties."[101]

The difficulties induced by the War of American Independence for the Habsburg government in Brussels continued long after the *Charming Peggy* affair. Indeed, complications arising from the fiasco became immediately apparent. On April 20, a British warship arrived in Ostend as part of British efforts to secure the abandoned *Peggy* in nearby Nieuwpoort. Zealous customs officers wished to inspect the ship as they did with every arriving vessel but the vice-consul protested that British warships were exempt from such scrutiny. Bemused, the officers sent off for clarification to councillors in Brussels.[102] Gordon, who by this point held nothing but bile and contempt for Starhemberg, festered in Brussels and used this latest incident as a test of loyalty.[103] Eager to avoid a new political storm with Britain, Starhemberg struck down the customs request and argued for British exemption.[104] The prospect of a rupture with Britain had forced the government of the Austrian Netherlands into appeasement.

The *Charming Peggy* affair is one example of the intense difficulties over the construction of neutrality in the Austrian Netherlands. Throughout the War of American Independence further disturbances occurred between an increasing array of belligerent actors. In this case, an American privateer caused the conflagration but in subsequent years naval encounters between French, Dutch, and Spanish ships with the British admiralty occurred on the Habsburg coastline on the North Sea. Firefights, raids, depositions, and hearings became part of the residential experience in places like Nieuwpoort and Ostend. Appeasement by ministers in Brussels followed a purely legalistic line. Regular ordinances forbade the transportation of munitions to the American colonies in name only from 1776 until 1778 when the French recognition of the United States prompted more muted responses from Starhemberg's officials to British demands for continued restrictions on the exportation of arms.[105] By then it mattered for little. Infractions continued throughout the period as American merchants continued to arrive and merchants in the Austrian Netherlands awoke to the possibilities across the Atlantic.

The Limits of the Law

Times of political turbulence are always good for lawyers. The American Revolution was no different. One of the central tenants of patriot resistance was to question the legality of the political order they sought to overturn. "No taxation without representation" was as much a condensed legal argument as it was a rallying call.[106] But the Revolutionary pursuit threw up legal questions beyond the thirteen colonies. The patriot need for arms and the British demand for soldiers provoked challenges to the authority of European states supplying these men and goods. Across the world's oceans and seas, captured ships—known as prizes—led to contested claims between captors and captured that demanded legal intervention and arbitration. Their mobility as transoceanic "legal spaces in motion" created collisions between imperial powers who sought to either use the law to their advantage or their defence.[107] Though static, neutral ports also became contested spaces as these ships entered them with their own conflicting legal traditions, priorities, and baggage.[108] The Habsburg Monarchy, with its neutral ports on the North Sea and in the Mediterranean, with its pool of military manpower, and its opportunities for trade, was deeply embroiled in these legal altercations. The proximity of Liège to its neutral ports made the Habsburg ports some of the most important entrepôts for sustaining the patriot war effort in the American Revolution. Without these shipments throughout the war, the conflict may have never resulted in a patriot victory. Even though the *Charming Peggy* caused a difficult legal and diplomatic dissensus to erupt in the Austrian Netherlands, it was a relatively simple case compared to the more protracted cases that emerged between the Habsburgs and belligerent powers as a result of the American Revolution.

Legal imbroglios affected the lives of ordinary people in the Habsburg Monarchy, not just the statesmen and bureaucrats in the corridors of power. When the inhabitants of Ostend stood along the shoreline to witness the dramatic fiery encounter between HMS *Kite* and *Le Cornichon* in 1778, they unwittingly became part of the legal process determined to settle the damage done to the town from the exchange of cannon fire. The British Admiralty as well as the Ostend Admiralty took depositions from the townspeople in the days afterwards in order to ascertain what had transpired exactly.[109] The same act of witness conscription occurred for the hundreds of Habsburg-born sailors aboard ships either seized or interrogated by British vessels during the War of American Independence. At least 132 subjects working on those vessels faced detention or interrogation by the British over fears of aiding the rebel and enemy economies.

These fears were sometimes justified as many Habsburg subjects did work on ships either belonging to or transporting goods to belligerent ports in France, the West Indies, or the Dutch Republic.[110] Yet guilty crews impelled innocent ones along with them. Even Habsburg trade between its ports suffered as the belligerent powers raided foreign ships without much regard. Such was the case for the ill-fated Dutch ship *De Goede Hoop* which sought to carry goods between two Habsburg ports, from Ostend to Trieste. Spanish ships captured the vessel and detained the crew in Cadiz for five months before they were again captured by a British warship off the Sicilian coast. The ship was impounded at Portsmouth and its cargo undelivered; the Habsburg stakeholders subsequently lost their investments.[111]

As a neutral power in the War of American Independence, the Habsburg authorities had recourse to seek justice, though this did not ensure either justice or compensation. Throughout the War of American Independence, the Habsburg consul in London, the Milanese-born merchant Antonio Songa, petitioned claims to British courts on behalf of merchants from across the Habsburg Monarchy. In fact, Songa's position had been created specifically for this reason.[112] Habsburg men and women lost vast sums from the misadventures incurred by the war. When the British captured St. Eustatius in 1781, Songa and his brother Bartolommeo Songa represented twenty-six disgruntled Habsburg investors, including three women, who lost goods stockpiled on the island.[113] The case lasted beyond the war itself and resulted in no compensation. The same occurred with the Habsburg consul in Cadiz, Paolo Greppi, who unsuccessfully protested the loss of one of his own ships in 1779.[114] Likewise, merchants at the Trieste Sugar Company lost several consignments of raw sugar to British warships in a single year without recompense.[115] The losses suffered by his subjects at the hands of the British navy infuriated Joseph II as he complained of the "incredible and unbearable" burden placed on his merchants by the British "despotism at sea."[116]

Joseph's frustration reflected the broader impact of the War of American Independence. It affected all maritime commerce with the Habsburg lands, not just the consignments destined for the Americas. Intra-European trade also suffered from the reverberations of the American Revolution. In May 1779, for example, the British captured a Dutch ship, the *Zeepart*, off the coast of Falmouth on its way to the Habsburg port of Fiume.[117] As a Dutch ship, several goods belonged to Dutch citizens but the Viennese merchant Johann Adam Bienenfeld had the lion's share of the cargo with over a thousand drums of saltpetre. Bienenfeld's cargo was worth a tremendous sum, which he sourced on behalf of the Habsburg military for the war over Bavaria.[118] Concerned that such a considerable consignment had been confiscated, Bienenfeld himself employed a representative to attest his case as a neutral subject and Belgiojoso, as ambassador, intervened to reclaim the costs.[119] Failing to disprove the innocence of the captain, they resorted to the next best alternative and offered to sell the valuable cargo of saltpetre to the British Board of Ordinance for a reasonable sum.[120] The offer turned sour as the British captured a second ship, carrying yet more saltpetre in Bienenfeld's name. Suspicions arose over whether this ship, *l'Union*, had intended to sail for France. Unwilling to trade with a smuggler, the British coyly frustrated the offer and the case dragged out between the two sides until the following year. By then, however, the War of the Bavarian Succession had ended and Bienenfeld gained only a fraction of the cargo's original worth.[121] In the context of his fellow compatriots, it was better than nothing at all.

The British threat was not the only danger for Habsburg traders. The War of American Independence generated greater possibilities for Habsburg merchants to trade within the Atlantic. For the first time, Ostend traders had extensive commerce with the Caribbean islands such as St. Eustatius and Dominica.[122] Yet these new avenues also exposed them to American privateers who preyed on vessels suspected of carrying enemy goods. One particular encounter between an American privateer and a Habsburg vessel led to a court case where the Habsburg subjects and their backers were defenceless. They had reached the limit of the law.

Troubles began on August 20, 1781, in the mid-Atlantic when the American ship *The Hope* seized the Ostend ship *Den Eersten*. The captain of *The Hope*, Daniel Darby, trawled the vessel along with its captain, Peter Thompson, and his sixteen-member crew back to Boston as a prize. Upon arrival, the Admiralty Court of Massachusetts convened a hearing on September 6 to decide whether the capture was lawful. Both men procured lawyers to make their case before a jury of twelve American peers. Darby claimed that the ship carried cargo belonging to English merchants destined for French-occupied Dominica that had originated in London and therefore, as property of the enemy, he was entitled to seize the goods. He further alleged that Thompson knew this fact and discarded the ship's papers by throwing them overboard during the capture.[123] Conversely, Thompson argued these claims were "false and groundless" and that Darby had forced him under duress to sign an English affidavit stating the goods had come from London.[124] The surviving documents found aboard *Den Eersten* proved incriminating, however. True, the ship belonged to the Ostend firm, *Liebaert, Baes, Derdeyn & Co.* but there were dozens of letters between English merchants and Dominican planters who sought to undermine the French blockade.[125] The ship's Ostend owners charged a hefty premium for transporting building materials to plantations which had suffered damage from the French invasion in return for usual Caribbean goods of rum, indigo, and sugar for London's mercantile houses.[126] In his cross-examination, the ship's supercargo, Johann Baptiste Pol, denied these claims and supported Thompson's defence that he "could not read two English words" and Darby had sought to trick them.[127] On November 24, both the jury and the presiding judge, Nathaniel Cushing, declared the ship's cargo to be a legal prize on the basis of the English letters. Cushing deemed the ship itself to be a neutral vessel and therefore not a legal prize.[128] Though mixed, the verdict meant another group of Habsburg merchants and sailors had lost out as a result of the Revolution but this time, and for the first time, in an American court.

The case did not stop in Massachusetts, however. Matters grew more contentious when Darby protested the judgement that the ship was neutral property and won the right to appeal in early 1782. Cushing passed the case to the newly created Court of Appeals in Cases of Capture, the first federal court in the United States, established two years earlier.[129] By the time of the *Eersten* appeal in January 1782, the court had only heard one previous case, meaning this Habsburg case was the second federal court case in American history.[130] Over three days in Philadelphia, Darby and his lawyers set against Thompson and Pol who acted as the attorneys for *Liebaert, Baes, Derdeyn & Co.*[131] The case revolved around whether or not the ship could be considered as a fair prize since, as Darby argued, they had breached the terms of the Dominican capitulation and, by transporting supplies to the English inhabitants, Thompson had not acted in a neutral way. Pol found it difficult to deny this claim since there had been plenty of evidence in the previous trial showing the consignments of British goods destined for the planters on Dominica. His only defence lay on the grounds that the ship had not reached Dominica before Darby had captured them and therefore had not broken any capitulation. In short, he conceded there may have been intent, but no law had been broken and the ship had still acted in a neutral manner. After a short recess, the presiding judges, Cyrus Griffin and William Paca, reached their verdict in early February 1782. The news was not good for Thompson, Pol, the Ostend firm, or the Habsburgs in general. Griffin and Paca found the *Eersten* fair game and therefore not a neutral vessel. They found Thompson and Pol had done "more than a mere intentional offence with regard to the capitulation."[132] In their eyes, the undertaking with British merchants had violated their neutrality in the first place before the ship had left Ostend. As Paca wrote in the final opinion,

The subjects of a neutral nation, cannot, consistently with neutrality, combine with British subjects, to wrest out of the hands of the United States and of France, the advantages they have acquired over Great Britain by the rights of war; for, this would be taking a decided part with the enemy.[133]

The result could not have been more damning for the merchants of the Habsburg Monarchy. The ruling of Griffin and Paca entailed that all Habsburg ships violated their neutrality which protected them against capture by American and allied vessels if they acted in league with British subjects. As Paca put it, such "fraud and stratagem" only resulted in the "garb of neutrality" rather than lawful neutrality.[134] Whereas Habsburg merchants had enjoyed neutral protection up until that point (because of the longstanding international observance that "neutral ships made neutral goods") this new precedent endangered their position.[135] It is not surprising that this verdict came months after the British envoy in Brussels made a similar charge against Habsburg neutrality:

> The fact indeed is that the Imperial flag is become [sic] almost as suspicious (not to use a stronger word), both in these seas and in those of America, as that of the Dutch was at the beginning of the war, the merchants of this country [are] treading very fast in the steps of their neighbours the Dutch, both in supplying the French West-India Islands with provisions and bringing home their produce.[136]

The news of American condemnation proved unsettling to the Habsburgs across the Atlantic. News quickly reached Vienna via the ambassador in Paris and ministers in Brussels.[137] The three owners at Ostend, Jean Baptiste Liebaert, Lieven Baes, and Alexandre Derdeyn launched a petition against the court's ruling with support from Brussels.[138] Their petition claimed Darby had captured the ship under false pretences and therefore this "direct act of piracy" ought to have precluded any jurisprudential process.[139]

Franklin warned chances of overturning the decision were low, especially since the firm lacked the financial resources in Philadelphia and Boston and had no means of proper representation.[140] Franklin's blunt warning ignited questions of whether the Habsburgs should establish a representative in the United States, and it certainly rang true for the trio in Ostend. In the following year, they submitted another petition and empowered an agent as their legal representative in anticipation of a rehearing.[141]

In the meantime, Thompson lost his own petition to reopen the case in May 1784.[142] The agent sent by the firm, Mark Prager, did not arrive until 1785 but he was immediately successful in urging Congress to allow the Court of Appeals the right to decide whether to retry the case.[143] The move backfired. During the hearing in November 1786, the opposing side mustered a lethal witness: John Baes, the nephew of Lieven Baes, who had left the company in 1783 and moved to Philadelphia. Baes testified that the company's directors knowingly entered into agreements with the British merchants and had set up further expeditions. Indeed, the ship's name, *Den Eersten (The First)*, implied it was one of many more to come. Alexandre Derdeyn, according to young Baes, had himself gone to London in order to procure cheap ex-British ships and fill them with British cargo before he sailed to Ostend to reship the goods and obtain clean papers for the vessel's voyage across the Atlantic.[144] "Founded upon a culpable reliance," the judges of the Court of Appeals found no issue in denying any rehearing and effectively upholding their original verdict.[145]

The *Eersten* case was the most high-profile court case between the Habsburg Monarchy and the United States during this period. It resulted from the lure of commercial opportunity offered to merchants in the Austrian Netherlands by the upheavals of American Revolution and their willingness to act as surrogates within imperial economies even if it meant supplying resources for plantation owners in the Caribbean. Jean Baptiste Liebaert, Lieven Baes, and Alexandre Derdeyn, of course, were not alone in acquiescing to this temptation. The trade in munitions and colonial goods skyrocketed in the ports of the Austrian Netherlands during the American Revolution, facilitating surrogate trading lines from there to the Caribbean, Africa, and the United States. Hundreds of firms, businessowners, and investors like *Liebaert, Baes, Derdeyn & Co.* participated in this Habsburg interjection into the colonial maritime world of the Atlantic during the American Revolution and its immediate aftermath.[146] Not all endeavours lasted but historians who have recently pointed to the complicity of Habsburg merchants, industrialists, and officials partaking in colonial economies of the nineteenth century may do well to dwell upon the eighteenth-century precedents of such actions and connivances.[147]

Conclusions

The War of American Independence embroiled many Habsburg subjects into difficult, often lethal situations. British "despotism at sea," as Joseph II called it, and the audacity of American privateers to supply the patriot struggle brought these subjects into the disruptive arena of international conflict. To be certain, Habsburg smugglers were aware of the risks and chose to compete within a contested imperial commercial world.

For officials in the Austrian Netherlands and in the Grand Duchy of Tuscany, the complexities of international commerce and the legal entanglements arising from it were a treacherous political minefield. The American Revolution produced domestic changes in the ways these regions operated. The Grand Duke of Tuscany declared a strict neutrality in the port of Livorno which reconfigured the prior trading relationships of the merchants there. In the Austrian Netherlands, officials found it difficult to appease both sides. Prince Starhemberg, as head of the regional government, exacerbated the situation by inflaming British suspicions of his pro-American bias. Accusations of bias also occurred in the opposite direction as American admiralty and appellate courts ruled against Habsburg merchants as agents of British aid and called into question the sincerity of Habsburg neutrality.

Throughout the War of American Independence, officials in the Habsburg Monarchy encountered challenges arising from the conflict; it was not a war they could easily disentangle themselves from, nor was it a war confined solely to the Atlantic powers. The American Revolution took place in the Mediterranean and the North Sea. It was a war in Europe as well as North America, the Caribbean, India, and further afield. It was, as a result, an inescapable challenge for the Habsburg Monarchy.

CHAPTER FIVE

"The Long, Laborious, and Most Odious Task"

*The First Struggle for Recognition between the Habsburg Monarchy and
the United States of America, 1776–1779*

U NDER THE COVER OF darkness on the night of Saturday, May 23, 1778, a carriage clattered along the road before the glacis of Vienna. The worn-down wheels kicked up dirt along the way, adding to the "dust desert" which often hindered the firing line of the armaments adorning the embankments, bastion walls, and watchtowers overlooking the approach. Inside the carriage, the sole occupant tried his best to shield his face from the lanterns which faintly illuminated the way, hiding his visage from the multitude of guards defending the city's entryway. If he could look outside, the growing shape of the city's defences would have been his only distinguishable destination. The first contact came at the mouth of the sconce where a guard from within the small sentry stepped out. Toll paid, luggage fumbled, books—some suspiciously in English—thoroughly thumbed, and his French papers presented, the occupant and his driver were allowed to proceed across the first bridge into the huge triangular monolith of the Schottentor. At the second checkpoint a paid informer clocked the new arrival and sent word into the bowels of the city. As the carriage proceeded along the second and final bridge over the defensive ditches and into the protective welcome of the streets near Schottenhof, the traveller breathed a momentary sigh of relief. The long journey had come to an end, but his task had just begun. Vienna, his goal, was a fortress city: impregnable to conquerors, safe harbour to the imperial dynasty. Except, as far as the Habsburgs were concerned, the most dangerous man in Europe had just slipped in. The first American envoy had arrived in Vienna.[1]

Why did William Lee, this first envoy, enter Vienna under darkness? Why did the Habsburgs see him as a threat? The first diplomatic mission between the Habsburg Monarchy and the United States is one of the most fascinating and illuminating episodes in their rich historical relationship. Lee's mission not only reflected the embryonic state of American diplomacy but also the cultural clash between entrenched court etiquette and "militia diplomacy"—the American practice of sending uninvited envoys to European states. This clash is one reason, but not the only reason, for the ultimate failure in the American struggle for recognition from the Habsburg Monarchy during the War of American Independence. The fact that Lee's mission failed has often been the point of fixation in largely one-sided accounts of this episode. The simplified narrative holds Lee accountable for the mission's failure. One historian deemed Lee's diplomatic character was "better suited to the role of prosecuting attorney than peacemaker."[2] Others have felt content to argue that his sour demeanour led him to "whiling away [his] time in Paris, venting [his] frustrations on Franklin."[3] Some have stumbled in determining which Lee brother made it to Vienna[4]—in fact both William and his brother Arthur Lee made the journey—whilst some believed Lee never reached the Habsburg capital despite copious material evidence.[5] When faced with assigning who or what caused the failure of the mission, one historian concluded, "such a question is, of course, difficult to answer conclusively."[6] The futility expressed here, however, underscores the misdirection such a focus on Lee's character brings.

If we decentre William Lee from the story and focus instead on the wider context of his mission and time spent in Vienna, a far more interesting and refreshing tale emerges: a tale of the unlikely successes of the first American experiments in statecraft at the court of Vienna. It was here that militia diplomacy created a cult of fascination. In breaking diplomatic norms, American patriots also broke new diplomatic ground. Indeed, it goes against Horst Dippel's still accepted remark that "The sporadic appearance of American negotiators in Berlin and Vienna does not seem to have had any noteworthy influence."[7] Focusing only on Lee's handling at court dilutes this wider perspective and the overall importance of his mission. By adopting an expanded viewpoint, I highlight the impact of an official American visitor on Viennese society and individuals within the Habsburg lands. Lee's mission, his interactions, his supporters, his detractors, his enemies, his visitors, and even those who only heard of him and never got to meet him, demonstrate the wider influence of Lee's mission in Vienna as well as the continued openness of Viennese elites towards the American Revolution and its cause. Rather than reducing Lee's mission to an episode of failure, this more complex encounter illustrates the wider stakes at play in the in first struggle for recognition between the Habsburg Monarchy and the United States.

From Normandy Shores to Bohemian Fields

When members of the Continental Congress resolved on July 4, 1776, to establish a "separate and equal station" for the thirteen colonies of mainland North America, they also established the need for diplomatic recognition. In the political transition towards independence, the new United States of America required international recognition to obtain legitimacy for itself and to engage with other nations on the world stage.[8] The leaders of the self-proclaimed United States understood the necessity of these external relations since they were fighting a war of survival against the preeminent military power of the day. Therefore, uninvited patriots, the "militia diplomats," attempted to force themselves into European courts in the hope of procuring recognition, military resources, and perhaps alliances.[9] Vienna, the capital of the Habsburg dynasty, was one of these targeted courts.

From the outset, the patriot strategic view included the Habsburg Monarchy, but most narratives of the American Revolution do not acknowledge this fact. Yet it is imperative to recognise that the patriot revolutionaries incorporating one of Europe's most powerful dynasties into their political plan made complete sense. The Habsburg monarchs, after all, ruled a vast European territory with the second largest European population, commanded a substantial military, and owned the lands surrounding one of the largest weapon manufactories in the world at Liège.[10] Given that the exigencies of the war forced the patriots to seek military supplies such as uniforms, gunpowder, and monetary loans from across Europe, approaching the power that controlled the transit network around Liége became a high priority. Moreover, Joseph II's role as Holy Roman Emperor, and therefore nominal head of all the German princes, including the Duke-Elector of Brunswick-Lüneberg (Britain's King George III), was a considerable weight in the scale of patriot consideration. Joseph, the revolutionaries came to hope, could halt the flow of Hessian mercenaries that swelled the British forces in North America using this position. Indeed, since the Hanoverian succession in 1714 had rendered Great Britain not only an Atlantic power but also a continental one in Europe, George III's German holdings in Brunswick would constitute an exposed front if the Habsburgs—the ally of their ally France—could be brought onto the patriot side. The British would have to divert additional resources to defend it. Tensions between George III as an elector and Joseph II as emperor within the Holy Roman Empire was another noted weakness by Americans.[11] Combined, these British weaknesses and the strengths of Joseph II appeared as favourable incentives to target the Habsburg Monarchy.

The Grand Duke of Tuscany provided another impulse for patriots to approach the Habsburg Monarchy. Prior to Pietro Leopoldo's edict of neutrality in 1778, he and his ministers had attempted to keep vital trading lanes with North America open for business. Tuscan merchants in Livorno had traded extensively with British North America for cod from the New England fisheries long before the outbreak of revolution. By 1775, Livornese merchants traded in Baltimore, Charleston, New York, Philadelphia, and Norfolk, Virginia.[12] When hostilities flared between colonists and the British in 1775, Pietro Leopoldo declared Livorno open to all traders. One of the American commissioners in Europe, Silas Deane, interpreted this as a friendly overture to the patriot cause, although it was not intended as one. Deane described Pietro Leopoldo as "being zealously in favour of America," whose actions to take off "all duties on American commerce, [were] to give it encouragement."[13] The Tuscan agent Filippo Mazzei, who had arrived in Virginia in 1773, encouraged the emerging leaders of the American Revolution to conduct a private mission to Florence, which he suggested would be "very beneficial to us in our present struggles."[14] At the same time, Thomas Jefferson, in contact with Mazzei and various Tuscans, mused on whether loans could be obtained given this sincerity.[15] In early 1777, a patriot supporter published a *Memoire and Supplemental Observations* which argued, "the wisest plan of Conduct will be to engage some of the powers of Europe to recognize the Independancy of the Colonys [sic]; Perhaps the Emperor, the King of Prussia, with the Grand Duke of Tuscany, might be induced to Concur with France in making such a recognition."[16] From Pietro Leopoldo's simple action, intended to protect trade, patriots gained the impression that the Habsburg dynasty, by extension, had shown support for their cause. One of the Americans' major convictions to bring about relations between the United States and the Habsburg Monarchy rested on the assumption that Pietro Leopoldo's actions reflected a sentiment shared by his brother Joseph.

In the spring of 1777, Arthur Lee travelled unofficially to investigate the German courts. He followed in the footsteps of Deane's secretary William Carmichael who Deane had sent to Hamburg and Berlin to gather intelligence in the autumn of 1776.[17] Lee's mission included Frederick II's court at Berlin, which, patriots generally believed, had also shown sympathetic signs.[18] Lee travelled with another patriot revolutionary, Stephen Sayre, who served as his secretary.[19] Lee and Sayre left Paris on May 12 and arrived in Vienna around May 27, 1777. They became the first patriot revolutionaries to reach Vienna. The British ministry in London knew of their plans—even to the point that they travelled in a carriage "painted deep green"—but this information never reached the British representatives in Vienna.[20] Lee and Sayre spent three days in the city before leaving on May 29, for Berlin. During their stay the pair met with commercial agents in and around Vienna. A few months later, from nearby Eisenstadt, a Jewish textile merchant by the name of Barruch Pincus wrote in order to answer Lee's enquiry about the quality, quantities, and relative costs of his fabrics which could be used for uniforms.[21] Since Lee had no commission to deal with the Habsburgs, it is unlikely he attempted to meet with any Viennese officials. In one of the two short letters that he wrote to Benjamin Franklin from Vienna, Lee conveyed the error of earlier impressions about the Habsburgs. "There is," he remarked, "a Cold tranquillity here, that bodes us no good" and added in French, "We cannot warm up the German coldness."[22] His warnings came too late. Congress had already issued a dual commission to the courts of Vienna and Berlin, along with one for Florence, *before* Lee's cautionary reports arrived. The ill-founded hunch about the Habsburgs had become an objective of patriot diplomacy.

The man chosen for the dual venture was Arthur's elder brother, William Lee. This elder Lee is one of those figures relegated to the margins of history, largely because, as his biographer Alonzo T. Dill concludes, his abilities went "unfulfilled by the wartime tasks imposed upon him."[23] Although Lee belonged to the illustrious Lee dynasty, he was overshadowed by the more familiar exploits of his older siblings Richard Henry Lee and Francis Lightfoot Lee. After growing up at Stratford Hall situated on the tidewaters of the Potomac River along the Northern Neck of Virginia, in the 1760s he relocated to London and established himself as a businessman in the city. There he stayed with his uncle in a "nice house on Craven Street, next door to Franklin."[24] By the 1770s, Lee, along with his brother Arthur, had become immersed in the liberal politics of the day. As the situation between Britain and the colonies became increasingly agitated, Lee found fertile ground to make powerful allies amongst those who defended the rights of the colonists. His influential associates, mainly the radical John Wilkes, promoted him and Sayre, then a merchant in London, for election as sheriffs. In 1773, William Lee and Sayre became the first American-born sheriffs of London. Franklin wrote to his son in astonishment: "The new Sheriffs-elect are—could you believe it?—both Americans!"[25]

Election as sheriff of London strengthened Lee's political experience.[26] As conflict escalated in the colonies, however, Lee's high office and colonial heritage became a focal point of contention. Twice he was attacked and denounced before the end of his term in 1774. Undeterred, Lee ran unsuccessfully again and again for public office in numerous parliamentary by-elections. In one, the

Southwark constituency, one witness noted how people were "whipped into a Republican frenzy" after Lee entered the running.[27] On May 19, 1775, Lee regained his political standing by winning a wardmote at the Ironmonger's Hall to become the first and only American-born alderman of the City of London.[28] Yet this office earned him greater vilification as worsening news of revolutionary conflict reached the metropole. Lee faced a personal crisis as the prejudice against him made his public presence untenable. After war had broken out, Lee "guessed that American tobacco would be pouring into France" and saw an opportunity to exit London.[29] In the summer of 1776 he travelled for the first time to Paris where he discovered the impossibility of trading tobacco against the monopoly of the French government.[30] A further blow came from his painful first encounter with Deane, who had taken a dislike to William's brother Arthur and opposed any "meddling" with his own trading and political efforts in Paris.[31]

Upon his lamentable return to London, Lee sowed the seed for his role in the interaction between the Habsburg Monarchy and the United States of America. Along the exposed Normandy shores at the town of Dieppe, he penned a desperate plea to his brother in Congress, Richard Henry Lee. "Can't you fix upon some employment for a certain friend of yours," the younger Lee insisted, referring to himself, "[something] that is equal in his station of life, and his capacity, such as it is?" Given that Lee faced returning to London in the wake of the publication of the Declaration of American Independence, he sought to make use of his brother's congressional influence to save himself, hinting to him that "it would have been prudent to have had the Declaration of Independence authoritatively proclaimed to every Court in Europe."[32] As Lee crossed the channel back to London, he had little idea what this letter would set in motion.

Congress originally appointed Lee as a commercial agent for Nantes a few months later in February 1777. Discord among the American diplomats in Paris boiled over around this time, especially between Deane and Arthur Lee, whose personal difficulties arose from their competing aims and culminated in Lee accusing Deane of fraud and embezzlement.[33] Their spat had severe repercussions for William Lee's new career. Most importantly, Congress sent his commission to Paris rather than directly to London for fear of interception. Deane took responsibility to inform him but exercised little urgency. On March 3, Deane forwarded the commission via ordinary, vulnerable post and consequently word of the appointment spread through London before Lee himself received confirmation on April 21, adding to his vilification as one of the "aliens and improper people [put] to office."[34] Lee endured this hostility in London until the birth of his first daughter Portia Lee in early June, after which he felt free to move to Paris.

In Paris, Lee discovered his first appointment was as commercial co-agent to the ineffective and often drunken Thomas Morris. Moreover, Deane had conspired with Franklin to replace Lee with Franklin's grandnephew. To solidify their attempt, Deane persuaded Lee to wait in Paris rather than go directly to Nantes, arguing that another agent there, John Ross, should settle Morris's accounts beforehand. Without any allies—both his brother Arthur and Sayre were abroad—Lee reluctantly remained in Paris throughout the summer of 1777, but after realising Deane's ploy and the unlikelihood of Ross finishing anytime soon, he left embittered for Nantes. On August 4, Lee arrived to find Morris a "strange lost man," who was blind drunk and had barricaded himself in his room. Distressed, Lee wrote to his brothers to complain of the rotten situation and fumed at Deane for the debacle, likening the appointment of Franklin's grandnephew to "ordering your Servant to take my Coat off my back and put it on your own!"[35] Seeing no good in Nantes, he returned to Paris on October 6, 1777. There, the situation had declined further. Accusations of fraud amongst the commissioners had reached an unresolvable point. Franklin despaired how "in a court [. . .] where every word is watched and weighed [. . .] one of them is offended if the smallest thing that is done without his consent."[36] The Lee brothers agreed the best solution would be to rid themselves of Deane by sending him to Amsterdam and Franklin to Vienna. They began petitioning their contacts in Congress for such an outcome.[37]

Instead, Lee learned that Congress had already entrusted him to be the representative to both the courts of Vienna and Berlin back on July 1, 1777. Congress instructed him to petition Joseph as Holy Roman Emperor to stop German princes providing Britain with mercenaries; to gain Habsburg "acknowledgement of the independence of these States," and finally, to "propose treaties of friendship and commerce."[38] The day after he returned from Nantes, Lee accepted his newest commission but warned that he had not been able to "conference on the subject with the commissioners." At the same time, he offered his resignation as an alderman of London.[39]

Winter precluded any immediate travel and instead Lee set to work preparing his affairs. He received the indirect help from the Habsburg ambassador Count Florimond Mercy-d'Argenteau in Paris, who observed immediately an "imperfection" in the commission. As it was, Lee's papers permitted him only to deal with Joseph and not Maria Theresa, whom Lee informed Congress was "extremely jealous of her power and authority, not permitting her son to interfere in any manner."[40] Such a transgression of courtly protocol became an increasingly common feature of the first American interaction with the Habsburgs.

The difficulties of his task emerged over successive months. Lee confided to one brother how, as a commercial agent, "I could and assuredly should have been of great use to the Public," but as a diplomat he had grave concerns. He confessed:

> I doubt my abilities, for however anxious and zealous, it must require both much time and more capacity than is common for a man not versed in the crooked paths of courts to get into the mysteries of the most subtle cabinets of Europe and besides [at] about 40 years old, it is somewhat awkward to go to school to learn languages.[41]

Lee's own acknowledgement of his inadequacies for the mission stemmed from his unfamiliarity with German and, by Viennese accounts, his poor command of French. Lee also faced financial pressures, earning little as a commercial agent.[42] In 1777, he attempted to use his knowledge of political events to manipulate the stock market but his trading order transacted too late and lost him his hedge.[43] To compound matters, his wife Hannah Philippa Ludwell Lee arrived in France with their children which precipitated the move to larger, more expensive premises on the Parisian outskirts at Chantilly.[44] In desperation, Lee pressed Congress for additional funds citing Vienna as "such a gay and lavish court as any," but receiving no answer, he took out a personal loan of 3,000 French livres to cover the costs of the mission.[45] No ordinary diplomat in Europe faced such difficulties, and Lee's financial difficulties would have a profound effect on the first diplomatic interaction between the Habsburg Monarchy and the United States.

Further problems emerged as soon as the new year dawned. On January 31, Morris finally succumbed to alcoholism, which forced Lee, now sole agent for commerce, to dash once again to Nantes to resolve commercial affairs. There, Lee clashed again with Ross over documents that belonged to Morris. Ross accused Lee of unrightfully meddling by confiscating Morris's papers, which Lee did regardless before he returned to Paris on February 25—only to face the same dispute with Franklin.[46] Deane, aided by an angered Franklin, delayed Lee further by withholding documents provided by Congress, which Lee thought necessary to take to Vienna.[47] They also attacked Lee's legitimacy of holding two positions.[48] Indeed Lee faced an uphill battle in asserting his legitimacy as a diplomat. George Mercer, an American military officer, who sojourned at Paris that year, wrote to his old friend George Washington,

> Neither Chance [n]or Accident could ever have named William Lee a Commissioner to the first Court in Europe or indeed to any Court in

FIGURE 9. Portrait of the first American envoy to
the Habsburg Monarchy, William Lee

the World. America herself cannot believe—tell it not in the Streets of
Philadelphia nor let it be known in Virginia: William Lee an *Ambassador*
to Vienna and Arthur Lee an *Ambassador* to France—but to do Justice to
Arthur Lee, he has every Kind of Sense and Knowledge, expect common
Sense and a Knowledge of the World, and he is a Man of Learning, but
what Apology can be made for the Appointment of William Lee?[49]

Lee's time in service at Paris and Nantes had been the most testing period
of his life so far, and it made for ill-preparation ahead of a more trying time
in Vienna.

At the same time, Vienna increasingly became the fulcrum of European diplomacy as foreign ministers competed to influence the Habsburgs. The fact
that the Americans were not at all alone in their designs on the Habsburg court
exacerbated Lee's naivety and ill-preparedness. Many European powers, particularly Britain and France, were desirous to steer the Habsburgs to their own ends.
In the last major European conflict, the Seven Years' War, the position of the
German powers had heavily determined the outcome, so much so that William
Pitt the Elder famously quipped, "America was conquered in Germany."[50] As the
Revolutionary war escalated, the same, it seemed, would be the case again. The
British desire to induct the Habsburgs towards their side in the fight was not a
sudden development. Rather it was a theme that had long dominated British

diplomatic aims on the continent. From 1763, the British lamented the loss of their powerful ally, and reversing the outcomes of the so-called Diplomatic Revolution of 1756—when the Habsburgs became allies of France and Britain allied with Prussia—became an outright objective. In 1765, then Secretary of State John Montagu, the fourth Earl of Sandwich, had informed the Habsburg ambassador "how much it was to be wished that the union which formerly subsisted with the House of Austria might be re-established." "We were," Sandwich concluded, "the natural allies of each other," especially since the British sought security for their Hanoverian interests and an additional bulwark against French expansionism in Germany.[51]

It was a persistent belief. In 1771, George III declared that "England, in conjunction with the House of Austria and the [Dutch] Republic" seemed the "most secure barrier" against France and Spain.[52] As the situation intensified and open war with France ebbed closer towards reality, British efforts increasingly centred on Vienna. There, the British ambassador Sir Robert Murray Keith wrote proudly to his superiors that anti-French temperament existed in Joseph II who, he argued, "is so totally unlike a Frenchman, above all, a French monarch."[53] The Habsburgs seemed an ideal counterweight. If they could be dislodged from the French alliance and wed to British interests, then the French might reconsider their involvement in the American war, British Hanover would be less strategically exposed, and Britain would gain a powerful military ally on the continent. By 1778, the Secretary for War, Charles Jenkinson, remarked how Britain's fate now lay with those "great military powers in the interior parts of Europe."[54]

French policy makers were acutely aware of this situation and sought to isolate the British from any continental connection, especially Vienna. The French ambassador, Louis Auguste le Tonnelier, Baron de Breteuil, repeatedly attempted to convince the Habsburg monarchs of British aggression as responsible for the outbreak of hostilities. The initial clash between *La Belle Poule* and HMS *Arethusa* in 1778 was, Breteuil claimed, the result of such British belligerence and justified the defensive actions of France.[55] Yet this narrative did not wash with the Habsburgs, particularly the emperor, who during his recent journey through France had noted thousands of uniforms being smuggled across the Atlantic.[56] To Joseph, British aggression was in fact retaliation in a war already begun by French action.[57]

The French situation deteriorated further following the death of the Bavarian Elector Maximilian Joseph. By late 1777, French officials had committed themselves to supporting the American cause despite the consequences with Britain. News of the elector's death in late December arrived in Paris by January 5, 1778.[58]

The timing proved troublesome for French strategy. The elector's passing had extinguished the main Wittelsbach line before the question over the inheritance of Bavaria had been settled. Habsburg forces were now poised to take the Bavarian lands, which the dynasty had claimed for decades.[59] Concerned by the potential Habsburg acquisition of Bavarian territory along with its revenue, and, importantly, the electoral role within the Holy Roman Empire, Frederick II of Prussia immediately protested against Habsburg claims in favour of a more agreeable, if not neutral succession.[60] The succession crisis pitted the two competing German dynasties, the Habsburgs and Hohenzollerns, against one another and had severe consequences for the stability of continental Europe. By April, both sides had raised armies and Frederick marched his troops into Bohemia.

The French foreign minister, Charles Gravier, comte de Vergennes, had worked to avoid this very situation for years. In 1775, he had sought to curb Joseph's expansionist tendencies when the emperor gained the province of Bukovina from the Turks. Vergennes had made it clear that the French would not support any further acquisitions.[61] He maintained this policy, knowing any war between Austria and Prussia would sap France's ability to deal a decisive blow to Britain through the opportunity afforded by the rebellion in America.[62] In the eyes of Vergennes and other French ministers, Joseph had no legal right to the Bavarian lands. As much as Joseph would not recognise the French interpretation of the War of American Independence, King Louis and Vergennes would not support the Habsburg outlook on the War of the Bavarian Succession. This geopolitical tit-for-tat imperilled the French alliance with the Habsburgs, who argued that Frederick's invasion of Bohemia had invoked their defensive alliance of 1757 and, accordingly, France now owed 20,000 troops to the Habsburg cause. As 1778 wore on, the alliance weakened and both sides insisted on neutrality vis-à-vis Prussia and the Americans, respectively, to spite the other.

Lee's mission to the Habsburg court thus came at a fortuitous moment for France. The American mission offered a chance to break the Bourbon-Habsburg stalemate by potentially persuading the Habsburgs towards the American side without risking a French commitment to the Bavarian issue. At the very least, any acceptance of the patriot emissary would signal sympathy towards the Americans. The stakes were even higher since the French had officially recognised the thirteen colonies as the sovereign United States of America in the Franco-American alliance. Any degree of Habsburg recognition, even tacitly through accepting an envoy, became the biggest concern for Britain's minister at Vienna, Keith, who, upon first hearing of Lee's mission, sought immediate assurances from Habsburg ministers that an audience with Lee would be refused.

He worked to avoid such a situation where France, as he put it, could build "a thousand false stories upon that single circumstance."[63] The French meanwhile offered all means of assistance for the mission. Breteuil would chaperon Lee in Vienna, hopefully gaining him an audience with either monarch. The American mission presented France with a golden opportunity to widen the American conflict and further isolate Britain with little political risk attached. War was coming to Vienna.

These strategies created a precarious international situation for the Habsburgs. A few weeks before Lee left Paris for Vienna, Joseph II engaged Breteuil in conversation at a Viennese dinner party. The pair discussed the two major wars now facing Europe: one for America, the other for Bavaria. Each of them held contrasting views. For Breteuil, the two conflicts were inextricably linked; for Joseph, they were two distinct events.[64] The French conflagration held little interest for the emperor. First and foremost, Habsburg policy had grown divergent from French strategic interests as Eastern territories had become a greater political magnet for Joseph's ambitions. He had acquired Galicia through the First Partition of Poland in 1772, Bukovina from the Ottomans in 1777, and further Ottoman territories remained a continual object of future aspirations.[65] By contrast, French fixation on the Atlantic counted for little except for potential disturbances to the balance of power. Maria Theresa's reflections on this situation to her daughter, Marie Antoinette, should be remembered here. In order to achieve success in Bavaria, the Habsburgs needed to avoid any involvement in the Anglo-French dispute. Hence Joseph preferred to view the two wars as two distinct confrontations. Neutrality became the only viable Habsburg position out of necessity given their own aims.

Given this broader European context, certain aspects of Lee's mission were already pre-determined by wider geopolitical events. The Habsburgs, increasingly wary and displeased by the French, looked upon his mission before it even began as an extension of Bourbon policy to press them into a conflict in which they did not desire to partake. The French meanwhile considered it an opportunity to break the diplomatic logjam. The British, for their part, would stop at nothing to prevent it from succeeding. The American patriots showed no awareness of these troublesome aspects, however. From their viewpoint, Lee's mission was merely part of a broader strategy to attempt to secure support from any European court in their struggle. It was only later that Lee and his colleagues became aware of this paralysing geopolitical climate. Lee, therefore, was not the overall decisive element in determining the mission's success. To be sure, his personal suitability for the position of envoy was questionable, ranging from his inabilities in French to his frictions with other Americans in Paris. This ill-fated setup of militia diplomacy made the task at hand even more arduous, but it would have always been a Sisyphean task. Little wonder then, that as Lee left Paris in the spring of 1778, he was beginning the journey he would later describe as the "long, laborious, and most odious task" of his life.[66]

"You Know Mr Lee is In Town?"

William Lee set out from Paris on March 24, 1778, without any real aim. Aware of the growing rupture between the Habsburgs and Hohenzollerns, Lee sensed war over the Bavarian crisis was on the horizon. His last report to Congress a day before his departure had laid out his concerns. He explained how Berlin represented the greater chance of success given Frederick II's earlier overtures to recognise the United States as soon as France had done so, but, he warned, "at this critical moment it is impossible for any man in the world to form a decisive opinion because the issue will depend on events that are yet in the womb of time." Lee elected to move to a midpoint in the German lands instead and wait for "the first opening that is made on either side in our favour."[67] He reached the Free Imperial City of Frankfurt in early April. There, he hesitated further about the war, which, "if once commenced," he believed, "promises to be the most bloody and desolating that Europe has known for this century past."[68] Berlin remained Lee's primary objective but in Frankfurt, word reached him that Frederick had reneged on his vow, and so Lee's plan shifted towards Vienna. An anxious letter sent to his brother Arthur at the end of the month revealed his indecisiveness and worries:

> If [I] should not be properly received at Vienna, in case the course should be bent that way, do you think [I] ought to remain there, to wait the course of events? Perhaps it may not be improper to stay and the point of indignity may be got over from the mistake in the commission.[69] No decided resolution can be taken yet for some days in consequence of what was communicated [on] the 23rd [to Congress] but as far as any judgement can be formed at present Vienna will be the course at last.[70]

Lee's Viennese mission was completely ad hoc. Not only had he settled on prioritising Vienna at the eleventh hour, but his reordering set his affairs in further disarray. In the first week of May, Lee desperately urged the commissioners back in Paris for help in securing his French host in Vienna but he had little hope that Franklin and Deane would comply. On May 10, Lee confided to a

friend, "One line from [them] would make everything go smoothly, but without it very little can be expected in the present situation of things . . . [and] unless Franklin can be counteracted, I am not to expect anything."[71] The next day,
exactly one month after his arrival, Lee finally left for Vienna. The time spent
deliberating in Frankfurt added to the complexity of Lee's mission. During his
stay there, the *Wienerisches Diarium* had announced Lee's role in Vienna. The
newspaper identified Arthur and William Lee, "the brothers of Heinrich Richard Lee [*sic*], the famous member of Congress," who were assigned respectively
to Spain and "some other court."[72] Of course certain members of the Habsburg
court had been well aware of Lee's intended mission from rumour and espio-
nage. The British were aware, too. Keith had already informed his superiors in
London on April 22 that "Lodgings are taken here for Mr William Lee, who
is daily expected."[73]

Lee's numerous delays in Paris and in Frankfurt afforded Keith ample time
to prepare for his arrival. He successfully sought assurances from the State
Chancellor Prince von Kaunitz that Lee would be denied an audience. Kaunitz gave these willingly as he resented the French imposition in the first place.
King George found them to be "very satisfactory" and instructed Keith to "take
an Opportunity of assuring the Prince that His Majesty is very sensible of this
Mark of Her Imperial Majesty's Attention and friendly disposition, which the
King is ever desirous to procure."[74] By early May 1778, Keith and his superiors
in London had placed their trust in Kaunitz and were quietly confident Lee's
mission would result in abject failure. However, they overinterpreted this goodwill to mean the "court is desirous of breaking off the Connection with France,
and renewing the Old System."[75] The British deluded themselves by thinking a
Habsburg alliance against France in the War of American Independence was
within reach. Lee's mission in Vienna would prove the ultimate test for such an
alliance, and so Keith monitored the situation with great attention.

As Lee arrived under the cover of darkness on the evening of Saturday, May
23, Keith received "immediate information of his Arrival" from one of his informers at the gates. For his part, Breteuil, his French equivalent, sought out
Kaunitz at one of his usual billiard parties. He shared the news of Lee's arrival
towards the end of his conversation with Kaunitz by mentioning how he would
"take the liberty to present [a] gentleman traveller, Mr William Lee, who has
brought recommendations." It seemed as if Breteuil had underestimated Kaunitz's foreknowledge of the mission. The next day Keith, ever anxious, paid Kaunitz a visit. "You know Mr Lee is in town?" Kaunitz asked to raise the matter.
"I am sorry for it," he added, "[since] I am surprised at the Court of France

FIGURE 10. Portrait of Sir Robert Murray Keith, the British
ambassador in Vienna during the American Revolution

persisting in sending such a Person to Vienna." As Kaunitz explained the French ambassador's desire to present Lee as a "gentleman traveller," it became clear to Keith that this would wreck any attempt to keep Lee out of the court entirely. The plot hinged on the freedom of any ambassador to present private persons rather than having to request an official audience in order to present a foreign emissary. In devising such a plan, Breteuil knew it counted for very little to observers whether Lee would be met as a traveller or as an American emissary since any reception would be enough for their aims. For the British, it was vital that Lee not be received at all, and so Keith replied, "I shall be very sorry, Sir, if you receive Lee under any Shape or Denunciation."[76] Kaunitz had been warned and Keith pressed further the stakes involved by meeting Lee.

It was at that point in their conversation that Breteuil arrived at the scene. Keith naturally avoided his French counterpart, which allowed Breteuil and Kaunitz to resume their conversation from the night before. Keith later noted how the "conversation was not very long, and the Ambassador seemed uneasy at quitting the Prince." In order words, he sensed Breteuil's desperation. Before Kaunitz left, he confidentially told Keith, "I have not been able to dissuade Mr de Breteuil from taking this rash step; He says he has positive orders . . . and must obey them by presenting [Lee] to me."[77] Kaunitz was caught between both sides.

The manoeuvres of Breteuil and Keith already affected Lee's chances of success. Keith held the advantage. He was a gifted linguist and experienced diplomat in Vienna since 1773 who had fostered great respect among his Viennese colleagues. The only chink in Keith's armour was the relationship with his superiors in London. His constant lack of sufficient instruction or information from them hampered his effectiveness at court. "I am forced to feed upon the scraps," he decried to one friend.[78] Keith's dilemma became more acute during Lee's mission because of the ill-health of his direct superior, Henry Howard, twelfth Earl of Suffolk, whose sickness prevented him from responding in full or within time. By July 1778, Suffolk had become so incapacitated that Thomas Thynne, Viscount Weymouth took responsibility for instructing Keith.[79] Breteuil by contrast enjoyed a good line of communication to and from the French court.[80] He was, however, severely disadvantaged when it came to his relationship with the ministers in Vienna. His interactions with Kaunitz had turned sour when Breteuil had rebuffed Kaunitz over the legitimacy of Habsburg actions in the Bavarian crisis. Kaunitz "at first smouldered, then he flew into a rage" according to eyewitnesses.[81] It was one of several instances when Kaunitz lost his temper at the French representative.[82] By April 1778, it had become impossible to hide the "coldness between the cabinets of Versailles and Vienna."[83]

For all his occasional outbursts, Kaunitz was a brilliant statesman. His experience had accrued over some twenty-five years by 1778.[84] The Viennese, however, noted his peculiar personality. Kaunitz was by all accounts a paranoid hypochondriac, prone to sudden headaches and illnesses that would remove him from courtly life, and from which sprang a pedantic vegetarian diet. His predilection for brushing his teeth after every meal was another point of eccentricity noted by his acquaintances.[85] Yet Kaunitz was quite sociable despite his unusual mannerisms. The British traveller Sir Nathanial Wraxall provided a rich portrait of Kaunitz during his visit to Vienna in the late 1770s, a city he believed "offers more resources to a stranger" than any other.[86] Wraxall experienced Viennese social life centred upon the "common rallying point of pleasure and relaxation" at Kaunitz's townhouse at Freyung, which was "open every evening for the reception of company and constitutes a principal source of amusement at Vienna."[87] Kaunitz was easily accessible, "usually engaged at billiards . . . or in conversation as his inclinations may lead." "Everything," declared Wraxall, "conduces to put a foreigner at his ease, and insensibly to divest him of the awkwardness or embarrassment . . . in the midst of a society, with whose habits and common topics of conversation he is unacquainted."[88] This was a far cry away from the type of reception William Lee would encounter at Kaunitz's home.

When Breteuil took Lee to meet with Kaunitz after dinner on May 26, 1778, Mr. Ernest, the British chargé d'affaires, was intentionally present to keep watch on the meeting. "The Prince," reportedly "without speaking one Single Word to either, made Lee the coldest Bow possible & turned away, leaving the Room a moment after and taking no taking no farther notice of the Ambassador or of his Traveller."[89] Although other visitors also found Kaunitz "remarkably cold and inattentive to strangers, sometimes scarcely deigning to speak," Breteuil's actions led Kaunitz to act deliberately cold in this instance.[90] Duped, Kaunitz wrote furiously to Maria Theresa about the encounter, stating he "received [Lee] with a simple politeness but without saying a word." "I will give him no invitation to dinner," he added, "and will continue to receive him coldly if he comes again" and so advised his sovereign "under no circumstance grant audience to this man in his capacity or as a private individual."[91] Keith summarised the event to his superiors by noting how Kaunitz seemed "a good deal nettled" and was "not much pleased with the Ambassador."[92]

Other dinners went smoother for Lee. After taking leave of the awkward situation, Breteuil and Lee went house-calling to leave visit cards among the local Viennese nobility and foreign dignitaries before they headed to the ambassador's box at the theatre.[93] Fortunately for the cash-strapped Lee, Breteuil was "the only member of the diplomatic corps whose establishment enables him to entertain in a style of magnificence."[94] Accordingly, two days later Breteuil hosted a dinner party to honour and introduce the Viennese to his foreign guest. First impressions fixated on Lee's appearance as "rich, thoroughly ugly, [and] marked by the smallpox."[95] Lee's popularity declined as his inability to converse fluently in French became apparent.[96] Under scrutiny from Count Johann von Saint-Julien, "a great partisan of the Americans" who "continuously questioned the said American about hundreds of things of his country," Lee's communicative abilities came undone.[97] Another observer noted, Lee "possesses a good head and reasons very well," but "speaks little French and expresses himself very badly."[98] This dinner was Lee's first exposition, but more were to follow. Despite linguistic mishaps, however, Lee acquired a level of notoriety amongst Viennese socialites.

The dinners connected Lee to a sympathetic Viennese audience, hailing from a variety of important offices and backgrounds. Among his fellow diners were Count von Saint-Julien who, at the age of twenty-one, was starting a promising career in the imperial army, and Countess Maria Elisabeth von Waldstein.[99] Countess Maria Carlotta von Hatzfeld was married to the influential statesman Count Karl Friedrich von Hatzfeld, the imperial chamberlain. Lee had obviously charmed the latter as she later introduced him to her husband. Another notable guest at the dinner table was Prince Wenzel Johann Joseph Paar, a well connected noble and the imperial postmaster general.[100]

The obvious absentees, however, were the courtiers who had already expressed their sympathies for the American cause. The most significant absence was Jan Ingenhousz, who had left for London in order to present the Baker Lectures at the Royal Society.[101] Ingenhousz, who had been the most forceful advocate for the Americans, was completely unaware of Lee's mission. The animosity between Franklin and the Lees had robbed the mission of a vital ally in Vienna. Similarly, Lee's name was unknown to Count Karl von Zinzendorf who, with equally unintended misfortune, had departed for Trieste three weeks before Lee's arrival.[102] That summer in Trieste, he began to read *Common Sense* just as the Revolution's representative resided a few hundred miles away. Emperor Joseph II was also away on military manoeuvres in upper Bohemia. Joseph's time away from court and his frequent disagreements over the Bavarian crisis meant foreign policy lay effectively in the hands of his mother and Kaunitz.[103] This afforded Maria Theresa a greater level of autonomy in her son's absence; a further disadvantage for Lee's success. On May 31, she responded to Kaunitz's memorandum on his encounter with Lee by venting her anger at the French ambassador. She instructed her own, Mercy-d'Argenteau, to reaffirm to the French court that she "cannot possibly receive him ... not even as a simple traveller." Such a meeting, she fretted to Kaunitz, would "breed factionalism and cause incivility."[104] For Maria Theresa, the anxiety that she would be "driven against her will" by the American issue, as she had expressed already to her daughter, seemed a plausible reality.

Lee had, after all, come knocking on her door. On May 27—in between the disastrous nocturnal encounter with Kaunitz and the first dinner party the night after—Lee and Breteuil had travelled to the palace of Schönbrunn outside the city walls. The pair "made all the usual Visits there to the *Grandes Maitresses* of the Empress and Her Daughters as likewise to the Great Chamberlain in the manner which is customary [for] the Presentation of a Stranger patronised by a Foreign Minister." These conventional greetings were as far as Lee was permitted. Kaunitz reassured an increasingly concerned Keith the next day by reconfirming "Her Royal Mistress's firm Resolution that Lee should have no Admission whatever either publick or private to Her Presence." "Since," Kaunitz continued, "she is so sincerely disposed to cultivate with His Majesty, [and] had thought proper to render Her Determination as clear indubitable and peremptory as possible to preclude all false surmises and Conjectures of distant nations." Within just five days of Lee's arrival, the door at Schönbrunn had shut.

Keith declared, with a sigh of relief, "I believe that I may now look upon the Affair as wholly terminated."[105]

Lee's own inabilities combined with the embryonic nature of patriot diplomacy had forced him to rely upon the French ambassador, whose shambolic efforts jeopardised the mission. By so hastily forcing Lee upon the court, Breteuil had gambled away the American's chances. As Keith supposed, "His Excellency probably imagined that by this means he would leave little Time for deliberation and procure Access to the Empress before any Resolution could be taken to shut the Door against Mr Lee." Ostracised by Kaunitz since the Bavarian crisis, Breteuil could have hardly been aware of the extent of Kaunitz's preparedness and the sincerity of his guard against Lee. To attempt to bypass courtly etiquette in Vienna, where "little is ever to be gained by surprise," was to provide the fatal blow to Lee's mission overall.[106] Besides, Lee himself realised the ruse of masquerading as a simple traveller would not work: "all the world knows my design," he wrote to Arthur.[107]

In a second effort to speak with the court gatekeeper, Lee made another appearance at Kaunitz's home on June 2, but crucially, without Breteuil. Even without him, this latest ploy failed as he "remained in the room for a considerable Time but Prince Kaunitz took no Notice."[108] A week later, Breteuil devised a new strategy by presenting Lee to the ageing Imperial Vice Chancellor, Prince Rudolf Joseph von Colloredo, who harboured deep misgivings about the French and argued with Kaunitz for a rapprochement with the British. The meeting, predictably, did not go well. Lee presented himself to the "Prince and Princess and to most of the principal People present" at the same time as they were receiving English guests through Keith. "The unexpected Appearance at that house and in that Place," Keith reported later, "stirred up an Indignation in my Breast which I was at no Pains to conceal."[109] Within no time, the whole court heard of "a real comic scene [filled] with sourness and emotion."[110] Kaunitz, in his latest memorandum on French indecency, informed Maria Theresa, "it was a deliberate indiscretion on [France's] part, designed to compromise us vis-à-vis England."[111] The Colloredo debacle seemed to cement the impossibility of Lee's mission.

Perhaps revealing his inexperience, Lee appeared blissfully unaware of his perilous situation and the gross insults done to the court by his repeated unwelcome appearances. The next day, on June 10, Lee wrote jubilantly to his brother: "the American cause seems to engage conversation much more than the differences in this country."[112] Lee did not admit this resulted from his controversial actions. As for Breteuil, Lee naïvely expressed admiration for the man "who is polite, able, and extremely well-versed in the management of such an intricate business...and has in short done everything that I could wish."[113] The irony was completely lost on Lee. Breteuil's decision to force Lee into several high-profile encounters within the first few days of his mission had endangered the whole undertaking. But controversy at the soirees of Princes Colloredo and Kaunitz gave Lee an unexpected second wind. Whoever could enrage the high nobility of the capital was suddenly of great interest to the Viennese nobles. As the Swedish ambassador wrote home, "Mr Lee is causing quite a stir here."[114]

During the first half of June, Lee's celebrity reached a zenith. On June 13, Keith lamented, "It has been a matter of great Uneasiness to me, to remark within these few Days, that the Treatment of Mr Lee is very much changed in his Favour." Lee "has not only been well received in several visits to Count Colloredo,"[115] Keith bemoaned, "but he has dined with very large Companies at Count Hatzfeld's and is to have the same Honour at Prince Schwarzenberg's, Great Master of the Household."[116] The latter two were particularly influential. Both Count Karl Friedrich von Hatzfeld and Prince Joseph Adam von Schwarzenberg were members of the Privy Council and advisors to Maria Theresa. Interestingly, Schwarzenberg's daughter was married to Count Ludwig von Zinzendorf. American interest travelled further. Prince Johann Rudolf Chotek von Chotkow und Wognin, for example, had erected a "maison américaine" at one of his Bohemian estates.[117] Lee also met with Antonia Elisabeth Susanna Forster, daughter of the celebrated naturalist Johann Reinhold Forster, who worked as a governess for a rich mercantile family in Vienna.[118] Lee had finally made a breakthrough.

Lee's controversy in Vienna served to make the American Revolution more widely known in the Habsburg lands. His unorthodox methods of diplomacy garnered him an air of notoriety which extended beyond the city. News of Lee's activities travelled to all parts of the Monarchy. In Habsburg Lombardy, a friend of the wife of the imperial commissioner in Milan kept her abreast of Lee's disastrous encounters at the Viennese court, describing in detail Lee's animus for such clashes, and the American cause.[119] In Buda, the aspiring scholar Johann Zinner heard of Lee's presence in Vienna and desired to meet him in order to compile his books on the American Revolution, but could not make it to Vienna in time.[120] In Vienna itself, Lee's brash behaviour elevated him to an object of curiosity among the Viennese who invited him to dinner after dinner in early June. Whereas Lee's mission to pry open the imperial court and obtain support from the Habsburg monarchs for the America cause was certainly a near-impossible task given Kaunitz's reservations and Keith's talent for keeping British interests front and centre, Lee's blunders at court ensured the American Revolution remained a topic of special interest among courtiers and their networks throughout the summer of 1778. Failure at court boosted his success in the salons and at the dinner tables of the Viennese elites.

Fortunately for Keith, Lee's success stopped at the dinner table. Despite his tenacity at "having appeared three or four Times" at Kaunitz's home, Keith was still able to take comfort in the fact that "the Prince has not hitherto opened his Lips to him."[121] This included one occasion when Kaunitz attended Breteuil's recurring dinner parties on June 12. Keith now felt exasperated at the "gall to be daily exposed to meet with Lee at Houses, from which [he could] not wholly withdraw." Keith had identified his rising popularity among courtiers who could not be persuaded to shun the Virginian. Yet before long, Keith reported with satisfaction how Lee "had thought it proper not to make his Appearance at Prince Kaunitz's," and that Lee had become alienated from the diplomatic corps which Keith managed to press into line.[122]

The shift came from Lee's own melancholy about his prospects in Vienna. On June 24, as Keith presented more English guests to Maria Theresa at Schönbrunn, Lee whiled away writing letters.[123] He lamented in one how his "Austrian associates have become somewhat cooler toward him . . . [especially] since the Emperor and King have taken their high line, mouths are in some measure shut."[124] In another, he revealed how his mind was turning to Sweden and Denmark as more likely allies, especially as they "will be much more useful than either Austria or Prussia."[125] By the end of the month, Vienna was awash with rumours that Lee would soon depart the city but with little idea about his next destination.[126] Keith of course was more spirited to report home, "Mr Lee appears very little in Publick, never at Prince Kaunitz's; and the other Colloredo is in the Country. It is said that Lee's stay here will be very short."[127]

Lee had indeed decided to move on. As June began to end, Lee thought the unending stalemate over Bavaria was "sapping attention towards Germany from the American situation," reducing his opportunities in Vienna.[128] There seemed little sense to remain when the ardently isolated Maria Theresa was his only hope, especially as she would soon become even more reclusive during her annual period of mourning for her late husband. Towards the start of July, Keith noted how Lee "has been shut up [for] several Days and constantly writing," but he suspected Lee would leave "in the Hands of a private Person some wild project of Commerce, a Bait for all others, which the People of this Country are the most ready to swallow."[129] Keith was half-right. Lee lingered on for the arrival of his new secretary Samuel Stockton, who reached Vienna around late June.[130]

In the meantime, Lee had tried to compel other diplomats at court to listen to his case. Filippo Vivalda, Marquess of Castellino, the ambassador for the Kingdom of Sardinia, became a focus of Lee's efforts. Prior to Lee's arrival, Castellino had been instructed to follow the prevailing opinion about Lee in Vienna; if Lee were to be recognised by a majority, then he would follow suit.[131] Over the course of June, Lee set himself to dissuade Castellino of his instructions and, by July, he had almost succeeded. Castellino agreed to meet Lee but only in an unofficial capacity as a "Virginian merchant." The pair discussed the prospects of trade between Sardinia and the United States—but without much substance in Castellino's mind, the talks amounted to nothing.[132] Once Stockton had arrived, the pair attempted to convince another target with only a modicum of success. Confirming Keith's intelligence, Lee and Stockton delivered papers to Nils Bark, the Swedish envoy at Vienna, who was not in when they called.[133] On suspicion of their interaction, Bark was later called to Schönbrunn and "passed a considerable time with her Imperial Majesty [and] the French Ambassador with whom he had a long conference."[134] The climate of fear surrounding Lee prevented any further diplomatic initiatives in Vienna.

On July 4, Keith, who had not heard from London since May, finally received instructions. In his reply he triumphantly noted how Lee and Stockton had already left for "the post road back to the Empire and Frankfurt." Relishing Lee's defeat, Keith wrote how it was rightly so; Lee "was losing Ground instead of gaining it" as his "publick Mission must certainly have proven fruitless as it was contemptible."[135] Indeed, Lee had left Vienna on July 2, 1778. This departure, however, was not the end to the effects of the American Revolution in Vienna but merely a continuation. In many ways, Lee's visit had stimulated further the keen interests of the Viennese, imparting to them a tangible example of the Revolution.

Conclusion

American diplomatic failure in Vienna resulted from multiple factors, not just one man's deficiencies. Lee functioned precisely as we would expect from an inexperienced diplomat thrust into the most rigidly ceremonial court in Europe. Failure instead arose largely from two decisive factors: one, the miscalculations made by the French ambassador, Breteuil; and two, inroads made by the British minister resident, Keith, to obtain political promises, which impressed upon the Habsburgs the wider gravity of the situation. The Habsburgs could not acknowledge Lee because doing so risked a delicately established neutrality, created to protect Habsburg interests. In part, because they also wished to spite the French. Sheer bad luck did play a role in Lee's demise as well—notable sympathisers were not in town—but geopolitical exigencies proved more fatal. Diplomats in the court understood this. The Ragusan ambassador reported extensively on Lee's predicament and dismissal by the court, where, he noted, "most people believe he won't be received," but crucially added, "this is an effect of the harmony that reigns between the courts of Vienna and London."[136] The personalities of Breteuil and Keith were pivotal in the first interaction between the United States and the Habsburg Monarchy.

However, just as we assign blame, we should also acknowledge success, and this is a crucial point: there was success in Lee's mission. First, if nothing else, his weeks in Vienna demonstrated the resolve of patriot intentions to form their own diplomatic connections within the European system. It bolstered American sovereignty. Secondly, Lee's visit to Vienna kindled a further degree of interest in the American Revolution. Lee's culinary companions were powerful figures within the court; their informal receptions of him were enough to drive Keith to despair. Even through failure, Lee triumphed. His celebrity increased after his diplomatic faux pas with ministers. Lee left Vienna with nothing to show, but his legacy was the intangible, indelible impression he left behind. The first struggle for recognition may have been mismanaged, it may have failed in its aims, but it was the beginning of a connection between the United States and the biggest continental European power.

CHAPTER SIX

"Wedded to the System They Have Embraced"

The Habsburgs as Mediators and Profiteers in the War of American Independence, 1780–1783

T HE FINAL YEARS of the War of American Independence created new possibilities for the Habsburg Monarchy. In the Austrian Netherlands, Ostend flourished in the later years of the conflict as the only neutral port in northwestern Europe. The influx of foreign ships and investments carried with them new prospects for local firms and business. Trading opportunities, which had been impossible due to the British monopoly before then, now became reality as Habsburg firms reaped the benefits of supplying the Caribbean and North American markets for the first time. For as long as peace remained elusive, profit would continue. Elsewhere in the Habsburg Monarchy, merchants desired the same fortunes. Traders and bankers in the city of Trieste, the major Habsburg free port in the northern Adriatic, clamoured for a share in trade. Many of them attempted to create the first direct trading routes between Trieste and the North American mainland. In doing so, their profits rivalled those of the imperial expeditions to India and China. Overall, private enterprise and economic expansion in the Habsburg Monarchy benefitted greatly from the disruption of the American Revolution and the prospect of an independent United States.

New political challenges and opportunities also emerged for the Habsburgs during the War of American Independence. In 1779, the Habsburgs suffered a humiliating conclusion to the War of the Bavarian Succession, which thwarted Joseph II's designs on Bavaria and heralded a Prussian victory within the eyes of European powers. Co-mediation of the Peace of Teschen assured the Russians the prestige of arbiter of the Holy Roman Empire. Relations between the Habsburgs and France waned as a result of French participation in the peace process. For the Habsburgs, the War of American Independence offered the possibility to correct this humiliation in failing to secure Bavaria. Maria Theresa dreamed of bringing about a general peace within Europe, and State Chancellor Prince von Kaunitz and Joseph II worked tirelessly to realise this aim after her death. Chasing a conclusion to the American Revolutionary war, therefore, took precedence over the economic advantages presented by its continuance. At stake was a restoration of dynastic pride, an opportunity to control the fortunes of Europe, and the chance to inflict painful revenge upon the French and Prussians. Yet few today recall Maria Theresa's dying dream of peace or Kaunitz's longed-for Congress of Vienna which, had it come to pass, would have supplanted Paris as the diplomatic birthplace of a recognised United States of America.

"We Must Bide Our Time" – Ostend and the Atlantic

Across Europe, merchants vied for new commercial opportunities occasioned by the War of American Independence. Nowhere was this rush more present than in the port of Ostend. As the only neutral port on the European mainland at the ligature between the North Sea and Atlantic Ocean, Ostend's mercantile classes benefitted immensely from the conflict. British raids first brought French merchants to Ostend to protect their vessels under the neutral imperial ensign. Dutch merchants followed suit during the Fourth Anglo-Dutch War. Between 1778 and 1780, Ostenders witnessed an almost seven-fold increase in the number of ships using their harbour.[1] Exports to the British Isles, where British merchants also utilised imperial neutrality for their vessels to the Caribbean, soared in same period: Ostend-England trade more than doubled by 1780 whilst exports to Scotland rose from virtually nothing to £45,803 in 1781 and doubled in 1782.[2] The meteoric rise of Ostend as a commercial entrepôt arose from two main factors, both of which were influenced by the American Revolution. First, Ostenders supplied munitions to belligerents owing to its neutrality and proximity to Liège, one of the largest munition manufactories in eighteenth-century Europe; and secondly, masking ships under imperial colours and ownership protected against foreign infractions at sea. Throughout the American Revolution, Ostend was an indispensable port of call for all warring powers.

The independent Prince-Bishopric of Liège was the source of Ostend's tremendous success during the Revolution. The capital Liège, as well as the towns and hamlets in the environs surrounding the city, bisected the Austrian Netherlands and were a manufacturing hub for small arms, rifles, muskets, bayonets, and occasionally cannons. Powder mills, nail factories, and rifling workshops signified the town's way of life. Along the Vesdre River alone, forty different workshops carved out barrels for rifles. The region produced 240,000 guns on average per year for export abroad.[3] All belligerents sourced weapons from Liège. The thirteen American colonies were the most in need. They suffered from the lack of powder mills and ammunition producers in general. Consequently, procuring arms became a major patriot priority. In little more than two months in 1775, the Committee of Safety in Pennsylvania spent nearly £25,000 procuring necessary weapons for their militia.[4] This was excellent news for Liège—and for Ostend. Benjamin Franklin, as a Pennsylvanian agent, fulfilled orders with weapons from Liège and before long, he received unsolicited samples and promises from Liègeois manufacturers hoping for a "channel of arms for the Free States of America."[5]

The completion of the system of canals and roadways connecting Liège with Ostend on the eve of the Revolution allowed for easy transportation of the munitions, especially after the Dutch prohibited military exports.[6] Initial arms traffic between Liège and North America took a circuitous route via Lisbon. British, French, and Habsburg agents in the Portuguese capital tracked the consignments destined for North America.[7] In 1776, the Mayor of Liège declared, "our traders, great and small, are giving work to our men; we see nothing but crates of guns in the streets."[8] Liège's bustling streets in 1776 actually represented a low point of munitions exports. In subsequent years, an extraordinary amount of weaponry transited the Austrian Netherlands to supply the War of American Independence. By the end of the war, Ostend had shipped around two million pounds of munitions.[9] The War of American Independence turned the region into a profitable powder keg.

From 1781 until the end of the war, Ostend was the only neutral port along the northwestern European coastline. The maritime convention of "neutral ships made neutral goods" protected any ships sailing under the Habsburg flag. Ostend merchants offered to "neutralise" foreign vessels through use of the flag. This "neutralisation" trade operated in several ways. The simplest measures involved ships entering Ostend where goods would be unloaded and then reloaded, which involved new cargo papers stating the goods came from the Austrian Netherlands. English ships utilised this method extensively through so-called "Algerian passports" obtained at Ostend, which cleared any cargo heading past the Iberian Peninsula irrespective of the destination.[10] The other method involved re-registering ownership whereby Ostend merchants took ownership of a vessel in name only. The owners were neutral, but the ship, captain, and cargo remained the de facto property of foreigners. These "paper" companies operated through merchants in the Austrian Netherlands who acted as commissioners for large international syndicates. But foreign merchants also relocated to Ostend or established shell companies to reap the same benefit. Merchants from Dunkirk were the first wave of such competitors. One Dunkirk trader, François de Vinck, masked a fleet of 157 ships. His company *De Vinck & Co.* became the major commissioner for European traders to the Atlantic during the Revolution.[11]

Neutralising ships and masking ownership became so prevalent that a new verb emerged: *Ostendisieren* (to Ostendize).[12] This process precipitated an explosion of ship traffic around Ostend. From 1780 to 1783, between 6,000 and 9,000 ships entered Ostend. This was a remarkable increase from the roughly 480 ships which entered each year from 1775 to 1778.[13] In 1782, over fifty foreign firms registered their operations in Ostend and the entirety of the Dunkirk fishing fleet had swapped their flag for the imperial one. Ostend authorities issued 1,944 passports that year and the Admiralty granted firms 268 new passes between 1781 and 1783. The rise was so great that the walls of Ostend had to be torn down and a new neighbourhood and harbour facilities constructed.[14] The American Revolution ushered in an era of considerable economic growth for Ostend and the Austrian Netherlands.

The growth in trade volume increased Ostend's Atlantic connections. New trade avenues opened in the West Indies where the British, Danish, Dutch, French, and Swedish sought to supply their colonies through the neutral imperial flag. In 1782 alone, 126 ships listed the Greater Antilles as their destination in the *Gazette van Gent*. From 1778 until 1785, a constant flow of ships travelled between Ostend and the Caribbean.[15] British traders maintained vital supplies of gin, tea, and tobacco from Caribbean plantations to London by migrating to Ostend. In 1781, a government report noted how, on a single day, 68,970 pounds of tea arrived in London from Ostend.[16] Ostend's merchants even encompassed slave traders. Friedrich Romberg became one of the most successful in this trade in the Austrian Netherlands.[17] Romberg first sought to capitalise on the burgeoning munitions trade to America under his new maritime company *Romberg Fils & Ricour* in Ostend but his request to transport arms to St. Thomas was denied by the authorities in 1782.[18] Romberg expanded his fleet, with almost half of his 327 ships under ownership by established merchants in the Austrian Netherlands.[19] He then founded a maritime insurance company in Bruges and founded two further companies to enter the slave trade; *Romberg & Cie* in Ghent, which focused on forced transportation to Cuba and Saint-Domingue, and *Romberg, Bapst & Cie* at Bordeaux with a German financier and help from Brussels-based bankers, which Romberg fronted through his son Henry. This firm rose to become one of the major slaving houses in France.[20] The Ghent-based branch sent ten ships from Ostend in 1782 destined for Angola and West Africa.[21] Joseph II ennobled Romberg in 1784 for his pioneering efforts, but it was the American Revolution to which Romberg owed his success.[22]

Whilst connections between Ostend and the Atlantic embedded trade links with the Caribbean, fewer merchants dared to enter the warzone directly around mainland America. Direct trade between the United States and Ostend only occurred towards the close of the war, when safer passage seemed assured. Ostend merchants were eager to start, however. John Fottrell, one of the longstanding Irish merchants in Ostend, exemplified this cautious excitement. Fottrell planned to send a ship, *De Stad Weenen*, under imperial colours to Philadelphia but feared an American ban on British products. He solicited Franklin for advice before he continued.[23] Franklin could not help Fottrell against the importation ban, but he did provide a list of wares and contacts in the United States.[24] In his letter to Franklin, Fottrell explained how trade with the United States was a matter of particular interest for local Ostend magistrates. "In consequence of orders from Government," Fottrell noted, the local authorities wished for him to "acquaint all my friends" with Franklin's information so that "every encouragement and facility that can be desired will be granted to the American trade here."[25]

Fottrell's successful trade with the United States spread among Ostend merchants.[26] Franklin received numerous petitions from them in quick succession. In late January 1783, Jean-Guild Wets, a merchant at Bruges, wrote on behalf of a consortium "composed of fourthy of the most Substantial marchants of Flandres [*sic*]," desiring direct trade with the United States.[27] The next day, on January 31, another representative of *Veuve d'Aubremé & Fils* from Brussels wrote on the occasion of "a striking and glorious Epoch in the Annals of the Century" and begged of him to send a list of contacts in Boston and Philadelphia.[28] A few days later, an Irish firm based in Dunkirk and Ostend, *Connelly Sons & Arthur*, informed Franklin of their plan to divert ships from the West Indies towards Boston, Charleston, Philadelphia, and New York with linens in exchange for tobacco. They also asked to become American consuls and included a portfolio of ten references from American and European merchants.[29]

Administrators in the Austrian Netherlands were keen to oversee the continuation of profiteering from the American Revolution. When the first wave of emigrant merchants came to trade out of Ostend following the French entry into the war in 1778, Prince Georg Adam von Starhemberg, the minister plenipotentiary in Brussels, ordered the Council of Finance to start preparing suggestions for how to develop a market presence in North America.[30] The short memorandum, submitted by Councillor Denis-Benoît, baron de Cazier, argued American commerce would benefit the Austrian Netherlands but the merchants would organise this themselves. Starhemberg expected more, especially on the prospects for direct trade, so he proposed that the treasurer general have it more "thoughtfully debated" at the Council of Finance. In the meantime, he forwarded the memorandum to Kaunitz as "a work of foresight." Kaunitz's response was muted.[31] Unlike Starhemberg, he was more aware of the perilous state of neutrality since Lee visited Vienna at the same time Starhemberg forced these discussions. Kaunitz thought any advances by Brussels towards the Americans would undermine their neutral position, so he ignored further discussion.[32] But Starhemberg did not relent. After further deliberation with his councillors, he urged enticements for American traders in order to stimulate business.[33] Pressed again by Starhemberg, Kaunitz acquiesced at the end of October 1778 but he limited Starhemberg's actions to merely pursuing a commercial relationship with the Americans, nothing political.[34]

Starhemberg felt dissatisfied with his remit and over the next few years, he pushed its limits. For a time, he pursued a channel to Franklin through Jan Ingenhousz, but this plan failed due to Ingenhousz's sojourn to London.[35] Kaunitz would not countenance any overtures to the dozens of Americans living in the Austrian Netherlands so Starhemberg turned instead to the consul in Bordeaux for ideas, but nothing came of it.[36] By 1781, the conversation had no clear direction without accepting a political connection via representation and a treaty of commerce.

The issue seemed more urgent than ever following the Fourth Anglo-Dutch War and the highpoint of Ostend's commercial influence. Profits ran so high that it was inconceivable and impractical to relinquish it. Franklin's indirect response to the legal dispute over the *Eersten* case in the American courts seemed to offer a solution. In his letter on the matter, Franklin pointed out that legal representation could be ensured through a consul general, who "might at all times assist his compatriots with his Counsels and Protection in any Affairs they might have in that Country."[37] Ministers in Brussels interpreted this as an invitation to send a consul but without requiring a treaty or recognition. On March 24, 1782, the Council of Finance met in Brussels to discuss Franklin's idea.[38] Their lengthy memorandum considered the logistical ramifications of such an undertaking, but unanimously agreed a consul general should be established, since it would provide "useful information" and could "support the general interests of commerce and direct the speculations of traders in the various provinces of the monarchy." In conclusion, they envisaged a grand system of several vice-consuls "given the scope of the United Colonies"; one for each American state, under the direction of a Consul General, a "learned man" from the mercantile class who "would be the means by which the government, either here [in Brussels] or in Vienna, would gather good information on the local circumstances [in America], especially in relation to trade."[39] Starhemberg approved the council's measure and sent it to Kaunitz for deliberation with the emperor. His adjoining comment, however, highlighted the problem of recognition which was inherent in establishing any formal consular network. Starhemberg sensed Franklin's plan was "to get our Court to recognise the Independence of the United Colonies" which he felt unable to recommend "as long as the fate of the Colonies remains undecided."[40] On April 13, 1782, Kaunitz discussed the recommendations in an audience with the emperor and afterwards replied to Starhemberg. Kaunitz agreed to the necessity of a consul for ensuring the future trade with the United States but he could not allow any appointment to occur since it risked ruining his role as a mediator. "We must first bide our time," Kaunitz argued, "until we will see what the fate of the colonies will be."[41]

The Peace that Would Have Been

May 13, 1779, is not a date well remembered by historians of the American Revolution, but it should be. The Peace of Teschen sealed the fate of Central Europe on that day, bringing an end to the War of the Bavarian Succession and preventing any European war from distracting the Atlantic powers. British dreams of a German confrontation which would sap French resources had not materialised and thus the aim of forcing France to fight on multiple fronts vanished. Joseph II's hopes were also dashed. His plan to exchange the Austrian Netherlands for the Bavarian territories had been thwarted under the terms of the treaty. His recompense was a sliver of land called the Innviertel, now incorporated into the Archduchy of Austria above the Enns. Joseph and his ministers had spent nearly 100 million florins in financing the war.[42] The 2,200 square kilometres of the Innviertel was a bitter and meagre compensation in return.

May 1779 influenced the course of the American Revolution in another way, too. In her customary note of thanks to the co-mediators of the peace, Maria Theresa offered the same service to bring about peace between the French King Louis and King George in the War of American Independence.[43] The offer of mediation to an ally who had just arbitrated a humiliating peace seemed a strange act. A bemused French ambassador Breteuil certainly thought so. He outlined his suspicions to ministers in Paris, believing the Habsburgs sought to humble the French and to extract a warmer relationship with Britain at France's expense.[44] The French decided inaction was the best course and simply chose to ignore the polite suggestion. A cordial remark maybe, but Maria Theresa had made the offer with sincerity. It was a sentiment she expressed to her daughter Marie Antoinette.[45] Advancing in age, she desired peace and stability for her dynasty in Europe.

But the mediation offer was also a calculated ploy. Maria Theresa still feared the influence of Prussia's Frederick II, especially as she believed he manoeuvred to dislodge her strained, but still necessary, alliance with France.[46] A mediator role between the Atlantic powers had a lot to offer her. In this role, the Habsburgs would be able to raise themselves above Prussia after such a calamitous war. Whether or not the Americans would gain independence, being the arbitrator would put the Habsburgs in a position of strength among the European powers at a time when alliances and rivalries seemed to be shifting. The war against Prussia may have ended in Teschen, but the struggle resumed in the diplomatic realm. Maria Theresa accordingly set about convincing the French of her honest intentions through indirect means. She urged her ambassador to portray it as a "courtly compliment" from one monarch to another.[47] She was, as usual, blunter in discussing the matter with Marie Antoinette. She declared how her interests were the same as those of the French crown and pressed the young queen to ensure the king would accept only her offer.[48] Maria Theresa's efforts were utterly in vain, however. On May 27, 1779, King Louis graciously declined the invitation citing the prior refusal of Britain to accede to a similar Spanish-led mediation.[49] In reality, rejection stemmed from the French foreign minister Vergennes's distrust of his Habsburg allies since he sensed the upset in Vienna caused by the Peace of Teschen.[50]

Joseph II's posturing did not help his mother's efforts any either. The emperor had disliked Breteuil's obstinate attitude over Bavaria from the beginning. His regard for the French ambassador had declined following the impertinence of the Lee affair, and his barely dry signature on the humiliating treaty at Teschen was the final straw. Joseph disparaged Breteuil whenever he could and mentioned as much in his letters to Marie Antoinette so courtiers in Versailles would know too.[51] Rumours swirled whether Breteuil would quit his post but he endured the abuse for several years more—the unfortunate man went on to become the French monarchy's last prime minister on the eve of the French Revolution.[52] In 1783, Joseph aired his grievances about France in a striking letter to his sister. He believed France had always undermined Habsburg interests within and outside the Holy Roman Empire. Joseph had not done the same to them. He had not complained even when French enlargements were harmful to Habsburg interests such as the acquisition of Corsica "which had been very prejudicial to the interests of the House of Austria and its branches in Italy."[53] Joseph's frustration with French actions had smouldered before 1779 and then severely impaired the French willingness to hand him or his mother primacy in potential peace negotiations over America. Joseph's actions, furthermore, gave the French little confidence in a fair mediation. During a lengthy conference with the Dutch ambassador, for example, Joseph argued for them to abandon their anti-British approach, warning of the dangers if the French and Spanish were to unseat the British in the Atlantic.[54] Making matters worse, Joseph also planned a visit to England, which never materialised and perhaps had no other reason than to antagonise the French further.[55]

Whereas Habsburg overtures had fallen on deaf French ears, the situation in Vienna gave some encouragement that the British would take up the offer. In May 1779, Maria Theresa—acting through Kaunitz—ventured the same proposition to the British ambassador Sir Robert Murray Keith, who reported back to London that the offer was cordial and open, meaning if they were to decline, it would do no harm.[56] Months went by before Keith received further instruction. The British ministers were willing to accept the invitation but stipulated in mid-July that foreign support of the colonies must be dropped before negotiation could begin; a demand designed to preclude any chance of negotiating their independence. Conditional acceptance reflected British good faith in the Habsburgs, who, they thought, were more pro-British than anything else. But this did not mean complete trust was forthcoming. Keith's first objective was apprehending the origin of the offer. Had Maria Theresa thought of it herself or had the French some part in it? The answer was paramount as the British suspected France would not (or could not) betray American independence, and so any intermediary power agreed by them might have accepted this premise already.[57]

Keith acted quickly. He rushed to the countryside palace at Laxenburg where Kaunitz was staying to make his enquiry and signal the conditional acceptance. His secretary accompanied him so that he could produce a verbatim report of what happened next. Kaunitz confirmed the independent origin of the offer. France had no part in it. Instead, the Habsburgs were animated by the desire to tend to the "increasing flame," as Kaunitz characterised the American Revolution.[58] His next words were music to British ears. Kaunitz offered to work in total "candour and openness" with Keith for a mediation under Habsburg supervision. His plan involved renewing the overtures to France and Spain without informing the courts of the British tacit acceptance. Instead, Kaunitz would instruct his ambassadors to merely insinuate that the British were willing to accept and that terms of peace must be put forward by all parties. Kaunitz's plan met British expectations since he spoke plainly of the "three courts" (Britain, France, and Spain) as the intended participants, ignoring the Americans. Kaunitz then moved on to matters more delicate for the Habsburgs: would there be a co-mediator and where would such a negotiation be held? Kaunitz made clear that the Prussians could not be contemplated, but some other state might join if so wished. The venue would be Vienna, pending confirmation. The final obstacle was Breteuil, whose spies, Kaunitz knew, had followed Keith and who would raise suspicions about their extraordinary meeting in the countryside. Together they concocted a plausible explanation about Keith handing over papers of ill-consequence from his latest despatch. Plans concluded, Keith took his leave.[59] And so in the idyllic settings of Palace Laxenburg just outside Vienna, the first real hopes had been kindled for an end to the War of American Independence.

Meanwhile, Maria Theresa had lost all hope for the mediation. Winning over one side was not enough. She felt British interests were too strong in Vienna and knew the French would not trust Joseph over the fate of North America.[60] "The predilection here for England is always manifesting itself more and more," she lamented to her ambassador in Paris.[61] In the intervening months, both Maria Theresa and Joseph sounded out the opinion of Marie Antoinette concerning the French position. Only a handful of the letters between her and Joseph survived the destruction of another revolution, so we are left to wonder what they might have discussed during this period.[62] Maria Theresa's enquiries, however, did survive.[63] Their letters reveal a mother and daughter of the same mind on the importance of peace for Europe. "My heart desires it more than anything else in the world," Marie Antoinette wrote.[64] She did not expect peace any time soon, however. In 1779, France had just secured Spanish entry into the war, pitting Britain against two continental enemies with a superior combined force at sea. From the French perspective, it was time to strike whilst the iron was hot rather than time to strike a deal.

Kaunitz pondered the impasse with his subordinates in Paris and Madrid. News from the latter was promising. Despite initial rejection, the Habsburg ambassador in Madrid, his son Count Dominik Andreas von Kaunitz-Questenberg, was optimistic in September 1779.[65] He had immediately gone to Spain's chief minister José Moñino y Redondo, conde de Floridablanca, who responded well to the idea. Floridablanca tentatively accepted the invitation but would only confirm Spain's participation after consultation with France.[66] Kaunitz-Questenberg prodded for an answer two months later but without much luck. In an empty memorandum, Floridablanca confirmed general desires for peace and insisted

FIGURE 11. Portrait of Prince Wenzel Anton von Kaunitz-Rietberg

on a congress but revealed precious little in terms of Spain's demands or think-ing about how such a meeting could be achieved.[67] It had become clear that the Spanish would not act alone and would only follow France's lead, which would then entail American participation and in turn scupper any British involvement.

The question became, therefore, how likely was American independence and could the British withstand the revolutionaries' demands for their separation? More exposed to the pro-American euphoria around Franklin at the French court, Count Florimond Mercy-d'Argenteau believed that the American side held the upper hand. At best, their position afforded them "absolute indepen-dence" and at worst, a modified existence within the British empire. The recent troubles in Ireland over the anti-papist acts passed by the British Parliament strengthened his opinion.[68] Kaunitz thought otherwise. He was more suscepti-ble to Keith's opinions on the matter.[69] From Kaunitz's perspective, American independence was not at all assured. The British could withstand the financial stresses of the war better than the other belligerents. Prolonged conflict would lead the powers involved to peace eventually, but he supposed Britain's situation would improve before then.[70] As 1779 drew to a close, Kaunitz resolved to await any changes in the fortunes of the belligerents, which would then bring about the prospects of peace.

Events in 1780 exacerbated Maria Theresa's failure to secure a Habsburg me-diation. The Habsburgs had been one of the first to issue such a proposition among the European powers, but they were no longer alone. In December 1779, the Russian Empress Catherine II sought to build upon her prestige at Teschen by instructing her foreign minister Count Nikita Ivanovich Panin to pursue a Russian-mediated peace.[71] In March 1780, King Ferdinand IV of Naples-Sicily made similar overtures through his representative in London.[72] Indeed, by then some peace talks had begun. The Spanish had entered the war with limited objectives—primarily the conquest of Gibraltar and Minorca—and were willing to concede their participation as leverage towards these aims in secret negotiations started with an informal British delegation.[73] Habsburg officials tracked the course of these meetings intently but sensed nothing would come of them.[74] New military developments in North America further frustrated the prospects of peace. When the Siege of Charleston ended with the British occupation of the city, both Maria Theresa and Marie Antoinette despaired. They were not distraught for the American loss—the "miserable defence" of the Americans was to be expected from "such bad troops" in Marie Antoinette's opinion—instead, they feared the British victory would protract the war further and diminish the chances of Maria Theresa's "long-hoped for" peace.[75]

Despite renewed pessimism, obstacles, and competition, Kaunitz pursued a solo Habsburg mediation throughout 1780. He sought in vain to appease all sides by tempting each of them to the table with incompatible or incredible offers. In Paris, Mercy-d'Argenteau reportedly proposed an immediate armistice to last nine years upon the current status quo.[76] In Vienna, Breteuil faced audience after audience with the monarchs on the issue. He conceded nothing and was repulsed by the good-cop, bad-cop tactics of Maria Theresa and Joseph, where the former pleaded for peace on behalf of Europe's salvation and the latter threatened Breteuil—over the course of a three-hour interview—with tales of how the British would never accept a sovereign United States and the Spanish would never allow such an example in the Americas.[77] At home and abroad, the indefatigable efforts to secure a sole mediation under the Habsburgs failed time and again.

Events soon took away the initiative from Kaunitz. In January 1780, Admiral Rodney relieved the Gibraltar garrison following defeat of the Spanish fleet. In March, Catherine II founded the League of Armed Neutrality as an open international system for neutrals to fend off harassment of their mercantile fleets by belligerents. The League was detrimental to the British capacity to wage war. It marked a stunning failure for the British aim to secure an alliance with Russia, while it brought France's Vergennes further pleasure to see Russia not only maintain neutrality but to defend it.[78] The League's creation prompted neutral powers to join in order to protect their commerce and profits from carrying war supplies to the belligerents. In quick succession, the northern neutrals entered the system.[79] In November, the Dutch Republic seemed poised to join, but the British could not allow one of the largest foreign carrying fleets to supply their enemies, and so a confiscated plan for American aid from a few Dutch financers was trumpeted as a breach of their neutrality and the British declared war before the authorised Dutch delegation to St. Petersburg could subscribe to the League.[80] The beginning of the Fourth Anglo-Dutch war, alongside the War of American Independence, marked the lowest point in Britain's estrangement from the European powers.[81] The Dutch conflagration came at an inopportune time for the French. Exhausted by the costs of the war and fearful that Spain would abandon the fight given the failure to take Gibraltar, the French council decided in December 1780 that the need for peace had arrived.[82] Peace, at last, seemed assured.

Although the belligerents in the war had arrived at the point which Kaunitz had long awaited, a sole Habsburg mediation was not guaranteed. In fact, it now seemed more unlikely. For one, the belligerent powers had all viewed the proposal as Maria Theresa's invention. Her death on November 29, 1780, weakened the credible impartiality of her son and increased French distrust towards his intentions. In his private correspondence, Keith wrote candidly about the positive change in British fortunes after Maria Theresa's death. "Our Emperor has behaved like an angel ever since his accession," he exclaimed as he boasted of his "friendly disposition to this country, which at this hour is in a state it never found itself before."[83] French ministers sought out an effective counterweight. The earlier Russian offer (from December 1779) appeared to solve both problems; France could sue for peace under a more favourable power, and it would aid their standing with Catherine II.[84] The Franco-Russian plan was no secret among Europe's courts before the offer had been accepted and widened to Britain and Spain. Both Kaunitz in Vienna and British ministers in London had heard the rumours from multiple sources and both sides hoped for a compromise.[85]

Meanwhile, Keith's new superior in London, David Murray, Viscount Stormont was an Austrophile. Throughout the summer of 1780, Stormont tried to curry favour with the Habsburgs in the hopes of an alliance.[86] In September, Keith offered Kaunitz British support for the reopening of the River Scheldt, a vital economic waterway in the Austrian Netherlands which had been shut off to maritime commerce by Dutch forts since the sixteenth century.[87] In return, Keith demanded Habsburg co-mediation if the Franco-Russian initiative became real.[88] Keith's overtures chimed perfectly with the Habsburg position. Joseph and Kaunitz viewed co-mediation as a success. Not only would it honour the wish of Joseph's late mother, but it would allow a recovery of their prestige after Teschen and included the possibility to make the French wince as terms were deliberated. Moreover, a co-mediation with Russia furthered the diplomatic pivot pursued by Joseph who favoured warmer relations with Russia, working toward an alliance, even, which would enable them to focus on joint expansion against the Ottomans.[89] Positive reception in Vienna allowed Stormont to demand co-mediation when the Russian offer arrived in London, which the Russians readily accepted. The Congress of Vienna seemed, at last, to be confirmed. Kaunitz rejoiced at the news, reportedly declaring, "Lord Stormont has baptised the baby!"[90]

Kaunitz worked tirelessly to ensure the Congress of Vienna would be held in the summer of 1781. He insisted on all parties putting forward terms for a mediation. In a memorandum issued to all courts involved, he tasked them with devising terms which they would only accept if they were in the opposing position.[91] The British were pleased by the call. Stormont endeavoured to influence the co-mediators further towards his cause by offering the Russians the island of Minorca and the reopening of the River Scheldt for the Habsburgs.[92] A plan to award the Habsburgs the island of Tobago was also mooted at one point but nothing came of it.[93] Kaunitz rebuffed Keith for such obvious bribes.[94]

For their part, the French were dismayed by the suggestions emanating from Vienna. In mid-February 1781, Breteuil confronted Kaunitz about the trickiest question of all: what was to be the fate of the Americans? Kaunitz understood that the French position demanded their independence but he also realised this was incompatible with British aims. The middle ground, the two men realised, might be partition. If some colonies were to become independent and others returned to the British, then perhaps both sides could be appeased.[95] Kaunitz forwarded the plan to Mercy-d'Argenteau wherein Canada would be returned to the French, Britain would retain the Carolinas and Georgia, and the rest would form a sovereign American republic.[96] It is notable that Kaunitz was indifferent to American independence. From his perspective, it was merely a hurdle to surpass in the negations; if a diminished American state were the result, then it would be up to the Americans to survive. Vergennes agreed with the idea but felt that it could not originate from the French as it would be too painful to the Americans, it would have to come from the mediators instead.[97]

In March, Joseph met with Breteuil to thrash out the problem of American attendance at the Congress of Vienna. Joseph could not reconcile admission of the Americans with British opposition. If any congress were to be successful, then it had to be restricted to the three powers plus the two mediating courts. Joseph mused through possible solutions with Breteuil.[98] What if a separate peace could be arranged? What if the British regained America in exchange for Gibraltar? Such thoughts were infeasible but demonstrated Joseph's different thinking. Whereas Kaunitz perceived that the Americans had a plausible chance as a reduced state, Joseph saw their independence as a bargaining chip. Years before he would wage a short war against the Dutch over the issue of the River Scheldt, Joseph seemed tempted by the bait laid out by the British.[99] John Adams thought as much from rumours he heard in Amsterdam. In June 1781, he shrewdly called out Joseph's position. "The Emperor," he declared, "appears to be more intent at present upon taking a fair Advantage of the present Circumstances, to introduce a flourishing Commerce into the Austrian Flanders, than upon making Treaties with England or waging War in its favour."[100] Meanwhile, Kaunitz continued to work on the American conundrum. In a conversation with Breteuil, he hit upon the idea of each state sending its own representative rather than a single American representative.[101] The idea was shrewd. The Americans would be present, perhaps even as plenipotentiaries rather than actual delegates, but they would be so divided among themselves that the British could have their separate peace, picking off the Carolinas and Georgia following the preferred plan of partition. John Adams described this idea decades later as "the most insidious and dangerous Plott that was ever laid to insnare Us and deprive Us of our Independence"; but for the time being, he had no idea of what Kaunitz planned nor how he close he came to seeing it become reality.[102]

On May 21, 1781, after many months of diplomatic wrangling, Kaunitz and the Russian representative in Vienna, Prince Dmitry Mikhailovich Golitsyn, sent off the preliminary terms for peace at Vienna. The Americans were to be invited and a separate peace worked out exclusively between them and Britain unless either side requested mediation. In trying to please everyone, however, Kaunitz pleased none. The call for a one-year armistice upset the French who feared the British would consolidate their position, while the absence of anything about Gibraltar alienated the Spanish.[103] The British raged at the American invitations. Count Belgiojoso, the Habsburg envoy in London, received a thorough dressing down for the impertinent terms.[104]

This harsh awakening meant that the British outright refused any participation on these terms and placed their hopes instead on the summer campaigns of 1781. The result was disastrous for them as much as it was for concluding peace in Vienna. On October 18, 1781, General Charles Cornwallis surrendered after a lengthy siege at Yorktown. The decisive blow collapsed British hopes for subjugating America and preventing independence. The defeat also signalled a death knell for the Congress of Vienna. The British had lost the ability to hold out and so peace, it seemed obvious, would take place under American, French, and Spanish terms. Upon hearing the news, the Spanish special envoy sent to Vienna as the provisional representative packed up his bags and left.[105] Kaunitz attempted in vain to keep alive the prospects for an international summit in Vienna. The fall of the North ministry in London in March 1782 confirmed the new reality when his successor despatched an envoy to Paris to sue for peace.[106] Kaunitz could do little more than concede the ultimate loss of the Habsburgs' cherished congress.

Cold-shouldered by the victors, Kaunitz and Joseph resented the new peace plans and abhorred the French disregard for their earnest attempt to secure a universal peace. In 1783, Joseph still spoke bitterly of it. "Could France have achieved the same and come out of the last war with England with such advantages," he scorned, "if not for the assuredness and security of my involvement."[107] Stormont had failed to accommodate any meaningful role for his perceived saviour in the new negotiations; the Americans and French refused any mediation outright. Besides, Joseph and Kaunitz wanted nothing to do with the new congress. "I am afraid no real assistance can be expected from the Court of Vienna," Stormont despaired, "who are wedded to the system they have embraced, and will not suffer themselves to see how much their own interests are concerned in the great contest in which we are engaged."[108] The great contest over America ended not in Vienna but instead in Paris.

Philadelphia in Europe

Writing from Philadelphia almost twenty-five years after the end of the Revolution, Count Charles-Albert de Moré—a nobleman and former aide-de-camp to Lafayette and Washington—responded with great elation to the news of his older brother's intention to emigrate from Switzerland. His brother's choice of destination, the younger Moré commended, "is the most suitable and certain for success," one where "true pioneers [are] flocking from the most diverse of lands in order to make a new life for themselves." This attractive place, he continued with praise, "is the port in which castaways find shelter and a new, promising life." Despite the resemblance, the port Moré spoke so highly of was not his own Philadelphia but instead a place which Moré concluded "is the Philadelphia of Europe"—Trieste.[109] Trieste merited such a comparison; in 1700 it had still been a sleepy trading village nestled along the northernmost end of the Adriatic Sea. By the end of the century, it had transformed into a vibrant cosmopolitan centre of interregional and international commerce. Such transformation came from the policies of the Habsburgs, who saw the ports of Trieste and Fiume as natural entrepôts for international trade. In 1718, Maria Theresa's father removed tariffs to make Trieste a free port in emulation of the Spanish trading hubs on the Atlantic coast.[110] In 1775 during one of his visits, Joseph II named Trieste the main port for the hereditary lands and Fiume as the primary outlet for Hungarian goods. In this way, his reforms established a geographically closer trade hub and lowered reliance on the faraway ports on the North Sea. Triestines received even further privileges; a mercantile college and a new stock exchange alongside one of the largest docks along the Adriatic coastline.[111] By the time of the American Revolution, the sleepy harbour had woken up.

The American Revolution excited Triestine merchants for the opportunity to trade directly with North America. Previously, Triestine goods went via the Atlantic ports, especially Cadiz, and American goods arrived via the British Isles and the Austrian Netherlands.[112] An independent United States opened direct trading avenues for Trieste's merchants for the first time. Habsburg consuls across Europe were assiduous to this fact and urged the Triestine governor to explore this trade. Christian Ludwig Hofer, one such consul in Hamburg, reported sales of Bohemian and Silesian goods from there to America, which, he suggested, could be more cheaply supplied from Trieste.[113] Within twelve months, Hofer sent four more detailed reports including extracts of goods demanded by the president of the Congress.[114] Merchants in Trieste were supremely aware of such possibilities themselves. Months before the adoption of the Declaration of American Independence one informed authorities in Vienna that "the current situation of the English Colonies in America seems to me to merit considerable attention, and more than ever before [. . .] to have commerce, which has especially made the Dutch and English so rich and respectable."[115] Such insistence was not a singular occurrence. Ministers received numerous petitions agitating to exploit the revolutionary turmoil. Petitions came from serious members of Habsburg society. During the summer of 1782, amid rumours of a definitive peace, Jean Gabriel, comte de Raineval et de Fauquembergue proposed a Central and North American trading mission to Kaunitz, but received refusal days later.[116] Johann Zollikofer von Sonnenberg, member of a large Swiss mercantile dynasty, proposed several ships for an expedition from Trieste to the United States. Joseph personally scrutinised the proposal but eventually rejected it because of the "extraordinary claims necessary" to fund the operation.[117]

Domestic petitioners for new transatlantic trade were not alone. Petitions for direct trade between Trieste and the United States reached all sides. In November 1779, a local captain introduced the Governor of Trieste Karl von Zinzendorf to Dr. George Logan, a Pennsylvanian medical graduate of the University of Edinburgh who toured Europe after his studies.[118] Zinzendorf surmised Logan was an unofficial "agent of Congress" who "without an audience in Vienna [...] now comes here to inquire if trade relations between this port and the United States might be born after the peace."[119] In January 1782, Franklin noted an extraordinary meeting in his diary. Willem Bolts, the architect of Habsburg trade with the Far East, came to propose how a circumnavigational route might take goods from Trieste to China and from there to the United States and back to Trieste. Franklin entertained "much Discourse" about the idea and gave Bolts "Hopes of it upon a Peace," but nothing more.[120] At the same time, François Emmanuel Joseph Baraux, an Antwerp merchant who had relocated to Trieste, wrote to John Adams on behalf of the Imperial Privileged Trading Company in Trieste. He requested "an extensive list of the best Merchants in the different towns of America" so his company could "get into a reciprocal, advantageous connection."[121] In his reply, Adams noted how after peace "there will probably be a considerable Trade between the several Ports of the United States of America and Trieste, through which place I fancy several American Productions will find their Way into the Interior of the Austrian Dominions."[122] In both encounters, Adams and Franklin expressed their belief that commerce with Trieste could only establish itself once a general peace had been concluded.

Triestine merchants were rather more impatient, however. Ignaz Verpoorten, another merchant who had swapped Antwerp for the Adriatic, became the first pioneer. As director of the Trieste and Fiume Sugar Company since 1776, Verpoorten had an obvious interest in American markets, but his position also afforded him important contact within the local and Viennese administrations.[123] Through these channels, he urged for peace in the Americas and support for a trading mission to the United States. He met with Zinzendorf to discuss the expedition in January 1782.[124] In order to realise this scheme, Verpoorten had to obtain a patent for the ship's use of the imperial ensign, granted only by the Aulic Chamber (*Hofkammer*) in agreement with the vessel owners, the captain, and local officials—in this case Zinzendorf and the head of the municipal stock exchange. Verpoorten applied for the imperial patent for his ship *l'Americano*, which the authorities approved on May 31, 1782, long after his intended departure.[125] The *Americano* set sail for the northern Caribbean and Carolinas a few weeks later with a crew of twenty and 286 tonnes of goods.[126] The *Americano* became the first ship to sail directly between Trieste and the New World. The cargo featured textiles, metalwares, glass, and wines for export and imported sugar, rum, and indigo from the Caribbean and Carolinas.[127] It was a risky but profitable venture. Verpoorten established a new company to solidify his gains. The *Verpoortische Assecuranz und Handlungs-Compagnie* received its imperial grant on June 21, 1782, and became the first American-Triestine company as a result. The company's charter reflected the seriousness of the ambition to trade with the United States. An endowment of four million florins, imperial protections, and tax exemption on domestic goods set to last for twenty years ensured considerable interest in the new firm. News of its announcement made front-page headlines in the *Wienerisches Diarium* and featured in mercantile journals in Hamburg and Weimar.[128] In early November 1782, Verpoorten sent two further ships from Trieste to North America.[129]

Verpoorten was the first merchant to trade directly between Trieste and North America, but only just. In 1781 three additional applications arrived at the Aulic Chamber but they had faltered for one reason or another. In March, the Serbian-Greek merchant Jovo Kurtovič had applied for his ship *La Città di Vienna* (or *La Bella Vienna*) but fell foul to scrutiny.[130] Safeguarding neutrality, Aulic Chamber officials prevented merchants from trading military contraband without official sanctions. The respected merchant Count Johann Berchtold de Proli, who was part of a famous mercantile dynasty in the Austrian Netherlands, scuppered Kurtovič's application with a disapproving report raising concerns over contraband.[131] Proli's damaging report was likely a dubious manoeuvre since he had intervened—this time favourably—in another proposal by Johann Jakob Kick, the imperial consul in Marseilles and a close associate of the Proli family. Kick's plan intended for the *Comte de Cobenzl* to sail from Trieste to Africa and onwards to North America. Yet there was a hitch with the captain and main financiers of the expedition who were not natural-born imperial subjects. Strict maritime laws prohibited foreign-born subjects from enjoying imperial protections—in Verpoorten's *l'Americano* mission, six merchants signed an affidavit to confirm the Italian captain owed his allegiance to the emperor.[132] Proli's interjection argued that Kick and other financiers were imperial subjects and constituted a majority of the interested parties, and, therefore, the mission should go ahead. But officials remained unconvinced. Kick received an outright refusal in mid-August.[133]

A week after Kick's application failed, Zinzendorf met with the director of the Imperial Privileged Trading Company in Trieste, Johann Heinrich Frohn, who, together with Baraux and Proli, proposed another American scheme.[134] The new plan involved *La Città di Trieste*—perhaps the hastily renamed *La Città di Vienna*—under a Milanese captain and backed by prominent Triestine and Hungarian nobles such as Count Samuel Gyulay von Maronsnémeth.[135]

Recommendation by Zinzendorf preceded official approval in Vienna but despite success with the court bureaucracy, no further records exist of their mission to America. By 1783, the Aulic Chamber had received four proposals for direct trade between Trieste and America, two of which gained approval.

Direct trade with North America arose out of its perceived profitability, but how valuable was this new trade? Statistical tables showing Trieste's imports and exports are patchy throughout the eighteenth century, but thankfully a statistical table compiled in 1783 upon the arrival of a new governor shines light on the initial year of Triestine-American commerce.[136] Administrators already recognised the economic contributions of North America by listing it under a separate heading, *l'Amérique Septentrionale*, which they further subdivided into the "Antilles" or "America Septentrionale." The table also allows for precise valuation as it shows the amount and value of each product. In 1783, forty-nine products featured under the "America Septentrionale" heading, ranging from ironware to gypsum, and from quicksilver to luxury woods. Textiles formed the largest export group (thirty-two percent of American exports) with a value of 30,400*fl*. Textiles combined with glassware (fourteen percent) and agricultural equipment (seven percent) comprised the majority of exported goods to the United States. It is likely that this table reflects Verpoorten's voyages to North America in 1782 since he carried a large amount of agricultural and metalwares for a Boston firm.[137]

Table 1 below reveals Verpoorten's strategy of carrying diverse goods to America, as forty-six other products constituted the remaining fifty percent of export value. On a national scale, this trade already represented the size of a large-scale firm. The firm *Artaria & Co.*, for example, was the first major music publishing house in the Vienna. In 1787, the company's stock value totalled 74,373*fl* and made the owner Domenico Artaria one of "the richest merchants in Vienna."[138] The twofold larger income from the United States made Verpoorten and other merchants in Trieste comparatively richer and underlines the reasons behind the popularity and excitement over his new American trading company.

Triestine merchants sourced a mix of domestic and foreign products to export to the United States. Administrators distinguished goods between "*prodotti della Germania*" and "*commercio di Economia*" to delineate products imported from abroad (commercio) and those sourced from markets within the Holy Roman Empire (Germania).[139] Domestic products featured textiles from Bohemia and metalwares from Carinthia and Styria whilst foreign products included *dolci* (currants, raisins, sultanas) and *legno bosso* or *legno scodano* (boxwood and unseasoned wood). Wood products originated from around the Adriatic region whilst

TABLE 1. Highest Valued Exports to the United States from Trieste, 1783

Product Name (Orig.)	Product Name (Eng.)	Percentage of Total Exports to US	Value (fl)
Telerie Diversi di Germania	German Linens	31.6	30,400
Vetri e Cristalli	Glass and Crystals	13.7	13,200
Ferramenta Lavorata	Agricultural Tools	7.0	6,750
Rame	Copper	3.6	3,497
Lanerie	Wools	3.4	3,200
Setarie	Millet	3.1	3,000
Cordami	Rigging/Cording	2.7	2,613
Acciaro	Steel	2.7	2,600
Uvapassa	Raisins	2.4	2,331
Solfo	Sulphur	2.2	2,118

SOURCE: FHKA, NHK, Kommerz Litorale Akten, Generalia, K. 850 (1780-1785), fols. 1003-1020.

currants came from the Eastern Mediterranean. Merchants sourced these goods to export almost exclusively to American markets. Table 2 below highlights goods for which at least one-fifth of the total import into Trieste was then reshipped to the United States. These products were predominantly industrial or luxury goods.

The commercial importance of the United States is underscored when compared with other international destinations. In 1783, the value of exports to the United States amounted to 96,177fl or less than one percent of total export value. This sum might not appear very high, but it is substantial, especially for a nascent trading route. Among Triestine export destinations that year, the United States ranked twelfth out of twenty total countries. Triestine merchants exported more commercial value to the United States than Holland, the West Indies, Malta, England, Flanders, Sicily, the Barbary States, or the Republic of Ragusa. The Habsburg Monarchy had begun trading ventures to India and China in 1775. No separate values were given for either India or China but the combined value of exports to these two markets in 1783 was only 26,161fl higher than those to the United States. In other words, within the first year of direct American trade, Triestine merchants obtained seventy-eight percent of the value of the expeditions to India and China. It was a testament to the profitability and desirability of the new transatlantic route within the Habsburg ambition to trade globally.

TABLE 2. Triestine Exports to the United States procured from foreign markets, 1783

Product Name (Original)	Product Name (English)	Percentage of Product's Total Original Import to Trieste	Value (fl)
Spongie	Sponges	74.9	250
Solfo	Sulphur	64.2	2,118
Verderame	Copper sulphate	29.8	382
Cordami	Rigging/Cording	24.0	2,613
Galla	Gall	23.9	1,560
Vino ordinario	Ordinary Wines	21.7	299
Capari [Capperi]	Capers	21.4	126

SOURCE: FHKA, NHK, Kommerz Litorale Akten, Generalia, K. 850 (1780-1785), fols. 1003-1020.

Trieste remained a predominantly Mediterranean port, however. The vast majority of export value lay in the Italian regions around Venice, Ferrara, Lombardy and the Papal States. No more than five percent of total export value flowed beyond the Mediterranean. These destinations included India, China, the United States, the West Indies, England, the Dutch Republic, the Austrian Netherlands, Hamburg, and the United States. When compared to these other extra-Mediterranean destinations, however, the importance of the United States market becomes clearer; the United States ranked first in value.[140] It cannot be doubted that for such initial commercial connection, the United States quickly outperformed other trade routes which had been established for far longer. This rapid rise validates the interest of Triestine merchants to capitalise on new transatlantic commerce and to gain profits from the newly independent United States of America.

Conclusion

The later years of the American Revolution provided two ports of the Habsburg Monarchy with unparalleled economic opportunities. Neutrality had been a difficult position to maintain in the early stages of the war, but as new belligerents entered the war, neutrality became an increasingly beneficial stance. New direct trading routes, either through novel mercantile initiatives in Trieste or the influx of masked shipping via Ostend, allowed Habsburg merchants the unique chance to profit from the chaos of revolution. Access to Atlantic markets opened

opportunities for Habsburg merchandise. The desire to maintain these new avenues of trade fuelled debates among Habsburg ministers on the best methods
to secure it for the long term. The first ideas of official relations between the
Habsburg Monarchy and the United States were born out of these debates which
rested upon the establishment of diplomatic ties through treaties of commerce
and consular representation.

Yet the impatience to recognise the United States did not outweigh the consideration for international conventions. If peace remained elusive, so did any prospect of Habsburg interaction with an independent United States. The same elusive
peace evaded the best efforts of the Habsburg rulers themselves along with Prince
Kaunitz who ardently sought to utilise the international desire for peace to their
benefit. The failed hopes for a Congress of Vienna in 1782 represented the end to a
serious initiative on behalf of the Habsburgs to end the War of American Independence under their mediation in Vienna. The rationale for doing so included little
consideration for American independence and was more concerned with appeasing the belligerents into entering peace talks which remained the primary aim of
Kaunitz's efforts. He failed in this process and in doing so, ensured the Peace of
Vienna became the Peace of Paris as we remember it today.

CHAPTER SEVEN

"A New Set of Merchants"

The Development of Postwar Commerce between the Habsburg Monarchy and the United States of America, 1783–1785

O N FEBRUARY 4, 1783, Great Britain recognised the independence of the United States of America and agreed to an armistice. The news reached Vienna within two weeks.[1] On February 18, the emperor pondered this news in his correspondence with his ambassador in Paris. Joseph II did not concern himself with the political fallout at all. "The object of trade with the Americans," he noted instead, "will be of the greatest importance for the future."[2] These words foreshadowed the primacy that economic interests would assume when it came to the relationship between his lands and those of the new United States. In other words, attentiveness to the importance of transatlantic commerce replaced difficult political considerations of neutrality. As a result, the years between 1783 and 1785 witnessed growing mercantile speculation across the whole Habsburg Monarchy, from Ostend to Trieste, from Fiume to Florence. Joseph's memorandum initiated a new policy for a new age, as economic concerns trumped the ideological gulf between monarchy and republic. Benjamin Franklin's America and Joseph's Austria no longer seemed so far apart.

Central to this new world of opportunity for the Habsburg Monarchy were those who sought to bridge the transatlantic divide: the traders, the fundraisers, the businessmen, the sailors, and the chancers. Together they embarked upon commercial ventures which bound together Habsburg ports and American cities. Collectively they were what Franklin deemed "a new set of merchants [who] have grown up into business."[3] In some cases, these undertakings consolidated trading lines forged during wartime. Others resurrected older pre-war economic ties that had been disrupted by revolutionary mayhem. Yet for many, trading with America meant something ground-breaking, untested, tempting, and now possible for the first time. Merchants at all of the major Habsburg ports of

Livorno, Ostend, and Trieste were ready to reframe, renew, or to establish for the first time commercial ties to the newly independent United States.

Integrating events and a flurry of activities in these ports into the picture of early American independence reveals the wider connectedness that independence ushered forth for the former thirteen colonies. The American Revolution was not just an event with political ramifications, but also one with deeply interwoven economic reverberations. In creating a new nation, the American Revolution also created a new state with commercial interests to be incorporated into the balance of power in eighteenth-century Europe. American independence was a new world replete with new friends, new foes, and among them, a new set of merchants.

Livorno: Attempts at Reconnection

Commercial connections had existed between Livorno and North America long before the outbreak of the American Revolution. North American vessels were a frequent sight at the Tuscan port; fifty of them had arrived between 1770 and 1774 alone.[4] Many carried cod from New England fisheries along with a small amount of American goods. Dating back to the 1740s, this trade, modest at first, had been cemented by a generation of sailors and merchants by the time of the Revolution. And then it all came to a halt. War disrupted these trade flows, and merchants crossing the seas in either direction found it increasingly hard to avoid predatory British, Spanish, and French ships seizing their wares. For Filippo Mazzei, the most ardent proponent of Tuscan-American trade, nothing could be done until the cessation of fighting came about officially in 1783.[5]

The man who led the Livornese charge to return to American markets was Antonio Francesco Salucci. The firm he fronted, *Salucci & Figlio*, had lost the ship *La Prosperità* to the British already in 1779 and his associate Sebastino V. Salucci had been embroiled in a court case over another ship, the *Teti*, captured by the Spanish in 1780. Spurred on by peace, Antonio was determined to reignite Tuscan transatlantic commerce. He purchased a large brig and christened it *Il Diligente,* which set sail for Philadelphia in May 1783. When it successfully returned to Livorno in December with a cargo of tobacco, wax, and dyewood, it became the first successful Tuscan ship to sail to the United States for some time.[6] Confidence restored, Salucci wrote to Franklin with excitement in August 1784. He was proud to inform him about the "flourishing Commerce between our Tuscan State and your united States of America."[7] He was certain "no State in Europe is better calculated" for such commerce "as we have almost every article Europe furnishes and can take off in Return every American produce." Success emboldened Salucci. He sent further ships to the United States. *Il Diligente* repeated its transatlantic journey in February 1784, this time to Virginia.[8] *l'Etruria* left Terricciola (near Livorno) for Philadelphia and followed a more innovative route, selling Tuscan goods in Philadelphia before sailing up to Boston for cod and arriving back in Livorno in January 1785. The largest of the three ships, the 500 tonne *Teresa Geltrude* repeated the same route between 1784 and 1785.

Ministers in Vienna followed the success of these voyages intently. Although the Grand Duchy of Tuscany fell under a secundogeniture ruled by the emperor's younger brother, the representatives of the Viennese court kept ministers aware of the latest developments.[9] Officials in Vienna hoped to understand the vitality and nature of commerce with the sovereign United States and Tuscany. They wished to know the substance of this direct trade and its prospects for enriching the lives of the Tuscan inhabitants. The actions of Tuscan merchants, after all, could inform similar projects of traders in the hereditary lands of the Habsburg Monarchy. Moreover, as subjects of an autonomous state, these merchants were also competitors for the domestic vendors in the Habsburg lands. Such concerns spoke to the tight nexus between the economic and political realms where mercantilist instincts of one nation could jeopardise the political interests of another, even between states ruled under the same dynasty.

In 1785, Salucci expanded his prospective voyages: *La Cinque Sorelle* and *Il Diligente* to Virginia; *l'Etruria* and the *Teresa Geltrude* to Boston.[10] *Salucci & Figlio* had clearly established a foothold in the transatlantic trade with the United States, and his firm's promoters felt potential gains were still to be made. That year, Salucci selected a young associate within the firm, Filippo Filicchi, as the company's representative in the United States. Filicchi received a share of the profits under a new subsidiary company, *Filicchi & Co.*, and the support for a three-year mission in America. Prior to Filicchi's departure, *Salucci & Figlio* had used the New York house *William Seton & Co.* as their primary contact and goods handler in the United States. Filicchi arrived in New York in mid-summer but did not stay there for long. He undertook trips to Philadelphia, Boston, and Providence, Rhode Island, in order to scout out lucrative trades and send back valuable reports.[11]

Filicchi's tenure in the United States certainly benefitted *Salucci & Figlio* through the supply of information but upon his return to Livorno in 1788, he learned that the pioneering firm had gone bankrupt. The legal battle over the *Teti* in the Spanish courts had rumbled on since 1780 and the mounting legal costs ruined company finances.[12] From the ashes of one company grew another, however. The collapse allowed Filicchi to act with full autonomy and he returned to the United States a year later as the partner in a new firm, *F. & A. Filicchi*, established with his brother. The new firm picked up the American trade from *Salucci & Figlio* and, thanks to Filicchi's firsthand knowledge, became the most successful transatlantic company in Livorno.[13] In a testament to his importance, Filicchi became the American consul for Livorno in 1794, after years of repeated attempts to gain that office.[14] The Filicchi and Salucci endeavours were the success stories of the initial postwar years in Tuscan-American relations. On the official level, however, the outlook was less optimistic.

Attempts at a commercial treaty between Tuscany and the United States began in October 1783 when members of Congress instructed American commissioners to pursue treaties with several European nations, including various Habsburg territories. Recognising the sovereignty of Tuscany under the terms of Habsburg secundogeniture, the Americans pursued a separate treaty with the Grand Duchy. Yet all of these schemes were beset with difficulties. In the Tuscan case, the American commissioners—Benjamin Franklin, John Adams, and Thomas Jefferson—sounded out feelings in Florence through Francesco Favi in late September 1784.[15] Finding a warm reception to the idea, they forwarded the treaty proposal to Favi in December. The proposed draft was in fact a copy of the semi-concluded treaty with Prussia, which they hoped would serve as a model for Tuscany and elsewhere.[16] The Tuscans responded enthusiastically and returned an amended version in April of the following year.[17] Jefferson led the deliberation on the counter-proposals and compiled a summary on the alterations.[18] Further debates within the American circles rolled on until they submitted their *Observations* to Favi in response.[19] Another round of wrangling came from the Tuscan side in the form of a forty-six-page *Nuova minuta del trattato* (New treaty draft) with further revisions.[20] By the time Jefferson and Adams came to study the latest proposals, nearly a year had elapsed since the initial offer to Tuscany. Jefferson seemed displeased. "The order of the articles," he complained to Adams, "is entirely deranged and their direction almost totally changed."[21] Jefferson believed nothing could be rescued from the Tuscan negotiations. In a letter Jefferson wrote to Filippo Mazzei in the summer of 1785, he noted how any prospect of a "rational connection" with Tuscany was now "barren."[22]

Difficulties on the Tuscan side had arisen as soon as the American commissioners had made overtures in September 1784. Although Pietro Leopoldo was receptive to schemes aimed at enhancing his dominion, he first sought the opinion of local officials.[23] One of them, a Livornese tax inspector named Fierallmi, expressed doubts that any worthwhile offer could be made to the Americans.

Tuscans could not give them much incentive beyond proposing equal status with all other merchants in the city, he argued.[24] This issue became more pressing when the American proposals reached Florence. Favi had insisted to his superiors that the Americans understood the concerns of Fierallmi and that no extraordinary privileges could be granted to American merchants; their latest response, however, seemed unaware of this limitation. Things came to a head when the governor of Livorno Count Federigo Barbolani di Montanto received the draft treaty and proceeded to comb through the articles individually.[25] Barbolani found many points to be entirely incongruent with Tuscan customs. His extensive commentary on Article Four laid out this dissonance clearly. One provision stated that trading benefits were to occur for Tuscan and American ships arriving in the ports of the two nations. Barbolani pointed out how this undermined the Tuscans who lacked a sufficient fleet and would trade many goods indirectly aboard vessels belonging to other nations.[26] Furthermore, he worried that American vessels would hold an unequal advantage over Tuscan merchants since they would have the benefits of the treaty in addition to the rights of every nation at Livorno. In effect, he argued, this would also go against the American insistence, according to Favi, that both Tuscany and the United States would be equals in the treaty. The only solution Barbolani saw was to establish an "unlimited reciprocal freedom" between them which would include Tuscan and American goods on any vessel and only to the degree which Tuscany held with other nations already.[27] Barbolani and Fierallmi's insights, as part of the *Nuova minuta di trattato*, were what Jefferson likely referred to as the "deranged" order and "changed" direction of the negotiations. Both sides had reached an impasse.

Barbolani resisted further overtures. In February 1785, an intrepid American entrepreneur, Eliphalet Brush, visited Tuscany. John Quincy Adams described him as "full of vivacity and life."[28] Indeed he was. Originally from Connecticut, where he had served during the early part of the war, Brush had turned to a commercial life in New York.[29] Brush had met the Adamses—father and son—in Amsterdam in 1781 when he first toured Europe on behalf of his New York firm *Broome, Platt & Brush*.[30] Four years later, Brush travelled again to drum up trade for the company. Livorno seemed a prime target. Brush regarded Tuscany as an "emporium" of Mediterranean goods, which sold wares "better calculated for our [American] market than any other."[31] In Livorno, Brush met with Barbolani as well as with the Grand Duke in Florence.[32] He spoke of the "great advantages" of trade between the United States and Tuscany.[33] Brush even presented a list of suitable goods; Tuscan oil, hemp, and silks offered for American cod, tobacco, and spermaceti.[34] But the mission created the impression that the American commissioners had sent Brush to restart the stalled negotiations. Pressed by Tuscan officials, Brush explained how he lacked any official powers to conclude a treaty and acted purely as a private agent. Nevertheless, he had made a good impression in Tuscany, since several individuals supported his subsequent mission to Naples where he chased the same scheme.[35]

Agents such as Brush were part of a concerted effort to re-establish and expand the pre-war economic ties between North America and Tuscany. The enthusiasm for this reinvigorated connection came from both sides as Tuscans such as Salucci and Filicchi tried to enact the wartime dreams of Mazzei. Motivated by potential success, these venture capitalists sought out old and new markets and contacts on the other side of the Atlantic. Yet this mercantile impulse did not translate into a tangible political connection in the form of a commercial treaty. The stumbling block for any such agreement lay in the personal negotiations between American and Tuscan officials. As will be discussed later, Jefferson's outlook on the entirety of the Habsburg Monarchy clouded his approach to such dealings. Meanwhile, Tuscan officials like Barbolani interpreted American demands as incompatible with their own pre-existing arrangements. The Tuscan case is the first instance—but not the last—in US-Habsburg relations where a disconnect appeared between two sides and between economic entrepreneurs and political representatives.

Ostend: Prosperity or Poverty?

In 1783, the postwar fate of Ostend erupted onto the pages of the *Augspurgische Ordinari Postzeitung*. It was an open question for one of the largest official newspapers of the Holy Roman Empire: would prosperous Ostend survive the Peace of Paris? An April edition carried the first murmurings of impending ruin. "One can easily discern that they are partisan," noted the editors who reported on the relocation of many Dutch traders following the peace. "Whilst it is true that Ostend cannot remain so prosperous," they conceded, "American independence will certainly keep Ostend afloat."[36] By the end of the year, reports began to contradict this prediction, though the editors attempted to minimise the negativity: "Ostend's trade has fallen since the end of the war, as foreseen, but not by so much that the trade is not higher than before the war began."[37] Another issue detailed how Ostend had become one of "the most spacious and convenient ports in Europe."[38] In Vienna, the newspapers there had little to say about the rumours of harder times for Ostenders. As far as the public were informed, one of the richest Habsburg ports would continue to thrive. Indeed, one article noted how America "drunken with joy" about peace continued to import vast amounts from Ostend.[39] So what did, in fact, lay ahead for Ostend? Prosperity or poverty?

The answer depended in part on the actions of officials who sought to maintain the benefits gained during the Revolution. In 1781, the Brussels government elected to found a new committee to oversee the recent surge in international trade.[40] Under the superintendence of the Secretariat of State and War, the six members of the new *Comité de Commerce Maritime* had dealt with the inundation of paperwork associated with the blossoming trade. Now the committee would play a leading role in defining the port's postwar position. On January 23, 1783, Minister Plenipotentiary Prince Georg Adam von Starhemberg ordered committee members to investigate ways "to render permanent a portion of the advantages already existing, to multiply resources and relations, and to make greatest use possible of the current circumstances, namely the imminent peace and, seemingly, the independence of the United States of America."[41] Starhemberg's request reveals the apparently low ambition—or, perhaps, realism—with which the Brussels officials approached the matter: he aimed to preserve "a *portion*" of the advantages. It was already taken as a matter of fact that not all the wartime gains could be sustained.

Three of the six committee members responded to Starhemberg's request.[42] Two of them proposed standard measures such as lowering tariffs on American goods and ensuring domestic cargo suitable for Atlantic markets.[43] One of them proposed something quite different. Henri Deplancq had been a member of the committee since its inception and, like the others, held high-ranking positions elsewhere in the Brussels government. In his case, he also served on the Council of Finance and as the director of the Board of Customs.[44] In pondering the Ostend question, Deplancq explored the situation with great scope and pragmatism. In his *Mémoire* submitted to Starhemberg, there were opportunities as well as challenges.[45] First of all, Deplancq argued some countries should be written off without hesitation. Russian trade amounted to nothing more than a small exchange in sawdust whilst trade with Denmark-Norway centred on crayfish. Great Britain and the Dutch Republic always presented the greatest challenges from their dominant commercial positions, which was "very ruinous" for the Austrian Netherlands unless importations from these nations could be reduced.[46] The stagnant position with France, Portugal, and the Mediterranean states was unlikely to change except negatively as French traders moved back to Dunkirk. Spain represented a small hope for improvement since port duties were low enough to allow a sliver of profitable trade in places like Cadiz, so Deplancq saw North America as the only real chance for growth.

Deplancq advocated shifting interests from the Caribbean to the United States. He predicted that before long, France and Britain would raise tariffs to protect their islands as the Dutch had already done. As he concluded, "with this uncertainty, it seems to me that is premature to form any policy on Caribbean trade and that it is enough to merely watch for what happens next."[47] The stabilised position of the United States of America as a fully independent and sovereign nation allowed for more opportunity. Deplancq felt American trade was "extremely interesting" as it gave all European traders an equal playing field. This meant Flemish textiles would fare well. In return, rice and tobacco could be sourced from the Carolinas and Virginia. He noted that American tobacco might harm the nascent Flemish tobacco industry which had sprung up to meet domestic demand during the war, but that it could be reshipped for a profit if the American price was low enough.[48] To these ends, he argued it was necessary to gain representation and a treaty with the Americans as soon as possible. He even envisioned a system where there would be three consuls in the United States: one each in New York and Charleston with a central authority in Philadelphia to oversee them.[49] In Deplancq's view, a focus on the United States clearly demarcated the way forward.

In deciding the best course for the economy of the Austrian Netherlands, Starhemberg had chosen not to rely solely on his councillors. His directive also included merchants. Seven responded, with the imperial consuls in London, Antonio Songa, and Dunkirk, François Joseph de Lattre, also providing input.[50] As for the merchants, William Herries of the firm *Herries, Keith & Co.* in Ostend suggested the founding of a national bank in order to serve as guarantor on prospective voyages to North America.[51] Others sought government support in terms of subsidies and lower tariffs.[52] The most interesting proposition was the desire to acquire an island in the Caribbean. Several respondents backed the idea including Herries and de Lattre along with Charles André Melchior de Proli, the widow (*Veuve*) van Schoor, and Friedrich Romberg in Brussels.[53] The latter two seemed especially keen, perhaps given their slave trading activities.[54] They insisted anywhere would do and Van Schoor included a list of suitable places from Curaçao to Honduras, and from Mexico to Suriname. De Lattre held the island of Tobago more firmly in mind. All proponents argued this would ensure continued access to the Caribbean, maintain a competitive advantage, and would open a beachhead into the United States markets and possibly into Spanish North America via the Mississippi river. In spite of these perceived benefits, the Brussels government declined further consideration on the grounds that foreign pressures to abandon colonial ambitions had been too great in the past and the sums needed to purchase an island such as Tobago, if the French could even be persuaded of re-linquishing it, as well as the non-existent navy to protect it, would be enormous.[55]

Starhemberg may have felt his grand survey of opinions had been a failure, but he dutifully sent the reports on to Vienna. There, as in Brussels, the merchants' either tepid or harebrained schemes met with little enthusiasm. In this light, De-plancq's more calculated approach appeared the most reasonable and suitable way forward. The need for a solution had become more urgent in Brussels following the news that Spanish port authorities had begun making conditions increasingly unfavourable for foreign traders. The singular hope for improved European com-merce receded with news of complications in selling Flemish cargo onboard the Danish ship *Anne Sophie* in March 1783. To make matters worse, the ship had been sailing to Philadelphia via the Spanish ports and, as one Ghent merchant involved in the transaction claimed, costs had now risen by twenty to twenty-five percent as a result.[56] Officials struggled to find alternatives but nothing appeared practical beyond Deplancq's suggestion to send consular representatives.

In the meantime, the prevailing thought was that the merchants themselves would preserve trade with North America. This notion was not without merit. Merchants had a clear incentive to continue transatlantic trade. Flemish firms es-tablished partnerships in the United States to secure their presence in American markets. This involved either starting business associations with American firms or sending a representative to the United States. The first Ostend firm to take this direction was *Herries, Keith & Co.* run by two Englishmen, George Keith and William Herries. They sent over John Paterson—about whom little is known—to travel between Charleston and New York for one to two years. In anticipation of his mission, they focused on their contacts in England to reach out to Americans, most notably through an associate to William Temple Franklin.[57]

In the immediate postwar period at least four additional Flemish companies followed the example of *Herries, Keith & Co.* The firm of *Liebaert, Baes, Derd-eyn & Co.* established a partnership with Mark Prager in Philadelphia, the son of the Amsterdam-London family conglomerate run by Yehiel Prager, which had traded through Ostend during the Revolution.[58] Prager proved highly effective in Philadelphia. George Washington described him as a "gentleman engaged extensively in trade" and recommended him to his friends after Prager had won Washington's approval within a year of his arrival.[59] It was one of many useful friendships throughout Prager's time in America.[60] Whereas during the war *Liebaert, Baes, Derdeyn & Co.* had sent ships along the lucrative route to the Caribbean, their new partner advised them of better opportunities. In this case, *Liebaert & Prager*—as the new association was known—specialised in trading

American wheat to Lisbon in exchange for Portuguese wines to Ostend.[61] Prager's efforts were diluted, however, by the ongoing court case over the *Eersten*, which sapped his energies and forced him to lobby Congress on at least one occasion.[62] In 1785, the firm suffered another court case involving another ship, *l'Empereur*, diverting Prager's attention yet again.[63] Beset with difficulties, the partnership did not outlast the 1780s as Mark Prager traded under his own company by 1791.[64] Its existence, however short, still demonstrated the tenacity and new direction of Ostend firms postwar.

Firms across the Austrian Netherlands mirrored the new American initiatives of *Herries, Keith & Co.* and *Liebaert & Prager.* In Antwerp, *De Heyder, Veydt & Co.* formed a close connection through the insurance house of James Vanuxem in Philadelphia.[65] Vanuxem functioned as the main insurer and his son's future father-in-law, Herman Joseph Lombaert of *Ghovaere & Lombaert*, served as the clearinghouse for *De Heyder, Veydt & Co.* in North America.[66] Through these two unofficial partners, *De Heyder, Veydt & Co.* sold large amounts of textile goods from Lier and Antwerp and earned a profit of around twenty-five percent on their North American sales.[67] New connections such as these required a great deal of trust and transatlantic cooperation between firms without formal business ties or which lacked a connubial link.[68] The *De Heyder, Veydt & Co.*--Vanuxem–*Ghovaere & Lambaert* trading nexus ultimately proved too deficient in trust as business ceased in 1787 and arguments erupted over the payment of debts.[69] Seeking to continue their exports to the United States, *De Heyder, Veydt and Co.* sold off their remaining stock via *Samuel Wetherill & Sons* in Philadelphia but failed to attract any other substantial partnerships.[70] The failure to sustain such bonds of business confirmed what the British envoy in Brussels, George Byng, Viscount Torrington, had to say about the trade with the United States: "The want of faith in the Americans—and the various stories told of the dishonesty of their merchants, will prove a great obstacle to any confidence [as] these wary people here are not easily inclined to risk their money."[71] Given the British reluctance towards American independence and the efforts in the 1780s to regain much of the lost American commerce, Torrington was undoubtedly prejudiced against such endeavours. His words, however, reflected the difficult reality in establishing viable long-term connections across the Atlantic in the late eighteenth century.

Philadelphia attracted the greatest postwar interest, but other American cities became prospective sites also. One Ostend ship, the *Ceres*, arrived in Norfolk, Virginia, in 1786, for instance.[72] The largest port in the southern states, Charleston, became the focal point of other concerted efforts to establish a beachhead in American markets. Two Flemish firms established connections with companies in the city. These connections proved rather poor, however. In the first instance, Charleston functioned as an indirect port of call for the Ostend firm *De Kuyper,* which sailed its namesake ship to Philadelphia in 1784. There, the company's associates, Pennsylvanian partners *Biddle & Tellier,* sold the Flemish goods and loaded the *De Kuyper* with flour and other provisions for sale in Charleston and Curaçao before it would return from South America to Ostend a year later.[73] This exchange meant that whilst an Ostend ship technically arrived in Charleston, it was carrying on an intra-American trade rather than beginning a new transatlantic venture between Charleston and Ostend. The second case attempted to achieve direct transatlantic trade but failed to sustain it. A native of Ghent founded the firm *De Surmont* in Charleston sometime in late 1783 or early 1784 and received the ship *Jacoba et Isabella* from Ostend in mid-1784 carrying a variety of Flemish goods to exchange for tobacco.[74] The expedition faltered in profitability since the company's director understood little about the tariffs in South Carolina and barely made anything from the trade. He sold his wares at cost and returned home with the ship.[75] South Carolina seemed too distant an opportunity for the merchants of the Austrian Netherlands.

Whilst the firms *De Kuyper* and *De Surmont* failed in their attempts to trade with a second American city, there were other merchants in the Austrian Netherlands who traded with North America but did not establish any lasting presence. At least fifteen ships sailed from Ostend to the United States between July 1783 and 1788.[76] Compared to four ships that sailed to the Caribbean from 1783 to 1785, this number was significantly higher and represented the shift away from the Caribbean for Ostend traders.[77] Merchants in the Austrian Netherlands sensed the new direction in trade. Applications to be the Habsburg consul in the United States arrived on Deplancq's desk from 1782 onwards.[78] But Deplancq recommended that these pleas be left unanswered until the American situation had stabilised and a policy regarding consular presence had been worked out in Vienna.[79]

At the same time, merchants approached American representatives to open Flemish trade with the United States. Sir Robert Herries penned a forty-eight-page memorandum on the prospects of British and Flemish goods in American markets which he sent to Silas Deane in 1783.[80] Edward Browne, a British subject in Ostend, approached John Adams for the position of American consul and enlisted other merchants in London to support his cause.[81] Browne's desire rested on the wish to continue trade with William Lee, who had retired to his Green Spring plantation in Virginia during the summer of 1783.[82] Their bond was one of friendship as well as business. Lee's wife Hannah Philippa Ludwell

Lee and their children moved in with the Browne family at Ostend and Lee entrusted a large sum of money to Browne, which he could draw upon more easily than sending remittances from across the Atlantic.[83] Together with Dennis de Berdt, a merchant friend from Lee's London days, the trio sought to rehabilitate Virginian trade through exporting Flemish and British goods via Ostend in return for cheap tobacco from Lee's Virginian neighbours.[84]

Yet by 1785, the venture had produced little. Lee suffered a wave of personal tragedies; first, the death of his wife as she was about to embark from Ostend to America in 1784 and then the slow erosion of his eyesight which had worsened upon his return to Virginia, so much so that he could not read by candlelight. Plans were waylaid by the unhelpful nature of transatlantic communication, too. In 1785, Lee had already complained to Browne that he had not heard from him for over a year when he wrote bluntly and painfully,

> It seems that added to the other misfortunes that have persecuted me in a successive habit for two years past, I have lost a friend; a loss that at my time of life is generally not easy to be repared [sic] and in my Case perhaps it is impossible, but I will still address you by that sacred title.[85]

Lee's loss subsided with his receipt of a handful of letters from Browne during the years up to 1788. They reveal how little of their plans actually transpired. Through Browne's company *Browne & Perryman*, Lee managed to trade Madeira wines instead, meaning the trade had nothing to do with Ostend except for Browne's presence as his European agent.[86] The Madeira trade, however, did not prove successful as Lee's contacts in Brussels reported that they suffered losses on the venture.[87] By the late 1780s, Lee seemed unable to lead a new direction. In 1791, he underwent a rudimentary cataract operation which rendered his eyes useless. Blind, enfeebled by the many years of travel and the personal devastation of his wife's death, Lee died in 1795. The man who had once been a celebrity in Vienna, the first representative of the United States to the Habsburg lands, and a self-exiled resident in Brussels, could achieve no further meaningful connection in the postwar years.

Lee and Browne were not the only American merchants to attempt transatlantic trade from Ostend, however. The New York merchant Nicholas Low made a concerted effort. Prior to the end of the war, Low had no commercial ties with Ostend. But an unsolicited letter from an English mercantile firm in Ostend, *William Williams & Co.*, got his attention, even though Low did not reply to the opportunity to sell "tobacco, rice, turpentine, slaves, and indigo" through the firm.[88] Instead, by 1785, Low had made contact with the Antwerp firm of

Werbrouck & Mellerio through whom he procured hats to sell in Philadelphia.[89] The venture made good returns and *Werbrouck & Mellerio* sent a representative to Philadelphia the following year to act as their representative with Low and his associate, Joseph Lacoste.[90] At its peak, however, the collaboration abruptly ended, perhaps because *Werbrouck & Mellerio* operated through their new Philadelphian representative. Low's Antwerp business dealing was the rare instance of an American-led interaction with Ostend.

Most other American merchants shut up shop in Ostend. Thomas Barclay had commanded a large presence in Ostend's American wartime trade but relocated to Paris where he embarked upon a diplomatic career.[91] Three merchants, William Bingham, Samuel Ingliss, and Robert Gilmor, had likewise benefitted from directing ships from Ostend to Philadelphia during the war as *Bingham, Ingliss & Gilmor*. Gilmor operated out of Amsterdam during that period and from there he sought to continue direct trade to the United States, particularly to his native Baltimore.[92] The initiative did not last long as the trio liquidated their endeavours in February 1784.[93] One American firm showed interest in establishing a trade in Ostend but only to a limited degree. In 1784, the Baltimore firm *Samuel & John Smith* sent out a circular advertisement titled "A New Scene of Commerce has opened with the Country" to thirty-eight European port-cities. Re-establishing ties with Great Britain was clearly the priority for them but Ostend featured as one of the six non-British ports featured on their roster. Nothing came of it.[94]

No American presence lasted in Ostend beyond 1786. Symptomatic of the attitude by the late 1780s, a petition to Thomas Jefferson to use Ostend as the main entrepôt for Irish commerce in 1785 went without reply.[95] The heydays of American trade at Ostend ended in these postwar years. Whereas wartime produced a boom for Ostend's transatlantic trade through the international use of a neutral naval flag, the peace that followed brought hardship and ruin as foreign merchants upped sticks and returned to their respective countries. In most cases, it was a foreseeable result—one questioned openly in the Augsburg press and resoundingly answered by poverty rather than prosperity. What was unforeseen, however, was the tenacity of local merchants to continue the good times and to fight for a piece of the lucrative American trade. Like many Habsburg moments in the American Revolution, Ostend and its transatlantic trade was a brief episode of boom and bust, but it was one which mattered greatly and affected the course of action vis-à-vis the Americans during this decade. Ostend's commercial rise was instrumental in shaping the urgency from ministers in the Austrian Netherlands for a political connection between the Habsburg Monarchy and the United States. Its fall would cement an eventual malaise about the utility of America on the eve of a homegrown revolution in the Austrian Netherlands. Ultimately, it would not be until the Napoleonic Wars that commerce would again pick up and Congress would deem a consular representative necessary in the former Austrian Netherlands.[96]

Trieste: The Maturity of Direct Trade

By the time of the Treaty of Paris, only two groups of Triestine merchants had been successful in their aims to established direct trade between America and the Adriatic: Frohn and Baraux on the one hand, and Verpoorten and his new company on the other. Verpoorten was in fact the only Trieste trader to complete a roundtrip with the crossing of his *l'Americano* in 1782. He was among the new set of merchants but by no means alone. The voyages of *La Città di Trieste* and *l'Americano* during the war (see chapter 6) signalled new opportunities to other merchants in Trieste. Spurred by his example, this new generation of postwar merchants now sought to consolidate and expand the direct transatlantic trade between Trieste and the United States.

Domenico Francesco Belletti, a merchant of considerable repute, became one of the most enthusiastic merchants for transatlantic trade. Belletti directed Trieste's Mercantile Insurance Chamber and headed the firm *Belletti & Zaccar Compagnie* which traded extensively in the Levant.[97] Belletti began a furious letter campaign to Franklin in order to secure his appointment as the official consul for the United States.[98] Belletti's first letter, written in February 1783, spoke of his admiration for the American republic.[99] Belletti obviously intended to flatter Franklin, wishing to be "employed in the service of your respectable Republic here and across the whole Austria Littoral in the role of a Consul General, through which [flows] the commerce of your states with that of our august Monarch."[100] Belletti received no response from Franklin but persisted regardless. In April, Belletti sent Franklin four letters within eighteen days, demonstrating his seriousness in establishing his own trade with the United States. In his first letter, Belletti outlined his lobbying efforts to convince the emperor of the viability of American trade and his company's preparations to trade goods from the hereditary lands and the Levant.[101] His final three letters took an increasingly desperate tone, pleading with Franklin for a letter of recommendation and at least a show of support for his commercial expedition. Met again with silence, Belletti mustered support from the French consul in Trieste but this letter arrived too late to help.[102]

Despite Belletti's inclusion of two recommendations—including one by Count Karl von Zinzendorf—Franklin did not seem to care.[103] His rescue came from intervention by Charles André Melchior de Proli, an influential merchant and banker in the Austrian Netherlands, who lobbied Franklin successfully in May 1783 to procure American contacts for Belletti's venture.[104]

Belletti's commercial expedition had many backers. A conglomeration of successful merchants formed around him including Antonio Rossetti along with Giacomo Francesco Maria Gabbiati and the Flemish-born Ambrosius von Strohlendorf, the head of the Triestine stock exchange. These sophisticated pioneers acquired the right connections both geographically and politically to obtain trade with the United States. Rossetti and Gabbiati functioned as Levantine contacts, Belletti pushed Franklin for support though Proli, and Strohlendorf provided the ship for the mission, *La Capricieuse*.[105] This ship had crossed the Atlantic from Ostend in 1781 but Stohlendorf repurposed it to "go to America."[106] For the expedition, the quartet planned to sail under imperial colours and therefore had to first navigate treacherous court scrutiny before navigating ocean waves. Belletti once again began a furious campaign. He personally travelled to Vienna to submit the application to the Aulic Chamber in May 1783. One immediate problem occurred. The intended captain of the ship, George Simpson was a Scottish-born sailor and not an imperial subject. The quartet arranged for Frohn and Baraux to exert their influence. In their attestation, they praised Simpson's qualities and argued for honourary citizenship.[107] The directors also addressed secondary concerns over smuggling arms since, as one treasury official noted, America was still "presently full of soldiers from all over the world."[108] Eventually the officials granted the patent but, as in previous cases, it included a list of prohibited goods.

With clearance awarded for the mission, Belletti wrote to Franklin again in September 1783. "It is certain," he declared, "the Port of Trieste has *more than any other port* a very solid commercial enterprise with America."[109] Simpson set sail that month with Franklin's letters of introduction.[110] *La Capricieuse* became the largest Triestine vessel to sail directly to the United States with 350 tonnes of cargo. Upon arrival in Philadelphia, Simpson brokered contact with the influential merchant and financier Robert Morris, the Superintendent of Finance, and with the trading house *Bache & Shee*, operated by Franklin's son-in-law Richard Bache and his associate John Shee. *Bache & Shee* handled most of the goods from *La Capricieuse*. Franklin's son-in-law was delighted at this opportunity and thanked his father-in-law for,

Your kind introductions in the Mercantile line [which] have thrown a pretty large scene of business into Bache & Shee's hands, and we have a good prospect before us of its being profitable, [as] our connections with Trieste in the Empire of Germany [Holy Roman Empire], are likely to be very considerable, and our prospects very flattering.[111]

Bache & Shee operated as distributors, selling the Triestine products easily. On December 10, 1783, the *Pennsylvania Gazette* listed the first advert of goods from *La Capricieuse* featuring "dates, spices, and currants" brought from the Levant and sold by the shopkeeper Samuel Garrigues in Philadelphia.[112]

Simpson and the quartet developed an ingenious strategy for increasing their yields from the American trade. Sailing out of Trieste with Simpson was a Captain Wouters, a native of Antwerp who travelled to Baltimore over the winter of 1783 and purchased an American ship which they renamed the *Comte de Brigido* in honour of the new governor of Trieste, Pompejus Brigido von Bresowitz.[113] Wouters took command of this vessel laden with American products, and they left their respective ports in late summer 1784. Both ships arrived in Trieste on November 9, 1784.[114] News of their arrival and the success of the venture, especially the method of one-out, two-back travelled fast through the Habsburg lands. Governor Brigido wrote a letter to *Bache & Shee* thanking them "for their friendship and support which they [gave] Cap. Simpson during his stay." In it, he expressed his joy at "our commerce between our countries which has been started and will become more considerable" given "the remarkable boundaries of the New Republic and the New World."[115] Belletti, Simpson, and the other backers shared the same opinion and embarked on planning their next voyage.

The success of *La Capricieuse* depended upon the quality and suitability of the merchandise for sale. Fortunately, the statistical table of 1783 provides an insight into which wares sold well. Although it is unclear which voyages the table includes, the figures allow for some indication of overall trends commensurate with the *Capricieuse* expedition. Firstly, metalwares from Carinthia and Styria produced some of the largest profits (see table 3 below).

Most of these metal goods focused on agricultural use and accounted for a tenth of the net worth exported to the United States in 1783. Metalwares sold exceedingly well in Philadelphia. According to Wouters, iron strips used for constructing barrels achieved a fifty percent return on their original value.[116] American traders purchased these products since iron manufacturing in the United States had not yet matched the Austrian standard. The rich opportunities of the American markets prompted one of the Styrian sailors to write home to an acquaintance in Graz. He shared his "absolute conviction that the American trade

TABLE 3. Metalware exported to the United States from Trieste, 1783

Product Name (Orig.)	Product Name (Eng.)	Quantity (Tonnes)	Value (fl)	Percentage of Trieste-US Export
Acciaro	Steel	26	2,600	0.8
Ferramenta lavorata	Agricultural tools	21	6,750	7.0
Ferro in ancore	Iron weights/anchors	4	480	0.5
Ferro in fasci	Iron straps/strips	17.50	1,571	1.6
Ferro in filati	Iron rods	5.25	499	0.5
Ferro in vom-ere e badilla	Iron ploughs/shovels	9	1,344	1.4
	Total	82.75	13,248	11.8

SOURCE: FHKA, NHK, Kommerz Litorale Akten, Generalia, K. 850 (1780-1785), fols. 1003-1020.

offers the biggest advantages possible for the emperor's merchants," especially, he noted, because "it is commonly known that American factories desperately need Austrian goods [and] what is more, few factories even occupy this Republic." Editors of the *Wienerisches Diarium* published the letter, commenting that other merchants were following suit.[117]

Indeed, another ship from Antwerp, *La Poste*, arrived on July 21, 1784, laden with iron strips and bands (*fer spaté en ruban*) produced by one of the best iron manufactories in the Austrian Netherlands.[118] The official Habsburg representative in Philadelphia (discussed in the next chapter) explained that the high quality of these goods as well as the comparatively low wages in Austrian mines gave ironware a significant advantage over the competition from British and Swedish iron producers.[119]

Carinthia, Styria, and the Austrian Netherlands were not the only Habsburg provinces to absorb the new American trade. Manufactories in Bohemia as well as the former Habsburg territory of Silesia benefitted from direct transatlantic trade. These provinces predominantly accessed Atlantic markets through Hamburg, but Prussian aggression drove Bohemian merchants to trade along southern routes via the Mediterranean.[120] Under this old system, merchants constantly complained of their profits being eroded by Spanish trading houses.[121] Direct trade from Trieste to American markets proved one of the simplest and most cost-effective avenues for inland Central European manufacturers, so much so that Silesian manufacturers under Prussian rule also elected to redirect their commerce towards Trieste. Textiles and glass products were the principal goods exported to the United States from these areas. Glass products included crystal goblets and various tumblers that were already noted across Europe for their fine quality. Textiles—hats, fine cloths, clothing, drapes, and linen—became the second most successful product overall.[122] The direct trading value of linens amounted to 30,400 Austrian Gulden (*fl*) alone in 1783.[123] *Bache & Shee* initially produced returns of around forty percent on these goods. Such business attracted considerable interest. Karl Anton Fitz, a textile factory owner in Budišov, Moravia, brokered personal contact with *Bach & Shee* in Philadelphia through the Simpson-Wouters mission, for example.[124] The ability to trade directly proved irresistible.

Simpson and Wouters reinvested profits from exports to purchase the main import from the United States: tobacco. Eighteenth-century Europeans imported large quantities of tobacco, and inhabitants of the Habsburg Monarchy were no different. Domestic production of tobacco in the Habsburg lands centred around the Hungarian plains. However, Hungarian producers cultivated a different species that was less desirable than the American variety. Europeans preferred the taste of "English" tobacco to the so-called "*Bauern-Tabak*" (farmer's tobacco) grown in Hungary.[125] Tobacco cultivation and selling was also heavily regulated in the Habsburg Monarchy. The government legalised tobacco in 1701 but exercised a state monopoly over sales and the distribution of licenses in the Austrian lands for much of the century. In 1783, the state monopoly became a permanent feature, ending only with the Republic of Austria's accession to the European Union in 1995.[126]

In the Hungarian lands, a more liberal regime persisted despite attempts to install the same state-controlled monopoly. Looser regulation and private industry enabled constant cultivation following the first tobacco factory in 1722, but also exposed Hungarian producers to greater effects in market fluctuations. There was both opportunity and peril at stake. When war interrupted production and exportation from North America, Hungarian tobacconists rushed to supplant the fall in American supplies which forced European consumers to accept whatever variety of tobacco was on offer. There was still a preference for American tobacco when it could be had, which caused some shipments of Hungarian tobacco to be cancelled or returned, but scarcity of American tobacco created a significant boom for Hungarian merchants.[127] Tempted by easy success, the director of the Austrian tobacco monopoly, even resigned his post in order to devote himself to trading tobacco out of the Hungarian port of Fiume in 1777.[128] By 1783, revenues from Hungarian tobacco reached the unseen heights of nearly three million florins in value.[129] For entrepreneurs in Hungary, the boom was a golden opportunity since many other Hungarian products received harsh tariffs from Vienna in order to protect Austrian industry.[130] Yet, with the cessation of hostilities, boom inevitably turned to bust as American exportation resumed and Hungarian suppliers could not compete with the influx of cheaper, more popular American tobacco, which traders like Simpson and Wouters now returned through local ports.[131]

Merchants and Hungarian officials did not relinquish their hopes of reviving the Hungarian tobacco sector, however. As part of a programme to stimulate the Hungarian economy in anticipation of his great institutional reforms of 1785, Joseph II allowed some efforts to alleviate the position of the tobacco farmers in their postwar plight.[132] Tolls were lowered on the main road to Fiume and a new watermen's guild enabled smoother transit on rivers.[133] The man overseeing these improvements was the new Governor of Fiume, Count Pál Almásy von Zsadány who thought the Simpson-Wouters expedition offered Hungarian farmers a renewed opportunity. Almásy requested the pair gather tobacco seeds from Virginia and Maryland so that they might be used and tested in Hungarian fields where, he hoped, the better American species would thrive and could compete in European markets.[134] Though Almásy got his seeds, it was too late. The tonnes of tobacco leaf Simpson and Wouters brought back confirmed the insurmountable inferiority of Hungarian tobacco. The new direct trade between Trieste and America guaranteed the plentiful and cheap supply of American tobacco and ensured that Hungarian production would only serve smaller domestic and regional markets within the Habsburg lands and Central Europe.[135] Fond memories of the boom times during the American Revolution remained firm in many Hungarian minds into the nineteenth century and many hoped to still challenge the American predominance in European markets.[136] By then, however, Southern politicians and planters sent out "special tobacco agents" to ensure their hegemony continued in places like the Habsburg Monarchy.[137]

Although results of the Simpson-Wouters mission proved hard for Hungarians, it was an all-round achievement for Triestine merchants. The quartet was keen to continue their exploits and so, as 1785 began, both ships again sailed for Philadelphia and Baltimore, reaching their destinations by March 1785 with a similar but more refined cargo.[138] This was the first time Trieste merchants had directly exported to Baltimore and before the year was out, advertisements for Bohemian glassware appeared in the city's newspaper.[139] Triestine merchants now had a foothold in two ports of the United States. Based on this success, there was enough conviction to form an entirely new company specifically designated for transatlantic trade. In July 1785, Belletti, Simpson, and Strohlen-dorf formed a new "quartet'" alongside newcomer Karl von Maffei, the Maltese and Papal consul in Trieste. Together they established the *Compagnia di Commercio per l'America Settentrionale* also known as the *Compagnia Austriaco-Americana* (Austrian-American Trading Company), and served as its board of directors.[140] Announcements reverberated across Austria and America that summer.[141] The founding of the Society was a massive undertaking with an initial fund of 500,000*fl* divided into 1,000 shares costing 500*fl* each. Participation in such a firm was therefore restricted to the wealthy mercantile and noble classes. The first general assembly took place in Trieste in November 1785. The founding of the Austrian-American Trading Company and its stock offer made news in Vienna and across continental Europe.[142]

In order to establish such an undertaking, privileges and permission had to be obtained from the Aulic Chamber. The quartet submitted a charter for approval at the same time they went public with the initiative. Governor Brigido supported their application. In August, Brigido wrote to the emperor personally about the company and petitioned him to grant them official privileges. Brigido explained in the most positive terms how the "several well-meaning, intelligent and experienced merchants" came together to form the company after the successful Philadelphia mission, which had "by no means completely satisfied their patriotic zeal."[143] In addition, Brigido stressed how the firm's previous mission had "exported almost exclusively domestic products, of which there is the greatest abundance" and added,

> The important utility of [this] impending enterprise, and the honesty with which the direction of the new commenced trading society is arranged, impresses me so much that I cannot refrain from recommending this new enterprise of the highest grace and mercy unquestionably.[144]

Brigido went a step further than simply endorsing the latest mercantile project with the United States. Given the numerous applications, missions, and ferment then present in Trieste, he advised the emperor,

> A new commerce on such firm grounds and for the greatest mutual utility may not fail, especially if Your Majesty, with all righteousness, permits maximum protection, and in the meantime achieves at establishing friendly agreement with the Republic of the United States of America much wanted on the most permanent footing.[145]

FIGURE 12. View of the free port of Trieste
by Ferdinand Runk and Anton Herzinger (ca. 1800)

The application met with success in Vienna. Joseph sanctioned the status of
a privileged company in early September 1785, thereby acknowledging their endeavours as something of value to the state.[146] In essence, the conferment seemed
a realisation of Joseph's original aim of extending trade with the Americans back
in 1783. By 1785, he had been fully convinced of the merits of such a trade. At the
same time as Joseph received Brigido's petition, he held an audience with Gilbert
du Motier, marquis de Lafayette, who later, with joy, informed Jefferson that
American commerce "was a great object" in the emperor's mind. Indeed, Joseph
was not the only one in Vienna fixated on this topic. Lafayette also informed
Jefferson of a visit from Kaunitz who had come to speak to him "very willingly"
about the substance of American trade.[147] Lafayette's visit was coincidental; the
court had already set on the priority of trade with the new United States, and
Trieste had played a fundamental role in establishing that conviction.

The maturity of direct trade between Trieste and the United States represented a fundamental cornerstone in the Habsburg attitude towards pursuing
a political connection between the two states. Triestine merchants had been
equally tenacious as Ostend and Livornese traders in forging direct ties with
North America and, crucially, in convincing local and Viennese officials of the
worthiness of their endeavours. The Austrian-American Trading Company

embodied the new, emboldened spirit of transatlantic opportunity rife in Trieste and with official imperial support of its missions. The rapidity and intensity of transatlantic trade with the United States in these postwar years ensured the United States remained one of the most valuable commercial routes outside of the Mediterranean for the imperial entrepôt on the Adriatic.

Conclusion

The development of postwar commerce between the Habsburg lands and the United States of America took place in the three major ports of Livorno, Ostend, and Trieste. In those towns, new merchant adventurers aimed to profit from the opportunities ushered in by American independence. Major American ports, from Charleston to Boston, became targets of Habsburg mercantile ambitions. In several cases, Habsburg merchants established considerable footholds in the American economy by sending representatives, entering partnerships, and creating contacts with American businesses. Though in some cases these connections proved short-lived, their existence testifies to the extensive commercial spaces in which both the Habsburgs and Americans operated.

In spaces beyond the Atlantic—in the Mediterranean, the Adriatic, and the North Sea—merchants created new trade flows, and, in the case of Tuscany, expanded upon the earlier trading scene. The effects of this postwar commerce emanated from these centres and affected wider regional markets. In the Habsburg Monarchy, this produced positive and negative effects. The hopes of reviving a Hungarian tobacco market crashed after the reintroduction of cheap, popular American tobacco. Yet, in Transylvania, new ventures inspired local businessmen to seek out their own routes to American markets.[148] As Franklin had put it, a "new set of merchants" had come into existence. The zeal and determination of the mercantile classes to exploit the new situation in North America impressed the ruling elites who supported such initiatives at the state level. In Trieste, officials even wrote to the emperor in support of the newly established trading company. The belief in an independent United States as a source of economic potential emerged from the mercantile world, moved into the political realm, and combined to create an urgency to nourish this nascent trade.

In the postwar aftermath, the question of American commerce loomed large in the minds of administrators across the Habsburg Monarchy. Emperor Joseph II pondered its "greatest importance" already in 1783 and Prince von Kaunitz sought out Lafayette to parley with him about the subject a few years later. The successful missions of traders both during and after the war convinced a previously hesitant bureaucracy of the need for a political connection in order to defend and sustain the profitable commercial ties to the United States. The emerging urgency was, however, one-sided. Although American merchants attempted trade with Habsburg markets such as Ostend, these efforts paled in comparison to the overwhelming interest of Habsburg merchants and administrators in the United States. It was a significant development given the American insistence on brokering contact with the Habsburgs during the War of American Independence and the mission of William Lee in 1778. During the American Revolution, the question for Habsburg officials had been how to mitigate against the negative effects while profiting from the neutral carrying trade. Now, in a time of peace, the question had become how to secure Habsburg trade as one among equals. The time for action had arrived.

CHAPTER EIGHT

"If His Imperial Majesty Should Think Fit"

The First Habsburg Representatives in the United States of America,
1783–1789

A N ORDINARY HOUSE in New York City hosted an extraordinary meeting in the late summer of 1785. A middle-aged father and his seventeen-year-old son entered a parlour room fitted with a large wooden table in the centre. On top were eleven glasses of finest Madeira wine. Their host, who towered over them at an impressive 6'6", rose to greet them but failed to offer the opulent drink on display. Instead, he boasted how the wine had been a personal gift from the marquis de Lafayette, given to his colleague who sat stubbornly in one corner of the room, his facial scars on show. Two more men looked on from the leisure of a chaise lounge. All of them, the father noted later, "mutilated" their ears with silver pendants and pierced each nostril with large silver rings which distracted from faces covered in bear's grease and black hair powdered copiously, but unevenly, with dazzling red vermillion. The host's attire also struck him as worthy of record; the gentleman who stood throughout the entire meeting wore a dark blue robe overlaid with delicate red, yellow, and white lines whilst around his neck hung a solid gold English gorget and fourteen rows of decorative brown beads. The gentleman also showed off these beads to his guests, pressing them into their hands for a short while. When asked where someone might acquire such ornaments, the gentleman faced the son and with a piece of chalk drew a large map on the table, pointing out to the boy the distances from his house to Fort Schuyler and from there to Schenectady, to Albany, and finally, to the lands of his own Oneida Nation. "370 miles," the boy counted. But the Oneida chief had not realised the distance his two guests had already come; he had just lectured the son of the first representative of the Habsburg Monarchy to the United States.[1]

Such an encounter resulted from the Habsburg desire to secure trade with the United States, and the fear of losing it. At the start of 1783, the Habsburg Monarchy had no commercial representatives in the United States for its avid mercantile traders whatsoever. By the end of that year, three individuals resided permanently in the new United States for this purpose, but only one functioned in any official capacity as far as the Habsburgs were concerned. None of them, however, gained bilateral recognition and likely for this reason, their presence in the early republic has been overlooked by historians. These individuals, their families, their missions, and their fates, however, merit a detailed account. The establishment of commercial representation in the United States was a major step for the Habsburg Monarchy in acquiring formal ties with the Americans and protecting the nascent trading links between both lands. Prior to 1783, only two other places beyond the Mediterranean commanded enough attention to warrant consular representation form the Habsburg Monarchy. Both places were in East Asia. The missions of 1783 were the first representations of the Austrian Habsburgs in the Americas.[2] The pivot towards North America, and the efforts undertaken to create an official presence there, reflected the new primacy of commercial interests for Habsburg officials beyond Europe. Following the conclusion of peace, the United States became the focus of economic aspirations beyond European seas.

Representation brought the Habsburgs more gains than anticipated. New contacts, such as the meeting with the Oneida leaders, created opportunities previously unimagined in Vienna. The window into American society, commerce, and industry also brokered new understandings of fragility and competition within the American economy. Yet the highly compartmental nature of the Habsburg Monarchy affected the ability to construct effective policy that would take advantage of these economic opportunities. Divisions over representation in North America between regional officials in the Austrian Netherlands and imperial officials in Vienna was an important symptom of this discord. Distrust within the bureaucracy and mercantile communities of the Habsburg Monarchy not only resulted in more commercial representation in the United States than anywhere else beyond Europe but also exposed the continued importance of American commerce and the rising struggle to retain its benefits. The first Habsburg representatives in the United States signified the scramble to harness the bounty of transatlantic trade among imperial ministers and merchants alike.

The Internal Debate over Representation

Commercial connections forged by merchants during and after the Revolution indicated the potential richness of the American market. In the Austrian Netherlands, the carrying trade produced an exuberant wealth and the same gains incentivised merchants at Trieste towards the first direct trading ventures with American ports. These merchants were not alone, however. Across Europe, merchants and government officials recognised the need to solidify their share of lucrative transatlantic trade with the United States and to impede the share of other nations. Habsburg merchants like Bertin de Jaure were the first to panic at the mercantilist manoeuvres of other European states. He petitioned the regional government in Brussels for action by opening up direct relations with the Americans and securing representation in the United States.[3] In April 1782, the minister plenipotentiary in Brussels, Prince Georg Adam von Starhemberg recognised the threat, siding with merchants who begged for some kind of treaty protection by arguing for representation in the United States.[4] His plan chimed with the recommendations of the Council of Finance in Brussels which advocated a large consular system in the United States with the aim of directing trade from the individual states to the Habsburg lands. A system of several vice-consuls, one for each American state, under the direction of a consul general, ideally in Philadelphia, would be enough in their opinion.[5]

Benjamin Franklin's apparent support spurred on Starhemberg's actions. For his part, it seemed that Franklin invited treaty negotiations and a consular system from the Habsburgs.[6] Yet Franklin could not speak for the Americans entirely. American diplomacy was still a rather ad hoc business throughout this period when the lack of unified central institutions hampered the development of concrete foreign representation. During the War of American Independence, members of the Continental Congress had appointed several envoys to the European powers but did not enjoy fully reciprocal relations with many of them. Franklin became the first accredited diplomat to France in 1779 but he continued to respond to other matters and foreign requests.[7] Under the Articles of Confederation and Perpetual Union adopted by Congress in March 1781, a new Department of Foreign Affairs would oversee the administration of diplomatic ties and the creation of American consuls abroad. Yet the system proved weak and ineffective given the lack of empowerment for the secretary of foreign affairs and his ministers overseas. Such problems would not be solved until the introduction of the federal constitution in 1787.[8] By the effective conclusion of the war, very little had cemented the American diplomatic presence in Europe or smoothened the process of conducting foreign relations back home in Philadel-phia.[9] Expanding commerce remained at the heart of American foreign interests but, given the nature of American diplomacy, the urgency had to come from the Habsburgs side in order to broker relations.[10]

The timing seemed right in 1782, but without the consent of the emperor or State Chancellor Prince von Kaunitz, nothing could be done. The problem for the ministers and merchants of the Austrian Netherlands was that the Viennese officials did not share the same sense of urgency. From their view, North Ameri-can trade was in a nascent state. Although Kaunitz agreed it would be "advanta-geous for the [Austrian] Netherlands, and for the other States of his Majesty, to have a Consul in the United American Colonies," he remained steadfast on his decision to wait "to see what the fate of the colonies will be."[11] The disapproval dampened ambitions but also raised concerns in Brussels.

On November 30, 1782, Great Britain concluded the Preliminary Articles of Peace with the United States, now internationally recognising its former colo-nies as a sovereign and independent state. For ministers in the Austrian Nether-lands, the news removed any doubts over treating with the Americans. In Brus-sels, Starhemberg was convinced the Habsburgs needed to act soon in order to secure their share. Merchants continued to press for representation; the latest, Pierre-Jean Bouvier from Namur, who established his apothecary business in Port-au-Prince in Saint-Domingue, nominated himself for the role of "Consul Imperial" for the Americas.[12] On January 22, 1783, Starhemberg wrote another letter, but not to Kaunitz, whose cool feelings he remembered. Instead, he di-rectly contacted the imperial ambassador Count Florimond Mercy-d'Argenteau in Paris to set the wheels in motion. Starhemberg concocted the story that the emperor had asked him to report on the possibilities and necessities of trade with the Americans, but he hinted,

> It would be easy to respond effectively to one or the other of these issues if we had *here*, as there also, some sort of emissary or US agent, who I can con-fer secretly or at least discuss this important subject with, but the failure of this means I will only be able to tell His Majesty of general things and not provide a concise enough answer.[13]

Starhemberg explained to Mercy-d'Argenteau how Franklin once suggested such an arrangement but because "we had too much to fear from England," the discussion was dropped. Starhemberg urged Mercy-d'Argenteau to open channels with the Americans and make insinuations towards beginning such an arrangement. Yet such actions without official sanction from Vienna were dangerous. Seemingly aware of this, Starhemberg instructed Mercy-d'Argenteau not to make "mention of anything" to courtiers in Vienna and, secondly, any "insinuations with Mr Franklin ought to be only in the manner of a conversation which could never comprise yourself." Finally, perhaps most tellingly of all, Starhemberg ordered Mercy-d'Argenteau to "kindly burn this letter."[14]

Starhemberg's ploy was risky on multiple levels. First, he acted without permission. His actions subverted imperial authority. If Mercy-d'Argenteau's insinuations on his behalf came across as an offer of Habsburg recognition before the official treaty of peace had been concluded, then it would change the emperor's policy without his consent. Second, Starhemberg's actions ignored diplomatic norms. Unlike other European powers, the Habsburgs could not approach another nation, especially leaders of a recent rebellion and new republic, unless it was in response to a solicited offer.[15] Joseph II was Holy Roman Emperor and held dozens of other titles. His position as an emperor, a king of kings, was intended to outrank all other rulers.[16] In essence, the emperor could not go knocking on the door of the Americans, although Starhemberg seemed to be prying the door open already.

Given the risks associated with Mercy-d'Argenteau's delicate operation, it is not known what exactly occurred. Any mission report Starhemberg would have received most assuredly burned in his fireplace—presuming he followed his own instructions. Mercy-d'Argenteau likely received the letter in early February of 1783 and did indeed raise the conversation with Franklin, but again, no material proof or correspondence from either side survives. This scenario, however, explains Starhemberg's next action. A few weeks later, he sent off a proposal to his superiors in Vienna arguing for "the conclusion of a Treaty of Commerce and Amity with the American States without delay and the prompt sending of an accredited Minister or Resident to America" in order to represent the Habsburgs.[17] Starhemberg outlined his reasoning, noting that the Americans would be friendly to such an offer but without giving away his actions with Mercy-d'Argenteau. Starhemberg even nominated his preferred candidate for the position of consul general. Indeed, the ministers in Brussels had already run an internal search for suitable candidates.[18]

Starhemberg's rashness troubled Kaunitz. In presenting the proposal to the emperor on March 19, Kaunitz appended a large memorandum outlining his concerns. Although Kaunitz agreed it was "desirable to both sides for the swift connection to be made, it cannot be done for the time being." Kaunitz cautioned, "It is necessary for the American States to take the first steps to your Imperial Majesty on account of their status of recognition, until then there can neither be an accredited person sent to the United States nor a Treaty concluded with them."[19] The question of recognition posed a problem in Kaunitz's mind, especially since diplomatic etiquette and rank held sway over Habsburg officials' desire to obtain American commerce. At the same time, Kaunitz acknowledged the rising need to secure American trade for the Monarchy and meditated an interim solution to this issue:

> In order not to lose any time for all practical and preparatory steps towards a trade connection, however, between the hereditary lands (*Erblände*) and the American States, it would be best in my opinion, to send an official Commercial Advisor to America entrusted to learn about the terrain and to prepare the first principles for mutual recognition and commerce, and only then, when the recognition of American sovereignty has been made by Your Majesty, will he be bestowed with a ministerial character.[20]

Kaunitz masterfully articulated several profound changes to Starhemberg's strategy within these few lines. First, he reoriented the focus to the hereditary lands and, by their sole mention, promoted their interests over the Austrian Netherlands. Secondly, Kaunitz effectively divorced representation from the conclusion of a commercial treaty. The new title of "commercial advisor" rather than consul general absolved any requirement for Habsburg recognition since it became a non-diplomatic undertaking. This stopgap, in essence, solved the troublesome issue of American recognition and imperial diplomatic hierarchy whilst, hopefully, laying the groundwork for commercial connections between the Habsburg Monarchy and the United States.

Kaunitz, however, held reservations about Starhemberg's suggestion of who should be sent, and his objections again reflected the rising sense of competition between the different regions of the Habsburg Monarchy. Starhemberg had nominated Baron Frederick Eugene de Beelen-Bertholff. Beelen, an experienced bureaucrat in the provincial administration for over twenty years, served as secretary for the Council of Finance in Brussels where he drafted official reports, copied letters, and understood the commercial interests of the Austrian Netherlands as a result.[21] He also spoke several languages, including English.[22] Starhemberg knew Beelen had served as a secretary to Kaunitz during his ambassadorship in Paris in the 1750s and hoped this would secure favour for Beelen in Vienna. He was mistaken. Kaunitz strongly advised against his old colleague's promotion to the new post. Kaunitz feared that Beelen would represent only the Austrian Netherlands at the expense of the interests of the hereditary lands. He argued that Beelen "is someone wholly unsuited for the position, since the entire hereditary lands

and their mercantile interests are completely unknown to him."[23] Kaunitz had
a major problem in dislodging Beelen as the main candidate, however, as Beelen
had officially applied for the post in February.[24] Kaunitz hastily nominated one of
his civil servants, Franz Anton von Blanc, but the emperor approved Beelen as his
new "Counsellor of Commerce and Navigation" for North America on March
22, 1783.[25] Kaunitz had lost the first battle but did not give up the fight.

The administrations in Brussels and Vienna also clashed over the instructions
for Beelen's unique mission to Philadelphia. The Habsburg Monarchy had not
established a position in such a capacity ever before. In Brussels, Starhemberg
set to work immediately and deliberated in conjunction with the Privy Council
and the Committee of Maritime Commerce *before* news of Beelen's acceptance
by the emperor had reached them.[26] Together they drafted a set of twenty-two
points for Beelen's projected five-year term. The first nine articles explained Beel-
en's presumed role, with the very first instruction being entirely incongruent
with Kaunitz's view. It stated the primary aim of "the Imperial Minister" was
the creation of a treaty of commerce and amity with the Americans on principle of mutual reciprocity. The subsequent eight points clarified Beelen was
to report on the sales of listed goods which the Austrian Netherlands wished
to trade with North America and the goods which might interest merchants
in Ostend for importation. These opening articles also outlined two sensitive
objectives. Firstly, Beelen was to negotiate a reduction of the two-and-a-half-
percent American tariff on exports for Ostend merchants. Secondly, he was to
discover whether any commercial treaty could extend their rights to trade with
the Antilles via American ships. Caribbean trade was, after all, an important
consideration given the intense commerce between there and Ostend during
the war. However, Starhemberg noted that France's commercial treaty with the
Americans did not afford such privileges.

Articles ten to thirteen highlighted Beelen's role and seniority. Although he
was subservient to the Privy Council in Brussels, he would enjoy superiority
over all imperial subjects and merchants as the sole "sovereign officer" in North
America. His designation, other than that of "Imperial Minister," was "Consul
General" as he would advise on how to establish future vice-consuls. Articles
fourteen to sixteen allowed him to speculate on any mercantile enterprise during
his tenure, and he would also report any potential speculative ventures to Brussels. Beelen's main task was to supply Brussels with constant reports on relevant
American commercial developments. The final five articles dealt extensively with
these reports' structure and composition. Firstly, he was to order them into topics concerning either regions or specific goods and the news relating to them.

Article eighteen stipulated that all reports should be written in French as to avoid the delay of translation or inaccuracies in expression. Two articles outlined that he was to keep a rolling record of all European ships entering American ports and to collect all American trade ordinances. The final instruction contained the only mention of the hereditary lands, ordering reports into two categories, one for the Austrian Netherlands and one for the hereditary lands, with duplicates of the latter to be sent to Vienna. In short, the instructions compiled by Starhemberg and his associates focused entirely upon the advantages and representation of merchants in the Austrian Netherlands with very little attention to the concerns of those in the hereditary lands.

Unsurprisingly, Kaunitz amended these instructions. He made several alterations before he returned them to Starhemberg. Beelen's instructions grew to a total of thirty-eight points. Specific references to merchant circumstances in the Austrian Netherlands gave way to equal provisions made for merchants in Austria, Bohemia, Moravia, and Hungary. In the first redraft, perhaps as a concession, Beelen provisionally received "the commission of consul of the emperor and the honour of an accredited person by His Majesty to the Congress of the United States of America."[27] This description ensured Beelen's status as the first Habsburg representative to the United States. The first five instructions retained many of the general points: to communicate American commercial opportunities for the emperor's subjects and render any assistance for his merchants and their interests in North America. Articles six to twelve now referred exclusively to the Austrian Netherlands whilst the interests of the hereditary lands featured in the remaining twenty-six articles. It took until June for his formal instructions to be accepted by the Brussels and Viennese administrations, but Brussels officials began preparing for Beelen's departure in late May already.[28] In the decision to appoint a Habsburg representative to the new United States, Brussels officials had forced the issue and led the way. In doing so, an internal division arose over the mission in the Habsburg Monarchy.

The Mission of Baron de Beelen-Bertholff

On July 6, 1783, Beelen left Brussels for Paris with his secretary Pierre Gourland.[29] Beelen's wife Jeanne-Marie Thérèse (née de Castro-y-Toledo) and his two sons, François Eugène and Constantin Antoine, and their daughter Clemencé Auguste accompanied them.[30] The departure severed a family as the Beelens left behind their other two daughters, Thérèse Eugénie de Beelen-Bertholff and Philippine Josephine de Beelen-Bertholff.[31] In Paris, the Beelens stayed with

Mercy-d'Argenteau close to the Tuileries Palace. Mercy-d'Argenteau instructed Beelen further, procured letters of recommendation, and introduced the family to John Adams.[32] On August 1, they arrived at Le Havre and boarded the *George Washington*. From there, they first sailed to Poole, England, before sailing to Philadelphia.[33] However, Beelen was not the only European commercial agent heading across the Atlantic. That month, the Saxon representative Philipp Thieriot also made his crossing.[34] In September, the Portuguese representative departed as well.[35] The haste in Brussels had not been in vain; the Habsburg Monarchy ensured their representative became one of the first to arrive. Yet the infighting between Brussels and Vienna made Beelen's mission harder than those of his contemporaries who worked for a single administration.

On September 9, the Beelen-Bertholff family reached the United States—a week after the country formally obtained independence following the Treaty of Paris. The voyage was difficult, especially for Beelen. His situation deteriorated upon arrival in Philadelphia.[36] The city convulsed under the "Fall Fever" which at its height that autumn claimed the lives of thirty people per day. Less than twenty-four hours before their arrival, Franklin's son-in-law warned that "more frequent changes to Hot and Cold were never known in America."[37] Weakened by the transatlantic crossing and now in the midst of an epidemic, Beelen fell ill. Matters were complicated further by their accommodation. First, the family lodged with a well-known hotelier James Oellers—a trader from Aachen whose brother, a priest in Brussels, might have been their only connection. In the spring, they moved into their own house at 578 Front Street on the banks of the Delaware River.[38] Luckily, Beelen made a recovery a few short weeks after his arrival, but if he had died, the mission and the family's new American life would have been over before it began.

Philadelphia in the 1780s must have been an unfamiliar sight to the Beelens. There was a simple charm compared to the elaborate surroundings they had left behind: the grand boulevards of Paris, the medieval streets of Brussels, or their ancestral Bellenhof manor house. This was certainly the impression for the younger son, Constantin Antoine, who had reportedly played with the dauphin of France during his father's tutelage with Mercy-d'Argenteau.[39] Young Constantin kept a record of his impressions in his sketchbook.[40] The local flora and wildlife surrounding his new rustic homestead piqued his interest as did the figure of George Washington whose likeness he also sketched.[41] Appearance was everything for the family. Beelen made good use of his title in all correspondence and kept his private life in the same vein. He noted in a letter to his relatives back home that his living room was the only one in Philadelphia to be covered in damask wallpaper.[42]

FIGURE 13. Baron Frederick Eugene de Beelen-Bertholff, the first official representative of the Habsburg Monarchy in the United States of America

Before long, Beelen got to work. On September 24, 1783, he met with Ralph Izard, the former envoy to Tuscany. Beelen and Izard had a mutual acquaintance in common, the Tuscan representative Francesco Favi, who had prepped Izard ahead of his Tuscan mission and had now supplied Beelen with his letter of introduction. That evening, Izard presented Beelen at a dinner party in the home of Robert Morris, an important Philadelphian merchant and the superintendent of finance in the United States. The French ambassador, Anne-César de la Luzerne also attended. In Philadelphia, just as in Vienna, the dinner table was an important site of conversation and connection, but this could also be an embarrassing site for hierarchy. During the meal, Morris confronted Beelen with a difficult question: what exactly was his role in the United States? Not wanting to tread on the toes of la Luzerne, an official ambassador, Beelen stuck to Kaunitz's prescribed line that he was a trade commissioner seeking to encourage commerce with the Habsburg Monarchy.[43] The resulting conversation went well enough for Beelen to have something to write home about. The following day he began the first of his numerous reports.

Meanwhile, antagonisms continued over Beelen's mission in Vienna. The Viennese press took a sceptical view. The *Wiener Blättchen* newspaper referred pointedly to Beelen as the "Niederlander" ("the Dutchman") and remarked how he was "without any accreditation" in America.[44] Earlier in the month, the *Wienerisches*

Diarium had noted a major problem for Beelen's mission: the American Congress was not in the city.[45] One of the fundamentals of Beelen's mission was to enable a treaty of commerce between the two countries and report on American legislative activities. However, in the months before Beelen's arrival, a band of militiamen had gathered in protest and marched on Philadelphia because the almost-bankrupted government had not honoured their service payments. The event became known as the "Philadelphia Mutiny" and caused congressmen to flee first to Princeton, New Jersey and later to Annapolis, Maryland.[46] Congress became an itinerant assembly moving between cities and would not meet again in Philadelphia until the constitutional convention was organised four years later in 1787.

Throughout the turmoil of the early republic's politics, Beelen did his utmost to follow congressional events, however. By October 1783 he compiled the first list of congressional acts related to commerce for his superiors in Brussels. Beelen also collected regional ordinances from state assemblies. These changes in regulations were of great importance in order to inform Habsburg merchants of fluctuations in American prices or tariffs.[47] In the early years of Beelen's mission, the port of Charleston became a particular concern where merchants enjoyed a booming trade fuelled by the postwar reconstruction of plantations. Importation of necessary agricultural equipment was a particular object of interest. Merchants in Ostend responded quickly to Beelen's advice, sending the *Jacoba et Isabella* in mid-1784. Beelen wrote favourably of this venture and recommended further voyages from Ostend and Trieste.[48]

Beelen's mission reflected the need for rapid responses to changing economic situations. In South Carolina, French merchants from the Antilles created a financial bubble by using illicit tactics to undercut foreign merchants in the plantation reconstruction business.[49] As a result, they oversaturated the market, depressed export prices, and threatened the economy. Charleston officials responded with ordinances restricting imports, which naturally harmed the opportunity for Habsburg trade with the southern states. Concerned for potential trade, Beelen received further instructions to provide solutions for the Charleston ordinance. Although Beelen met with Secretary of Foreign Affairs John Jay whilst in New York to protest on behalf of the Ostend trading companies, he reported that nothing more could be done.[50] By mid-1785, Beelen reported similar initiatives by the state legislatures in Massachusetts and North Carolina and called strongly on the emperor to secure a treaty of commerce to avoid any further exclusion from American trade.[51] American economic volatility represented a continual concern for Beelen and his superiors. Beelen voiced concerns over paper money and its susceptibility to counterfeiting, and the Brussels administration looked sceptically at the health of American finances as a result.[52] In expressing unease over the circulation of paper money, the Habsburgs were no different from other European observers who fretted over the instability of paper notes compared to hard currency. Saddled with debt after the War of American Independence, state legislatures resorted to raising money by fiat through the issuing of printed notes and raising loans. Americans were aware of the negative connotations and the effect on foreign relations, but the problem persisted until the ratification of the Constitution and the consolidation state debts into a national deficit.[53] Yet Habsburg officials were willing to overlook these concerns as long as reasonable returns could be made on trade with the United States. Beelen's reports were an influential factor in deciding on the probability of those returns.

Through his friendship with Morris, Beelen gained privileged knowledge on the commercial state of the union, but in 1784 Congress abolished Morris's position as superintendent of finances. Beelen wrote to Brussels dismayed that three financers in New York, whom he did not know, were now in charge.[54] Yet Beelen did befriend several congressional presidents including Richard Henry Lee and Elias Boudinot.[55] Beelen's reputation spread quickly, thanks in part to Morris's letter of endorsement to Congress. In November 1784, Henry Lee stopped in Philadelphia where Beelen "took the opportunity to spread promotions for the Ostend merchants."[56] One of the earliest instances of Beelen's renown came from Commodore John Paul Jones who visited Beelen before he departed for Paris and requested letters of recommendation to the emperor since he intended to travel to Vienna.[57] Such instances reveal how Beelen's reception by Americans in Philadelphia was more on par with the reception of an official representative rather than just a mere "commercial advisor." In other words, Americans interpreted Beelen's mission as a de facto form of representation despite his best intentions (and instructions) to act in a non-diplomatic manner.

Important friends mattered, but Beelen also ventured to the new congressional location in New York City in September 1785 in order to monitor the situation more closely. Beelen brought along his eldest son. It was at this point the father-and-son duo met with the leaders of the Oneida, the Native American nation who travelled there to petition Congress about encroachments on their lands.[58] Beelen described the opportunity as "too favourable to let it escape" and arranged the meeting under "the pretence of a foreign traveller" wishing to learn more about the Oneida.[59] His true motive, however, aimed at finding new avenues of trade between the Native Americans and the Habsburg Monarchy. In his reports afterwards, he propositioned the emperor continually about opening direct trade with the Oneida. One of his main arguments stemmed from their importance in the fur trade:

> The fact that peace between the many different and numerous wild nations has occurred, seems worthy of our attention, given the amount of interest in furs of Your August Monarch's subjects in several of Your kingdoms and Hereditary States [and because] they will soon be able to get the best price from our direct navigation from Trieste.[60]

Beelen's suggestion might seem fanciful, but it was entirely serious and entirely in accordance with his instructions to find new commercial opportunities. Beelen argued for the suitability and viability of such a trade. In his meeting with the four Oneida gentlemen, he learned what products might be exchanged with them "and neighbouring friends" for furs, vermillion, and jewellery. Beelen left the meeting inspired but "with still many questions to ask."[61]

Beelen maintained his fascination for direct trade between the Habsburg Monarchy and Native American nations. His frequent reports featured details about Indigenous developments and economic situations as a result. Beelen monitored and described, for instance, the American commercial endeavours with the Chippewa, Delaware, Ottawa, and Wyandotte Nations which culminated in the Treaty of Fort MacIntosh in 1785.[62] In a private letter to Count Belgiojoso, the new minister plenipotentiary in Brussels, he stressed the peace between the formerly warring nations.[63] He later expanded this report to include a full summary of the political alliances between the Mohawks and Cohnawaghans which "brought peace to the Great Lakes Region" and bode well for future trade.[64] And to drive home the point, Beelen studied their treaties with the British and argued that these could serve as a model, should the emperor be willing to agree to it. In doing so, Native American trade appeared to be a consequential advantage for the Habsburgs based on its one official's interaction with the United States.

In addition to his observations of Native American nations, Beelen also maintained a strict surveillance of other European nations' political interactions with the United States. Beelen listed all foreign consuls who resided in the United States by the end of 1784 and informed his superiors each time a significant development occurred.[65] One of his earliest reports that year detailed Thieriot and the Saxon project for a commercial treaty with the United States.[66] In November, he followed the arrival of Antoine René Charles Mathurin, comte de Laforêt as the French Consul in Charleston and covered the nomination of John Temple as the British Consul General.[67] In September 1785, Beelen filed a lengthy

TABLE 4. Distribution of Topics in Baron de Beelen-Bertholff's
Reports, 1784–1789

Year	Date	Topics	Pages	Trade	Politics	Foreign	Misc.
1784	25 Apr.	19	96	13	4	0	2
	12 Aug.	12	83	7	3	2	0
	22 Sep.	11	77	6	0	3	2
	14 Nov.	11	74	4	2	5	0
	13 Dec.	9	37	4	1	3	1
	Total	**62**	**367**	**34**	**10**	**13**	**5**
1785	21 Mar.	17	175	11	1	3	2
	17 Jun.	40	135	15	8	15	2
	10 Sep.	17	152	9	4	4	0
	20 Oct.	3	20	2	0	0	1
	Total	**77**	**482**	**37**	**13**	**22**	**5**
1786	25 Feb.	24	166	15	3	4	2
	19 Jun.	25	141	16	3	5	1
	12 Sep.	16	100	6	1	6	3
	22 Dec.	15	88	4	4	6	1
	Total	**80**	**495**	**41**	**11**	**21**	**7**
1787	20 Mar.	17	70	8	4	0	5
	24 May	16	81	7	5	2	2
	28 Jul.	12	82	7	2	1	2
	7 Nov.	11	35	9	1	1	0
	Total	**56**	**268**	**31**	**12**	**4**	**9**

(Cont.)

Year	Date	Topics	Pages	Trade	Politics	Foreign	Misc
1788	22 Mar.	13	81	4	3	3	3
	31 May	13	64	7	2	3	1
	28 Sep.	12	35	8	1	3	0
	27 Dec.	13	56	4	3	4	2
	Total	**51**	**236**	**23**	**9**	**13**	**6**
1789	27 Mar.	12	28	6	4	2	0
	22 Jun.	11	55	4	3	2	2
	Total	**23**	**83**	**10**	**7**	**4**	**2**
	Grand Total	**349**	**1,564**	**176**	**62**	**77**	**34**

SOURCE: HHStA, Belgien, DDB Rot, K. 182a, K. 182b, K. 182c, K. 182d, and K. 182e.

memo on the "public character" of Don Diego de Gardoqui, who became the first Spanish envoy to the United States.[68] Beelen even monitored Spanish policies within South America.[69] In 1786, he provided Vienna with information regarding the conclusion of the Treaty of Commerce between Prussia and the United States, which (as discussed in the next chapter) had profound consequences for US-Habsburg relations.[70] Beelen also monitored European trade with the individual states. He scoured almanacs, newspapers, and local advertisements for lists of ships in major American ports and collated these into his quarterly reports. At first, he only covered Philadelphia, but he rapidly began to monitor most major ports such as Baltimore, New York, and Charleston but also smaller hubs like New London, Connecticut, and Hampton, Virginia.[71] Beelen's exhaustive efforts to catalogue maritime trade in America undoubtedly made his reports one of the most insightful views into early American economic life for ministers and merchants in the Habsburg lands.

Beelen's reports resulted from the diligence of a man who did the job of the entire consular system which had been envisaged in Brussels in 1782. He sent detailed information drawn from first-hand inquiries, carefully curated material, and painstakingly summarised these details into comprehensive memoranda. Although many other European nations established consular and diplomatic relations with the United States during this period, their correspondences do not appear to match the quality and quantity of Beelen's reports. Neither the British consul John Temple nor the Swedish representatives supplied their respective courts with more information than Beelen.[72] As a result, Beelen's mission ensured that the Habsburg Monarchy was among the most well-informed of the European powers on the political, domestic, international, and economic developments of the early United States. It might be hard to imagine the breadth and depth of Beelen's efforts, but table 4 above shows a breakdown of Beelen's reports from the United States.

It is clear that Beelen maintained a high level of commitment and professionalism in his role in the United States. He sent 1,564 pages back to Europe during his mission. Half related to trade, in accordance with his main role as a commercial advisor, but the second most important topic of discussion regarded the actions of other foreign representatives, reflecting Beelen's political purpose as well. Beelen's reports usually travelled via Le Havre and Bordeaux to Mercy-d'Argenteau who forwarded them to Brussels. This communication route was slow. On average, Beelen's reports took about four months to arrive. On a few occasions, Beelen used ships going directly to Ostend or asked trustworthy captains sailing to London to pass reports to the Habsburg embassy there.[73] In 1784, he sent five bundles back to the Austrian Netherlands, but from then on settled into the regular rhythm of one large quarterly report. Although Viennese ministers were privy to these reports, not all arrived at the State Chancellery—early reports from 1783 are still missing from the Viennese archive as a result.[74] Beelen had only one direct interaction with Kaunitz, concerning Triestine competition with French and Swedish merchants.[75] For the entirety of the mission, Beelen received orders directly from Belgiojoso in Brussels and addressed reports to him.

In Brussels, Beelen's reports were treated with great interest and seriousness. During the planning stage for the mission, several members of the Committee for Finances had suggested founding a completely new committee which would compile the results of Beelen's reports and see to their implementation.[76] Henri Deplancq, the high-ranking bureaucrat and director of the Board of Customs, received the task of combing through Beelen's recommendations.[77] From Deplancq and Belgiojoso in Brussels, Beelen's reports were disseminated across the Habsburg lands. In the Austrian Netherlands, the administration shared Beelen's suggestions with local industrialists such as the owners of a fabric factory in Tournai who received a copy of Beelen's report on "the use of carpets in North America."[78] Likewise, Kaunitz forwarded relevant duplicates to the Aulic Chamber as well as to governors in Trieste and Fiume, who shared these amongst local merchants.[79] Indeed, Beelen followed his instructions to send reports concerning the whole geographic spread of mercantile interests for the emperor's subjects. In fact, from 1783 to 1786 the majority of his reports dealt specifically with the commerce of Habsburg lands outside the Austrian Netherlands.[80] Several reports detailed prospects for Hungarian or Tuscan trade in the United States.[81] Beelen also responded to requests from the hereditary lands, such as Governor Pál Almásy von Zsadány's request for tobacco seeds in Fiume. Beelen, in this regard, took seriously his role as representing all imperial subjects. He even supported efforts fostering cooperation between the regions of the Habsburg Monarchy. For instance, when it became clear iron goods were extremely profitable in American markets, Beelen informed Belgiojoso that it would be prudent for manufacturers in Namur to contact merchants in Trieste to learn from their experiences and not to compete against one another.[82]

Beelen jealously guarded his position as the official representative of all Habsburg subjects, and nowhere is this more clearly demonstrated than in his interactions with the Simpson-Wouters mission from Trieste. When *La Capricieuse* arrived in late 1783, Simpson called on Beelen in Philadelphia. Both men seemed threatened by each other's presence and mission. Simpson, although courteous, clearly saw Beelen's presence as an obtrusion from the Brussels administration. During his stay in Philadelphia over the harsh winter of 1783, George Simpson attempted to build his own connections outside of Beelen's circle, through his contact with the firm *Bache & Shee*. In a subsequent report to Belgiojoso, Beelen complained that Simpson had been so active that local merchants confused him for the representative from Trieste. The final straw came when the *Pennsylvania Gazette* also confused the pair on two occasions, and Beelen requested confirmation that he was still the only legitimate imperial representative.[83] It was a telling symptom of the compositional nature of the Habsburg Monarchy playing out in North America. Although plagued by difficulties arising from the internal tensions between different regions of the Habsburg Monarchy, Beelen's mission fulfilled its brief. Beelen acted as the diligent observer for Habsburg officials in North America. His mission represented the concerted effort to scout out American trading possibilities and to secure the ties already existing between Habsburg lands and the sovereign United States of America.

Rival Imperial Missions

Beelen faced a more serious challenge to his authority from subsequent individuals who acted as additional representatives for trade between the Habsburg Monarchy in the United States. One of them disembarked from *La Capricieuse*.

Franceso Taddeo Reyer represented various merchants in Trieste but predominantly worked as the main contact for the Austrian-American Trading Company (see chapter 7). When Simpson and Captain Wouters left for Trieste, Reyer acted as their spokesman. His primary preoccupation concerned the distribution of goods through *Bache & Shee* and helping to expand this enterprise with their new associate Charles Lennox in Baltimore. Reyer spent several years in Philadelphia as their agent.[84] Upon his return to Trieste in 1786, Reyer kept in touch with his American colleagues who became instrumental for his later career. In 1788, Reyer founded a new firm to trade in the West Indies, which made him one of the major traders in Trieste. He also invested in a cane sugar manufacturing business near Wiener Neustadt and relied upon his American associates to act as blockade runners during the Napoleonic Wars, when he shipped goods from the United States and Britain to Eastern and Central Europe. He subsequently established company branches in London, Spain, the United States, and the Far East by sending family members to act as his informers and representatives. The house of *Reyer & Schlick* developed into one of the largest importers of colonial goods for Habsburg markets, acquiring sugar, coffee, cotton, rum, and spices.[85] In the 1830s, Reyer became the first president of the Austrian Lloyd.[86] If it were not for Reyer's formative experiences in the United States, the Austrian Lloyd would not have developed into such a successful worldwide enterprise.

Reyer's departure from Philadelphia wrought great difficulties for the merchants of the Austrian-American Trading Company and testifies to the independence Reyer held from Beelen. In 1787, now without their self-appointed representative, two merchants, Antonio Righettini and Giacomo Serera, wrote to Beelen on behalf of the company since they had not heard from *Bache & Shee* for over six months. "The great distance does not serve them an excuse for their silence," they complained, "since it is our opinion that a more exact correspondence is required than if we were situated closer to each other."[87] The rest of the letter conveyed the seriousness of the situation. *Bache & Shee* had failed to pay their share of the latest sales. Distressed, Righettini and Serera empowered Beelen "for this purpose, as for any other ... [with] full power and declare that all steps taken by you will be recognised and well received by us."[88] This promotion for Beelen reflects how the merchants of the Austrian-American Trading Company had not seen Beelen as their representative beforehand.

A further challenge to Beelen's authority in the United States came from another representative. Not content with Beelen as sole representative, Kaunitz supported the parallel mission of the wealthy Austrian warehouser and commercial advisor to the emperor in Vienna, Joseph Paul von Weinbrenner.[89] Weinbrenner was eager to establish his own trading ties with the United States, and he tried to secure Franklin's help in creating a commercial presence in America. In February 1783, he informed Franklin that he and others in Vienna desired to trade freely with American merchants who are "happy and abundant" with goods like cotton and tobacco.[90] Weinbrenner needed solid information, however. He asked Franklin for a list of suitable mercantile houses in Boston, Philadelphia, and New York that would entertain his business. Franklin ignored this request, as he did so many other merchant pleas, but Weinbrenner tried again a few months later.

In this second attempt, Kaunitz supported Weinbrenner by enlisting the help of Jan Ingenhousz, the great American partisan in Vienna who had Franklin's ear. Kaunitz instructed him to pass on Weinbrenner's message again and Ingenhousz did as ordered, explaining to Franklin how he was to "press [you] for the favour of an answer."[91] This time Franklin responded, but not with the merchant list the trio hoped for in Vienna. Instead, Franklin insisted his absence from America "for these last twenty-five years" had robbed him of all useful acquaintances.[92] By the time Franklin's reply arrived in June, Weinbrenner had selected the Bohemian-born Joseph Donath, a fellow freemason, to be his agent in America.[93] Donath had sufficient experience from his work in one of Vienna's mercantile houses.[94] Before the end of the month, the Ingenhousz-Weinbrenner team again pressed Franklin, this time for letters of recommendation for this new commercial agent, who, they informed him, "will set out in a few weeks for Philadelphia, New York, and Boston, where he will spend two years."[95] Donath duly travelled to Hamburg where he departed on August 15 for Philadelphia, just two weeks after Beelen had commenced his trip. He arrived carrying samples of Weinbrenner's products of shoes, hats, fabrics, and Bohemian glassware, which he intended to sell or trade for furs. He set up a shop on a corner of Chestnut Street and reported back on the sales directly to Weinbrenner and Kaunitz in Vienna.

Beelen and Donath failed to strike an amicable chord. The two men met in person sometime before April 1784 and although Beelen described him as an "intelligent man," he was dismayed that Donath had not registered with him upon arrival.[96] Beelen extracted the details of Donath's mission, which he then reported to his superiors in Brussels. Donath's instructions, Beelen noted, stipulated he should explore the fur markets of North America and try to establish a connection directly to these markets for the Bohemian lands. Beelen had little faith that he would succeed, given Donath's paltry salary and harsh winter, which prevented any venture until the summer months. "For these reasons," he concluded, "this is a lost year, and Mr. Weinbrenner would have been wiser to send his emissary three months sooner."[97] Beelen gave Donath little encouragement whatsoever.

Donath, by contrast, cooperated well since he offered Beelen the use of his prospectus of fabrics. Beelen secured samples, which he passed along to Belgiojoso, noting how "our Flemish fabric merchants might find them useful when deciding their cargoes for America."[98] Beelen monitored Donath's activities throughout the successive months. In one report, he noted how Donath's products performed well and Weinbrenner made a thirty percent profit on Bohemian fabrics, but remarked this was lower than the forty percent margin attained by the Bohemian and Silesian drapes brought over on *La Capricieuse.*[99] The pair met again where Donath explained his urgent need to procure furs. Beelen delighted in demonstrating his advanced knowledge over Donath. He informed Brussels how he had to explain that the cheapest but highest quality furs were to be found in upstate New York. This scheme was, in other words, Beelen's idea to trade with the Oneida. Donath subsequently travelled several times along the line the Oneida chief had drawn for Beelen's son, through New York to Albany and Schenectady. Donath planned future ventures to Fort Pitt and Fort Detroit in search of suitably inexpensive fur producers amongst the Native Americans, but his time was up as Weinbrenner's original commission expired in 1785.

Donath chose to remain in the United States, however. He continued life as a merchant in Philadelphia, eventually forming his own business as *Donath & Co.*, which acted as a conduit for Habsburg goods. In October 1786, Donath recognised his indebtedness to Franklin by presenting him with a case of Hungarian wines.[100] In time, Donath's Bohemian wife Rosalia joined him in Philadelphia where they raised three children as Donath expanded his commercial empire.[101] At Spring Mill on the Schuylkill River, he acquired several acres of land and dabbled for a while in apiary.[102] He traded extensively but above all handled wares from Central Europe.[103] Though he maintained commercial ties in the Habsburg lands, his intellectual world shifted firmly towards the American republic. In a series of letters to his friend František Antonín Steinský—who had befriended Franklin in 1780—Donath pondered the difference between his former and adopted homelands. He called out Steinský, somewhat playfully, as being complicit in an intolerable regime. "As a public professor," he declared, "it is your duty to keep out every ray of light and darken even darkness itself." By contrast, Donath enjoyed "the birth right of every American," namely freedom.[104] Donath's choice to remain and continue his new life in the United States would not be the last time a Habsburg national made this decision.

The representative missions of Reyer and Donath were a continuation of private firms establishing their own contacts in the United States. Firms in Tuscany and Ostend had utilised their own partners and employees as commercial representatives in the United States; Reyer and Donath's missions, however, were more direct challenges to the imperial authority of Beelen. The directors of the Austrian-American Trading Company preferred Reyer's handling of their business affairs and only turned to Beelen once he returned whereas Donath's presence represented a direct rebuke to Beelen's position. Weinbrenner's posting of Donath to Philadelphia with Kaunitz's support reflected the perceived fears of Beelen's suitability to serve the interests of all of the Habsburg lands equally and not just the Austrian Netherlands. These fears were of course unwarranted and Beelen demonstrated a clear desire to improve the commerce of all the emperor's territories, but the existence of these concerns in 1783 had resulted in two rival private representatives who sought to improve trade for their respective employers above all else.

The Demise of the Beelen-Bertholff Mission

In 1787, Beelen's tenure as the official commercial advisor in the United States came up for review since his instructions stipulated a five-year term. On February 29, 1787, Henri de Crumpipen, Vice-President of the Privy Council instructed Count Balthazar de Proli, the brother of Charles André Melchior de Proli who interceded for Belletti's *La Capricieuse* expedition in 1783, to compile a summary report on Beelen's mission within a year. Initially, the plans from 1782 called for a renewal or replacement to be made, but in light of the deteriorating relationship Proli's report would influence whether the mission would continue at all. One year later, Proli submitted his initial findings followed by a more detailed report in April 1788.[105] The first prognosis seemed favourable: Beelen had dutifully fulfilled his office and supplied Brussels with a steady and valuable stream of information. Proli, however, was critical. Although Beelen's diligence and assessments had their value, the results did not justify the enormous costs of the mission especially in light of collapsing trade between the Habsburg lands and North America.[106] "It is certain the stay of Mr Beelen in this distant country has never produced any advantage proportionate to the expense which it causes," he argued, and he was uncertain whether a treaty of commerce could now change anything.[107] Proli drove home this fact with a table enumerating the origins of all the ships entering American ports according to Beelen's reports.[108] "Out of

1,076 foreign vessels," Proli declared, "only seventeen of His Majesty's ships have arrived there in four years."[109] The futility seemed clear.

When Beelen's half-brother Maximilien de Beelen visited Vienna in 1787, he learned that the Brussels administration contemplated recalling Beelen and reappointing him to a lower position. Maximilien failed to disclose his conversation directly to Beelen but did mention it to his son-in-law Charles François Maurice de Janti who immediately warned Beelen. As a result, or perhaps because his commission neared its projected end, Beelen began to stress the state of his poor health in the covering letters of his reports. In September 1788, Beelen explained, "I have, Sir, the misfortune of not being able by fault of ill-health to produce for Your Excellency a more extensive and refined work under my usual zeal" and divulged news of a surgery he had undergone to alleviate a tumour "which compresses my stomach and must be cleared."[110] Beelen's strategy was to appear too sick to once again cross the Atlantic.

In June 1790, a final report ended Beelen's mission. The "unfortunate Beelen" had been "abandoned" without payment or instructions since the official end of his mission in 1787, though his reports continued until the last was sent on June 22, 1789. In spite of his diligence and the copious information provided to the Habsburg administration, US-Habsburg trade by the close of the decade was negligible. Beelen's mission was "therefore without object" and the recommended policy became a reliance on merchants to "make their own arrangements with the United States."[111] The need for representation had ended. On July 30, 1790, Brussels notified Beelen of his mission's termination. He was commended for "the ardour and intelligence shown" in his mission, but it was over and he must prepare to return home. Beelen's mission represented in many ways the pinnacle of the Habsburg determination to establish a commercial footing in North America during the 1780s. The demise of the mission ensured Beelen remained the sole official Habsburg representative to the United States in the eighteenth century.

In February 1791, Beelen received his contractual termination but he protested any journey to the Austrian Netherlands, citing his ill-health and debts which he still owed in America.[112] By 1792, he had won the fight for his future. After Joseph II's death in 1790, his brother Pietro Leopoldo succeeded him briefly as Leopold II before his own sudden demise led to his son becoming emperor in July 1792. The new Emperor Francis II granted Beelen a state pension and the freedom to choose whether or not to return. Beelen had good reason to forsake Europe. Life in the United States had been a glorious foundation for the Beelen family. Confirming the suspicions of some in Brussels, Beelen had invested in American land speculation.[113] He bought and developed a large plot of land in Pennsylvania straddling Chester and Lancaster counties where he constructed several sawmills and established a botanical garden. The main house became known by locals as "the castle" on account of its grandeur and style.[114] In addition to this estate, Beelen owned ten land tracts in Philadelphia County, a vast 2,100 acres in Western Pennsylvania, and a further 2,000 acres each along the Scioto River in Ohio and the Green River in Kentucky. In the 1790 census his "castle" property listed thirty-four occupants alone. The spending spree also included a two-hundred-and-fifty-dollar property in Hellam, Pennsylvania which Beelen purchased in February 1798. The Beelens even helped finance the building of a local Catholic church. In the late-1790s, the Beelens relocated to another lavish property in Bottstown, West Manchester—then on the edge of York Town in York County, Pennsylvania—a red brick house surrounded by groves of Lombardy poplar trees. The house no longer stands, but along South Forrest Road in the old Bottstown section of nowadays York, Pennsylvania, some of these trees still grow.[115] Around that time, Lewis Miller, a local folk artist, witnessed the Beelens driving in their "fine phaeton" coach to Sunday mass at Conewago Chapel. He later sketched the impressive sight from memory.[116] On his estates, Beelen acquired many indentured servants. His household of thirty-four individuals likely counted many whom he owned in this fashion. In March 1795, for example, Beelen leased one of his servants, Amos Michael, to another local landowner for $19.10s.[117] His final estate accounts of 1805–1806 listed his fortune at $10,471.[118] All this proves to an undeniable extent that the Beelens lived a prosperous lifestyle after the termination of his mission.

Wealth did not shield the Beelens from disease. In summer 1804, yellow fever swept the United States and the Beelen family fell sick. On September 11, the baroness died before her son Francis, who lived in faraway Millerstown, arrived on horseback despite suffering from the disease himself. Though Francis missed his mother's last moments, he witnessed the agonising decline of his father over the next six months. On the morning of April 5, 1805, Frederick Eugene de Beelen died of kidney failure brought on by the fever. His body was taken to Conewago Chapel immediately and left outside for fear of contamination. That evening, the parish priest arranged for two enslaved people to bury the body and erect a marble slab over the gravesite.[119] It was enslaved people who interred the first representative of the Habsburg Monarchy to the United States. When Beelen died, the Habsburgs had no official representation in the United States. It took thirty-three years until another baron, Wenzel Philipp de Mareschal, presented his credentials in October 1838 that the Habsburgs finally had full representation in the United States.[120]

Conclusion

Baron Frederick Eugene de Beelen-Bertholff represented the Habsburg Monarchy as a commercial advisor in the United States for almost six years. He went beyond his brief to seek out new economic opportunities for the Habsburgs in North America. His detailed reports facilitated a direct exchange between Habsburg ministers and merchants with their counterparts and interested parties in the United States. His mission manifested the concentrated efforts to gain a foothold in the United States by the Habsburgs. Beelen, the sole state-appointed representative, was the vanguard of this new venture, and his diligent investigations fuelled the interests of others in the Habsburg Monarchy. It placed the Habsburg Monarchy on par with other European powers seeking to reap the benefits of commerce with a new sovereign American republic. Although those benefits proved to be elusive and ultimately marginal, the lure of expectation drew Habsburg ministers to take bold steps and considerable expense in establishing a permanent mission in the Americas for the first time.

Beelen's responses to the Simpson and Donath infringements illustrate the tensions that haunted the Habsburg initiatives in the United States. It was a dynamic also at work between Brussels and Vienna. It is telling of not only the importance of American commerce but also the difficulties in dealing with an emerging nation. Habsburg efforts to secure part of American trade involved both state-led and privately initiated endeavours. Merchants in Trieste as well as industrialists in Vienna like Weinbrenner launched their own crusade to secure transatlantic trade with the United States. From Ostend to Trieste, Namur to Styria, Brussels to Fiume, there was an insurmountable wave of interest in the United States developing in the mercantile and political classes within the Habsburg Monarchy. This broad economic interest had large repercussions for the development of the relationship between the new United States and the Habsburg Monarchy. Up until now, economics had been the driver, but the government in Vienna felt compelled to take the lead. A treaty of commerce had to be achieved.

CHAPTER NINE

"A Trifling Personage"

*Thomas Jefferson and the Second Struggle for Recognition between the
Habsburg Monarchy and the United States of America, 1785–1786*

O N MARCH 30, 1826, less than a hundred days before his death,
Thomas Jefferson wrote his last letter to then President of the United
States John Quincy Adams. Adams, as he so often did, had sought
advice from Jefferson; this time, he had inquired about the elder statesman's
role as a diplomat in Europe and procuring commercial treaties with the European powers in the 1780s.[1] Jefferson replied with an extensive summary of the
international situation then facing the new republic. In a moment of openness
with his New England colleague, Jefferson made a curious admission about the
Habsburg Monarchy. "Austria," he noted, "became desirous of a treaty with us,
and her Ambassador pressed it often on me, but our commerce with her being
no object, I evaded his repeated invitations."[2] Jefferson wrote no more on the
subject. Yet both his actions and attitudes towards the Habsburg Monarchy echo
louder than these elusive words and illuminate the fatal struggle in the relationship between the new United States and the Habsburg Monarchy; one in which
Jefferson played the most decisive, but destructive of roles.

Jefferson is widely acknowledged as a central figure in the establishment of
the United States of America, perhaps even *the* central figure for some, as he
was the primary author of the Declaration of American Independence and an
enigmatic emblem for the new nation proclaiming freedom whilst also enslaving
thousands. But without doubt, Jefferson was the pivotal figure in determining
American relations with the Habsburg Monarchy.[3] It was largely in his hands
that the issue fell during his time serving as the United States' minister plenipotentiary in France. Yet in the popular mind, his flirtations with Maria Cosway
seem all too often his only discernible activity in Paris.[4]

That said, as crucial a figure as Jefferson was for the shape that US-Habsburg relations ultimately took, he was not the only factor. Great difficulties lay in navigating diplomatic norms between an entirely new nation on the one hand and states of the *ancien régime* on the other; one endowed with a cohort of inexperienced diplomats up against life-long aristocratic politicos. These two worlds collided on Jefferson's watch in the mid-1780s. For centuries, Europe had acclimatised to the New World, but it had always been a subservient relationship. Now, largely under Jefferson's management, the Old World had to accept a new-world member as an equal. None found this process more treacherous than the Habsburgs, but they trod this path diligently, inveigled by visions of economic enhancement.

Attempts Towards a Commercial Treaty

Throughout the 1780s, Joseph II's foreign policy oscillated between half-realised plans. First was his reignition of the project to trade away the territory of the Austrian Netherlands for the Bavarian lands, which came to nought. Second, he attempted to reopen the River Scheldt to commerce—which had been denied by international fiat since the late sixteenth century, crippling Antwerp's commerce—despite the tensions it created with the Dutch Republic. Third, a new alliance with Russia in 1781 brought with it unfinished schemes for Joseph, such as the so-called "Greek Project" of Catherine II, which would carve up Ottoman territory in the Balkans and restore the Byzantine Empire under her grandson. The period was a turbulent shifting between Joseph's expansive reform agenda at home and semi-realised plans abroad, which Joseph's biographer Derek Beales acknowledges was "contemptible in its manner as in its achievement."[5] One goal remained constant, however. The aim of securing American trade was a continual focus. In February 1783, he outlined his desire to shore up transatlantic commerce with the United States and noted how American trade "will be of the greatest importance for the future."[6] The early months of 1783 witnessed the turnaround in US-Habsburg relations when the Habsburgs committed to sounding out ties with the United States.

The only problem, however, was the Habsburgs could not be seen to initiate contact with the Americans. For one thing, the cessation of hostilities had not yet been converted into an internationally ratified treaty. The Treaty of Paris was signed in September 1783 and ratified by the Americans in January and the British in April 1784 during which time European powers scrambled to secure a share of commerce with the new sovereign American state. International legal norms of European states had emerged earlier in the century as more concrete codifications of the laws of war and nations.[7] In this line of thinking, the American entry into the European international system had to follow the established doctrines of international law and relations. Intervention in another state's affairs—in this case, in Britain's affairs via the recognition of the United States by approaching them for a commercial treaty—broke the accepted norms of the inherent rights of nations and of the international *jus gentium*.[8] There could be no formal conversations between the Americans and Habsburgs in early 1783 until a formal peace had been pronounced. Moreover, the preeminence of the Habsburg dynasty as elected rulers of the Holy Roman Empire caused further problems. The conventional diplomatic order of preference among European powers dictated that the Holy Roman Empire—and by extension, Joseph II— traditionally took precedence before all other Christian nations and was only below the Roman papacy in order of preference as a universalist and imperial title.[9] In other words, the Habsburgs as an imperial dignity took precedence over the new American state and were the higher power. Such ranks and deference mattered to the Habsburg dynasty, especially in dealings with other imperial dignities such as Russia, Persia, and later, Napoleonic France, although these norms were not properly stablished until the early nineteenth century.[10] They, therefore, could not be seen to interact with a lesser power—especially former "rebels." No matter how much they desired American commerce, the Americans had to be seen to make the first offer.

Americans were aware of this obstacle. Back in 1779, John Adams had explained to members of Congress how international concerns meant Joseph "will be one of the last Powers to acknowledge our Independence."[11] In April 1783, he renewed his warning. "The Emperor has an inclination to treat with us," he informed his friends at home, "but the House of Austria never makes the first Advances."[12] Yet Congress neglected to act and initiate the first step by the early months of 1783. With pressure mounting from the fears of losing the lucrative commerce gained during the war, the imperial ambassador in France, Count Mercy-d'Argenteau, had no option but to find a discreet and indirect channel with the Americans and try to provoke an offer to negotiate.

In early 1783, Mercy-d'Argenteau attempted to broker these indirect channels. He first sought communication through the Tuscan representative in Paris, Francesco Favi, and the Tuscan legation. Favi acted as the representative for the viceroys of the Austrian Netherlands and consul for the Republic of Ragusa.[13] These three roles gave Favi the flexibility to contact the Americans, unlike Mercy-d'Argenteau. On his insistence, Favi cultivated a close friendship with Benjamin Franklin. The

FIGURE 14. Portrait of the imperial ambassador to France, Count Florimond Claude Mercy-d'Argenteau by an unknown artist.

link provided much information. Even Jan Ingenhousz was surprised to learn from Favi's reports, which passed from Tuscany to Vienna, that Franklin was determined to make a southern tour of Europe and stop in Vienna before his final departure back to the United States.[14] Three of Favi's reports from January and February detailed the Americans' European treaty efforts.[15] Through Favi, Mercy-d'Argenteau created the backchannel which enabled him to correspond with the Americans without breaking diplomatic norms.

Mercy-d'Argenteau's headache, however, was that Franklin as minister to France and Adams as minister to the Dutch Republic had no powers to deal with the Holy Roman Empire or the Habsburg Monarchy. His second option was more convoluted but aimed at securing a connection with someone who he believed to be the empowered minister: Francis Dana. Congress had appointed Dana to St. Petersburg with instructions to treat with the powers of the League of Armed Neutrality, which included the Habsburg Monarchy.[16] Mercy-d'Argenteau's counterpart there, Count Johann Ludwig von Cobenzl, would lead the negotiations whilst Adams advised Dana "immediately to communicate your Mission to the Minister of the Emperor" to ensure wheels started turning.[17] Unknown to Adams and Mercy-d'Argenteau, however, Dana was not properly empowered. He declined Adams's request since he believed he had "no authority to make any commercial Treaty with the Emperor."[18] Adams did not receive Dana's letter until May 1783, by which time Mercy-d'Argenteau had reported gleefully to Starhemberg, "I regard the communication between these gentlemen and myself as open."[19] Miscommunication, as always, seemed to threaten the relationship between the Habsburg Monarchy and the United States.

Believing Mercy-d'Argenteau had a diplomatic channel, ministers across the Habsburg Monarchy worked towards an American treaty. In Brussels, Starhemberg and his councillors hosted William Lee.[20] On February 18—the same day Joseph issued his American priorities to Mercy-d'Argenteau—Lee wrote to Adams with the news, "I am advised from very good authority that the Emperor is desirous of entering into a treaty of commerce with the United States of America on terms of quality and mutual advantage." Lee explicitly warned Adams about the issue of the order of preference,

> It is an invariable rule with the Court of Austria never to make Officially the first advances to any other Sovereign Power, therefore if Congress approve of a Commercial Treaty being enter'd into with his Majesty, it is necessary that the formal Proposition for that purpose shou'd be first made on the part of America.[21]

In Vienna, when Ingenhousz wrote to Franklin about the Weinbrenner mission, he also hinted that propositions about a commercial treaty from Vienna were imminent since it was the court's wish "to get a share of that source of riches, enjoyed formerly by England alone."[22] Meanwhile, news broke across Europe of Beelen's mission to the United States. The overtures from the Habsburg side were hard to ignore.

When the Dana-Cobenzl route appeared closed, however, Adams did not admit to his mistake nor did he alert Mercy-d'Argenteau to the problem.[23] Mercy-d'Argenteau waited but broke his silence as negotiations for the Treaty of Paris concluded. On the evening of July 3, 1783, Adams sat at his desk drafting his latest report to Secretary of Foreign Affairs Robert R. Livingston, when his servant interrupted him with the arrival of a guest. Mercy-d'Argenteau came in response to Adams's previous unannounced visit whilst Mercy-d'Argenteau was out in order to thank the imperial ambassador for his role in the peace negotiations. The fact that Adams had called on him first gave Mercy-d'Argenteau the pretext of returning the favour as if the Americans had initiated contact—it had only taken from January to July. Mercy-d'Argenteau made it clear he visited in a personal rather than official capacity to form "an acquaintance" with Adams, which he hoped would be improved into "a more intimate one." The pair quickly "fell into a Conversation of an hour" and ran "over a variety of Subjects" including migration to the United States and the "sober, frugal & industrious Character" of the inhabitants of the Habsburg Monarchy.

Mercy-d'Argenteau's friendliness surprised Adams since Mercy-d'Argenteau spoke frankly throughout.[24] One subject dominated the conversation: potential trade. Adams shared Mercy-d'Argenteau's ideas about it advantages and routes via Trieste, Fiume, and the Austrian Netherlands. Mercy-d'Argenteau's experience as an estate owner appealed to Adams's farmer side and impressed upon Adams the value in such a trade.[25] The amicable session ended with Adams's invitation to a future dinner. His newfound friendship bewildered him. He got back to his report, where the last line he had written talked of "a Treaty of Commerce with Great Britain."[26] Adams, however, turned his mind to securing one with the Habsburgs as well.

Ten days later, on July 13, 1783, Adams wrote the first of two memoranda on his ideas and impressions about such an opportunity with the Habsburgs. Adams had considered a commercial treaty seriously in the intervening days. He believed Joseph had clearly "caused to be intimated, several ways, his inclination to have a Treaty of Commerce with us" and he outlined five reasons why such a deal would be advantageous,

1. Because, as Emperor of Germany, and King of Bohemia & Hungary, he is at the head of one of the greatest Interests & most powerfull Connections in Europe [. . .]
2. Because the present Emperor is one of the greatest men of this Age [. . .]
3. Because that, if England should ever forget herself again so much as to attack us, she may not be so likely to obtain the Alliance or Assistance of this Power against us [. . .]
4. Because the Countries, belonging to this Power upon the Adriatic Sea, & in the Austrian Flanders, are no inconsiderable Sources of Commerce for America [. . .]
5. Because, altho' we have at present a pleasant & joyfull prospect of friendship & uninterrupted Alliance with the House of Bourbon, which I wish may never be obscured, yet this friendship & Alliance will be the more likely to continue unimpaired for our having the friendship & Commerce of the House of Austria: [. . .] we may find in the Alliance of Austria, England and Holland a resource against the Storm. Supernumerary Strings to our Bow & provisions against possible Inconveniences, however improbable, can do us no harm—[27]

Adams made clear his reasoning for a commercial treaty with the Habsburgs in these lines. He recognised the true importance and influence of the Habsburgs among the European states. From the American perspective, Adams regarded the Habsburg Monarchy as one of the greatest powers in Europe. Joseph II's titles were not only reflections of his own power but were also markers of how deeply enmeshed the Habsburg Monarchy was within the European balance of power. Moreover, Adams saw him as a suitable and respectful ally whose character he admired. He was also convinced of the wealth of the Austrian Netherlands as a result of his repeated visits on his way back and forth to the Dutch Republic from Paris. His reasoning also demonstrated the effects of his friendly conversation with Mercy-d'Argenteau who evidently assured Adams of the value of commerce in places such as Trieste in Adriatic. Finally, a Habsburg alliance allayed Adams's own concerns about the French influence in American international strategy. He famously disagreed with the French foreign minister Vergennes during his time as a commissioner at the French court and, unlike some other American leaders (Jefferson in particular), he was not of a French persuasion or outlook.[28] Anticipating the emerging split between Federalists and Democratic Republicans in later years, Adams already voiced his concerns over the true intention of France and sought other European allies to counteract French influence over American diplomatic and commercial relations with other powers. In this effort, Adams considered the Habsburg Monarchy a worthy and appropriate partner.

Adams urged this connection to be made as soon as possible, even suggesting sending an American envoy to Vienna. He had clearly been taken in. Joseph was "one of the greatest men of this Age," Adams extolled.[29] In his second memorandum, sent the following day, Adam continued his praise. "The Emperor is vastly powerful" and, Adams predicted, would soon expand his dominion into the Ottoman territories alongside Russia, in reference to the growing sabre rattling against the Turks and the "Greek Project" of the Empress Catherine II.[30] Adams believed this would produce "a great Revolution in the Commerce of Europe," where trade would revolve around the Danube, Don, and Dnieper Rivers flowing into the Black Sea. If successful, Adams foresaw "this would be such an Accession of Wealth, Commerce and Naval Power" that it certainly merited the consideration of fostering relations with the Habsburgs in case these plans ever became a reality.[31]

Franklin also recommended a commercial treaty with the Habsburgs. A week after Adams, he also wrote to Livingston. "I have it also from a good hand at the Court of Vienna," Franklin informed him, "that the Emperor is

FIGURE 15. Portrait of John Adams as a diplomat by John Singleton Copley (1783)

desirous of establishing a Commerce with us from Trieste as well as Flanders, and would make a Treaty with us if proposed to him."[32] There is no mystery who Franklin's "good hand" was. Back in April, Ingenhousz had informed him of Mercy-d'Argenteau's new powers to treat with the Americans. He divulged more, sharing the news that the "Emperour is ready to acknowledge the united states as a souverain and independent power as soon as you or any one authorised makes any Steps towards that purpose [*sic*]."[33] It was another indirect route utilised by the Habsburgs to prod the Americans into action. Franklin, in a very similar vein to Adams, noted his excitement over the prospect of a commercial connection. "Many useful Productions and Manufactures of Hungary may be had extremely cheap there" he argued to Livingston.[34] Both Adams and Franklin were convinced of the necessity to conclude a treaty with the Habsburgs and lobbied their insistence with Congress.

In late October 1783, Congress members decided to empower Adams and Franklin to enter into negotiations with Joseph's representatives. They ordered them to announce "the high sense which the United States in Congress assembled entertains of his exalted character and eminent virtues, and their earnest desire to cultivate his friendship, and to enter into a treaty of amity and commerce for the mutual advantage of the subjects of his Imperial Majesty, and the citizens of these United States."[35] The sedentary pace of transatlantic communication subsequently delayed arrival of these new and crucial instructions, however.[36] Mercy-d'Argenteau began to question the sincerity of his American counterparts in the meantime. Had they ignored the emperor's overtures? On October 1, 1783, he had confronted the French foreign minister Vergennes about the lack of American rapidity. Mercy-d'Argenteau recorded Vergennes's response verbatim and forwarded it to State Chancellor Prince von Kaunitz in his latest update on the situation. The reason, he echoed, was Franklin, "who is old, tired of business, and careless," and the other commissioner, John Jay, "lacks energy and vivacity," leaving only Adams "who cannot be entirely trusted since his veins are filled with English blood."[37] Vergennes was of course biased given his ill rapport with Adams but Mercy-d'Argenteau lacked any other clue or answer on the state of the negotiations.

Franklin ended Mercy-d'Argenteau's diplomatic purgatory nine months later on July 30, 1784. "By various Circumstances been long delayed," Franklin stated unashamed, he could now communicate the desire to "cultivate the friendship of his Imperial Majesty" and begin negotiations.[38] To add to Mercy-d'Argenteau's probable relief, Franklin informed him "the late Governor of Virginia," Thomas Jefferson, would join Adams as a commissioner. Mercy-d'Argenteau acted hastily to account for the lost time. First, he responded magnanimously to Franklin's letter. "The sentiments which the Emperor entertains for the United States of America," he replied, "make me foresee the satisfaction which his Majesty will have in entering into engagements with them."[39] He quickly informed Kaunitz and requested new instructions for negotiating.[40] Kaunitz's response took another month since he had to consult the emperor about his final decision first, and to do so required a full account of the situation. In his report, Kaunitz reiterated the problem of recognising a former "rebel" nation, especially since the Treaty of Paris still awaited proper ratification.[41] Kaunitz maintained only when American sovereignty was assured "in a legal manner throughout the whole of Europe by the peace treaty" could negotiations begin."[42] In addition, he reaffirmed the order of international precedence whereby "the American States should make the decent first steps to be recognised by Your Majesty as true independent sovereigns."[43] Such comments demonstrated the Habsburg commitment to upholding the international norms and diplomatic conventions among European powers. Kaunitz, who had absorbed the ideas of leading theorists on international order during his education, valued these norms in his interaction with the Americans.[44] Furthermore, Kaunitz articulated how representatives of the United States had to respect the order of preference enjoyed by the imperial dignity of the Habsburgs. In his mind, an advance by the Americans had to be made formally to the Habsburgs. This rigidity of diplomatic etiquette reflected the difficult incorporation of a new nation into the international order of the *ancien régime*.

Kaunitz, however, thought it prudent to prepare terms for a hypothetical treaty despite the unrecognised status of the United States. He recommended any agreement must "for the most part consist of only generalised stipulations."[45] Any special articles of the negotiation, Kaunitz opined, needed discussion with the composite regions of the Habsburg lands, including the Bohemian and Hungarian Chancelleries and especially the Austrian Netherlands.[46] The emperor regarded Kaunitz's proposal lukewarmly. "A Commercial Treaty with those Americans," he scribbled in the margins, "will not be much use for our country, but the conditions may be discussed."[47] Joseph's tepidness belied his earlier enthusiasm over American commerce and his support of the official mission of Baron de Beelen-Bertholff to Philadelphia but reflected his latest intention to exchange Bavaria for the Austrian Netherlands, his realm which stood arguably the most to gain from such a treaty. Such an exchange project had been a perennial preoccupation for Joseph, who had failed to acquire the Bavarian lands during the War of the Bavarian Succession in 1778, as it would have granted him a more solidified border to the West and an additional elector within the Holy Roman Empire.[48] Nevertheless, he consented to the preparations for an American treaty.

Kaunitz forwarded the good news to Mercy-d'Argenteau in early September 1784.[49] In Kaunitz's version it was indeed good news; he omitted the emperor's lukewarm response and instead instructed Mercy-d'Argenteau to inform Franklin that Joseph "had gladly heard the demand of the United States, and would gladly offer his hands to all these states, as the foundation of a mutually friendly agreement and the commercial interactions of subjects on both sides."[50] Simultaneously, Kaunitz informed the various regional chancelleries of the negotiations. He requested information be shared with officials in the Austro-Bohemian, Hungarian, and Transylvanian regions so they might offer their specific "insight and early expressions" on any future treaty with the United States.[51] This consultation of the entire Habsburg lands not only resulted from the compositional nature of the monarchy but also reflected the belief of officials in Vienna that American trade might benefit the Monarchy as a whole. Lastly, Kaunitz issued orders to Count Ludovico Barbiano di Belgiojoso, who replaced the retiring Starhemberg as the minister plenipotentiary in Brussels, to contact, instruct, and advise Mercy-d'Argenteau during negotiations with the Americans.[52]

In late September, Mercy-d'Argenteau acknowledged his new powers from Kaunitz, but in his reply he noted three problems. The first was the health of

Franklin, whom he explained "is very sick on sand and stone," a reference to Franklin's troublesome problems with gout. The second was the appointment of Jefferson, who Mercy-d'Argenteau did not know because Jefferson had failed to report to him after his arrival.[53] This was the first news of Jefferson's arrival to reach Vienna as well as the first sign of disconnect between the two men. The final issue was Kaunitz's deferral to Belgiojoso and requests from the various chancelleries, which left Mercy-d'Argenteau with "no other choice but to await these further orders."[54] In the meantime, Mercy-d'Argenteau forwarded a copy of his new powers to Franklin. Crucially, Mercy-d'Argenteau informed him of Kaunitz's decision to delegate to Belgiojoso and to gather information from the chancelleries. "When the Particulars respecting this Matter shall be sent me," he wrote, "I shall instantly communicate them and I avail myself of this opportunity to renew the Assurances."[55] Franklin interpreted this as an instruction to wait on Brussels before anything could be done further.[56] This simple misunderstanding threatened the entire undertaking, but nobody realised it at the time.

Thomas Jefferson Lies

On September 13, 1784, the new minister plenipotentiary in Brussels, Count Belgiojoso, received his new instructions. He turned to the Treasurer General and member of the *Comité de Commerce Maritime*, Baron de Cazier, who helped process Beelen's reports. Cazier presented his preliminary drafts of commercial expectations for a treaty on October 21, 1784.[57] A week later, Belgiojoso sent on the results to Mercy-d'Argenteau who informed Kaunitz of the draft for the first time on November 6. Kaunitz responded with provisions particular to the merchants in Trieste and Fiume.[58] The internal competition over the regional interests of the Habsburg Monarchy had not ceased. Yet, from a wider perspective, everything had begun to take shape. It only required the Americans to respond in kind. At this point, however, the Habsburg dynasty could still not be seen to initiate such negotiations as their imperial dignity and order of preference outranked the Americans. Mercy-d'Argenteau received everything by late November, but he did not pass the stipulations onto the Americans since it was their turn and duty to start the negotiations proper. Any action by him would jeopardise Habsburg preeminence. As 1784 turned into 1785, the pressure to conclude a treaty with the Americans rose ever higher; that year the Austrian-American Trading Company had begun in Trieste and Beelen's reports detailed the endless potential in North America. No overture came from the American side, however. And this was the moment when Jefferson entered the fray.

FIGURE 16. Portrait of Thomas Jefferson as Minister to France by Mather Brown (1788)

Jefferson had arrived in Paris in August 1784 as a representative in commercial negotiations and then succeeded Franklin on May 17, 1785, as the American minister to France. Jefferson's first introduction to the French court had been relaxed. His enjoyment came more through the salons where Franklin's influence had won him "a door of admission [...] to the circle of literati."[59] His friends were primarily these literati.[60] As Franklin departed France in July 1785, and after Adams's appointment to London, Jefferson became the sole American representative. This situation gravely affected the negotiations with the Habsburgs.

Jefferson's original outlook on American commercial relations recognised the postwar challenges facing the United States in 1783. At this time, Jefferson acknowledged the necessity in re-establishing international commerce but viewed foreign commercial connections as supplementary to the agrarian basis of the American economy. International trade was not the path to prosperity, but a secondary motor, in his thinking. Jefferson's primary concern was preventing reconnection with British merchants since, he feared, such a commercial reunion could reduce the Americans' hard-won independence. Jefferson, as part of the congressional "Committee of Three" responsible for drafting the new commercial strategy, favoured a wide engagement with as many friendly European nations as possible in order to preserve their economic independence from Britain. This strategy aimed at converting Europe to the "commercial principles of the

American Revolution"—that is, foreign relations predicated upon mutually advantageous trade.[61] Congress, as a result, listed sixteen nations, practically most of Europe, for American representatives to treat with equally. Jefferson saw this goal as "part of a system, wise and advantageous if executed in all its parts," that would achieve the economic connections needed to guarantee continued independence.[62] In some sense, when Jefferson succeeded Franklin and inherited his half-negotiated plans in the summer of 1785, his political outlook still engendered him towards treating with all European powers, including the Habsburg Monarchy.

Yet Jefferson's thoughts changed during his negotiations for commercial treaties. He neither stuck to his idealistic vision of an agrarian America nor acted in a strict realist fashion. Instead, Jefferson reacted to commercial offers from European nations with a rationalist mindset, driven above all by his sense of whether it was in the best interests for the ideal future of the United States. Such pragmatism came to define Jefferson's later statecraft, but it was brought home to him during these years in Paris when he began to appreciate the relative weakness of the United States.[63] It was a lesson other Americans were learning as they adjusted to the new American borders in the Midwest and encountered stiff opposition from European neighbours.[64] Jefferson's own humble pragmatism is clear in his diplomatic negotiations with the European states. He soon felt the principle of mutually advantageous trade should necessitate treaties with powers most valuable to the United States: powers with territory in the Americas. Trade benefits from these nations, he believed, were numerous and bountiful. As a result, he gave greater importance to the Portuguese treaty than a Habsburg deal; Portugal was an Atlantic power whereas the Habsburgs were not. Sweden, owning the island of St. Eustatius in the Caribbean, also superseded the Habsburgs whose lack of Atlantic possessions led him to dismiss their commerce as inconsequential. Jefferson's hierarchical thinking certainly guided his actions in the negotiations.

Jefferson's aversion towards treating the Habsburg Monarchy as a priority began to show immediately. In September 1785, Jefferson received a letter from the marquis de Lafayette, which detailed his friendly audience with Joseph (see chapter 7). Lafayette had seized this opportunity to act as an unofficial trade ambassador for the young republic. "I directed, and sometimes forced the conversation," he revealed to Jefferson, resulting in the discovery of the emperor's preference for "liberal treaties, [which] would open the door to American importations in order to pay for Austrian goods." That same evening, Kaunitz had approached Lafayette. The pair discussed the situation of American and Austrian goods—Kaunitz knew already from Beelen's reports—but Lafayette noticed he was bemused. "Why," asked Kaunitz in cutting straight to the point, "don't they make advances to us?" Lafayette could only respond that the Americans had done so, but as Kaunitz clarified, their "demand had been an indirect one." In other words, Kaunitz was dissatisfied with the American initiation since it had largely been Mercy-d'Argenteau who orchestrated contact and requests up until then. Habsburg ministers were meant to be responders not the initiators. He made clear to Lafayette that nothing could go on "without reciprocity."[65] In his eyes, it was a matter of fairness and of mutual respect. Lafayette recommended swift action but relied on Jefferson to communicate the news to Adams in London and to Congress across the Atlantic.[66]

Jefferson, at first glance, complied. On September 24, he conveyed Lafayette's findings to Adams. Yet the placement—a few short lines sparing any detail at the end—and his overall tone reveal his hesitation about a Habsburg treaty. "In the present unsettled state of American commerce," Jefferson declared, in reference to the new opportunities and challenges for trade with Europe, he wanted to "avoid all further treaties except with American powers. If Count Merci [*sic*] therefore does not propose the subject to me, I shall not to him nor do more than decency requires if he does propose it."[67] Jefferson's words here are striking. He openly declared his intention to counteract congressional instructions "to cultivate the Friendship of his imperial majesty" with a treaty. Jefferson also demonstrated his disdain for such a treaty owing to the limited influence of the Habsburg Monarchy in the Atlantic and the Americas. Lastly, Jefferson's playing dumb to Mercy-d'Argenteau's request was rather coy, since he was fully aware of the diplomatic etiquette that dictated the interactions with the Habsburg ambassador. Jefferson's deceit emerged again a few weeks later as he reported Lafayette's letter to John Jay, Congress's new foreign secretary. In the sole line Jefferson spared for the news, he mentioned "a possibility of an overture" from the Habsburg court. He omitted a full explanation of the present state of the negotiations.[68] In this initial action by Jefferson, we can already discern the sentiments he expressed to John Quincy Adams forty years later.

Jefferson had a problem, however. Lafayette's visit to Vienna had not only revealed the deadlock but had sprung Kaunitz into action. Lafayette informed Jefferson, "I am apt to think he [Kaunitz] may order His Ambassadors to talk with you or Mr. Adams."[69] Indeed the order came. On October 1, 1784, Kaunitz informed Mercy-d'Argenteau about the Austrian-American Trading Company in Trieste which required better trading terms in order to compete successfully with foreign merchants in the United States. Kaunitz requested that he discuss this matter urgently with Jefferson.[70] For Mercy-d'Argenteau, this provided yet another headache. By mid-October he admitted his difficulties to Kaunitz. He had been unable to fulfil these instructions due to Jefferson's "continued lengthy absences."[71] Although Jefferson undertook several tours of Europe during his time as minister in France, these absences were in fact Jefferson's attempts to "avoid all further treaties" with non-Atlantic powers.[72]

The evasion worked. Jefferson's preference for the salons and infrequent attendance at the regular diplomatic corps events made it easy for him to elude Mercy-d'Argenteau. It took until January 1786 for Mercy-d'Argenteau to meet with Jefferson and discuss the situation. Mercy-d'Argenteau's frustration must have eroded his usual decorum since the confrontation was not very diplomatic by Jefferson's account. "The imperial ambassador took me apart the other day," he complained to Adams. He explained Mercy-d'Argenteau's anger that he had not received anything for "about eighteen or twenty months" since corresponding with Franklin in September 1784. The seriousness of the deadlock became clear to all. Mercy-d'Argenteau had promised to pass on the preliminary articles once his superiors in Brussels and Vienna had finalised them, but he still expected the next move to come from Franklin, or Franklin's replacement on the American side. Jefferson refused to take accountability for this mishap. He explained to Mercy-d'Argenteau that "we had always supposed it [the offer to negotiate] was unanswered and had therefore expected the next step from [you]." Mercy-d'Argenteau became angry, especially since Jefferson informed him that his negotiation powers were set to expire.[73] Mercy-d'Argenteau and Jefferson ended their conversation without either one accepting fault but with plenty of animosity. That evening, Mercy-d'Argenteau sent his secretary, Franz Paul von Blumendorf, to deliver to Jefferson a copy of his last correspondence with Franklin to extricate any negligence from his side.[74]

Jefferson fretted over the next steps since he still wished to avoid concluding a treaty with the Habsburgs. He relied upon Adams in London for instruction, especially as Mercy-d'Argenteau continued to "make advances" and he endeavoured to "evade" until he could receive word from Adams.[75] Jefferson's fears were becoming real. Mercy-d'Argenteau's assiduity made him "anxious" to receive Adams's advice. Unfortunately for Jefferson, Adams's response was slow. By early February, he had still not heard anything. He prodded Adams again, stressing how he was "anxious" to receive an answer.[76] Finally, Adams's reply came a few weeks later. He implored Jefferson to act without delay. "I am clearly for treating with the Emperor's Ambassador immediately," he explained, "and even for the [Austrian] Netherlands only, although it would be better to extend it to all the rest of his Dominions." Adams could not have given a clearer line of instruction to Jefferson, especially with his final lines on the matter, "I pray you to proceed in the Business, *as fast as you please*. Treaties commercial with the two Imperial Courts [meaning Brussels and Vienna] cannot possibly do us any harm that I can conceive."[77] Adam's sentiment contrasted sharply with Jefferson's. Adams had experienced the Austrian Netherlands in person and had been convinced of commerce with the Habsburg lands from his interactions with Mercy-d'Argenteau. On the other hand, Jefferson, who had no such experience, felt the opposite and continued to stall.

Jefferson interpreted Adams's line "as fast as you please" liberally. He received Adams's response amid his preparation for one of his first European tours.[78] He left Paris for London in mid-March without a single word to Mercy-d'Argenteau. In a letter to Jay, Jefferson later accounted for his inaction, explaining, "Tho I received Mr Adams's opinion in favour of our proceeding in the treaty [. . .] those which called me to London, a treaty with Portugal, was more important."[79] Here Jefferson clearly articulated how the the Atlantic dimension was of greater importance in his commercial calculations. For Jefferson, this was a matter of priority and the Habsburgs counted for little in his mind compared to the potential trade from a country such as Portugal. His own personal preferences overrode the advice from Adams to seal the treaty with the Habsburgs and his trip to London allowed gave him the perfect excuse to stall yet again. Notwithstanding his personal preferences, there was little excuse for his failure to inform Mercy-d'Argenteau. Jefferson was away for seven weeks.

In the meantime, Mercy-d'Argenteau prepared for Jefferson's return. He reported to Kaunitz on the latest developments, hinting at Jefferson's duplicity. After explaining their first meeting, he mentioned Jefferson's revelation that his commission would expire on May 12 but he hoped "something definite" could be accomplished by then.[80] Kaunitz too had been diligent. The final treaty proposal had been confirmed by the various chancelleries and laid before the emperor as the basis for negotiations.[81] "His Majesty has deigned to approve the conclusion of a treaty of amity and commerce with the United States," he declared to Belgiojoso and Mercy-d'Argenteau.[82] The highly compartmental nature of the Habsburg Monarchy made for a convoluted process, but one which could have come to a happy conclusion if not for the expiration of Jefferson's commission.

Jefferson returned to Paris twelve days before his powers were due to expire. Mercy-d'Argenteau sought him out urgently but when they did meet, he was gravely disappointed. Jefferson protested that no negotiation could be completed in the time remaining. Mercy-d'Argenteau pleaded for an extension or for the negotiations to continue until Congress could renew them, but Jefferson signalled that nothing could be done.[83] Jefferson's mind had been firmly fixed. On May 10, he reported the meeting to James Monroe, reiterating his belief that "no great good" could be gained from such a treaty despite his congressional instructions and Adams's optimism.[84] Jefferson's economic prejudice deterred him from completing the treaty negotiations with the Habsburg Monarchy. In the end, his determination prevailed and Mercy-d'Argenteau admitted defeat. It was like a game of chess where one grandmaster had won by running out the clock.

Relations deteriorated between Mercy-d'Argenteau and Jefferson from this point onward, reflecting the greater dissolution of Habsburg interest in the United States. The Prussians had some indirect role in this divergence. They concluded a commercial treaty with the United States in September 1785. Belgiojoso heard of this from Beelen, who relayed the news from New York in February 1786, when Congress was poised to ratify the treaty.[85] How could the Americans finalise a deal with the Prussians and not the Habsburgs? Mercy-d'Argenteau received fresh orders to confront Jefferson again. "[One of the] greatest deceptions," decried Mercy-d'Argenteau in his report to Kaunitz, "the American Minister, Mr Jefferson, as I asked him, seemingly would not admit to this actuality!"[86] Jefferson indeed denied all knowledge of the Prussian-American treaty despite his signature on the parchment. In other words, he lied. And his response outraged the Habsburg minister and cemented the end of their interaction.

There were several reasons behind the failure to conclude a commercial treaty between the Habsburg Monarchy and the United States. Miscommunication existed on both sides. Officials from both states awaited replies without realising their own need to act. Almost a year was lost between 1784 and 1785 because Mercy-d'Argenteau waited on Franklin's reply and vice versa. Protocol was another reason. Kaunitz's adherence to diplomatic preeminence undoubtedly caused these delays. Yet the Americans were cognizant of this practice and certainly knew the onus fell on them. But the political arrangement of both states also caused delay. On the one hand, negotiations with the Americans were a matter for the whole Habsburg Monarchy and entailed input from various regional administrations. Ministers in other nations obtaining treaties (Denmark, Prussia, Portugal, Sweden for instance) did not encounter such an obstacle.

On the other hand, the American situation caused similar delays. Congress worked through three commissioners before Jefferson and Adams became responsible for negotiating with European courts. Added to this were the slow communications between them and across the Atlantic as well as the need to consult Congress. The two-year commission period proved a decisive element, curtailing negotiators and allowing Jefferson an excuse. His critical delays brought on either through absence or aversion exacerbated this time constraint. Crucially, Jefferson's decision to travel to London to finalise the Portuguese treaty not only constituted delay at a critical juncture but was a conscious evaluation of its importance over a treaty with the Habsburgs. Jefferson's actions make clear his negativity toward a potential treaty with the Habsburg Monarchy and his deliberate action to avoid its realisation. Jefferson's predisposition and his actions ultimately undermined the efforts to bring together the Habsburg Monarchy and the United States after three years of attempted negotiations.

Jefferson and Joseph

Jefferson's actions clearly wrecked the chances of a conclusive commercial treaty between the Habsburg Monarchy and the United States of America in the 1780s. His actions helped set back the progress of US-Habsburg relations for a generation. In the immediate period before the outbreak of revolutionary maelstrom across Europe, this decade represented the opportune moment for such commercial ties to be cemented before the convulsions of war waylaid any Habsburg interest or ability in transatlantic trade with the Americans. Jefferson's deliberate mishandling, therefore, derailed the negotiations and ultimately set the Habsburgs on the path to be the last European great power to recognise and establish formal ties with the United States.

Jefferson's aversion seemingly arose from his prioritisation in concluding treaties with European powers which had possessions in the Atlantic. The Habsburgs, without much of a foothold in the Atlantic, could not offer Americans very much in his mind. Unlike Adams, he did not have the conviction of potential Habsburg commerce in the eastern Mediterranean or along the Danube nor did he share Franklin's positive outlook formed by years of incessant mercantile enquires from the Habsburg lands and his friendship with people like the court physician Jan Ingenhousz. Instead, Jefferson acted upon his own instincts and according to his own sense of political economy and commercial utility.[87] Rather than outright deny the Habsburgs a right to negotiate, Jefferson shied away from interpersonal conflict and preferred to undermine the negotiations via dilatoriness and deception. To be sure, Jefferson's thoughts on international commerce were influential, but he was not entirely consistent with his own priorities. Seeing this thinking as the reason for his aversion to a Habsburg treaty is plausible but does not account why Jefferson concluded a treaty with Prussia in September 1785—a power without any American stakehold.[88] Why, then, did Jefferson allow a treaty with Prussia but not one with the Habsburg Monarchy?

Considering only Jefferson's geopolitical thought is an incomplete explanation of his foreign policy as minister in France. It was only one calculation among many in his mind at the time. Jefferson's personal outlook also heavily shaped his negotiations with European powers. Jefferson was informed not just by his interactions as a diplomat but also as an observer and individual living in Europe. His digestion of news, politics, and personal relations also shaped his diplomatic outlook. His perception of contemporary events gave rise to an intrinsic "mental map" of European powers that influenced his interaction as a diplomat. An individual's mental map reflects the cognitive biases and environmental framework constructed from the world around them.[89] In Jefferson's case, such worldviews may have been unwarranted or misinformed but were nonetheless his perception and outlook. Jefferson's interaction with the Habsburg Monarchy is a clear articulation of this influence. Jefferson's views of the Habsburg Monarchy fundamentally affected his interactions in negotiating a treaty with the Habsburg Monarchy. Nowhere is this more acute than in his discussions of Joseph II through his private and personal correspondence.

The figure of the emperor was pivotal in shaping Jefferson's perception of the wider Habsburg Monarchy as a potential economic partner. Joseph, as a head of state, signified the values and position of the Habsburg Monarchy. At the beginning of the 1780s, there were many commonalities between the two men. They were both men of the enlightenment and believed in its core values. Joseph's reform efforts in domestic matters impressed Jefferson greatly. His Tolerance Patents, for example, issued first by Joseph in 1781 granted limited freedoms to religious non-Catholic minorities for the first time.[90] Similarly, Joseph's ardent anti-papal inclination reduced the monastic influence in education and chimed with Jefferson's sensibilities on the separation of church and state, something which he formulated in his *Notes on the State of Virginia* around the same time.[91] From these "public acts," Jefferson concluded on more than one occasion that Joseph's character was "far above the level of common men."[92] There were other Americans who agreed with Jefferson about Joseph's early reign. Adams and Franklin both let their positive opinions be known. Jay wrote well of Joseph's reforms and how "he seems to be seriously preparing to be great and formidable."[93] Gouverneur Morris, a Massachusetts congressman and later successor to Jefferson in Paris, viewed Joseph's eastern ambitions as something beneficial to the United States, especially if a commercial connection with the Habsburg Monarchy could be obtained through a treaty. "As an American," he declared, "it is my hearty wish that she [Catherine II] and the Emperor may effect their schemes, for it will be a source of great wealth to us, both immediate and future."[94] Jefferson, however, viewed these plans with disapproval. If they did come to pass, then he likened it for people there as an exchange of "one set of Barbarians for another."[95] Although Jefferson had seen some good in the emperor at the beginning of the 1780s, he increasingly acknowledged some poorer tendencies of Joseph II.

As the 1780s progressed, Jefferson gradually viewed Joseph as an unwise and ineffective figure. "We have here under our contemplation," he wrote in December 1784, "the future miseries of human nature, like to be occasioned by the ambition of a young man, who has been taught to view his subjects as cattle."[96] Jefferson viewed Joseph's diplomatic efforts critically. "It is a pity," Jefferson remarked, "the emperor would not confine himself to internal regulation, in that way he has done much good."[97] Jefferson witnessed the news of half-completed designs on Europe with disapproval. As he confided to one friend, Joseph "is a restless, ambitious character, aiming at everything, preserving in nothing, taking up designs without calculating the force which will be opposed to him, and dropping them on the appearance of firm opposition."[98] Jefferson viewed this lack of attentiveness in Joseph's foreign policy as indicative of a man oddly "whimsical," "bizarre, and eccentric, particularly in the dog-days."[99] Jefferson saw these flaws transpire into "perilous" situations for the emperor as he "dwindles to that of a petty bully, and is marked, as his enemies denote it, with eccentricity and inconsistence." "If he persists," Jefferson concluded in a letter to George Washington, "the probable combination against him seems to threaten his ruin."[100]

As Jefferson's time in Paris continued, his views of Joseph diminished further. This "trifling personage," as he referred to him, seemed to grow weaker by his endless schemes, especially, Jefferson noticed, in the Holy Roman Empire. In 1785, the rulers of Prussia, Saxony, and Hanover joined together to form what became known as the *Fürstenbund* or League of Princes aimed as a bulwark against the emperor's expansionist policies as espoused in his desires on Bavaria and the corrupt election of Joseph's brother to the powerful Electorship of Cologne.[101] The more Jefferson learned of the *Fürstenbund* from the salons and newspapers of Paris, the more Jefferson realised it weakened Joseph, leaving him in "a solitary situation" and "much wounded."[102] As a union of smaller provinces united against the tyranny of an overbearing figurehead, the *Fürstenbund* certainly enjoyed some sympathy from Jefferson who delighted at the successive victories that thwarted Joseph's plans on Bavaria and within the Holy Roman Empire. To Jefferson, the League was perhaps a vindication of the belief in the success of confederacy against tyranny and resonated with own part in the struggle against

Great Britain. In August 1785, Jefferson believed Joseph had been tarnished by the *Fürstenbund*. "In truth," Jefferson concluded, "he undertakes too much."[103]

Jefferson perceived Joseph's ambitious nature as his most glaring detraction as it often brought him into disadvantageous conflagrations. Joseph's preoccupation with reopening the River Scheldt to free commerce caused an international scene. The resulting small war between the Austrian Netherlands and the Dutch Republic in October 1784, known as the "Kettle War" since only an iron kettle was struck by cannon fire, was one clear example in Jefferson's mind. From his viewpoint, Joseph's decision to sail two warships into Dutch waters in protest of the closed River Scheldt had escalated an already precarious situation.[104] Jefferson's perception of Joseph increasingly became one of a despot and warmonger as a result. He complained of Joseph's bellicose nature to several friends. "Not a circumstance can be produced, not a symptom mentioned in the conduct of the emperor which does not breathe a determination for war," he declared.[105] Jefferson acknowledged Joseph as a particular threat to European stability. Joseph's schemes would sooner or later provoke further war.[106] He explained to Franklin that it was merely a question of "with whom the emperor will pick the next quarrel."[107]

Taken together, these impressions were a consistent feature of Jefferson's time in Europe. From his arrival in August 1784 to the failure of the treaty in May 1786, Jefferson digested contemporary events and, with increasing disdain, conceived of an insolent emperor determined to destabilise the international community through his grand designs. The emperor's reputation and actions affected Jefferson's perception of the viability of the Habsburg Monarchy as an international partner. These geopolitical concerns eroded Jefferson's confidence in Ostend and Trieste as desirable trading locations.

Further south, Jefferson's Mediterranean views were undoubtedly influenced by Filippo Mazzei, his neighbour in Virginia during the early to mid-1770s. In 1778, Jefferson had written to Richard Henry Lee,

> In the present very prosperous situation of our affairs I have thought it would be wise to endeavour to gain a regular and acknoleged [*sic*] access in every court in Europe, but [of all] the Southern [ones]. The countries bordering on the Mediterranean I think will merit our earliest attention. They will be the important markets for our great commodities of fish, wheat, tobacco, and rice. [. . .] I have been led the more to think of this from frequent conversations with Mazzei, whom you know well, and who is well acquainted with all those countries.[108]

By 1785, Jefferson's Mediterranean views had altered. In Europe, he had come to increasingly appreciate (and abhor) the threat of piracy sanctioned by the Barbary States along the north African coastline. "Our trade to Portugal, Spain, and the Mediterranean is annihilated," he despaired. The alternative trading option (in Jefferson's mind) was Ostend. But the war clouds over the nearby River Scheldt persuaded Jefferson against such an entrepôt for trade. In his response to William Wenman Seward's scheme to make Ostend the major trading conduit to the United States for Irish goods, Jefferson explained he could not think why the more "dangerous" port offered any more benefit than the French port Lorient, "which," Jefferson argued, "is a freeport and in great latitude, which is nearer to both parties."[109] The major ports of the Habsburg Monarchy dealing in transatlantic trade were therefore of little interest to Jefferson.

Moreover, Jefferson was personally far more insulated from the Habsburg lands. "I know of none, have no correspondent or even acquaintance at Ostend," he wrote at one point.[110] True, Jefferson did not command the attention of Europe in the same way as Franklin. As a result, he did not inherit the same networks as Franklin. Compared to him, Jefferson had very few attachments to Vienna. The main conduit for Franklin had been Jan Ingenhousz but as Franklin ended his time in Paris so did this vital interpersonal link. Although Franklin and Ingenhousz relied on Jefferson to relay their correspondence, Jefferson did not strike up any personal friendship with Ingenhousz. This disconnect was despite his regard for the scientist to "whose researches the lovers of science are so much indebted."[111] In contrast to the scores of letters exchanged between Franklin and Ingenhousz, Jefferson's writing to Ingenhousz amounted to a mere two letters and were simple expressions of regard attached to the latest parcel or letter from Franklin. Jefferson clearly did not make use of Ingenhousz despite Franklin's advice that Ingenhousz was "a proper Correspondent in case he [Jefferson] should have anything to insinuate to that Court."[112] The loss of Ingenhousz for Jefferson severely limited his connection to Vienna.

Jefferson's relative obscurity in comparison to Franklin also exacerbated this disconnection. The vast volume of correspondents Franklin enjoyed from across the Habsburg lands were not so interested in Jefferson, a man of far less renown in Vienna than his predecessor. Whereas Franklin had received over two hundred letters from Habsburg inhabitants during his time in Europe, Jefferson could count only a handful. Moreover, Jefferson's only impressions of the inhabitants of Vienna were secondary through Lafayette's 1785 letter and a conversation with John Adams's son-in-law Colonel William Stephens Smith, who had travelled to Vienna in late 1785 with the future South American revolutionary

Francisco de Miranda.[113] Smith had been captivated by Joseph's simple manner and disregard for pomp during his observations of him at the opera. "You very rarely see any person, not even the military looking," he noted, "this is very singular." Smith spent the duration of the entire opera wondering how such a towering dynastic figure could be so normal and humble. "In a republic," he noted, "Washington is reverenced and adored by all[; . . .] in a tyrannical government, as Prussia, *Le Roi*, is their terrestrial God and his subjects will freely sacrifice their lives to his caprice and humour." The fact that Joseph "laid aside the pomp and parade" yet still commanded such respect from his subjects greatly impressed Smith and rattled his developing political views. A military man, Smith previously felt that display, rank, and pageantry were essential to a ruler's persona, but he now began to question whether this was entirely correct. Joseph II, who ruled a "mild government though not republican but not tyrannical either," could have important "lessons for republicans" back home, he concluded.[114]

If Smith shared these imperial impressions with Jefferson during his stop in Paris on his return to London, then they did not produce any effect. Federalists like Adams and Smith might have been wooed by the figure of the emperor but Jefferson, a republican, was not.[115] Jefferson became diametric to Joseph. His perception of the Habsburg Monarchy during the 1780s gave rise to his apathy for any kind of political connection. This reason in addition to his developing thoughts on political economy is a more complete explanation for his lethargic and dilatory tactics used in his interactions with Mercy-d'Argenteau.

Conclusion

Jefferson's intercession in the struggle for recognition via a commercial treaty between the Habsburg Monarchy and the United States underscores how personalities and styles of diplomacy undermined the economic interests of two states. Jefferson occupied a pivotal role in the negotiations for a treaty. Under Franklin, negotiations had progressed comparatively smoothly. Franklin's interactions with Mercy-d'Argenteau as well as his informal network in Vienna provided a comfortable base for both the American and Habsburg negotiators to work from. This situation changed suddenly following Jefferson's arrival. His absence and then personal awkwardness in the encounters with Mercy-d'Argenteau were detrimental. As we have seen, his evolving personal biases certainly informed these interactions as well; Jefferson's disdain for the emperor and his actions combined with his thoughts on the future political economy of the United States to produce an ardently negative attitude towards a treaty of commerce with the Habsburg Monarchy. Jefferson's attitude stood in stark contrast to the more open and favourable perspective of his joint negotiator John Adams, but his role as the main interlocutor in Paris enabled him to dodge, stall, and ultimately derail negotiations. The result was great annoyance on the Habsburg side, exacerbated by the discovery of the conclusion and then deceitful concealment of the treaty with Prussia by Jefferson. As a consequence, Jefferson's interactions with the Habsburg Monarchy marked a watershed moment in US-Habsburg relations. No longer would the Habsburg Monarchy seek a diplomatic connection with the United States. No longer would the Habsburg reach into the Atlantic be pursued. The interests of the revolutionary era had come to a close and a new era of divergence had begun. It would last well into the next century.

"I Am Happy Only When I Can Find a New World for Myself"

The Residue of Revolution in the Habsburg Lands, 1787–1795

W HEN THOMAS JEFFERSON RETURNED to the United States in late 1789, he harboured plans to renovate his mountain-top home at Monticello and his other property at Poplar Forest, Virginia. He was inspired by the classical architecture of Europe in his designs for more lavish plantation houses. Although delayed by his appointment as the first Secretary of State, Jefferson realised his architectural plans over the course of the 1790s and much of the early 1800s. Both houses at Monticello and Poplar Forest made extensive use of natural light.[1] At Monticello, Jefferson masterfully employed architectural designs to allow for an abundance of light. Standing in the central hallway, one can view the outside in four directions thanks to Monticello's multiple glass doors and windows. For Jefferson, the harmony of natural light satisfied not just the practical purpose of illumination but also reflected the man himself as an enlightened thinker in tune with the natural world.[2] Throughout his renovations, Jefferson relied upon Joseph Donath to meet his construction needs. Donath, the former representative of the Weinbrenner firm in Vienna, supplied much of the glass needed for the windows of Jefferson's estate. Jefferson used Donath's company in Philadelphia because he preferred the quality of Bohemian glass to any other.[3] Beginning in 1792, he made the first of several orders which continued over two decades. In total, Jefferson obtained at least 1,630 panes of Bohemian glass and paid Donath hundreds of dollars for his service.[4] There was a certain amount of irony in this transaction as well. Jefferson, the man who viewed Habsburg trade as having little value, now imported one of the staple Habsburg products at an inflated price since Donath secured his glass orders through Hamburg rather than Trieste merchants.[5] It was the price Jefferson paid for having subverted the commercial treaty with the Habsburg Monarchy.

Jefferson's subversion helped usher in a long period of malaise in US-Habsburg relations, a period which stretched deep into the nineteenth century and arguably characterised the entirety of the relationship.[6] Jefferson's snub of Count Mercy-d'Argenteau undoubtedly produced economic consequences. By the time the treaty negotiations between him and Mercy-d'Argenteau failed, many other European states had already or were beginning to benefit from official relations with the United States: France (1778), the Dutch Republic (1781), Sweden (1783), Prussia (1785), and Portugal (1786). As other nations also established relations with the United States in the 1790s and 1800s, such as Denmark (1796) and Russia (1803), the Habsburg Monarchy increasingly diverged from the transatlantic world. Without the advantages and protection of a treaty of commerce, Habsburg merchants found themselves unable to compete in North American markets. Styrian iron was more costly than comparable Swedish ironware; Levantine goods flowed more cheaply to the United States via ports in France and Spain which enjoyed lower tariffs; and Flemish merchants realised their textiles could not compete with the mass of other products. Bohemian glass proved the sole outlier. Besides Jefferson, Donath also supplied the architect Henry Latrobe with Bohemian glass for many new federal buildings in Washington, DC, including the White House.[7] But Bohemian glass was not enough to sustain an entire trade route alone, especially one which now relied upon ports to the North rather than Trieste.

From 1786 onwards, direct transatlantic ventures from the lands of the Habsburg Monarchy slowly ceased operating. In Trieste, Ignaz Verpoorten's company collapsed spectacularly with debts of over 200,000*fl* in 1786. That same year, the Austrian-American Trading Company ended. Its leaders sought emergency capital from Vienna, but with profits waning and the four directors deemed too "greedy and unscrupulous" by locals in Trieste, no rescue came.[8] The situation in Ostend fared little better. Ephrain Murdoch, a "furious partisan of the American cause" who traded from there to Philadelphia and Virginia, moved his business to Dunkirk in 1787. Francis Bowens, who had carried mail for Franklin during the war and sent ships to Philadelphia and Baltimore, declared bankruptcy at the same time. By the end of the decade, the agreement between the firm *Liebaert, Baes, Derdeyn & Co* in the Austrian Netherlands and their associate Mark Prager in Philadelphia had collapsed.[9] Undermined by private representation and diminishing official belief in the benefit of American commerce, the Habsburg Monarchy's designated representative in the United States, Baron Frederick Eugene de Beelen-Bertholff, ended his mission in 1789. Meanwhile his brother Maximilian de Beelen-Bertholff advised the minister plenipotentiary in Brussels that the port of Ostend would be ruined imminently "if measures are not taken to prevent it."[10] The brief window of opportunity for Habsburg entrepreneurs in the Atlantic created by the turbulence of the American Revolution was over by the end of the 1780s.

Habsburg interest in transatlantic trade waned in subsequent years. Dynastic succession changed the outlook in some ways. After Joseph II died unexpectedly in 1790, his younger brother Pietro Leopoldo (the Grand Duke of Tuscany) who had favoured American constitutional ideals succeeded him as Leopold II. However, he too died suddenly in March 1792. His son and Joseph's nephew, Francis II, reigned during the heady years of the French Revolution and the subsequent Napoleonic Wars that briefly brought the Habsburg Monarchy to its knees with humiliating military defeats and several territorial losses including the coastline along the Adriatic. Waging war against the revolutionary turmoil in Europe defined Francis II's early reign and sapped his attention for much else. American interests, which once commanded serious attention at the Viennese court, now took a back seat. After Beelen's mission ended, Giuseppe Mussi, a Milan-born merchant residing in Philadelphia, petitioned the Aulic Chamber to become Beelen's replacement, but his application was refused. In their concluding response, ministers explained the new Emperor Francis's view that "no advantage would be gained from formally accrediting any person with the Congress which had been so favoured by his late Majesty Emperor Joseph."[11] Francis did not alter his view in 1794 when Mussi reapplied or in 1796 when another merchant requested the same honour.[12] Habsburg merchants evidently remained more intrigued by North American commerce than the state did.

Across the Atlantic, the opposite was true. American officials sought to secure trade with the Habsburg port of Trieste. In 1797, Washington appointed Konrad F. Wagner as the first American consul.[13] A few years later, the first documented American vessel arrived to unload cotton, sugar and coffee.[14] The growth of American imports in subsequent years convinced Viennese officials of the need for an American representative. In 1804, Francis received the proposition again but declined to act.[15] It was not until after the restoration of the Illyrian provinces and the acquisition of Venetian territory following the Congress of Vienna that ended the Napoleonic wars in 1815 that Francis decided to entertain the idea.[16] However, the process of finding and appointing a consular representative proved difficult as the lead candidate did not wish to end up in the United States.[17] The issue was finally resolved in 1820 with a consular officer officially named in New York but by then Habsburg representation in the Americas functioned through Count Emanuel Joseph Eltz, the first ambassador to Brazil.[18]

By that time the Habsburgs lagged behind other European powers in establishing American representations. Helvetia (Switzerland), for example, enjoyed an official representative presence in the United States long before the Habsburgs.[19] Much like the time of the American Revolution, Central European firms became impatient and arranged their own private representatives. The Imperial Tobacco Monopoly (*Österreichische Tabakregie*) named Antonio E. Perez as a representative in New Orleans after 1815. Perez was so effective that he even provided Viennese officials with reports and made suggestions for the further expansion of Habsburg diplomatic posts in the Americas.[20]

The economic imperative to connect with the United States of America declined concurrently with the political belief in the United States as a viable sovereign nation. During the 1780s, Viennese newspapers discussed at length the poor state of the American economy and political system. The new republic seemed enfeebled and beset with political calamities. The Philadelphia mutiny of 1783, Shay's rebellion of 1786–1787, as well as reports of paper money further compounded the image of a destitute situation.[21] Some Hungarian and Flemish newspapers featured similar disparagements.[22] The negative depiction of America angered John Adams who decried how "all the Gazettes of Germany teem with Lies to our Disadvantage."[23] Fictitious or not, the air of negativity stuck. Beelen's reports painted a dire picture. In 1785, he commented how the president-elect of Congress was "in such tottering state of health" that it was doubtful "whether and when" he would be able to assume office. By contrast, Beelen, besotted with the idea of Habsburg-Native American commerce, forwarded laudatory descriptions of the Muscogee Creek and a portrait of their former leader Mico-Clucco whose title was "equivalent to our title of emperor."[24] The impression of instability and weakness rendered through these mediums further eroded the Habsburg resolve to form any political connection with the United States. By 1787, Joseph II asked, "What has the Revolution given them?" during the height of the Constitutional Convention that summer. "Nothing," he retorted, "but general imbecility, confusion, and misery."[25]

By the late 1780s, Habsburg ministers became increasingly weary of the negative effects of American independence. Concerns rose over emigration in the direction of the Atlantic rather than to the Habsburg provinces in the East. Throughout the eighteenth century, recruitment plans to populate the *neo acquista* of the eastern Habsburg territories competed against transoceanic destinations.[26] After independence, the desire to emigrate to the new American republic increased. From his vantage point in London, Adams sincerely believed that "half of Germany," which to Adams included the Habsburg territories, was on "tiptoe" ready "to fly to America for relief."[27] The writer Dositej Obradović from the Banat of Temesvar desired to emigrate to America, as did Jan Ingenhousz from Vienna.[28] A sovereign United States seemed a temptation even to members of the imperial court. In 1783, a member of the Imperial Aulic Council (the *Reichshofrat*), one of the most powerful institutions within the Holy Roman Empire, petitioned Franklin for help in retiring to the United States since he knew the new nation would need "experienced and accomplished men" such as himself. His preference was for Georgia, either of the Carolinas, or even Virginia, "if it were not too remote."[29]

In London, the Habsburg consul Antonio Songa sounded alarm over the siren calls of transatlantic migration. In February 1783 already, he argued how the issue of emigration was more pressing than ever as "Americans will try in every possible way to induce people from all the countries of Europe." Songa foresaw how, post-Revolution, the United States would expand its industry and require an even greater skilled workforce. "[This] emigration, which the independence of America may cause, is perhaps the first point which Europe must endeavour to prevent," he noted. The second point Songa observed had to do with the futility of ordinances and laws to prevent emigration. "There are always ways to escape these laws," he reminded his superiors. Instead, Songa suggested Habsburg officials should be braced to sacrifice their "lowest inferior workers" to "American temptations."[30] Confirmation of Songa's fears and predictions rang true following similar reports by Beelen. Within a year of his arrival in September 1783, Beelen observed the effects of American westward expansion into the newest counties of North Carolina annexed from Cherokee lands. The soil there was rich, the rivers plentiful, and the air clean but the land sparsely populated. The solution for the landholders, Beelen reported with alarm, rested on recruiting migrants from the Habsburg lands. "It is my knowledge," Beelen stated, "that seven emigrant subjects of Your Majesty the Emperor—natives of the environs of Ghent, Kortrijk, Brussels and further—have already arrived at Philadelphia since my sojourn in this country."[31] Combined with the perceived political instability of the post-independent United States, such fears stoked the emerging negative view of America among Habsburg officials.

In the war's aftermath it became increasingly clear that all of Europe had cause to fear the repercussions of the American Revolution. Beginning in the 1780s, successive waves of revolutionary ferment stalked the Habsburg lands. These rebellions were either reactive against the far-reaching Josephine reforms or the perceived injustices within Habsburg society. All of them were united by parallels to the American example. In 1784, an uprising broke out among villagers in the mountains of Transylvania where tensions between the different ethnic groups in the region—Hungarian Szekels, German-speakers (known as Transylvanian Saxons), and Romanians often referred to as Wallachians—reached a tipping point. Wallachians had first appealed to the Habsburg monarch for a redress of grievances via several delegations to Vienna but when the imperially sanctioned extension of privileges proved difficult to enact back in Transylvania, the fighting started.[32] Although Joseph had been sympathetic to their pleas, he now instructed the imperial army to restore order and end the bloodshed. In December 1784, two of the Wallachian leaders of the rebellion faced execution after they issued a proclamation demanding an end to the excessive abuses by feudal lords and the distribution of their lands to local peasants.[33]

Although the Principality of Transylvania had suffered several spikes of social unrest in the eighteenth century,[34] observers in and outside the Habsburg Monarchy regarded Horea's rebellion, as it became known, as something different. In 1785, the sensationalist writer Jacques-Pierre Brissot drew the most obvious parallels between the Transylvanian situation and the American Revolution. He penned an imputation against Joseph II, alleging the emperor had denied the right of protest to the Wallachians by crushing the rebellion. In Brissot's eyes, the revolt was a "beautiful monument erected to liberty" which followed the American example before them. "They [the Wallachians] must say," he argued "if the American has been able, why not I?"[35] If the propositions of the Wallachians were unjust, Brissot further explained, "it must also be said that the declarations of the United States of America were equally unjust for they are exactly the same."[36] Brissot's comparison of the two rebellions in defence of peoples' rights echoed louder in Europe than the actual uprising itself. German and Italian translations quickly followed, bringing the criticism of the emperor's policy more directly to his subjects. In doing so, Brissot not only made Habsburg inhabitants aware of the parallels between their situation and the successful American Revolution, but he also made clear the rights Americans now enjoyed as a result of their independence. Article IV of the Maryland constitution of 1776 adorned the frontispiece of his pamphlet.[37] Purposefully selected by Brissot, it spoke directly to the Wallachian struggle: "Whenever the ends of government are perverted and public liberty manifestly endangered, and all other means of redress are ineffectual, the people may and, of right, ought to reform the old or establish a new government."[38]

Inspiration from the American Revolution existed across the Habsburg lands. The War of American Independence, in the eyes of many Habsburg inhabitants, had not been a bloody conflict or civil war but rather the just defence of liberty against tyranny and a virtuous struggle to protect the inherent rights of the governed. Nowhere was this impression of the American Revolution stronger than in the Austrian Netherlands, where the inherent rights of subject became a flashpoint in the late 1780s. At the beginning of that decade, Joseph had endeavoured to reform the ancient customs and archaic privileges of the various estates under his dominion in order to create "just one body, uniformly governed."[39] In the Austrian Netherlands this entailed sweeping reforms aiming to rid the region of, as one historian has candidly phrased it, the "museum of late-medieval corporate liberties."[40] Joseph's centralising crusade overhauled judicial, political, and religious apparatuses, provoking severe discontent at first and then open disagreement with the provincial estates. Aware of the mounting resistance to his plans, Joseph consoled his ministerial representative in Brussels by saying "do not be discouraged, dear Count, we will struggle together for the good of the state."[41] The people of the Duchy of Brabant within the Austrian Netherlands, however, saw to it that they were discouraged. Students' protests erupted over the proposed changes to the seminary in Louvain/Leuven and they were joined before long by the estates themselves who issued a defiant proclamation against the continual abrogation of their endowed rights.[42]

Amid the growing furour in Brabant, many leaders of the resistance drew parallels to their situation with the American Revolution. Information coming to subjects in the Austrian Netherlands via newspapers had been more pro-American in tone than elsewhere in the Monarchy. American constitutionalism seemed a realistic model based on coverage in the pages of the *Courrier de l'Escaut,* among others.[43] Those opposed to the Josephinian reforms emphasised the favourable results of the American Revolution, an event which had enriched the Austrian Netherlands, after all. At the outbreak of unrest in early 1787, Charles Lambert d'Outrepont, a member of the provincial council of Brabant, gave a rousing speech which later reached the populace in print. In his view, the eighteenth century was one of revolution. Liberty had shone in Corsica and Poland before being extinguished; only America had been successful and now it was the time for the inhabitants of Brabant to decide whether or not to lift the torch.[44] D'Outrepont expounded the opportunities awaiting the people of the Austrian Netherlands if they would only follow the "American example" and embrace a "government which approaches republicanism rather than despotism."[45]

D'Outrepont was the first among a chorus of resistors who lauded the American cause as their rightful counterpart. A flood of lyrical verses hit the streets which Habsburg officials collected assiduously before forwarding them to ministers' desks in Vienna.[46] "Be born free, fear the shackle, imitate America!"

instructed one placard; "I invite you without mercy, Poor Belgians, [and] Tyrannical Emperor, follow America," demanded one more; and "Poor Belgian people," announced another, "do as in America: shake off the yoke of your emperor!"[47] In Vienna, Kaunitz fretted they would actually succeed in imitating the Americans. If such a situation were to pass, he worried, then the people of the Austrian Netherlands who, he thought, enjoyed "so many attractive prospects for independence," could join the Americans as "the happiest peoples in the universe."[48]

Two major anti-reformist groups emerged in the spring of 1787: the "traditionalists" and the "democrats."[49] Common to both parties was a consensus on the relevance of the American example.[50] The first group called for the defence of the ancient privileges against Joseph's modernising reforms and coalesced around the Estate of Brabant member Hendrik van der Noot, whose nickname—perhaps derogatorily—in Vienna was "the Franklin of the Austrian Netherlands."[51] The second group centred on the more radical jurist Jan-Frans Vonck who argued in favour of reform but not without the democratic consent of those he governed. The "Vonckist" or "Democrats," as this group became known, clung more tightly to the American model.[52] Some within this circle had either attempted to fight for the Revolution or had seen action in the War of American Independence.[53] Leading pamphleteers advocated emulation of the United States as resistance turned towards revolt and open rebellion throughout 1788 and 1789.[54] When the Vandernootists and Vonckists merged to form a revolutionary committee in 1789, they issued a manifesto on behalf of Brabanters in October 1789 "written in the spirit of the American Declaration of Independence."[55] The declaration led to the short-lived United Belgian States (*Verenigde Nederlandse Staten/États-Belgiques-Unis*) a few months later. Both the name and the resulting constitution directly referenced the American beacon across the Atlantic.[56]

Revolution in the Austrian Netherlands helped the American Revolution to resonate even more loudly through the Habsburg lands. Although ultimately crushed by Habsburg forces within a year of existence, the road to the United Belgian States had created a lasting impression on Habsburg inhabitants. A young Hungarian noble named Gergely Berzeviczy passed through Brussels during the first stirrings of rebellion in 1787 and remarked how "uplifting" it was to witness the "courage and resolve" among the people "for the sake of freedom."[57] The scenes in Brussels only served to strengthen the democratic convictions of Berzeviczy, who was returning to Hungary after a sojourn to the British Isles. "England," he noted at the same time as he watched with interest the "ferment" in Brussels, had "shaped my political understanding and opinions, which had previously been unclear."[58] Upon arrival in Buda, Berzeviczy became an ardent advocate of consensual governance at a time when Hungarians defended their relationship and rights under Habsburg rule.

Like many of his fellow Hungarian noblemen, Berzeviczy believed in purported parallels between Hungary under the Habsburgs and the Americans formerly under British rule. The idea was so widespread that one Göttingen professor, who had taught many Hungarians, bemoaned how much he had suffered from hearing about this "pet idea of the Hungarian aristocracy."[59] Hungarian nobles clung to the persistent fiction that Hungary was an independent kingdom ruled only via a personal union with a member of the House of Habsburg.[60] Rulership existed only with consent of the ruled in this train of thinking. When abuses by the ruler forced the ruled to break that contract, then any dissent was lawful and even necessary, as the Americans had shown. Joseph's imposition of reforms prejudicial to the Hungarian people constituted, so the logic ran, a rejectable abuse of power.

In the summer of 1789, Berzeviczy gave a speech in which he advanced the notion that Joseph had repeatedly infringed upon the rights of Hungarians; his list of grievances was a clear imitation of the Declaration of American Independence, of which he had obtained a handwritten copy during his travels.[61] He elaborated on these charges after Joseph's death in early 1790 when effective change in Hungary seemed possible. His pamphlet *De dominio Austriae in Hungaria* (On the rule of Austria in Hungary) specifically referenced the United States and United Belgian States as examples of people "blessed by freedom" after years of subjugation. When rule turned to tyranny, their rebellions seemed "natural" and righteous in Berzeviczy's eyes.[62]

By the time Berzeviczy's *De dominio Austriae* passed privately among liberal circles in Hungary, the revolutionary scene in Europe had changed, however. The French Revolution in July 1789 captivated many Hungarians much like the American Revolution had previously done. One Hungarian poet, János Nagyváthy, considered the present moment in 1790 as the beginning of a future utopia for Hungarians. Imagining himself as an observer in the year 1900 and looking back on history, he saw how freedom had begun first with the English, then the Americans, followed by the French, and finally the "noble-hearted" Hungarians.[63] There were those who were determined to bring the example of the American Revolution to Hungary sooner than Nagyváthy envisioned.

Radical elements within Hungarian society were labelled "Jacobin" at the time for their inspiration by the French Jacobin faction of anti-royalists. This group, however, also took considerable inspiration from the Americans. Among them was the legal theorist József Hajnóczy, whose pamphlets urged liberal civic and juridical reform in the Hungarian lands. His ties to American revolutionary thought stretched back earlier than his political writings. During the War of American Independence, Hajnóczy had received a commission from the Hungarian magnate Ferenc Széchényi to assemble a library for his county seat. Today it forms the core of the Hungarian National Library and contains some of the rarest Americana from this period, which means that Hajnóczy took an avid interest in obtaining American works.[64] Hajnóczy also utilised his employer's assembled materials for his own personal systematic study.[65] His fascination with American political principals continued up to the French Revolution, when he supplied material and articles to the periodical *Hadi és Más Nevezetes Történetek* (Military and other notable stories), which had looked favourably on the new American republic throughout the 1780s. Hajnóczy supplied the editors with his personal copy of the French translation of Thomas Paine's *The Rights of Man* for reprinting in 1791.[66] Reflecting his legal background, Hajnóczy also published his own works extolling the wisdom and virtue of the American laws. In one, he recommended introducing a Hungarian version of the Virginia statute for religious freedom. "There is no doubt," he declared, "that this law, breathing with humanity, could take root here just the same as there."[67]

Hajnóczy's admiration for American laws and his desire to implement them in Hungary brought him into contact with the future "Jacobin" circles. Central to this group was Ignác Martinovics, who, while less intellectual than Hajnóczy, was just as passionate about the American example. Historians generally identify Martinovics as the first embodiment of the Age of Revolutions in the Habsburg Monarchy, without realising his proper motivations or his alleged "conspiracy" movement.[68] Descended from a Habsburg-Serbian family, Martinovics taught natural sciences at the University of Lemberg (Lviv) where he was admitted as a Freemason in the "Honest Man" lodge. He became engrossed in masonic mythology and helped propagate the proliferation of lodges across Hungary in the 1780s. Martinovics led a double life, however. He had been recruited by the court intelligence service in Vienna to infiltrate and report on the masonic movement. In 1792, Martinovics filed a report with the director of court intelligence, alleging a list of names of the Viennese Illuminati who swore oaths to defend "in writing, in speech and with arms the current situation of France and America against all despots."[69] In other reports, he warned of a growing "French-American fever" in the Habsburg lands.[70]

Although Martinovics worked as an informer for the Habsburg court, he remained loyal to revolutionary ideas, explicitly referring to the United States

FIGURE 17. The execution of the Hungarian "Jacobins" in 1795

as the "immortal American Republic" and ranking foreign rulers against Washington or Paine.[71] In one of his most incendiary pamphlets, Martinovics encouraged aristocrats to introduce changes "in the Pennsylvanian way," and lauded the results of the American constitution. "I adore the Philadelphia Convention," he stated openly.[72] The boldness of his prose had alienated Martinovics from the court and cost him his position as an informer, but it did not matter much. In 1794, he began actively recruiting members for his own societies, modelled after the Jacobin clubs in France.[73] He named Hajnóczy as one of four directors and co-authored pamphlets calling for the overthrow of monarchism. According to the radicals, sovereignty rested entirely within the people, who were responsible to exercise it themselves, and not the monarchy.[74] Habsburg authorities might have tolerated allusions to American constitutionalism and the defence of rights but emulating the seditious extremism of the French Jacobins triggered a crackdown. Faced with arrest and certain death, Martinovics surrendered himself and betrayed his accomplices who were subsequently located and arrested. In May 1795, he and six others—including Hajnóczy—were publicly executed in Buda.

The execution of the Hungarian Jacobins marked a point when the American Revolution could no longer serve as an open ambition. Works by the most prominent American revolutionaries that had been permitted during the 1770s and 1780s now entered censorship lists for the first time. Franklin's novel *The Speech of Polly Baker* from 1747 received a retroactive ban in 1794, followed by a French translation of his autobiography.[75] Books published as late as 1827 on American themes showed evidence of censorship.[76] Following the executions, the Bishop of Agram (Zagreb) Miska Verhovacz, a councillor named Jakob Szecsenacz, and the jurist Paul Lukács were all arrested for their ownership of texts by Thomas Paine or for publishing works related to Franklin.[77] The poet, Mihály Vitéz Csokonai, expressed his despair at the changing freedom in 1795. In a letter to a friend following his expulsion from the Reformed College of Debrecen on account of his liberal ideas, he wrote:

> I, an exile in my own country, carry on my days in boredom. I am happy only when I can find a New World for myself, and build there a Republic, a Philadelphia. At least there, like Franklin, I can snatch lightning from heaven and the sceptres from tyrants.[78]

The conservatism of the 1790s and 1800s could not completely eradicate the legacy of the American Revolution in the Habsburg Monarchy, however. "I still hold to the great American sage, Franklin," Csokonai admitted privately to a liberal friend in 1803.[79] And adherents of American ideals discovered new ways of conveying its ideas. Berzeviczy, who had narrowly avoided the fate of Hajnóczy and Martinovics, focused instead on the economic power of the United States and frequently used it as validation for his free-trade plans for the Hungarian lands.[80] Praise of American military figures such as George Washington became the new focal point as he embodied the more positive virtue and patriotic good of the Revolution. When Hungarian-Americans later chose to erect a monument to a prominent American in Budapest, they chose Washington who best represented "the embodiment of both American ideals, and of the ideal of Hungarians on both sides of the Atlantic."[81] Franklin, who throughout this period was the paragon of the Revolution, underwent a sanitised retelling during the early years of the post-Napoleonic order. A biographical account by Ferenc Szilágyi, published in Transylvania in 1818, presented Franklin first and foremost as a scientist and publicist who happened to play some role in the Revolution's course.[82] For a generation of later Hungarian nationalists and revolutionaries such as Count István Széchenyi and Lajos Kossuth, Franklin represented only a moral figure through his writings and sayings.[83] His revolutionary activity no longer mattered in the way it once had.

RESIDENTS IN THE Habsburg Monarchy never lost sight of the American Revolution. Its flame smouldered but was not extinguished. The dilution of the explosiveness of the first revolutionary experience in Central Europe during the early nineteenth century ultimately gave way to a period of greater unrest. In the revolutions of 1848–1849, the United States again became a symbol of a utopia created out of courageous adherence to righteous, unalienable principles.[84] Kossuth, the new "Washington of Hungary," solicited American support by nurturing a Hungarian martyrology in which the Emperor Francis Joseph I became George III and the Hungarians were either the Puritans seeking freedom and liberty or republicans in search of their independence.[85] In Habsburg Lombardy, protagonists agitating for reform and Italian nationalists aiming for independence both drew inspiration from the American example. They aimed to break the lucrative state monopolies in order to gain political leverage. The tobacco boycott, begun on New Year's Day in 1848, allowed an easy parallel to the infamous Boston Tea Party. "Franklin's fellow citizens abstained from tea; as of today you ought to refuse tobacco," ran the refrain.[86] For moderates like Carlo Cattaneo, who initially resisted Italian unification in favour of greater autonomy for Lombardy within the Habsburg system, American federal government served a possible blueprint for the future. Like many Milanese publicists and jurists, Cattaneo interpreted the American Revolution as a useful justification for federalisation and as a balm against the more fervent calls for secession and unification with the Italian peninsula.[87] Cattaneo and his companions were not alone in finding an American model. In 1849 and in 1906, two separate plans would have reformulated the Habsburg Monarchy towards a federalised American structure.[88] From the immediate post-Napoleonic aftermath known as the *Vormärz* to the twilight decades of Habsburg rule in Central Europe, the American political example and its republican style of government continually beckoned.[89]

The American experiment shone gradually brighter as the antithesis to the old regime in Europe. At his nadir after successive defeats by Napoleon, Emperor Francis reportedly said that he should emigrate to America to atone for his political failings.[90] If true, the emperor was implying that the United States was a suitable punishment for his inability to defend the principles of monarchy and his imperial power. Many of his subjects were inclined to disagree. Travellers and migrants from the Habsburg Monarchy in the United States recognised it as a land entirely different to their own. Some, like Joseph Donath, began to question their former homeland. People there, in his estimation, were "deprived of civil liberty" and "vassals" who required "the flame of liberty" to spread among them.[91] Writing from Philadelphia in his "happy hemisphere," he looked upon the scene of Europe and Francis's coronation in July 1792 with great haughtiness. "What animal is the emperor?" Donath asked his friend in Prague before concluding that the emperor was, "in plain English, a butcher of men."[92] Being in America confirmed or awoke such bias in Habsburg migrants looking back on their land of origin. Maria von Born, daughter of the celebrated Transylvanian mineralogist Ignaz von Born, spent twenty years in the United States. She returned to Vienna in 1815 and disapproved of its poor education system, its lack of public welfare, and the insufficient intelligence of its inhabitants. "How has Vienna fallen behind," she exclaimed, "because young America is growing up fast!"[93]

The lure of America as a promised land, a free land, became increasingly stronger throughout the nineteenth century. The Austrian poet Nicholas Lenau characterised his emigration to the United States as a journey "towards freedom."[94] István Széchenyi extolled America as "the country where the Rights of Mankind are most equal and where the constitution is best."[95] He desired most of all to travel to the United States in the 1830s but like many compatriots, he faced discouragement and prevention from Viennese authorities who distrusted the influence of the American republic in an era after the French Revolution. The Austrian Chancellor Prince Klemens von Metternich thought Széchenyi bizarre for wanting to visit America and viewed his travel plans with suspicion. In his personal diary, Széchenyi decried such derision. "By heaven, there are people who do not understand that some want to visit a free country!"[96] Though Metternich and his colleagues could dissuade Széchenyi from his American travels, subsequent generations of Habsburg minsters could not prevent the ever-rising tide of movement between the Habsburg lands and the United States. Széchenyi's oldest son, Béla Széchenyi, realised his father's dream by touring the northern United States during the American Civil War and publishing an instructive account of his journey in Hungarian, which extolled the marvels of American progress.[97] In the second half of the nineteenth century, the trickle of migration turned into a flood. By the outbreak of World War I in 1914, nearly four million Habsburg subjects had crossed the Atlantic for a new life in the nation forged by the American Revolution. Few were aware, however, that tens of thousands of them migrated along the Adriatic-Atlantic route first established during the selfsame revolutionary period.[98]

Like them, we too may have lost sight of the Habsburg moment in the American Revolution, but simply because it is forgotten does not reduce its importance. If we are to understand the Age of Revolutions, we must appreciate the areas where revolutionary sentiments smouldered for longer rather than erupted on short fuses. The American Revolution exerted a profound influence on the eighteenth-century Habsburg Monarchy. Lives were shaped by its war, fortunes were made in its shadow, and policies altered in its wake. The Revolution was a difficult opportunity, a challenge of adaptation for the Habsburgs as much as it was an invitation to emulate the Atlantic powers of Europe. The American Revolution and its influence in the Habsburg lands did not come out of nowhere, but rather through a sustained and intensive interest by people made curious by the events and rhetoric from across the ocean. The impulse to chase economic gains cemented the Monarchy's interests further into the Atlantic, but this imperial outreach was short-lived. The Habsburg exigency of securing new relations with a sovereign United States faltered at the hands of Thomas Jefferson, who, unlike some of his contemporaries, viewed the monarchy with a critical eye. Nevertheless, in the later decades of the eighteenth century, the embers of revolutionary zeal smouldered on to flare up on distinct occasions throughout the Monarchy's existence. Infused with the radicalism of the French revolutionary movement, the original American imprint within the Habsburg mentality could no longer continue unchallenged. The once revolutionary pull, which had animated so many individuals across the Habsburg lands during the 1770s and 1780s, succumbed to the ideological pressure of the 1790s and emergence of a new reactionary conservatism at the dawn of a new century.

When young Benjamin Silas Arthur Schuster came of age during this period, his world was fundamentally different from the one of his parents. In theirs, the American example shone like a beacon, and they were unafraid to declare openly their enthusiasm for its cause, bold enough to name their "petit Américain" after its illustrious leaders and daring enough to inform Franklin of their prayers for him and his fellow revolutionaries. In place of their world was a new regime, tighter and more reactionary to the revolutionary murmurings such actions could divulge. It was a stark cry from the Habsburg Monarchy of the 1770s and 1780s which harboured interested enthusiasts such as the Schusters and where even the rulers themselves read the latest thoughts of American leaders. We may never know whether Benjamin S. A. Schuster lived on with pride in his name, becoming a "grand Américain," or whether he chose to conceal it, shunning his godfathers in absentia. But we do know the reality of an expansive revolutionary movement which affected greatly the inhabitants of the Habsburg lands and, for a time, compelled many of them towards a more open, oceanic, and expansive interaction with the world. Though the Habsburg moment in the American Revolution was brief, it was intense and influential.

Introduction

1. Domarchiv St. Stephan, Wien, Geburts und Taufbuch der Dompfarre St. Stephan, Tomus 94, fol. 153r.

2. The original letter is lost but referenced in the next citation below.

3. Library of the American Philosophical Society [APS], Franklin Papers, Series VI, Letter No. XXVII, 92.5, Jean-Chrétien Schuster to Franklin, 8 February 1783.

4. I have found no trace of Maria Schuster's death in the *Sterbebücher* of the appropriate diocese. Johann Schuster, according to the baptismal register, worked for *Steiner & Co*, the sabre and blade manufactory belonging to the Swiss-born Melchior Steiner, see Mentschl, "Steiner, Melchior (II.) von (1762–1837), Großhandler, Fabrikant und Banker," in *Österreichisches Biographisches Lexikon*, 13:176.

5. John Adams, diary entry of 10 October 1782 following a study of the journal of Guy Claude, comte de Sarsfield through Bruges and Ostend in *The Adams Papers*, 3:10–40; *Magyar Hírmondó*, 17 November 1780; Klíma, "Glassmaking Industry and Trade in Bohemia, 520.

6. Diekmann, Lockruf der Neuen Welt; O'Reilly, *Agenten, Werbung und Reisemodalitäten*, 109–120; O'Reilly, *Alluding to Alternatives*, 159–184.

7. Sir Robert Murray Keith to Thomas Bradshaw, 5 March 1774, in Smyth, *Memoirs and Correspondence*, 1:461.

8. Singerton, "Knowledge of and Sympathy for the American Cause," 128–158; Singerton, "A Revolution in Ink," 91–113.

9. Dippel, *The American Revolution and the Modern Concept of 'Revolution'*, 124–129; Bödeker, *The Concept of the Republic in Eighteenth-Century German Thought*, 35–52; Stourzh, Liberal Democracy as a Culture of Rights, 11–41.

10. Kazinczy, "Pályám emlékezete [Remembrance of My Career]," in *Versek, műfordítások, széppróza, tanulmányok* [Poems, Translations, Belles-Lettres, and Studies], ed. Mária Szuander, 1:252; Závodszky, American Effects, 29.

11. O'Reilly, "Lost Chances," 53–70; O'Reilly, *A Life in Exile*, 66–90; Ingrao, The Habsburg Monarchy, Ingrao, The Habsburg Monarchy, 118–167.

12. Pace, "Franklin and Italy since the Eighteenth Century," 243–244; Szilassy, "America and the Hungarian Revolution," 180–196; Halácsy, "The Image of Benjamin

Franklin in Hungary," 9–25; Katona, "The Hungarian Image of Benjamin Franklin," 43–60; Závodszky, American Effects, 15–16, 20–24.

13. Hochedlinger, Austria's Wars of Emergence, 281 and 300–301; Dickson, Finance and Government, 2:Appendix, fig. A:1.

14. De Dorlodot, "Les ports d'Ostende et de Nieuport," 141–157; Van Gucht, *"De trans-Atlantische handel vanuit Oostende"*; Huibrechts, *"Swampin' Guns and Stabbing Irons."*

15. Ronkard, "Les répercussions de la Guerre Américaine," 51–90; Parmentier, *Profit and Neutrality*, 206–226.

16. Dull, A Diplomatic History of the American Revolution; Ferreiro, American Independence and the Men of France and Spain.

17. Murphy, Charles Gravier, Comte de Vergennes, 393; Scott, British Foreign Policy.

18. Armitage, The Declaration of Independence; Gould, Among the Powers of the Earth.

19. On Russia: Golder, "Catherine II. and The American Revolution," 92–96; Griffiths, "Nikita Panin, Russian Diplomacy, and the American Revolution,", 1–24; Bolkhovitinov, *Rossiia i voina SShA za nezavisimost' 1775 - 1783* [Russia and the War of the United States of America for Independence]; Bolkhovitinov, "The Declaration of Independence," 1389–1398. On Sweden: Benson, Sweden and the American Revolution; Johnson, Swedish Contributions to American Freedom; Elovson, Amerika i svensk litteratur; Johnson, "Swedish Officers in the American Revolution," 33–39; Barton, "Sweden and the War of American Independence," 408–430. On Poland: Marraro, "Philip Mazzei and His Polish Friends," 757–822; Libiszowska, "Polish Opinion of the American Revolution," 5–15; Sokol, "The American Revolution and Poland," 3–17; Tazbir, "Knowledge of Colonial North America in Mid-Eighteenth-Century Poland," 99–109. On the German lands (in addition to those cited below): Kapp, Friedrich der Grosse und die Vereinigten Staaten von Amerika; Gallinger, Die Haltung der deutschen Publizistik; Haworth, "Frederick the Great and the American Revolution," 460–478; Dippel, "Die Wirkung der amerikanischen Revolution," 101–121; Overhoff, "Die transatlantischen Bezüge der hamburgischen Aufklärung," 57–84. This list here is far from extensive.

20. Atwood, The Hessians; Crytzer, Hessians; Szyndler, Tadeusz Kościuszko, 1746–1817; Pula, Tadeusz Kościuszko; Wrangel, *Lettres d'Axel de Fersen*; Barton, Count Hans Axel von Fersen.

21. Bailyn, "The Idea of Atlantic History," 19–44; Bailyn, Atlantic History; Canny, "Atlantic History: what and why?" 399–411; Elliot, *Afterword: Atlantic History: A Circumnavigation*, 233–249, esp. 239.

22. Games, "Atlantic History: Definitions, Challenges, and Opportunities," 741–757.

23. "It is possible that we are reaching the limits of its [Atlantic History] utility for historians of the Revolution." Cogliano, Revolutionary America 1763-1815, xv; Games, et al., "Forum: Beyond the Atlantic," 675–742.

24. Calderón and Thibaud, Revolucion en el mundo Atlántico; Griffin, American Leviathan; Saunt, West of the Revolution; DuVal, Independence Lost; Taylor, American

Revolutions, 4–5; Spero, Frontier Rebels; Langley, The Long American Revolution; McFarlane, *The American Revolution and Spanish America*, 37–61.

25. Gould, "Entangled Histories, Entangled Worlds," 764–786; Cohen, "Was there an Amerindian Atlantic?" 388–410; Bushnell, *Indigenous America and the Limits of the Atlantic World*, 191–221.

26. Wulf, "No Boundaries? New Terrain in Colonial American History," 7–12; Wulf, "Vast Early America."

27. Archives générales du Royaume de Belgique/Algemeen Rijksarchief van België [ARB], Secrétaire d'État et Guerre [SEG], 2151/2, Rapports du 18 Juillet et du 26 Septembre 1782 sur un projet d'acquisition de l'Isle de Tobago; Nicolaus Fontana, "Tagebuch der Reise des k.k. Schiffes Joseph und Theresia nach den neuen österreichischen Pflanzorten in Asia und Afrika," orig. trans. Joseph Eyerel, Joseph (Leipzig, 1782) in G. Pilleri, ed., *Maria Teresa e le Indie orientali: La spedizione alle Isole Nicobare della nave Joseph und Theresia e il diario del chirurgo di bordo* (Bern: Verlag de Hirnanatomischen Institutes, 1982), 9; Bolts, Précis de l'Origine, 14.

28. The same can be said for the Baltic and other ports on the North Sea, see Pohl, *Die Beziehungen Hamburgs*; Weber, *Deutsche Kaufleute im Atlantikhandel*; Evans and Rydén, *Baltic Iron*.

29. Haus-, Hof und Staatsarchiv [HHStA], Staatskanzlei [StK], Spanien, Karton [K]. 109–1, Paolo Giusti, 'Considérations sur l'état présent de l'Espagne' (1 April 1780), Part XXVIII 'Examen de la question s'il serait de l'intérêt de la cour impériale que Gibraltar tombât au pouvoir de l'Espagne.'

30. Armitage, Bashford, and Sivasundaram, Oceanic Histories.

31. For a good example of this, see Abulafia, The Great Sea.

32. Randa, Österreich in Übersee; Babudieri, Trieste e gli interessi austriaci; Markov, "L'expansion autrichienne," 281–329. The recent work of Dr. Klemens Kaps is especially illuminating in this respect, see, for example, his "Handelsverflechtungen," 445–464; and his *A Gateway to the Spanish Atlantic?*, 246–264.

33. Weber, *Deutsche Kaufleute*; Kossok, *Die Bedeutung des spanisch–amerikanischen Kolonialmarktes*, 210–218: Zeuske and Ludwig, "Amerikanische Kolonialwaren in Preußen und Sachsen," 257–301; Steffen and Weber, *Spinning and Weaving*, 87–108.

34. For a useful discussion on the hybrid imperial nature of the Habsburg Monarchy, see Frank, "Continental and Maritime Empires," 783.

35. Hertz, "England and the Ostend Company," 255–279; Narang, "The Ostend Company's Records," 17–37; Everaert, *Willem Bolts*, 363–369.

36. De Dorlodot, "Les ports d'Ostende et de Nieuport," 141–157; Huibrechts, *"Swampin' Guns and Stabbing Irons."*

37. *Magyar Hírmondó*, 1 November 1780.

38. Two notable exceptions are: Strohmeyer, *Die Habsburger Reiche* and Rady, *The Habsburgs*.

39. Pollack-Parnau, Eine österreich-ostindische Handelskompanie; Tschugguel, *"Österreichische Handelskompanien"*; Hatschek, *Sehnsucht nach fernen Ländern*, 85–99; Navrátilová and Míšek, "Austrian Diplomacy in the Orient," 199–204; Botez,

"Maximilian Hell," 165–174; Klemun, "Space, State, Territory, Region, and Habitat," 414–415; Madriñán, Jacquin's American Plants; Walsh, *"Between the Arctic & the Adriatic"*; Do Paço, L'Orient à Vienne; Do Paço, "Patronage and Expertise," 48–64.

40. Brechka, Van Swieten and His World; Lindner, Ignaz von Born; Schmidt, "Franz von Dombay," 75–168; King, "William Bolts," 1–28; Aspaas and Kontler, Maximilian Hell. We need only to think how apparent this is in the field of music with many composers imbibing new cultural dimensions in Vienna.

41. O'Reilly, *Habsburg Eighteenth-Century Global Contexts*. I am grateful to the author for sharing his preliminary draft. For now, see O'Reilly, "Global, Regional and Small Spaces," 201–211.

42. Knott, "Narrating the Age of Revolution," 3–36; McDonnell, "Rethinking the Age of Revolution," 301–314.

43. Faÿ, L'esprit révolutionnaire en France; Echeverria, Mirage in the West; Appleby, "America as a Model," 267–286; Hulliung, Citizens and Citoyens; Whatmore, *"The French and North American Revolutions,"* 219–238.

44. Palmer, The Age of the Democratic Revolution; Adelman, "An Age of Imperial Revolutions," 319–340; Armitage and Subrahmanyam, The Age of Revolutions in Global Context.

45. Dubois, Avengers of the New World; Gaspar and Geggus, A Turbulent Time; Landers, Atlantic Creoles in the Age of Revolutions; Paquette, Imperial Portugal in the Age of Atlantic Revolutions.

46. Polasky, "Traditionalists, Democrats, and Jacobins," 227–262; Polasky, Revolutions without Borders; Polasky, "Revolutionaries between Nations," 165–201.

47. Venturi, The End of the Old Regime in Europe. Less influential but still useful is the edited volume: Newman, Europe's American Revolution.

48. Palmer, Age of Democratic Revolution, 1:103–110, 263–265; 2:156–173.

49. Palmer, Foreword to Dippel, Germany and the American Revolution, ix.

50. Dippel, Americana Germanica 1770–1800; Dippel, Germany and the American Revolution.

51. Israel, The Expanding Blaze, 606.

52. Wangermann, Von Joseph II. zu den Jakobinerprozessen; Körner, "Franz Hebenstreit," 39–62; Reinalter, Jakobiner in Mitteleuropa. An outlier is of course: Loft, "The Transylvanian Peasant Uprising," 209–218.

53. John Adams to Robert R. Livingston, 13 July 1783, *The Papers of John Adams* [PJA], 15:106–109; Barlow, Conspiracy of Kings, 9.

54. Goger, *"Die Beziehungen der Habsburgermonarchie zu den Vereinigten Staaten von Amerika von 1838 bis 1867,"*; Curti, "Austria and the United States," 141–220; Loidolt, *"Die Beziehungen Österreichs"*; Szilassy, "America and the Hungarian Revolution," 180–196.

55. Metternich quoted in Sofka, "Metternich's Theory of European Order," 148n64.

56. Coolidge, The United States as a World Power, 224; Schwartz, "Roundtable Review," 6. A similar line is taken by the politician-cum-historian Heinrich Drimmel in his Die Antipoden.

57. Singerton, *175 or 235 Years of Austro-American Relations?*, 13–30.

58. Quote from Agstner, Austria-Hungary and its Consulates, 36. "Between 1776 and 1829, the United States and the Habsburg Empire had very little to do with one another [. . .]" in Phelps, U.S.-Habsburg Relations, 40. Cf. Singerton, "'A Story of Benign Neglect'?" 56–68.

59. Zahra, The Great Departure; Steidl, Fischer-Nebmaier and Oberly, From a Multiethnic Empire.

60. Mettauer, "American Studies in Austria"; Wagnleitner, Coca-Colonization; Gassert, *The Spectre of Americanization*," 189.

61. Abádi-Nagy, "Not an Untroubled Bliss," 3–13; Frank and Kövecses, "American Studies in Hungary"; Federmayer, "American Studies in Hungary"; Jařab, "American Studies in the Czech Republic and Slovakia."

62. Benna, Contemporary Austrian Views; Benna, "Österreichs erste diplomatische Vertretung,", 215–240; Fichtner, *Viennese Perspectives*, 19–32; Gorman, America and Belgium; Dvoichenko-Markov, "A Rumanian Priest," 383–389. See also Halácsy, Katona, and Závodszky, American Effects.

63. Dippel, Germany and the American Revolution; Király and Barany, East Central European Perceptions; Tazbir, "The Discovery of America in East-Central Europe," 263–283.

64. Kunec, "Hungarian Participants," 41–57.

65. Elliott, "A Europe of Composite Monarchies," 48–71. For this reason, I do not prefer the term Habsburg Empire in this book, see Strohmeyer, "*Ein Problemaufriss*," 1027–1056.

66. HHStA, Sonderbestände, Nachlass Schlitter, K. 16, 'Selbstautobiographie', fols. 40–41; Schlitter, *Beziehung*.

67. Schlitter, ibid., 102–105.

Chapter 1

1. Molnár Basa, "English and Hungarian Cultural Contacts," 209; Hoff, *Kurze Lebensabriße*, 2–22.

2. O'Reilly, *Habsburg Eighteenth-Century Global Contexts*. I am grateful to the author for sharing his preliminary draft with me.

3. Bray, "Crop Plants and Cannibals," 298.

4. Feest, *Von Kalikut nach Amerika*, 367–375. For Maximilian's claim to universal monarchy, see Madar, *Maximilian and the Exotic*, 237–238.

5. Appelbaum, Triumph, 19.

6. Madar, *Maximilian and the Exotic*, 238; MacDonald, "Collecting a New World," 649.

7. Kleinschmidt, Ruling the Waves, 24–25, 117–118, 188–192.

8. Feest, "The People of Calicut," 295. The artist was Jörg Kölderer.

9. Madar, *Maximilian and the Exotic*, 239–240; Kleinschmidt, Ruling the Waves, 196–208.

10. Laubenberger and Rowan, "The Naming of America," 92–93.

11. For Charles V, see Vandenbroeck, *Amerindian Art*," 99–104, 110–117. For Maximilian II and Rudolf II, see Gschwend, *The Emperor's Exotic*, 76–103.

12. MacDonald, "Collecting a New World," 653, 659, and 663.

13. Turpin, *The New World Collections*, 65–66; Laferl, Die Kultur der Spanier in Österreich, 169–171.

14. Pieper, Die Vermittlung einer Neuen Welt, 21n112 and 201.

15. Pieper, ibid., 29; Rudolph, "Kunstbestrebungen," 170.

16. Heger, "Altmexikanische Reliquien," 379–400; Brezina, "Der mexikanische Federschild," 138–140; Feest, "Vienna's Mexican Treasures," 1–64; Meadow, *The Aztecs at Ambras*, 349–368.

17. O'Reilly, "Lost Chances," 59; O'Reilly, *A Life in Exile*, 66–90.

18. O'Reilly, "Lost Chances," 66–70; Döberl, *The Royal and Imperial Stables*, 197–232.

19. Page, "Music and the Royal Procession," 104; Yonan, Politics of Imperial Art, 31–41.

20. Ács, Reformations in Hungary, 228–229.

21. Gschwend, *The Emperor's Exotic*, 98; Belozerskaya, *Menageries*, 71; Zedinger, Franz Stephan, 249–253.

22. Simáková and Macháčková, Teatralia, 1:215, figures XXII-XXIII; Polleroß, *Amerika in der Wissenschaft*, 243; Sommer-Mathis, *Amerika auf der Bühne*, 290.

23. Cesky Krumlov, Státni Hrad a Zámek, Inv. No. 2173.

24. Ivanič, Cosmos and Materiality, 30; Hanß, *Making Featherwork*, 148.

25. Oliván, "Two Imperial Ambassadresses," 95–118.

26. Hyden-Hanscho, *France as an Intermediary for Atlantic Products*, 153–167; Hyden-Hanscho, "Invisible Globalization," 11–54.

27. This occurred with the relative decline in popularity of exotic feathers by seventeenth century, see Johnson, Cultural Hierarchy, 256-258 and 264. Cf. Rublack, "Befeathering the European," 43–51.

28. Schmale, Romberg, Köstlbauer, The Language of Continent Allegories; Romberg, Die Welt im Dienst des Glaubens.

29. I extrapolate this number from the Continental Allegories in the Baroque Age database https://erdteilallegorien.univie.ac.at/ (October 2018).

30. Romberg, *Did Europe Exist in the Parish before 1800?*, 101–102.

31. Otruba, "Österreichische Jesuitenpatres," 31.

32. Otruba, ibid., 31; Otruba, "Der Anteil österreichischer Jesuitenmissionäre," 430–445; Rynes, "Los Jesuitas Bohémicos," 193–202.

33. Boglár, "XVIII. Századi magyar utazók Dél-Amerikában," 449–461; Babarczi, "*Magyar jezsuiták Braziliában*."

34. Gagliano and Ronan, Jesuit Encounters.

35. Po-Chia Hsia, "Jesuit Foreign Missions," 58–59.

36. Křížová, "Meeting the Other," 37–38.

37. Kristóf, *Diabolized Representations*, 38–73; Kristóf, *The Uses of Demonology*, 161–182.

38. "Dissertatio philologica de homine" in *Calendarium 1709* cited in Kristóf, *Local Access to Global Knowledge*, 209.

39. Neumann, *Historia seditionum*. Neumann was born in Brussels but came to the Bohemian province for training in the 1660s; see Christelow, "Father Joseph Neumann," 423–442; Rodríguez, "Joseph Neumann," 237–259.

40. Quoted in and translated by Křížová, "Meeting the Other," 42.

41. Kristóf, *Local Access to Global Knowledge*, 208.

42. "Dissertatio geographica altera" in *Calendarium 1681*; "Admiranda plantarum, Viridarium philosophicum" in *Caldendarium 1691*; "Descriptio avium peregrinarum" in *Calendarium 1695* cited in Kristóf, ibid., 209.

43. Szentiványi, *Curiosiora et Selectiora*; Angyal, *Martin Szentiványi*, 152–163.

44. Martini Szentivany [*sic*], "Dissertatio physica curiosa de plantis" and "Viridarium Philosophicum" in *Calendarium Cassoviense ad annum Jesu Christi* (Košice, 1754), 63–84.

45. The title of Bertalanffi's work was *Világnak két ren-beli rövid ismerete* [*A brief introduction to two colonies of the world*] (Trnava/Nagyszombat, 1757). See Závodszky, American Effects, 10.

46. The first editions between the years 1726 and 1736 were printed in Augsburg as well as Graz; the later editions from 1748 to 1761 were printed in Vienna. See Anhang 2: Die jesuitische Missionszeitschrift der "Neue Welt-Bott" in Borja González, Jesuitische Berichterstattung, 277–278.

47. Borja González, ibid., 124–166; Dürr, "The World in the German Hinterlands," 148–153.

48. Strasser, *Jesuit Migrations*, 104–106.

49. Dürr, "Der 'Neue Welt-Bott'," 441.

50. "Anhang 3: Berichterstattung im "Neuen Welt-Bott" nach Regionen," in Borja González, Jesuitische Berichterstattung, 279–281.

51. Borja González and Strasser, *German Circumnavigation*, 73–92

52. Strasser, *Jesuit Migrations,* 107.

53. Oppermann, *Conceptions of Space*, 111–121.

54. Strasser, *Jesuit Migrations*, 105.

55. Duhr, *Deutsche Auslandssehnsucht*, 47.

56. Borja González, Jesuitische Berichterstattung, 167.

57. Many turned to academic positions, see Shore, *Enduring the Deluge*, 148–161. For the Habsburg Italian provinces, see Guasti, *Spanish Jesuits in Italy*, 248–261.

58. Borja González, Jesuitische Berichterstattung, 180–186; Stolley, *East from Eden*, 243–262.

59. Tirsch assembled these into the so-called *Codex Pictoricus Mexicanus* located in the Czech National Library; Národní knihovna České republiky, Oddělení rukopisů a vzácných tisků, Sign. XVI B 18.

60. Beales, *Joseph II*, 1:460–464.

61. Lüsebrink, *Between Ethnology and Romantic Discourse*, 129.

62. Dobrizhoffer, *An Account of the Abipones*, 1:iii–iv.

63. Dobrizhoffer, *Historia de Abiponibus equestri*; Dobrizhoffer, *Geschichte der Abiponer*.

64. Dobrizhofer, *An Account of the Abipones*, 1:v.

65. De Asúa, Science in the Vanished Arcadia, 32; Altic, "Post-Expulsion Jesuit Cartography," 108; Borja González, Jesuitische Berichterstattung, 232–236.

66. Shore, Jesuits and the Politics of Religious Pluralism, 163–174.

67. Fertig, *Transatlantic Migration*, 195.

68. Fertig enumerated 130,000 between 1683 and 1800, see his Lokales Leben, atlantische Welt, 79.

69. Melton, Religion, Community, and Slavery; Gillespie and Beachy, Pious Pursuits; Engel, Religion and Profit.

70. O'Reilly, *Salzburg to the New World*, 120; Thirring, "Die Auswanderung aus Ungarn," 1–29.

71. Bartlett and Mitchell, *State-Sponsored Immigration*, 91–114; O'Reilly, *Agenten, Werbung und Reisemodalitäten*, 109–120.

72. O'Reilly, Competition for Colonists: Europe and Her Colonies in the Eighteenth Century (University of Galway, n.d.), 6; https://www.histecon.magd.cam.ac.uk/docs/o'reilly_competition_octo4.pdf [December 2019].

73. Diekmann, Lockruf der Neuen Welt; Görisch, Information zwischen Werbung und Warnung.

74. O'Reilly, "Competition for Colonists," 14.

75. O'Reilly, *Salzburg to the New World*, 119.

76. Schelbert and Rappolt, Alles ist ganz anders hier; O'Reilly, *Bridging the Atlantic*, 25–44.

77. Anon., Der Steyerische Robinson, ii–iii.

78. Gerbi, The Dispute of the New World, 3–34 and 52–156.

79. Frisi, *La colombiade*, vii–xx.

80. Quoted and translated by Gerbi, The Dispute of the New World, 110.

81. Carli, *Le lettere americane:*, 2nd ed., 1:197–198, 207; 2:16.

82. Miller, "Some Early Italian Histories," 103–106. German translation appeared in 1785, French in 1788.

83. Benjamin Franklin to Lorenzo Manini, 19 November 1784. The original was published by Manini in the *Gazzetta di Cremona* (1785: no. 72). A transcription appears in Pace, Benjamin Franklin and Italy, 395–396. For the dedication, see APS, Franklin Papers Series, Mss.B.F.85, 7, XXX, 9, Lorenzo Manini to Benjamin Franklin, 9 October 1783.

84. Quoted in Del Negro, Il mito americano, 178–179.

85. *Taube, Friedrich Wilhelm von*, Allgemeine Deutsche Biographie, 37:420–422. The earliest origin for this seems to be a eulogy by Anton Friedrich Büsching, see his Beiträge, 4:221.

86. Taube, Thoughts. Mentioned in, for example, Baur, Kleines historisch-literarisches Wörterbuch, 2:731.

87. Entry under "Taube" in Aikin and Johnston, *General Biography*, 330.

88. *Taube*, Allgemeine Deutsche Biographie, 37:420–422.

89. Taube, Historische und politische Abschilderung.

90. Ibid., 261.

91. Ibid., 261.

92. Ibid., 263.

93. Ibid., 266–267.

94. Ibid., 268.

95. Taube, Geschichte der Engländischen Handelschaft. The appended essay was titled: *Mit einer zuverlässigen Nachricht von den wahren Ursachen des jetzigen Krieges in Nordamerika*.

96. Ibid., iii.

97. Taube, Abschilderung der Engländischen Manufacturen; Taube, Historische und politische Abschilderung der Engländischen Manufacturen.

98. "Gewältig Veränderungen" in Taube, Abschilderung der Engländischen Manufacturen, 2:i.

99. Ibid., s.n. (final page of the preface).

100. Bowd, "Useful Knowledge or Polite Learning?," 190.

101. Zinzendorf, entry dated 13 December 1778 in Klingenstein et al, Zwischen Wien und Triest, 2:318.

102. Entry dated 12 December 1778, in ibid., 2:317.

103. Entry dated 8 January 1779, in ibid., 2:346; entry dated 20th December 1780, in ibid., 2:776.

104. "Serionne, Joseph Accarias" in Biographisches Lexikon des Kaiserthums Österreich, 34:148; Accarias, "Un publiciste dauphinois."

105. Astigarraga, *Spain and the Economic Work*, 607–634; Astigarraga, "L'Économie Espagnole en Débat," 357–389.

106. Hasquin, Population, commerce et religion, 155–167.

107. Astigarraga, *Spain and the Economic Work*, 615.

108. Sérionne, *Les intérêts des nations*; Sérionne, *La richesse*.

109. Sérionne, *La richesse*, 51–52.

110. Ibid., 93.

111. Ibid., 94.

112. Ibid., 94.

113. Ibid., 94.

114. Lindemayr, *Der engländische Patriotismus*. I am grateful to Dr. Thomas Stockinger for pointing me to this play.

115. Neuhuber, *Maurus Lindemayr*, 1:353 and 355. All quotations come from this edition.

116. Ibid., 354.

117. Ibid., 359.

118. Ibid., 360.

119. Ibid., 375.

120. Ibid., 375.

121. Lindner, "Sozial-, Gesellschafts- und Herrschafts-kritische Reflexionen," 195–268; Senigl, *Haydn und seine Beziehungen zum Kloster Lambach*, 145–148.

122. [Joseph Marius Babo], *Das Winterquartier in Amerika*. The play was written by Babo in Mannheim and published by him in Vienna in 1778 but premiered there in 1786, see Adam, Germany and the Americas, 1044–45.

123. "Die Pantomime; betitelt: Arlequin - Der Neue Abgott in Amerika," attached to Kurz's *Der Krumme Teufel* ([Vienna], 1759), 1–13.

124. Ibid., 12–13.

125. Tar, Deutschsprachiges Kindertheater, 35–36; Scherl and Rudin, *Joseph Anton Stranitzky*, 666–670.

126. Buch, Magic Flutes and Enchanted Forests, 254 and 382.

127. Betzwieser, *Kurz-Bernardon, Haydn und die theatrale Anderwelt*, 193–208.

128. Known as Friedrich Augustus Brischdower (Bridgetower), who claimed to be from a line of African princes and whose son George Bridgetower became a famous violinist. See Wright, "George Polgreen Bridgetower," 65–82; Thurman, "*Black Musicians in Germany and Austria*," 37; Corfield, *Bridgetower, George (1780-1860)*, 1:85–86. For Haydn's tutoring of George, see Walter, Haydn in seiner Zeit, 313.

129. Detering, Kolumbus, Cortés, Montezuma; Winkler, "Alzire, ou les Américains' de Voltaire," 47–62; Rice, *Montezuma at Eszterház*, 231–242.

130. Sisman, "Haydn's Theater Symphonies," 332–340.

131. Hörwarthner, "*Haydn's Library*: 415 and 442n178; Van Boer, *Undermining Independence*, 39–60.

132. Melton, *From Courts to Consumers*, 438–460.

133. Polzonetti, "Quakers and Cowboys," 28.

134. Chinatti, "Calzabigi's Vision of an Enlightened America," 135–142.

135. Chinatti provides this synopsis in ibid., 136–137.

136. Polzonetti, Italian Opera, 236.

137. Ibid., 242–243

138. Quoted in Stefania Buccini, Americas in Italian Literature, 115.

139. Sauer, "Habsburg Colonial," 5–23.

140. Hunter, *Bourgeois Values*, 171–172; Polzonetti, Italian Opera, 234n11.

141. Polzonetti, Italian Opera, 247–250.

142. Ibid., 255–256.

143. Ibid., 326.

Chapter 2

1. Sir Robert Murray Keith to Thomas Bradshaw, 15 September 1774, in Smyth, Memoirs and Correspondence, 1:474–482.

2. William Lee to Edmund Jennings, 24 June 1778, in Ford, *Letters of William Lee* [LWL], 2:454–455.

3. Press, "The Habsburg Court," 23–45.

4. Cerman, Habsburgischer Adel und Aufklärung, 9.

5. APS, Franklin Papers Series, Mss.B.F.85, XIV, 169, Bek to Franklin, 10 June 1779. For Karl von Zinzendorf's reading of Robertson's *History of America*, see HHStA, Kabinettsarchiv [KA], Kabinettskanzlei [KK], Nachlass Zinzendorf [NZ], Tagebücher Zinzendorf [TZ], Bd. 30, 15 January 1785, fol. 8 and 5 October 1785, fol. 178. For Zinzendorf's meeting in Edinburgh, see Rill, "*Die Reise des Grafen Karl von Zinzendorf*," 14–31.

6. Dickson, "Count Karl von Zinzendorf's 'New Accountancy,'" 26. N.B. Karl's half-brother Ludwig von Zinzendorf was more likely the author of the recommendation.

7. The catalogue was of Louis César de La Baume Le Blanc, the duc de Vallière's library, see Wolf and Hayes, The Library of Benjamin Franklin, entry 1941, 479. For Strattmann, see Hüttel-Herbert and Reiterrer, *Strattmann, Paul (1755–1821), Bibliothekar und Geistlicher*, Österreichisches Biographisches Lexicon, 13:370.

8. APS, Franklin Papers Series, Mss.B.F.85, XXXI, 104, Strattmann to Franklin, 5 March 1783; Strattmann to Franklin, 15 March 1784, *The Papers of Benjamin Franklin* [PBF], 42:20.

9. APS, Franklin Papers Series, Mss.B.F.85, XXXIV, 184, Birkenstock to Franklin, 29 December 1786; Franklin to Birkenstock, 15 February 1788, unpublished, "Franklin Papers project at Yale University."

10. APS, Franklin Papers Series, Mss.B.F.85, XXXIV, 184, Birkenstock to Franklin, 29 December 1786.

11. Both Birkenstock and Strattmann were members of the censorship committee during the American Revolution: Birkenstock from 1774 and Strattmann from 1782.

12. Klingenstein, Staatsverwaltung und kirchliche Autorität, 161–178.

13. Sashegyi, Zensur und Geistesfreiheit; Bodi, Tauwetter in Wien.

14. Bachleitner, Die literarische Zensur in Österreich, 73–75.

15. Ibid., 78 and 83.

16. Figures obtained from the "Verdängt, verpönt—vergessen?" database.

17. For a full breakdown and discussion, see Singerton, "Knowledge of and Sympathy for the American Cause," 138–141.

18. Puttemans, La censure dans les pays-bas autrichiens; Delpiano, Il governo della lettura; Syrovy, *Die italienischsprachigen Gebiete*, 218–220.

19. For censorship ducking by the nobility, see Gates, "Aristocratic Libraries," 23–41.

20. Sierens, "*De Amerikaanse Revolutie in de Gazette van Gend*"; Lapeera, "*De Amerikaanse Revolutie in enkele Brusselse kranten*"; Köpf, "*Wir Haben Nachricht aus Amerika*"; Vincenzi, "*La rivoluzione Americana*"; Singerton, "Knowledge of and Sympathy for the American Cause," 130–137.

21. Köpf, "Daß alle Menschen gleich erschaffen sind," 183–196.

22. Wienerisches Diarium [WD], 3 April 1779.

23. WD, 24 December 1774, Anhang, 9–11.

24. Köpf, *"Wir haben Nachricht aus Amerika,"* 27.

25. WD, 31 August and 11 September 1776. The *Nuove di diverse corti e paesi* in Lombardy published it in full because the newspaper technically fell under Swiss jurisdiction as it was based in Lugano. The full print appeared also in Florence and Milan in the *Notizie del Mondo* and *Gazzetta Universale,* 3 September 1776 and *Gazzetta di Milano,* 11 September 1776 respectively. Anna Vincenzi suggests the Grand Duke of Tuscany's relaxed governance permitted it in Tuscany, see her "The Many American Revolutions of Italian Public Opinion" (Paper present at the conference on "Propaganda, Persuasion, the Press and the American Revolution, 1763-1783," organized by the University of Hong Kong and the Thomas Jefferson Foundation, Hong Kong, China, April 2016). I am grateful to Dr. Vincenzi for sharing this paper with me.

26. *Magyar Hírmondó,* 31 January 1781.

27. WD, 20 December 1777.

28. Benna, Contemporary Austrian Views, 36–37.

29. Nowak, "Christian August Graf Seilern," 51–99.

30. HHStA, StK, Provinzen, Niederösterreich, K. 1, Report dated 22 Christmonats [December] 1777, fols. 162–167.

31. Landriani to Franklin, 9 November 1783, PBF, 41, 187–189.

32. Cerman, Habsburgischer Adel und Aufklärung, 385–446.

33. APS, Franklin Papers Series, Mss.B.F.85, XXXIII, 26, Windischgrätz to Franklin, 9 February 1785. A copy can be found in the Czech State Archives at Plzeň, see SOA v Plzni, Rodinny Archiv Windischgrätzu, No. 931/16.

34. APS, Franklin Papers Series, Mss.B.F.85, XXXIII, 68, Windischgrätz to Franklin, 1 April 1785. Windischgrätz had made a similar request in 1783: APS, Franklin Papers Series, Mss.B.F.85, XLIII, 245, Windischgrätz to Franklin, 10 August [1783].

35. APS, Franklin Papers Series, Mss.B.F.85, XXXIII, 121, Windischgrätz to Franklin, 1 June 1785.

36. Ondo-Grečenková, *Le réseau épistolaire,* 289–305.

37. Franklin to Ingenhousz, 29 April 1785 in Sparks, *The Works of Benjamin Franklin,* 6:533.

38. Beales, Joseph II, 2:579.

39. Windisch-Graetz, *De l'âme,* 80–85; Cerman, *Moral Anthropology,* 182.

40. Cerman, ibid., 188–189.

41. Beales, Joseph II, 2:579.

42. The "five dames" were: 1. Princess Maria Josepha Clary-Aldringen; 2. Princess Maria Sidonia Kinsky; 3. Princess Marie Leopoldine von Liechtenstein; 4. Countess (Princess after 1794) Marie Leopoldine von Kaunitz-Rietberg; and 5. Princess Eleonore von Liechtenstein. The latter two were sisters of Oettingen-Spielberg originally and the two Liechtensteins (3 and 5) were sisters-in-law. Joseph II and his two close friends, Field Marshall Count Franz Moritz Lacy and Count Franz Xavier Orsini-Rosenberg were frequent attendees from 1769 onwards. See Gates-Coon, The Charmed Circle.

43. Beales, Joseph II, 1:323.

44. HHStA, KA, KK NZ, TZ, Bd. 30, 18 December 1785, fols. 214–215.

45. Beales, Joseph II, 1:324.

46. Ibid., 326; Wolf, Liechtenstein, 42–43.

47. Gates-Coon, The Charmed Circle, 194. For the general view of the *Dames* on Joseph's foreign policy, see ibid., 175–200.

48. Ibid., 282–283.

49. Ingenhousz relayed the whole affair to Franklin in a letter dated 15 August 1783, PBF, 40:475–484. On sequestration of the family's property, see Catanzariti, *The Papers of Robert Morris*, 7:549; Jenkins, *The Family of William Penn*, 425.

50. APS, Franklin Papers Series, Mss.B.F.85, 6, XXVI, 70, Juliana Penn to Franklin, 23 November 1782. She also wrote to John Jay at the same time as Morris and also to John Adams on 24 December 1782, so it seems likely that the Liechtensteins were part of the same campaign.

51. Klingenstein et al, Zwischen Wien und Triest, 2:169.

52. See, for example, British Library [BL], Add. MS 35525, fols. 301-302, Pergen to Keith, 25 June 1782.

53. Gates-Coon, "Anglophone Households," 133–134.

54. Wraxall, Memoirs, 2:241.

55. Diary entries 5 December 1777 and 17 March 1778 in Klingenstein et al, Zwischen Wien und Triest, 2:76 and 160.

56. Ibid., 26 January 1778, 2:127.

57. Thun to Hugh Elliot, 24 August 1775 in Minto, A Memoir 47–48.

58. This was the unpublished and privately written *Memoires de Romina Grobis* (Memoirs of a Fat Cat), a fictional travel account critical of America written by Princess Alexandrine von Dietrichstein (née Shuvalov) in around 1830. Musilová, "*"Gâtée par le Monde" Literárni dílo Kněžny Alexandry z Dietrichsteina,"* 63n339; for a transcription see ibid., 132-138. The original manuscript is to be found in Moravsky Zemsky Archiv Brno, Rodinny Archiv Dietrichsteinů, K. 584, Signatur 1264, Inv. C. 2455, 'Literárni tvorba Alexandry z Dietrichsteina.' I am grateful to Dr. Ivo Cerman for this example.

59. Klingenstein et al, Zwischen Wien und Triest, 3:822–823, 16 February 1781. The discussion might have had an added effect as two months later, Auersperg bought an American atlas, see entry dated 28 April 1781, in ibid., 3:637.

60. For Seilern's role, see HHStA, StK, Provinzen, Niederösterreich, K. 1, fols. 162–167.

61. Klingenstein et al, Zwischen Wien und Triest, 1: 13–22.

62. "Fact-finding missions" as Elisabeth Fattinger has called them; see her *Conflicting Identities in an Age of Transition*, 113.

63. HHStA, KA, KK, NZ, T, Bd. 13, fol. 110r; Gürtler, "Impressionen einer Reise," 333–370.

64. HHStA, StK, England, Varia, K. 11, *Observations*, "Colonies Angloises dans l'Amerique Septentrionale et dans l'Archipel des Antilles," fols. 639–733.

65. Klingenstein et al, Zwischen Wien und Triest, 2:155, 200, and 206.

66. HHStA, KA, KK, NZ, TZ, Bd. 39, 18 October 1794, fols. 260v-261; Bd. 41, 22 October 1796, fol. 287v.

67. Klingenstein et al, Zwischen Wien und Triest, 3:599, 11 February 1780.

68. Ibid., 2:288, 21 October 1778.

69. For example "Les consuls de Venise, de France, d'Angleterre dont le dernier me conta beaucoup de l'Amérique, des anciens troubles à Boston." Ibid., 2:125, 1 January 1777.

70. For his meetings with the British ambassador about the Revolution, see 3 and 21 April 1778 in ibid., 2:171 and 184.

71. HHStA, KA, KK, NZ, TZ, Bd. 20, 3 October 1775, fol. 131; Ibid., Bd. 30, 15 January 1785, fol. 8 and 5 October 1785, fol. 178.

72. Klingenstein et al, Zwischen Wien und Triest, 2:83, 18 December 1777.

73. This was a circle of twelve gentlemen clustered around Thomas Bradshaw. The twelve were all political-military types who occupied prominent positions in government, banks, and the military. They wrote in a candid, often jocular manner to each other. Keith's closest friend within the group was Anthony Chamier, the under-secretary to the southern secretary of state and brother of Daniel Chamier, the commissary general to the army in North America, see Bradshaw, Thomas Bradshaw, 91–92.

74. Keith to Thomas Bradshaw, 16 September 1774 in Smyth, *Memoirs*, 1:476–477.

75. Keith to Anthony Chamier, 21 January 1775, ibid., 2:35–36.

76. Keith to Chamier, 17 December 1774, ibid., 2:34; Keith to Bradshaw, 16 September 1774, ibid., 1:476–477; Keith to Chamier, ibid., 21 January 1775, 2:35–36.

77. BL, Add. MS. 35511, fols. 248-249, Morton Eden to Keith, 5 April 1777; BL, Add. MS. 35511, fols. 162–163, George Cressener to Keith, 31 January 1777.

78. BL, Add. MS. 35504, fol. 111 and Add. MS. 35506, fol. 141.

79. National Records of Scotland [NRS], Papers of the Scot Family of Gala, Family Letters of Sir Henry Hay-Makdougall and Henry Hay-Makdougall 1770-1777, GD/477/407/Nos. 12, 13, 15, 14, 16, 17 and 18, Sir Henry Hay-Macdougal to Henry Hay-Macdougal, 1 November 1776, 18 November 1776, 2 December 1776, 16 December 1776, 30 December 1776, 6 January 1777, 20 January 1777 respectively; BL, Add. MS. 35512, fols. 77, 152, Sir Henry Hay-Macdougal to Keith, various. The relative was a Sandy Campbell. "You made me truly happy with good accounts of Sandy Campbell." in NRS, Papers of the Scot Family of Gala, Family Letters of Sir Henry Hay-Makdougall and Henry Hay-Makdougall 1770-1777, GD/477/407/No. 29, Henry Hay-Macdougal to Sir Henry Hay-Macdougal, 5 October 1776.

80. NRS, Papers of the Scot Family of Gala, Family Letters of Sir Henry Hay-Makdougall and Henry Hay-Makdougall 1770-1777, GD/477/407/No. 33, Henry Hay-Macdougal to Sir Henry Hay-Macdougal, 7 December 1776. Further requests in NRS, ibid., GD/477/407/Nos. 30, 31 and 35, Henry Hay-Macdougal to Sir Henry Hay-Macdougal, 6 November 1776, 16 November 1776, and 11 January 1777.

81. Keith to Bradshaw, 29 August 1774 in Smyth, *Memoirs*, 1:474.

82. Keith to Bradshaw, 5 March 1774, ibid., 1:461. Original emphasis.

83. Keith to Andrew Drummond, 14 October 1780, ibid., 2:109–110.

84. Keith to Bradshaw, 16 September 1774, ibid., 1:476–477.

85. Zinzendorf acts as a good example here since he constantly lists news of America from liberal papers such as the *Gazette de Leyde*.

86. NRS, Papers of the Campbell Family (Earls of Breadalbane), GD/112/74/3/13, John Campbell (future fourth Earl of Breadalbane and Holland) to Elizabeth Campbell, 12 December 1781.

87. NRS, Papers of the Campbell Family (Earls of Breadalbane), GD/112/39/335/4, Colin Campbell to Elizabeth Campbell, 18 March 1782. Spanish forces recaptured the island of Menorca in January 1782.

88. Keith to Anne Murray Keith of Murrayhall, 1 December 1780, in Smyth, *Memoirs*, 2:112.

89. Ibid., 112.

90. Jan Ingenhousz to Franklin, 4 and 29 January 1777, PBF, 23:115–117 and 255-257; Lewin, *Französische Botschaft*, 5-6.

91. Jean-François Georgel to Franklin, 9 April 1777, PBF, 23:574–575.

92. APS, Franklin Papers Series, Mss.B.F.85, XLIX, 21, Hennessienne to Franklin, 28 September 1778.

93. Ingenhousz to Franklin, 4 January 1777, PBF, 23:115–117.

94. Szabo, Kaunitz and Enlightened Absolutism, 37.

95. Dickson, Finance and Government, 1:255; Szabo, Kaunitz and Enlightened Absolutism, i; Beales, Joseph II, 1:92–93. Szabo has since considered this designation more thoroughly in Szabo, *Favorit, Premierminister oder "drittes Staatsoberhaupt"?*, 345-362.

96. Szabo, ibid., 33; Kroupa, *Fürst Wenzel Anton Kaunitz-Rietberg*, 360-382; Lenderova, "Correspondance de Mme Geoffrin," 309–316.

97. Benna, Contemporary Austrian Views, 6

98. Beer, *Joseph II., Leopold II. und Kaunitz*, passim; Brunner, Correspondances intimes de l'empereur Joseph II, passim.

99. For example "die amerikanischen Insurgenten," in HHStA, StK, Frankreich, Berichte, K. 155, Mercy-d'Argenteau to Kaunitz, 18 December 1776, fol. 123 and HHStA, StK, Frankreich, Weisungen, K. 157, Kaunitz to Mercy-d'Argenteau, 31 July 1777. For the use of the term, see Roider, "William Lee," 166; Benna, Contemporary Austrian Views, 49.

100. Whereas Kaunitz maintained his terminology until the end of the war, Mercy-d'Argenteau and Count Georg Adam von Starhemberg, for example, called them "Americans" from around 1781 onwards.

101. TNA, SP80/218, Keith to Lord Suffolk, 30 December 1776.

102. HHStA, StK, Frankreich, Weisungen, K. 157, Kaunitz to Mercy-d'Argenteau, 31 July 1777.

103. Similar to Kaunitz's reaction to the French Revolution, see Hochedlinger, *Dass Aufklärung das sicherste Mittel ist*, 62–79.

104. HHStA, StK, Provinzen, Niederösterreich, K. 1, Report of 22 Christmonats [December] 1777, fols. 162–167.

105. Maria Theresa to Marie Antoinette, 3 February 777 in Arneth and Geoffroy, *Correspondence secrète*, 3:16–17.

106. Ingenhousz to Franklin, 14 December 1777, PBF, 25:286–290.

107. Ingenhousz to Baron von Pichler, 29 December 1777, PBF, 25:369–372.

108. Ibid., 25: 370.

109. Ingenhousz to Franklin, 29 November 1782, PBF, 38:364–366.

110. Ingenhousz to Franklin, 20 August 1782, PBF, 38:25–28.

111. Ingenhousz to Franklin, 4 January 1777, PBF, 23:115–117.

112. For the term "revolutionary emperor," see Szabo, "Changing Perspectives," 111–138.

113. Archivio di Stato di Firenze [ASF], Affari di Stato [AdS], Affari Esteri, C. 2335, esp. reports dated 16 and 23 December 1776.

114. Niccoli to Franklin with note in Franklin's hand, 26 May 1777, PBF, 24:84–85.

115. Franklin to Ingenhousz, 26 April 1777, PBF, 23:613–614.

116. Franklin to Ingenhousz, 29 April 1785, unpublished, "Franklin Papers Project at Yale University."

117. See note in Franklin's hand affixed to Niccoli to Franklin, 26 May 1777, PBF, 24:84–85.

118. HHStA, Hausarchiv, Hofreisen, K. 9, Konv. 2-1, Journal der Reise Kaiser Josephs II. nach Paris, entry dated 26 May 1777.

119. "Mercredi 28. Sa Majesté étant allé le matin faire quelques visites de congé, je fus déjeuné chez l'Abbé Nicoli où j'avais donné rendez-vous au docteur Francklin." In Philipp Cobenzl, *Journal de mon voyage en France avec l'Empereur Joseph en 1777* (1777). The manuscript is in the possession of the antiquarian specialist Steffan Völkel to whom I am grateful for sharing with me the extract on Cobenzl and Franklin's meeting. I provide the exact quotation here since it may not be readily available to other researchers.

120. Ingenhousz to Franklin, 28 June 1777, PBF, 24:239–242.

121. Playfair, *Joseph and Benjamin*, advertisement, s.n.

122. For Playfair's publishing presence in Paris in the 1790s, see New York Public Library, T. B. Myers Collection, #1435, fol. 1, Stephen Rochefontaine to Ben Walker, 28 January 1792; Furstenberg, *When the United States Spoke French*, 251–252.

123. David R. Bellhouse, The Flawed Genius of William Playfair: The Story of the Father of Statistical Graphics, (in press, 2021), Chp. IV "Some Politics and Political Writing," s.n. I am grateful to Dr. Bellhouse for sharing his forthcoming work with me.

124. Dippel contends this first came from a private letter sent in the mid-1790s—see Dippel, Germany and the American Revolution, 63n75—this most certainly arose from Joseph's 1777 trip, see Duval-Pyrau, Journal et Anecdotes and Beales, Joseph II, 1:384n94.

125. To give but a few examples: Williams, Europe and America in 1821, 1:98; Everett, *An Address*, 34; Craik and MacFarlane, *Pictorial History*, 1:473; Bent, *Short Sayings*, 314–315. Most recently by Fairlie, "The Shot Heard Round the World."

126. Mercy-d'Argenteau to Maria Theresa, 15 July 1777 in Arneth and Geffroy, *Correspondance Secrète*, 3:95.

127. Archivio di Stato di Milano [ASM], Archivio Belgiojoso [AB], C. 571, no. 13, Joseph II to Belgiojoso, 15 April 1782.

128. ASM, AB, C. 571, no. 17, Joseph II to Belgiojoso, 14 August 1782.

129. Joseph II to Pietro Leopoldo [Leopold], 14 September 1780 in Arneth, *Maria Theresia und Joseph II.*, 3:312.

130. Joseph to Catherine, 13 November 1780, in Arneth, *Joseph II. and Katharina von Russland*, 16.

131. Joseph to Catherine, 13 November 1780, ibid., 16; Joseph to Catherine, 10 January 1781, ibid., 34–35.

132. Joseph to Catherine, 13 November 1780, ibid., 16.

133. I adopt the Italian spelling of his name here until his ascension, where I will refer to him as Leopold II.

134. Marraro, "Mazzei's Correspondence," no. 3, 275–301; ibid., no. 4, 361–380.

135. Pace, Franklin and Italy, 116.

136. Huber-Frischeis, Knieling, and Valenta, Die Privatbibliothek, 48–49.

137. Wandruszka, Leopold II, 1:346; Balázs, *Pierre-Léopold et la Hongrie*, 151. Pietro Leopoldo penned his thoughts in a famous text now edited, see Beales and Pasta, Relazione.

138. HHStA, Hausarchiv, Sammelbände, K. 12, Konv. 12, fols. 267–301.

139. Wandruszka, Leopold II, 1:371 and 375; Cochrane, "Le riforme leopoldine," 199–215; Boutier, "Les imprimés," 423–468.

140. HHStA, Hausarchiv, Sammelbände, K. 12, Konv. 12, fols. 272–273; Gabrieli, *The Impact of American Political Ideas*, 197.

141. *Gazzetta Universale: O Sieno, Notizie Istoriche, Politiche, di Scienze, Arti, Agricoltura* (Florence) and *Notizie del Mondo* (Florence), both 14 September 1776. See Gabrieli, *The Impact of American Political Ideas*, 196; Armitage, The Declaration of Independence, 70.

142. Article 1 of Declaration of Rights, 12 June 1776. For the Virginian influence, see Palmer, Democratic Revolution, 1:386; Noether, "As Others Saw Us," 129–134; Zimmerman, Das Verfassungsprojekt; and Billas, American Constitutionalism, 80, 100–102, and 417.

143. In contrast to the works cited above, only a few historians have correctly identified that it is indeed the Pennsylvanian Constitution of 1776 which influenced Pietro Leopoldo's constitutional project: Wandruszka, Leopold II, 1:372–373; Schuener, *Constitutional Traditions*; Fichtner, *Viennese Perspectives*, 19–32; Davis, "Observations," 373–380. The original manuscripts in the HHStA confirm the Pennsylvania constitution was Pietro Leopoldo's primary object of fascination; see HHStA, Hausarchiv, Sammelbände, K. 13, no. 10, "Observations sur les Constitution de la République de Pennsylvanie.'

144. HHStA, Hausarchiv, Sammelbände, K. 13, nos. 10 and 11. It is conceivable that he had access to a printed edition of Rochefoucauld's translation: "Constitution de la Republique de Pensylvanie, telle qu'elle a ete etablie par la Commission generale extraordinaire, elue cet effet, & assemblee a Philadelphie, dans ses seances, commencees

le 15 Juillet 1776, & continuees par des ajournemens successifs, jusqu'au 28 Septembre suivant," in Rochefoucauld, Affaires de l'Angleterre.

145. HHStA, Hausarchiv, Sammelbände, K. 13, no. 10, fol. 1; translation provided by Davis, "Observations," 377.

146. HHStA, Hausarchiv, Sammelbände, K. 13, no. 10, fol. 1.

147. Their exchanges are in HHStA, Hausarchiv, Sammelbände, K. 12, nos. 13–21.

148. See Gianni's *Memorie sulla Constituzione di governo immaginata del granduca Pietro Leopoldo de servire all'istoria del suo regno in Toscana* in ASF, Carte Gianni, N. 221. Gianni later published his remarks as *La Constituzione Toscana imaginata dal Granduca Pietro Leopoldo: memoria del Senatore F. M. Gianni scritta nell'anno 1805* (Siena, 1805).

149. *Relazioni sul Governo della Toscana* (1770) as quoted in Becattini, "La lezione," 105.

150. HHStA, Hausarchiv, Sammelbände, K. 13, no. 10.

151. In 1784, Joseph planned to abrogate the Tuscan secundogeniture, ultimately uniting it with the Monarchy, forcing Pietro Leopoldo to see the futility of his plans until his brother's declining health, and heirless condition, made imminent imperial succession revitalise his constitutional ambitions between 1787 and 1789. See Beales, Joseph II, 2:355–359.

152. Pasta, *The Enlightenment at Work*, 41–62.

Chapter 3

1. Universitätsarchiv Wien, S. 94.9, Wiesner's Note to the k.k. Ministerium für Kultur und Unterricht, 11 July 1903.

2. Most notably Palmer, Democratic Revolution, 2:135–174; Venturi, End of the Old Regime, 2:605–763; Israel, The Expanding Blaze, 606–609.

3. Dippel, Germany and the American Revolution, 62 and 223. An earlier version of this section appears in my "A Revolution in Ink," 91–113. Two more letters have since come to light after that publication but these have not materially changed my analysis. (Both letters belonged to Count Joseph O'Donnell).

4. Franklin received a total of 37 letters from 22 Prussian individuals. My estimations come from the overview catalogue of the Franklin Papers based at Yale University.

5. There were undoubtedly lost letters which are mentioned in other letters. For a fuller breakdown of this correspondence, see my "A Revolution in Ink," 91–113.

6. Caroline Winterer, "Where is America in the Republic of Letters?" 608.

7. Polišenský, Benjamin Franklin, američtí Moravané a čeští čtenáři, 315–322; Baťha, Fragment literární, 1–2; Singerton, "Science, Revolution, and Monarchy," 145–150.

8. See my "A Revolution in Ink," 117–118: APS, Franklin Papers, Mss.B.F.85, 7, XXIX, 68, Steinský to Franklin, 3 August 1783.

9. APS, Franklin Papers, Mss.B.F.85, 4, XXXVI, 142, Steinský to Franklin, 17 June 1789; Literární Archiv Památníku národního písemnictví [LA PNP], Fonds F. A. Steinského 1760–1811, 15/5, Franklin to Steinský, 23 November 1782; Korty, "Franklin's World of Books," 310.

10. *Transactions of the American Philosophical Society*, 137.

11. Landriani to Franklin, 9 November 1783, PBF, 41:187–198; Pace, Franklin and Italy, 39–41.

12. APS, Franklin Papers, Mss.B.F.85, 8, XL, 128, Nekrep to Franklin, 12 June 1784.

13. APS, Franklin Papers, Mss.B.F.85, 7, XXVII, 190, Anthony Mikoviny to Franklin, 13 March 1783; APS, Franklin Papers, Mss.B.F.85, 2, LIX, 83, Baron Carl von Emerich to Franklin, 4 December 1777; APS, Franklin Papers, Mss.B.F.85, 5, XIX, 51, Baron Philippe-Charles de Pfortzheim to Franklin, 2 August 1780; APS, Franklin Papers, Mss.B.F.85, 2, LXII, 106, Rihm to Franklin, 19 December 1777; Guillaume, Régiment de Clerfayt, 40.

14. APS, Franklin Papers, Mss.B.F.85, 2, LXX, 88, Kováts to Franklin, 13 January 1777.

15. Gaisberg and Stahel to Franklin, 29 March 1780, unpublished, "Franklin Papers Series at Yale."

16. APS, Franklin Papers, Mss.B.F.85, 2, VII, 189, Comte Leopold Barbo to Franklin, 25 December 1777.

17. APS, Franklin Papers, Mss.B.F.85, 4, XIV, 151, Hyppolite de Verité to Franklin, 2 June 1779.

18. Oberleithner to Franklin, 9 January 1778, PBF, 25.460–461.

19. APS, Franklin Papers, Mss.B.F.85, 7, XXX, 83, Franz Rudolph von Großing (also Grossinger) to Franklin, 10 November 1783.

20. APS, Franklin Papers, Mss.B.F.85, 7, LIX, 50, Gräventiz to Franklin, 26 Jun 1783. He had joined the Aulic Council in November, 1772, see HHStA, Obersthofmeister-amt, Ältere Zeremonialakten, K. 86, Konv. 20, nos. 3 and 4. He retired from there in 1785, see HHStA, RHR, RK, Verfassungsakten, K. 27-28-43.

21. APS, Franklin Papers, Mss.B.F.85, 7, XXVII, 68, *Veuve d'Aubremé & Fils* to Franklin, 31 January 1783; Ibid., 106, *De Vinck et Compagnie* to Franklin, 13 February 1783; *Antonio Salucci & Sons* to Franklin, 5 February 1779, 7 March 1783, PBF, 39:302–303; APS, Franklin Papers, Mss.B.F.85, 7, XXVII, 65, Wets to Franklin.

22. APS, Franklin Papers, Mss.B.F.85, 2, VII, 169, Dujardin to Franklin, 14 March 1778.

23. Ingenhousz to Franklin, 15 November 1776, PBF, 23:7–12.

24. Ingenhousz to Franklin, 23 May 1781, PBF, 35:97–100.

25. Ingenhousz to Franklin, 12 June 1782, PBF, 37:467–69.

26. Ingenhousz to Franklin, 28 June 1777, PBF, 24:239–42.

27. Ingenhousz to Franklin, 18 October 1777, PBF, 25:85–86.

28. Ingenhousz to Franklin, 2 January 1784, PBF, 41:401–404.

29. Ingenhousz to Franklin, 15 November 1776, PBF, 23:7–12.

30. Ingenhousz to Franklin, 1 September 1783, PBF, 40:562–563.

31. Ingenhousz to Franklin, 15 November 1776, PBF, 23:7–12.

32. Ingenhousz to Franklin, 28 June 1777, PBF, 24:239–242.

33. BL, Add. MS. 35511, Hardwicke Papers, Sir Robert Murray Keith Personal Correspondence, fol. 294, Ingenhousz to Keith, [28 June 1777]. The letter is undated in the original, but Ingenhousz listed it as 28 June 1777 in his personal letterbook held at the Koninklijke Bibliotheek in The Hague. I have relied here upon the microfilm duplicate at the APS, Philadelphia, Mss.H.S. Film.23.

34. Ingenhousz to Franklin, 7 April 1781, PBF, 34:521–523.

35. Skemp, Making of a Patriot.

36. HHStA, Handschriftensammlung, HS-Weiß, No. 443, Remarques sur les affaires présente de l'Amérique Septentrionale, [s.d.] September 1777.

37. HHStA, KA, KK, NZ, TZ, Bd. 20, 3 October 1775, fol. 131.

38. Ingenhousz to Franklin, 14 December 1777, PBF, 25:287.

39. Österreichische Nationalbibliothek [ÖNB], Handschriften, 6/97-3, "Bericht an Maria Theresa über zwei Briefe Franklins, 18 Mai 1777"; a French translation of Franklin's *Comparison of Great Britain and the United States in Regard to the Basis of Credit in the Countries*, (ca. 1777). See also Dippel, Germany and the American Revolution, 62.

40. Cauffman referenced in Hennesey, American Catholics, 60.

41. Rodenbough, Autumn Leaves, 17.

42. Willcox, "Some Notes," 83–84 and Willcox, "Historical Sketches," 422–427.

43. Joseph Cauffman to Joseph T. Cauffman, 28 March 1775 in Rodenbough, Autumn Leaves, 26.

44. There was contact between the Cauffman family and Bishop Carroll later, see University Archives of Notre Dame, Catholic Church Archdiocese of Baltimore [CABA] Manuscripts, 1/17, Mary Cauffman to Bishop Carroll, 9 May 1810.

45. Joseph Cauffman to Joseph T. Cauffman, 28 March 1775 in Rodenbough, Autumn Leaves, 26.

46. Joseph Cauffman to Joseph T. Cauffman, 28 March 1775, ibid., 28.

47. Joseph Cauffman to Joseph T. Cauffman, 15 July 1776, ibid., 29.

48. Joseph Cauffman to Joseph T. Cauffman, 28 March 1775 and 15 July 1776, ibid., 26–29.

49. "De Cauffmann Josephus ex Philadelphia in Pennsylvania Americanus Med. Auditor" Altes Universitätsarchiv Wien [AUW], Akten der Medizinische Fakultät der Universität Wien, rotokoll der Medizinische Fakultät VIII. His graduation certification is held under AUW, Rigorosenprotokolle, Med. 9.5 Rigorosenprotokoll der Mediziner dated 2 September 1777.

50. Joseph Cauffman to Joseph T. Cauffman, 15 July 1776, in Rodenbough, Autumn Leaves, 28–29.

51. APS, Franklin Papers, Mss.B.F.85, 2, V, 163, Cauffman to Franklin, 23 April 1777. The letter is also published in "Cauffman Applying for Service," 77–82; and PBF, 23:603–606.

52. Cauffman to Franklin, 23 April 1777, PBF, 23:603–606.

53. Cauffman to Franklin, 23 April 1777, PBF, 23:603–606.

54. Ingenhousz to Franklin, 15 November 1776, PBF, 23:7–12.

55. Ingenhousz to Franklin, 28 June 1777, PBF, 24:239–242.

56. Only the ship's surgeon is listed, not Cauffman, see "Cauffman Applying for Service," 80–82.

57. Cauffman to Franklin, 23 April 1777, PBF, 23:603–606.

58. APS, Franklin Papers, Mss.B.F.85, 4, XV, 52, Joseph Pelligrini to Franklin, 19 July 1779.

59. For this phenomenon and term, see Bailyn, Ideological Origins, 50th Anniversary Edition, 230–320.

60. For the recent figures see Conway, Britannia's Auxiliaries, 50. The most detailed account still remains Atwood, The Hessians.

61. Taylor, "'Patrimonial' Bureaucracy and 'Rational' Policy," 33–56.

62. O'Reilly, *Migration, Recruitment and the Law*, 119–137. For the "evil" attribution, see next citation.

63. Kriegsarchiv, Zentralstellen, Wiener Hofkriegsrat, Protokolle, Hofkriegsrat Memorandum, 9 September 1780, G.2677, No. 5113; see other debates in G.756, No.1433 and G.958, No.1852. I am grateful to Dr. Ilya Berkovich for his help finding these documents.

64. I have relied upon the ongoing *Hessian Information System on Regional History* (LAGIS) project run by the Hessisches Landesamt für geschichtliche Landeskunde in Marburg which digitises muster lists of recruited Hessian soldiers under the HETRINA (Hessian Troops in North America) project and which provides the basis for this estimate.

65. Information from ibid., HETRINA database.

66. Oberösterreichisches Landesarchiv, Herrschaftsarchiv Weinburg, A-IV, Bd. 182.

67. Grüll, "Aus dem Tagebuch," 297. See also *Bericht des Leutnants Johann Justus Eggertt* in Siegfried Haider, Berichte aus der Neuen Welt, 14–30.

68. See above as well as the *Militär Schematismus des österreichischen Kaiserthumes* (Vienna: K.K. Hof- und Staatsdruckerei, 1824), 503.

69. In the few scholarly works on Johann Zinner, historians have been content to refer to him by a variety of names: Johann Zinner, Johann Carl Zinner and János Zinner being the most frequent. The "Carl" in his name stems from the letter written by him to Franklin (cited in the following footnote). Hungarian scholars have tended, incorrectly, to prefer the Hungarian variant of his name (János) despite the fact he never personally used this variant. In the archival material cited below, I have seen him referred to multiple times as Ioanne Baptiste Zinner as well as Johann Zinner. Given that Johann Zinner was the name which he most frequently and consistently used, this seems to be the most appropriate. For "Carl" see Winter, "Johann Carl Zinner," 55–61.

70. APS, Franklin Papers, Mss.B.F.85, 3, XII, 84, Jean-Claude de Zinnern [sic] to Franklin, 26 October 1778.

71. There is no surviving letter from Franklin to Zinner, but Zinner gave confirmation of their meeting in his book, Merkwürdige Briefe, last page of the "Vorbericht."

72. Announced in the *Magyar Hírmondó*, 4 October 1789, no. 80, 649 as "Janos Czinner" but Zinner was not on the rollcall of the staff that year. He first appears on the staff of the Royal Academy in 1781, see Archiv Mesta Košice, Košická Univerzita Katalóg, vol. I, 1781, fols. 431–432.

73. The others were Gyor, Nagyszombat-Pozsony, Nagyvarad, Zagreb: see, Brnardić, *The Enlightenment's Choice of Latin*, 119–151.

74. Archív Mesta Košice, Košická Univerzita Katalóg, vol. I, 1781, fols. 431–439.

75. See discussion of the *Notitia* below.

76. Zinner, Merkwürdige Briefe.

77. Ibid., 40 and 45–48.

78. Ibid., Vorbericht, s.n.

79. Ibid., 40 and 45–46.

80. Ibid., 142.

81. Ibid., 142.

82. Ibid., 1–3; see also Závodszky, American Effects, 21 and Lévai, *The Relevance of the American Revolution*, 100.

83. Zinner, Merkwürdige Briefe, 229–234.

84. Ibid., 177–181.

85. Ibid., 173–174.

86. "Brief VII: Generals Lee Meynung von den gegenwärtigen Unruhen an General Bourgoyne," ibid., 25–39; "Brief IX: Antwort des Generals Lee an Bourgoyne," ibid., 49–50.; Mazzagetti, Charles Lee, 101–102.

87. Zinner, Merkwürdige Briefe, 34.

88. Ibid., 38.

89. "Rede des Samuel Adams an die Versammlung zu Philadelphia, gehalten den 1. August 1776," Ibid., 64–67. For an overview of the Americana banned by Habsburg censors, see my "Knowledge of and Sympathy for the American Cause," 128–158.

90. Zinner, Merkwürdige Briefe, 312–325. He misattributed it to Samuel Adams, as was common at the time.

91. Most notably the "last asylum of mankind" refrain is missing.

92. See the section beginning with "I have heard it asserted by some, that as America hath flourished…" which includes "I answer roundly, that American would have flourished as much, and probably much more, had no European power had anything to do with her" which Zinner translated as "Gesetzt auch, das wäre wahr, so behaupte ich, dass Amerika eben so würde geblühet haben, wenn es auch in gar keiner Verbindung stünde." Zinner, Merkwürdige Briefe, 316–317.

93. The different handwriting between the *Notitia* and *Versuch* suggests that Zinner had student helpers aid his completion. Given Zinner's German-speaking background, it is likely he wrote the *Versuch* in his own hand.

94. Both works are held at the Jána Bocatia Library. The several manuscripts written by Zinner here are as follows: *Abhandlung von Europäischen Käyserthümen* (1782), *Acta academis regina cassoviensis* (s.d.), *Ius publicum hungaria* (1781), *Notitia historica de*

coloniis americae septemtrionalis (1783), *Præcipua prælia secundi belli punici: observationibus militaribus illustrata* (s.d. [ca. 1782]) and *Versuch einer Kriegsgeschichte der verbündenen Staaten von Nordamerika* (1784) in Verejná Knižnica Jána Bocatia v Košiciach, Rukopisné diela Jána Zinnera.

95. Verejná Knižnica Jána Bocatia v Košiciach, Rukopisné diela Jána Zinnera, *Notitia Historica*, Pars I. Completems coloniasum america septemtrionalis ord. et progressum usq. ad initium bello hodierni; Pars II. De bello americano usque ad foedus cum gallis per americanus initium; Pars III. De bello americano ad inito cum gallis foedere usq. ad pacem parisium.

96. Štátny oblastny archív v Košiciach, Hlavné Riaditelstvo Školského Obvodu v Košiciach, Akadémia v Košiciach 1788–1793, B, K. 21 (97–101), dated 12 January 1789, fol. 480.

97. Archív Mesta Košice, Košická Univerzita Katalóg, vol. 1, 1784. fols. 454–456.

98. Verejná Knižnica Jána Bocatia v Košiciach, Rukopisné diela Jána Zinnera, *Versuch einer Kriegsgeschichte der verbündenen Staaten von Nordamerika* (1784).

99. APS, Ms.BF.85, 3, XII, 84, Jean-Claude de Zinnern to Benjamin Franklin, 26 October 1778.

100. Jean Zinner to Franklin, 23 September 1783, PBF, 41:30–31.

101. Jean Zinner to Franklin, 23 September 1783, PBF, 41:30–31. I am grateful to Lukas Stelzhammer for producing a German translation from the original Latin for me.

Chapter 4

1. Testimony of Giovanni Jacapo Giusti in TNA, SP98/81, fols. 23–29 enclosed in Sir John Dick to Lord Weymouth, 29 February 1776.

2. HHStA, StK, Portugal, Berichte, K. 10, Count Adam von Lebzeltern to Kaunitz, 31 March 1778; TNA, SP89/85, fol. 107, Robert Walpole to Lord Weymouth, 1 February 1778.

3. Action of HMS *Apollo* and the *Stanislaus*, 15 June 1780, described in Osler, *Viscount Exmouth*, 30–31.

4. Hildebrand, Den svenska kolonin St Barthélemy, 315; cf. Johnson, Swedish Contributions, 1:546, 551–552, and 564–565.

5. Barton, "Sweden and the War of American Independence," 424; Syrett, *Royal Navy*, 103–106.

6. TNA, SP98/81, fols. 37–38, Weymouth to Lords of the Admiralty, 18 March 1776.

7. TNA, SP98/81, fol. 39, Weymouth to Dick, 22 March 1776.

8. Ibid., fol. 60, Dick to Weymouth, 8 April 1776.

9. Ibid., fols. 77–78, Dick to Weymouth, 3 May 1776.

10. TNA, SP98/82, fol. 6, Sir Horace Mann to Weymouth, 13 January 1777.

11. Ibid., fols. 15–16, Lords of the Admiralty to Sir John Undy, 5 February 1777. These instructions were much delayed and Undy received instructions only at the end of May,

see ibid., fols. 65–65r, Undy to Weymouth, 29 May 1777; and ibid., fols. 57–57r, Undy to Pietro Leopoldo, 4 April 1777.

12. TNA, SP 98/81, fols. 57–57r, Dick to Weymouth, 5 April 1776.

13. Ibid., fols. 57r–58, Dick to Weymouth, 5 April 1776.

14. Ibid., fol. 58.

15. TNA, SP98/81, fol. 59, Dick to Weymouth, 8 April 1776. See also, "Cargoe of a Danish Ship from Trieste consigned to *Messr. Frank & Comp.* arrived at Leghorne April 6, 1776," "Cargoe of the Dutch Ship consigned to *Messr. Frank & Comp.*," and "Cargoe of the French Ship from Trieste consigned to *Messr. Frank & Comp.*," attached to Mann to Weymouth, 20 April 1776, ibid., fols. 70–70r.

16. Dick to Weymouth, 8 April 1776, ibid., fol. 59r.

17. Ibid., fol. 58.

18. Ibid., fol. 60. Original emphasis.

19. Ibid., fol. 71, Dick to Weymouth, 15 April 1776.

20. Bolts, Considerations on India Affairs; Hallward, William Bolts, 103–106; Everaert, *Willem Bolts*, 363–369; Gough and King, "William Bolts," 8–28.

21. HHStA, Staatenabteilungen, Ostindische Kompanien, Triest-Antwerpen, K. 4, Konv. 1, Diplomatischen Korrespondenzen der Staatskanzlei 1774–1776, fol. 2, Belgiojoso to Kaunitz, 1 November 1774; Bronza, "Preparations of the Austrian Expedition," 63–76.

22. *Otto Frank & Co.* was based in Hamburg.

23. HHStA, Ostindische Kompanien, Triest-Antwerpen, K. 4, Konv. 1, Diplomatischen Korrespondenzen der Staatskanzlei 1774–1776, fol. 8.

24. TNA, SP98/81, fols. 68–69, Mann to Weymouth [in cipher], 20 April 1776.

25. Hallward, William Bolts, 137.

26. TNA, SP98/81, fols. 68r–69, Mann to Weymouth, 20 April 1776.

27. See "Extrait de l'article cinquième de l'octroi accord par S. M. I. & R. Apostolique à Monsieur Guillaume Bolts, sous la date de Vienne due 5me Jour Juin 1775," in ibid., fol. 116, Dick to Weymouth, 3 July 1776. It is a remarkable clause given this was written in June of 1775, see FHKA, NHK, Kommerz Litorale, K. 902, Oktroi, fols 195r–198r.

28. TNA, SP98/81, fols. 61–62, Weymouth to Dick, 23 April 1776; ibid., fol. 65, Weymouth to Mann [in cipher], 30 April 1776.

29. For talk of resignation, see ibid., fols. 96–97r, Dick to Weymouth, 7 June 1776; for acceptance, see ibid., fol. 102, Weymouth to Dick, 12 July 1776; and for Dick's confirmation to Weymouth, ibid., fols. 125–126, 3 August 1776.

30. Copied in ibid., fols. 110–110r, Dick to Weymouth, 21 June 1776.

31. "To the printer of the London Chronicle," enclosed within ibid., fols. 112–112r, Dick to Weymouth, 21 June 1776.

32. Ibid., fols. 156–156r, Undy to Weymouth, 6 November 1776. He presented his credentials to Pietro Leopoldo in mid-November, see ibid., fol. 162, Mann to Weymouth, 16 November 1776.

33. Ibid., fol. 65, Weymouth to Mann [in cipher], 30 April 1776.

34. Ibid., fol. 91, Mann to Weymouth [in cipher], 25 May 1776.

35. ASF, AdS, Affari Esteri, C. 901, Belgiojoso to Piccolomini, 11 September 1772.

36. Becattini, *Filippo Mazzei*, 32–33.

37. Codignola, *Blurred Nationalities*, 30n44.

38. Addobbati, "Filippo Mazzei e Guiseppe Bettoia," 133–194.

39. Thomas Woodford to Giovanni Fabbroni, 18 December 1775 in Idzerda, Marchione, and Scalia, *Mazzei: Selected Writings*, 1:86–87.

40. For Bettoia's strategy, see Codignola, *Blurred Nationalities*, 31.

41. Codignola, *Blurred Nationalities*, 30n46.

42. Idzerda et al, *Mazzei: Selected Writings*, 1:262.

43. TNA, HCA 32/430/9, Documents relating to the capture of the ship *La Prosperita* (formerly the *Norfolk* and the *Friendship* [*l'Amicizia*]), 1778, fols. 1–110.

44. Addobbati, *Oltre gli intermediary*, 145–183; cf. Codignola, *Blurred Nationalities*, 32n60.

45. TNA, HCA 32/360/5, Documents relating to the capture of the ship *l'Immacolata Concezione*, 1780, fols. 1–141.

46. TNA, SP98/82, fol. 196, Mann to Weymouth, 18 August 1778.

47. Ibid., fol. 145, Mann to Weymouth, 31 March 1778.

48. Ibid., fols. 139–139r, Mann to Weymouth, 14 March 1777. Mann suspected that the French had been withholding American news, see ibid., fol. 122, Mann to Weymouth, 3 January 1778.

49. Ibid., fols. 192–192r, Undy to Weymouth, 10 August 1778.

50. TNA, SP98/81, fols. 169–169r, Mann to Weymouth, 14 December 1776; TNA SP98/82, fols. 106r–107, Mann to Weymouth, 21 October 1777.

51. TNA, SP98/82, fol. 384r, Mann to Weymouth, 3 August 1778.

52. Ibid., fol. 385, Mann to Weymouth, 3 August 1778.

53. This and "Gianni regarded Livorno as a foreign colony in Tuscan territory," in Tazzara, *Free Port of Livorno*, 225n73 and 226; Wandruskza, *Pietro Leopoldo*, 302–303.

54. HHStA, HA, SB, K. 10, Konv. 5-1, fol. 5r, Maria Carolina to Pietro Leopoldo, 28 April 1778; Beales, *Joseph II*, 1:395–419; Wandruszka, *Leopold II*, 1:324–331.

55. Angiolini, *Neutrality*, 82–100; Addobbati, "L'espace de la guerre et du commerce," 233–249.

56. Angiolini, *Neutrality*, 83 and 97–98.

57. A copy can be found in in TNA, SP120/76, "Volendo noi provvedere che nel nostro porto di Livorno, e negli altri porti e scali della Toscana," dated 1 August 1778.

58. Holldack, "Neutralitätspolitik Leopolds von Toskana," 733–739; Wandruszka, *Leopold II*, 1:323.

59. Angiolini, *Neutrality*, 97.

60. Translation and comments in TNA, SP98/82, fols. 198–200, Mann to Weymouth, 18 August 1778.

61. Marginalia in Mann's copy of the Edict in TNA, SP98/82, fols. 199–199r enclosed in, Mann to Weymouth, 18 August 1778.

62. Marraro, "Mazzei's Correspondence," no. 3, 275–301; ibid., no. 4, 361–380. Mazzei penned several essays for Pietro Leopoldo, including *Reasons why the American States cannot be accused of having rebelled* (1781) and *Reflections tending to predict the outcome of the present war* (1781), see Idzerda et al, *Mazzei: Selected Writings*, 1:293–299 and 300–308.

63. Ibid., 1:171.

64. Venturi, End of the Old Regime, 1:92.

65. Ralph Izard to Henry Laurens, 18 October 1774, in Izard-Deas, *Correspondence of Mr. Ralph Izard*, 1:15–18.

66. Niccoli to Izard, 28 January 1778 in Sparks, *Diplomatic Correspondence*, 1:689–691; Antonucci, *Consuls and* Consiglieri, 80.

67. Izard to Laurens, 21 December 1777, in "Izard-Laurens Correspondence," 50.

68. Codignola, *Relations*, 30–31.

69. Lampredi, Dal commercio, 1:26–27 and 38–39; Meeks, Revolutionary Western Mediterranean, 30–31.

70. Zedinger, *Kaunitz und Cobenzl*, 197–217.

71. Wilden-Neeser, *Letters and Papers*, xxi.

72. TNA, SP78/297, fols. 272–272r, Frazer to Weymouth, 29 December 1775; TNA, SP78/298, fol. 11, Frazer to Stormont, 2 January 1776; Archives des Affaires Etrangère [AAE], Correspondence Politique [CP], Angleterre, 514, Stormont to Vergennes, 2 January 1776.

73. TNA, SP78/298, fol. 39, Frazer to Stormont, 19 January 1776.

74. Wilden-Neeser, *Letters and Papers*, 10.

75. Entry for *Eendragt* in the list of ships departing from Texel dated 16 March 1776 in TNA, SP84/552, Yorke to Suffolk, 23 April 1776.

76. TNA, SP78/298, fols. 338–339r, Frazer to Stormont, 30 March 1776.

77. Ibid., fols. 340–341, Frazer to Stormont, 2 April 1776.

78. Archives générales du Royaume de Belgique/Algemeen Rijksarchief van België [ARB], Conseil Privé [CP], 1154B, De Brauwere to Starhemberg, 13 April 1776.

79. Conyngham recalled (in Wilden-Neeser, *Letters and Papers*, 9) that the *Eendragt* arrived late but reports such as De Brauwere's contradict him; see Huibrechts, "Swampin' Guns and Stabbing Irons." I am grateful to Dr. Huibrechts for sharing her dissertation with me. We have conducted similar research in the ARB but our emphases on events are different.

80. ARB, CP, 1154B, reports of De Brauwere and Patrice de Nény to Starhemberg, 13 April 1776.

81. Absent between April and August 1774; January to June 1775; and September onwards, see TNA, SP 77/107, fols. 1–300 passim.

82. HHSA, Belgien, DDA, Berichte, K. 212, Starhemberg to Kaunitz, 12, 16, 19, 26, and 30 September 1775.

83. TNA, SP77/107, Joseph Fry to William Eden, 3 November 1775.

84. TNA, SP77/108, Peter to Suffolk, 7 April 1776.

85. HHStA, Belgien, DDA, Berichte, K. 216, Starhemberg to Kaunitz, 13 April 1776.

86. Copy enclosed in TNA, SP77/108, Gordon to Suffolk, 10 April 1776; original in ARB, CP, 1154B.

87. "dans une forme fort déplacée" in report of Nény, ARB, CP, 1154B.

88. HHStA, Belgien, DDA, K. 216, Starhemberg to Belgiojoso, 12 April 1776.

89. Ibid., Gordon to Starhemberg, 11 April 1776.

90. ARB, CP, 1154B, Starhemberg to Gordon, 11 April 1776.

91. TNA, SP77/108, Gordon to Suffolk [in cipher], 12 April 1776.

92. Depositions of Michel Meynne, Gustavus Conyngham, Jonathan Nesbitt and Louis Loot in ARB, CP, 1154B, report by Nény.

93. ARB, CP, 1154B, report of De Brauwere to Starhemberg, 13 April 1776.

94. Ibid., De Brauwere to Starhemberg, 16 April 1776; TNA, SP77/108, Peter to Suffolk, 13 April 1776.

95. De Brauwere's report. The *Industry* arrived from New England and again Frazer had suspected false papers stating Spain as the origin, see TNA, SP78/297, fol. 272, Frazer to Weymouth, 29 December 1775.

96. TNA, SP77/108, Peter to Suffolk, 13 April 1776.

97. ARB, CP, 1154B, De Brauwere to Starhemberg, 18 April 1776.

98. TNA, SP77/108, Gordon to Suffolk, 27 April 1776.

99. HHStA, Belgien, DDA, Weisungen, K. 35, Kaunitz to Starhemberg, 30 April 1776.

100. ARB, Secretaire d'Etat et Guerre [SEG], 1640, Henri de Crumpipen to Nény, 5 July 1776; TNA, SP77/108, Peter to Suffolk, 6 July 1776.

101. Wilden-Neeser, *Letters and Papers*, 10.

102. ARB, CP, 1154B, Crumpipen to Neny, 26 April 1776 (containing the 24 April petition by customers officers).

103. Memoir by Gordon copied in HHStA, Belgien, DDA, K. 216, Starhemberg to Kaunitz, 27 April 1776, annex.

104. HHStA, Belgien, DDA, K. 216, Starhemberg to Kaunitz, 27th April 1776.

105. Huibrechts, "*Swampin' Guns and Stabbing Irons*," 444–475.

106. Pole, "Law and the American Revolution," 126.

107. Perl-Rosenthal, "On Mobile Legal Spaces and Maritime Empires," 184–185 and 194.

108. Crawford, "The *Hawke* and the *Dove*, a Cautionary Tale," 49–66.

109. Memoire attached to HHStA, Belgien, DDA, K. 233, Starhemberg to Kaunitz, 15 September 1778; HHStA, Belgien, DDA, K. 232, report of the Grand Pensionary of Ostend, 13 August 1778.

110. Results from the "Brill Prize Papers Dataset."

111. TNA, High Court Admiralty [HCA] 32/343/6, fols 1–33.

112. Schnaubelt, "*Österreich und England*," 355–356.

113. TNA, HCA42/149/1, Claim of Anthony Songa, 20 November 1781; TNA, HCA42/150/1, Claim 17 of 6 June 1782; TNA, HCA42/150/2, Claim of Anthony and Bartholomew Songa, 24 June 1783; TNA, HCA42/150/3, Claim of 26 June 1784; TNA, HCA42/152/1, Claim of 26 June 1784.

114. HHStA, StK, England, Weisungen, K. 128, fols. 16–17, Kaunitz to Belgiojoso, 13 September 1779; HHStA, StK, England, Berichte, K. 119, fols. 31–34, Belgiojoso to Kaunitz, 1 October 1779; Kaps, *Entre el Servicio y los Negocios Transnacionales*, 231.

115. HHStA, StK, England, Weisungen, K. 128, fols. 16–17, Kaunitz to Belgiojoso, 25 September 1780; ibid., fols. 24–30, Kaunitz to Belgiojoso, 17 December 1780; ibid., fols. 33–34, Kaunitz to Belgiojoso, 18 December 1780; HHStA, StK, England, Berichte, K. 120, fols. 53–56, Belgiojoso to Kaunitz, 29 December 1780.

116. ASM, AB, C. 571, Joseph II to Belgiojoso, 3 July 1781.

117. HHStA, StK, England, Weisungen, K. 128, fols. 1–2, Kaunitz to Belgiojoso, 5 May 1779.

118. TNA, SP 100/13, 'Account delivered by Mr Sarkolzy to the King's Proctor,' 1 July 1779.

119. TNA, SP 100/13, Belgiojoso for Bienenfeld and Paul Sorkolzy to Weymouth, 8 July 1779.

120. TNA, SP 100/13, 'Account of saltpetre shipped at Lorient aboard of the Zeepart,' 12 July 1779; HHStA, StK, England, Berichte, K. 118, fol. 18r, Belgiojoso to Kaunitz, 13 July 1779. The final sum paid (including interest) was £31,352, see TNA SP 100/13, Belgiojoso to Weymouth, 4 August 1779.

121. HHSTA, StK, England, Berichte, K. 120, fol. 33v, Belgiojoso to Kaunitz, 28 March 1780.

122. De Dorlodot, "Les ports d'Ostende et de Nieuport," 141–157; Ronkard, "Les répercussions de la Guerre Américaine," 51–90.

123. The court files relating to the entire case from the American side, numbering some four hundred pages, can be found under National Archives and Records Administration [NARA], Record Group [RG] 267, Records of the United States Supreme Court [SC]: Records of the Court of Appeals in Cases of Capture [CA], Entry 1 – Revolutionary War Prize Case Files, 1776–1786 and Entry 2 Misc. Case Papers, 1772–1784; Microfilm Publication M162. I am grateful to Robert Ellis, archivist at the Federal Judicial Record Office, Washington DC.

124. NARA, RG267, SC, CA, 1-2, Court Proceedings, 22 November 1781.

125. Ibid., Exhibits, Richard Neave to Jacob Kladen, 1 May 1781; Richard Neave to Duncan Campbell of St. Vincent's, 1 May 1781; Kender Mason to James Morson, 12 May 1781; James Blundell to James Waddington, 12 June 1781; and Jonathan Blundell to William Author, 12 June 1781.

126. Ibid., Exhibits, *Liebaert, Baes, Derdeyn & Co.* to Vivian Home, 21 June 1781; ibid., *Liebaert, Baes, Derdeyn & Co.* to *Messrs Henry Pinchin & Co.*, 25 June 1781; ibid., copies of ship manifest and goods of *Den Eersten*, notarised 20 September 1781.

127. Ibid., Interrogation of Pol, s.d. [November 1781].

128. Ibid., Judgements of Judge Cushing, 6 and 19 December 1781.

129. Bourguignon, The First Federal Court, 116–119; Mask and MacMahon, "Revolutionary War Prize Cases," 480–483 and 486–495.

130. Resolution, 2 U.S. 1 (1781): Miller et al Libellants and Appellants v. The Ship Resolution, and Ingersoll, Claimant and Appellee & Miller et al Libellants and Appellants v. The Cargo of the Ship *Resolution* and O'Brien and Appellant. The court reheard the case in December 1781 as Resolution, 2 U.S. 19 (1781).

131. NARA, RG267, SC, CA, 1-2, Court Proceedings, 28 January 1782.

132. Ibid., Decree of Condemnation in the Court of Appeals, 5 February 1782.

133. Ibid., Decree of Condemnation in the Court of Appeals, 5 February 1782.

134. Ibid., Order by Cyrus Griffin on 22 March 1782 endorsed by Nathaniel Cushing.

135. Kulsrud, Maritime Neutrality to 1780; Bourguignon, "Incorporation of the Law of Nations," 270–295.

136. TNA, FO26/2, Alleyne Fitzherbert to Stormont, 3 August 1781.

137. HHStA, StK, Frankreich, Berichte, K. 160, Mercy to Starhemberg, 10 March 1782; HHStA, Belgien, DDA, Berichte, K. 260, Starhemberg to Kaunitz, 2 April 1782.

138. Memoire de Monsieurs *Liebaert, Baes, Derdeyn & Co.* enclosed in Vergennes to Franklin, 18 July 1782, PBF, 36:446–447; transcribed and translated in *The Works of Dr. Benjamin Franklin*, 5:122–126.

139. Ibid., 5:124.

140. Franklin to Vergennes, 18 January 1782, PBF, 36:447–448; HHStA, Belgien, DDA, Korrespondenz Frankreich, K. 9, Mercy-d'Argenteau to Starhemberg, 20 January 1782.

141. The second petition (undated) by *Liebaert, Baes, Derdeyn & Co.* addressed to Franklin is labelled B in the apostilled collection of documents by Peter Stephen du Ponceau in NARA, RG267, SC, CA, 1-2, Court Proceedings; Vergennes to Franklin, 22 March 1783, PBF, 39:367–368. The enclosures believed to be missing by the Franklin Papers are contained in the court records.

142. NARA, RG267, SC, CA, 1-2, Court Proceedings, Documents relating to the Petition for Review of Darby v. *Eersten* filed on 10 May 1784; ibid., Refusal of a Rehearing heard before the Court of Appeals on 24 May 1784.

143. Ibid., Memorial by *Liebaert, Baes, Derdeyn & Co.* presented to Congress by Prager, 9 February 1785; ibid., John Jay to President of Congress, 13 February 1785.

144. NARA, RG267, SC, CA, 1-2, Court Proceedings, Deposition of John Baes, 1 March 1787.

145. Ibid., Verdict of Judges Griffin and Read, 11 May 1787.

146. Bergmans, *"Handelsbetrekkingen,"* 29–88.

147. Frank, "The Children of the Desert and the Laws of the Sea," 410–444; Sauer, "Habsburg Colonial," 5–23.

Chapter 5

1 Based upon an account provided by Sir Robert Murray Keith in TNA, SP80/220, Keith to Suffolk, 27 May 1778.

2. Morris, Peacemakers, 151.

3. Hutson, Adams and Diplomacy, 54.

4. Edward Gibbon even believed Silas Deane travelled to Vienna, see Gibbon to J. B. Holroyd, 21 March 1778, in Prothero, *The Private Letters of Edward Gibbon*, no. 342.

5. "William never got to carry out his commission to Berlin and Vienna" in Van Vlack, Silas Deane, 138. The inaccuracy of Arthur Lee travelling to Vienna in 1778 is present in Mustafa, Merchants and Migrations, 149–150. Paul B. Bernard mistakes Arthur Lee and William Carmichael going on their German mission in 1776 when Carmichael travelled there in 1776 and Arthur Lee went in 1777 to say nothing of William Lee, see Bernard, Joseph II and Bavaria, 22. In his repertorium of American diplomats, Walter Burges Smith lists Lee as an envoy to Berlin but not under Vienna, see Smith, America's Diplomats and Consuls, 76–78.

6. Roider, "William Lee," 167.

7. Dippel, Germany and the American Revolution, 39.

8. Bukovansky, Legitimacy and Power Politics, 3.

9. My analysis here benefits from Gould, Among the Powers of the Earth, 2.

10. The Habsburgs maintained 57 infantry and 32 calvary regiments during this period (1775–1783), see Table 13 in Hochedlinger, Austria's Wars of Emergence, 301; Szabo, Kaunitz and Enlightened Absolutism, 3.

11. "The Elector of Hanover and the Emperor are on exceedingly ill terms" in Chandler, *A friendly address*, s.n.; Black, The Continental Commitment, 156.

12. Codignola, *Relations*, 29.

13. Deane to John Jay, 3 December 1776, in Isham, *The Deane Papers*, 1:396; Deane to the Committee of Secret Correspondence, 26 November 1777, in Sparks, *Diplomatic Correspondence*, 1:64–65.

14. Mazzei to Franklin, 5 September 1777, PBF, 24:502–503.

15. Jefferson to Adams, 21 August 1777, *The Papers of Thomas Jefferson* [PTJ], 2:27–29.

16. Stevens, *Facsimiles of Manuscripts in European Archives*, 2: nos. 149–150. Likely authored by Edward Bancroft, see Dull, Diplomatic History, 90.

17. As historian Jonathan R. Dull states, Carmichael "remains a remarkably mysterious figure" and his Berlin mission even more so, see Dull, Franklin the Diplomat, 37. The best account of Carmichael's mission is to be found in Kapp, Friedrich der Grosse, 18–21 with additional material in Kite, "Revolutionary Correspondence," 1–11; and Connecticut Historical Society, Silas Deane Papers, Box 1, Folder 33, Carmichael's letters dated 11, 12, 25 and 26 November 1776 from Hamburg and Berlin.

18. Haworth, "Frederick and the American Revolution," 460–478.

19. Wharton, *Diplomatic Correspondence*, 2:316 and 319–20; Alden, Stephan Sayre, 97–121.

20. Browning, "Hugh Elliot in Berlin," 88.

21. Houghton Library, Harvard University, Arthur Lee Papers, Ms. Am. 811-811.7, MJ811.2.III, fol. 61, Pincus to Lee, 20 July 1777. I am grateful to librarian Micah Hoggart. There is no other trace of Pincus despite searches in local and regional archives.

22. Lee to Franklin, 27 May 1777, in Wharton, *Diplomatic Correspondence*, 1:327.

23. Dill, Militia Diplomat, 46. Historian Pauline Maier saw great value in Lee, casting him as someone who sorely needs "closer examination." Maier, From Resistance to Revolution, 248.

24. Tsapina, "*The Strange Case of Philipp Ludwell*," 3.

25. Franklin to William T. Franklin, 14 July 1773, PBF, 18:385.

26. Public Addresses, LWL, 1:11.

27. Morgan, Dr Johnson's "Dear Master", 94.

28. Jenings-Lee, The Lees of Virginia, reprint, 236–237.

29. Lee to Charles Dumas, 10 September 1776, LWL, 1:183.

30. Lee to Barbeu Dubourg, 27 August 1776, LWL, 1:180–182.

31. Dill, Militia Diplomat, 33.

32. Lee to Richard Henry Lee, 15 October 1776, LWL, 1:184–90.

33. Clark, Silas Deane, 133–159; Abernethy, "The Origin of the Franklin-Lee Imbroglio," 41–52; Goldstein, "Silas Deane: Preparation for Rascality," 75–97.

34. Public Ledger, 22 July 1777, LWL, 1:197; BL, Add. Mss. 34414, George Lupton to William Eden, June to July 1777.

35. Dill, Militia Diplomat, 37–38.

36. Franklin to James Lovell, 22 July 1778, PBF, 27:54.

37. Arthur Lee to Richard Henry Lee, 4 October 1777; "My idea of adapting characters and places is this - Dr. F[ranklin] to Vienna, as the first, most respectable, and quiet; Mr Deane to Holland . . . France remains the [sic] center of political activity, and here, therefore, I should choose to be employed." Sparks, *Diplomatic Correspondence*, 1:625.

38. President of Congress to Lee, 1 July 1777, ibid., 1:591–592.

39. Lee to the President of Congress, 7 October 1777, ibid., 1:592–593; Dill, Militia Diplomat, 41.

40. Lee to Charles Thompson, Secretary of Congress, 2 January 1778, in Sparks, *Diplomatic Correspondence*, 1:596–598; Lee to President of Congress, 22 January 1778, LWL, 1:345.

41. Lee to Francis Lightfoot Lee, 4 January 1778, LWL, 1:325–329.

42. Lee to Richard Henry Lee, 2 January 1778, LWL, 1:314–319.

43. Lee to Edward Brown, 12 January 1778, LWL, 1:341–342.

44. Dill, Militia Diplomat, 43.

45. Lee to Richard Henry Lee, 2 January 1778 and Lee to President of Congress, 22 January 1778, LWL, 1:314–19; 345; Lee to Brown, 26 February 1778, LWL, 2:368.

46. Lee to Richard Henry Lee, 13 and 28 February; Lee to Franklin, 25 February, 12 and 13 March; Lee to Deane, 16 March; and Lee to President of Congress, 28 February 1778, LWL, 2:355–362, 370–373, 367, 395–396, 397–398, 399, 384–386.

47. Lee to American Commissioners 8 and 14 May 1778, LWL, 1:429, 431.

48. Dill, Militia Diplomat, 44. Lee held three offices concurrently as he was also a commercial agent for Virginia.

49. Mercer to Washington, 28 November 1778, *The Papers of George Washington* [PGW], 18:321–325. Original emphasis.

50. Simms and Riotte, Hanoverian Dimension, 31.

51. Simms, Three Victories, 524–525.

52. Scott, *'The True Principles of the Revolution'*, 51–91.

53. Keith to Chamier, 11 April 1777, in Smyth, *Memoirs*, 2:76–77.

54. Simms, Three Victories, 621.

55. Murphy, Vergennes, 258.

56. Benna, Contemporary Austrian Views, 40.

57. Murphy, Vergennes, 259.

58. Bemis, Diplomacy, 70–71n1. The French minister in Munich sent word at 7 p.m. on December 30, 1777; it arrived in Paris on January 4, 1778.

59. Beales, Joseph II, 1:77 and 349.

60. Frederick protested on January 3, 1778, at the convention at Ratisbon (Regensburg). Murphy, Vergennes, 295–296.

61. Ibid., 292n9; Dull, French Navy and American Independence.

62. Bernard, Joseph II and Bavaria, 31.

63. Keith to Drummond, 3 June 1778, in Smyth, *Memoirs*, 2:82–84.

64. Murphy, Vergennes, 291.

65. Elliot, Hufton and Scott, Emergence of the Eastern Powers.

66. Lee to Richard Henry Lee, 7 October 1777, LWL, 2:254.

67. Lee to President of Congress, 23 March 1778, LWL, 2:411–412. For Frederick II's overtures, see Haworth, "Frederick the Great and the American Revolution," 460–478.

68. Lee to Jenings, 11 April 1778, LWL, 2:416.

69. Referring to the flaw pointed out by Mercy-d'Argenteau.

70. Lee to Arthur Lee, 30 April 1778, LWL, 2:426.

71. Lee to Izard, 10 May 1778, LWL, 2:430–431.

72. WD, 2 May 1778.

73. TNA, SP80/220, Keith to Suffolk, 22 April 1778. Keith suspected Lee was in Prussia, see TNA, SP80/220, Keith to Suffolk, 16 May 1778.

74. TNA, SP80/220, Suffolk to Keith, 12 May 1778.

75. Ibid., Suffolk to Keith, 3 April 1778.

76. Ibid., Keith to Suffolk, 27 May 1778.

77. Ibid.

78. Keith to Chamier, 11 April 1777, in Smyth, *Memoirs,* 2:65.

79. TNA, SP80/220, Weymouth to Keith, 3 July 1778. The Secretaries for the Northern and Southern Departments directed British foreign policy over separate geographical areas in Europe. Both political appointments, these ministers defended governmental policy in Parliament and reported to the king, see Black, British Politics and Foreign Policy, 11–52.

80. AAE, CP, Autriche, 336.

81. Murphy, Vergennes, 298 and 537.

82. Ibid., 298; Vergennes issued a memorandum to all French ambassadors outlining the case against the Habsburg position which offended Kaunitz.

83. TNA, SP80/220, Keith to Suffolk, 25 April 1778.

84. Bernard, Joseph II, 3.

85. Ibid., 4; Fulton, Dr John Moore, 296.

86. Wraxall, Memoirs, 2:235.

87. Ibid., 2:236–237.

88. Ibid., 2:238.

89. TNA, SP80/220, Keith to Suffolk, 27 May 1778.

90. Fulton, Dr John Moore, 295.

91. HHStA, StK, Vorträge, K.126, fol. 132, Kaunitz to Maria Theresa, 28 May 1778. The British chargé d'affaires commended Kaunitz for his reception of Lee and repeated Keith's request to ensure that the "Door of the Empress's Apartment might be positively locked against him." TNA, SP80/220, Keith to Suffolk, 27 May 1778.

92. TNA, SP80/220, Keith to Suffolk, 27 May 1778.

93. Ibid.

94. Wraxall, Memoirs, 2:237.

95. HHStA, Sonderbestände, Khevenhüller-Metsch Familienarchiv, Reigersburg, K. 183, Bd. 2, Count Franz-Xaver Koller to Princess Anna Khevenhüller-Metsch, 28 May 1778. I am grateful to Count Bartolomäus Khevenhüller for his permission to access these family papers.

96. For the mishaps, see Benna, Contemporary Austrian Views, 26; Schlitter, Beziehung, 6–7.

97. HHStA, SB, Khevenhüller-Metsch Familienarchiv, Reigersburg, K. 183, Bd. 2, Koller to Khevenhüller-Metsch, 1 June 1778.

98. Ibid., Koller to Khevenhüller-Metsch, 8 June 1778.

99. Schmidt-Brentano, Kaiserliche und k. k. Generale, 86.

100. Roider, "William Lee," 164; Kneschke, Adels-Lexicon, 7:25.

101. Ingenhousz to Franklin, 6 March, 14 May, and 15 June 1778, PBF, 26:67–70, 457–458, and 625.

102. Klingenstein et al, Zwischen Wien und Triest, 1:177–183.

103. Beales, Joseph II, 1:298.

104. Maria Theresa to Mercy-d'Argenteau, 31 May 1778 in Arenth, Geschichte Maria Theresias, 10:434–444.

105. TNA, SP80/220, Keith to Suffolk, 30 May 1778.

106. Ibid.

107. Virginia Historical Society Library [VHS], Mss.1.L51.F.417, Section 118, William Lee to Arthur Lee, 29 May 1778.

108. TNA, SP80/220, Keith to Suffolk, 3 June 1778.

109. Ibid., Keith to Suffolk, 10 June 1778; Benna, Contemporary Austrian Views, 41.

110. HHStA, SB, Khevenhüller-Metsch Familienarchiv, Reigersburg, K. 183, Bd. 2, Count Koller to Princess Maria Amalia Khevenhüller (née Liechtenstein), 15 June 1778.

111. HHStA, StK, Vorträge, K. 126, fol. 139, Kaunitz to Maria Theresa, 18 June 1778.

112. VHS, Mss.1.L51.F.417, Section 118, Lee to Arthur Lee, 10 June 1778.

113. Lee to Arthur Lee, 29 May 1778 in Roider, "William Lee," 166.

114. Riksarkivet Stockholm, Diplomatica, Germania, Kartong 453, Report of Nils Bark dated 30th May 1778. I am grateful to archivist Örjan Romefors for sending this report and to Prof. Ellinor Forster for her translation from Swedish into German for me.

115. To avoid confusion, this was Count Franz Paula Karl von Colloredo (1736–1806).

116. TNA, SP80/220, Keith to Suffolk, 13 June 1778.

117. Cerman, *Každodenní život Chotků v parku Veltrusy*, 12–17. I am grateful to Dr. Ivo Cerman for this information.

118. Johann Reinhold Forster to Franklin, 30 July 1778, PBF, 27:181–182; Uhlig, Georg Forster, 168.

119. See the letters of Count Koller to Princess Maria Amalia Khevenhüller (née Liechtenstein) throughout May and June in HHStA, SB, Khevenhüller-Metsch Familienarchiv, Reigersburg, K. 183, Bd. 2. Her husband was Prince Johann Sigismund Friedrich von Khevenhüller (1732–1801), *kaiserlicher und Reichsbevollmächtigter Generalcommissär* in Milan.

120. APS, Franklin Papers, Mss.B.F.85, 3, XII, 84, Jean-Claude de Zinnern [*sic*] to Franklin, 26th October 1778.

121. TNA, SP80/220, Keith to Suffolk, 13 June 1778.

122. Ibid., Keith to Suffolk, 17 June 1778. Keith's earlier exhaustion had begun to show; on June 3, he wrote, "I can hardly guide the pen, my fingers are so tired with scribbling!"

123. Ibid., Keith to Suffolk, 24 June 1778.

124. Lee to Edmund Jenings, 24 June 1778, LWL, 2:454–455. Lee wrote at least six lengthy letters that day.

125. Lee to Arthur Lee, 24 June 1778, LWL, 2:454–455.

126. TNA, SP80/220, Keith to Suffolk, 20 June 1778.

127. Ibid., Keith to Suffolk, 24 June 1778.

128. Matthäus Graf von Vieregg to Joseph Franz Xaver Freiherr von Haslang, 15 July 1778, quoted in Dippel, Germany and the American Revolution, 38.

129. TNA, SP80/220, Keith to Suffolk, 27 June 1778.

130. Stockton to Franklin, 3 June 1778, PBF, 26:582–583; TNA, SP80/220, Keith to Suffolk, 4 July 1778.

131. Codignola, Blurred Nationalities, 63.

132. Ibid., 64.

133. Riksarkivet Stockholm, Diplomatica, Germania, Kartong 453, report of Nils Bark, 12 June 1778. Forster translation.

134. TNA, SP80/220, Keith to Suffolk, 18 July 1778.

135. Ibid., Keith to Suffolk, 4 July 1778.

136. Croatian State Archives Dubrovnik, Acta Sanctae Mariae Majoris, XVIII, Series 31.3062/53, 3, Sebastian d'Ayala to Ragusan Senate, s.d [June 1778]. I am grateful to Dr. Anna Vincenzi for helping decode d'Ayala's difficult script.

Chapter 6

1. Houtte, Contribution, 350–353; Davis, Joseph II, 6.

2. Van Bruyssel, Histoire, 3:294n1; NRS, Customs Records, RH20/23.

3. Gaier, Four Centuries, 45.

4. Salay, "The Production of Gunpowder," 423.

5. Deuborne to Franklin, 10 November 1778, PBF, 28:12–15.

6. Miller, Sir Joseph Yorke, 38; Serruys, "The Port and City of Ostend," 325.

7. HHStA, StK, Portugal, K. 9–10, fols. 45–46, Lebzeltern to Kaunitz, 14th June 1777.

8. Gaier, Four Centuries, 73.

9. Huibrechts, "*Swampin' Guns and Stabbing Irons*," 510. Huibrechts calculated estimates for the level of exports based upon the transit ledgers of internal customs houses, which recorded the weights and types of military goods, to arrive at this number.

10. Parmentier, *Profit and Neutrality*, 207–208.

11. Kent History & Library Centre [KHLC], Cobb of Margate, Family and Business Papers, *De Vinck & Co.* Correspondence, KCA, EK-U1453/B5/1706, fols. 6–11.

12. Bergbohm, Die bewaffnete Neutralität, 212.

13. Farasyn, De 18de eeuwse bloeiperiode, 68–86; Houtte *Histoire économique*, 2:65, 100, 121, and 169; cf. Van Gucht, "*De trans-Atlantische handel vanuit Oostende*," 74.

14. ARB, SEG, 2151 (1–2), 'Rapport du Comité du 28 Avril 1781 sur le projet de l'Agrandissement du bassin d'Ostende.'

15. Everaert, "Le pavillon impérial," 64–65.

16. ARB, SEG, 2151/2, 'Rapport du Comité du 8 8bre 1781 au Sujet des artisans et ouviers Angloix, qui Vivement et établir dans ce Päis-ci.'

17. Koninklijke Bibliotheek van België/Bibliothèque Royale de Belgique, Manuscripts Division, no. G2077, *Mémoire des faits de Frédéric de Romberg* (Brussels, 1810).

18. ARB, SEG, 2152, 4 November 1782, Rapport au Comité de Commerce; TNA, FO 95/8/2, Petition of Messers Romberg et Compagnie to Belgiojoso, 15 January 1781.

19. Weber, Deutsche Kaufleute, 195–8; Parmentier, *Profit and Neutrality*, 214.

20. Meissner, Mücke, and Weber, Schwarzes Amerika, 94; Schulte-Beerbühl and Weber, *From Westphalia to the Caribbean*, 89.

21. Parmentier, *Profit and Neutrality*, 214.

22. Weber, "Linen, Silver, Slaves, and Coffee," 7; Weber, Deutsche Kaufleute, 196.

23. Fottrell to Franklin, 21 February 1783, PBF, 39:195; Parmentier, "The Irish Connection," 31–54.

24. Fottrell to Franklin, 29 October 1781, PBF, 35:664–665.

25. Fottrell to Franklin, 21 February 1783, PBF, 39:32.

26. KHLC, Cobb, EKU1453/B3/5/687 fols. 1–31.

27. Wets to Franklin, PBF, 38:693.

28. *Veuve d'Aubremé & Fils* to Franklin, 31 January 1783, PBF, 38:701.

29. *Connelly & Sons* to Franklin, 4 February 1783, PBF, 38:693.

30. ARB, CP, 1154B, Circular, 25 July 1778.

31. HHStA, Belgien, DDA, Berichte, K. 232, fols. 175–181, Starhemberg to Kaunitz, 25 July 1778, which contains Cazier's memorandum.

32. HHStA, Belgien, DDA Weisungen, K. 40-1, Kaunitz to Starhemberg, 5 August 1778.

33. HHStA, Belgien, DDA, Berichte, K. 232, Starhemberg to Kaunitz, 15 August 1778.

34. HHStA, Belgien, DDA, Weisungen, K. 40-1, Kaunitz to Starhemberg, 31 October 1778 and 1 December 1778.

35. HHStA, Belgien, DDA, Berichte, K. 234, Starhemberg to Kaunitz, 26 November 1778; HHStA, Belgien, DDA, Weisungen, K. 41, Kaunitz to Starhemberg, 6 January 1779.

36. ARB CAPB 499, D106, Starhemberg and the Committee of Maritime Commerce deliberated for two days between 14–15 February 1781.

37. Franklin to Vergennes, 18 January 1782, PBF, 36:447–448.

38. HHStA, Belgien, DDA, Berichte, K. 260, Avisé au Comité à Bruxelles, 24 March 1782.

39. HHStA, Belgien, DDA, Berichte, K. 260, Avisé au Comité à Bruxelles, 24 March 1782.

40. HHStA, Belgien, DDA, Berichte, K. 260, Starhemberg to Mercy [to Kaunitz], 31 March 1782.

41. HHStA, Belgien, DDA, Weisungen, K. 47, Kaunitz to Starhemberg, 13 April 1782.

42. Beales, *Joseph II*, 1:421–422.

43. The offer was made on 19 May 1779. I have been unable to find the original but it is referenced in Flassan, *Histoire générale*, 7:300.

44. AAE, CP Autriche, 339, Breteuil to Vergennes, 26 May 1779.

45. Maria Theresa to Marie Antoinette, 1 July 1779, in Arneth and Geoffrey, eds., *Correspondance secrète*, 3:327.

46. Ibid., 3:327–328.

47. Maria Theresa to Mercy-d'Argenteau, 31 July 1779, ibid., 3:336.

48. Maria Theresa to Marie Antoinette, 1 December 1779, in Arneth, *Maria Theresia und Marie Antoinette*, 292–293.

49. AAE, CP, Autriche, 340, fols. 222–223, Louis XVI to Maria Theresa, 27 May 1779. The King of Spain reiterated the same: AEE, CP, Espagne, 594, fols. 225–226, Charles III to Maria Theresa, s.d. June 1779.

50. AAE, CP, Autriche, 340, fols. 237–238 and 302–306, Vergennes to Breteuil, 9 June and 17 June 1779; AAE, CP, Autriche, 340, fol. 345, Breteuil to Vergennes, 12 July 1779; Murphy, *Vergennes*, 311–312 and 331.

51. Maria Theresa to Mercy-d'Argenteau, 31 July 1779, in Arneth and Geoffrey, eds., *Correspondance secrète*, 3:335.

52. TNA, SP80/221, fol. 152, Keith to Weymouth, 19 June 1779.

53. Joseph II to Marie Antoinette, 9 September 1783, in Arneth, *Marie Antoinette, Joseph II und Leopold II*, 32.

54. Maria Theresa to Mercy-d'Argenteau, 31 July 1779, in Arneth and Geoffrey, *Correspondance secrète*, 3:335–336. Keith wrote: "Baron Breteuil has received less Thanks in this Capital, than ever any Mediator did after having finished his Work." TNA, SP80/221, fols. 142r–143, Keith to Weymouth, 2 June 1779.

55. Mentioned in Maria Theresa to Marie Antoinette, 30 June 1780 and Marie Antoinette to Maria Theresa, 13 July 1780, in Arneth and Geoffrey, eds., *Correspondance secrète*, 3:444–445. For Joseph II's earlier contemplation, see Beales, Joseph II, 1:252.

56. TNA, SP80/221, fol. 125–128r, Keith to Weymouth, 19 May 1779.

57. TNA, SP80/221, fols. 176–181r, Weymouth to Keith, 16 July 1779, nos. 9 and 10.

58. Ibid., fol. 197, Keith to Weymouth, 31 July 1779.

59. Ibid., fols. 196–203r.

60. Maria Theresa to Mercy-d'Argenteau, 31 July 1779, in Arneth and Geoffrey, *Correspondance secrète*, 3:336.

61. Maria Theresa to Mercy-d'Argenteau, 4 August 1779, ibid., 3:338.

62. HHStA, Familienakten, Sammelbände, K. 7, fols. 293–300; HHStA, Familienakten, Sammelbände, K. 26 and K. 27a passim. The few which have survived, have been incorporated into Alfred Ritter von Arneth's edition. Here, there is only one letter from 1778, and the next comes in 1780, see Arneth, *Marie Antoinette, Joseph II und Leopold II*, 20–22; Nougaret, "Marie-Antoinette dans les fonds des Archives nationales," 129–136.

63. Maria Theresa only retained some of the letters from the regular monthly interchange between her and her daughter. Those that do survive are best served in three editions where each editor omitted certain parts (such as the sexual relations between Marie Antoinette and King Louis). The Arneth edition (quoted above) including Mercy-d'Argenteau's correspondence offers the most political discussion. The other editions are: Arneth, ed., *Maria Theresia und Marie Antoinette: Ihre Correspondenz* and Girard, ed., *Correspondance entre Marie Thérèse et Marie Antoinette*.

64. Marie Antoinette to Maria Theresa, 16 August 1779, in Arneth and Geoffrey, *Correspondance secrète*, 3:338.

65. HHStA, StK, Spanien, Berichte, K. 111, Konv. 5, fols. 25–26, Kaunitz-Questenberg to Kaunitz, 17th June 1779.

66. HHStA, StK, Spanien, Berichte, K. 112, Konv. 1, fols. 1–2, Kaunitz-Questenberg to Kaunitz, 1 September 1779. This was obviously dilatory as well as honest since Floridablanca did the same to the Russians when a mediation offer from St. Petersburg was forthcoming, see AAE, CP, Russie, 105, Charles Olivier de Saint-Georges, marquis de Vérac to Vergennes, 8 September 1780.

67. Floridablanca to Kaunitz-Questenberg, 28th November 1779, contained within Kaunitz-Questenberg's report to Kaunitz, 6 December 1779, HHStA, StK, Spanien, Berichte, K. 112, Konv. 1, fols. 138-139r. Kaunitz-Questenberg's follow-up came on 13 November 1779, ibid., fols. 136–137r.

68. Mercy-d'Argenteau to Kaunitz, 16 November 1779 in Arneth and Flammermont, *Correspondance secrète du comte de Mercy Argenteau*, 543.

69. See, for example, TNA SP80/221, fols. 171–172, Keith to Weymouth, 14 July 1779.

70. Kaunitz to Mercy-d'Argenteau, 3 August 1779 and 1 September 1779 in Flammermont, *Correspondance secrète*, 540–542.

71. De Madariaga, *Armed Neutrality*, 223.

72. Archivio di Stato di Napoli, Fondo Ministero Affari Esteri, Inghilterra, Busta 33, Count Michele Pignatelli to Francesco d'Aquino Prince di Caramanico, 28 March 1780.

73. Bemis, The Hussey-Cumberland Mission; Morris, Peacemakers, 43–66; Dull, The Miracle of American Independence, 113–118.

74. HHStA, StK, Spanien, Berichte, K. 112, Konv. 4, Kaunitz-Questenberg to Kaunitz, 28 April 1780; HHStA, StK, Spanien, Berichte, K. 113, Konv. 6, Kaunitz-Questenberg to Kaunitz, 17 July 1780; ibid., Kaunitz-Questenberg to Kaunitz, 7 September 1780; HHStA, StK, Spanien, Berichte, K. 113, Konv. 7, Kaunitz-Questenberg to Kaunitz, 16 October 1780. There was also a close monitoring of the British and French responses to these talks, see HHStA, StK, England, Berichte, K. 120, fols. 15–16, Belgiojoso to Kaunitz, 27 July 1780; HHStA, StK, Frankreich, Berichte, K. 162, Mercy-d'Argenteau to Kaunitz, 16 August 1780.

75. Maria Theresa to Marie Antoinette, 30 June 1780, and Marie Antoinette to Maria Theresa, 13 July 1780 in Arneth and Geoffrey, eds., *Correspondance secrète*, 3:444–445.

76. The insinuation must have been verbal as only Prussian reports confirm it, see Morris, Peacemakers, 159.

77. AAE, CP, Autriche, 341, fols. 310–314, Breteuil to Vergennes, 5 October 1780.

78. De Madariaga, Armed Neutrality, 172–215.

79. Af Malmborg, Neutrality and State-Building, 36–39; Müller, *Sweden's Neutrality*, 203–224.

80. Murphy, Vergennes, 284–287; De Madariaga, Armed Neutrality, 234–238.

81. Simms, Three Victories, 636–661.

82. Murphy, Vergennes, 325.

83. Keith to Sir Joseph Yorke, 20 January 1781 in Smyth, *Memoirs*, 1:116; Keith to Richard Rigby, 21 January 1781, ibid., 1:119.

84. Murphy, Vergennes, 331; Bemis, Diplomacy, 181.

85. De Madariaga, Armed Neutrality, 264–265.

86. TNA, SP80/223, fols. 31–32r, Stormont to Keith, 25 August 1780.

87. TNA, SP80/223, fol. 3, Stormont to Keith, 8 August 1780; ibid., fols. 37–38, Keith to Stormont, 2 September 1780; and ibid., Keith to Stormont, 6 September 1780, fols. 40–44.

88. Ibid., fols. 167–179, Stormont to Keith, 1 December 1780.

89. Mayer, "The Price for Austria's Security: Part I," 257–299; Beales, Joseph II, 2:104–132.

90. TNA, FO 7/1, Keith to Stormont, 10 January 1781.

91. Kaunitz to Mercy-d'Argenteau [and Belgiojoso], 21 May 1781 in Arneth and Flammermont, *Correspondence secrète du comte de Mercy Argenteau*, 1:35. Cf. De Madariaga, Armed Neutrality, 325n66.

92. De Madariaga, Armed Neutrality, 239–263.

93. A persistent idea; see ARB, SEG, 2151/2, 'Rapports du 18 Juillet et du 26 Septembre 1782 sur un projet d'acquisition de l'Isle de Tobago.'

94. TNA, FO 7/1, Keith to Stormont, 7 February 1781.

95. AAE, CP, Autriche, 342, fol. 56, Breteuil to Vergennes, 11 February 1781.

96. HHStA, StK, Frankreich, Weisungen, K. 164, Kaunitz to Mercy-d'Argenteau, 8 February 1781.

97. Bemis, Diplomacy, 181–182.

98. AAE, CP, Autriche, 342, fol. 127, Breteuil to Vergennes, 5 March 1781.

99. TNA, FO 7/1, Stormont to Keith, 9 January, 4 February, and 27 February 1781.

100. Adams to President of Congress, 26 June 1781, PJA, 11:396–398.

101. AAE, CP, Autriche, 342, fol. 237, Breteuil to Vergennes, 19 April 1781.

102. Adams to Joseph Ward, 15 April 1809, early access document via *"Founders Online."*

103. HHStA, StK, Frankreich, Weisungen, K. 164, Kaunitz to Mercy-d'Argenteau, 23 May 1781. Summarised in de Madariaga, Armed Neutrality, 325.

104. HHStA, StK, England, Berichte, K. 120, Belgiojoso to Kaunitz, 8 June and 16 July 1781; TNA, FO 7/1, Stormont to Keith, 12 June 1781.

105. Morris, Peacemakers, 188.

106. Black, British Foreign Policy, 11–12; Stockley, Britain and France, 35–36.

107. Joseph II to Marie Antoinette, 9 September 1783 in Arneth, *Marie Antoinette, Joseph II und Leopold II*, 32.

108. TNA, FO 7/4, Stormont to Keith, 15 January 1782.

109. De Incontrera, Trieste e l'America, 99–101; Reill, Nationalists who feared the Nation, 81–82.

110. O'Reilly, "Lost Chances," 53–70; Faber, Litorale Austriaco; Gasser, "Österreichs Levantenhandel," 120–130; Kaltenstadler, "Seehandel über Triest," 55:482–497 and 56:1–104.

111. Bosetti, De Trieste à Dubrovnik, 63.

112. Finanz und Hofkammerarchiv [FHKA], Neue Hofkammer [NHK], Kommerz Litorale, Akten, K. 992 (1749–1796); British consul Nathanial Green's reports to London held at BL, Manuscripts, Keith Papers, Add. Mss. nos. 35508-35542 and Drake Papers, Add. Mss. 46826; TNA, SP97/61, Green to Keith, 3 April 1775; see also Kaps, "Small But Powerful," 427–455.

113. Archivio di Stato di Trieste [AST], Deputazione di Borsa poi Camera di Commercio e d'Industria di Trieste (1751–1921) [DB], Serie VII, 'Tramissione da parte del Governo della relazione di Felice Carli sul commercio con le Province americane' in Carteggio [C] no.105, fol.88; 'Transmissione del Governo del rapporto inviato dal console in Nantes sulle cause dell'insuccesso del commercio tra Francia e America' in C.156, fol. 45.

114. AST, DB, Serie VII, C.67, fol. 49, 'Communicazione del Governo per il rapporto inviato inviato da Hofer relativo al commercio con l'america'; C.160, fol. 59, 'Transmissione del Governo del rapporto del console in Amburgo sul commercio con gli Stati Uniti d'America'; C.60, fol. 40, 'Communicazione del Governo per la relazione inviata da Hofer sul commercio con l'america'; C.128, fol. 14, 'Transmissione del rapporto

inviato dal console in Amburgo sui rapporti commerciali con l'America'; and C.74, fol. 57, 'Transmisisone da parte del Governo del rapporto del console in Amburgo sul commercio con le 13 Province Americane Indipenti'.

115. Christoph Beller to the Hofkammer, 7 August 1776, FHKA, NHK, Kommerz Abteilung, Noten, K. 616, fols. 365–367. The *Hofkammer* was the main administrational organ of the financial matters; see Sapper, "Das Hofkammerarchiv als Forschungstätte," 309–314.

116. FHKA, NHK, Kommerz Litorale, Akten, K. 903, fols. 897-901, Kaunitz, Memorandum, 11 July 1782.

117. HHStA, StK, Vorträge, K. 137, Kaunitz, Memorandum with Joseph's marginalia, 30 June 1782.

118. Bell, "Philadelphia Medical Students," 10.

119. HHStA, KA, KK, NZ, TZ, Bd. 24, 5 November 1779, fol. 275. The Logan family papers at the Historical Society of Pennsylvania archives yielded no trace of a congressional commission.

120. Franklin's Journal, 2 January 1782, PBF, 36:354–356.

121. Baraux to Adams, 21 March 1782, PJA, 12:342.

122. Adams to Baraux, 7 April 1782, PJA, 394.

123. FHKA, NHK, Kommerz Litorale, Akten, Triestiner und Fiumer Handlung – Zucker, Fasz. 103, K. 893, e.g. fol. 388.

124. HHStA, KA, KK, NZ, TZ, Bd. 26, 12 June 1781, fol. 199.

125. FHKA, NHK, Kommerz Litorale, Akten, Flaggenpatente, Fasz. 113v, K. 957 'Verpoorten Band' (1750–1800).

126. Stock, Trieste e l'America nascente, 7.

127. *Historisches Portefeuille*, Year One, 9th edition, September 1782, X, 'Abriss der Begebenheiten,' 1168; Babudieri, Trieste e gli interessi austriaci, 91–92.

128. WD, 29 June 1782; *Politisches Journal*, "VIII: Nachrichten aus verschiedenen Ländern," VIII (1782), 175–176; *Der Teutsche Merkur*, "VI: Octroy der neuen Triester Assecuranz-Handels-und Disconto-Compagnie," I (1783), 88–93.

129. WD, 4 November 1782; Babudieri, Trieste e gli interessi austriaci 92.

130. Popularly reported as *Das Schöne Wien* but the application states *La Città di Vienna*.

131. FHKA, NHK, Kommerz Litorale, Akten, K. 903, fols. 669–685.

132. FHKA, NHK, Kommerz Litorale, Akten, Flaggenpatente, K. 957 'Verpoorten Band' (1750–1800).

133. FHKA, NHK, Kommerz Litorale, Akten, K. 903, fols. 696–701.

134.HHStA, KA, KK, NZ, TZ, Bd. 26, 19 August 1781, fol. 260.

135. FHKA, NHK, Kommerz Litorale, Kommerz nach Ost- und Westindien, K. 903, fols. 721–740.

136. For the most recent overview, see Kaps, *A Gateway to the Spanish Atlantic?*, 177–132; FHKA, NHK, Kommerz Litorale Akten, Generalia, K. 850 (1780–1786) fols. 1003–1020. I was pleased to make this discovery during the course of my doctoral research and to see the table's valuable information of use elsewhere.

137. Babudieri, Trieste e gli interessi austriaci, 92.

138. Ridgewell, *Economic Aspects – The Artaria Case*, 110; Dickson, Finance and Government, 1:426–427.

139. Dr. Alessandra Sambo found a similar Germania classification in Venetian statistical tables defining it as "a vast area that could be defined as Austro-Prussian, perhaps with some extension into the Caucasus region." ("la Germania, une vaste aire qu'on pourrait définir austro-prussienne, avec peut-être quelques extensions dans le Caucase.") Sambo, "La balance de commerce," 387. I am grateful to Prof. Silvia Marzagalli for this information.

140. Based on calculations derived from the FHKA, NHK, Kommerz Litorale Akten, Generalia, K. 850 (1780–1786), fols. 1003-1020 Two caveats are needed: first, India and China are not broken down separately, and so obscure an individual valuation, but collectively represented more than just the United States alone; second, the French ports are not listed but likely included ports in the Mediterranean and on the Atlantic coastline (Marseille and Bordeaux) and so this cannot be definitely counted either.

Chapter 7

1. WD, 15 February 1783.

2. Arneth and Flammermont, *Correspondance secrète du comte de Mercy Argenteau*, 1:165.

3. Franklin to Ingenhousz, 16 May 1783, PBF, 40:8–13.

4. Codignola, Blurred Nationalities, 31.

5. Codignola, *Relations*, 29.

6. Ibid., 30.

7. APS, Franklin Papers, Mss.B.F.85, XXXII, 84, *Salucci & Fils* to Franklin, 20 August 1784.

8. *Salucci & Fils* to Franklin, 7 March 1783 and 6 June 1783, PBF, 39:302–303 and 40:119–120; Codignola, Blurred Nationalities, 32.

9. HHStA, StK, Toskana, K. 20, Veigl to Kaunitz, 26 October 1784, "Notizie dell'America Settentrionale: Le Navi Toscane che cola sono andate da Livorno."

10. Codignola, Blurred Nationalities, 33–34.

11. Codignola, *La lettera*, 205–214.

12. Ibid., 34n78; Codignola *Relations*, 31n9.

13. Codignola, Blurred Nationalities, 142–149.

14. Codignola, Blurred Nationalities, 124 and 150; Antonucci, *Consuls and* Consiglieri, 80–82.

15. Favi to American Commissioners, 10 October 1784, PTJ, 7:437–438.

16. Burnett, "Note on American Negotiations," 584. They also sent this version to Denmark and Portugal.

17. Favi to American Commissioners, 26 April 1785, PTJ, 8:104.

18. Jefferson, "Notes on Alterations Proposed by Favi," PTJ, 8:105–110.

19. Jefferson, "Observations on the alterations proposed on the part of His Royal Highness the Grand Duke of Tuscany in the articles of treaty offered by the Commissioners of the United States of America," enclosed in American Commissioners to Favi, 8 June 1785, PTJ, 8:187–195.

20. Favi to Jefferson, 10 November 1785, PTJ, 9:280; *Nuova minuta del trattato* in PTJ, 8:105–110.

21. Jefferson to Adams, 19 November 1785, PTJ, 9:41–47.

22. Original missing. Jefferson made a note of it in his *Summary Journal of Letters*, 12 May 1785, PTJ, 8:152.

23. Favi to Commissioners, 16 November 1784, PJA, 16:430–431.

24. ASF, AdS, Affari Esteri, C. 930, Fierallmi to Pietro Leopoldo, 26 November 1784.

25. ASF, AdS, Affari Esteri, C. 930, Piccolomini to Count Federigo Barbolani di Montanto, 11 January 1785. Transcribed in Cortese, "Le prime relazioni," 14. I have seen the original but refer to Cortese's transcription.

26. Cortese, "Le prime relazioni," 16.

27. Ibid., 17.

28. John Quincy Adams to Abigail Adams [sister], 18 August 1785, Adams Family Correspondence [AFC], 6:255.

29. Brush served as a colonel in the Connecticut militia between May 1776 and January 1781, see *Fourth Report of the National Society of the Daughters of the American Revolution*, 191.

30. For Amsterdam: Diary of John Quincy Adams, AFC, 1, entry dated 10 June 1781. For friendship with Adams family: Abigail Adams to John Adams, 29 September 1781, AFC, 4:220. For Europe in 1782: Brush to Adams, 19 November 1782, PJA, 14:72–73. For firm: Broome-Semans and Broome-Schwarz, Broome, Latourette and Mercereau Families, 105. For background: Mann, "Thomas and Richard Brush," 132.

31. Brush to Adams, 4 February 1785, PJA, 16:515.

32. Codignola, Blurred Nationalities, 33.

33. Brush to Adams, 4 February 1785, PJA, 16:515–516.

34. Brush to Adams, 4 February 1785, PJA, 515; Cortese, "Le prime relazioni," 9. This seems to be the same list he presented to the ministers in Naples-Sicily, see Brush to Giovanni [John] Acton, 25 March 1785, Archivio di Stato di Napoli, Affari Esteri, Busta 4210 and Codignola, Blurred Nationalities, 55n14.

35. Cortese, "Le prime relazioni," 9; Codignola, Blurred Nationalities, 267n14. Brush returned to America after Naples, see John Quincy Adams to Abigail Adams [sister], 20 August 1785, AFC, 6:287.

36. *Augspurgische Ordinari Postzeitung*, no. 82, 7 April 1783, last page.

37. *Augspurgische Extra-Zeitung*, no. 288, 2 December 1783, first page.

38. *Augspurgische Ordinari Postzeitung*, no. 289, 3 December 1783, second page.

39. *Wiener Zeitung*, 25 June 1783, 6.

40. Ronkard, "Les répercussions de la Guerre Américaine," 57.

41. Starhemberg to Deplancq, 23 January 1783, transcribed in Schlitter, *Berichte*, 230–231.

42. The six members of the Committee were Gaspar Baudier, Nicolas Botte (secretary), Denis Benoît de Cazier, Henri Deplancq, Ferdinand Grégoire Paradis and Thomas François Grysperre. The three who responded were Deplancq, Grysperre, and Paradis.

43. ARB, CAPB, 512 and SEG, 2162, memoranda of Grysperre, 23 February 1783 and Paradis, 20 March 1783 respectively.

44. Levfevre, Documents, 385; Pricken, Deplancq. Huibrechts, "*Swampin' Guns and Stabbing Irons*," 530n128. Huibrechts states he died in 1785 but Levfevre (p. 350) gives 1791.

45. ARB, CAPB, 512, *Mémoire sur les effets de la Paix relativement au Commerce des Etats de Sa Majesté l'Empereur et sur les combinaisons auxquelles cet événement pourrait donner lieu*, 17 February 1783, transcribed by Houtte, "Contribution," 363–379. Huibrechts has located another (annotated) version in ARB, CP, 1154B, presumably by the council members or Starhemberg himself. I have only seen the earlier version and quote from Houtte's version.

46. Houtte, "Contribution," 363–366.

47. Ibid., 373–374; Everaert, "Le pavillon impérial," 60–61.

48. Houtte, "Contribution," 370–371.

49. Ibid., 376.

50. ARB, SEG, 2150/2, Songa, 16 March 1783; ARB, CAPB, 152, De Lattre, 31 January 1783. Some discrepancy on the response numbers: Houtte found nine including Baudier, Deplancq, de Lattre, and Songa whereas Huibrechts found responses from Bedene de Jenne, Friedrich Romberg, Veuve van Schoor, Charles de Proli, Hollier, De Looze, and William Herries. I can confirm her findings.

51. ARB, CAPB, 512, Report, 18 February 1783.

52. ARB, CAPB, 512, Report, 23 February 1783.

53. ARB, CAPB, 512, Report, 6 and 10 February 1783; ARB, SEG, 2162, Report, 4 February 1783.

54. Verhaegen, "Le commerce des esclaves en Belgique," 254–262; Anspach, "Frédéric baron de Romberg," 161–181; Huibrechts, "*Swampin' Guns and Stabbing Irons*," 476.

55. ARB, SEG, 2151/2, 'Rapports du 18 Juillet et du 26 Septembre 1782 sur un projet d'acquisition de l'Isle de Tobago.'

56. ARB, SEG, 2150, Charles Kersemans to Kaunitz, 6 March 1783 in 'Rapport du Comité le 20 Mars 1783 concernant l'Annonce d'une augmentation de Droits en Espagne'; ARB, SEG, 2154, Starhemberg to Kaunitz, 6 March 1783; ARB, SEG, 2154, 'Rapport du Comité sur diverses lettres du Secrétaire de légation à Madrid, Hambourg, et du Consul Impérial à Cadix, Comte de Greppi, relatives au nouveau Tarif des Douanes en Espagne, 31 May 1783.'

57. APS, William Temple Franklin Papers, Mss.B.F.86, CV, 72, James Drummond to William Temple Franklin, 13 June 1783 and APS, William Temple Franklin Papers, Mss.B.F.86, CV, 71, James Elphinston to William Temple Franklin, 13 June 1783.

Drummond was a school friend of William Temple Franklin and associated with *Herries, Keith & Co.* until its restructuring in 1784 when Charles Herries took over, see APS, William Temple Franklin Papers, Mss.B.F.86, CV, 60, *Robert Herries & Co.* Circular to William Temple Franklin, 31 July 1784.

58. The family settled in Amsterdam in the 1740s with a branch in London, *Israel Levin Salomon's*, which relocated to Ostend during the Revolution. Mark was one of three Prager sons to travel to the United States, see Marcus, United States Jewry, 1:146–147.

59. Library of Congress [LoC], George Washington Papers, Series 2, Letterbooks 1754–1799: Letterbook 11, 243, Washington to William Fitzhugh, 23 July 1784.

60. Library of Congress [LoC], George Washington Papers, Series 4, General Correspondence, Series 4, MSS 44693: Reel 098, 141–142, Prager to Washington, 27 October 1788, which was written from Amsterdam following his father's death in early 1788, see TNA, PROB 11/1162/253, Will of Israel Levin Salomon [Yehiel Prager], 21 February 1788.

61. HHStA, Belgien, DDB Rot, K. 182b, Report of Baron de Beelen-Bertholff, 17 June 1785, Add. JJ, fol. 117. The Pragers were part of the Portuguese Jewish community in Amsterdam and used their connections in Lisbon, tapping into a longstanding wheat and wine trade, see Fisher, The Portugal Trade, 42–43. They were lucky to operate when the trade was depressed pending a US-Portuguese trade agreement, see Reeder, Smugglers, Pirates and Patriots, 90–91.

62. HHStA, Belgien, DDB Rot, K. 182c, Report of Baron de Beelen-Bertholff, 25 February 1786, Add. K, fols. 55–68.

63. University of Chicago Library, Special Collections, Butler-Gensaulus Collection, Box 1, fol. 74, Note of John Dickinson, 3 October 1785.

64. Marcus, United States Jewry, 1:147.

65. Hagley Library and Museum, Wurts Family Papers, Section I, James Vanuxem Papers, Promissory Notes, Box 1, Folder 15. N.B. sometimes spelled as the Dutch variant *De Heijder, Veijdt & Co.*

66. James Vanuxem Jr. (1790–1877) was born in Philadelphia. He married Susannah Lombaert, daughter of Herman Joseph Lombaert and Margaretta Wynkoop Lombaert, see ibid. under miscellany and the historical note to the collection.

67. HHStA, Belgien, DDB Rot, K. 182a, Report of Baron de Beelen-Bertholff, 14 November 1784, Add. B, fols. 55–68 and K. 182b, 17 June 1785, Add. C, fol. 12; Du Plessis, Transitions to Capitalism, 298.

68. Lamikiz, Trade and Trust, i.

69. HHStA, Belgien, DDB Rot, K. 182d, Report of Baron de Beelen-Bertholff, 20 March 1787, Add. M, fols. 51–54.

70. Winterthur Museum, Joseph Downs Collection of Manuscripts, Coll. Mic. 187, Ledgerbook of Samuel Wetherill and Sons, fol. 180. They also sold goods under their own name, see advertisement of *De Heyder, Veydt & Co.* in *The Pennsylvania Packet*, 16 November 1787.

71. TNA, FO 26/3, Torrington to Lord Carmarthen, 22 January 1786.

72. HHStA, Belgien, DDB Rot, K. 182c, Beelen-Bertholff to Belgiojoso, 24 November 1786, fols. 447–457.

73. HHStA, Belgien, DDB Rot, K. 182a, Report of Baron de Beelen-Bertholff, 14 November 1784, Add. C, fols. 121–143. *Biddle & Tellier* was Clement Biddle and Rudolph Tellier.

74. HHStA, Belgien, DDB Rot, K. 182a, Report of Baron de Beelen-Bertholff, 14 November 1784, Add. M, fols. 177–180; Van Winter, American Finance and Dutch Investment, 1:177.

75. HHStA, Belgien, DDB Rot, K. 182a, Report of Baron de Beelen-Bertholff, 14 November 1784, Add. M, fols. 177–180; HHStA, Belgien, DDB Rot, K. 182a, 13 December 1784, Add. J, fol. 220.

76. Hasquin, Joseph II, 62.

77. Farasyn, De 18de eeuwse bloeiperiode and Ronkard, "Les répercussions de la Guerre Américaine," Tableau I. Mouvement portuaire: Ostende & Bruges/Antilles, 64–65;

78. Two applications dated 3 July 1782 and 11 January 1782 in ARB, SEG, 2173, 'Demandes pour des Places de Consuls avec un Inventaire des Rapports et Pieces 1781–1786.'

79. Deplancq's memorandum, 18 July 1782 in ARB, SEG, 2173, 'Rapport sur la requête de F. J. Bouvier natif de Namur tendante a nomme Consul General Imperial en Amérique.'

80. Connecticut Historical Society, Silas Deane Papers, Box 7, Folder 21, Sir Robert Herries, 'Observations on Commerce.' Herries, a major trader in tobacco, saw success in reshipping Flemish linens, laces, and hats to the United States.

81. Browne to Adams (27 January 1784) is missing but was forwarded by Dennis de Berdt to Adams, 6 February 1784, PJA, 16:17–18. Adams forwarded the letters to Franklin and Jay on 27 March 1784 (PBF, 42:78) and Franklin acknowledged that he had sent the letter on to Congress on 16 April 1784, PJA, 16:165–166. Nothing more came of it.

82. Dill, Militia Diplomat, s.n.

83. Browne and Lee had cooperated throughout the war and had traded with one another since at least 1775, see the Jessie Ball duPont Memorial Library at Stratford Hall [SH], The Archives of the Robert E. Lee Memorial Foundation, Papers of the Lee Family, William Lee Letterbooks [WLLB], Box 9, Lee to Francis Lightfoot Lee, 23 September 1775.

84. Lee had known De Berdt since 1771, see SH, WLLB, Box 9, Lee to Anthony Stewart, 1 April 1771. For Lee's desire to see commerce restored, see Lee to Arthur Lee, 2 April 1783; Lee to Samuel Thorpe, 11 April 1783; Lee to Adams, 24 April 1783, LWL, 3:939–945. For Lee's scheme with Browne, see VHS, William Lee Letterbooks, Mss.51.f.421, fols. 148–150, Lee to Browne, 26 April 1785.

85. VHS, William Lee Letterbooks, Mss.51.f.421, fol. 153, Lee to Browne, 11 May 1785.

86. Ibid., fols. 265–268, Lee to Browne, 6 May 1786 and Lee to Frederick Grand, 6 May 1786.

87. Ibid., fols. 270–271, Lee to Brothers Overman, 6 May 1786.

88. LoC, Nicholas Low Papers, "Ostend, Belgium," Box 3, William Williams to Nicholas Low, 10 September 1783.

89. LoC, Nicholas Low Papers, "Anvers, Belgium," Box 7, *Werbrouck & Mellerio* to Nicholas Low, 22 March 1785 and 1 August 1785.

90. LoC, Nicholas Low Papers, "Anvers, Belgium," Box 9, *Werbrouck & Mellerio* to Joseph Lacoste, 20 January 1786.

91. Roberts and Roberts, Thomas Barclay (1728–1793), 158–171.

92. *The Papers of Robert Morris* [PRM], 9:xxxvii; Maryland Historical Society, Robert Gilmor Collection, Series 1, Box 1, Folder 29, George Gibson to Gilmor, 15 June 1785.

93. Robert Morris to Gilmor, 14 February 1784, PRM, 9:120–121.

94. Rabuzzi, *Cutting Out the Middleman?*, 184.

95. William Wenam Seward to Jefferson, 25 October 1785, PTJ, 8:672–674.

96. The first representatives were Francis L. Taney in Ostend (1801–1803) and James Blake in Antwerp (1801–1804), see Smith, America's Diplomats, 67.

97. FHKA, NHK, Kommerz Litorale, Akten, Fasz. 105, K. 905 'Borse', fols. 260–261 (1775); fols. 271–272 (1776); fols. 278–279 (1777); fols. 286–287 (1779); fols. 415–416 (1783) and fol. 392; Anon., Handbuch für Kaufsleute, 1:254.

98. Singerton, "New World, New Market," 65–72.

99. Dominique François Belletti to Franklin, 21 February 1783, unpublished, "Franklin Papers Project at Yale University.".

100. Belletti to Franklin, 21 February 1783, unpublished, "Franklin Papers Project at Yale University."

101. APS, Franklin Papers, Mss.B.F85, 7, XXVIII, 11, Belletti to Franklin, 7 April 1783; APS, Franklin Papers, Mss.B.F85, 7, XXVIII, 26, Belletti to Franklin 11 April 1783; APS, Franklin Papers, Mss.B.F85, 7, XXVIII, 39, Belletti to Franklin, 14 April 1783; and APS, Franklin Papers, Mss.B.F85, 7, XXVIII, 62, Belletti to Franklin, 25 April 1783.

102. Antoine-Madeleine Bertrand to Franklin, 15 September 1783, PBF, 40:362.

103. APS, Franklin Papers, Mss.B.F85, 7, XXVIII, 39, Zinzendorf for Belletti, 19 January 1780.

104. APS, Franklin Papers, Mss.B.F85, 7, XXVIII, 90, Proli to Franklin, 14 May 1783. Franklin's letter of introduction (14 May 1783) is in FHKA, NHK, Kommerz Litorale, Akten, K. 903, fol. 1107.

105. Spellings varied.

106. HHStA, KA, KK, NZ, TZ, Bd. 26, 30 August 1781, fol. 274.

107. FHKA, NHK, Kommerz Litorale, Akten, K. 903, fol. 1046r–1047.

108. FHKA, NHK, Kommerz Litorale, Akten, K. 903, fol. 1046r.

109. APS, Franklin Papers, Ms.B.F85., 7, XXIX, 147, Belletti to Franklin, 15 September 1783. Original emphasis.

110. Ibid.

111. APS, Franklin Papers, Ms.B.F85, 8, X, 11, Richard Bache to Franklin, 7 March 1784.

112. *Pennsylvania Gazette*, 10 December 1783.

113. HHStA, Belgien, DDB Rot, K.182a Report, 25 April November 1784, Add. O, fols. 59–64; HHStA, Belgien, DDB Rot, K.182a, Report, 14 November 1784, Add. A., fols. 114–120.

114. HHStA, Belgien, DDB Rot, K.182a, Report, 21 March 1785, Add. J, fols. 276–298.

115. Ibid., fols. 280–281.

116. Ibid., fols. 276–298.

117. WD, 18 September 1784. Original letter dated 12 February 1784.

118. HHStA, Belgien, DDB Rot, K. 182a, Report, 14 November 1784, Add. A., fols. 114–120; Houtte, *Histoire économique*, 1:32–33.

119. HHStA, Belgien, DDB Rot, K. 182a, Report, 14 November 1784, Add. A., fols. 118–120, 'Lettre à Mons. Jaumenet maître des forges à Namur,' September 1784; Hildebrand, "Foreign markets for Swedish iron," 3–52.

120. Leos Müller and Michal Wanner, "Bohemian Textiles and Glass in Eighteenth-Century Global Trade" presented at *The Third European Congress on World and Global History*, 14–17 April 2011, London School of Economics; Kellenbenz, *Der deutsche Außenhandel*, 4–60; Ramcke, *Die Beziehung zwischen Hamburg und Österreich*.

121. HHStA, Belgien, DDB Rot, K. 182e, No. 3, fol. 32.

122. HHStA, Belgien, DDB Rot, K. 182a, Report 25 April 1784, Add P., fols. 65–66.

123. HHStA, Belgien, DDB Rot, K. 182a, Report 25 April 1784, Add P., fol. 66.

124. HHStA, Belgien, DDB Rot, K. 182c, Letter, fols. 287–295.

125. The two species were *Nicotiana Tabacum* commonly called "Virginia tobacco," grown in America, and *Nicotiana Rustica* also called "Aztec tobacco," grown in Hungary. For attitudes towards tobacco, see Maxwell, "Tobacco as Cultural Signifier," 1–19.

126. Maxwell, Everyday Nationalism, 60–61.

127. In 1777, for example, word of a new consignment of American tobacco arriving in France compelled one Dutch merchant to cancel his order of Hungarian tobacco, see Zinzendorf, diary entry 6 August 1777 in Klingenstein et al, *Zwischen Wien und Triest*, 2:24.

128. Maxwell, Everyday Nationalism, 62.

129. Ibid., 61.

130. Marczali, Hungary in the Eighteenth Century, 28–29.

131. Ibid., 77; Márki, Amerika és a magyarság, 4.

132. On Joseph's journey to the Banat see Beales, Joseph II, 1:366–367 and Kulcsár, *The Travels of Joseph II*, 34–57.

133. Marczali, Hungary in the Eighteenth Century, 78.

134. Almásy to Beelen-Bertholff, 4 December 1783 in HHStA, Belgien, DDB Rot, K. 182a, Report 25 April 1784, Add. L, fols. 52–56.

135. Mérei, "Marktverhältnisse im Außenhandel," 378.

136. Maxwell, Everyday Nationalism, 63–64.

137. Phelps, U.S.-Habsburg Relations, 43–44.

138. HHStA, Belgien, DDB Rot, K. 182a, Report, 21 March 1785, Add J, fols. 276–298; cf. Codignola, Blurred Nationalities, 70.

139. Lanmon, "The Baltimore Glass Trade," 21 and 26.

140. HHStA, StK, Provinzen, Küstenland, K. 1, 'Prospetto di una Compagnia di commercio per l'America Settentrionale.' In German the company was called the *Österreichisch-Amerikanische Gesellschaft*. For the Italian name see Codignola, Blurred Nationalities, 69.

141. 'V. Handlungsanzeigen' in *Salzburger Intelligenzblatt*, 28 September 1785; HHStA, Belgien, DDB Rot, K. 182b, fol. 313–316, Beelen-Bertholff to Kaunitz, 18 October 1785.

142. For example: 29 October 1785, *Journal Général de France* (Paris, 1785), 524.

143. HHStA, StK, Vorträge, K. 141, Brigido to Joseph II, 12 August 1785.

144. Ibid.

145. Ibid.

146. HHStA, StK, Noten der Vereinigten Hofkanzlei, K. 14, Nota der vereinigten Hofkanzlei to the Staatskanzlei, 5 September 1785.

147. Lafayette to Jefferson, 4 September 1785, PTJ, 8:478–480.

148. "III. Siebenbürgen. Anfang eines Handels mit Amerika" in *Provinzial Nachrichten aus den Kaiserl. Königl. Staaten*, 17 April 1784, 483–484.

Chapter 8

1. HHStA, Belgien, DDB Rot, K. 182c, 25 February 1786, Add. J, fols. 24–35.

2. Agstner, *Consulates South of the Rio Grande*, 85–117. The two Asian posts were in Canton (1781) and Mauritius (1783) followed later by one in Bengal (1787).

3. ARB, SEG, 2150, No. 76, Requête du sieur Bedene de Jaure, 18 March 1782.

4. HHStA, Belgien, DDA, Berichte, K. 260, Starhemberg to Kaunitz, 2 April 1782.

5. HHStA, Belgien, DDA, Berichte, K. 260, Avisé au Comité à Bruxelles.

6. Franklin to Mercy-d'Argenteau, 18 January 1782, PBF, 36:447–448.

7. Dull, "Franklin and the Nature of American Diplomacy," 346–363; Perkins, *American Foreign Relations*, 1:26–41.

8. Elkins and McKitrick, The Age of Federalism, 65–89; Kaplan, Colonies into Nation, 158–161; Edling, A Revolution in Favor of Government, 131–134.

9. See Guinta and Hargrove, The Emerging Nation, 2: *"Trials and Tribulations."*

10. Gilje, "Commerce and Conquest," 735–770.

11. HHStA, Belgien, DDA, Weisungen, K.47, Kaunitz to Starhemberg, 13 April 1782.

12. ARB, SEG, 2173, No. 145, Requête de Bouvier, 11 January 1783.

13. HHStA, Belgien, DDA, Korrespondenz Frankreich, K. 33.

14. Ibid.

15. For American awareness of this issue, see Lee to Adams, 18 February 1783, PJA, 14:276–277.

16. Habsburg ambassadors simultaneously represented both the imperial dignity and the various other dignities held by the Habsburg monarch, see Hochedlinger, Austria's Wars of Emergence, 46–47.

17. HHStA, StK, Vorträge, K.137, fol. 167-173, Kaunitz to Joseph, 19 March 1783.

18. ARB, CAPB, 512, Report, 25 February 1783.

19. HHStA, StK, Vorträge, K.137, fol. 170, Kaunitz to Joseph, 19 March 1783.

20. Ibid. fol. 171.

21. Mallon, "Beelen-Bertholff," 149.

22. For Beelen's experience: ARB, CP, 1067, 20 December 1777.

23. HHStA, StK, Vorträge, K. 137, Kaunitz, Memorandum, s.d.

24. ARB, CAPB, 512, Beelen to Starhemberg, 25 February 1783.

25. HHStA, Belgien, DDA, Berichte, K. 275, Belgiojoso to Kaunitz, Nos. 63 and 69.

26. ARB, SEG, 2162, fol. 156, 'Project de Points pour server de matériaux au Instructions concernant le commerce de donner au Ministre et au Consul qui seroient envoyées de la part de S.M. l'Empereur auprès des États Unis de l'Amérique Septentrionale,' 6 April 1783.

27. HHStA, Belgien, DDA, Weisungen, K. 49, 'Projet d'instructions pour N.N. declare consul imperial et royal dans l'Amérique Septentrionale,' s.d.

28. ARB, SEG, 2161, fol. 165. 'Sur divers points de directions ultérieures à fixer avant le départ du Baron de Beelen vers les États-Unis,' 25 May 1783.

29. ARB, CAPB, 512, Memoire de Beelen, 14 May 1783.

30. For their marriage: Hellin, *Histoire chronologique*, 482–483.

31. Family information drawn from Historical Society of Pennsylvania [HSP], Beelen Family Papers [BFP]. Two daughters had married by the time of the mission: Philippine married Edouard de Dorlodot in 1781, and Thérèse married Charles François Maurice Villeneuve de Janti. Descendants in the Dorlodot line, especially Baron Albert de Dorlodot—Beelen's great-great-great grandson—attempted to compile a family history and a sketch of the Beelen Mission, see his "Analysis of documents on Baron de Beelen-Bertholff and his mission in America, his life there and his children." in HSP, BFP. From Constantin Antoine stems the Gazzam line, whose descendants also compiled a historical account of the family, see Anton de Beelen Mackenzie, *History of the Gazzam Family—together with a sketch of the American branch of the family of de Beelen* (Reading, PA: 1894). I am grateful to further descendants of both American and European lines for sharing their family story with me.

32. ARB, SEG, 2163, fol.198, Memorandum, 22 July 1783.

33. Alison, "Baron de B," 30–35.

34. Thieriot was shipwrecked and made it to Philadelphia in March 1784. He returned the following year, see Lingelbach, "Saxon-American Relations," 525–30.

35. WD, 29 September 1784.

36. Five Habsburg agents forming an imperial botanic mission to the United States were onboard and recorded the terrible journey. ÖNB, Codex Series, no. 3517 'Expedition Märter', no. 1596, and HHStA, Wissenschaft und Kunst, K. 6 'Märter Schriften.' I have refrained from discussing this interesting episode in the early US-Habsburg relationship since Dr. Heather Morrison is currently working on a monograph on the subject. See her "Open Competition in Botany," 107–119.

37. APS, Franklin Papers, Mss.B.F85, 7, XXIX, 133, Bache to Franklin, 8 September 1783.

38. Mallon, "Beelen-Bertholff," 150.

39. Young, "The Baron de Beelen-Bertholff," 1–7.

40. Untitled Sketchbook in the HSP, BFP.

41. He also composed a short *Treatise on the Use of Colour* in the HSP, BFP.

42. De Dorlodot, "*Analysis*," 6.

43. PRM, 8:568.

44. 'Erbländische Nachrichten,' *Wienerblättchen,* 25 September 1783.

45. WD, 17 September 1783.

46. HHStA, Belgien, DDB Rot, K. 182a, Report, 21 March 1785, Add. E, fols. 252–255.

47. 'Projet d'un Édit soumis par la législation de la Pensylvanie à la considération du public tendant à imposer un droit d'entrée additionnel sur les objets et sur le pied y repris.' in HHStA, Belgien, DDB Rot, K. 182b, Report, 17 June 1785, Add. R, fols. 49–52; 'Etat de Rhode Island Douannes.' in HHStA, Belgien, DDB Rot, K. 182b, 10 September 1785, Add. D, fols. 177–180; 'Douannes Innovations de Massachusetts.' in HHStA, Belgien, DDB Rot, K. 182b, 10 September 1785, Add. C, fols. 173–176; 'New York.' in HHStA, Belgien, DDB Rot, K. 182b, 10 September 1785, Add G., fols. 191–194.

48. HHStA, Belgien, DDB Rot, K. 182a, Report, 14 November 1784, Add M, fols. 17–180; 'Exportations of Charleston' in HHStA, Belgien, DDB Rot, K. 182b, 17 June 1785, Add. P, fols. 46–47; and Piat Lefebvre to Beelen, in HHStA, Belgien, DDB Rot, K. 182c, Report, 19 June 1786, Add. T, fols. 295–306.

49. Hill, French Perceptions, 90–94; HHStA, Belgien, DDB Rot, K. 182c, Report, 22 December 1786, Add. A, fol. 460.

50. HHStA, Belgien, DDB Rot, K. 182a, Report, 21 March 1785, Add. F, fols. 266–269; HHStA, Belgien, DDB Rot, K. 182b, 17 June 1785, Add. N, fol. 38; Beelen to Jay, [before 14] September 1785 in Nuxoll, *Selected Papers of John Jay,* 4:177–179.

51. HHStA, Belgien, DDB Rot, K. 182b, fols. 313–320, Beelen to Kaunitz, 18 October 1785. Beelen warned the situation in North Carolina could be severe in his report of 25 February 1786 in HHStA, Belgien, DDB Rot, K. 182c, Add. M, fols. 71–94.

52. HHStA, Belgien, DDB Rot, K. 182b, Report, 17 June 1785, Add. Q, fol. 48.

53. Edling, A Hercules in the Cradle, 24–25; Edling, "'So Immense a Power in the Affairs of War,'" 287–326; Van Cleve, "The Anti-Federalists' Toughest Challenge," 529–560.

54. HHStA, Belgien, DDB Rot, K. 182a, Report, 14 November 1784, Add. E, fol. 157.

55. Boudinot to Franklin, 1 November 1783, PBF, 41:169.

56. HHStA, Belgien, DDB Rot, K. 182a, fols. 183–188, Beelen to Belgiojoso, 13 December 1784.

57. HHStA, Belgien, DDB Rot, K. 182a, fols. 1–5, Beelen to Belgiojoso, 25 April 1784.

58. Hauptmann and McLester, Onedia Indian Journey, 10.

59. HHStA, Belgien, DDB Rot, K. 182c, Report, 25 February 1786, Add. J, fols. 24–35.

60. HHStA, Belgien, DDB Rot, K. 182a, Report, 21 March 1785, Add. J, fols. 276–298.

61. HHStA, Belgien, DDB Rot, K. 182c, Report, 25 February 1786, Add. J, fols. 24–35.

62. HHStA, Belgien, DDB Rot, K. 182a, Report, 25 April 1784, Add. E, fols. 22–39.

63. HHStA, Belgien, DDB Rot, K. 182c, fols. 183–188, Beelen to Belgiojoso, 13 December 1784.

64. HHStA, Belgien, DDB Rot, K. 182a, Report, 21 March 1785, Add. J, fol. 277.

65. HHStA, Belgien, DDB Rot, K. 182a, Report, 13 December 1784, Add. H, fol. 219.

66. HHStA, Belgien, DDB Rot, K. 182a, Report, 25 April 1784, Add. A, fol. 15.

67. For Temple: HHStA, Belgien, DDB Rot, K. 182c, Report, 25 February 1786, Add. Z, fols. 148–149.

68. HHStA, Belgien, DDB Rot, K. 182a, Report, 10 September 1785, Add. K, fols. 225–228.

69. HHStA, Belgien, DDB Rot, K. 182c, Report, 19 June 1786, Add. C, fols. 237–240.

70. HHStA, Belgien, DDB Rot, K. 182c, Report, Add. BB, fols. 341–345.

71. HHStA, Belgien, DDB Rot, K. 182c, Report, 12 September 1786, Add. O, fols. 401–404.

72. See Temple's reports in *Bowdoin and Temple Papers*, vols. 1-3; Müller, "Swedish-American Trade," 173–188. Hans Schlitter published Beelen's reports, as *Die Berichte des ersten Agenten Österreichs in den Vereinigten Staaten von Amerika* (Vienna: Tempsky, 1891). Schlitter heavily edited the correspondence and chose selected reports from the collection, however. By my calculations he published the following fractions: K.182a (31%), K. 182b (41%), K. 182c (32%), K. 182d (29%), K. 182e (15%).

73. HHStA, Belgien, DDB Rot, K. 182b, fols. 292–295, Beelen to Belgiojoso, 20 October 1785.

74. Thus rendering Schlitter's edition more incomplete, see Houtte, "American Commercial Conditions," 567–578.

75. HHStA, Belgien, DDB Rot, K. 182b, fols. 313–320, Beelen to Kaunitz, 18 October 1785.

76. Proposals of Cazier, Deplancq and Müllendorf in Starhemberg to Kaunitz, 12 April and 6 May 1783 in HHStA, Belgien, DDA, Berichte, K. 270, fols. 34 and 126 respectively.

77. The committee reports are HHStA, Belgien, DDB Rot, K. 182e, fols. 1–135.

78. HHStA, Belgien, DDB Rot, K. 182e, fols. 49–96, 'Rapport du Committee sur les Deux Reports de Beelen en Philadelphie,' 16 September 1784.

79. AST, DB, Serie VII, C.75, fol. 58 'Communicazione del Governo per la nomina del Barone di Bellen a Consigliere di Commercio presso di Congresso Americano.'; AST, DB, Serie VII, C.127, fol.13 'Trasmissione del Governo delle tabelle inviate dal consiglieri Barone de Beelen, dei prezzi delle merci in Filadelfia.'; FHKA, NHK, Kommerz Litorale, Akten, K. 904, fols. 1245, 1272–1278, 1299; FHKA, NHK, Kommerz Litorale, Akten, Generalia, K. 850, fols. 886-890; FHKA, NHK, Kommerz Böhmen, Akten, K. 1205, Teil III – Vorträge, fols. 708-709.

80. HHStA, Belgien, DDB Rot, K. 182a, Report, 14 November 1784, Add. L, fols. 171–176.

81. HHStA, Belgien, DDB Rot, K. 182a, Report, 13 December 1784, Add. G, fols. 207–218; HHStA, Belgien, DDB Rot, K. 182c, Report, 19 June 1786, Add. B, fols. 235–236.

82. HHStA, Belgien, DDB Rot, K. 182a, Beelen to Belgiojoso, 14 November 1784, Add. A, fols. 114–120.

83. HHStA, Belgien, DDB Rot, K. 182a, Report, 25 April 1784, Add. O, fols. 59–64; *Pennsylvania Gazette*, 12 February and 13 September 1784.

84. Incontrera, Trieste e l'America, 124; Codignola, *Le prime relazioni*, 25–38.

85. Pühringer-Gräf, 'Reyer, Franz Thaddäus von,' *Neue Deutsche Biographie*, 21 (2003), 482.

86. Coons, Steamships, Statesmen, and Bureaucrats, 6–9.

87. Righettini and Serera to Beelen, 23 February 1787 in HHStA, DDB Rot, K. 182d, Report, 24 May 1787, Add. M, fols. 110–118.

88. HHStA, DDB Rot, K. 182d, Report, 24 May 1787, Add. M, fols. 110–118.

89. Wurzbach, *Biographisches Lexikon*, 54:23–26; Adler, *Political Economy in the Habsburg Monarchy*, 213.

90. Quoted in Ingenhousz to Franklin, 26 February 1783, PBF, 39:188–189.

91. Ingenhousz to Franklin, 8 April 1783, PBF, 39:444–446.

92. Franklin to Ingenhousz, 16 May 1783, PBF, 40:8–13.

93. Donath was born to Anton Donath and Anna Catharina Hübner in St. Georgenthal (today Jiřetín pod Jedlovou) in northern Bohemia. He studied at Prague from 1772 to 1775 and entered the civil service in Vienna. His personal papers are at the University of Pennsylvania, Kislak Special Collections, Misc. Manuscripts, Box 6 'Donath Manuscripts.' For his freemasonry: HHStA, KA, VA, K. 70, Nos. 4 & 5, 8 and 13 July 1783, fols. 52–57.

94. Donath seems to have worked for the firm *Kohler & Kern* according to his letter to Steinský, dated 19 April 1790 in Archiv Národního muzea Praha [ANM], Fond Steinský.

95. Ingenhousz to Franklin, 23 June 1783, PBF, 40:216–217. Weinbrenner's letter is missing.

96. HHStA, Belgien, DDB Rot, K. 182a, Report, 25 April 1784, Add. P, fols. 65–66.

97. HHStA, Belgien, DDB Rot, K. 182a, Report, 25 April 1784, Add. P, fol. 65.

98. HHStA, Belgien, DDB Rot, K. 182a, Report, 25 April 1784, Add. P, fol. 66. The report Donath carried was entitled "Nota über die Musterkarte," but it is missing.

99. HHStA, Belgien, DDB Rot, K. 182a, Report, 14 November 1784, Add. L, fols. 171–176.

100. APS, Franklin Paper Series, 8, Mss.B.F85, XXXIV, 161, Donath to Franklin, 27 October 1786.

101. See the family burial plot in the graveyard of St. Mary's Catholic Church, Philadelphia.

102. APS, Mss.Ms.Coll.200, Journal of Bee-Keeping at Spring Mill (1787–1788); Singerton, "A Bumbling Beekeeper from Bohemia."

103. Hagley Library and Museum, Accession no. 38, *Donath & Co.* Letterbooks, 1801–1802; A. McElroy, *Philadelphia Directory for 1839* (Philadelphia, 1839), 65; Winterthur Museum, Delaware, Bernard M. Bloomfield Papers.

104. LA PNP, Fonds F. A. Steinského 1760–1811, Donath to Steinský, 20 July 1792.

105. 'Observations concernant la Correspondance du Gouvernement des Pais Bas Autrichiens avec le Conseiller de Commerce Baron de Beelen depuis l'arrivée de celui-ci en Amérique en 1783 jusqu'à la fin de 1787,' 24 April 1788 in HHStA, DDB Rot, K.182e, Rapport au Beelen, fols. 39–90r.

106. Proli to Henri de Crumpipen, 10 February 1788 in HHStA, DDB Rot, K.182e, Rapport au Beelen, fol. 19.

107. Ibid., fol. 20.

108. HHSTA, DDB Rot, K. 182e, Rapport au Beelen, Appendix B, fol. 32.

109. Proli to Henri de Crumpipen, 10 February 1788 in HHStA, DDB Rot, K. 182e, Rapport au Beelen, fol. 20.

110. HHStA, Belgien, DDB Rot, K. 182e, fols. 256-259, Beelen to Ferdinand von Trauttmansdorff, 28th September 1788.

111. HHStA, Belgien, DDB Rot, K. 182e, fols. 11–18.

112. De Dorlodot, "*Analysis*," 5.

113. In February 1785, Colonel Jean-Pierre Ransonnet wrote to Pierre de Reuss, assistant to then Secretary of War De Crumpipen, upon his return home to Liège from Pennsylvania. Ransonnet had travelled to the United States in order to surveil Beelen's mission. In his report, he noted how Beelen had invested in Pennsylvanian land and included a general prospectus aimed at enticing European investment and migrants. ARB, CAPB, 303, Ransonnet to Reuss, 8 February 1785.

114. The main habitation became known as "the castle" and the area today is known as Barons Mills. De Dorlodot, "*Analysis*," 5; Young, "The Baron de Beelen-Bertholff," 4.

115. The Hellam deeds are contained within Gazzam, History of Gazzam Family, 61–65. Young, "Beelen-Bertholff," 4; Andes, "Honey Brook's only nobleman," 347–348. Address 2301 South Forrest, York PA is the likely location of Beelen's last home.

116. York County Historical Society Collections, Lewis Miller, *Chronicles of York, 1790–1870*, 2 vols.

117. Gazzam, History of Gazzam Family, 65.

118. York County Archives, Administration Accounts and Inventory of Baron de Beelen-Bertholff.

119. Young, "Beelen-Bertholff," 5. Originally the chapel honoured the Beelens with a burial inside near the altar, but at some point, the slab was relocated outside; their bones still rest somewhere beneath the chapel floor.

120. Benna, "Österreichs erste diplomatische Vertretung," 215–240.

Chapter 9

1. Adams to Jefferson, 20 March 1826, Thomas Jefferson Retirement Series – Early Access, *Founders Online*, National Archives: http://founders.archives.gov/documents/Jefferson/98-01-02-5970 (December 2016).

2. Jefferson to Adams, 30 March 1826, ibid., http://founders.archives.gov/documents/ Jefferson/98-01-02-5995 (December, 2016).

3. Jefferson's role has been acknowledged by Burnett, "Note on American Negotiations," 579–587; Houtte, "American Negotiations with Austria," 567–578; Benna, Contemporary Austrian Views, 12; Schlitter, Beziehungen; Friebel, "*Österreich und die Vereinigten Staaten*," 81–88.

4. The most famous popular depiction is of course the James Ivory film *Jefferson in Paris* (1995) and his infatuation with Maria Cosway is most recently examined by Kukla, Mr. Jefferson's Women. Jefferson's period in Paris is well covered but not exclusively from a foreign policy perspective, see Kimball, Jefferson: The Scene in Europe; Rice, Thomas Jefferson's Paris; Adams, The Paris Years; Wilson and Stanton, Jefferson Abroad among others. The best account of Jefferson's foreign policy in Paris remains Woolery, The Relation of Thomas Jefferson to American Foreign Policy which highlighted that Jefferson's period as minister plenipotentiary in France witnessed "the highest point of technical service that he performed for the United States." (p. 65). The best overview of Jefferson's diplomacy is now Francis D. Cogliano, Emperor of Liberty.

5. Beales, Joseph II, 2:397. Beales's Chapter 11 (pp. 373–402) in this biography is one of the best summaries in English of Habsburg foreign policy under Joseph II but as Michael Hochedlinger notes "there is no satisfying treatment of Habsburg foreign policy concepts in the second half of the eighteenth century," in his Austria's Wars of Emergence, 374–375.

6. Arneth and Flammermont, *Correspondance secrète du comte de Mercy Argenteau*, 1:165.

7. Nakhimovsky, "Vattel's Theory of the International Order," 157–173; Holland, "The Moral Person of the State," 438–445.

8. The idea of a *jus gentium* or "law of nations" harkened back to Roman legal conventions in the western juridical tradition. It was a customary expression of natural rights (*jus naturale*) which governed the interaction of members within a system between different *gentes* or peoples and nations. In sixteenth and eighteenth centuries, the devastation and instability of confessional wars drove Europeans to reigniting ideals of international conduct. One of the leading theorizers was Christian Wolff who applied the novelties of empiricism and logic to the function of international relations and derived the *jus gentium* as a moral imperative of states as part of their natural and sacred power. An influential disciple of Wolff was the Swiss jurist Emer de Vattel, whose ideas expanded upon Wolff's ideas and sought to define the reasonable limits of territoriality of states. Though influential, Vattel's propagation of Wolff was by no means universally accepted by the late eighteenth century, see Stapelbroek, "Universal Society, Commerce and the Rights of Neutral Trade," 63–89.

9. Whaley, Germany and the Holy Roman Empire, 2:13–14; Wilson, *The Meaning of Empire in Central Europe around 1800*, 22–42; see also Tanner, The Last Descendant of Aeneas.

10. The Holy Roman Emperor acknowledged the imperial dignity of the Russian Tsar in 1742 but the issue had been a thorny one for some time, see Hennings, Russia and Courtly Europe, 44–46 and Wilson, Heart of Europe, 153–155. For the dispute with Persia, see the sixteenth-century complaints of imperial ambassadors at the Ottoman court at Constantinople in Stoyanova, *The Benefits and Limits of Permanent Diplomacy*, 152–171. The imperative to still outrank France after Napoleon's self-proclamation as an emperor and his coronation sanctified by the presence of the Pope forced Francis II to elevate the dignity of the Austrian realms in 1804 to an imperial level, see Wilson, "Bolstering the Prestige of the Habsburgs," 722–724.

11. Adams to President of Congress, 4 August 1779, PJA, 8:108–120.

12. Adams to James Warren, 12 April 1783, PJA, 14:401–402; Lee to Adams, 18 February 1783, PJA, 276–277.

13. Vucinich, Dubrovnik and the American Revolution, 1–23.

14. Ingenhousz to Franklin, 26 February 1783, PBF, 39:217–222.

15. ASF, AdS, Affari Esteri, no. 2335, fols. 372–373; fol. 377; fols. 383–384, Favi to Piccolomini, 20, 27 January and 3 February 1783, respectively.

16. Adams was mistaken: "[Dana] has a Commission which Authorises him to treat with the Emperor, as well as with all the other Powers, who compose the Armed Neutrality," in Adams to Lee, 23 February 1783, PJA, 14:290–291.

17. Adams to Dana, 22 February 1783, PJA, 14:285–287. It seems Dana did not correspond with Cobenzl, see the Dana Papers at the Massachusetts Historical Society and Cresson, Francis Dana.

18. Dana to Adams, 16/27 March 1783, PJA, 14:368–369. Dates reflect the Gregorian and Julian calendars.

19. ARB, SEG, 2162, Mercy-d'Argenteau to Starhemberg, 19 April 1783. A few days prior, Mercy-d'Argenteau had asked Franklin for passports for the botanical mission led by Franz Joseph Märter, see Mercy-d'Argenteau to Franklin, 12 April 1783, PBF, 39:474–475.

20. HHStA, Belgien, Korrespondenz Frankreich, K. 33, Starhemberg to Mercy, 9 April 1783.

21. Lee to Adams, 18 February 1783, PJA, 14:276–277.

22. Ingenhousz to Franklin, 8 April 1783, PBF, 39:444–446.

23. Adams to Dana, 1 May 1783, PJA, 14:464–465. The only mention Adams made between May and July was to James Warren: "The Emperor has an Inclination to treat with Us but the House of Austria never makes the first Advances," Adams to Warren, 12 April 1783, PJA, 14:401–402.

24. Adams to Livingston, 3 July 1783, PJA, 15:76–81.

25. Mercy-d'Argenteau inherited estates from his natural father and foster father. For details of the familial estates, see LoC, Mercy-d'Argenteau Estate Papers.

26. The dinner took place on 9 August 1783, but Adams did not go. Adams to Livingston, 13 August 1783, PJA, 15:220–223.

27. Adams to Livingston, 13 July 1783, PJA, 15:106–109.

28. Bauer, "With Friends Like These," 664–692.

29. Adams, *The Works of John Adams*, 8:95.

30. Adams to Livingston, 14 July 1783, PJA, 15:109–111; Beales, Joseph II, 2:376–384.

31. Adams to Livingston, 14 July 1783, PJA, 15:110–111.

32. Franklin to Livingston, 22–26 July 1783, PBF, 40:355–370.

33. Ingenhousz to Franklin, 8 April 1783, PBF, 39:444–446.

34. Franklin to Livingston, 22–26 July 1783, PBF, 40:355–370.

35. Hunt, *Journals of the Continental Congress,* 25:754.

36. A continual problem that year, see Franklin's complaint in Franklin to Livingston, 15 April 1783, PBF, 39:467–472.

37. HHStA, StK, Frankreich, Notenwechsel, K. 13, Mercy-d'Argenteau to Kaunitz, 1 October 1783.

37. William Temple Franklin to Adams, 1 August 1784, PJA, 16:287–288n1. The existent copy of Franklin's letter held in the HHStA was presented by Austrian Chancellor Leopold Figl to the Library of Congress, see "Manuscripts," *Quarterly Journal of Current Acquisitions*, 10, no. 3 (1953), 162.

38. Mercy-d'Argenteau to Franklin, 20 July 1783, PBF, 42:73.

39. HHStA, StK, Frankreich Berichte, K. 169, Mercy-d'Argenteau to Kaunitz, 1 August 1784.

40. The treaty came into full effect in May 1784.

41. HHStA, StK, Vorträge betreffende Akten, K. 2–3, Kaunitz, Vortrag an den Kaiser, 15 August 1784.

42. HHStA, StK, Vorträge betreffende Akten, K. 2–3, Kaunitz, Vortrag an den Kaiser, 15 August 1784.

43. Kaunitz had studied Wolff under his tutor Johann Friedrich von Schwanau, see Klingenstein, *Der Aufstieg des Hauses Kaunitz*, 169–171.

44. HHStA, StK, Vorträge betreffende Akten, K. 2–3, Kaunitz, Vortrag an den Kaiser, 15 August 1784.

45. HHStA, StK, Vorträge betreffende Akten, K. 2–3, Kaunitz, Vortrag an den Kaiser, 15 August 1784

46. See marginalia on HHStA, StK, Vorträge betreffende Akten, K. 2–3, Kaunitz, Vortrag an den Kaiser, 15 August 1784.

47. Bernard, Joseph II and Bavaria, 151–165.

48. HHStA, StK, Frankreich, Weisungen, K. 167, Kaunitz to Mercy-d'Argenteau, 4 September 1784.

49. HHStA, StK, Frankreich, Weisungen, K. 167, Kaunitz to Mercy-d'Argenteau, 4 September 1784.

50. HHStA, StK, Notenweschel, Hofkanzlei, K. 13, [Kaunitz] Nota an die Vereinigte Hofkanzlei, 4 September 1784.

51. HHStA, Belgien, DDA, Weisungen, K. 52, Kaunitz to Belgiojoso, 5 September 1784. Starhemberg received the largely ceremonial position as *Obersthofmeister* (Grand Master of the Household) when he returned to Vienna.

52. HHStA, StK, Frankreich, Berichte, K. 169, Mercy-d'Argenteau to Kaunitz, 25 September 1784.

53. HHStA, StK, Frankreich, Berichte, K. 169, Mercy-d'Argenteau to Kaunitz, 25 September 1784.

54. HHStA, StK, Verträge betreffende Akten, K. 2 (1747/1751–1784) – 3, Konvulut 2 'B' 1784, Letter of Mercy-d'Argenteau, s.d.

55. Commissioners to President of Congress, 11 November 1784, PTJ, 7:493–500.

56. Drafts of the treaty have been identified first by Van Houtte in the ARB and Hans Schlitter in the HHStA: see Van Houtte, "American Negotiations with Austria," and Schlitter, *Beziehungen,* 175–183. A copy of the preliminary treaty drawn up by Cazier here is contained within HHStA, StK, Verträge betreffende Akten, K. 2–3, Fol. C, along with the comments by Antonio Songa, possibly by Kaunitz (unidentified hand), and possibly by Karl von Zinzendorf. There are a total of three drafts found to date, ranging from 27 stipulations to 25 stipulations (with 5 extraordinary) to 24 stipulations (with 2 extraordinary). I believe the ARB holds the final treaty draft finalised in 1786, contrary to Van Houtte's suggestion of HHStA, Belgien, *"DD Vorträge, K. 13."* I have been unable to verify this, however.

57. HHStA, Belgien, DDA, Weisungen, K. 52, Kaunitz to Belgiojoso, 20 November 1784.

58. Jefferson to Abigail Adams, 21 June 1785, PTJ, 8:241.

59. Gordon-Reed and Onuf, Most Blessed of the Patriarchs, 97–134.

60. Peterson, "Thomas Jefferson and Commercial Policy," 592. For Jefferson's agrarian vision, see Harrison, "Thomas Jefferson and Internal Improvement," 335–349; Sofka, "American Neutral Rights Reappraised" 599–622. For the primacy of this strategy, see Kaplan, Entangling Alliances with None; Ben-Atar, The Origins of Jeffersonian Commercial Policy and Diplomacy; Gilje, "Commerce and Conquest," 735–770.

61. Jefferson to Jay, 27 January 1786, PTJ, 9:233–236.

62. Cogliano, Emperor of Liberty, 10 and 79.

63. Horsman, *Diplomacy of the New Republic,* 110–120; Merritt, "Sectional Conflict and Secret Compromise," 117–171; Carroll, A Good and Wise Measure, 6–19; Gilje, The Making of the American Republic, 286–290.

64. Lafayette to Jefferson, 4 September 1784, PTJ, 8:478–480.

65. He wrote of the same audience to Washington, but much less than to Jefferson, see Lafayette to Washington, 3 September 1784, PGW, 3:224–225.

66. Jefferson to Adams, 24 September 1785, PJA, 17:466–470.

67. Jefferson to Jay, 6 October 1785, PTJ, 8:592–593.

68. Lafayette to Jefferson, 4 September 1784, PTJ, 8:480.

69. HHStA, StK, Frankreich, Weisungen, K. 167, Kaunitz to Mercy-d'Argenteau, 1 October 1784.

70. HHStA, StK, Frankreich, Berichte, K. 171, fol. 90–91, Mercy-d'Argenteau to Kaunitz, 18 October 1784.

71. Jefferson's tour of northern and southern France as well as the northern Italian states took place in 1787, see Kimball, Jefferson: The Scene of Europe, 184–235.

72. Jefferson supposed Congress could have no objections to renew them, or perhaps to send some person to Brussels to negotiate the matter there, see Jefferson to Adams, 12 January 1786 [First letter], PTJ, 9;165–167. Mercy-d'Argenteau agreed, see HHStA, StK, Berichte, K. 171, fols. 4–7, Mercy-d'Argenteau to Kaunitz, 9 January 1786; HHStA, StK, Berichte, K. 171, fols. 90–91, Mercy-d'Argenteau to Kaunitz, 18 October 1785; and HHStA, StK, Berichte, K. 171, fols. 34–36, Mercy-d'Argenteau to Kaunitz, 31 January 1786.

73. Jefferson to Adams, 12 January 1786 [Second letter], PTJ, 9:167.

74. Jefferson to Adams, 12 January 1786 [First letter], PTJ, 9:166.

75. Jefferson to Adams, 7 February 1786, PTJ, 9:258–260.

76. Adams to Jefferson, 28 January 1786, PTJ, 9:238. Original emphasis.

77. Shackelford, Jefferson's Travels in Europe, 43–64.

78. Jefferson to Jay, 12 May 1786, PTJ, 9:514–516.

79. HHStA StK, Frankreich, Berichte, K. 171, Mercy-d'Argenteau to Kaunitz, 12 February [Hornung] 1786.

80. HHStA, StK, Frankreich, Weisungen, K. 170, Kaunitz to Mercy-d'Argenteau, 19 February [Hornung] 1786. Kaunitz had received the responses from the regional chancelleries that month, see HHStA, StK, Notenwechsel, Hofkanzlei, K. 108, Noten von der Hofkanzlei, 31 March 1786 and HHStA, StK, Vorträge, K. 142, Kaunitz, Vortrag an der Kaiser, 22 March 1786.

81. HHStA, Belgien, DDA, Weisungen, K. 55, Kaunitz to Belgiojoso, 22 March 1786; HHStA, StK, Frankreich, Weisungen, K. 170, Kaunitz to Mercy-d'Argenteau, 22 March 1786; HHStA, Belgien, DDA, Berichte, K. 198, Belgiojoso received confirmation on 1 April 1786; Belgiojoso forwarded his confirmation to Mercy-d'Argenteau on 13 May 1786, see HHStA, Belgien, DDA, Korrespondenz Frankreich, K. 38.

82. HHStA, StK, Frankreich, Berichte, K. 171, fols. 19–20, Mercy-d'Argenteau to Kaunitz, 20 August 1786. The earlier report is missing.

83. Jefferson to Monroe, 10 May 1786, PTJ, 9:499–504.

84. HHStA, Belgien, Berichte, DDB Rot, K. 182c, fols. 1–4, Beelen to Belgiojoso, 25 February 1786.

85. HHStA, StK, Frankreich, Berichte, K.173, Mercy-d'Argenteau to Kaunitz, 20 August 1786.

86. Historian Csaba Lévai concludes Jefferson's ideas on political economy and the commercial utility were his biggest motivators at this time, see Lévai, *Efforts to Establish Political and Commercial Relations*, 111–126; Lévai, "Van esély a nyitásra a császár részéről," 20–48.

87. Reeves, "The Prussian-American Treaties," 475–510 is the most important account of the commercial treaty between the Kingdom of Prussia and the United States alongside Kapp, Friedrich der Grosse, 86–150.

88. Henrikson, "'Mental Maps,'" 495 and 498.

89. A series of toleration measures issued between 1781 and 1787 removed the obstacles for non-Catholics to worship more freely in society and to participate to a greater extent in industry but under certain conditions. Protestants, for example, could construct prayer houses but nothing exactly like a church and they could not conduct weddings. Jews were allowed into commercial professions but lost autonomy on taxation, judicial matters, and schools, meaning they had to send their children to state secondary schools and educate them in German-language primary schools. All Jews had to adopt surnames and were eligible for military conscription following the 1782 Edict of Tolerance. See O'Brien, "Ideas of Religious Toleration," 5–80; Karniel, Toleranzpolitik.

90. For Joseph's enlightened reforms, see Beales, Enlightenment and Reform, 227–255; Dickson, "Reshaping of the Austrian Church," 89–114. For Jefferson and religion, see Onuf, The Mind of Thomas Jefferson, 139–168; Gordon-Reed and Onuf, Most Blessed of the Patriarchs, 267–299.

91. Jefferson to Madison, 8 December 1784, PTJ, 7:557–560; Jefferson to Monroe, 10 December 1784, PTJ, 7:562–565.

92. Jay to Henry Knox, 10 December 1781 in Johnson, *Correspondence and Public Papers*, 2:159–161.

93. Gouverneur Morris to Jay, 25 September 1783 in Johnson, *Correspondence and Public Papers*, 3:85–89.

94. Jefferson to Richard Henry Lee, 12 July 1785, PTJ, 8:286–288; Jefferson to Ezra Stiles, 17 July 1785, PTJ, 8:298–301.

95. Jefferson to Horatio Gates, 13 December 1784, PTJ, 8:571.

96. Jefferson to James Currie, 27 September 1785, PTJ, 8:558–560.

97. Jefferson to John Page, 20 August 1785, PTJ, 8:417–419.

98. Jefferson to Madison, 8 December 1784, PTJ, 7:557–560; Jefferson to Monroe, 10 December 1784, PTJ, 7:562–565.

99. Jefferson to Washington, 10 December 1784, PTJ, 7:566–567.

100. Blanning, "'That Horrid Electorate' or 'Ma Patrique Germanique'?" 311–344.

101. Jefferson to Page, 20 August 1785, PTJ, 8:417–419; Jefferson to James Monroe, 28 August 1785, PTJ, 8:444–446.

102. Thomas Jefferson to Page, 20 August 1785, PTJ, 8:444–446.

103. Murphy, Vergennes, 405–416.

104. Jefferson to Francis Hopkinson, 13 January 1785, PTJ, 7:602–603.

105. Jefferson to Charles Thomson, 21 June 1785, PTJ, 8:245–246; Jefferson to Madison, 18 March 1785, PTJ, 8:38–41.

106. Jefferson to Franklin, 5 October 1785, PTJ, 8:585–586.

107. Jefferson to Richard Henry Lee, 30 August 1778 in Idzerda et al, *Mazzei: Selected Writings*, 1:135.

108. Jefferson to Seward, 12 November 1785, PTJ, 9:27–28.

109. Jefferson to William Stephens Smith, 13 September 1786, PTJ, 10:362–363.

110. Jefferson to Ingenhousz, 14 July 1785, PTJ, 8:295; 'supplemental documents,' PTJ, 27:749.

111. Franklin to Jefferson, 11 July 1785, PTJ, 8:282.

112. Von Hase, "Eine amerikanische Kritik," 372–393.

113. Diary entry, 20 October 1785 in Dávila, ed., *Archivo del General Miranda: Viajes, Diarios 1750–1785*, 1:428.

114. Klingenstein, *Lessons for Republicans*, 181–212. I am grateful to Prof. Klingenstein for providing me with a copy.

Epilogue

1. McDonald, "Constructing Optimism," 182.

2. Wilson, Jefferson on Display, 224–225.

3. One reason why Jefferson preferred Bohemian glass was for its "stout" quality of thickness which suited the exposed hill-top location of Monticello, see Jefferson to Donath, 4 December 1796, PTJ, 29:212–213.

4. For his orders, see Jefferson to Donath, 16 November 1792, 12 August 1795, 16 September 1795, 2 October 1796, 9 October 1807, in PTJ, 24:622; 28:436; 28:469; 29:187 respectively; and via "Early Access, Founders Online". There are also multiple mentions of Donath's payments in Jefferson's Memorandum books and his Remodelling Notebook.

5. Hagley Library and Museum, Donath Letterbooks, vol. 2, fol. 162, Donath to H. van der Juissen, 11 August 1804.

6. Friebel, *"Österreich und die Vereinigten Staaten"*; Curti, "Austria and the United States," 137–206; Davis, *"Diplomatic Relations."*

7. LoC, Henry Latrobe Papers, Box 3 'Correspondence relating to the Capitol,' vol. 1, Latrobe to Donath, 4 October 1803 and 19 September 1805; Latrobe to Donath, 4 October 1803 and 19 September 1805, in Carter et al, *Papers of Benjamin Henry Latrobe*, fiches 26 and 44.

8. Andreozzi, *From the Black Sea to the Americas*, 79–81.

9. HHStA, Belgien, DDB, Rot. K. 182d, Report, 27 November 1787, Add. K, fol. 267; HHStA, Belgien, DDB Rot, K. 182e, Report, 27 December 1788, Add. N, fol. 346; HHStA, Belgien, DDB Rot, K. 182e, Report, 27 March 1789, Add. L, fols. 373–375; HHStA, Belgien, DDB Rot, K. 182e, Report, 22 June 1789, Add. L, fols. 435–437.

10. Allgemeines Verwaltungsarchiv, Familienarchiv Trauttmansdorff, Fürst Ferdinand, K. 276, fol. 89, Maximilien de Beelen-Bertholff to Count Ferdinand von Trauttmansdorff, 31 March 1789.

11. HHStA, Staatskanzlei, Notenwechsel, Hofkammer, K. 8, fols. 310–312.

12. FHKA, NHK, Kommerz Littoral, K. 984, (Second) Application of Mussi, fols. 827–832; FHKA, NHK, Kommerz Littoral, K. 984, Application of Franz von Silbernagel, fols. 835–852.

13. Codignola, Blurred Nationalities, 71. Cf. Phelps, U.S.-Habsburg Relations, 113 and Agstner, Austria (-Hungary) and Its Consulates, 71, who both mistake John Lamson as the first US consul in Trieste. Lamson had been appointed in 1799 but was absent from his duties and much delayed in getting to Trieste. He arrived at the end of 1801, but Jefferson replaced him with William Riggin in 1802.

14. The *Sukey* arrived in February 1800, see Stock, Trieste e l'America nascente, 15.

15. HHStA, StK, Vorträge, K. 168, VI–IX, fol. 108, Vortrag an den Kaiser, 26 June 1804.

16. Agstner, Austria (-Hungary) and Its Consulates, 73–77.

17. Agstner, Austria(-Hungary) and Its Consulates, 77–87.

18. HHStA, StK, Brasilien, Berichte, K. 1–9, "Instruktionen an Graf Eltz" (1817).

19. The first Swiss consul took office in Philadelphia in 1816, see Schnyder, "Das schweizerische Konsularwesen," 37.

20. HHStA, StK, Brasilien, K. 1–6, "Mémoire von A. E. Perez betreffend Handel mit Brasilien" (1818); Agstner, *Consulates South of the Rio Grande*, 87.

21. Singerton, *"Empires on the Edge,"* 217–220.

22. For example: *Ungarische Staats- und Gelehrte Nachrichten*, no. 12, 10 February 1787; *Gazette van Gend*, 13 August and 5 November 1787.

23. Adams to Mazzei, 29 December 1785 in Idzerda et al, *Mazzei: Selected Writings*, 1:509.

24. O'Reilly, Competition for Colonists.

25. BL, Add. MS. 35539, fol. 1, Keith to Carmarthen, 3 August 1787.

26. HHStA, Belgium, DDB, Rot, K. 182c, Report, 25 February 1786, Add. E, fol. 49n.

27. Adams to Mazzei, 15 December 1785 in Idzerda et al, *Mazzei: Selected Writings*, 1:504.

28. Ingenhousz to Franklin, 1 September 1783, PBF, 40:562–563; APS, Franklin Papers, VIII, 33, 115, Franklin to Ingenhousz, 29 April 1785; Dimitrije Obradović, 210. I am grateful to Dr. Wladimir Fischer-Nebmaier for the latter information.

29. APS, Ms.B.F85, 7, LIX, 50, Count Friedrich Grävenitz[-Walhm] to Franklin, 26 June 1783. It appears Grävenitz-Walhm never made the journey.

30. HHStA, Belgien, DDA Berichte, K. 176, Songa to Starhemberg/Kaunitz, 8 February 1783.

31. HHStA, Belgien, DDB Rot, K. 182b, 'Emigration de Européens,' 14 November 1784, Add. G, fols. 159–160.

32. Prodan, Supplex Libellus Valachorum.

33. For accounts see Auner, Bauernaufstandes in Siebenbürgen; Edroiu, Horea's Uprising; Shapiro, "The Horea Rebellion," 65–93; Prodan, "Joseph II and Horea's Uprising," 135–144.

34. In 1744 a revolt led by Visarion Sarai and the Orthodox unrest between 1759–1761 led by Sofronie of Cioara (Stan Popovici). See Hitchins, History of Romania, 61.

35. Brissot, *Seconde lettre d'un défenseur du peuple*, 50.

36. Ibid., 79.

37. Ibid., 16–19 and 87.

38. Ibid., frontispiece.

39. Quoted from Beales, Joseph II, 2:477.

40. Palmer, Democratic Revolutions, 1:341.

41. Venturi, End of the Old Regime, 2:711.

42. Davis, Joseph II, 246–260.

43. Smeyers, *De Amerikaanse vrijheidsoorlog*, 153–163; Gorman, America and Belgium, 32–35.

44. KU Leuven Main Library Tabularium Politiek – België 23/3/1787-13/12/1787, (Leuven, Belgium), 3, D'Outrepont, Considérations, 11, 21–22, and 32. I am grateful to Dr. Jane Judge for providing me with a copy.

45. D'Outrepont, Considérations, 14.

46. Schlitter, Regierung Josefs II, 1:223.

47. All quoted in Gorman, America and Belgium, 153–154; Polasky, Revolution in Brussels, 55.

48. Kaunitz to Joseph, 20 June 1787 in Schlitter, Regierung Josephs, 1:249.

49. Polasky, "Traditionalists, Democrats, and Jacobins," 227–262.

50. Vercruysse, " Révolution Brabançonne," 1098–1108.

51. Georg Forster, the explorer-botanist resident in Vienna, used the phrase in print, see Forster, *Ansichten vom Niederrhein*, 194. For the name otherwise, see Gorman, America and Belgium, 176–190.

52. Polasky, Revolution in Brussels, 94–95.

53. Antoine d'Aubremez, a wine merchant, had fought out in America whereas Jean-André van der Mersch had not successfully found a way to fight for the patriots, although he was nicknamed *"Washington Belgique"* during this time. See Polasky, Revolution in Brussels, 102 and Judge, The United States of Belgium, 125.

54. Judge, The United States of Belgium, 214–219.

55. Polasky, Revolution in Brussels, 120.

56. Judge, The United States of Belgium, 164–195.

57. Quoted in Balázs, Hungary and the Habsburgs, 262.

58. Balázs, Hungary and the Habsburgs, 262.

59. August von Schlözer, *Staatsanzeigen* quoted in Rényi, *A századforduló (18.-19. század) Angliája*, 199–215; Lévai, *In between and within Great Powers*, 129–141.

60. Szakály, *Managing a Composite Monarchy*, 205–220.

61. Balázs, Reformpolitikus, 145.

62. Lévai, *Within Two Systems*, 41.

63. Nagyváthy, *A Nagy-szivüségnél* (1790) quoted in Závodovsky, American Effects, 46.

64. Katona, "American Influences," 15. Katona cites Benda, *A Magyar jakobinus mozgalom iratai*, 1:46–49. He relied upon an extensive Viennese network, including the editor of the *Wienerisches Diarium,* Conrad Dominik Bartsch, to source his Americana, see, HHStA, KA, VA, Correspondentiae Heinoczianae, K. 48-1, especially, Bartsch to Hajnóczy, 12 May 1789, fol. 193.

65. Kókay, *Hajnóczy József és Széchenyi Ferenc Kapcsolata*, 91.

66. Závodovsky, American Effects, 41–42.

67. Závodovsky, American Effects, 44.

68. Palmer and Kenez, "Two Documents," 423–442.

69. Martinovics, "Beobachtungen über geheime demokratische Verbindungen in Wien von 21ten bis 26ten Jänner 1792," in Benda, *Magyar jakobinusok iratai*, 1:578–586.

70. Benda, *Jakobinusok*, 454–468, 700, and 788.

71. Martinovics, *A Magyarország gyülésben egyben-gyűlt méltóságos és tekintetes nemes rendekhez 1790-ik esztendőben tartatott beszéd*; Benda, *Magyar jakobinusok iratai*, 1:125; 144.

72. "Ad normam pensylvanorum" and "Adora Philadelphiae coetum" in Benda, *Magyar jakobinusok iratai*, 1:125 and 147.

73. These were called the "Society of the Reformers" and "Society of Liberty-Equality-Fraternity."

74. "A True Patriot" [Martinovics], *Felhívás Zemplen megye egybegyűlt rendeihez hogy rázzák le az ausztriai ház igáját* (1794).

75. Singerton, "Knowledge of and Sympathy for the American cause," 139.

76. Such was the case with József Péczeli, *Summarium Retenioris Europaeae a Detectione Americae ad Revolutionem Gallicum* (Debrecen, 1827). According to Katona, the line about an American standing army was censored, see Katona, "Hungarian Image," 27n36.

77. Martinovics had informed on Verhovacz's ownerships of Paine's *Droit de l'Homme* in his Zagreb library which he allegedly used to teach seminary students, see Fraknói, *Martinovics élete*, 253 for the information and for Verhovacz's notes, see Benda, *Magyar jakobinusok iratai*, 2:796–797. For the others, see Benda, *Magyar jakobinusok iratai*, 2:279, 359, and 705.

78. Csokonai to Sándor Bessenyei, s.d. [1795], in Balázs, *Csokonai Vitéz Mihály minden munkája*, 2:809–810.

79. Csokonai to Countess Mária Erdődy (née Festetics), 19 May 1803, in Debreczeni, *Levelezés*, 263.

80. Lévai, *Within Two Systems*, 42.

81. Lévai, *The Relevance of the American Revolution*, 112.

82. Halácsy, "Franklin in Hungary," 14.

83. Viszota, "Gróf Széchenyi István a gimnaziumban," 915; Gál, "Széchenyi and the U.S.A.," 95–119.

84. Szilassy, "America and the Hungarian Revolution," 180–96; Freifeld, Nationalism and the Crowd, 115–116.

85. Komlos, Louis Kossuth in America; Johnson, "*Magyar*-mania in New York City," 237–249.

86. Peruta, Milano nel Risorgimento, 132.

87. Körner, America in Italy, 130–138.

88. For comparison of the 1849 Kremsier constitutional draft and the American constitution see, Macartney, The Habsburg Empire, 418 and Murad, Franz Joseph, 130. For

Aurel Popovici and his plan of a United States of Greater Austria, see Popovici, Die Vereinigten Staaten von Groß-Österreich, and its inspiration (among others) from the American model, see Gusejnova, European Elites and Ideas of Empire, 74.

89. Brauneder, *America's Influence*, 673–681. More generally, Fröschl, *Amerika in den Verfassungsdiskussionen*, 43–44; Angermann, "Frühkonstitutionalismus und das amerikanische Vorbild," 1–32.

90. Walter, *Die österreichische Zentralverwaltung*, Part II, 5:12, no. 3a.

91. ANM, Fond Steinský, Donath to Steinský, 19 April 1790. See also Petráňová, "Z korespondence Františka Steinského," 101–112. For a full transcription and more analysis of the Donath-Steinský corrrspondence, see Singerton, "Science, Revolution, and Monarchy," 145–164.

92. LA PNP, Fonds F. A. Steinského 1760–1811, Donath to Steinský, 20 July 1792.

93. Det Kongelige Bibliotek, NKS 1698-2, Münter Arkiv, Letter 328, Maria Bassegli [von Born] to Friedrich Münter.

94. Sturmberger, *Amerika-Auswanderung aus Oberösterreich*, 65.

95. Barany, "The Interest of the United States in Central Europe," 298.

96. Ibid., 283. Translation mine.

97. Glant, "A Hungarian Aristocrat in Civil War America," 287–301.

98. Around 47,450 migrants emigrated via Trieste between 1870–1900 and seven per cent of all Austrian immigrants to the US went via Trieste between 1907–1912. See Brunnbauer, *Globalizing Southeastern Europe*, 80; Boyd, "Initiating Mass Movement," 36. For the millions of transatlantic migrants from the Habsburg lands to the United States in the late nineteenth and early twentieth centuries, see Steidl, On Many Routes, 20–21 and 101–162.

BIBLIOGRAPHY

Archives

Austria

Allgemeines Verwaltungsarchiv, Vienna
  Familienarchiv Trauttmansdorff
    Fürst Ferdinand, K. 276
Altes Universitätsarchiv, Vienna
  Akten der Medizinische Fakultät der Universität Wien
    Protokoll der Medizinische Fakultät VIII
  Rigorosenprotokolle
    Med. 9.5 Rigorosenprotokoll der Mediziner
Domarchiv St. Stephan, Vienna
  Geburts- und Taufbuch der Dompfarre St. Stephan, Tomus 94 (1778)
Finanz- und Hofkammerarchiv, Vienna
  Neue Hofkammer
    Generalia Akten, K. 850
    Kommerz Böhmen, K. 1205
    Kommerz Litorale, K. 850, K. 893, K. 902, K. 903, K. 904, K. 905, K. 957,
    K. 984, K. 992
    Kommerz Noten, K. 616
Haus-, Hof- und Staatsarchiv, Vienna
  Handschriftensammlung
    HS-Weiß
      No. 443 *Remarques sur les affaires présente de l'Amérique Septentrionale*
    Wissenschaft und Kunst, K. 6 'Märter Schriften.'
  Hausarchiv
    Hofreisen, K. 9, Konv. 2-1, Journal der Reise Kaiser Josephs II. nach Paris.
    Sammelbände, K. 7, K. 10, K. 12, K. 13, K. 26, K. 27a
  Hofarchiv
    Oberstmeisteramt
      Ältere Zeremonialakten, K. 86

Kabinettsarchiv
  Vertrauliche Akten, K. 48, K. 70
  Nachlaß Zinzendorfs
    Tagebücher
      Vols. 13, 20, 24, 26, 30, 39, 41
Staatenabteilungen Belgien
  DDA, Berichte, K. 176, K. 198, K. 212, K. 216, K. 232, K. 233, K. 234, K. 260, K.
    270, K. 275
  DDA, Weisungen, K. 35, K. 40, K. 41, K. 47, K. 49, K. 52, K. 55
  DDA, Korrespondenz Frankreich, K. 9, K. 33, K. 38
  DDB, Rot, K. 182a, K. 182b, K. 182c, K. 183d, K. 184e
Ostindische Kompanien, Triest-Antwerpen, K. 4
Staatskanzlei
  Brasilien
    Berichte, K. 1
  England
    Berichte, K. 118, K. 119, K. 120
    Weisungen, K. 128
    Varia, K. 11
  Frankreich
    Berichte, K. 155, K. 160, K. 162, K. 169, K. 171, K. 173
    Notenwechsel, K. 13
    Weisungen, K. 157, K. 164, K. 167, K. 170
  Noten der Vereinigten Hofkanzlei, K. 14
  Notenwechsel, Hofkammer, K. 8
  Notenwechsel, Hofkanzlei, K. 13, K. 108
  Portugal
    Berichte, K. 9, K. 10
  Provinzen
    Niederösterreich, K. 1
    Küstenland, K. 1
  Spanien
    Berichte, K. 109, K. 111, K. 112, K. 113
  Toskana
    Berichte, K. 20
  Vorträge, K. 126, K. 137, K. 140, K. 141, K. 142, K. 168
  Vorträge betreffende Akten, K. 2, K. 3
  Sonderbestände
    Nachlass Schlitter, K. 16
    Khevenhüller-Metsch Familienarchiv, Reigersburg, K. 183
Kriegsarchiv, Vienna
  Zentralstellen, Wiener Hofkriegsrat
    Protokolle

Hofkriegsrat Memoranda

> G.756, No.1433
>
> G.958, No.1852
>
> G.2677, No. 5113

Oberösterreichisches Landesarchiv, Linz

Herrschaftsarchiv Weinburg, A-IV, Band 182, Justus Eggertt Tagebuch.

Österreichische Nationalbibliothek, Vienna

Handschriftensammlungen und Alte Drucken

Johann Ferdinand Baumgartner, *Das Mittel reich zu werden* (Vienna, 1777)

Anonymous, *Nützliches Adreß- und Reisebuch oder Archiv der nöthigsten Kenntnisse von Wien für Fremde und Inländer* (Vienna, 1792)

Benjamin Franklin, *Comparison of Great Britain and the United States in Regard to the Basis of Credit in the Countries.* Translated by Jan Ingenhousz (1777)

Franklin to Marsilio Landriani, 14 October 1787, B6/96-2

Franz X. Huber, *Franklins freier Wille* (Leipzig, 1787)

Anton Satori, *Discours sur la Grandeur et importance de la dernière Révolution de l'Amerique septentrionale: Sur les causes principals qui l'ont determine: et sur son influence vraisemblable sur l'Etat Politique et sur le commerce des Puissances Européennes* (1783)

Ingenhousz-Franklin Correspondence, Cod. Ser. No. 4062

Ingenhousz, *Bericht an Maria Theresa über zwei Briefe Franklins*, 18 May 1777, B6/97

Rudolf Valltravers, *Bericht für diejenigen welche nach Nord Amerika sich begeben und alldort ansiedeln wollen* ('Hamburg' [Vienna], 1786)

Codex Series No. 3517 'Expedition Märter', No. 1596

Belgium

Archives générales du Royaume de Belgique/Algemeen Rijksarchief van België, Brussels

Chancellerie Autrichienne des Pays-Bas à Vienne, Coll. 303, 499, 512, D106

Conseil Privé, Coll. 479, 1067, 1154A, 1154B

Secretaire d'État et Guerre, Coll. 1464, 1640, 2150, 2151/1-2, 2160, 2161, 2162, 2163, 2173

Bibliothèque Royale de Belgique/Koninklijke Bibliotheek van België, Brussels

Manuscripts Division

Mémoire des faits de Frédéric de Romberg (Brussels, 1810) Ms. No. G2077

Croatia

Državni Arhiv, Dubrovnik

Acta Sanctae Mariae Majoris, XVIII, Series 31.3062/53-3.

Sebastian d'Ayala Correspondence

Czechia

Archiv Národního muzea, Prague
    Fond Steinský
Literární archiv Památníku národního písemnictví, Prague
    Fonds F. A. Steinského 1760-1811
Moravsky Zemsky Archiv, Brno
    Rodinny Archiv Dietrichsteinů, K. 584
Státni Hrad a Zámek, Český Krumlov
    Inv. No. 2173

Denmark

Det Kongelige Bibliotek
    Münter Arkiv, NKS 1698-2

France

Archives des Affaires Etrangère, Paris
    Correspondence Politique
        Angleterre, 514
        Autriche, 336, 339, 340, 341, 342
        Russie, 105

Hungary

Magyar Nemzeti Levéltár, Budapest
    Családi Levéltárak, P53 - Berzeviczy Gergely iratai, 1789/b. fasc. 19a-23a

Italy

Archivio di Stato di Firenze, Florence
    Affari di Stato
        Affari Esteri, C. 901, C. 930, C. 2335
Archivio di Stato di Milano, Milan
    Archivio Belgiojoso, C. 571
Archivio di Stato di Napoli, Naples
    Fondo Ministero Affari Esteri, Busta, 33, Busta, 4210
Archivio di Stato di Trieste, Trieste
    Deputazione di Borsa, Serie VII
        C. 60, C. 67, C. 74, C. 75, C. 105, C. 128, C. 156, C. 160

Slovakia

Achív Mesta v Košiciach, Košice
  Košická Univerzita Katalóg, vol. 1
Štátny oblastny archíve v Košiciach, Košice
  Hlavné Riaditelstvo Školského Obvodu v Košiciach
    Akadémia v Košiciach 1788-1793, B
    K. 21 (97-101).
Verejná Knižnica Jána Bocatia v Košiciach, Košice
  Rukopisné diela Jána Zinnera
    Abhandlung von Europäischen Käyserthümen (1782)
    Acta Academis Regina Cassoviensis (s.d.)
    Ius Publicum Hungaria (1781)
    Notitia Historica de Coloniis Americae Septemtrionalis (1783)
    Præcipua Prælia Secundi Belli Punici: Observationibus Militaribus Illustrata
      (s.d. [1782])
    Versuch einer Kriegsgeschichte der verbündenen Staaten von Nordamerika (1784)

Sweden

Riksarkivet, Stockholm
  Diplomatica
    Germania, K. 453

United Kingdom

British Library, London
  Drake Papers
    Add. Mss. 46826
  Hardwicke Papers
    Add. MS. 35504, 35506, 35511, 35512, 35525, 35539
  William Eden Manuscripts
    Add. MS. 34414
Kent History & Library Centre, Maidstone
  Cobb of Margate, Family and Business Papers
    De Vinck & Co. Correspondence
      EK-U1453/B5/1706
    J. Fottrell of Ostend Correspondence
      EK-U1453/B3/5/687
    Liebaert, Baes, Derdeyn & Co. Correspondence
      EK-U1453/B5/4/797a-d

National Records of Scotland, Edinburgh
  Customs Records
    RH20/23
  Papers of the Campbell Family (Earls of Breadalbane)
    GD/112/74/3/13
    GD/112/39/335/4
  Papers of the Scot Family of Gala
    Hay-Makdougall Family Letters 1770-1777
      GD/477/407
The National Archives at Kew, London
  Foreign Office Papers, 7/1
    Series 07 (Austria from 1782) 1, 4
    Series 26 (Flanders), 2, 3
    Series 95 (Miscellanea), 8/2
    Series 97 (Supplements to General Correspondence)
  High Court of Admiralty
    Prize Court (32), 360/5, 430/9, 434/6
    Appeals for Prizes (42), 149/1, 150/1, 150/2, 150/3, 152/1
  Prerogative Court
    Probate 11/1162/253
  State Papers Series
    Series 77 (Flanders), 107, 108
    Series 78 (France), 297
    Series 80 (Holy Roman Empire to 1782), 218, 220, 221, 223
    Series 81 (German States)
    Series 84 (Holland), 552
    Series 89 (Portugal), 85
    Series 97 (Turkey), 298, 61
    Series 98 (Tuscany), 81, 82
    Series 100 (Foreign Ministers in England), 13
    Series 120 (Gazettes and Pamphlets: Italian States), 76

United States of America

Alderman Library, University of Virginia, Charlottesville, VA
  Jefferson and Madison Correspondence (Jefferson Retirement Series Papers)
    Correspondence regarding Joseph Donath (1792-1804)
American Philosophical Society Library, Philadelphia, PA
  Franklin Papers Series, Mss. B.F. 85
    Series II, III, IV, V, VI, VII
  Journal of Bee-Keeping at Spring Mill, MSS.MS.Coll.200
  Microfilm Collection
    Mss. H.S. Film 23 (Jan Ingenhousz Letterbook)

William Temple Franklin Papers, Mss.B.F.86
   CV, 71, 72
   CVI, 60
Connecticut Historical Society, Hartford, CT
  Silas Deane Papers, Boxes 1, 7
Hagley Library and Museum, Wilmington, DE
  Donath & Co. Letterbooks, (1801-1802), Accession No. 38
  Wurts Family Papers, Section I
    James Vanuxem Papers
      Promissory Notes, Box 1
Historical Society of Pennsylvania, Philadelphia, PA
  Beelen-Bertholff Family Papers
  Fox Family Papers
  Logan Family Papers
Houghton Library, Harvard University, Cambridge, MA
  Arthur Lee Papers, Ms. Am. 811-811.7, MJ811.2.III
The Jessie Ball duPont Memorial Library at Stratford Hall, VA
  The Archives of the Robert E. Lee Memorial Foundation
    Papers of the Lee Family
      William Lee Letterbooks, Box 9
Library of Congress, Washington DC
  George Washington Papers
    Series 2, Letterbooks 1754-1799
      Letterbook No. 11
    Series 4, General Correspondence
      MSS. 44693: Reel 098
  Henry Latrobe Papers, Box 3
  Mercy-d'Argenteau Estate Papers
  Nicholas Low Papers
    "Ostend, Belgium," Box 3
    "Anvers, Belgium," Boxes 7, 9
Maryland Historical Society, Baltimore, MD
  Robert Gilmor Collection, Series 1, Box 1, Folder 29
Massachusetts Historical Society, Boston, MA
  Amory Financial Papers, MS. N-2024
  Francis Dana Papers, MS. N-1088
  Winthrop Family Papers, MS. N-262
National Archives and Records Administration, College Park, MD
  Record Group 267
    Records of the United States Supreme Court
      Records of the Court of Appeals in Cases of Capture
        Revolutionary War Prize Case Files, 1776-1786
          Miscellaneous Case Papers, 1772-1784

Miscellaneous Court Records, 1777- 1789
Microfilm No. M162
New York Public Library, New York City, NY
T. B. Myers Collection, #1435
University Archives of Notre Dame
Catholic Church Archdiocese of Baltimore
Manuscripts, 1/17
University of Chicago Library, Chicago, IL
Special Collections
Butler-Gensaulus Collection, Box 1
University of Pennsylvania, Philadelphia, PA
Kislak Special Collections
Miscellaneous Manuscripts
Box 6 'Donath Manuscripts'
Virginia Historical Society, Richmond, VA
William Lee Letterbook, Mss. 1L51f417
Winterthur Museum & Library, Winterthur, DE
Joseph Downs Collection of Manuscripts, Coll. Mic. 187
Ledgerbook of Samuel Wetherill and Sons
Bernard M. Bloomfield Papers
York County Archives, York, PA
Administration Accounts and Inventory of Baron de Beelen-Bertholff
York County Historical Society, York, PA
Lewis Miller, *Chronicles of York, 1790 – 1870*, 2 vols

Private Collection

Journal de mon voyage en France avec l'empereur Joseph en 1777 by Philipp Cobenzl.

Printed Sources

Aikin, John and William Johnston. *General Biography; or Lives Classical and Historical* . Vol. 19. London: Robinson, 1814.

American Philosophical Society. *Transactions of the American Philosophical Society*. Philadelphia: American Philosophical Society, 1838.

Anon. *Der Steyerische Robinson oder Reisen und besondere merkwürdige Begebenheiten des Joseph Müller*. Vienna: Johann Georg Mößle, 1791.

Anon. *Handbuch für Kaufsleute im Jahren 1785-86*. vol. 1. Leipzig, 1786.

Babo, Joseph Marius. *Das Winterquartier in Amerika*. Vienna: Logenmeister, 1778.

Joel Barlow. *Conspiracy of Kings: A poem addressed to the Inhabitants of Europe from another Quarter of the Globe*. London, 1792.

Baur, Samuel. *Kleines historisch-literarisches Wörterbuch über alle denkwürdige Personen.* vol. 2. Ulm, 1814.

Bent, Samuel Arthur. *Familiar Short Sayings of Great Men.* Boston, 1882.

Bolts, Guillaume. *Précis de l'Origine, de la marche et de la chûte de la Compagnie d'Asie et d'Afrique dans les ports du Littoral Autrichien.* Liège, 1785.

Bolts, William. *Considerations on India Affairs.* vols. 1 & 2. London, 1772, 1775.

Brissot, Jacques-Pierre. *Ein Vertheidiger des Volks – an Kaiser Joseph den Zweyten in Betreff seiner Auswanderungs-Verordnung.* Translated by Anonymous. s.l., 1785.

Brissot, Jacques-Pierre. *Seconde lettre d'un défenseur du peuple à l'empereur Joseph II sur soin règlement concernant l'émigration et principalement sur la révolte des Valaques; où l'on discute à fond le droit de révolte de Peuple.* 'Dublin', 1785.

Brissot, Jacques-Pierre. *Un défenseur du peuple à l'empereur Joseph II.* 'Dublin', 1785.

Büsching, Anton Friedrich. *Beiträge zu der Lebensgeschichte denkwürdiger Männer.* vol. 4. Halle, 1786.

Carli, Gian Rinaldo. *Le lettere americane: Nuova edizione corretta ed ampliata con l'aggiunta della parte III, ora per la prime volta impressa.* 2nd ed. 2 vols. Cremona: Lorenzo Manini, 1781.

Chandler, Thomas Bradbury. *A friendly address to all reasonable Americans, on the subject of our political confusions.* Boston, 1774.

Craik, George L. and Charles MacFarlane. *The Pictorial History of England.* London, 1841.

Dobrizhoffer, Martin. *An Account of the Abipones, an Equestrian People of Paraguay.* Translated by Sara Coleridge. 3 vols. London: Murray, 1822.

Dobrizhoffer, Martin. *Geschichte der Abiponer, einer berittenen und kriegerischen Nation in Paraguay.* Translated by Anton Kreil. 3 vols. Vienna: Kurzbeck, 1784.

Dobrizhoffer, Martin. *Historia de Abiponibus equestri, bellicosaque Paraquarieae natione.* 3 vols. Vienna: Kurzbeck, 1784.

D'Outrepont, Charles-Lambert. *Considérations sur la Constitution des Duchés de Brabant et de Limbourg et des autres provinces des Pays-Bas Autrichens lues dans l'Assemblée Générale des États de Brabant le 23 mai 1787.* Brussels, 1787.

Duval-Pyrau, Henri-François. *Journal et anecdotes intéressantes du voyage de la monsieur le Falckenstein.* Paris, 1777.

Everett, Alexander Hill. *An Address to the Literary Societies of Dartmouth College on the Character and Influence of German Literature.* Boston, 1839.

Fezer, Johann Jakob. *Wahrscheinlichkeiten.* 'Philadelphia', 1785.

de Flassan, Gaétan de Raxis. *Histoire générale et raisonnée de la Diplomatie française: depuis la fondation de la monarchie jusqu'à la fin du règne de Louis XVI.* vol. 7. Paris: Treuttel et Würtz, 1811.

Fontana, Nicolaus. "Tagebuch der Reise des k.k. Schiffes Joseph und Theresia nach den neuen österreichischen Pflanzorten in Asia und Afrika." Translated by Joseph Eyerel. Leipzig: 1782. In *Maria Teresa e le Indie orientali: La spedizione alle Isole Nicobare della nave Joseph und Theresia e il diario del chirurgo di bordo,* edited by G. Pilleri. Bern: Verlag de Hirnanatomischen Institutes, 1982.

Forster, Georg. *Ansichten vom Niederrhein, von Brabant, Flandern, Holland, England und Frankreich im April, Mai und Juni 1790.* Berlin, 1791).

Frisi, Paolo. *La Colombiade poema di Madama du Boccage tradotto dal francese in Milano.* Milan: Marelli, 1771.

Gianni, Francesco Maria. *La Costituzione Toscana imaginata dal Granduca Pietro Leopoldo: memoria del Senatore F. M. Gianni scritta nell'anno 1805.* Siena, 1805.

Hellin, Emmanuel Auguste. *Histoire Chronologique des Évêques et du Chapitre Exemt de l'Eglise Cathédrale de S. Bavon à Gand.* Ghent, 1772.

Hoff, Heinrich Georg. *Kurze Biographien oder Lebensabriße merkwürdiger und berühmter Personen neuerer Zeiten von unterschiedlichen Nazionen und allerley Ständen.* Brünn/Brno: Neumanns Schriften, 1782.

Kazinczy, Ferenc. "*Pályám emlékezete* [Remembrance of My Career]," in *Versek, műfordítások, széppróza, tanulmányok* [Poems, Translations, Belles-Lettres, and Studies]. Edited by Mária Szuander. vol. 1. Budapest: Szépirodalmi Könyvkiadó, 1979.

Kurz, Joseph Felix von. *Der Krumme Teufel.* [Vienna], 1759.

Lampredi, Giovanni Maria. *Dal commercio dei populi in tempo di guerra.* vol. 1. Florence, 1788.

Nagyváthy, János. *A nagy-szivüségnél.* 1790.

Neumann, Joseph. *Historia seditionum quas adversus Societatis Iesu missionarios, eorumque auxiliares moverunt nationes Indicae, ac potissum Tarahumara in America Septentrionali.* Prague, 1728.

Péczeli, József. *Summarium Retenioris Europaeae a Detectione Americae ad Revolutionem Gallicum.* Debrecen, 1827.

Playfair, William. *Joseph and Benjamin – A Conversation.* London, 1787.

de La Rochefoucauld d'Enville, Louis Alexandre, *Affaires de l'Angleterre et de l'Amérique* (Paris, 1778)

de Sérionne, Jacques Accarias. *La richesse de l'Angleterre, contenant les causes de la naissance & des progrès de l'industrie, du commerce & de la marine de la Grande-Bretagne, les causes de leur decadence, & l'etat de ses forces actuelles & de ses ressources.* Vienna: Trattner, 1771.

de Sérionne, Jacques Accarias. *Les intérêts des nations de l'Europe, dévelopés relativement au commerce.* Florence, Leiden, Leipzig, London, and Naples, 1761–1766.

Szentiványi, Márton. *Curiosiora et selectiora variarum scientiarum miscellanea. In tres partes divisa.* Trnava/Nagyzombat, 1689–1708.

Szentivany, Martini [sic]. *Calendarium cassoviense ad annum Iesu Christi.* Košice, 1754.

Taube, Friedrich Wilhelm. *Abschilderung der Engländischen Manufacturen, Handlung, Schifffahrt und Colonien, nach ihrer jetzigen Einrichtung und Beschaffenheit: Theils aus eigener Erfahrung, theils aus zuverläßigen und glaubwürdigen sowohl schriftlichen als mündlichen Nachrichten.* 2 vols. Vienna: Kraus, 1777–1778.

Taube, Friedrich Wilhelm. *Historische und politische Abschilderung der Engländischen Manufacturen, Handlung, Schiffahrt und Colonien nach ihrer jetzigen Einrichtung und Beschaffenheit: Theils aus eigener Erfahrung, theils aus zuverlässigen und glaubwürdigen, sowohl schrifftlichen als mündlichen Nachrichten, im Grundrisse entworfen*. Wien, 1774.

Taube, Friedrich Wilhelm. *Thoughts on the present state of our Colonies in North America on their Behaviour to the Mother Country and on the true interest of the Nation in regard of the Colonies*. London, 1766.

Török, Lajos [formerly attributed to Adalbert Barics] *Conspectus regiminis formae regnorum Angliae et Hungariae*. 1790.

Wekherlin, Ludwig Wilhelm. "Über den Aufruhr der Wallachen in Siebenbürgen: Ein Paragraf," in *Das graue Ungeheuer*, 3, no. 7 (1784), 185–188.

Williams, J. D. *Europe and America in 1821 – Translated from the French of the Abbé de Pradt*. vol. 1. London, 1822.

Windisch-Grætz, Johann Joseph, comte de. *De l'âme, de l'intelligence et de la liberté de la volonté*. Strasbourg: Chez J. G. Treuttel, 1790.

Wrangel, F. U., ed. *Lettres d'Axel de Fersen à son pere pendant la Guerre d'Amérique*. Paris, 1929.

Wraxall, Nathaniel, *Memoirs of the Courts of Berlin, Dresden, Warsaw and Vienna in the Years 1777,1778, and 1779*. vol. 2. London: Cadell and Davies, 1800.

Zinner, Johann. *Merkwürdige Briefe und Schriften der berühmtesten Generäle in Amerika nebst derselben beygefügten Lebensbeschreibungen*. Augsburg: Kletts, Wittwe und Franck, 1782.

Editions

Abbot, W. W., ed. *The Papers of George Washington*. Confederation Series. vol. 3. Charlottesville: University of Virginia Press, 1994.

Adams, Charles F., ed., *The Works of John Adams*. vols. 3 and 8. Boston, MA: Charles Little and James Brown Publishers, 1856 and 1875.

Arneth, Alfred von, ed., *Joseph II. and Katharina von Russland, ihr Briefwechsel*. Vienna: Braumüller, 1869.

Arneth, Alfred von, ed., *Marie Antoinette, Joseph II und Leopold II: Ihr Briefwechsel*. Vienna: Braumüller, 1866.

Arneth, Alfred von, ed., *Maria Theresia und Joseph II: Ihre Correspondenz und sammt Briefen Josephs an seinen Bruder Leopold*. Vienna: Carl Gerold's Sohn, 1868.

Arneth, Alfred von, ed., *Maria Theresia und Marie Antoinette: Ihr Briefwechsel während der Jahre 1770-1780*. Vienna: Braumüller, 1865.

Arneth, Alfred von, and Jules Gustave Flammermont, eds., *Correspondance secrète du Comte de Mercy-Argenteau avec l'empereur Joseph II et de prince de Kaunitz*. vol. 1. Collection de documents inédits sur l'histoire de France. Paris: Imprimerie Nationale, 1889.

Arneth, Alfred von, and Auguste Geoffroy, eds., *Maria Antoinette – Correspondance secrète entre Marie-Thérése et le comte de Mercy-Argenteau*. vols. 1–3. Paris: Firmin-Didot, 1875.

Anon. "Izard-Laurens Correspondence from South Carolina Historical Society Collection." *The South Carolina Historical and Genealogical Magazine* 22, no. 2 (April 1921): 39–52.

Balázs, Vargha, ed., *Csokonai Vitéz Mihály minden munkája*. vol. 2. Budapest: Szépirodalmi Könyvkiadó, 1973.

Beales, Derek E. D., and Pasta, Renato, eds., *Pietro Leopoldo d'Asburgo Lorena, Relazione sullo stato della monarchia (1784)*. Rome: Edizioni di Storia e Letteratura, 2013.

Beer, Adolf, ed., *Joseph II., Leopold II. und Kaunitz: ihr Briefwechsel*. Vienna: Braumüller, 1873.

Benda, Kálmán, ed., *A Magyar jakobinus mozgalom iratai*. vol. 1. Budapest: Akadémiai Kiadó, 1957.

Boyd, Julian P., et al, eds., *The Papers of Thomas Jefferson*. vols. 2, 7, 8, 9, 10, 27, 24, 28, and 29. Princeton, NJ: Princeton University Press, 1950–1972.

Brunner, Sebastian, ed., *Correspondances intimes de l'empereur Joseph II avec son ami le comte de Cobenzl et son premier ministre le prince de Kaunitz*. Mainz: Kirchenheim, 1871.

Butterfield, L. H., ed., *The Adams Papers: Diary and Autobiography of John Adams*. vol. 3: Diary, 1782–1804. Cambridge, MA: Harvard University Press, 1961.

Carter II Edward C., et al, eds., *The Papers of Benjamin Henry Latrobe*. Edited microfiche copies. Clifton, NJ: The Maryland Historical Society, 1976.

Catanzariti, John, ed., *The Papers of Robert Morris*. vols. 7–9. Pittsburgh, PA: University of Pittsburgh Press, 1989.

Cohn, Ellen R., et al, eds., *The Papers of Benjamin Franklin*. vols. 18, 23, 24, 25, 26, 27, 28, 35, 37, 24, 25, 35, 36, 38, 39, 40, 41, and 42. New Haven, CT: Yale University Press, 1990–2017.

Dávila, Vicente, *Archivo del General Miranda*: *Viajes, Diarios 1750-1785*. vol. 1. Caracas: Archivio Nationales/Editorial Sur-América, 1929.Debreczeni, Attila, ed., *Csokonai, Levelezés, sajtó alá rendezte és a jegyzeteket írta*. Budapest: Akadémiai, 1999.

Flammermont, Jules Gustave, ed., *Correspondance secrète du comte de Mercy Argenteau avec l'empereur Joseph II et le prince de Kaunitz*. Paris: Imprimerie Nationale, 1891.

Ford, Worthington Chauncy, ed., *The Letters of William Lee*. vols. 1–3. Brooklyn, NY: Historical Printing Club, 1891.

Grayson Allen, David, Robert J. Taylor, and Marc Friedlaender, eds., *The Adams Papers: Diary of John Quincy Adams (Nov. 1779–Mar. 1786)*. vol. 1. Cambridge, MA: Harvard University Press, 1981.

Lint, Gregg L., et al, eds., *The Papers of John Adams*. vols. 11, 12, 14, 15, 16, and 17. Cambridge, MA: Harvard University Press, 1996–2014.

Girard, Georges, ed., *Correspondance entre Marie Thérèse et Marie Antoinette*. Paris: Grasset, 1933.

Haider, Siegfried, ed., *Berichte aus der Neuen Welt: Die Vereinigten Staaten von Amerika zwischen Unabhängigkeits-und Bürgerkrieg aus (ober)österreichischer Sicht*. Linz: Landesverlag, 2000.

Hunt, Gaillard, ed., *Journals of the Continental Congress, 1774-1789*. vol. 25. Washington, D.C.: US Government Printing Office, 1922.

Idzerda, Stanley J., Margherita Marchione, and S. Eugene Scalia, eds., *Philip Mazzei: Selected Writings and Correspondence*. Prato: Cassi di Risparmi e Depositi di Prato, 1983.

Isham, Charles, ed., *The Deane Papers*. New York, NY: New York Historical Society, 1886.

Izard-Deas, Anne, ed., *Correspondence of Mr. Ralph Izard of South Carolina*. vol. 1. New York, NY: Charles Francis & Co., 1844.

Johnson, Henry P., ed., *The Correspondence and Public Papers of John Jay*. vols. 2–3. New York, NY: G.P. Putnam's Sons, 1890–1893.

Lengel, Edward G., ed., *The Papers of George Washington*. Revolutionary War Series. vol. 18. Charlottesville, VA: University of Virginia Press, 2008.

Lengyel, Réka and Gábor Tüskés, eds., *Learned Societies, Freemasonry, Sciences and Literature in 18th-Century Hungary: A Collection of Documents and Sources*. Budapest: MTA Bölcsézettudományi Kutatóközpont Irodalomtudományi Intézet, 2017.

Klingenstein, Grete, Antonio Trampus, and Eva Faber, eds., *Europäische Aufklärung zwischen Wien und Triest: Die Tagebücher des Gouverneurs Karl Graf Zinzendorf 1776-1782*. vols. 1–4. Vienna: Böhlau, 2009.

Levfevre, Jean, ed., *Documents sur le personnel supérieur des Conseils Collatéraux du Gouvernement des Pays-Bas pendant le XVIIIe siècle*. Brussels: Commission Royale d'Histoire, 1941.

Mályusz, Elemér, ed., *Sándor Lipót főherceg iratai 1790-1795*. Budapest: Magyar Történelmi Társulat, 1926.

Marraro, Howard R. "Mazzei's Correspondence with the Grand Duke of Tuscany during His American Mission." *The William and Mary Quarterly* 22, no. 3 (1942): 275–301.

Marraro, Howard R. "Mazzei's Correspondence with the Grand Duke of Tuscany during His American Mission." *The William and Mary Quarterly* 22, no. 4 (1942): 361–380.

Mátrai, László, ed., *Martinovics, Filozófiai írások*. Budapest: Magvető Könyvkiadó, 1956.

Minto, Emma Eleanor Elizabeth Elliot-Murray-Kynynmound, countess of. ed., *A Memoir of the Right Honourable Hugh Elliot*. Edinburgh: Edmonston and Douglas, 1868.

Neuhuber, Christian, ed., *Maurus Lindemayr – Die hochdeutschen Komödien: Kritische Ausgabe.* vols. 1–2. Vienna: Praesens Verlag, 2006.

Nuxoll, Elizabeth M., ed., *The Selected Papers of John Jay.* vol. 4. Charlottesville, VA: University of Virginia Press, 2015.

Prothero, Rowland E., ed., *The Private Letters of Edward Gibbon 1753-1794.* vols. 1–2. London: John Murray Publisher, 1896.

Schlitter, Hanns, ed., *Die Berichte des ersten Agenten Österreichs in den Vereinigten Staaten von Amerika Baron de Beelen-Bertholff an die Regierung der Österreichischen Niederlande in Brüssel 1784-1789.* Fontes rerum Austriacarum. 2. Abtheilung: Diplomataria et acta. Vienna: F. Tempsky, 1891.

de Serrione, Jacques Accarias. *Un publiciste dauphinois du XVIIIe Siècle: Jacques Accarias de Sérionne, sa famille, sa vie, ses ouvrages.* Bulletin de l'Académie Delphinale. no. 3. Grenoble: F. Ailler Père et Fils, 1889.

Smyth, Gillespie, ed., *Memoirs and Correspondence (official and familiar) of Sir Robert Murray Keith, Envoy Extraordinary and Minister Plenipotentiary at the Courts of Dresden, Copenhagen, and Vienna from 1769 to 1792.* vols. 1–2. London: Henry Colburn, 1849.

Sparks, Jared, ed., *The Diplomatic Correspondence of the American Revolution.* vol. 1. Boston, MA: Hale, 1829.

Sparks, Jared, ed., *The Works of Benjamin Franklin.* vol. 6. Chicago, IL: Townsend, 1882.

Stevens, Benjamin F., ed., *Facsimiles of Manuscripts in European Archives Relating to America, 1773-1783.* London: Malby & Sons, 1889.

Walter, Friedrich, ed., *Die österreichische Zentralverwaltung.* Part II. vol. 5: Die Zeit Franz II. (I.) und Ferdinands I. (1792–1848), Aktenstücke. Vienna: Veröffentlichungen der Kommission für Neuere Geschichte Österreichs, 1956.

Wharton, Francis, ed., *The Revolutionary Diplomatic Correspondence of the United States.* vols. 1–2. Washington D.C.: U.S. Government Printers, 1889.

Wilden-Neeser, Robert, ed., *Letters and Papers relating to the Cruises of Gustavus Conyngham 1777-1779.* New York, NY: De Vinne Press, 1915.

Secondary Literature

Abádi-Nagy, Zoltán. "Not an Untroubled Bliss: The Post-Early-Phase Post-Communist Situation of English Studies in Hungary." *Hungarian Journal of English and American Studies* 2, no. 1 (1996): 3–13.

Abernethy, Thomas Perkins. "The Origin of the Franklin-Lee Imbroglio." *The North Carolina Historical Review* 15, no. 1 (1938): 41–52.

Abulafia, David. *The Great Sea: A Human History of the Mediterranean.* London: Allen Lane, 2011.

Ács, Pál. *Reformations in Hungary at the Age of the Ottoman Conquest.* Göttingen: Vandenhoeck & Ruprecht, 2019.

Adam, Thomas, ed., *Germany and the Americas: Culture, Politics, and History: A Multidisciplinary Encyclopedia.* Santa Barbara, CA: ABC-Clio, 2005.

Adams, William Howard. *The Paris Years of Thomas Jefferson.* New Haven, CT: Yale University Press, 1997.

Addobbati, Andrea. "Filippo Mazzei e Giuseppe Bettoia: une relazione d'affari all'ombra della Rivoluzione Americane, 1773–1781." *Nuova Studi Livornesi* 11 (2004): 133–194.

Addobbati, Andrea. "L'espace de la guerre et du commerce: réflexions sur le Port of Trade polanyien à partir du cas de Livourne." *Cahiers de la Méditerranée* 85 (2012): 233–249.

Addobbati, Andrea. "Oltre gli intermediary: La Anton Francesco Salucci & figlio alla conquista dei mercati americani, 1779-1788." In *Storia e attualità della presenza degli Stati Uniti a Livorno e in Toscana,* edited by Paolo Castignoli, Luigi Donolo, and Algerina Neri, 145–183. Pisa: Plus, 2003.

Adelman, Jeremy. "An Age of Imperial Revolutions." *The American Historical Review* 113, no. 2 (April 2008): 319–340.

Adler, Simon. *Political Economy in the Habsburg Monarchy 1750-1774: The Contribution of Ludwig von Zinzendorf.* London: Palgrave Macmillan, 2020.

Agstner, Rudolf. "Austria(-Hungary) and her Consulates South of the Rio Grande (1828-1918): A Survey." In *Transatlantic Relations: Austria and Latin America in the 19th and 20th Centuries,* edited by Günter Bischof and Klaus Eisterer, 85–117. Innsbruck: Studienverlag, 2006.

Agstner, Rudolf. *Austria(-Hungary) and its Consulates in the United States of America since 1820.* Münster: LIT Verlag, 2012.

Alden, John Richard. *Stephan Sayre: American Revolutionary Adventurer.* Baton Rouge, LA: Louisiana State University Press, 1983.

Alison, Henry. "Baron de B: A Forgotten Man in American History." *Pennsylvania Traveller* (1968): 30–35.

Altic, Mirela. "Changing the Discourse: Post-Expulsion Jesuit Cartography of Spanish America." *Journal of Jesuit Studies* 6, no. 1 (2019): 99–114.

Andes, Martin L. "Honey Brook's only nobleman." *Chester County Collections* 10 (s.d.): 347–348.

Andreozzi, Daniele. "From the Black Sea to the Americas. The Trading Companies of Trieste and the Global Commercial Network (18th Century)." In *Mediterranean doubts Trading Companies, Conflicts and Strategies in the Global Spaces XV-XIX Centuries,* edited by Daniele Andreozzi, 79–81. Palermo: New Digital Press, 2017.

Angermann, Erich. "Der deutsche Frühkonstitutionalismus und das amerikanische Vorbild." *Historische Zeitschrift* 219, no. 1 (1974): 1–32.

Angiolini, Franco. "From the Neutrality of the Port to the Neutrality of the State: Projects, Debates and Laws in Habsburg-Lorraine Tuscany." In *War, Trade and Neutrality: Europe and the Mediterranean in the Seventeenth and Eighteenth Centuries,* edited by Antonella Alimento, 82–100. Milan: Franco Angeli, 2011.

Angyal, Andreas. "Martin Szentiványi: Ein ungarisches Gelehrtenleben des ausgehenden 17. Jahrhunderts im Rahmen der deutsch-slawisch-ungarischen

Wissenschaftsbeziehungen." In *Ost und West in der Geschichte des Denkens und der kulturellen Beziehungen: Festschrift für Eduard Winter zum 70. Geburtstag*, introduction by A. P. Juškevič, edited by W. Steinitz, P.N. Berkov, B. Suchodolski, and J. Dolanský, 152–163. Berlin: Akademie-Verlag, 1966.

Anon. "Dr. Joseph Cauffman Applying for Service during the Revolutionary War." *Records of the American Catholic Historical Society of Philadelphia* 21, no. 2 (1910): 80–82.

Anon. *Fourth Report of the National Society of the Daughters of the American Revolution*. Washington D.C.: U.S. Government Printing Office, 1902.

Anspach, Claude. "Frédéric baron de Romberg: Seigneur de Machelen Sainte-Gertrude 1729–1819." *Le Parchemin*, no. 291 (1994): 161–181.

Antonucci, Anthony J. "Consuls and Consiglieri: United States Relations with the Italian States." In *Rough Waters: American Involvement with the Mediterranean in the Eighteenth and Nineteenth Centuries*, edited by Silvia Marzagalli, James R Sofka, and John J. McCusker, 77–100. St. John's, Newfoundland: International Maritime Economic History Association, 2010.

Appelbaum, Stanley. *The Triumph of Maximilian I*. New York, NY: Dover Publications, 1964.

Appleby, Joyce. "America as a Model for the Radical French Reformers of 1789." *The William & Mary Quarterly* 27, no. 2 (1971): 267–286.

Aretin, Karl Otmar Freiherr von. "Russia as a Guarantor Power of the Imperial Constitution under Catherine II." *The Journal of Modern History* 58, Supplement: Politics and Society in the Holy Roman Empire, 1500-1806 (1986): 141–160.

Armitage, David, Alison Bashford, and Sujit Sivasundaram, eds., *Oceanic Histories*. Cambridge: Cambridge University Press, 2018.

Armitage, David, and Subrahmanyam, Sanjay, eds., *The Age of Revolutions in Global Context, ca. 1760-1840*. Basingstoke: Palgrave Macmillan, 2009.

Armitage, David. *The Declaration of Independence: A Global History*. Cambridge, MA: Harvard University Press, 2007.

Armitage, David. "Three Concepts of Atlantic History." In *The British Atlantic World 1500-1800*, edited by David Armitage and Michael J. Braddick, 11–27. Basingstoke: Palgrave Macmillan, 2002.

Arenth, Alfred von. *Geschichte Maria Theresias*. vol. 10. Vienna: Braumüller, 1879.

Aspaas, Per Pippin and László Kontler. *Maximilian Hell (1720–92) and the Ends of Jesuit Science in Enlightenment Europe*. Leiden and Boston: Brill, 2019.

Astigarraga, Jesús. "L'économie espagnole en débat: l'oeuvre d'Accarias de Sérionne et sa réfutation par campomanes." *Revue Historique* 2, no. 662 (2012): 357–389.

Astigarraga, Jesús. "Spain and the Economic Work of Jacques Accarias de Serionne." In *The Economic Turn: Recasting Political Economy in Enlightenment Europe*, edited by Sophus A. Reinert and Steven L. Kaplan, 607–634. London: Anthem Press, 2019.

Asúa, Miguel de. *Science in the Vanished Arcadia: Knowledge of Nature in the Jesuit Missions of Paraguay and Río de la Plata*. Leiden and Boston, MA: Brill, 2014.

Atwood, Rodney. *The Hessians: Mercenaries from Hessen-Kassel in the American Revolution*. New Edition. Cambridge: Cambridge University Press, 2002.

Auner, Michael. *Zur Geschichte des rumänischen Bauernaufstandes in Siebenbürgen 1784*. Hermannstadt (Sibiu): Krafft & Drotleff, 1935.

Babudieri, Fulvio. *Trieste e gli interessi austriaci in asia nei secoli XVIII e XIX*. Padova: Milani, 1966.

Bachleitner, Norbert. *Die literarische Zensur in Österreich von 1751 bis 1848*. Vienna: Böhlau, 2017.

Bailyn, Bernard. *Atlantic History: Concept and Contours*. Cambridge, MA: Harvard University Press, 2005.

Bailyn, Bernard, and Patricia L. Denault, eds., *Soundings in Atlantic History: Latent Structures and Intellectual Currents 1500-1830*. Cambridge, MA and London: Harvard University Press, 2009.

Bailyn, Bernard. "The Idea of Atlantic History." *Itinerario* 20, no. 1 (1996): 19–44.

Bailyn, Bernard. *The Ideological Origins of the American Revolution*. 50th Anniversary Edition. Cambridge, MA: Harvard University Press, 2017.

Balázs, Éva H. "A Magyar jozefinisták külföldi kapcsolataihoz." *Századok* 97, no. 6 (1963): 1187–1203.

Balázs, Éva H. *Berzeviczy Gergely: A Reformpolitikus 1763-1795*. Budapest: Akadémiai Kiadó, 1996.

Balázs, Éva H. *Hungary and the Habsburgs 1765-1800: An Experiment in Enlightened Absolutism*. Translated by Tim Wilkinson. Budapest: Central European University Press, 1997.

Balázs, Éva H. "Pierre-Léopold et la Hongrie." In *Venezia, Italia, Ungheria fra Arcadia e Illuminismo: Rapporti Italo-Ungheresi dalla Presa di Buda alla Rivoluzione Francese*, edited by Béla Köpeczi and Péter Sárközy, 147–154. Budapest: Akadémiai Kiadó, 1982.

Barany, George. "The Interest of the United States in Central Europe: Appointment of the First American Consul to Hungary." *Papers of the Michigan Academy of Science, Art, and Letters* 47 (1962): 275–298.

Bartlett, Roger and Bruce Mitchell, "State-Sponsored Immigration into Eastern Europe in the Eighteenth and Nineteenth Centuries." In *The German Lands and Eastern Europe*, edited by Roger Bartlett and Karen Schönwälder, 91–114. Basingstoke: Macmillan Press, 1999.

Barton, Hildor A. *Count Hans Axel von Fersen: Aristocrat in an Age of Revolution*. Boston, MA: Twayne Publishers, 1975.

Barton, Hildor A. "Sweden and the War of American Independence." *The William and Mary Quarterly* 23, no. 3 (1966): 408–430.

Basa, Enikő Molnár. "English and Hungarian Cultural Contacts in the 16th Century." *Hungarian Studies* 10, no. 2 (1995): 205–234.

Bat'ha, František. *Fragment literární pozůstalosti Fr. S. Ant. Steinského.* Prague: Literární archiv Národního muzea, 1960.

Bauer, Jean. "With Friends Like These: John Adams and the Comte de Vergennes on Franco-American Relations." *Diplomatic History* 37, no. 4 (2013): 664–692.

Beales, Derek E. D. *Enlightenment and Reform in Eighteenth-Century Europe.* London: I. B. Tauris, 2005.

Beales, Derek E. D. *Joseph II*, vol. 1: In the Shadow of Maria Theresa, 1741–1780. Cambridge: Cambridge University Press, 1987.

Beales, Derek E. D. *Joseph II*, vol. 2: Against the World, 1780–1790. (Cambridge: Cambridge University Press, 2009.

Becattini, Giacomo. "La lezione di Pietro Leopoldo." *Moneta e Credito* 65, no. 258 (2012): 103–111.

Becattini, Massimo. *Filippo Mazzei: mercante italiano a Londra 1756-1772.* Prato: Pentalinea, 1997.

Bell, Whitfield J. "Philadelphia Medical Students in Europe 1750-1800." *Pennylvania Magazine of History and Biography* 67, no.1 (January 1943): 1–29.

Bellhouse, David R. The Flawed Genius of William Playfair: The Story of the Father of Statistical Graphics (forthcoming, 2021).

Belozerskaya, Marina. "Menageries as Princely Necessities of their Times." In *Oudry's Painted Menagerie: Portraits of Exotic Animals in Eighteenth-Century Europe*, edited by Mary Morton, 59–74. Los Angeles, CA: J. Paul Getty Museum, 2007.

Bemis, Samuel Flagg. *The Diplomacy of the American Revolution.* 2nd edition. Bloomington, IN: Indiana University Press, 1957.

Bemis, Samuel Flagg. *The Hussey-Cumberland Mission and American Independence: An Essay in the Diplomacy of the American Revolution.* Princeton, NJ: Princeton University Press, 1931.

Ben-Atar, Doron S. *The Origins of Jeffersonian Commercial Policy and Diplomacy.* New York, NY: Palgrave Macmillan, 1993.

Benna, Anna Hedwig. *Contemporary Austrian Views of American Independence: A Documentary on the Occasion of the Bicentennial.* Translated by Cheryl Bernard-Vienna: Federal Press Service, 1976.

Benna, Anna Hedwig. "Österreichs erste diplomatische Vertretung bei den Vereinigten Staaten von Amerika." *Mitteilungen des Österreichischen Staatsarchivs* 29 (1976): 215–240.

Bender, Thomas, Laurent Dubois, and Richard Rabinowitz, eds., *Revolution! The Atlantic World Reborn.* New York, NY: New York Historical Society, 2011.

Benson, Adolph B. *Sweden and the American Revolution.* New Haven, CT: Tuttle, Morehouse & Taylor Company, 1926.

Bergbohm, Carl. *Die bewaffnete Neutralität 1780-1783: Eine Entwickelungsphase des Völkerrechts im Seekriege*. Berlin: Puttkammer & Mühlbrecht, 1884.

Bernard, Paul B. *Joseph II and Bavaria: Two Eighteenth-Century Attempts at German Unification*. The Hague: Nijhoff, 1965.

Betzwieser, Thomas. ""Die Wilden wohnen gar nicht weit": Kurz-Bernardon, Haydn und die theatrale Anderwelt." In *Joseph Haydn und die Neue Welt: Musik- und kulturgeschichtliche Perspektiven*, edited by Walter Reicher, 193–208. Vienna: Hollitzer Verlag, 2019.

Billas, George Athan. *American Constitutionalism Heard Around the World 1776-1989: A Global Perspective*. New York, NY: New York University Press, 2009.

Black, Jeremy. *British Foreign Policy in an Age of Revolution 1783-1793*. Cambridge: Cambridge University Press, 1994.

Black, Jeremy. *British Politics and Foreign Policy, 1744-1757: Mid-Century Crisis*. London and New York, NY: Routledge, 2015.

Black, Jeremy. *The Continental Commitment: Britain, Hanover, and Interventionism 1714-1793*. London and New York, NY: Routledge, 2012.

Blanning, Tim C. W. ""That Horrid Electorate' or 'Ma Patrique Germanique'? George III, Hannover, and the Fürstenbund of 1785." *The Historical Journal* 20, no. 2 (1977): 311–344.

Bödeker, Hans Erich. "The Concept of the Republic in Eighteenth-Century German Thought." In *Republicanism and Liberalism in America and the German States 1750-1850*, edited by Jürgen Heideking and James A. Henretta (with Peter Becker), 35–52. Cambridge and Washington D.C.: Cambridge University Press and the German Historical Institute, 2004.

Bodi, Leslie [László]. *Tauwetter in Wien: Zur Prosa der österreichischen Aufklärung 1781-1795*. Frankfurt am Main: Fischer, 1977.

Boer, Bertil van. "Undermining Independence: The English Political and Cultural Views of America during Haydn's London Sojourns." In *Joseph Haydn und die Neue Welt: Musik- und kulturgeschichtliche Perspektiven*, edited by Walter Reicher, 39–60. Vienna: Hollitzer Verlag, 2019.

Boglár, Lajos. "XVIII. Századi magyar utazók Dél-Amerikában." *Ethnographia* 63 (1952): 449–461.

Bolkhovitinov, Nikolai N. *Rossiia i voina SShA za nezavisimost' 1775 - 1783* [Russia and the War of the United States of America for Independence]. Moscow: s.n., 1976.

Bolkhovitinov, Nikolai N. "The Declaration of Independence: A View from Russia." *The Journal of American History* 85, no. 4 (1999): 1389–1398.

Borja González, Galaxis. *Jesuitische Berichterstattung über die Neue Welt: Zur Veröffentlichungs-, Verbreitungs- und Rezeptionsgeschichte jesuitischer Americana auf dem deutschen Buchmarkt im Zeitalter der Aufklärung*. Göttingen: Vandenhoeck & Ruprecht, 2011.

Borja González, Galaxis, and Ulrike Strasser, "The German Circumnavigation of the Globe: Missionary Writing, Colonial Identity Formation, and the Case of Joseph Stöcklein's Neuer Welt-Bott." In *Reporting Christian Missions in the Eighteenth Century: Communication, Culture of Knowledge and Regular Publication in a Cross-Confessional Perspective*, edited by Markus Friedrich and Alexander Schunka, 73–92. Leipzig: Harrassowitz Verlag, 2017.

Bosetti, Gilbert. *De Trieste à Dubrovnik: Une ligne de fracture de l'Europe*. Grenoble: ELLUG, 2006.

Botez, Elvira. "Maximilian Hell and the Northernmost Transit of Venus Expedition of 1769." *Journal of Astronomical Data* 10, no. 7 (2004): 165–174.

Bourguignon, Henry J. "Incorporation of the Law of Nations during the American Revolution: The Case of the San Antonio." *The American Journal of International Law* 71, no. 2 (1977): 270–295.

Bourguignon, Henry J. *The First Federal Court: The Federal Appellate Prize Court of the American Revolution 1775-1787*. Philadelphia, PA: American Philosophical Society, 1977.

Boutier, Jean. "Les imprimés révolutionnaires français en Toscane: paradoxes d'une liberté surveillée 1789-1792." *Mélanges de l'école française de Rome* 102, no. 2 (1990): 423–468.

Bowd, Rebecca. "Useful Knowledge or Polite Learning? A Reappraisal of Approaches to Subscription Library History." *Library & Information History*. 29, no. 3 (2013): 182–195.

Boyd, James David. "Initiating Mass Movement: Questions of Commercial Information in Atlantic Migration from Central Europe 1870-1900." *Journal of Austrian-American History* 2, no. 1 (2018): 31–50.

Bradshaw, Richard Lee. *Thomas Bradshaw (1733-1774): A Georgian Politician in the Time of the American Revolution*. Bloomington, IN: Xlibrus US Press, 2011.

Brauneder, Wilhelm. "America's Influence on Constitutional Development in the Habsburg Monarchy." In *Constitution et Révolution aux États-Unies d'Amérique et en Europe 1776-1815*, edited by Robert Martucci, 673–681. Macerata: Laboratorio di storia costituzionale, 1995.

Bray, Wawrick. "Crop Plants and Cannibals: Early European Impressions of the New World." *Proceedings of the British Academy* 81 (1992): 289–326.

Brechka, Frank T. *Gerard van Swieten and His World 1700–1772*. Berlin: Springer Verlag, 1970.

Brezina, Anna "Der mexikanische Federschild aus Ambras." *Archiv für Völkerkunde* 14 (1959): 138–140.

Brnardić, Teodora Shek. "The Enlightenment's Choice of Latin: The Ratio Educationis of 1777 in the Kingdom of Hungary." In *Latin at the Crossroads of Identity: The*

Evolution of Linguistic Nationalism in the Kingdom of Hungary, edited by Gábor Almási and Lav Šubarić, 119–151. Leiden and Boston: Brill, 2015.

Bronza, Boro. "Preparations of the Austrian Expedition towards India, 1775-1776." *Istraživanja: Journal of Historical Researches* 29 (2018): 63–76.

Broome-Semans, Barbara and Letitia Broome-Schwarz, *Broome, Latourette and Mercereau Families of New York and Connecticut: 17th to 19th Centuries*. New York, NY: Xlibris, 2013.

Browning, Oscar. "Hugh Elliot in Berlin." *Transactions of the Royal Historical Society* 4 (1889): 85–101.

Brunnbauer, Ulf. *Globalizing Southeastern Europe: Emigrants, America, and the State since the late Nineteenth Century*. Washington, D.C.: Lexington Books, 2016.

Bruyssel, Ernst van. *Histoire du commerce et de la marine en Belgique*. vol. 3. Brussels: Lacroix, 1864.

Buccini, Stefania. *The Americas in Italian Literature and Culture 1700-1825*. Philadelphia, PA: Penn State Press, 1997.

Buch, David J. *Magic Flutes and Enchanted Forests: The Supernatural in Eighteenth-Century Musical Theater*. Chicago, IL: University of Chicago Press, 2008.

Bukovansky, Mlada. *Legitimacy and Power Politics: The American and French Revolutions in International Political Culture*. Princeton, NJ: Princeton University Press, 2002.

Burnett, Edmund C. "Note on American Negotiations for Commercial Treaties, 1776-1786." *The American Historical Review* 16, no. 3 (1911): 579–587.

Bushnell, Amy Turner "Indigenous America and the Limits of the Atlantic World, 1493–1825." In *Atlantic History: A Critical Appraisal*, edited by Jack P. Greene and Philip D. Morgan, 191–221. New York, NY: Clarendon for Oxford University Press, 2009.

Calderón, María Teresa and Clément Thibaud, eds., *Revolucion en el mundo Atlántico*. Bogotá: Universidad Externado de Colombia, 2006.

Canny, Nicholas. "Atlantic History: What and Why?" *European Review* 9, no. 4 (2001): 399–411.

Carroll, Francis M. *A Good and Wise Measure: The Search for the Canadian-American Boundary, 1783-1842*. Toronto: University of Toronto Press, 2001.

Cerman, Ivo. *Habsburgischer Adel und Aufklärung: Bildungsverhalten des Wiener Hofadels im 18. Jahrhundert*. Stuttgart: Steiner Verlag, 2010.

Cerman, Ivo. "Každodenní život Chotků v parku Veltrusy." In *Kronika Schola naturalis: Projekt revitalizace zámku Veltrusy a centrum Evropské úmluvy o krajině*, edited by Kamil Kristen Brzák, Petr Hudec, Jan Kadeřábek, and Dušan Michelfeit, 12–17. Prague: Národní památkový ústav, územní památková správa v Praze, 2015.

Cerman, Ivo. "Moral Anthropology of Joseph Nikolaus Windischgrätz." In *The Enlightenment in Bohemia: Religion, Morality, and Multiculturalism*, edited by Ivo

Cerman, Rita Krueger, and Susan Reynolds, 169–191. Oxford: Voltaire Foundation, 2011.

Chiantti, Luigi. "Calzabigi's Vision of an Enlightened America." *Comparative Literature Studies* 14, no. 2 (1977): 135–142.

Christelow, Allan. "Father Joseph Neumann, Jesuit Missionary to the Tarahumares." *The Hispanic American Historical Review.* 19, no. 4 (1939): 423–442.

Clark, George L. *Silas Deane: A Connecticut Leader in the American Revolution.* New York, NY: Putnam's, 1913.

Cochrane, Eric W. "Le riforme leopoldine nella corrispondenza degli inviati francesi 1766-1791." *Rassegna Storica del Risorgimento* 45 (1959): 199–215.

Codignola, Luca. *Blurred Nationalities across the North Atlantic: Traders, Priests, and their Kin Travelling between North America and the Italian Peninsula, 1763-1846.* Toronto: University of Toronto Press, 2019.

Codignola, Luca. "La lettera ai genitori del livornese Filippo Filicchi sui giovani Stati Uniti, 1785." In *Itinerari del libro nella storia. Per Anna Giulia Cavagna a trent'anni dalla prima lezione,* edited by Francesca Nepori, Fiammetta Sabba, Paolo Tinti, and Anna Giulia Cavagna, 205–214. Bologna: Pàtron editore, 2017.

Codignola, Luca. "Le prime relazioni tra il Nord America e la penisola italiana, 1750-1830: ciò che ancora non sappiamo." In *Flussi migratori e accoglienza tra storia e politiche di gestione,* edited by Pia Baldelli and Elena Baldassarri, 25–38. Rome: Aracne, 2009.

Codignola, Luca. "Relations between North America and the Italian Peninsula, 1763-1799: Tuscany, Genoa, and Naples." In *Rough Waters: American Involvement with the Mediterranean in the Eighteenth and Nineteenth Centuries,* edited by Silvia Marzagalli, James R Sofka, and John J. McCusker, 25–42. St. John's, Newfoundland: International Maritime Economic History Association, 2010.

Cogliano, Francis D. *Emperor of Liberty: Thomas Jefferson's Foreign Policy.* New Haven, CT: Yale University Press, 2014.

Cogliano, Francis D. *Revolutionary America 1763-1815: A Political History.* 3rd edition. London: Routledge, 2016.

Cohen, Paul. "Was there an Amerindian Atlantic? Reflections on the Limits of a Historiographical Concept." *History of European Ideas* 34, no. 4 (2008): 388–410.

Conway, Stephen *Britannia's Auxiliaries: Continental Europeans and the British Empire, 1740-1800.* Oxford: Oxford University Press, 2017.

Coolidge, Archibald Cary. *The United States as a World Power.* New York, NY: Macmillan, 1908.

Coons, Ronald E. *Steamships, Statesmen, and Bureaucrats: Austrian Policy towards the Steam Navigation Company of the Austrian Lloyd, 1836-1848.* Wiesbaden: Steiner, 1975.

Corfield, Justin. "Bridgetower, George (1780-1860)." In *Encyclopedia of Blacks in European History and Culture,* edited by Eric Martone, 1:85–86. Westport, CT: Greenwood Press, 2009.

Cortese, Nino. "Le prime relazioni tra gli Stati Uniti d'America e gli stati italiani." *Rassegna storica del Risorgimento* 58, no. 1 (1971): 3–20.

Crawford, Michael J. "The Hawke and the Dove, a Cautionary Tale: Neutral Ports and Prizes of War during the American Revolution." *Northern Mariner/Le Marin du Nord* 18, no. 3 (2008): 49–66.

Cresson, William Penn. *Francis Dana, a Puritan Diplomat at the Court of Catherine the Great.* New York, NY: The Dial Press, 1930.

Crytzer, Brady J. *Hessians: Mercenaries, Rebels, and the War for British North America.* Yardley, PA: Westholme Publishing, 2015.

Curti, Merle E. "Austria and the United States, 1848-1852: A Study in Diplomatic Relations." *Smith College Studies in History* 11, no. 3 (1926): 137–206.

Davis, Gerald. "Observations of Leopold of Hapsburg on the Pennsylvania Constitution of 1776." *Pennsylvania History: A Journal of Mid-Atlantic Studies* 29, no. 4 (1962): 373–380.

Davis, Walter W. *Joseph II: An Imperial Reformer for the Austrian Netherlands.* The Hague: Nijhoff, 1974.

Delpiano, Patrizia. *Il governo della lettura: Chiesa e libri nell'Italia del Settecento.* Bologna: Il Mulino, 2007.

Detering, Susanne. *Kolumbus, Cortés, Montezuma: Die Entdeckung und Eroberung Lateinamerikas als Literarische Sujets in der Aufklärung und im 20. Jahrhundert.* Weimar: VDG, 1996.

Dickson, P. G. M. "Count Karl von Zinzendorf's 'New Accountancy'. The Structure of Austrian Government Finance in Peace and War, 1781-1791." *The International History Review* 29, no. 1 (2007): 22–56.

Dickson, P. G. M. *Finance and Government under Maria Theresa, 1740–1780.* vol. 1: Society and Government. Oxford and New York, NY: Clarendon Press of Oxford University Press, 1987.

Dickson, P. G. M. *Finance and Government under Maria Theresa, 1740–1780.* vol. 2: Finance and Credit. Oxford and New York, NY: Clarendon Press of Oxford University Press, 1987.

Dickson, P. G. M. "Joseph II's Reshaping of the Austrian Church." *Historical Journal* 36, no. 1 (1993): 89–114.

Diekmann, Heiko. *Lockruf der Neuen Welt: Deutschsprachige Werbeschriften für die Auswanderung nach Nordamerika von 1630 bis 1760.* Göttingen: Universitätsverlag, 2005.

Dill, Alonzo T. *William Lee: Militia Diplomat.* Williamsburg, VA: Virginia Independence Bicentennial Commission, 1976.

Dippel, Horst. *Americana Germanica 1770-1800: Bibliographie deutscher Amerikaliteratur.* Stuttgart: Metzler, 1976.

Dippel, Horst. "The American Revolution and the Modern Concept of 'Revolution.'" In *New Wine in Old Skins: A Comparative View of Socio-Political Structures and Values Affecting the American Revolution*, edited by Erich Angermann,

Marie-Luise Frings, and Hermann Wellenreuther, 124–129. Stuttgart: Ernst Klett Verlag, 1976.

Dippel, Horst. "Die Wirkung der amerikanischen Revolution auf Deutschland und Frankreich." *Geschichte und Gesellschaft* 2 (1976): 101–121.

Dippel, Horst. *Germany and the American Revolution 1770–1800: A Sociohistorical Investigation of Late Eighteenth-Century Thinking*, translated by Bernhard Uhlendorf. Williamsburg, VA: Omohundro Institute, 1977.

Döberl, Mario. "The Royal and Imperial Stables of the Austrian Habsburgs during the Early Modern Period: A General Survey with Specific Reference to the Spanish Influence." In *Las Caballerizas Reales y el mundo del caballo*, edited by Juan Aranda Doncel and José Martínez Millán, 197–232. Córdoba: Litopress, 2016.

Do Paço, David. *L'Orient à Vienne au dix-huitième siècle*. Oxford: Voltaire Foundation, 2015.

Do Paço, David. Patronage and Expertise: The Creation of Trans-Imperial Knowledge, 1719-1848." In *Transnational Cultures of Expertise: Circulating State-Related Knowledge in the Eighteenth and Nineteenth Centuries*, edited by Lothar Schilling and Jakob Vogel, 48–64. Berlin: de Gruyter, 2019.

Dorlodot, Albert de. "Les ports d'Ostende et de Nieuport et les fournitures d'armes aux insurgents Américains 1774-1782." *Communications de l'Académie de Marine de Belgique* 7 (1953): 141–157.

Drimmel, Heinrich. *Die Antipoden: Die Neue Welt in den USA und das Österreich vor 1918*. Vienna: Amalthea, 1984.

Dubois, Laurent. *Avengers of the New World: The Story of the Haitian Revolution*. Cambridge, MA: Harvard University Press, 2004.

Duhr, Bernhard. *Deutsche Auslandssehnsucht im achtzehnten Jahrhundert: Aus der überseeischen Missionsarbeit deutscher Jesuiten*. Stuttgart: Ausland und Heimat Verlags-Aktiengesellschaft, 1928.

Dull, Jonathan R. *A Diplomatic History of the American Revolution*. New Haven, CT: Yale University Press, 1987.

Dull, Jonathan R. *Franklin the Diplomat: The French Mission*. Philadelphia, PA: American Philosophical Society, 1982.

Dull, Jonathan R. *The French Navy and American Independence: A Study of Arms and Diplomacy 1774-1787*. Princeton. NJ: Princeton University Press, 1975.

Dull, Jonathan R. *The Miracle of American Independence: Twenty Ways Things Could Have Turned Out Differently*. Lincoln, NE: University of Nebraska Press, 2015.

Dürr, Renate. "Der 'Neue Welt-Bott' als Markt der Informationen? Wissenstransfer als Moment jesuitischer Identitätsbildung." *Zeitschrift für historische Forschung* 34 (2007): 441–446.

Dürr, Renate. "The World in the German Hinterlands: Early Modern German History Entangled." *The Sixteenth Century Journal* 50, no. 1 (2019): 148–153.

DuVal, Kathleen. *Independence Lost: Lives on the Edge of the American Revolution.* New York, NY: Random House, 2015.

Dvoichenko-Markov, Demetrius. "A Rumanian Priest in Colonial America." *The American Slavic and East European Review* 14, no. 3 (1955): 383–389.

Echeverria, Durand. *Mirage in the West: A History of the French Image of American Society to 1815.* Princeton, NJ: Princeton University Press, 1957.

Edroiu, Nicolae. *Horea's Uprising: The 1784 Roumanian Peasants' Revolt of Transylvania.* Bucharest: Editura Ştiinţifică şi Enciclopedică, 1978.

Elliot, John H., Olwen Hufton, and Hamish M. Scott. *The Emergence of the Eastern Powers 1756-1775.* Cambridge: Cambridge University Press, 2001.

Elliot, John H. "Afterword: Atlantic History: A Circumnavigation." In *The British Atlantic World 1500-1800*, edited by David Armitage and Michael J. Braddick, 233–249. Basingstoke: Palgrave Macmillan, 2002.

Elliott, John H. "A Europe of Composite Monarchies." *Past & Present* 137, no. 1 (1992): 48–71.

Elovson, Herald. *Amerika i svensk litteratur 1750-1820.* Lund: Disputats, 1930.

Engel, Katherine Carté. *Religion and Profit: Moravians in Early America.* Philadelphia, PA: University of Pennsylvania Press, 2009.

Evans, Chris, and Göran Rydén, *Baltic Iron in the Atlantic World in the Eighteenth Century.* Leiden and Boston: Brill, 2007.

Everaert, John. "Le Pavillon Impérial aux Indes Occidentales: contrebande de guerre, et trafic neutre depuis le ports flamands 1778-1785." *Collectanea Maritima* 4 (1989): 43–67.

Everaert, John. "Willem Bolts, India Regained and Lost: Indiamen, Imperial Factories and Country Trade 1775-1785." In *Mariners, Merchants, and Oceans: Studies in Maritime History*, edited by K. S. Matthew, 363–369. New Delhi: Manohar, 1995.

Faber, Eva. *Litorale Austriaco: Das österreichische und kroatische Küstenland 1700-1780.* Graz: Steiermärkisches Landesarchiv, 1995.

Farasyn, Daniël. *De 18de eeuwse bloeiperiode van Oostende.* Ostend: Oostende Stadsarchief, 1998.

Fattinger, Elisabeth. "Conflicting Identities in an Age of Transition: The Autobiographical Writings of Karl Count Zinzendorf." In *Focus Austria: Vom Vielvölkerstaat zum EU-Staat. Festschrift für Alfred Ableitinger zum 65. Geburtstag*, edited by Siegfried Beer, Edith Marko-Stöckl, Marlies Raffler, and Felix Schneider, 112–129. Graz: Institut für Geschichte, 2003.

Faÿ, Bernard. *L'esprit révolutionnaire en France et aux États-Unis à la fin du XVIIIe siècle.* Paris: Champion, 1925.

Federmayer, Éva. "American Studies in Hungary." *European Journal of American Studies* 1, no. 1 (2006): 1-8.

Feest, Christian. "The People of Calicut: Objects, Texts, and Images in the Age of Proto-Ethnography." *Boletim do Museu Paraense Emilio Goeldi: Ciencias Humanas* 9, no. 2 (2014): 287–303.

Feest, Christian. "Vienna's Mexican Treasures: Aztec, Mixtec, and Tarascan Works from 16th-Century Austrian Collections." *Archiv für Völkerkunde* 44 (1990): 1–64.

Feest, Christian. "Von Kalikut nach Amerika: Albrecht Dürer und die "wunderliche künstliche ding" aus dem "neuen gulden land."" In *Dürer: Kunst, Künstler, Kontext*, edited by Jochen Sander, 367–375. Munich: Prestel, 2013.

Ferreiro, Larrie D. *American Independence and the Men of France and Spain Who Saved It*. New York, NY: Knopf, 2016.

Fertig, Georg. *Lokales Leben, atlantische Welt: Die Entscheidung zur Auswanderung vom Rhein nach Nordamerika im 18. Jahrhundert*. Osnabrück: Universitätsverlag Rasch, 2000.

Fertig, Georg. "Transatlantic Migration from the German-Speaking Parts of Central Europe, 1600-1800: Proportions, Structures, and Explanations." In *Europeans on the Move: Studies on European Migration 1500-1800*, edited by Nicholas Canny, 192–235. Oxford: Clarendon Press, 1994.

Fichtner, Paula S. "Viennese Perspectives on the American War of Independence." In *East Central European Perceptions of Early America*, edited by Béla K. Király and George Barany, 19–32. Lisse: De Ridder, 1977.

Fisher, H. E. S. *The Portugal Trade: A Study of Anglo-Portuguese Commerce 1700-1770*. Reprint. Adingdon: Routledge, 2006.

Fraknói, Vilmos. *Martinovics élete*. Budapest: Athenaeum, 1921.

Frank, Alison. "Continental and Maritime Empires in an Age of Global Commerce." *East European Politics and Societies* 25, no. 4 (2011): 779–784.

Frank, Alison. "The Children of the Desert and the Laws of the Sea: Austria, Great Britain, the Ottoman Empire, and the Mediterranean Slave Trade in the Nineteenth Century." *The American Historical Review* 117, no. 2 (2012): 410–444.

Frank, Tibor, and Zoltán Kövecses, "American Studies in Hungary." *EAAS Newsletter*, no. 32 (1994): s.n.

Freifeld, Alice. *Nationalism and the Crowd in Liberal Hungary 1848-1914*. London and Baltimore, MD: Johns Hopkins University Press, 2000.

Fröschl, Thomas. "Rezeption und Einfluss der American Constitution in den deutschen Verfassungsdebatten, 1789 bis 1949." *Journal of Modern European History* 6, no. 1 (2008): 38–57.

Fulton, Henry L. *Dr John Moore: A Life in Medicine, Travel, and Revolution*. Wilmington, DE: University of Delaware Press, 2015.

Furstenberg, François. *When the United States Spoke French*. New York, NY: Penguin Press, 2014.

Gabrieli, Vittorio. "The Impact of American Political Ideas in 18th-Century Italy." In *Contagious Conflict: The Impact of American Dissent on European Life*, edited by Arie N. J. den Hollander, 172–202. Leiden: Brill, 1973.

Gagliano, Joseph A., and Charles E. Ronan, eds., *Jesuit Encounters in the New World: Jesuit Chroniclers, Geographers, Educators and Missionaries in the Americas, 1549–1767*. Rome: Institutum Historicum Societatis Iesu, 1997.

Gaier, Claude. *Four Centuries of Liège Gunmaking*. Translating by F. J. Norris. London and Liège: Eugène Wahle and Sotheby Parke Bernet, 1976.

Gál, István. "Széchenyi and the U.S.A." *Angol Filológiai Tanulmányok/Hungarian Studies in English* 5 (1971): 95–119.

Gallinger, Herbert P. *Die Haltung der deutschen Publizistik zu dem amerikanischen Unabhängigkeitskriege 1775-1783*. Leipzig: Schmidt, 1900.

Games, Alison. "Atlantic History: Definitions, Challenges, and Opportunities." *The American Historical Review* 111, no. 3 (2006): 741–757.

Games, Alison, et al, "Forum: Beyond the Atlantic," *The William and Mary Quarterly* 63, no. 4 (2006): 675–742.

Gaspar, David B., and David P. Geggus. *A Turbulent Time: The French Revolution and the Greater Caribbean 1787-1804*. Bloomington, IN: Indiana University Press, 1997.

Gasser, Paul. "Österreichs Levantenhandel über Triest, 1740-1790." *Mitteilungen des Österreichischen Staatsarchivs* 7 (1954): 120–130.

Gassert, Philipp. "The Spectre of Americanization: Western Europe in the American Century." In *The Oxford Handbook of Postwar European History*, edited by Dan Stone, 182–201. Oxford: Oxford University Press, 2012.

Gates-Coon, Rebecca. "Anglophone Households and British Travellers in Late Eighteenth-Century Vienna: 'A Very Numerous and Pleasant English Colony.'" *Britain and the World* 12, no. 2 (2019): 130–150.

Gates-Coon, Rebecca. *The Charmed Circle: Joseph II and the "Five Princesses" 1765-1790*. West Lafayette, IN: Purdue University Press, 2015.

Gelder, Klaas van. "L'empereur Charles VI et « l'héritage Anjouin » dans les Pays-Bas Méridionaux, 1716-1725." *Revue d'histoire moderne et contemporaine* 58, no. 1 (2011): 53–79.

Gerbi, Antonello. *The Dispute of the New World: The History of a Polemic, 1750-1900*. Translated by Jeremy Moyle. Pittsburgh, PA: University of Pittsburgh Press, 2010.

Gilje, Paul A. "Commerce and Conquest in Early American Foreign Relations, 1750–1850." *Journal of the Early Republic* 37, no. 4 (2017): 735–770.

Gilje, Paul A. *The Making of the American Republic, 1763-1815*. New York, NY: Pearson, 2005.

Gillespie, Michele and Robert Beachy, eds., *Pious Pursuits: German Moravians in the Atlantic World*. New York, NY: Berghahn, 2007.

Glant, Tibor. "A Hungarian Aristocrat in Civil War America: Count Béla Széchenyi's 1862 study trip to the United States of America." *Studies in Travel Writing* 16, no. 3 (2012): 287–301.

Golder, Frank, A. "Catherine II and the American Revolution." *The American Historical Review* 21, no. 1 (1915): 92–96.

Goldstein, Kalman. "Silas Deane: Preparation for Rascality." *The Historian* 43, no. 1 (1980): 75–97.

Gordon-Reed, Annette and Peter S. Onuf. *Most Blessed of the Patriarchs: Thomas Jefferson and the Empire of the Imagination*. New York, NY: Liveright, 2016.

Gough, Barry M., and Robert J. King, "William Bolts: An Eighteenth-Century Merchant Adventurer." *The Journal of the British Records Association* 31, no. 112 (2005): 8–28.

Gould, Eliga H. *Among the Powers of the Earth: The American Revolution and the Making of a New World Empire*. Cambridge, MA: Harvard University Press, 2012.

Gould, Eliga H. "Entangled Histories, Entangled Worlds: The English-Speaking Atlantic as a Spanish Periphery." *The American Historical Review* 112, no. 3 (2007): 764–786.

Gorman, Thomas K. *America and Belgium: A Study of the Influence of the United States upon the Belgian Revolution of 1789-1790*. London: T.F. Unwin, 1925.

Grabbe, Hans-Jürgen. *Vor der großen Flut: Die europäische Migration in die Vereinigten Staaten von Amerika 1783 bis 1820*. Stuttgart: Franz Steiner Verlag, 2001.

Griffin, Patrick. *American Leviathan: Empire, Nation, and Revolutionary Frontier*. New York, NY: Hill & Wang, 2007.

Griffiths, David M. "Nikita Panin, Russian Diplomacy, and the American Revolution." *Slavic Review* 28, no. 1 (1969): 1–24.

Grüll, Georg. "Aus dem Tagebuch eines ewigen Soldaten." *Mitteilungen des oberösterreichischen Landesarchiv* 9 (1968): 291–297.

Gschwend, Annemarie Jordan. "The Emperor's Exotic and New World Animals: Hans Khevenhüller and Habsburg Menageries in Vienna and Prague." In *Naturalists in the Field: Collecting, Recording and Preserving the Natural World from the Fifteenth to the Twenty-First Century*, edited by Arthur MacGregor, 76–103. Leiden: Brill, 2018.

Guasti, Niccolò. "The Exile of the Spanish Jesuits in Italy, 1767-1815." In *The Jesuit Suppression in Global Context: Causes, Events, and Consequences*, edited by Jeffrey D. Burson and Jonathan Wright, 248–261. Cambridge: Cambridge University Press, 2015.

Guillaume, Gustav H. L. *Histoire du Régiment de Clerfayt*. Ghent: Busscher et Fils, 1865.

Gürtler, Gernot O. "Impressionen einer Reise: Das England-Itineraire des Grafen Karl von Zinzendorf 1768." *Mitteilungen des Instituts für Österreichische Geschichtsforschung*, 93, nos. 3–4 (1985): 333–370.

Gusejnova, Dina. *European Elites and Ideas of Empire 1917-1957*. Cambridge: Cambridge University Press, 2016.

Halácsy, Katalin. "The Image of Benjamin Franklin in Hungary." *Angol Filológiai Tanulmányok/Hungarian Studies in English* 10 (1976): 9–25.

Hallward, Norman L. *William Bolts, a Dutch Adventurer under John Company*. Cambridge: Cambridge University Press, 1920.

Hanß, Stefan. "Making Featherwork in Early Modern Europe." In *Materialized Identities in Early Modern Europe, 1450-1750: Objects, Affects, Effects*, edited by Susanna

Burghartz, Lucas Burkart, Christine Göttler, and Ulinka Rublack, 137-186. Amsterdam: Amsterdam University Press, 2021.

Harrison, Joseph H. ""Sic et Non": Thomas Jefferson and Internal Improvement." *Journal of the Early Republic* 7, no. 4 (1987): 335–349.

Hase, Alexander von. "Eine amerikanische Kritik am spätfriderizianischen System: zum Tagebuch von Col. William Stephens Smith, Adjutant von George Washington (1785)." *Archiv für Kulturgeschichte* 56, no. 2 (1974): 372–393.

Hasquin, Hervé. *Joseph II: Catholique anticlérical et réformateur impatient, 1741-1790*. Brussels: Edition Racine, 2007.

Hasquin, Hervé. *Population, commerce et religion au siècle des lumières*. Brussels: Éditions de Université de Brussel, 2008.

Hatschek, Christoph. "Sehnsucht nach fernen Ländern: Die Entdeckungsreisen der k. (u.) k. Kriegsmarine." In *Die Entdeckung der Welt, Die Welt der Entdeckungen: Österreichische Forscher, Sammler, Abenteurer*, edited by Wilfried Seipel, 85–99. Vienna and Milan: Kunsthistorisches Museum/Skira editore, 2001/2002.

Hauptmann, Laurence M., and L. Gordon McLester III, eds., *The Onedia Indian Journey: From New York to Wisconsin, 1784-1860*. Madison, WI: University of Wisconsin Press, 1999.

Haworth, Paul L. "Frederick the Great and the American Revolution." *The American Historical Review* 9, no. 3 (1904): 460–478.

Heger, Franz. "Altmexikanische Reliquien aus dem Schlosse Ambras in Tirol." *Annalen des k.k. Naturhistorischen Hofmuseums* 7 (1892): 379–400.

Hennesey, James. *American Catholics: A History of the Roman Catholic Community in the United States*. Oxford: Oxford University Press, 1981.

Hennings, Jan. *Russia and Courtly Europe: Ritual and the Culture of Diplomacy, 1648-1725*. Cambridge: Cambridge University Press, 2016.

Henrikson, Alan K. "The Geographical 'Mental Maps' of American Foreign Policy Makers." *International Political Science Review/Revue internationale de science politique* 1, no. 4 (1980): 495–530.

Hertz, Gerald B. "England and the Ostend Company," *The English Historical Review* 22, no. 86 (1907): 255–279.

Hildebrand, Ingegerd. *Den Svenska Kolonin St Barthélemy och Västindiska Kompaniet fram till 1796*. Lund: Lindstedts Universitetsbokhandel, 1951.

Hildebrand, K. G. "Foreign Markets for Swedish Iron in the Eighteenth Century." *Scandinavian Economic History Review* 6, no. 1 (1958): 3–52.

Hill, Peter P. *French Perceptions of the Early American Republic, 1783-1793*. Philadelphia, PA: American Philosophical Society, 1998.

Hitchins, Keith. *A Concise History of Romania*. Cambridge: Cambridge University Press, 2014.

Hochedlinger, Michael. *Austria's Wars of Emergence: War, State and Society in the Habsburg Monarchy 1683-1797*. London: Pearson Education/Longman, 2003.

Hochedlinger, Michael. "'Dass Aufklärung das sicherste Mittel ist, die Ruhe und An-hänglichkeit der Unterthanen zu befestigen.' Staatskanzler Kaunitz und die 'fran-ziszeische Reaktion' 1792–1794." In *Aufklärung – Vormärz – Revolution. Jahrbuch der Internationalen Forschungsstelle Demokratische Bewegungen in Mitteleuropa von 1770–1850 an der Universität Innsbruck*, vol. 16–17, edited by Helmut Reinalter, 62–79. Frankfurt am Main: Peter Lang, 1996/1997.

Holland, Ben. "The Moral Person of the State: Emer de Vattel and the Foun-dations of International Legal Order." *History of European Ideas* 37, no. 4 (2011): 438–445.

Holldack, Heinz. "Die Neutralitätspolitik Leopolds von Toskana." *Historische Viertel-jahrschrift* 30 (1936): 733–739.

Horsman, Reginald. *The Diplomacy of the New Republic, 1776-1815*. Wheeling, IL: Har-lan Davidson, 1985.

Hörwarthner, Maria. "Joseph Haydn's Library: An Attempt at a Literary-Historical Reconstruction." In *Haydn and His World*, edited by Elaine Sisman, translated by Katherine Talbot, 395–462. Princeton, NJ: Princeton University Press, 1997.

Houtte, Herbert van. "American Commercial Conditions and Negotiations with Austria, 1783-1786." *The American Historical Review* 16, no. 3 (1911): 567–578.

Houtte, Herbert van. "Contribution à l'histoire commerciale des états de l'empereur Joseph II." *Vierteljahrschrift für Sozial- und Wirtschaftsgeschichte* 8, nos. 2–3 (1910): 350–393.

Houtte, Herbert van. *Histoire économique de la Belgique à la fin de l'Ancien Régime*. Ghent: Van Rysselberghe & Rombaut, 1920.

Huber-Frischeis, Thomas, Nina Knieling, and Rainer Valenta. *Die Privatbibliothek Kaiser Franz' I. von Österreich 1784-1835*. Vienna: Böhlau, 2015.

Hulliung, Mark. *Citizens and Citoyens: Republicans and Liberals in America and France*. Cambridge, MA: Harvard University Press, 2002.

Hunter, Mary. "Bourgeois Values and Opera Buffa in 1780s Vienna." In *Opera Buffa in Mozart's Vienna*, edited by Mary Hunter and James Webster, 165–196. Cambridge: Cambridge University Press, 1997.

Hutson, James H. *John Adams and the Diplomacy of the American Revolution*. Lexing-ton, KY: University of Kentucky Press, 1980.

Hüttel-Herbert, Eva, and Hubert Reiterrer, "Strattmann, Paul (1755-1821), Biblio-thekar und Geistlicher." In *Österreichisches Biographisches Lexicon*, vol. 13, edited by members of the Österreichische Akademie der Wissenschaften, 370. Vienna: Aus-trian Academy of Sciences, 2010.

Hyden-Hanscho, Veronika. "Beaver Hats, Drugs and Sugar Consumption in Vi-enna around 1700: France as an Intermediary for Atlantic Products." In *Cultural Exchange and Consumption Patterns in the Age of Enlightenment: Europe and the Atlantic World*, edited by Veronika Hyden-Hanscho, Renate Pieper and Werner Stangl, 153–167. Bochum: Winkler Verlag, 2013.

Incontrera, Oscar de. *Trieste e l'America, 1782-1830*. Trieste: Zibaldone, 1960.

Ingrao, Charles W. *The Habsburg Monarchy, 1618–1815.* 3rd edition. Cambridge: Cambridge University Press, 2019.

Israel, Jonathan. *The Expanding Blaze: How the American Revolution Ignited the World 1775-1848.* Princeton, NJ: Princeton University Press, 2017.

Ivanič, Suzanna. *Cosmos and Materiality in Early Modern Prague.* Oxford: Oxford University Press, 2021.

Jařab, Josef. "American Studies in the Czech Republic and Slovakia." *European Journal of American studies* 1, no. 1 (2006): 1-6.

Jenings-Lee, Edmund. *The Lees of Virginia, 1642-1892.* Reprint. Baltimore, MD: Genealogical Publishing Co., 1974.

Jenkins, Howard M. *The Family of William Penn, Founder of Pennsylvania: Ancestry and Descendants.* Philadelphia, PA and London: Headley Brothers, 1899.

Johnson, Amandus. *Swedish Contributions to American Freedom, 1776-1783.* vols. 1–2. Philadelphia, PA: Swedish Colonial Foundation, 1953–1957.

Johnson, Amandus. "Swedish Officers in the American Revolution." *American Swedish Historical Foundation Yearbook* (1957): 33–39.

Johnson, Carina L. *Cultural Hierarchy in Sixteenth-Century Europe: The Ottomans and Mexicans.* Cambridge: Cambridge University Press, 2011.

Johnson, Herbert Alan. "*Magyar* mania in New York City: Louis Kossuth and American Politics." *The New York Historical Quarterly* (July 1964): 237–249.

Judge, Jane C. *The United States of Belgium: The Story of the First Belgian Revolution.* Leuven: Leuven University Press, 2018.

Judson, Pieter. *The Habsburg Monarchy: A New History.* New York, NY: Belknap Press, 2016.

Kaltenstadler, Wilhelm. "Der österreichische Seehandel über Triest im 18. Jahrhundert." *Vierteljahrschrift für Sozial-und Wirtschaftsgeschichte* 55, no. 4 (1968): 482–497.

Kaplan, Lawrence S. *Entangling Alliances with None: American Foreign Policy in the Age of Jefferson.* Kent, OH: Kent State University Press, 1987.

Kapp, Friedrich. *Friedrich der Grosse und die Vereinigten Staaten von Amerika.* Leipzig: Quandt und Händel, 1871.

Kaps, Klemens. "A Gateway to the Spanish Atlantic? The Habsburg Port City of Trieste as Intermediary in Commodity Flows between the Habsburg Monarchy in the Eighteenth Century." In *Globalized Peripheries: Central Europe and the Atlantic World, 1680-1860,* edited by Jutta Wimmler and Klaus Weber, 132–177. Woodbridge: Boydell Press, 2020.

Kaps, Klemens. "Entre el Servicio y los Negocios Transnacionales: El Caso de Paolo Greppi, Cónsul Imperial en Cádiz, 1774-1791." In *Los Cónsules de extranjeros,* edited by Marcella Aglietti, Manuel Herrero Sánchez, and Francesco Zamora Rodriguez, 225–235. Madrid: Doce Calles, 2013.

Kaps, Klemens. "Handelsverflechtungen zwischen der Habsburgermonarchie und dem Spanischen Atlantik im 18. Jahrhundert. Warenflüsse, Handelspolitik und merkantile Netzwerke." *Österreich in Geschichte und Literatur* 63, no. 4 (2019): 445–464.

Kaps, Klemens. "Small But Powerful: Networking Strategies and the Trade Business of Habsburg-Italian Merchants in Cadiz in the Second Half of the Eighteenth Century." *European Review of History* 23, no. 3 (2016): 427–455.

Karniel, Joseph. *Die Toleranzpolitik Kaiser Josephs II.* Gerlingen: Bleicher Verlag, 1986.

Katona, Anna. "American Influences on Hungarian Political Thinking from the American Revolution to the Centennial." *Canadian-American Review of Hungarian Studies* 5, no. 1 (1978): 13–28.

Katona, Anna. "The Hungarian Image of Benjamin Franklin." *Canadian-American Review of Hungarian Studies* 4, no. 1 (1977): 43–60.

Kellenbenz, Hermann. "Der deutsche Außenhandel gegen Ende des 18. Jahrhunderts." In *Die wirtschaftliche Situation in Deutschland und Österreich um die Wende vom 18. zum 19. Jahrhundert: Bericht über die erste Arbeitstagung der Gesellschaft für Sozial-und Wirtschaftsgeschichte in Mainz 4, 6. Marz 1963*, edited by Friedrich Lütge, 4–60. Stuttgart: Fischer, 1964.

Kimball, Marie Goebel. *Jefferson: The Scene in Europe.* New York, NY: Coward-McCann, 1950.

King, Robert J. "Heinrich Zimmermann and the Proposed Voyage of the Imperial and Royal Ship Cobenzell to the North West Coast in 1782-1783." *The Northern Mariner/Le marin du nord* 21, no. 3, (2011): 235–262.

King, Robert J. "William Bolts and the Austrian Origins of the Laperouse Expedition." *Terrae Incognitae* 40, no. 1 (2008): 1–28.

Kite, Elizabeth S. "Revolutionary Correspondence of Charles Carroll of Carrollton with William Carmichael." *Records of the American Catholic Historical Society of Philadelphia* 42, no. 1 (1931): 1–11.

Kleinschmidt, Harald. *Ruling the Waves: Emperor Maximilian I, the Search for Islands and the Transformation of the European World Picture ca. 1500.* Utrecht: Hes & De Graaf, 2008.

Klemun, Marianne. "Austrian Botanical Journeys (1783-1792). Network-Patterns in Expedition: Global Intentions Interwoven with Local Dimensions." In *International Networks, Exchange and Circulation of Knowledge in Life Sciences, 18th to 20th Centuries*, edited by Brigitte Hoppe, Sona Strbánová, and Nicolas Robin, 233–245. Paris: Archives Internationales d'Histoire des Sciences, 2006.

Klemun, Marianne. "Österreichische wissenschaftliche Sammelreisen nach den Amerikas, 1783-1789. Intentionen, Implikationen und Instruktionen." In *Wiener Zeitschrift zur Geschichte der Neuzeit*, vol. 5, no. 1: Österreich und die Amerikas, edited by Thomas Fröschl and Ursula Prutsch, 21–35. Innsbruck: Studienverlag, 2005.

Klemun, Marianne. "Space, State, Territory, Region, and Habitat: Alpine Gardens in the Habsburg Countries." *Studies in the History of Gardens & Designed Landscapes: An International Quarterly* 28, no. 3–4 (2008): 414–423.

Klíma, Arnošt. "Glassmaking Industry and Trade in Bohemia in the XVIIth and XVIIIth Centuries." *The Journal of European Economic History* 13, no. 3 (1984): 499–520.

Klingenstein, Grete. *Der Aufstieg des Hauses Kaunitz: Studien zur Herkunft und Bildung des Staatskanzlers Wenzel Anton.* Göttingen: Vandenhoeck & Ruprecht, 1975.

Klingenstein, Grete. "Lessons for Republicans: An American Critique of Enlightened Absolutism in Central Europe, 1785." In *The Mirror of History: Essays in Honour of Fritz Fellner,* edited by Solomon Wank, Heidrun Maschl, Brigitte Mazohl-Wallnig, Reinhold Wagnleitner and Fritz Fellner, 181–212. Oxford: Oxford University Press, 1988.

Klingenstein, Grete. *Staatsverwaltung und kirchliche Autorität im 18. Jahrhundert. Das Problem der Zensur in der theresianischen Reform.* Vienna: Verlag für Geschichte und Politik, 1970.

Kneschke, Ernst Heinrich. *Neues allgemeines deutsches Adels-Lexicon.* vol. 7. Leipzig: Voigt, 1867.

Knott, Sarah. "Narrating the Age of Revolution." *The William & Mary Quarterly* 73, no. 1 (2016): 3–36.

Kókay, György. "Patrióta vagy emberbarát? Hajnóczy József és Conrad Dominik Barstch, a Wiener Zeitung szerkesztője." In *Könyv, sajtó és irodalom a felvilágosodás korában,* edited by György Kókay, 82–98. Budapest: Akadémiai Kiadó, 1983.

Komlos, John. *Louis Kossuth in America 1851-1852.* Buffalo, NY: East European Institute, 1973.

Köpf, Paul. "Daß alle Menschen gleich erschaffen sind: Die Amerikanische Revolution im Spiegel zeitgenössischer Wiener Zeitungen." *Jahrbuch der Österreichischen Gesellschaft zur Erforschung des achtzehnten Jahrhunderts,* 24 (2010): 183–196.

Körner, Alfred. "Franz Hebenstreit (1747–1795): Biographie und Versuch einer Deutung." *Jahrbuch des Vereines für Geschichte der Stadt Wien* 30–31 (1974/75): 39–62.

Körner, Axel. *America in Italy: The United States in the Political Thought and Imagination of the Risorgimento, 1763-1865.* Princeton, NJ: Princeton University Press, 2017.

Korty, Margaret Barton. "Franklin's World of Books." *The Journal of Library History* 2, no. 4 (1967): 271–328.

Kossok, Manfred. "Die Bedeutung des spanisch–amerikanischen Kolonialmarktes für den preußischen Leinwandhandel am Ausgang des 18. und zu Beginn des 19. Jahrhunderts." In *Hansische Studien: Heinrich Sproemberg zum 70. Geburtstag,* edited by Gerhard Heitz and Manfred Unger, 210–218. Berlin: Akademie-Verlag, 1961.

Kristóf, Ildikó Sz. "Local Access to Global Knowledge: Historia Naturalis and Anthropology at the Jesuit University of Nagyszombat (Trnava) as Transmitted in Its Almanacs, 1676-1709." In *A Divided Hungary in Europe: Exchanges, Networks and Representations 1541-1699,* edited by Gábor Almási, Szymon Brzeziński, and Ildikó Horn, vol. 1 201–228. Newcastle: Cambridge Scholars Publishing, 2014.

Kristóf, Ildikó Sz. "Missionaries, Monsters, and the Demon Show: Diabolized Representations of American Indians in Jesuit Libraries of 17th-and 18th-Century Upper Hungary." In *Exploring the Cultural History of Continental European Freak Shows and 'Enfreakment'*, edited by Anna Kérchy and Andrea Zittlau, 38–73. Newcastle: Cambridge Scholars Publishing, 2012.

Kristóf, Ildikó Sz. "The Uses of Demonology: European Missionaries and Native Americans in the American Southwest." In *Centers and Peripheries in European Renaissance Culture: Essays by East-Central European Mellon Fellows*, edited by György Endre Szőnyi and Csaba Maczelka, 161–182. Szeged: JATE Press, 2012.

Křížová, Markéta. "Meeting the Other in the New World: Jesuit Missionaries from the Bohemian Province in America." *Historie – Otázky – Problémy* 8, no. 2 (2016): 35–46.

Kroupa, Jiří. "Fürst Wenzel Anton Kaunitz-Rietberg: Ein Kunstmäzen und Curieux der Aufklärung." In *Staatskanzler Wenzel Anton von Kaunitz-Rietberg 1711-1794: Neue Perspektiven zu Politik und Kultur der europäischen Aufklärung*, edited by Grete Klingenstein and Franz A. J. Szabo, 360–382. Graz: Andreas Schnider Verlagsatelier, 1996.

Kukla, Jon. *Mr. Jefferson's Women*. New York, NY: Knopf, 2007.

Kulcsár, Krisztina. "The Travels of Joseph II in Hungary, Transylvania, Slavonia, and the Banat of Temesvar 1768-1773." In *Intellectual and Political Elites of the Enlightenment*, edited by Tatiana V. Artemyeva and Mikhail I. Mikeshin, 34–57. Helsinki: Helsinki Collegium for Advanced Studies, 2014.

Kulsrud, Carl K. *Maritime Neutrality to 1780: A History of the Main Principles Governing Neutrality and Belligerency to 1780*. Boston, MA: Little, Brown & Co., 1936.

Kunec, Patrik. "The Hungarian Participants in the War of American Independence." *Cordul Cosminului*, 16, no. 1 (2010): 41–57.

Laferl, Christopher F. *Die Kultur der Spanier in Österreich unter Ferdinand I. 1522-1564*. Vienna: Böhlau, 1997.

Lamikiz, Xabier. *Trade and Trust in the Eighteenth-Century Atlantic World*. Woodbridge: Boydell Press, 2010.

Landers, Jane G. *Atlantic Creoles in the Age of Revolutions*. Cambridge, MA: Harvard University Press, 2010.

Langley, Lester D. *The Long American Revolution and Its Legacy*. Atlanta, GA: University of Georgia Press, 2019.

Lanmon, Dwight P. "The Baltimore Glass Trade 1780-1820." *Winterthur Portfolio* 5 (1969): 15–48.

Laubenberger, Franz and Steven Rowan, "The Naming of America." *The Sixteenth Century Journal* 13, no. 4 (1982): 91–113.

Leary, Lewis. "Phaeton in Philadelphia: Jean Pierre Blanchard and the First Balloon Ascension in America." *Pennsylvania Magazine of History and Biography* 67, no. 1 (1943): 49–60.

Lenderova, Milena. "Correspondance de Mme Geoffrin et de Wenzel Anton Kaunitz." *Dix-Huitième Siècle* 30 (1998): 309–316.

Lévai, Csaba. "In between and within Great Powers: The Comparison of Hungary and the British Colonies in North America in the 18th Century." In *Small Nations on the Borderlands of Great Powers*, edited by Attila Bárány and Satu Matikainen, 129–141. Debrecen: Kapitális Kft., 2013.

Lévai, Csaba. "The Relevance of the American Revolution in Hungarian History from an East-Central-European Perspective." In *Europe's American Revolution*, edited by Simon P. Newman, 94–122. Basingstoke: Palgrave Macmillan, 2006.

Lévai, Csaba. "Thomas Jefferson and his Efforts to Establish Political and Commercial Relations between the Habsburg Empire and the Early Republic." In *Europeans Engaging the Atlantic: Knowledge and Trade, 1500-1800*, edited by Susanne Lachenicht, 111–126. Frankfurt am Main: Campus Verlag, 2014.

Lévai, Csaba. "Van esély a nyitásra a császár részéről: Egy Habsburg-amerikai kereskedelmi egyezmény lehetősége az 1780-as években amerikai szemmel." *AETAS: Történettudományi Folyóirat* 27, no. 3 (2012): 20–48.

Lévai, Csaba. "Within Two Imperial Systems: Hungary and the British Colonies in North America Compared in the Writings of Gergely Berzeviczy (1763-1822)." In *Europe and its Empires*, edited by Mary N. Harris and Csaba Lévai, 31–45. Pisa: Pisa University Press, 2008.

Libiszowska, Zofia. "Polish Opinion of the American Revolution." *Polish American Studies* 34, no. 1 (1977): 5–15.

Lindner, Andreas. "Sozial-, Gesellschafts- und Herrschaftskritische Reflexionen im Musikschaffen der oberösterreichischen Stifte." *Studien zur Musikwissenschaft* 55 (2009): 195–268.

Lindner, Dolf. *Ignaz von Born: Meister der Wahren Eintracht*. Vienna: Österreichischer Bundesverlag, 1986.

Lingelbach, William E. "Saxon-American Relations, 1778–1828." *The American Historical Review* 27, no. 3 (1912): 525–30.

Liss, Peggy K. *Atlantic Empires: The Network of Trade and Revolution, 1713–1826*. Baltimore, MD: Johns Hopkins University Press, 1983.

Loft, Léonore. *Passion, Politics, and Philosophie: Rediscovering J.-P. Brissot*. Westport, CT: Praeger Publishers, 2002.

Loft, Léonore. "The Transylvanian Peasant Uprising of 1784: Brissot and the Right to Revolt – A Research Note." *French Historical Studies* 17, no. 1 (1991): 209–218.

Lüsebrink, Hans-Jürgen. "Between Ethnology and Romantic Discourse: Martin Dobrizhoffer's History of the Abipones in a (Post)modern Perspective." In *Jesuit Accounts of the Colonial Americas: Textualities, Intellectual Disputes, Intellectual Transfer*, edited by Marc André Bernier, Clorinda Donato, and Hans-Jürgen Lüsebrink, 127–143. Toronto: University of Toronto Press, 2014.

MacDonald, Deanna. "Collecting a New World: The Ethnographic Collections of Margaret of Austria." *The Sixteenth Century Journal* 33, no. 3 (2002): 649–663.

Mackenzie, Anton de Beelen. *History of the Gazzam Family—together with a sketch of the American branch of the family of De Beelen*. Reading, PA: Haage, 1894.

Madar, Heather. "Maximilian and the Exotic." In *Maximilian I. 1459-1519: Wahrnehmung - Übersetzung – Gender*, edited by Heinz Noflatscher, Michael A. Chisholm and Bertrand Schnerb. Innsbruck: Studienverlag, 2011: 233–250.

Madariaga, Isabel de. *Britain, Russia, and the Armed Neutrality of 1780: Sir James Harris's Mission to St. Petersburg during the American Revolution*. London and New Haven, CT: Hollis & Carter, 1962.

Madriñán, Santiago. *Nikolaus Joseph Jacquin's American Plants: Botanical Expedition to the Caribbean (1754–1759) and the Publication of the Selectarum Stirpium Americanarum Historia*. Leiden and Boston: Brill, 2013.

Maier, Pauline. *From Resistance to Revolution: Colonial Radicals and the Development of American Opposition to Britain, 1765-1776*. New York, NY: Knopf, 1972.

Mallon, Edward A. "Frederick Eugene, baron de Beelen-Bertholff." *Records of the American Catholic Historical Society of Philadelphia* 59, no. 2 (1948): 148–152.

Malmborg, Mikael af. *Neutrality and State-Building in Sweden*. Basingstoke: Palgrave Macmillan, 2001.

Mann, Conklin. "Thomas and Richard Brush of Huntington, Long Island." *New York Genealogical and Biographical Record* 67 (1936): 132.

Marcus, Jacob Rader, ed., *United States Jewry 1776-1985*. vol. 1. Detroit, MI: Wayne State University Press, 1989.

Marczali, Henry. *Hungary in the Eighteenth Century*. Cambridge: Cambridge University Press, 1910.

Márki, Sándor. *Amerika és a magyarság*. Budapest: n.p., 1893.

Markov, Walter. "L'expansion autrichienne outre-mer et les intérêts portugaises 1777-81." In *Congresso Internacional de Historia dos Descobrimentos*, Actas, vol. 5, part 2, 281–29. Lisbon: Comissão executiva das comemorações do V centenario da morte do Infante D. Henrique, 1961.

Marraro, Howard R. "Philip Mazzei and His Polish Friends." *Bulletin of the Polish Institute of Arts and Sciences in America* (April 1944): 757–822.

Marzagalli, Silvia, James R. Sofka, and John J. McCusker, eds. *Rough Waters: American Involvement with the Mediterranean in the Eighteenth and Nineteenth Centuries*. St. John's, Newfoundland: International Maritime Economic History Association, 2010.

Mask, Deirdre, and Paul MacMahon. "The Revolutionary War Prize Cases and the Origins of Diversity Jurisdiction.," *Buffalo Law Review* 63, no. 3 (2015): 477–547.

Maxwell, Alexander. "Tobacco as Cultural Signifier: A Cultural History of Masculinity and Nationality in Habsburg Hungary." e-*Journal of the American Hungarian Educators Association*, 5 (2012): 1–19.

Mayer, Franz Martin. "Zur Geschichte der österreichischen Handelspolitik unter Kaiser Karl VI." *Mitteilungen des Instituts für Österreichische Geschichtsforschung* 18 (1897): 129–145.

Mayer, Matthew Z. "The Price for Austria's Security: Part I. Joseph II, the Russian Alliance, and the Ottoman War, 1787–1789." *The International History Review* 26, no. 2 (2004): 257–299.

Mazzagetti, Dominick. *Charles Lee: Self before Country.* New Brunswick, NJ: Rutgers University Press, 2013.

McDonald, Travis C. "Constructing Optimism: Thomas Jefferson's Poplar Forest." *Perspectives in Vernacular Architecture* 8 (2000): 176–200.

McDonnell, Michael A. "Rethinking the Age of Revolution." *Atlantic Studies* 13, no. 3 (2016): 301–314.

McFarlane, Anthony. "The American Revolution and Spanish America, 1776-1814." In *Spain and the American Revolution: New Approaches and Perspectives,* edited by Gabriel Paquette and Gonzalo M. Quintero Saravia, 37–61. Milton: Routledge, 2020.

Meadow, Mark. "The Aztecs at Ambras: Social Networks and the Transfer of Cultural Knowledge of the New World." In *Kultureller Austausch: Bilanz und Perspektiven der Frühneuzeitforschung,* edited by Michael North, 349–368. Vienna: Böhlau, 2009.

Meeks, Joshua. *France, Britain, and the Struggle for the Revolutionary Western Mediterranean.* Basingstoke: Palgrave Macmillan, 2017.

Meissner, Jochen, Ulrich Mücke, and Klaus Weber. *Schwarzes Amerika: Eine Geschichte der Sklaverei.* Munich: C. H. Beck, 2008.

Meisterle, Stefan. "Country Trade unter kaiserliche Flagge: William Bolts und die zweite österreichische Ostindienkompanie." *Zeitschrift für Weltgeschichte* 9, no. 2 (2008): 63–87.

Melton, James van Horn. "From Courts to Consumers: Theater Publics in Eighteenth-Century Europe." In *European Theatre: Performance Practice, 1750-1900,* edited by James Davis, 438–460. Farnham: Ashgate, 2014.

Melton, James van Horn. *Religion, Community, and Slavery on the Southern Colonial Frontier.* Cambridge: Cambridge University Press, 2015.

Mentschl, J. "Steiner, Melchior (II.) von (1762–1837), Großhandler, Fabrikant und Bankier." In *Österreichisches Biographisches Lexikon.* vol 13, 176. Vienna: Verlag der Österreichischen Akademie der Wissenschaften, 2008.

Mérei, Gyula. "Marktverhältnisse im Außenhandel des Königreichs Ungarn 1790-1848." *Acta Historica Academiae Scientiarum Hungaricae* 27, no. 3–4 (1981): 359–424.

Merritt, Eli. "Sectional Conflict and Secret Compromise: The Mississippi River Question and the United States Constitution." *The American Journal of Legal History* 35, no. 2 (1991): 117–171.

Mettauer, Susanne. "American Studies in Austria." *European Journal of American Studies* 1, no. 1 (2006), 1–5.

Miller, Charles R. D. "Some Early Italian Histories of the United States." *Italica* 7, no. 4 (1930): 103–106.

Miller, Daniel A. *Sir Joseph Yorke and Anglo-Dutch Relations 1774-1780*. The Hague: Mouton, 1970.

Morgan, Lee. *Dr Johnson's "Dear Master" – The Life of Henry Thrale*. Lanham, MD: University Press of America, 1998.

Morris, Richard B. *The Peacemakers: The Great Powers and American Independence*. New York, NY: Harper & Row, 1965.

Morrison, Heather. "Open Competition in Botany and Diplomacy: The Habsburg Expedition of 1783." *Studies in Eighteenth-Century Culture* 46 (2017): 107–119.

Morrison, Heather. "'They Hear You Tell of Such Things as If They Were from America': Representations of the Newly Independent United States in an Austrian Botanist's Travelogue." *Austrian History Yearbook* 48 (2017): 74–90.

Müller, Leos. "Swedish-American Trade and the Swedish Consular Service, 1780-1840." *International Journal for Maritime History* 14, no. 1 (2002): 173–188.

Müller, Leos. "Sweden's Neutrality and the Eighteenth-Century Inter-State System." In *Sweden in the Eighteenth-Century World: Provincial Cosmopolitans,* edited by Göran Rydén, 203–224. Farnham: Ashgate, 2013.

Murad, Anatol. *Franz Joseph of Austria and His Empire*. New York, NY: Twayne, 1968.

Murphy, Orville T. *Charles Gravier, comte de Vergennes: French Diplomacy in the Age of Revolution: 1719-1787*. Albany, NY: State of New York University Press, 1982.

Mustafa, Sam A. *Merchants and Migrations: Germans and Americans in Connection 1776-1835*. New York, NY: Routledge, 2001.

Nakhimovsky, Isaac. "Vattel's Theory of the International Order: Commerce and the Balance of Power in the Law of Nations." *History of European Ideas* 33, no. 2 (2007): 157–173.

Narang, Indira. "The Ostend Company's Records and the 'Instructions' of Alexander Hume." *The Indian Economic and Social History Review* 4, no. 1 (1967): 17–37.

Navrátilová, Hana and Roman Míšek. "The Oriental Academy, Birth of a New Era of Austrian Diplomacy in the Orient." *Archiv orientální*. 71, no. 2 (2003): 199–204.

Negro, Piero del. *Il mito americano nella Venezia del settecento*. Padua: Liviana, 1986.

Newman, Simon P. *Europe's American Revolution*. Basingstoke: Palgrave Macmillan, 2006.

Noether, Emiliana P. "As Others Saw Us: Italian Views on the United States during the Nineteenth Century." *Transactions of Connecticut Academy of Arts and Sciences* 50 (1990): 129–134.

Nougaret, Christine. "Marie-Antoinette dans les fonds des Archives Nationales." *Annales historiques de la révolution française* 338 (October–December 2004): 129–136.

Obradović, Dositej. *The Life and Adventures of Dimitrije Obradović*. Los Angeles, CA: University of California Press 1953.

O'Brien, Charles H. "The Ideas of Religious Toleration at the time of Joseph II: A Study of the Enlightenment among Catholics in Austria." *American Philosophical Society* 59, no. 7 (1969): 5–80.

Oliván, Laura. "Judith Rebecca von Wrna and Maria Sophia von Dietrichstein: Two Imperial Ambassadresses from the Kingdom of Bohemia at the Court of Madrid, 1653–1674." *Theatrum Historiae* 19 (2016): 95–118.

Ondo-Grečenková, Martina. "Le réseau épistolaire scientifique européen de Joseph Nicolas von Windischgraetz." In *La plume et la toile: Pouvoirs et réseaux de correspondance dans l'europe des Lumières*, edited by Pierre-Yves Beaurepaire, 289–305. Arras: Artois Presses Université, 2002.

Onuf, Peter S. *The Mind of Thomas Jefferson*. Charlottesville, VA: University of Virginia Press, 2007.

Oppermann, Ira. "Conceptions of Space in the Missionary Periodical." In *Transcultural Imaginations of the Sacred*, edited by Klaus Krüger and Margit Kern, 111–121. Munich: Wilhelm Fink Verlag, 2019.

O'Reilly, William. "Agenten, Werbung und Reisemodalitäten. Die Auswanderung ins Temescher Banat im 18. Jahrhundert." In *Migration nach Ost- und Südosteuropa vom 18. bis zum Beginn des 19. Jhr*, edited by Matthias Beer and Dittmar Dahlmann, 109–120. Stuttgart: Jan Thorbecke Verlag, 1999.

O'Reilly, William. "Alluding to Alternatives: Sourcing and Securing Colonists in Eighteenth-Century Germany." In *Atlantic Understandings: Essays on European and American History in Honor of Hermann Wellenreuther*, edited by Claudia Schnurmann and Hartmut Lehmann, 159–184. Hamburg: LIT Verlag, 2006.

O'Reilly, William. "A Life in Exile: Charles Habsburg (1685-1740) between Spain and Austria." In *Monarchy and Exile: The Politics of the Absent Ruler from Marie de Medici to Wilhelm II 1631-1941*, edited by Philip Mansel and Torsten Riotte, 66–90. Basingstoke: Palgrave Macmillan, 2010.

O'Reilly, William. "Bridging the Atlantic: Opportunity, Information and Choice in Long-Range German Migration in the Eighteenth Century." In *Menschen zwischen zwei Welten: Auswanderung, Ansiedlung, Akkulturation*, edited by Walter G. Rödel and Helmut Schmahl, 25–44. Trier: Wissenschaftlicher Verlag, 2002.

O'Reilly, William. "Emigration from the Habsburg Monarchy and Salzburg to the New World, 1700-1848." In *The Atlantic World*, edited by D'Maris Coffman, Adrian Leonard, and William O'Reilly, 117–130. Abingdon: Routledge, 2015.

O'Reilly, William. "Global, Regional and Small Spaces in eighteenth-century Habsburg Europe." *Geschichte und Region/Storia e regione* 30, no. 1 (2021): 201–211.

O'Reilly, William. "Habsburg Eighteenth-Century Global Contexts." In *The Cambridge History of the Habsburg Monarchy*, edited by Howard Louthan and Graeme Murdock, s.n. Cambridge: Cambridge University Press, forthcoming.

O'Reilly, William. "Lost Chances of the House of Habsburg." *Austrian History Yearbook* 40 (2009): 53–70.

Osler, Edward. *The Life of Admiral Viscount Exmouth*. London: Routledge, 1854.

Otruba, Gustav. "Der Anteil österreichischer Jesuitenmissionäre am "heiligen Experiment" von Paraguay." *Mitteilungen des Instituts für Österreichische Geschichtsforschung* 63, no. 3–4 (1955): 430–445.

Otruba, Gustav. "Österreichische Jesuitenpatres des 17. und 18. Jahrhunderts in der Weltmission und als Erforscher der Erde." *Österreich in Geschichte und Literatur* 5 (1961): 29–39.

Overhoff, Jürgen. "Die transatlantischen Bezüge der hamburgischen Aufklärung, 1757-1817: Von Blitzableitern, Kommerz und republikanischen Idealen." *Zeitschrift des Vereins für Hamburgische Geschichte* 103 (2017): 57–84.

Pace, Antonio. "Franklin and Italy since the Eighteenth Century." *Proceedings of the American Philosophical Society* 94, no. 3 (1950): 243–244.

Palmer, Robert R. *The Age of the Democratic Revolution: A Political History of Europe and America, 1760-1800*. vol. 1: The Challenge. Princeton, NJ: Princeton University Press, 1959.

Palmer, Robert R. *The Age of the Democratic Revolution: A Political History of Europe and America, 1760-1800*. vol. 2: The Struggle. Princeton, NJ: Princeton University Press, 1964.

Palmer, Robert R. *The Age of the Democratic Revolution: A Political History of Europe and America, 1760-1800*. Updated edition with foreword by David Armitage. Princeton, NJ: Princeton University Press, 2014.

Palmer, Robert R., and Peter Kenez. "Two Documents of the Hungarian Revolutionary Movement of 1794." *Journal of Central European Affairs* 20 (1961): 423–442.

Page, Janet K. "Music and the Royal Procession in Maria Theresia's Vienna." *Early Music* 27, no. 1 'Music and Spectacle' (1999): 96–118.

Paquette, Gabriel. *Imperial Portugal in the Age of Atlantic Revolutions: The Luso-Brazilian World 1770-1850*. Cambridge: Cambridge University Press, 2013.

Parmentier, Jan. "Profit and Neutrality: The Case of Ostend 1781-1783." In *Pirates and Privateers: New Perspectives on the War on Trade in the Eighteenth and Nineteenth Centuries*, edited by David J. Starkey, 206–226. Exeter: University of Exeter Press, 1997.

Parmentier, Jan. "The Irish Connection: The Irish Merchant Community in Ostend and Bruges during the late Seventeenth and Eighteenth Centuries." *Eighteenth-Century Ireland/Iris an dá chultúr* 20 (2005): 31–54.

Pasta, Renato. "The Enlightenment at Work: Ideology, Reform, and a Blueprint for a Constitution." In *Florence after the Medici: Tuscan Enlightenment, 1737-1790*, edited by Corey Tazzara, Paula Findlen, and Jacob Soll, 41–62. New York, NY: Routledge, 2020.

Perl-Rosenthal, Nathan. "On Mobile Legal Spaces and Maritime Empires: The Pillage of the East Indiaman Osterley (1779)." *Itinerario* 42, no. 2 (2018): 183–201.

Peruta, Franco della. *Milano nel Risorgimento: dall'età napoleonica alle Cinque giornate*. Milan: Edizioni Comune di Milano, 1998.

Peterson, Merrill D. "Thomas Jefferson and Commercial Policy." *The William and Mary Quarterly* 22, no. 4 (October 1965): 584–610.

Petráňová, Alena. "Z korespondence Františka Steinského, prvního profesora pomocných věd historických na Karlově universitě." *Acta Universitatis Carolinae* 2 (1958): 101–112.

Phelps, Nicole M. *U.S.-Habsburg Relations from 1815 to the Paris Peace Conference: Sovereignty Transformed.* New York, NY: Cambridge University Press, 2013.

Pieper, Renate. *Die Vermittlung einer Neuen Welt: Amerika im Nachrichtennetz des habsburgischen Imperiums.* Mainz: Verlag Philipp von Zabern, 2000.

Pietschmann, Horst. "Die iberische Expansion im Atlantik und das Reich, ca. 1470-ca. 1530." In *Atlantic Understandings: Essays on European and American History in Honor of Hermann Wellenreuther,* edited by Claudia Schnurmann and Hartmut Lehmann, 43–60. Hamburg: LIT Verlag, 2006.

Plessis, Robert S. du. *Transitions to Capitalism in Early Modern Europe.* Cambridge: Cambridge University Press, 2019.

Po-Chia Hsia, Ronnie. "Jesuit Foreign Missions: A Historiographical Essay." *Journal of Jesuit Studies* 1, no. 1 (2014): 47–65.

Pohl, Hans. *Die Beziehungen Hamburgs zu Spanien und dem spanischen Amerika in der Zeit von 1740 bis 1806.* Wiesbaden: Steiner Verlag, 1963.

Pohlmann, Cornelia. *Die Auswanderung aus dem Herzogtum Braunschweig im Kräftespiel staatlicher Einflussnahme und öffentlicher Resonanz 1720-1897.* Stuttgart: Franz Steiner Verlag, 2002.

Polasky, Janet L. "Revolutionaries between Nations, 1776-1789." *Past & Present* 232, no. 1 (2016): 165–201.

Polasky, Janet L. *Revolution in Brussels, 1787-1793.* Brussels: Académie Royale de Belgique, 1987.

Polasky, Janet L. *Revolutions without Borders: The Call to Liberty in the Atlantic World.* New Haven, CT: Yale University Press, 2015.

Polasky, Janet L. "Traditionalists, Democrats, and Jacobins in Revolutionary Brussels." *The Journal of Modern History* 56, no. 2 (1984): 227–262.

Pole, J. R. "Reflections on American Law and the American Revolution." *The William and Mary Quarterly* 50, no. 1, 'Law and Society in Early America' (1993): 123–159.

Polišenský, Josef V. "Benjamin Franklin, američtí Moravané a čeští čtenáři." Afterword in, *Spoutané blesky,* edited by Endre Sós. Translated by Míla Zadražilová and Klára Vachulová, 315–322. Prague: Mladá fronta, 1972.

Pollack-Parnau, Franz von. *Eine österreich-ostindische Handelskompanie, 1775-1785: Beitrag zur österreichischen Wirtschaftsgeschichte unter Maria Theresia und Joseph II.* Stuttgart: Kohlhammer Verlag, 1927.

Polleroß, Friedrich, Andrea Sommer-Mathis, Christopher F. Laferl. *Federschmuck und Kaiserkrone. Das barocke Amerikabild in den habsburgischen Ländern.* Vienna: Bundesministerium für Wissenschaft und Forschung, 1992.

Polzonetti, Pierpaolo. *Italian Opera in the Age of the American Revolution*. Cambridge: Cambridge University Press, 2011.

Polzonetti, Pierpaolo. "Quakers and Cowboys: Italian Mythologies and Stereotypes of Americans from Piccinni to Puccini." *The Opera Quarterly* 23, no. 1 (2008): 22–38.

Popovici, Aurel. *Die Vereinigten Staaten von Groß-Österreich. Politische Studien zur Lösung der nationalen Fragen und staatsrechtlichen Krisen in Österreich-Ungarn*. Leipzig: Fischer, 1906.

Press, Volker. "The Habsburg Court as Center of the Imperial Government." *The Journal of Modern History* 58, Supplement: Politics and Society in the Holy Roman Empire, 1500-1806 (December 1986): 23–45.

Pricken, Jozef. *Deplancq, l'oublié*. Brussels: s.n., 1967.

Prodan, David. "Emperor Joseph II and Horea's Uprising in Transylvania." *Southeastern Europe* 3, no. 2 (1976): 135–144.

Prodan, David. *Supplex Libellus Valachorum or The Political Struggle of the Romanians in Transylvania during the 18th Century*. Bucharest: Academy of the Socialist Republic of Romania, 1971.

Pula, James S. *Tadeusz Kościuszko: The Purest Son of Liberty*. New York, NY: Hippocrene Books, 1999.

Puttemans, André. *La censure dans les pays-bas autrichiens*. Brussels: Palais des académies, 1935.

Rabuzzi, Daniel A. "Cutting Out the Middleman? American Trade in Northern Europe 1783-1815" In *Merchant Organization and the Maritime Trade in the North Atlantic 1660-1815*, edited by Olaf Uwe Janzen, 175–198. St. John's, Newfoundland: International Maritime Economic History Association, 1998.

Rady, Martyn. *The Habsburgs: The Rise and Fall of a World Power*. London: Penguin, 2020.

Ramcke, Rainer. *Die Beziehung zwischen Hamburg und Österreich im 18. Jahrhundert: Kaiserlich-reichsstädtisches Verhältnis im Zeichen von Handels-und Finanzinteressen*. Hamburg: Christians, 1969.

Randa, Alexander. *Österreich in Übersee*. Vienna: Herold, 1966.

Reeder, Tyson. *Smugglers, Pirates, and Patriots: Free Trade in the Age of Revolution*. Philadelphia, PA: University of Pennsylvania Press, 2019.

Reill, Dominique Kirchner. *Nationalists who Feared the Nation: Adriatic Multi-Nationalism in Habsburg Dalmatia, Trieste, and Venice*. Stanford: Stanford University Press, 2012.

Reinalter, Helmut, ed., *Jakobiner in Mitteleuropa*. Innsbruck: Studienverlag, 1977.

Rényi, Zsuzsa. "A századforduló (18.-19. század) Angliája, mint politikai és művelődési model a magyar kortársak számára." In *A felvilágosodás jegyében: Tanulmányok H. Balázs Éva 70. születésnapjára*, edited by Gábor Klaniczay, János Poór and Éva Ring, 199–215. Budapest: ELTE Soksz., 1985.

Rice, Howard C. *Thomas Jefferson's Paris*. Princeton, NJ: Princeton University Press, 1976.

Rice, John A. "Montezuma at Eszterház: A Pasticcio on a New World Theme." In *Joseph Haydn und Die Neue Welt: Musik- und kulturgeschichtliche Perspektiven*, edited by Walter Reicher, 231–242. Vienna: Hollitzer Verlag, 2019.

Ridgewell, Rupert. "Economic Aspects: The Artaria Case." In *Music Publishing in Europe 1600-1900*, Rudolf Rasch, 90-115. Berlin: BWV Verlag, 2005.

Roberts, Priscilla H., and Richard S. Roberts. *Thomas Barclay (1728-1793): Consul in France, Diplomat in Barbary*. Bethlehem, PA: Lehigh University Press, 2008.

Rodenbough, Theodore Francis. *Autumn Leaves from Family Trees*. New York, NY: Clark and Zugalla, 1892.

Rodríguez, Luis González. "Joseph Neumann: Un Mexicano desconocido (1648-1732)." *Anales de Antropología* 23, no. 1 (1986): 237–259.

Roider, Karl A. "William Lee: Our First Envoy in Vienna." *Virginia Magazine of History and Biography* 86, no. 2 (1978): 163–168.

Romberg, Marion. "Did Europe Exist in the Parish before 1800? The Allegory of Europe and her Three Siblings in Folk Culture." In *Contesting Europe: Comparative Perspectives on Early Modern Discourses on Europe 1400-1800*, edited by Nicholas Detering, Clementina Marsico, and Isabella Walser-Bürgler, 73–103. Leiden and Boston: Brill, 2020.

Romberg, Marion. *Die Welt im Dienst des Glaubens: Erdteilallegorien in Dorfkirchen auf dem Gebiet des Fürstbistums Augsburg im 18 Jahrhundert*. Stuttgart: Franz Steiner Verlag, 2017.

Ronkard, M. "Les répercussions de la Guerre Américaine et d'Indépendance sur le commerce et la pavilion belges." *Communication de l'Académie de Marine de Belgique* 7 (1953): 51–90.

Rublack, Ulinka. "Befeathering the European: The Matter of Feathers in the Material Renaissance." *The American Historical Review* 126, no. 1 (2021): 19–53.

Rudolph, Karl. "Die Kunstbestrebungen Kaiser Maximilians II. im Spannungsfeld zwischen Madrid und Wien: Untersuchungen zu den Sammlungen der österreichischen und spanischen Habsburger." *Jahrbuch der Kunsthistorischen Sammlungen in Wien* 91 (1995): 231–253.

Rynes, Václav. "Los Jesuitas Bohémicos trabajando en las Misiones de América Latina después de 1620." *Ibero-Americana Pragensia* 5 (1971): 193–202.

Salay, David L. "The Production of Gunpowder in Pennsylvania During the American Revolution." *Pennsylvania Magazine of History and Biography* 99, no. 4 (1975): 422–442.

Sambo, Alessandra. "La balance de commerce de la République de Venise: Sources et méthodes." *Cahiers de la Méditerranée* 84 (2012): 381–410.

Sapper, Christian. "Das Hofkammerarchiv als Forschungsstätte für den Wirtschaftshistoriker." *Scrinium* 26, no. 27 (1982): 309–314.

Sashegyi, Oszkár. *Zensur und Geistesfreiheit unter Joseph II: Beitrag zur Kulturges-chichte der habsburgischen Länder*. Budapest: Akadémiai Kiadó, 1958.

Sauer, Walter. "Habsburg Colonial: Austria-Hungary's Role in European Overseas Expansion Reconsidered." *Austrian Studies* 20, no. 1: Colonial Austria: Austria and the Overseas (2012): 5–23.

Saunt, Claudio. *West of the Revolution: An Uncommon History of 1776*. New York, NY: W. W. Norton, 2014.

Schelbert, Leo, and Hadwig Rappolt. *Alles ist ganz anders hier: Auswandererschicksale in Briefen aus zwei Jahrhunderten*. Freiburg: Walter Verlag, 1977.

Scherl, Adolf and Bärbel Rudin. "Joseph Anton Stranitzky." In *Theater in Böhmen, Mähren und Schlesien: Von den Anfängen bis zum Ausgang des 18. Jahrhunderts*, edited by Alena Jakubcová and Matthias J. Pernerstorfer, 666–670. Vienna: Verlag der Österreichischen Akademie der Wissenschaften, 2013.

Schlitter, Hans, *Die Beziehung Österreichs zu Amerika: 1. Theil - Die Beziehung Ös-terreichs zu den Vereinigten Staaten 1778-1787*. Innsbruck: Wagner'schen Universi-täts-Buchhandlung, 1885.

Schlitter, Hans. *Die Regierung Josefs II in den Österreichischen Niederlanden*. Vienna: Holzhausen, 1900.

Schmale, Wolfgang, Marion Romberg, and Josef Köstlbauer, eds., *The Language of Continent Allegories in Baroque Central Europe*. Stuttgart: Franz Steiner Verlag, 2016.

Schmidt, Jan. "Franz von Dombay, Austrian Dragoman at the Bosnian Border 1792-1800." *Wiener Zeitschrift für die Kunde des Morgenlandes* 90 (2000): 75–168.

Schmidt-Brentano, Antonio. *Kaiserliche und k. k. Generale 1618–1815*: Vienna: Öster-reichisches Staatsarchiv, 2006.

Schuener, Ulrich. "Constitutional Traditions in the United States and Germany." In *Deutsch-Amerikanische Verfassungsgeschichte Symposium 1976: Pressefreiheit und Finanzverfassung im Bundesstaat*, edited by Wilhelm A. Kewenig, 11–36. Berlin: Duncker und Humblot, 1978.

Schulte-Beerbühl, Margrit, and Klaus Weber. "From Westphalia to the Carib-bean: Networks of German Textile Merchants in the Eighteenth Century," In *Cosmopolitan Networks in Commerce and Society*, edited by Andreas Gestrich and Margrit Schulte-Beerbühl, 53–98. London: German Historical Institute London, 2011.

Schnyder, Matthias. "Das schweizerische Konsularwesen von 1798 bis 1895." *Politorbis* 36, no. 2 (2004): 5–71.

Schwartz, Thomas. "Roundtable Review of Phelps *U.S.-Habsburg Relations*: Introduc-tion." *SHAFR Passport* 45, no. 1 (2014): 6–7.

Scott, Hamish M. *British Foreign Policy in the Age of the American Revolution*. New York, NY: Clarendon Press of Oxford University Press, 1990.

Scott, Hamish M. "'The True Principles of the Revolution': The Duke of Newcas-tle and the Idea of the Old System." In *Knights Errant and True Englishmen:*

British Foreign Policy, 1660-1800, edited by Jeremy Black, 51–91. Edinburgh: John Donald, 1989.

Senigl, Johanna. "Der Bühnenkomponist Johann Michael Haydn und seine Beziehungen zum Kloster Lambach." In *Prima la danza! Festschrift für Sibylle Dahms*, edited by Gunhild Oberzaucher-Schüller, Daniel Brandenburg and Monika Woitas, 145–148. Würzburg: Königshausen & Neumann Verlag, 2004.

Serruys, Michael W. "The Port and City of Ostend and the Process of State Consolidation in the Southern Netherlands in the Seventeenth and Eighteenth Centuries: A Geopolitical Approach." *International Journal of Maritime History* 19, no. 2 (2007): 319–348.

Shackelford, George. *Thomas Jefferson's Travels in Europe 1784-1789*. Baltimore, MD: Johns Hopkins University Press, 1995.

Shapiro, Paul A. "The Horea Rebellion in Transylvania, 1784-1785." *Columbia Essays in International Affairs* 6 (1970): 65–93.

Shore, Paul. "Enduring the Deluge: Hungarian Jesuit Astronomers from Suppression to Restoration." In *Jesuit Survival and Restoration: A Global History, 1773-1900*, edited by Robert A. Maryks and Jonathan Wright, 148–161. Leiden and Boston: Brill, 2015.

Shore, Paul. *Jesuits and the Politics of Religious Pluralism in Eighteenth Century Transylvania: Culture, Politics and Religion 1693-1773*. Aldershot: Ashgate, 2007.

Simáková, Jitka, and Eduarda Macháčková. *Teatralia Zámecké Knihovny v Ceském Krumlově*. vol. 1. Prague: Knihovna Národního muzea v Praze, 1976.

Simms, Brendan, and Torsten Riotte, eds., *The Hanoverian Dimension in British History 1714-1837*. Cambridge: Cambridge University Press, 2009.

Simms, Brendan. *Three Victories and a Defeat: The Rise and Fall of the First British Empire*. New York, NY: Basic Books, 2007.

Singerton, Jonathan. "175 or 235 Years of Austro-American Relations? Reflections and Repercussions for the Modern Day." In *Austria and America: 20th-Century Cross-Cultural Connections*, edited by Joshua Parker and Ralph Poole, 13–30. Zurich: LIT Verlag, 2017.

Singerton, Jonathan. "A Revolution in Ink: Mapping Benjamin Franklin's Epistolary Network in the Habsburg Monarchy, 1776-1789." *Jahrbuch der österreichischen Gesellschaft zur Erforschung des 18. Jahrhunderts* 34 (2019): 91–113.

Singerton, Jonathan. "'A Story of Benign Neglect'? Die Gründungsgeschichte Amerikas und die Habsburgermonarchie 1776-1783." *Opera Historica: Zeitschrift für Geschichte der Frühen Neuzeit* 17, no. 1 (2016): 56–68.

Singerton, Jonathan. "New World, New Market: A Merchant's Mission to Trade between Philadelphia and Trieste in 1783." *Yearbook of the Society for 18th Century Studies on South Eastern Europe* 1, no. 1: Voices from an era of transition: South Eastern Europe in the 18th Century. (2018): 65–72.

Singerton, Jonathan. "Science, Revolution, and Monarchy in Two Letters of Joseph Donath to František Antonín Steinský." *Opera Historica: Zeitschrift für Geschichte der Frühen Neuzeit* 22, no. 1 (2021): 145–166.

Singerton, Jonathan. ""Some of Distinction Here Are Warm for the Part of America": Knowledge of and Sympathy for the American Cause in the Habsburg Monarchy, 1763–1783." *Journal of Austrian-American History* 1, no. 2 (2017): 128–158.

Sisman, Elaine R. "Haydn's Theater Symphonies." *Journal of the American Musicological Society* 43, no. 2 (1990): 332–340.

Smeyers, Jozef. "De Amerikaanse vrijheidsoorlog in de Nederlandstalige Zuidnederlandse bronnen uit de periode van de Brabantse Omwenteling."In *Revolutie in Brabant 1787-1793*, edited by Fernand Vanhemelryck, 153–163. Brussels: UFSAL, 1990.

Smith, Walter Burges. *America's Diplomats and Consuls of 1776 to 1865: A Geographic and Biographic Directory of the Foreign Service from the Declaration of Independence to the End of the Civil War.* Washington DC: U.S. Government Printing Office, 1986.

Sofka, James R. "American Neutral Rights Reappraised: Identity or Interest in the Foreign Policy of the Early Republic?" *Review of International Studies* 26, no. 4 (2000): 599–622.

Sofka, James R. "Metternich's Theory of European Order: A Political Agenda for 'Perpetual Peace'." *The Review of Politics* 60, no. 1 (1998): 115–149.

Sokol, Irene M. "The American Revolution and Poland: A Bibliographic Essay." *Polish Review* 12, no. 3 (1967): 3–17.

Spero, Patrick. *Frontier Rebels: The Fight for Independence in the American West, 1765-1776.* New York, NY: W. W. Norton, 2018.

Stapelbroek, Koen. "Universal Society, Commerce and the Rights of Neutral Trade: Martin Hübner, Emer de Vattel and Ferdinando Galiani." *COLLeGIUM: Studies Across Disciplines in the Humanities and Social Sciences* 3 (2008): 63–89.

Steeb, Christian. *Die Grafen von Fries: eine Schweizer Familie und ihre wirtschaftspolitische und kulturhistorische Bedeutung für Österreich zwischen 1750 und 1830.* Bad Vöslau: Stadtgemeinde, 1999.

Steffen, Anka, and Klaus Weber. "Spinning and Weaving for the Slave Trade: Proto-Industry in Eighteenth-Century Silesia." In *Slavery Hinterland: Transatlantic Slavery and Continental Europe, 1680-1850*, edited by Felix Brahm and Eve Rosenhaft, 87–108. Woodbridge: Boydell Press, 2016.

Steidl, Annemarie, Wladimir Fischer-Nebmaier, and James Oberly. *From a Multiethnic Empire to a Nation of Nations: Austro-Hungarian Migrants in the US, 1870-1940.* Innsbruck: Studienverlag, 2017.

Steidl, Annemarie. *On Many Routes: Internal, European, and Transatlantic Migration in the Late Habsburg Empire.* West Lafayette, IN: Purdue University Press, 2021.

Stock, Mario. *Trieste e l'America nascente.* Trieste: Société Arti Grafiche Industriali Trieste, 1985.

Stockley, Andrew. *Britain and France at the Birth of America.* Exeter: University of Exeter Press, 2001.

Stolley, Karen. "East From Eden: Domesticating Exile in Jesuit Accounts of Their 1767 Expulsion from Spanish America." In *Jesuit Accounts of the Colonial Americas: Textualities, Intellectual Disputes, Intellectual Transfer*, edited by Marc André

Bernier, Clorinda Donato, and Hans-Jürgen Lüsebrink, 243–262. Toronto: University of Toronto Press, 2014.

Stourzh, Gerald. "Liberal Democracy as a Culture of Rights: England, the United States and Continental Europe." In *Bridging the Atlantic: The Question of American Exceptionalism in Perspective*, edited by Elisabeth Glaser and Hermann Wellenreuther, 11–41. Cambridge and Washington D.C.: Cambridge University Press and the German Historical Institute, 2002.

Stoyanova, Aneliya. "The Benefits and Limits of Permanent Diplomacy: Austrian Habsburg Ambassadors and Ottoman-Spanish Diplomacy in the Second Half of the Sixteenth Century." In *Diplomatic Cultures at the Ottoman Court, 1500-1630*, edited by Tracey A. Sowerby and Christopher Markiewicz, 152–171. London: Routledge, 2021.

Stoye, J. W. "Emperor Charles VI: The Early Years of the Reign." *Transactions of the Royal Historical Society* 12 (1962): 63–84.

Strasser, Ulrike. "From "German India" to the Spanish Indies and Back: Jesuit Migrations Abroad and Their Effects at Home." In *Migration and Religion: Christian Transatlantic Missions, Islamic Migration to Germany*, edited by Barbara Becker-Cantarino, 91–109. Leiden and Boston: Brill, 2012.

Strohmeyer, Arno. "Die Habsburgermonarchie in der Frühen Neuzeit—ein Imperium? Ein Problemaufriss." In *Imperien und Reiche in der Weltgeschichte*, edited by Michael Gehler and Robert Rollinger, 1027–1056. Wiesbaden: Harrassowitz, 2014.

Strohmeyer, Arno. *Die Habsburger Reiche 1555–1740: Herrschaft, Gesellschaft, Politik*. Darmstadt: Wissenschaftliche Buchgesellschaft, 2012.

Sturmberger, Hans. "Die Amerika-Auswanderung aus Oberösterreich zur Zeit des Neo-Absolutismus, 1848-1861." In *Grundlagen transatlantischer Rechtsbeziehungen im 18. und 19. Jahrhundert*, edited by Wilhelm Brauneder, 65–128. Frankfurt am Main: Peter Lang, 1991.

Syrett, David. *The Royal Navy in European Waters during the American Revolutionary War*. Columbia, SC: University of South Carolina Press, 1998.

Syrovy, Daniel. "Die italienischsprachigen Gebiete der Habsburgermonarchie, 1768-1848." In *Die literarische Zensur in Österreich von 1751 bis 1848*, edited by Norbert Bachleitner, Daniel Syrovy, Petr Píša, and Michael Wögerbauer, 218–238. Vienna: Böhlau, 2017.

Szabo, Franz A. J. "Changing Perspectives on the "Revolutionary Emperor": Joseph II Biographies since 1790." *The Journal of Modern History* 83, no. 1, (2011): 111–138.

Szabo, Franz A. J. "Favorit, Premierminister oder "drittes Staatsoberhaupt"? Der Fall des Staatskanzlers Wenzel Anton Kaunitz." In *Der zweite Mann im Staat: Oberste Amtsträger und Favoriten im Umkreis der Reichsfürsten in der Frühen Neuzeit*, edited by Michael Kaiser and Andreas Pečar, 345–362. Berlin: Duncker & Humblot, 2003.

Szabo, Franz A. J. *Kaunitz and Enlightened Absolutism 1753-1780*. Cambridge: Cambridge University Press, 1994.

Szakály, Orsolya. "Managing a Composite Monarchy: The Hungarian Diet and the Habsburgs in the Eighteenth Century." In *The Eighteenth-Century Composite State:*

Representative Institutions in Ireland and Europe 1689-1800, edited by D.W. Hayton, James Kelly, and John Bergin, 205–220. Basingstoke: Palgrave Macmillan, 2010.

Szilassy, Sándor. "America and the Hungarian Revolution of 1848-49." *The Slavonic and East European Review* 44, no. 102 (1966): 180–196.

Szyndler, Bartłomiej. *Tadeusz Kościuszko, 1746–1817.* Warsaw: Wydawnictwo Bellona, 1991.

Tanner, Marie. *The Last Descendant of Aeneas: The Hapsburgs and the Mythic Image of the Emperor.* New Haven, CT: Yale University Press, 1993.

Tar, Gabriella-Nóra. *Deutschsprachiges Kindertheater in Ungarn im 18. Jahrhundert.* Münster: LIT Verlag, 2012.

Taylor, Alan. *American Revolutions: A Continental History, 1750-1804.* New York, NY: W. W. Norton, 2016.

Taylor, Peter K. "'Patrimonial' Bureaucracy and 'Rational' Policy in Eighteenth-Century Germany: The Case of Hessian Recruitment Reforms, 1762-93." *Central European History* 22, no. 1 (1989): 33–56.

Tazbir, Janusz. "Knowledge of Colonial North America in Mid-Eighteenth-Century Poland." *The Polish Review* 35, no. 2 (1990): 99–109.

Tazbir, Janusz. "The Popular Impact of the Discovery of America in East-Central Europe." *The Polish Review* 37, no. 3 (1992): 263–283.

Tazzara, Corey. *The Free Port of Livorno and the Transformation of the Mediterranean World.* Oxford: Oxford University Press, 2017.

Thirring, Gustav. "Die Auswanderung aus Ungarn: Beiträge zur Statistik und topographischen Verteilung der Auswanderung." *Bulletin de la Société hongroise de Géographie* (1902): 1–29.

Turpin, Adriana. "The New World Collections of Duke Cosimo I de'Medici and their Role in the Creation of a *Kunst- and Wunderkammer* in the Palazzo Vecchio." In *Curiosity and Wonder from the Renaissance to the Enlightenment*, edited by R. J. W. Evans and Alexander Marr, 63–86. Aldershot: Ashgate, 2006.

Uhlig, Ludwig. *Georg Forster: Lebensabenteuer eines gelehrten Weltbürgers.* Göttingen: Vandenhoeck & Ruprecht, 2004.

Vandenbroeck, Paul. "Amerindian Art and Ornamental Objects in Royal Collections: Brussels, Mechelen, Duurstede, 1520-1530." in *America, Bride of the Sun* [Exhibition Catalogue], 99–119. Antwerp: Royal Museum of Fine Arts, 1992.

Van Vlack, Milton C. *Silas Deane: Revolutionary War Diplomat and Politician.* Jefferson, NC: McFarland & Co., 2013.

Vasoli, Nidia Danelon. "Favi, Francesco Raimondo." In *Dizionario biografico degli italiani.* vol. 45. Rome: Istituto dell'Enciclopedia Italiana, 1995.

Venturi, Franco. *The End of the Old Regime in Europe 1776-1789: Republican Patriotism and the Empires of the East*, translated R. Burr Litchfield. vol. 2. Princeton NJ: Princeton University Press, 1991.

Vercruysse, J. "L'indépendance américaine et la Révolution Brabançonne." *Revue belge de philologie et d'histoire* 54 (1976): 1098–1108.

Veres, Madalina. "Putting Transylvania on the Map: Cartography and Enlightened Absolutism in the Habsburg Monarchy." *Austrian History Yearbook* 43 (2012): 141–164.

Verhaegen, Pierre. "Le commerce des esclaves en Belgique et à la fin du XVIIIe siècle." *Annales de la Société d'Archéologie de Bruxelles* 15 (1901): 254–262.

Viszota, Gyula. "Gróf Széchenyi István a gimnaziumban." *Századok* (1907): 915.

Vucinich, Wayne S. *Dubrovnik and the American Revolution*. Palo Alto, CA: Ragusan Press, 1977.

Wagnleitner, Reinhold. *Coca-Colonization and the Cold War: The Cultural Mission of the United States in Austria after the Second World War*. Chapel Hill, NC: University of North Carolina Press, 1994.

Walter, Horst. *Joseph Haydn in seiner Zeit*. Eisenstadt: Joseph Haydn Institut, 1982.

Wandruszka, Adam. *Leopold II: Erzherzog von Österreich, Großherzog von Toskana, König von Ungarn und Böhmen, Römischer Kaiser*. vols. 1–2. Vienna: Herold Verlag, 1963.

Wandruszka, Adam. *Pietro Leopoldo: Un grande Riformatore*. Florence: Vallecchi, 1968.

Wangermann, Ernst. *From Joseph II to the Jacobin Trials*. 2nd edition. Oxford: Oxford University Press, 1969.

Weber, Klaus. *Deutsche Kaufleute im Atlantikhandel, 1680-1830: Unternehmen und Familien in Hamburg, Cadiz und Bordeaux*. Munich: C.H. Beck, 2004.

Weber, Klaus. "Linen, Silver, Slaves, and Coffee: A Spatial Approach to Central Europe's Entanglement with the Atlantic Economy." *Cultural & History Digital Journal* 4, no. 2 (December 2015): s.n.

Whaley, Joachim. *Germany and the Holy Roman Empire*. vol. 2: The Peace of Westphalia to the Dissolution of the Reich, 1648-1806. Oxford: Oxford University Press, 2011.

Whatmore, Richard. "The French and North American Revolutions in Comparative Perspective." In *Rethinking the Atlantic World: Europe and America in Age of Democratic Revolutions*, edited by Antonino de Francesco and Manuela Albertone, 219–238. Basingstoke: Palgrave Macmillan, 2009.

Wiesner, Julius von, ed., *J. Ingen-Housz, sein Leben und seine Werken als Naturforscher und Arzt*. Vienna: Carl Konegen, 1905.

Willcox, Joseph. "Historical Sketches of Some of the Pioneer Catholics in Philadelphia and Vicinity." *Records of the American Catholic Historical Society of Philadelphia* 15, no. 4 (1904): 422–427.

Willcox, Joseph. "Some Notes Concerning Joseph Cauffman." *Records of the American Catholic Historical Society of Philadelphia* 21, no. 2 (1910): 83–84.

Williams, Greg H. *The French Assault on American Shipping, 1793-1813: A History and Comprehensive Record of Merchant Marine Losses*. London and Jefferson, NC: McFarland & Company, 2009.

Wilson, Douglas L., and Lucia C. Stanton. *Thomas Jefferson: Jefferson Abroad*. New York, NY: Modern Library, 1999.

Wilson, G. S. *Jefferson on Display: Attire, Etiquette, and the Art of Presentation.* Charlottesville: University of Virginia Press, 2018.

Wilson, Peter H. "Bolstering the Prestige of the Habsburgs: The End of the Holy Roman Empire in 1806." *The International History Review* 28, no. 4 (2006): 709–736.

Wilson, Peter H. *Heart of Europe: A History of the Holy Roman Empire.* Cambridge, MA: Harvard University Press, 2016.

Wilson, Peter H. "The Meaning of Empire in Central Europe around 1800." In *The Bee and the Eagle: Napoleonic France and the End of the Holy Roman Empire, 1806,* edited by Alan Forrest and Peter H. Wilson, 22–42. Basingstoke: Palgrave Macmillan, 2009.

Winkler, Daniel. "'Alzire, ou les Américains' de Voltaire et le Théâtre 'Sensible' dans le Contexte Transeuropéen." *Dalhousie French Studies* 106 (2015): 47–62.

Winter, Pieter J. van. *American Finance and Dutch Investment, 1780-1805 with an Epilogue to 1840,* translated by James C. Riley. vol. 1. New York, NY: Arno Press, 1977.

Winter, Peter. "Johann Carl Zinner." *Mesto a dejiny* 2 (2015): 55–61.

Winterer, Caroline. "Where is America in the Republic of Letters?" *Modern Intellectual History* 9, no. 3 (2012): 597–623.

Wolf, Adam. *Fürstin Eleonore Liechtenstein 1745-1812 nach Briefen und Memoiren ihrer Zeit.* Vienna: Verlag von Carl Gerold's Sohn, 1875.

Wolf, Edwin and T. Kevin J. Hayes *The Library of Benjamin Franklin.* Philadelphia, PA: American Philosophical Society and Library Company of Philadelphia, 2006.

Woolery, William Kirk. *The Relation of Thomas Jefferson to American Foreign Policy, 1783-1793.* Baltimore, MD: Johns Hopkins University Press, 1927.

Wright, Josephine B. "George Polgreen Bridgetower: An African Prodigy in England, 1789-1799." *The Musical Quarterly* 66, no. 1 (1980): 65–82

Wulf, Karin. "No Boundaries? New Terrain in Colonial American History." *OAH Magazine of History* 25, no. 1, (2011): 7–12.

Yonan, Michael E. *Empress Maria Theresa and the Politics of Imperial Art.* Philadelphia, PA: Penn State University Press, 2011.

Young, Henry J. "The Baron de Beelen-Bertholff." *Papers of the Historical Society of York County,* New Series, 1, no. 3 (s.d.): 1–7.

Zahra, Tara. *The Great Departure: Mass Migration from Eastern Europe and the Making of the Free World.* New York, NY: W. W. Norton, 2016.

Závodszky, Géza. *American Effects on Hungarian Imagination and Political Thought 1559-1848,* translated by Amy Módly. Highland Lakes, NJ: Atlantic Research and Publications Inc., 1995.

Závodszky, Géza. "Zinner János, az angol alkotmány első hazai ismeröje: A Dissertatio statistica de potestate exsequente Regis Angliae szerződéséről." *Magyar Könyvszemle* 103 (1987): 10–18.

Zedinger, Renate. *Franz Stephan von Lothringen (1708-1765): Monarch, Manager, Mäzen.* Vienna: Böhlau, 2008.

Zedinger, Renate. "'Kaiserliche Wunschliste': Die Instruktion für Nikolaus Joseph Jacquin." In *Jahrbuch der Österreichischen Gesellschaft zur Erforschung des achtzehnten Jahrhunderts*. vol. 23: Franz Stephan von Lothringen und sein Kreis, edited by Renate Zedinger and Wolfgang Schmale, 269–300. Bochum: Dieter Winkler Verlag, 2009.

Zedinger, Renate. "Kaunitz und Cobenzl: Zu den Zentralisierungstendenzen des Staatskanzlers im Wiener Verwaltungsapparat der Österreichischen Niederlande, 1753-1757." In *Staatskanzler Wenzel Anton von Kaunitz-Rietberg*, edited by Grete Klingenstein and Franz A. J. Szabo, 197–217. Graz: Andreas Schnider Verlag, 1996.

Zeuske, Michael and Jörg Ludwig. "Amerikanische Kolonialwaren in Preußen und Sachsen: Prolegomena." *Jahrbuch für Geschichte von Staat, Wirtschaft und Gesellschaft Lateinamerikas* 32 (1995): 257–301.

Zimmerman, Joachim. *Das Verfassungsprojekt des Großherzogs Peter Leopold von Toskana*. Heidelberg: Carl Winter, 1901.

Newspapers

Augspurgische Extra-Zeitung (Augsburg)
Augspurgische Ordinari Postzeitung (Augsburg)
Gazzetta Universale: O Sieno Notizie Istoriche, Politiche, di Scienze, Arti, Agricoltura (Florence)
Gazette van Gend (Ghent)
Historisches Portefeuille (Vienna)
Journal Général de France (Paris)
Magyar Hírmondó (Pozsony [Bratislava])
Notizie del Mondo (Florence)
Pennsylvania Gazette (Philadelphia)
Politisches Journal (Hamburg)
Provinzial Nachrichten aus den Kaiserl. Königl. Staaten (Vienna)
Salzburger Intelligenzblatt (Salzburg)
Der Teutsche Merkur (Leipzig, Frankfurt am Main, Weimar)
The Pennsylvania Packet (Philadelphia)
Ungarische Staats-und Gelehrte Nachrichten (Ofen [Budapest])
Wienerblättchen (Vienna)
Wienerisches Diarium/Wiener Zeitung (Vienna)

Unpublished Material

Babarczi, Dóra. "Magyar jezsuiták Brazíliában 1753-1760." Unpublished dissertation, University of Szeged, 2013.

Bergmans, Josiane. "Handelsbetrekkingen tussen de Zuidelijke Nederlanden, de Verenigde Staten van Amerika en de Antillen (1776-1794)." Parts I & II. Unpublished dissertation, University of Ghent, 1972.

Davis, Gerald H. "The Diplomatic Relations between the United States and Austria-Hungary 1913-1917." Unpublished dissertation, Vanderbilt University, 1958.

Friebel, Rudolf. "Österreich und die Vereinigten Staaten bis zum Gesandtenaustausch im Jahre 1838." Unpublished dissertation, University of Innsbruck, 1955.

Goger, Renate. "Die Beziehungen der Habsburgermonarchie zu den Vereinigten Staaten von Amerika von 1838 bis 1867." Unpublished dissertation, University of Vienna, 2010.

Gucht, Veerle van. "De trans-Atlantische handel vanuit Oostende van Amerikaanse tot Franse revolutie 1775-1790: Een kwantitatieve benadering." Unpublished dissertation, University of Ghent, 2008.

Huibrechts, Marion M. A. "Swampin' Guns and Stabbing Irons: The American Revolution, Liege Arms, and the Austrian Netherlands." Unpublished dissertation, KU Leuven, 2009.

Loidolt, Alfred. "Die Beziehungen Österreichs zu den Vereinigten Staaten zur Zeit des Amerikanischen Bürgerkrieges." Unpublished dissertation, University of Vienna, 1949.

Müller, Leos and Michal Wanner. "Bohemian Textiles and Glass in Eighteenth-Century Global Trade." Paper presented at the Third European Congress on World and Global History, London School of Economics, 14–17 April 2011.

Musilová, Martina. "'Gâtée par le Monde': Literární dílo Kněžny Alexandry z Dietrichsteina." Unpublished dissertation, University of South Bohemia, 2014.

Rill, Robert. "Die Reise des Grafen Karl von Zinzendorf und Pottendorf über die britischen Inseln im Jahre 1768 am Hand seiner Tagebuchaufzeichnungen." Unpublished dissertation, University of Vienna, 1983.

Schnaubelt, Ingeborg. "Die Errichtung eines Konsulates in London' in "Die Beziehungen zwischen Österreich und England von 1756 bis 1780." Unpublished dissertation, University of Vienna, 1965.

Singerton, Jonathan. "Empires on the Edge: The Habsburg Monarchy and the American Revolution, 1763-1789." Unpublished dissertation, University of Edinburgh, 2018.

Thurman, Kira. "A History of Black Musicians in Germany and Austria 1870-1961: Race, Performance, and Reception." Unpublished dissertation, University of Rochester, 2013.

Tsapina, Olga. "The Strange Case of Philipp Ludwell." Unpublished paper, The Huntington Library, 2012.

Tschugguel, Helga. "Österreichische Handelskompanien im 18. Jahrhundert und die Gründung der orientalischen Akademie als ein Beitrag zur Belebung des Handels mit dem Orient." Unpublished dissertation, University of Vienna, 1996.

Vincenzi, Anna. "La rivoluzione Americana e i primi anni della Repubblica Statunitense nell'opinione pubblica Italiana." Unpublished master's dissertation, Università Cattolica del Sacro Cuore, 2012-2013.

Vincenzi, Anna. "The Many American Revolutions of Italian Public Opinion." Paper present at the conference on "Propaganda, Persuasion, the Press and the American Revolution, 1763-1783," organized by the University of Hong Kong and the Thomas Jefferson Foundation, Hong Kong, China, April 2016. Shared with the author.

Walsh, Stephen. "Between the Arctic & the Adriatic: Polar Exploration, Science & Empire in the Habsburg Monarchy." Unpublished PhD dissertation, Harvard University, 2014.

Internet Sources

Brill Prize Papers Dataset, http://brc.brill.semcs.net/browse/prize-papers-part-1-online (July 2019).

Continental Allegories in the Baroque Age database https://erdteilallegorien.univie.ac.at/ (October 2018).

Fairlie, Henry, 'The Shot Heard Round the World,' *The New Republic*, 18th July 1988: https://newrepublic.com/article/90885/the-shot-heard-round-the-world (May 2019).

Franklin Papers, Yale University: http://franklinpapers.org/ (September 2018).

Hessisches Landesamt für geschichtliche Landeskunde, Marburg, *Hessian Information System on Regional History (LAGIS)*, HETRINA (Hessian Troops in North America), http://www.lagis-hessen.de/en/subjects/intro/sn/hetrina (June 2017).

O'Reilly, William, Competition for Colonists: Europe and Her Colonies in the Eighteenth Century, (University of Galway, n.d.), 6;
https://www.histecon.magd.cam.ac.uk/docs/o'reilly_competition_oct04.pdf (December 2019).

Singerton, Jonathan, "A Bumbling Beekeeper from Bohemia," American Philosophical Society Blog Series, https://www.amphilsoc.org/blog/aps-and-central-europe-bumbling-beekeeper-bohemia (October 2020).

Thomas Jefferson Retirement Series – Early Access, Founders Online, National Archives, http://founders.archives.gov/documents/Jefferson/98-01-02-5970 (December 2016).

Wulf, Karin, "Vast Early America: Three Simple Words for a Complex Reality," https://blog.oieahc.wm.edu/vast-early-america-three-simple-words/ (July 2020).

THE REVOLUTIONARY AGE

Embracing a broad chronology and geography, this series seeks to publish original scholarship on the revolutionary, and counterrevolutionary, upheavals—political, social, cultural, economic, intellectual, religious, military, and diplomatic—that transformed the Atlantic world between 1750 and 1850.

Navigating Neutrality: Early American Governance in the Turbulent Atlantic
Sandra Moats

Ireland and America: Empire, Revolution, and Sovereignty
Patrick Griffin and Francis D. Cogliano, editors

CPSIA information can be obtained
at www.ICGtesting.com
Printed in the USA
LVHW030723060123
736516LV00001B/36

Babar Ayaz has been associated with journalism for over 40 years. During this time he has worked for *The Sun*, Pakistan Press International (PPI), *Business Recorder* and *Dawn*. He has supervised the production of numerous TV programmes, including *Pakistan Business Update*, of which he was an editor for 11 years. It was the first private sector-produced television news programme in Pakistan dealing specifically with economic development.

At present he is a regular columnist for *Daily Times*, *Express* (Urdu daily) and *Awami Awaz* (Sindhi daily). He also contributes for some foreign newspapers and magazines. He has been the Pakistan correspondent of *Depthnews* (a feature service of the Press Foundation of Asia) as also for *The Hindu* and *Frontline* (both published from India).

He founded Mediators in 1988, the first independent public relations consultancy firm of Pakistan. He is a former chairman of the International Public Relations Association (IPRA), Pakistan chapter. As the head of the Mediators' Conferences, he conceptualized, organized and compered a number of international conferences. He has participated in various international and national seminars and workshops and has lectured at various forums on the political, economic and social problems of Pakistan.

What's wrong with
PAKISTAN?

Babar Ayaz

HAY HOUSE INDIA

Australia • Canada • Hong Kong • India
South Africa • United Kingdom • United States

Hay House Publishers (India) Pvt. Ltd.
Muskaan Complex, Plot No.3, B-2 Vasant Kunj, New Delhi-110 070, India
Hay House Inc., PO Box 5100, Carlsbad, CA 92018-5100, USA
Hay House UK, Ltd., Astley House, 33 Notting Hill Gate, London W11 3JQ, UK
Hay House Australia Pty Ltd., 18/36 Ralph St., Alexandria NSW 2015, Australia
Hay House SA (Pty) Ltd., PO Box 990, Witkoppen 2068, South Africa
Hay House Publishing, Ltd., 17/F, One Hysan Ave., Causeway Bay, Hong Kong
Raincoast, 9050 Shaughnessy St., Vancouver, BC V6P 6E5, Canada

Email: contact@hayhouse.co.in
www.hayhouse.co.in

ISBN 978-93-81431-59-7

Designed and typeset at Hay House India

Printed and bound at
Thomson Press (India) Ltd., Faridabad, Haryana (India)

To
the millions who became the
victims of terrorism

Contents

CONTENTS

CONTENTS

PART - V

PART - VI

Harf-e-haq, dil mey khatakta hai jo kante ki tarah
Aaj iqrar karen, aur khalish mit-jae'e

– Faiz Ahmed Faiz

(The word of truth, which throbs in the heart like a thorn,
Let us today accept, and the anguish be wiped out.)

– Translation: Victor Kiernan

PREFACE

When so much goes wrong with a country and it remains
a dysfunctional state even after 66 years of its inception, it
needs an unbiased and a dispassionate diagnosis.

NOT MUCH GOOD IS WRITTEN ABOUT PAKISTAN WITHIN THE country and abroad. Not much faith is expressed in Pakistan's future by its own people or by the world at large. *Newsweek* dubbed it as: 'Most dangerous state of the world'. Former British Prime Minister Gordon Brown says 75 per cent of terrorism cases, investigated in his country, have Pakistani connections. Present British Prime Minister David Cameron says 'Pakistan should stop exporting terrorism' and playing a dual role. US President Barack Obama's edict is that 'Pakistan is a fragile country'. Former US Secretary of State Hillary Clinton, former US chairman of the Joint Chiefs of Staff Admiral Mike Mullen, and leaked US official papers blame Pakistan for supporting the Taliban. The US government officials have hyphenated Pakistan with Afghanistan in their new policy to fight against the Taliban and the Al Qaeda and are calling Pakistan a part of the problem and not the solution. The Western countries' diplomats fear that Pakistan's nuclear assets can fall in the hands of the Taliban- and the Al Qaeda-backed extremists.

'Best friend' China has been telling Pakistan to take action against the Xinjiang province's Islamic militants who have links with Pakistani jihadis. Russia and Central Asian Republics (CARs) see Pakistan as a haven for the Islamic terrorists from Uzbekistan, Tajikistan and Chechnya. President Hamid Karzai of Afghanistan says that Pakistan should stop supporting the Taliban and interfering in his country's internal politics. Next-door neighbour India calls Pakistan the 'epicentre of terrorism' and its prime minister, Dr Manmohan Singh has linked future relations with Pakistan to the action taken against the terrorist groups like Lashkar-e-Taiba (LeT), who he believes is responsible for the Mumbai attacks. In fine, there is no major power in the world that does not hold Pakistan responsible for nurturing jihadi organizations with impunity.

Political analysts predicted in the early 1950s that the country would break as East Pakistan and West Pakistan would not be able to live together. The prediction was proven right within 24 years.[1] Tracing the roots of dictatorship in Pakistan, Hassan Gardezi and Jamil Rashid published a collection of papers by leading Pakistani intellectuals in 1983 titled *Pakistan: The Unstable State*. Founder of the Pakistan People's Party (PPP) Zulfikar Ali Bhutto, the most popular leader after Muhammad Ali Jinnah, who served as the ninth prime minister of Pakistan from 1973 to 1977, and prior to that as the fourth president of Pakistan from 1971 to 1973, was executed in 1979, predicted from the gallows: 'If I am assassinated, there will be deluge'.

Leftist leader Tariq Ali wrote 'Can Pakistan survive?' Najam Sethi, editor of a Pakistani weekly *Friday Times* commented at a seminar in India that 'Pakistan is a failing state'. He was arrested on returning home. Prominent journalist Khaled Ahmed too wrote in 2002 that Pakistan is a failing state. US think tank Fund for Peace ranked Pakistan tenth on the list of failing states. Somalia remains on the top of the 2010 list that is compiled annually on the basis of markings on:

Social Indicators

1. Mounting demographic pressures.
2. Massive movement of refugees or internally displaced.
3. Persons creating complex humanitarian emergencies.
4. Legacy of vengeance-seeking groups.
5. Grievance or group paranoia.
6. Chronic and sustained human flight.

Economic Indicators

1. Uneven economic development along group lines.
2. Sharp and/or severe economic decline.

Political Indicators

1. Criminalization and/or de-legitimization of the state.
2. Progressive deterioration of public service.
3. Suspension or arbitrary application of the rule of law and widespread violation of human rights.
4. Security apparatus operates as a 'state within a state'.
5. Rise of factionalized elites.
6. Intervention of other states or external political actors.

The establishment in Pakistan hates to admit that on all the counts the country's rating is quite realistic. However, the Pakistani media and educated classes talk about each of the failing attributes separately and not in a systematic and analytical way. The underlying factor, which has led the country to the brink is exploitation of religion to achieve political ends, is seldom discussed. Headlines that 'Pakistan is bankrupt and on the verge of default', are commonly seen and read in the media reports. No sooner is an elected government sworn-in, the common man starts talking about its ouster. The fact is the Asif Ali Zardari PPP-led coalition (2008–13) is the only civilian government to have completed its full term in office. This is indeed a good omen for Pakistan's democratic process, as it also shows maturity of major political forces.

Pakistan has had four military operations in Balochistan on one pretext or another. The one started by General Pervez Musharraf still continues. Pakistan is fighting a major war against local Taliban, though selectively, in the Khyber Pakhtunkhwa (KP). The whole country is infested with hundreds and thousands of religiously motivated trained militants. The younger generation is indoctrinated that jihad against the infidel is the duty of an 'Islamic State'. Muslim invaders are eulogized as heroes in the course books for waging jihad in the name of Islam, which draws moral sanction as history books do not mention real reasons of Muslim invasions.

The crime rate is alarmingly high. Every third person lives below the poverty line. The unprecedented 2010 floods further aggravated the situation, particularly for the rural poor.

* * *

'Trust deficit' is the most frequently used term in Pakistan, a country which does not trust the US though it is its biggest donor and a major market for its exports. Why? Because the majority of the population feels that the US administration is only with Pakistan to destroy the Al Qaeda and establish a government of its choice in Afghanistan. There are conspiracy theorists who think that US wants to break Pakistan and capture its nuclear bombs in cahoots with India. A vast majority is made to believe by the mullahs of all shades from the pulpit, week after week in Friday sermons, that there is a conspiracy against Islam, something the state, which was made in the name of Islam, too does not stop.

Hillary Clinton agrees that there is a trust deficit between the two countries and was never diplomatic about expressing her distrust either. She has reiterated many times that powers that be in the establishment knew where the Al Qaeda founder Osama bin Laden was in Pakistan.

Pakistan has a perennial distrust of India. Since its inception there has been a lurking fear that India does not want Pakistan to exist, this was based on some genuine fears in the early days. India, Pakistanis feel, is still active in destabilizing the country by supporting the Baloch separatist movement and by creating inroads in local terrorist groups through Afghan intelligence. Indian and Pakistani establishments are playing tit-for-tat games. The fact that the break-up of Pakistan is not in the interest of India any more is not accepted by the army-led establishment, while the big brotherly arrogance of India is not helping in building trust between the two countries. India does not trust Pakistan because of the two covert attacks against it – Kashmir in 1965 and Kargil in 1999. India has also suffered at the hands of the Pakistan-based jihadi organizations in Kashmir, Delhi, Mumbai and other cities, which gives it a reason to distrust Pakistani establishment.

Pakistan has a trust deficit with Afghanistan, as the establishment feels that the Karzai government is closer to India, and blames it for giving more space to India and for cooperating with its intelligence to destabilize Pakistan. On the other hand, Afghanistan does not trust

Pakistan because it has been interfering in its affairs for many decades. Pakistan's strong urge is to have strategic depth in Afghanistan by installing 'a favourable government' in Kabul. The fact that Taliban leaders are hiding in Pakistan and their forces are using Pakistan as a hinterland does not give us any excuse, when the Afghans say they don't trust our policies. The Taliban leaders who tried to enter into direct talks with Karzai and the US government were arrested to give the message that no solution without the blessing of Pakistan would be allowed.

Pakistan does not have a trust deficit with Iran, but has a strong suspicion that it finances and supports the Shiite militants in Pakistan. Iran on the other hand has a trust deficit with Pakistan as it thinks Pakistan is allowing the Saudi and US governments to use its land for destabilizing the Iranian government.

* * *

Internally, smaller provinces do not trust Punjab. They feel that, since population-wise it is the biggest province and has over 80 per cent of presence in the army, it has been exploiting the smaller provinces for the last 66 years. Though, lately, the situation has changed somewhat and Punjab politicians are becoming conscious that provincial autonomy would have to be respected, there are still many army co-evolutionists who do not trust the Baloch and Sindhi nationalists. To them anybody who is against the exploitation of the smaller nationalities and does not share their perception is a traitor, unless proved otherwise.

The army does not trust major politicians. It thinks that the 'bloody civilians' cannot be trusted with the national security policy and more recently for running the economy. So the army keeps running down the political governments in particular and politicians in general. Some of their co-evolutionists in the media readily oblige.

Ever since the present superior judiciary has been restored there is a mutual trust deficit between it and the elected government. While the judiciary feels that the civilian government is conspiring to undermine its powers, the civilian government does not trust the judiciary, as it feels its judgments destabilize the present dispensation. The result is that both the institutions are trying to claim more space in the polity of Pakistan.

The consequences are, Pakistan is caught in the whirlpool of trust deficits in which the country's boat is swirling at an uncontrollable speed. The establishment is not willing to accept that the national security policy, which it has followed with a slight difference of accent, is disastrous. Pakistan cannot get out of the present mess unless it accepts that the political formulation, that Muslims of India were a separate nation, was politically incorrect. Using religion as a means to achieve a political and economic end was a mistake which is resulting in large-scale loss of precious human lives, not to mention immense destruction of property, on virtually a day-to-day basis.

This book is an attempt to explain why Pakistan has been in a perpetual state of flux for the last six decades and more. When so much goes wrong with a country and it remains a dysfunctional state even after 66 years of its inception, it needs an unbiased and a dispassionate diagnosis. The critical analysis of its political history and the present precarious situation amply show that Pakistan was born with a genetic defect. Religious extremism and terrorism that Pakistan suffers from are the logical outcome of the communal politics of the pre-independence movement. I have attempted to suggest drastic treatment, without which the country would continue to fall. It is difficult to see where the bottom of the pit is.

May 2013 – Babar Ayaz

Acknowledgements

For four decades, while writing on political and economic issues as a journalist, I tried to diagnose what actually ails Pakistan. Most of the discourse in the country has been about the symptoms that torment it and not about the real ailment. My diagnosis is that Pakistan has a genetic defect. In Oriental culture a patient is normally not told about his/her serious ailment by the protective relations. Following this tradition I think Pakistanis avoid discussing this genetic defect openly. Consequently, real treatment i.e., genetic re-engineering, cannot be started. I owe writing this book to my love for the peoples suffering in Pakistan. They need to be told the truth straight-forwardly.

I am indebted to my father (the late) Shahzada Ayaz, who imbibed in me love and tolerance for all humanity without any prejudice.

I must thank many of my readers (of my articles as a journalist) and friends who encouraged me to write a book. Some even suggested publishing a selection of my columns. But I have always felt that journalese cannot take the place of the more serious and rigorous work needed to write a book.

I would have written this book at least two decades back but was unable to get the time off, from making a living and meeting my responsibilities to provide for my family. But as I turned 62 in 2011, I thought the time had come to write my first book. This could not have been possible without the support of my wife Dr Samia K. Babar, who took over the burden of running my PR agency that feeds the family. This allowed me to take a sabbatical to research for this book. She also read my first draft and subedited it. I am also thankful to my children Adarsh, Amar, Sarah and Myra for supporting me in writing the book, and for cautioning me that I should be careful not to invite the wrath of the religious extremists.

My research for this book owes a lot to the British Library in London, which keeps its door open for all and has very helpful staff. I am grateful to my close friends Dr Sarah Ansari and Professor Humayun Ansari (who teach history at the Royal Holloway, University of London) for their valuable advice.

I would be failing if I did not acknowledge my friend Professor Amin Mughal who edited the first draft and raised pertinent questions to crystallize my thesis. I would like to thank Ashok Chopra of Hay House Publishers for his useful editorial inputs. I am indebted to Tulika Rattan of Hay House who edited the manuscript closely and made useful suggestions.

I am also thankful to my brother-in-law Rafiq Khan who not only graciously allowed me to use his chalet near Murree* (where much of this book has been written), but also goaded me to finish it as soon as possible.

– Babar Ayaz

* A hill station in North Punjab.

PART - I

Chapter 1

THE GENETIC DEFECT OF PAKISTAN

What most politicians, who usually have short-term gains in sight, do not understand is that the 'end' does not always justify the 'means'; same 'means' that are used to achieve an 'end' mostly tend to dictate the subsequent 'end'. Pakistan is today being consumed by the religiosity that was whipped as a 'means' to achieve a separate homeland.

It was on the eve of the golden jubilee of Pakistan in 1997 that I made the following observation about the 'two-nation theory' while giving an interview to BBC World Service:

Although the Muslims were a small minority in India, they ruled the sub-continent for almost 650 years, and it never occurred to them that they were a separate nation. However, after 1857, it came to democracy, where numbers matter, the fear of being ruled by a Hindu majority suddenly started haunting the Muslim elite. And after centuries of convenient amnesia they realized that they were a separate nation.

While running away from democracy, the Muslim elite of India acted like a spoilsport. Here, the basic questionnaire is: What cured the Indian Muslims' amnesia and why did they realize that they were a separate nation? Why did they coin a 'two-nation theory' only when the British started reforms to allow limited self-rule to the Indians?

Many historians have given different reasons for the emergence of the demand for a separate homeland for the Muslims of India. The objective of this book, however, is to study the effects of the dangerous political formulation – 'two-nation theory' – on the political, economic and social growth of Pakistan since its inception. Adherence to this false theory has kept Pakistan unstable and has forced its 'peoples' to live under perennial nerve-racking uncertainty. (The word 'peoples' has been used here advisedly because Pakistan remains a multinational state – a fact consistently denied by its ruling establishment.)

However, before moving on to the current problems faced by Pakistan as a consequence of its basic political formulation, it would be useful to identify in this chapter the primary objective of the Muslim elite's movement in undivided India and, more importantly, the means they adopted to achieve their objective.

* * *

The 'two-nation theory' evolved from the basic fear that in a democracy the Hindu majority would subjugate the Muslim minority. In the Muslim-minority provinces of India at that time, the Muslim elite played a leading role in this movement, because they were upset by their diminishing share in government services and policy-making. East Bengal had taken the lead to invite the Muslim leaders on one platform for protecting their rights. Other Muslim majority provinces and principalities later joined the movement demanding maximum autonomy. This demand for special status was motivated by the fear of the Muslim elite that they would lose control of the provinces they ruled.

The Muslims had initially remained distanced from the British Raj, nursing a genuine grudge against them for having established their colonial rule by deposing the dying Muslim imperial rule in India. While these hostile feelings led to the isolation of the Muslims, their rejection of Western education stunted the growth of their middle class and business class. The great Muslim reformer and educator, Sir Syed Ahmad Khan had supported the British during the 1857 independence movement but, at the same time, realizing the backwardness of the Muslims pleaded that they should go in for modern education and remain loyal to the Raj. In 1875, he established the Mohammedan Anglo-Oriental (MAO) College (which in 1920 became Aligarh Muslim University), for promoting social and economic development of Indian Muslims. By this time the Muslim elite and the nascent middle class had started realizing that they were being left behind in almost all spheres of life by the Hindu majority who were once their subjects.

Pakistan's officially celebrated historian Dr Ishtiaq Hussain Qureshi has recorded: '[A] Muslim political organization came into being in Calcutta just one year after [the] establishment of the Indian Association. This was the Central National Muhammadan Association founded by Sayed Amir Ali in 1877 ... it proposed to work in harmony with western culture and progressive tendencies of the age.... In 1882 it presented to viceroy [Lord] Ripon a memorial which dealt exhaustively with the problems of Muslim education and with the grievances regarding their meagre representation in the government offices.' Towards the end of 1883 it presented views to the Government of Bengal on the pending Municipal Bill and suggested 'lowering of property qualifications to enfranchise a larger number of Muslims and the insertion of a provision in the Bill empowering the government to allow the minority to elect its own representatives where the state of communal feeling indicated the desirability of this expedient.' [1]

As the British government moved more towards self-rule, first through the Minto–Morley reforms resulting in the enactment of the Government of India Act 1919 and then as a result of the Government of India Act 1935, the Muslim elite's demand to ensure their share in the government on communal basis gathered momentum. They felt that since, in a democratic dispensation it was the numbers that mattered, there was clear indication that the Hindu majority would finally have more power after having been ruled by the Muslim invaders for about six centuries.

The Pakistani historian and scholar, Dr Mubarak Ali made the following observation at the very outset of his paper 'Consciousness of Muslim Identity in South Asia Before 1947': 'The concept of a Muslim political identity was a product of British rule when electoral process, of the so-called democratic institutions and traditions were introduced. British rule; that created a minority complex among Indian Muslims and thereby a consciousness of Muslim political identity. After passing through a series of upheavals, the Muslim community ... declared itself a nation, asserting its separateness.' [2]

The Muslims had started asking for a separate electorate as early as 1882, thus sowing the seed of Pakistan without realizing that ultimately it might lead them to seek a separate homeland – Pakistan.

To get the support of the masses the Muslim elite used religion unabashedly, particularly after the All India Muslim League's (AIML) defeat in the 1937 elections. After this, the Muslim poet and ideologue, Sir Muhammad Iqbal, in a letter to politician and statesman Muhammad Ali Jinnah advised: 'I have no doubt that you realize the gravity of the situation as far as Muslim India is concerned. The League will have to finally decide whether it will remain a body representing the upper class of Indian Muslims or Muslim masses who have so far, with good reasons, taken no interest in it. Personally, I believe that a political organization which gives no promise of improving the lot of the average Muslim cannot attract our masses.'[2] Iqbal then suggested that the solution to Muslim poverty was 'the enforcement of the Law of Islam and its future development in the light of modern ideas .... But the enforcement and development of the Shariat of Islam is impossible in this country without a free Muslim state or states.'[4]

Without understanding the consequences of the propaganda that a separate homeland was required for the Muslims to live according to Islamic values – the Sharia – the Muslim elite exploited religious feelings of the masses. What most politicians, who usually have short-term gains in sight, do not understand is that the 'end' does not always justify the 'means'; same 'means' that are used to achieve an 'end' mostly tend to dictate the subsequent 'end'. Pakistan is today being consumed by the religiosity that was whipped as a 'means' to achieve a separate homeland. Such are the dynamics of life, not only the politics. During the course of history both 'end' and 'means' get modified according to the objective and subjective conditions.

Notes and References

1. I. H. Qureshi, *A Short History of Pakistan*, Vols. 1–4, University of Karachi, Karachi, 1967.
2. Mubarak Ali, *Pakistan in Search of Identity*, Pakistan Study Centre, Karachi, 2009, p. 1.
3. Saleem Qureshi (compiler and editor), *Jinnah the Founder of Pakistan* (second edition), Oxford University Press, New York, 1998, p. 60.
4. Ibid., p. 61.

Chapter 2

Thrust of Pakistan Movement

Under the Government of India Act 1935, the British had retained power in Delhi, which in turn led the Congress to consolidate the powers in the party's centre. In response, the Muslim League came out with the 'two-nation theory' to protect the ruling elite of Muslim-majority provinces and the jobs in the Muslim-minority provinces.

To have a better understanding of the Muslim separatism in India, in the period that followed their rule over the country for centuries, a brief review of the relevant segment of history is needed.

The movement did not come out of the blue but evolved in a move to represent the privileged Muslim elite and middle-class interests in interaction with the policies of the Indian National Congress and, of course, the British. By the time the British dethroned the last emperor, Bahadur Shah Zafar, the Mughal Empire had crumbled, and each province and principality had assumed almost independent status. Like most feudal monarchies, the Mughal Empire's political structure even at its height rested on maximum autonomy of the constituent units. Where there were no local nawabs and rajas, governors were appointed who exercised powers on their behalf with little or no interference from the Centre. The monarchs only wanted the constituents to collect taxes and provide a force in times of war. The independent status of the territories was the basis of establishing Muslim empires that ruled India. The means of communications in those days were also not developed enough for the Centre to centralize the powers.

'The emergence of the Indian territories controlled by the Turks as an independent sultanate is usually dated back from the accession of Iltutmush .... The period from 1211 to 1526 was that of the Delhi Sultanate, although the Delhi Sultan rarely controlled all the territories conquered by the Turks. Major regions in extreme South, however had come under some form of control by the Turkish or other Muslim rulers.'[1]

The situation did not change during the Mughal period. As a matter of fact, by the time the British took over from the weak Mughal Empire, the provinces and principalities had enjoyed greater degree of autonomy. Delhi's writ was nominal. With the British the situation changed and the power got gradually concentrated in Delhi with the viceroy.

Meanwhile, the AIML entered into an agreement with the Congress in 1916, known as the Lucknow Pact. It was agreed that the Muslims would be given separate electorates in all provincial legislatures. Though the Muslims were only 14.3 per cent of the United Provinces (UP) population they were given 'substantial weightage' and accorded 30 per cent of the Indian seats in the Hindu majority provinces.

In the Government of India Act 1919, passed by the House of Commons, the British secretary of state for India, Edwin Montagu, had laid the foundation of self-government in India. Montagu had earlier told the House that 'The policy of His Majesty's Government, with which the Government of India are in complete accord, is that of the increasing association of Indians in every branch of the administration and the gradual development of self-governing institutions, with a view to the progressive realization of responsible government in India as an integral part of the British Empire.'[2] But this did not mean decentralizing the British Raj powers in India, which was home to many sub-nationalities and principalities.

Writer David Page has argued: 'British Raj attempted to manage the challenge of nationalism in that period [1920–32]. It looked particularly at the development of the representative institutions, which during those years provided partial and substantial provincial autonomy and it argued that these significant constitutional developments should not be seen simply as concessions to Indian nationalism but as Imperial control. According to this theory, the way in which political power is devolved – the balancing of rural against urban, of Muslim against non-Muslim, and the encouragement of the provinces at the expense of the national [government] played a role in shaping the character of politics, whether among Muslim separatists or the Congress nationalists …. [T]hat the manner in which power was devolved to the provinces without any corresponding devolution at the all-India level encouraged centrifugalism. The trend was discernible after 1920; it became crystal clear after 1937. Muslim separatism was reinforced by the emergence of autonomous Muslim majority provinces and the Congress had to develop … new strategies and mechanisms to keep the nationalist movement united…'³

Page has underlined that '[T]he Montagu–Chelmsford Reforms also changed the nature of all-India Muslim politics. Before 1920, Muslim political organizations at all India level had been in the hands of Muslims of the United Provinces, Bihar, and Bombay. In these provinces a Muslim educated elite had shared the political aspirations of the Hindu elite and had masterminded a political alliance with the Congress in pursuit of constitutional reforms.'³

It was after the provinces were given more powers in the reforms that the thinking in Muslim leadership started changing. The significant change in the politics of Punjab came from the fact that Montagu–Chelmsford reforms gave a bigger share to the rural Punjab in the power set up. The leadership accordingly shifted to the landed rural elite, which was friendlier to the British Raj. This was in conflict with the Congress strategy to keep the anti-colonial movement united. In this pursuit they 'set up a unitary party structure to control the Congress provincial governments.' Historian Robin Moore is quoted here by David Page as having stated that: 'Instead of the Congress provincial ministries operating as autonomous governments within the federal structure they accepted the Congress working committee as the legitimate directorate of a unitary government.'⁴

In a parallel development, the Muslim League too was ruled by Jinnah, leaving little room for decision-making with the League's provincial chapters. This aspect of Jinnah's centralization of power during the movement and after Pakistan gained independence will be discussed in the next chapter. Under the Government of India Act 1935, the British had retained power in Delhi, which in turn led the Congress to consolidate the powers in the party's centre. In response, the Muslim League came out with the 'two-nation theory' to protect the ruling elite of Muslim majority provinces and the jobs in the Muslim-minority provinces.

The Congress rejected the Government of India Act 1935 and demanded that a new Constituent Assembly be elected through adult franchise to frame the new Constitution of India. The 1935 scheme, on the other hand, envisaged 'division of monolithic Raj into quasi-autonomous units'. 'The constitutionalization of the Congress "Unitarianism" alarmed the Princes.'[5] The principalities wanted an Indian confederation with maximum autonomy. The Congress position was also alarming for the Muslims of India who ruled the Muslim majority areas. Although it was a good opportunity for them to join hands with the princes for attaining maximum autonomy, they did not pursue it. They seemed to be more interested in chasing the same objective on the basis of a communal slogan.

The pressure of Indian independence movement compelled the British government to reluctantly agree to partial autonomy in the Government of India Act 1935. However, whatever powers that were given to the provinces with one hand were taken back with the other by giving excessive powers to the governor of the province, who was to be appointed by the federal government.

The Indian Congress was not satisfied with the provisions of the act and felt that it would weaken the control of the central leadership on their provincial leaderships. On the other hand, the Muslim League leadership began to feel that even if they might be able to get limited powers in the Muslim majority areas under the 1935 Act, they would eventually be controlled first by the British Viceroy and then by the Congress administration after the transfer of power.

Notes and References

1. Ainslie T. Embree (editor), *Sources of Indian Tradition*, Vol. 2, Columbia University Press, New York, 1988.
2. David Page, *Prelude to Partition of India: The Indian Muslims and the Imperial System of Control 1920-1933*, Oxford University Press, India, 1999.
3. Ibid.
4. Ibid.
5. Ibid.
6. Ref: D.C.No.F.79/96/39, Pub Source: IOR: R/20/B/1591, documents in the British Library, London.

Chapter 3

TURNING POINT – AIML ELECTION DEFEAT

'The problem in India is not of an inter-communal character, but manifestly of an international one, and it must be treated as such .... If the British Government are really in earnest and sincere to secure [the] peace and happiness of the people of this sub-continent, the only course open to us all is to allow the major nations separate homelands by dividing India into "autonomous national states".'

The defeat of the Muslim League in the 1937 elections in most of the Muslim-majority areas led the party to rely more on the religious slogan to gather support of the Muslim masses. The autonomy movement was generally seen as a desire of the Muslim elite to gain power in their respective provinces. But once the religious leaders were approached with the warning that in an independent India they would not be able to live according to Islamic tenets, the Muslim League started getting the support of the pirs (the descendants of sufi saints who command influence on the followers) and religious leaders. The only opposition came from the Deoband school of thought – Jamiat-e-Ulama-e-Hind (JUH) – and Maulana Abdul Ala Maududi, twentieth century influential Islamist thinker. This was an unconvincing warning, because the Muslims had been living and flourishing in undivided India according to their religious norms and rituals for hundreds of years. Even today over 150 million Muslims are living and flourishing in India.

The concept of being a nation on the basis of religion is also in conflict with the history of Muslim rule in India as the Muslim invaders fought each other to gain control over it. If religion made people one nation, then why did they invade each other? At the same time these invasions of the sultanate of the same Islamic faith contradicts some biased Muslim historians' claim that India was conquered by Muslims to spread Islam. The Ghoris took over from the Ghaznavis and the Mughal Babur ousted the Lodhis. Was this to spread Islam?

A realistic view of the history of the Muslim invasions of India shows that their primary motive always was to exploit the economic wealth of the subcontinent, and hence, imperialistic. But this view is not shared by the majority of Muslims of South Asia even to this day. We will come back to this later in the chapter.

In Pakistan children are taught in schools that all Muslim invaders are heroes of Islamic history. For instance, even today the first Muslim invasion of Sindh in AD 712 by a 17-year-old general, Muhammad bin Qasim, is celebrated by the government. (At one such function where I was present, the eminent Sindhi intellectual Ali Ahmed Brohi noted that Qasim was made a general at the age of 17 only because he was the cousin of the Governor of Baghdad Al-Hajjaj ibn Yusuf, 'a clear case of nepotism in today's parlance'.) An attempt by a Sindhi nationalist poet and intellectual, Shaikh Ayaz, to eulogies Raja Dahar, who defended Sindh against this Arab invasion, was strongly criticized by all the Right-wing and pro-government intellectuals and officials. The history books in the syllabi of Pakistan amply demonstrate how the children are being imbibed with a distorted and biased version of history. Even non-Muslim invaders are glorified in the history books of the curriculum. Alexander is referred to as 'Alexander the Great', while the Punjabi Raja Porus, who defended Punjab, is treated indifferently.

Educationist Farzana Shaikh has referred to the two contradictory views of history: 'From the outset, the Muslim League campaigned for the protection of Muslim interests and openly questioned the validity of Indian nationalism .... Armed with opposing versions of Indian history and contrasting interpretation of significance of lines of social differences, they juxtaposed Indian nationalism against a Muslim community. Integral to this tension was the questionable privileging of an all-inclusive secular Indian nationalism over the exclusionary concerns of a Muslim communalism associated with narrow religious dogma.'[1]

The demand for a separate homeland for the Muslims of India was not raised during the 1857 uprising. For them it was a religious movement to begin with. What sparked the revolt was the news that the new bullets supplied to the sepoys were laced with pork fat. On the other hand, the Hindu and Sikh uprising was against the British rule. When the two strands of the movement converged into a war for independence, it was not for establishing a Muslim rule. The 'two-nation theory' did not exist at that time. The movement was suppressed by the British not without the support of many Muslim soldiers who did not side with the revolt. For many Muslim, Hindu and Sikh soldiers, the British Raj was just a change of masters and a matter of who paid better remuneration. It was substituting one invader of India with another.

Well-known Indian Researcher A. M. Zaidi maintains that after the 1857 uprising, 'two strands of Muslim thought diametrically opposite to each other emerged.' On the one side were ulema, Muslim religious scholars, who were inspired by Shah Waliullah and despised Western culture. His followers' 'hatred against [sic] the British and the Western culture became more pronounced and they laid [the] foundation of a school at Deoband (UP) for the propagation of their religious and political creed .... On the other side, Sir Syed Ahmed [Ahmad] Khan was able to read the signs of the time and could foresee the coming domination of Western civilization over his country.' These two strands of Muslim thought have worked in parallel – sometimes in collision and sometimes antagonistically – ever since Pakistan came into being. But the chink in Sir Syed's armour was that he tried to keep the Muslims away from the Congress, thus sowing the seeds of segregation between the Muslims and the Hindus. The idea of majoritarianizm was uppermost in the minds of the leaders of both strands of Muslim thought.

'Sir Syed formed the [United] India[n] Patriotic Association in 1888 and was asked to consider forming the All India Muslim Political Organization in 1893 with Agha Khan as the leader. In the process, Mohammedan Anglo-Oriental Defence Association was formed.'[2]

The decision by the British Raj to partition Bengal in 1905, after consulting the Dacca Muslim elite, provoked protest throughout India. The Muslim elite immediately welcomed this decision as it gave them an upper hand in the politics of the new province of East Bengal. This British move was intriguing as it divided the province that had the same language, history, culture (except for some religious rituals) and ethnicity on the basis of religion. Though the real motive was not made clear by the British, implicitly they showed the Muslims a path towards dividing India on communal lines. It was no coincidence that the British consulted the Nawab of Dacca, Sir Khwaja Salimullah Bahadur before the partition of Bengal. And after it was partitioned a delegation of the Muslims met the viceroy, Lord Minto, where they were assured that 'the political rights and interests of the Muslim minority would be safeguarded.'[3] This encouragement exposed the British motive, which was to divide the Indian anti-colonial movement.

Establishment of the AIML on 30 December 1906 by the Dacca elite and the subsequent division of Bengal was encouraged by Lord Minto (aka George Elliot-Murray Kynymound). It was presided by Nawab Viqarul Mulk, a prominent politician. The exclusionary demand to have a separate electorate was subsequently accepted by the British in 1909. The sequence of these events strengthens the case that the British policy to divide and rule eventually led to the division of India. The Muslim elite used the British need to win over the minority against the majority, who were leading the anti-colonial movement.

The Hindu rajas and Muslim nawabs who joined the freedom movement were also apprehensive about the British policies, which they perceived would lead to centralization of power. According to Professor Judith M. Brown:'The clearest contrast before and after 1947 was in the goals of the government. British rule had obviously been in the British interest – financial, strategic and in terms of expatriates careers …. The government was moreover aware that any major attempt to manage and intervene in society or the economy was both expensive and possibly dangerous if it touched religious and cultural sensibilities. However, the Second World War changed this non-interventionist stance. In order to mobilize Indian resources for the world-wide war efforts the British government in India became far more intrusive and directive of the economy; and British India officials, businessmen and politicians all began to think about a future pattern of industrialization and government planning and management of the economy …. To achieve this it had to tackle problems which the colonial regime would have never dared to touch – from reform of landholding, to abolition of the practice of treating those at the base of Hindu society as "untouchable", and change in the legal status and treatment of women.'[4]

The cultural changes regarding 'untouchables' and women were the need of an industrializing economy as it expanded the labour availability, which in turn helped in keeping the wages down. The

British colonization of India was to serve its rising industrial economy. They had brought with them a more centralized and oppressive taxation system – railways to carry the raw material from remote areas to the ports for shipping them to Britain, and the communication technology that helped in having a stronger control from Delhi. The introduction of organized state structure of an industrialized nation did upset the rulers of both Hindu and Muslim states. The transformation took away power from the rulers who had until now enjoyed its devolution.

This point is also underlined by the well-regarded intellectual and the co-founder of the Council of Social Sciences (Pakistan), Dr C. Inayatullah: 'After the end of the Muslim rule the limited political links between the Muslim elite and the masses snapped, the elite was becoming highly demoralized and disoriented. In such a situation up to the end of 19th century Muslim elite did form associations for educational reforms but not political parties ...'[5]

Writer Shahid Kardar also touched on the issue of the changing style of governance: 'The British, because of their own peculiar circumstances as colonizers, had installed a well-greased administratively efficient centralized system. These decision making structures and institutions are retained after political independence in complete contrast to one of the fundamental desires of the movement to create [a] Federal State.'[6]

The maximum autonomy agenda of the Muslim elite of India was reiterated by Jinnah many times at different forums: Jinnah's presidential address on 23 March 1940 epitomized the demand: 'The problem in India is not of an inter-communal character, but manifestly of an international one, and it must be treated as such .... If the British Government are really in earnest and sincere to secure [the] peace and happiness of the people of this sub-continent, the only course open to us all is to allow the major nations separate homelands by dividing India into "autonomous national states".'[6]

For example in Sindh, which was conquered by the British in mid-nineteenth century, the economic policies introduced by the Raj provoked the Sindhi feudal ruling class against the new rulers. These policies sowed the seeds of communal politics in the province as the balance of power between the Muslim elite and the rising Hindu mercantile and professional class began to shift. According to Dr Tanvir Ahmad Tahir, a researcher: 'The new rent receiving landlords, moneylenders, and businessmen came to form the middle class that emerged mainly from the Hindu community .... The Sindhi Muslims were essentially rural based community [and had] failed to avail the opportunity of socio-economic advancement offered by the British period.'[7]

The Sindhi rural elite, which had ruled the province as late as 1843, when the province was annexed by the British after the Talpurs lost the battle at Miani, were eager to regain control of their province. They resented the British move to merge Sindh with Bombay Presidency in 1847 and the imposition of Land Alienation Act. The merger took away the seat of power from Sindh to Bombay and increased the control of the Hindu urban classes; and the land act enabled the transfer of the mortgaged land to Hindu money lenders. These two factors eventually pushed the Sindhi Muslims to join the provincial autonomy movement led by the AIML at that time. Sindh was the first province to opt for Pakistan through an Assembly resolution.

In the Punjab, the rural landed elite were won over by Muslim League to win the 1946 elections and defeat the Unionist Party. It had become weaker after the Second World War once its utility to the British Raj, which had recruited thousands of soldiers for the war from Punjab, had diminished. In the Punjab religious slogans played a major part in winning the support of the masses. The landed elite of Punjab were also afraid that in an independent India ruled by the Congress land reforms would force them to part with their feudal jagirs.[8]

Notes and References

1. Farzana Shaikh, *Making Sense of Pakistan*, Hurst & Company, London, 2009, p. 17.
2. A. M. Zaidi (editor), *Evolution of Muslim Thought in India from Syed to Jinnah*, *Vol. 1, Indian* Institute of Applied Political Research, New Delhi, 1997.
3. Ibid.
4. Judith M. Brown (professor of Commonwealth History, Oxford University), 'India – 1947: The Making of a Nation State', South Asia Archives Library Group (SAALG), *SAALG Newsletter*, 1997.
5. C. Inayatullah, *State and Democracy in Pakistan*, Vanguard, Lahore, 1997.
6. Shahid Kardar, 'Notes on National Unity and Regional Imbalances', in Iqbal Ahmed (editor), *Fresh Perspective on India and Pakistan*, Bougainvillea Books, England, 1985.

7. Manzooruddin Ahmed, 'Iqbal and Jinnah on the "Two-Nations" Theory' in C. M. Naim (editor), *Iqbal, Jinnah and Pakistan: The Vision and the Reality*, Maxwell School of Citizenship and Public Affairs, Syracuse University, 1979.
8. Tanvir Ahmad Tahir, *Political Dynamics of Sindh*, Pakistan Study Centre, Karachi, 2010.

Chapter 4

INDIAN MUSLIMS' INTERPRETATION
OF HISTORY

'... It is quite clear that Hindus and Mussalmans derive their inspiration from different sources of history. They have different epics, their heroes are different, and they have different episode[s]. Very often the hero of one is a foe of the other, and likewise, their victories and defeat overlap.'

As Islam was used by the Muslim leaders of the Pakistan movement, Pakistan's rulers are hard-pressed to justify the Muslim invasions. As mentioned above, in Pakistan the Muslim invaders are eulogized in history text books. Mehmood Ghaznavi, who invaded India seventeen times, is painted as a great hero. His plundering 'lashkars' (mercenary army), which included recruits from the northern tribal belt, are presented as the warriors of Islam (jihadis) who destroyed temples, although their basic intention was to share the booty collected from the inhabitants of the river valleys of India. Pakistan's national poet, Allama Muhammad Iqbal and Sir Syed's lieutenant Maulana Altaf Hussain Hali's poetry praised the invasions and conquests of the Muslim rulers anywhere in the world. This rationalization of Muslim invasions, now in Pakistan, is the natural outcome of the dangerous political formulation on which the formation of Pakistan is based.

Even Muhammad Ali Jinnah, who had stuck to the secular demand of getting more autonomy for the Muslim elite of India during most of the early period of his career, succumbed to the temptation of using the Iqbalian argument in his 23 March 1940 speech, while supporting the Pakistan Resolution. His contention raises more questions than it answers: 'The Hindus and the Muslims belong to two different religious philosophies, social customs, and literature[s]. They neither inter-marry [he himself married a Zoroastrian] nor inter-dine together and, indeed, they belong to two different civilizations which are based mainly on conflicting ideas and conceptions. Their aspects on life and of life are different. It is quite clear that Hindus and Mussalmans derive their inspiration from different sources of history. They have different epics, their heroes are different, and they have different episode[s]. Very often the hero of one is a foe of the other, and likewise, their victories and defeat overlap.'

What Jinnah stated in this speech was half truth. Indeed, as he pointed out, Islam and Hinduism have two different philosophies. But there were many social, cultural and linguistic similarities among the Hindu and Muslim communities. Similarly the literature of different languages was not divided on the basis of religious beliefs – Rabindranath Tagore and Kazi Nazarul Islam were equally revered by all Bengalis irrespective of their religion. Mirza Asadullah Khan Ghalib, Mir Taqi Mir, Munshi Premchand, Krishan Chander, Josh Malihabadi, Amir Khusro and many others were part of a common heritage. Many Sufi poets and saints were and even today are revered both by Hindus and Muslims with equal fervour.

It is an unfortunate aspect of our reading of history that while the Muslim invaders and revivalist writers such as Iqbal are raised sky-high by the Muslims, those who resisted the Muslim invaders are heroes of the Hindus and other natives of India. But, as stated earlier, history is full of Muslim invaders who conquered India or a part of it from other Muslim rulers. So who is the hero in this case? Thus, the whole logic has been built on flimsy grounds. However, such arguments were given to incite the Muslims and gain their support.

Indeed, invasions were the norm of history. Wars were fought and conquests in human history have always been made and perhaps would be made in future in the name of either spreading a religion or for some other moral justification. The most recent example is that of the US invasion of Iraq, which was justified in the name of destroying weapons of mass destruction. When the weapons were not found the US government did not even apologize to the people of Iraq. They only changed the objective and claimed that they had removed a tyrant – Saddam Hussein.

However, the international law governing inter-state relations values today does not support invasions any more. The Muslim history of invasions or events like the crusades or any other wars should be interpreted on the basis of prevailing values and not on the touchstone of medieval period. They could be understood in terms of the value systems prevailing in their time, but value systems cannot be static, hence they should be evaluated in our times' values and accordingly reacted to. An objective analysis of history shows that the underlying motive for waging a war has mostly been economic gains, and not spreading a divine message. Reinterpretation of history is important to save our children and society from disinformation. Their present-day sensibility and the value system propagated by the world have no room for invasion of another country.

It is because of this distorted view of history that the Muslims of undivided subcontinent never questioned the phenomenon of invasion and the rule of a small minority over majority. On the contrary, to justify the 'two-nation theory' they have to support these invasions in the subcontinent. Historians may argue that the invasions and Muslim rule should be judged in the perspective of the political and social norms of the period in which they are placed. Justifying the redundant values provides sufficient space to the traditionalists and retrogressive forces to justify their obscurantist practices. They draw their strength from their reading of history, and those who want to look at chronicled happenings in a historical context only are caught in the time web. History has to be interpreted to draw the lessons for the progress of humankind, not for academic interest only or for personal aggrandizement.

It was a confused Iqbal, who '[a]fter rejecting modern theories of nationalism, constructed his own theory of Islamic nationalism. For him, the Islamic community [Millat] founded in faith of oneness of God could be the only legitimate principle of integration among the Muslims.' According to activist-scholar Eqbal Ahmad, 'Iqbal's political philosophy had no room for either secularism or democracy of the West.'[2] Brookings Institution scholar Stephen Philip Cohen has rightly underlined this factor: 'Iqbal's idea of Pakistan was not based on a European model of a nation-state, but on "an acute understanding that political power was essential to the higher end of establishing God's laws," like many of his co-religionists, including those who set the stage for today's Islamic parties, Iqbal saw territorial nationalism as a step towards a larger Islamic community, a vehicle for the perfection of Islam.'[3]

This kind of thinking provides space to the ideologues of the Al Qaeda, who wants to use Afghanistan and Pakistan for furthering their higher end of establishing God's laws i.e., Islamic Sharia across the world. Interestingly, Osama bin Laden said: 'I was ordered to fight the people until they say there is no god but Allah, and his prophet is Muhammed.' Notice how the initial political formulations that were used as a 'means' are holding people of Pakistan their hostage.

The Muslim leadership, which evolved the 'two-nation theory' did not dream it on one scary evening. The theory evolved over a period of time: From Sir Syed Ahmad Khan's attempt to prepare the Muslims for coming to terms with the British rulers and maintaining their position in the changing India, which was being transformed to meet the needs of a capitalist colonial structure; to the establishment of Muslim League in 1906 by the Muslim elite to plead their case to British that their share in power was shrinking and hence, it should be protected; to contesting the Muslim League case by Muhammad Ali Jinnah once he accepted the brief and pleaded that Muslims of India would be marginalized in a democratic India.

Initially as president of Muslim League, Jinnah endorsed these four points in 1927: [4]

1. Constitution of Sindh as a separate province.
2. Introduction of reforms in the North West Frontier Province and Balochistan.
3. Guarantee of Muslim majority in Punjab and Bengal legislatures.
4. Reservation of at least one-third of the seats in the central legislature for the Muslims.

If we look at these demands and Jinnah's subsequent fourteen points, one finds that the demands were secular in nature, while the Muslim elite sought to protect their right to rule with little interference of the Central Government. This was the over-riding political objective that the Muslim of India wanted to achieve till quite late within the framework of India.

42

A number of writers have now convincingly proved that the Jinnah-led Muslim League was against the unitary form of the government, which they feared, and perhaps rightly so, would make the Centre too powerful. But this over-centralization was irritating for all the provinces of India and even today they are fighting for more space within the framework of the Indian Union.

On the other hand, there was Iqbal's dream, which he espoused in his 1930 Allahabad address, for a separate autonomous homeland 'within India' for the Muslims.

Like Jinnah, General Pervez Musharraf, the tenth president of Pakistan from 2001 to 2008, who was secular in his private life, also succumbed to the same confused theory of Iqbal. On the one hand, they talk of Jinnah's secular Pakistan, and on the other, they praise Iqbal's idea where religion and the state should not be separated. This is true in the case of most political parties. They have failed either to deliberately or unwittingly understand that the modern nation-state is much different in essence from what Iqbal proclaimed.

Jinnah contested the Muslim League case like an astute advocate and even accepted the 1946 Cabinet Mission Plan, perhaps not because he felt it would work out but as a tactical move to show the British that he was willing to accept Muslim autonomous states within the Indian federation. However, it is another matter that the expanse of the autonomy demanded by Muslim League would have made India a confederation and not a federation. 'As late as March 1946 the India Office prepared a scheme for a "confederal system" as an alternative to complete partition. The Cabinet Mission [on 16 May 1946] gave its verdict against partition and proposed a Centre that restricted powers.'[5]

The Cabinet Mission Plan was the accession of the Muslim League's demands and provided for a right to secede and grouping of Muslim provinces in 'B' and 'C'. The Congress after having accepted this plan retracted in July 1946 with an assertion that the Constituent Assembly would be supreme and not bound by the restriction of the Cabinet Plan. This rescinding of an earlier understanding closed the doors to making India a loose federation and made the partition inevitable. One of the foremost leaders of Indian freedom struggle and a renowned scholar and poet Maulana Abul Kalam Azad characterized the Congress stand as 'one of those unfortunate events that changed [the] course of history.' He was not convinced with the idea of Pakistan and made an interesting observation: 'I must confess that the very term Pakistan goes against my grain. It suggests that some portions of the world are pure while others are impure. Such a division of territories into pure and impure is un-Islamic ... has been built up on the analogy of the Jewish demand for a national home.'[6]

More recently, the Bharatiya Janata Party (BJP) leader Jaswant Singh also expressed similar views in an interview with Karan Thapar on CNN-IBN regarding his book *Jinnah: India, Partition, Independence*. He highlighted two facts: One, that 'Muhammad Ali Jinnah did not win Pakistan as Congress leaders Jawaharlal Nehru and Sardar Vallabhai [Vallabhbhai] Patel "conceded" Pakistan to the Quaid-e-Azam with the English acting as a helpful midwife'; and two, Jinnah was a secular man and 'not a Hindu basher' or 'Hindu hater'. Some Indian writers have observed that the 'two-nation theory was a political contingent proposition rather than any religious grounded proposition.'

Another brilliant historian, Ayesha Jalal, has also concluded that Jinnah did not want a separate Pakistan when he campaigned for the autonomous provinces within the framework of a Union. His was the secular view which had nothing to do with Pan-Islamism. According to her, Jinnah wanted a Pakistan and a Hindustan, which could jointly take stands in the hostile world. She is right to conclude that Pakistan happened because Jinnah had no control over other forces and 'thus Pakistan was the strategic collapse of Jinnah's strategy.'[7]

The Muslim problem was the case of autonomy in the Muslim majority areas and affirmative action in favour of the Muslims of the Muslim-minority provinces because the elite feared the majority. Through the course of history and follies of both the Muslim League and the Congress India was divided.

What is wrong with Pakistan cannot be objectively analyzed without reviewing the political history of Pakistan. We cannot diagnose the chronic disease of the country without its medical history and running diagnostic tests. In the following chapters we would analyze what are harmful effects of the chronic disease on Pakistan.

Notes and References

1. Muhammad Ali Jinnah's speech at the Lahore Session of the Muslim League, 23 March 1940. (*Source*: Ministry of Information and Broadcasting, Government of Pakistan, Islamabad, 1983.)
2. Iqbal Khan (editor), *Fresh Perspective on India and Pakistan*, Bougainvillea Books, England, 1986.
3. Stephen Philip Cohen, *The Idea of Pakistan*, Brookings Institution Press, Washington, 2004.
4. A. C. Banerjee, *Two Nation Theory: The Philosophy of Muslim Nationhood*, Concept Publishing Company, New Delhi, 1981.
5. Ibid.
6. Maulana Abul Kalam Azad, *Indian Wins Freedom*, Orient Longman, Hyderabad, 1960.
7. Ayesha Jalal, *The sole Spokesman: Jinnah, the Muslim League, and the Demand for Pakistan*, Cambridge University Press, New York, 1985.

PART - II

Chapter 5

Objective Betrayed

Jinnah failed to fathom the ethno-linguistic diversity of the Pakistan he made, as he was no political scientist but simply an astute lawyer who believed strongly in his brief that Muslims were a nation. This led him to deny the existence of many nationalities in the country, which had emerged from tribalism to form the feudal national identity in their own right.

All through the movement for the economic and political rights of the Muslims of India the primary objective, as explained in chapter 1 was to get autonomy for the Muslim majority provinces and principalities, and better representation for the Muslims of the provinces where they were in a minority. Whether it was the Fourteen Points of Jinnah or the Pakistan Resolution of 1940, which became the manifesto of the AIML, the emphasis was on political and economic rights. First, Jinnah's Fourteen Points:

1. The form of the future Constitution should be federal with the residuary powers vested in the provinces.
2. A uniform measure of autonomy shall be granted to all provinces.
3. All legislatures in the country and other elected bodies shall be constituted on the definite principle of adequate and effective representation of minorities, in every province without reducing the majority in any province to a minority or even equality.

49

4. In the Central Legislative, Muslim representation shall not be less than one-third.

5. Representation of communal groups shall continue to be by means of separate electorate as at present, provided, it shall be open to any community at any time, to abandon its separate electorate in favour of a joint electorate.

6. Any territorial distribution that might at any time be necessary shall not in any way affect the Muslim majority in the Punjab, Bengal and the North-West Frontier Province (NWFP).

7. Full religious liberty, i.e., liberty of belief, worship and observance, propaganda, association and education, shall be guaranteed to all communities.

    (This was a secular clause, which was not much different from what was on agenda of the All India Congress).

8. No bill or any resolution or any part thereof shall be passed in any legislature or any other elected body, if three-fourths of the members of any community in that particular body oppose such a bill resolution or part thereof on the ground, that it would be injurious to the interests of that community or in the alternative, such other method is devised as may be found feasible and practicable to deal with such cases.

    (Once Pakistan was made no such right was given to the religious minority. Pakistan's Constitution has many clauses, which could have been opposed by the minorities if they were given the same power that the Muslim League demanded in the 14 points).

9. Sindh should be separated from the Bombay presidency.

10. Reforms should be introduced in the NWFP and Balochistan on the same footing as in the other provinces.

11. Provision should be made in the Constitution giving Muslims an adequate share, along with the other Indians, in all the services of the state and in the local self-governing bodies, having (giving) due regard to the requirements of efficiency.

12. *The Constitution should embody adequate safeguards for the protection of Muslim culture and for the protection and promotion of Muslim education, language, religion, personal laws and Muslim charitable institutions and for their due share in the grants-in-aid given by the state and by local self-governing bodies.* (Author's emphasis.)

13. No cabinet, either Central or provincial, should be formed without there being a proportion of at least one-third Muslim ministers.

14. No change shall be made in the Constitution by the Central Legislature except with the concurrence of the state's contribution of the Indian Federation.

This shows that only point 12 had demanded Muslims' religious freedom and protection. Similarly, the Pakistan Resolution's operative part demanded almost a confederation of the Muslim majority areas with India. The resolution was clear: 'No constitutional plan would be workable or acceptable to the Muslims unless geographical contiguous units are demarcated into regions which should be so constituted with such territorial readjustments as may be necessary. That the areas in which the Muslims are numerically in majority as in the North-Western and Eastern zones of India should be grouped *to constitute independent states in which the constituent units shall be autonomous and sovereign.'* (Author's emphasis, since it laid the foundation of almost a confederation arrangement.)

In a meeting on 23 June 1947, when the then chief of Indian Army, General Sir R. M. Lockhart asked Jinnah about the future Muslim League's policies, Jinnah told him: 'except for defence, foreign affairs and communications and perhaps one or two other subjects common to all provinces which would be controlled from the centre, provinces would have complete provincial autonomy.'[1]

The Muslim League leadership treated the provinces just as administrative units. There was no understanding that the provinces of India were based more or less on their respective ethno-linguistic identity which, most sociologists agree, are stronger than the religious ties. But contrary to the basic understanding of the socio-political structure, the irony is that once Pakistan was carved out of the sub-continent on the basis of Muslim majority provinces, the founders of Pakistan conveniently betrayed the basic objective of the whole movement.

Instead of giving maximum autonomy to the provinces, they centralized all powers. The rhetoric that the Muslims of India were one nation and as poet and politician Muhammad Iqbal, also known as

Allama Iqbal, had put it 'one ummah'*, took over the leaders. There was no understanding of the fact that Pakistan was a multi-ethnic and multi-structural society. The complexities of the different ethno-linguistic groups were over-simplified in the thesis that the Muslims of India were one nation, hence can be ruled under a centralist government. The Muslim ethnicity was artificial and temporary as it was based on the fear factor that once the one-man-one-vote democracy was introduced the Muslims would be at a disadvantage. This fear was not entirely misplaced. But it was exaggerated.

Muslims have flourished and expanded in many countries in which they are a minority. As a matter of fact, given a chance, a great number of Pakistanis today would prefer to migrate to the West for economic gains, leaving the so-called fortress of Islam and would be willing to live as a Muslim minority. Once Pakistan was made the 'fear thesis' of competition with the Hindu majority and other minorities of India was no more available for political exploitation Muslim ethnicity dissolved and the ethno-linguistic contradictions presented a new anti-thesis to the leadership.

Another challenge was homogeneous development of the country which was multi-structural – tribal, feudal and capitalist at the same time. Instead of resolving this contradiction by developing a new synthesis of equitable federating units, the leadership tried to suppress it. Stephen P. Cohen has pointed out: 'The leaders of the new state assumed that Jinnah's leadership and common faith would override any difference between the major ethno-linguistic groups. This was the real concern since support of Pakistan was tepid among Sindhis, Pakhtuns, and Baluch.'[2]

He was right. The Sindhis, who supported the Pakistan resolution in the Provincial Assembly led by G. M. Syed, realized before the country was made that Jinnah believed in a strong central control. The Pakhtuns were divided as the Frontier Gandhi, Khan Abdul Ghaffar Khan, had not supported a referendum with two options only. In Balochistan, the Muslim League party was led by a Pakhtun, Qazi Muhammad Essa. Young Nawab Akbar Shahbaz Khan Bugti was the only major

*Ummah in Arabic means nation or community. It is a synonym for *ummat al-Islamiyah* (the Islamic nation), and it is commonly used to mean the collective community of Islamic peoples. Source: Wikipedia.

tribal Baluch leader who supported the idea of Pakistan as they had no Hindu threat. As a matter of fact, the Khan of Kalat, Ahmad Yar Khan (1933–55) wanted the suzerainty that they had surrendered to the British under a treaty to be given back to him.

Even in the Punjab, the leadership jumped on to Pakistan bandwagon at the last moment, once creation of this country looked inevitable to the big Muslim landlords, and the public pressure was created by Muslim League through religious leaders and pirs. One of the major factors for supporting the Pakistan demand was that the feudal class of Bengal, Punjab and Sindh could see the red herring of land reforms in the socialistic manifesto of the Congress. They brought their middle classes and peasants along who were carried away by the religious slogans and hoped to get freedom from Hindu money lenders. The Muslim salariats wanted to take a bigger share in jobs and professions, which were dominated by Hindus.

To begin with, the supreme leader of the Muslim League, Muhammad Ali Jinnah, bade farewell to the idea of a real federation when he decided to be the all-powerful first governor-general of Pakistan, while in India Jawaharlal Nehru chose to be the prime minister keeping in line with the federalist and parliamentary tradition. Jinnah's step vested all powers in the hands of the top executive post, which was not directly responsible to the Constituent Assembly. As Syed has shown, Jinnah was empowered to adapt and modify any part of the 1935 India Act up to 31 March 1948 (later this date was extended by one year); the advice of ministers was not binding on him; he could overrule even the prime minister's orders .... Syed also uses the term "vice-regal system" to describe the centralization."[3]

Another shock for the provinces of the newly formed Pakistan was that of 'a new section 92A in the Constitution issued by the orders of the Governor-General, which empowered him [Jinnah] to dismantle the provincial administration in an "emergency", and establish the rule.'[4] This section was frequently used for dissolving the provincial governments of Sindh in 1951, the Punjab in 1953 and in Bengal in 1954.

Jinnah failed to fathom the ethno-linguistic diversity of the Pakistan he made, as he was no political scientist but simply an astute lawyer who believed strongly in his brief that Muslims were a nation. This led him to deny the existence of many nationalities in the country, which had emerged from tribalism to form the feudal national identity in their own right. They had a history of thousands of years before converting to Islam. These provinces were broadly based on an ethnic and linguistic basis and not on administrative. They also had provincial governments with required bureaucracies. It is therefore a distortion of history to claim that the peoples of Pakistan had no expertise to manage the affairs of their respective provinces on the eve of the partition of India. But Jinnah was almost allergic to the idea of multi-nationalities. He proclaimed: 'What we want, is not talk about Bengali, Punjabi, Sindhi, Baluchi, Pathan and so on. They are of course units. But I ask you: have you forgotten that lesson that was taught us thirteen hundred years ago. You have carved out a territory, a vast territory. It is all yours: it does not belong to a Punjabi, or a Sindhi or a Pathan or Bengali. It is all yours. You have got your central government where several units are represented. Therefore, if you want to build yourself up into a nation, for God's sake give up the provincialism.'[5]

The founders wanted to build a Pakistani nation at the cost of denying the reality that the country was composed of five major nationalities living within its boundary. And whenever, till this day, this reality hits the ruling establishment in the shin, they react sharply and sometimes violently. Military operations in Balochistan manifest this myopic approach. While mainstream politicians have started realizing the importance of autonomy for the federating units, the establishment still fails to understand that it is the denial of the due rights to the provinces that makes the federation weaker.

We have seen that in the case of the separation of East Pakistan, the denial that Pakistan is a multi-ethnic country was not just because of lack of political and social understanding; it was to promote the interest of the Punjabi–Mohajir* ruling classes. This approach was also the biggest impediment in the making of the Constitution for almost seven years after independence. The Pakistan Provisional Constitution Order 1947 was based on the 1935 India Act. Under this order, Pakistan was federal in name only; it concentrated powers in the Centre leaving little space for the provincial governments. Author Mehrunnisa Ali underlined this

*Mohajirs are immigrants who came to Pakistan from India after the Partition in 1947. It has been adopted by the Urdu- and- Gujarati-speaking population as a nomenclature to identify themselves.

fact: 'The interim Constitution established a highly centralized federal system in Pakistan as the Government of India Act 1935, adopted by the British government with colonial objectives, had provided for a strong centre. The central government's sphere was so strong that for all practical purposes, the country's governmental structure could hardly be described as truly federal.'[6]

As stated above, the long-term ramifications of the political formulation that Muslims of India were one nation were that the existence of different nationalities was denied, which, in fact, led to the separation of East Pakistan; four insurgencies for independence in Balochistan; a feeling of deprivation in Sindh, to the extent that, though weak, there is a separation demand by the Sindhi nationalists; and Pakhtunkhwa is under the fire of Islamic militants.

Reformist-writer and activist, known for his work on liberation theology in Islam, Asghar Ali Engineer has been less charitable while discussing the 'two-nation theory': 'The two-nation theory was deeply flawed and Jinnah formulated it as a sort of political revenge to [sic] the Congress leader Nehru.' This of course is the oversimplification of a complex political phenomenon, which had evolved since the mid-nineteenth century. He maintains that the 'two-nation theory was a political contingent proposition rather than any religious grounded proposition .... Jinnah opted for partition not as a part of his conviction but as political contingency.' For Jinnah it was like an advocate extending an argument to win the case although he may not believe it. His shortsighted political vision, in spite of the monocle he wore, was not able to view the consequences of his argument. And thus the baby he conceived is in pain to get rid of its genetic defect.

In the following chapters, I briefly review how the 'two-nation theory' and the slogan of an Islamic state impacted the provinces of Pakistan.

Notes and References

1. *The Transfer of Power*, Vol. XII (Sir R. M. Lockhart's Communication to Mountbatten), HMSO (Her Majesty's Stationery Office), London, 1983.
2. Stephen Philip Cohen, *The Idea of Pakistan*, Vanguard Books, Lahore, 2005, p. 203.
3. Mohammad Waseem, *Politics and State in Pakistan*, Progressive Publishers, Lahore, 1989, p. 94.

4. Ibid.
5. Akbar S. Ahmed, *Jinnah, Pakistan and Islamic identity: The Search for Saladin*, Routledge, London, 1977, p. 236.
6. Mehrunnisa Ali, *Politics of Federalism in Pakistan*, Royal Book Company, Karachi, 1966.

Chapter 6

BANGLADESH – A COLONY LOST

What Jinnah did not understand was that Bengali was the language of 54 per cent of Pakistanis and had a history older than that of Urdu. It was naïve to think that Bengali could be relegated to a secondary position while Urdu, the language of 3 per cent Pakistanis, could be given the status of the national language. It was true that Urdu was the link language in the western part of Pakistan, and continues to play this role effectively, but there was no harm in having two or more national languages. After all, India declared that all the major languages had a status equal to that of the national language.

The most painful example that illuminates the point that Jinnah's Muslim League betrayed the basic objective of the creation of Pakistan is the narrative of the separation of East Pakistan from Pakistan.

For a good 24 years after the creation of Pakistan, the ruling Punjabi–Mohajir establishment of Pakistan ruled East Pakistan as a colony. The Muslim League, Jinnah and the first prime minister of Pakistan, Nawabzada Liaquat Ali Khan, included, had no idea about the rights of the strong ethno-linguistic identity and consciousness of the nationalities residing in Pakistan. They also forgot that the Muslim elite of all the Muslim majority areas had supported the Pakistan movement for greater autonomy because they feared domination by a Hindu-dominated Centre. The theory, that all were one 'big happy Muslim nation' had overwhelmed them, and as a result they undermined the ground realities.

In the case of East Bengal, and in all other federating units, the Muslim League leaders joined hands with the big landlords and the Muslim aristocracy. The popular nationalist ethos of the peoples of the five provinces was not only ignored but also suppressed. If there was a voice of dissent, it was brow-beaten and labelled as a conspiracy inspired by the Indians and communists.

They misunderstood the fact that the division of Bengal by British viceroy, Lord George Nathaniel Curzon, after conspiring with the Muslim 'Ashrafia' (elite) in 1905, meant that the Muslim Bengalis were Muslims first and Bengalis later. It was a move to divide the people of Bengal and win the support of the Muslim Bengalis for the Raj, which was also in the interest of Muslim Bengalis, who felt deprived with the rising control of Hindus in government jobs and business. Lord Curzon toured East Bengal and addressing the Muslim landlords in Dacca at a lavish appointed assemblage he said in a lengthy speech that Bengal's partition would yield untold benefits to the Muslim community. The official and semi-official press invoked the partition scheme to protect the Muslim interests from 'Hindu pre-eminence'.[1] It can thus be said that the idea of a separate Muslim homeland was conceived by Lord Curzon and not by Iqbal or Chaudhry Rahmat Ali.

As mentioned earlier it was no surprise that soon after Bengal was divided, the Muslim elite of Bengal moved to protect the economic rights of the Muslim elite and the Muslim middle classes – the people who were once the rulers of Bengal. In return, they offered full support to the British rule, while the rest of the Indians were struggling against the imperial power. But the struggle for regaining Muslim pre-eminence at the cost of the division of Bengal did not mean that the Bengalis of East Bengal, which later became East Pakistan, had given up their Bengali nationalism. The Muslim card was played as a means to get autonomy for the Muslim elite and jobs for the middle classes.

***

Soon after Pakistan was established the Muslim League leaders thought it appropriate to impose Urdu as the only national language. The thinking at that time was, and it still exists in certain conservative circles, that Pakistan is one nation and hence should have one national language

– Urdu. Prime Minister Liaquat Ali Khan asserted in February 1948: 'Pakistan has been created because of the demand of a hundred million Muslims in this subcontinent and the language of [the] hundred million Muslims is Urdu.'[2] This was not acceptable to the Bengalis although many East Pakistani Urdu-speaking Ashrafia leaders also tried to sell the idea. It was strongly opposed by the Bengali middle classes, particularly the students.

Presuming that his charisma would work, Muhammad Ali Jinnah jumped into this debate, and on 21 March 1948 declared at the Race Course Maidan: 'Let me tell you in the clearest language that there is no truth that your normal life is going to be touched or disturbed so far as your Bengali language is concerned. But ultimately it is for you, the people of this Province, to decide what shall be the language of your province. But let me make it clear to you that the state language of Pakistan is going to be Urdu and no other language. Anyone who tries to mislead you is really an enemy of Pakistan. Without one state language, no nation can remain tied up solidly together and function.'[3] Instead of accepting the verdict of the governor-general, the Bengalis who had come to hear Jinnah went back enraged and rampaged on the way back.

What Jinnah did not understand was that Bengali was the language of 54 per cent of Pakistanis and had a history older than that of Urdu. It was naïve to think that Bengali could be relegated to a secondary position while Urdu, the language of 3 per cent Pakistanis, could be given the status of the national language. It was true that Urdu was the link language in the western part of Pakistan, and continues to play this role effectively, but there was no harm in having two or more national languages. After all, India declared that all the major languages had a status equal to that of the national language.

This was not just a provincial issue as Jinnah tried to explain. It was an issue vital for the people of East Bengal because they would have been placed in a disadvantageous position in competition with the Punjabi and Mohajir West Pakistanis, who had better understanding and command of Urdu. (But history was to show another side to the protagonists of both Urdu and Bengali – the economic value of English as the official language instead of Urdu and Bengali.)

This clearly meant supremacy of Urdu, over peoples of other nationalities residing in Pakistan, who spoke different languages. The

Bengalis were not prepared to accept this and continued protests, which took a violent turn on 21 February 1952 when the state government opened fire on the protesting students and, according to different accounts, seven to nine students died and several were injured. The attempt by the students to construct a memorial (Shaheed Minar) was also foiled, though eventually, the government had to give in. This memorial was also a rallying point for Bengali nationalists even during the liberation war against Pakistan.

***

After giving the East Bengalis its 'Shaheed Minar', now a symbol of nationalist struggle, it was finally agreed in the third draft of the Constitution in 1954 that Bengali and Urdu would be the official languages of the country. 'At the same time it provided for the use of English as the "official language of the country for twenty years".'[4] But it was an expensive trade off for the Bengalis as they had to accept the perfidious idea of 'one unit', thereby giving away their majority in the Assembly. Not only that, once all of West Pakistan was declared one province, what was called East Bengal in the official documents until 1954 was renamed East Pakistan. Commenting on the 'one unit', Shaikh Maqsood Ali, who served as a civil servant in Pakistan and Bangladesh, summed it well: 'The Bengalis suspected further that to prevent them from playing their due role in the politics of former Pakistan, the design of the West Pakistani power elite was to isolate East Bengal from the minority provinces of West Pakistan through consolidation of the four provinces of West Pakistan into "One Unit". Presumably, the West Pakistani feudal-military-bureaucratic power elite feared that without a One Unit, Bengalis would come as a united group, by winning the support of the minority provinces and by isolating Punjab, they would have sufficient majority to rule Pakistan.'[5]

This was the precise fear of the political leader Zulfikar Ali Bhutto, who represented the interest of the Punjab, as a result of having secured from this province a majority of seats in the 1970 election. After the break-up of the One Unit the election results had thrown up a leadership in the NWFP and Balochistan, which supported maximum autonomy for the federating units of the country. Leaders like Wali Khan and Ghaus Bakhsh Bizenjo showed an inclination to side with the Awami League. Many West Pakistani leaders had opposed boycott of the Constituent

Assembly that was suggested by Bhutto and demanded that power should be transferred to the Awami League. These leaders included two former air chiefs of Pakistan – Air Marshal Asghar Khan and Air Marshal Nur Khan; the former at that time was the head of Tehrik-e-Istiqlal Pakistan (TIP) and the latter was the leader of Muslim League (Council). The leaders of the two major religious parties, Mufti Mahmood of the Jamiat-e-Ulama-e-Islam (JUI) and Maulana Shah Ahmad Noorani of the Jamiat-e-Ulama Pakistan (JUP) said Pakistan was lost when Bhutto said it was saved after the postponement of the Assembly session. Jamaat-e-Islami (JI), however, sided with the military and its militant wing was involved in the pogrom of the Bengalis.

Even Sindh, where Bhutto was short by two seats in the Provincial Assembly, would have most probably voted for Sheikh Mujibur Rahman on his autonomy agenda. (It was only after the liberation of Bangladesh that independent candidates crossed over to the Pakistan People's Party – PPP.) Strong nationalist feelings and unrelenting struggle against the One Unit was fresh in the memories of Sindhis, which was evident by the widespread feeling among Sindhi-speaking people against the military operation in East Pakistan, and even when India entered East Pakistan to support the liberation war the Sindhis had hardly any sympathy for the Pakistani forces. Living in Sukkur, I witnessed this support for Bengali nationalism. However, the Punjabi settlers and Mohajir were not even willing to hear the other side of the story.

Bhutto wanted to agree with Mujib to an autonomy formula outside the Constituent Assembly, just like Jinnah did with the Cabinet Mission. On the other hand, though insistent on his six-point agenda that helped his party, the Awami League, sweep all the seats in East Pakistan, Mujib, like Nehru, wanted to discuss it in the Constituent Assembly. The six points were the outcome of the long list of economic and political grievances of the Bengalis and were based on the original political formulation of the 1940 Pakistan Resolution, which clearly mentioned that Pakistan would comprise 'autonomous states'. The parliamentary committee of the Muslim League had quietly changed the plural 'states' to the singular 'state'. In 1946 this change was never accepted by the supporters of autonomy to this day.

The use of word 'provinces' in place of 'states' was either a conscious move or it just reflected the mindset of the Muslim League leadership, which wanted a strong West Pakistan-based Centre. Mujib had argued that in the USA, the USSR and India the federating units were called states, then why not in Pakistan? But the ruling elite have always given the impression that these provinces are basically administrative units and are not based on their ethno-linguistic identity. In his speech on 15 February 1971 in Peshawar, Bhutto announced the boycott of the first session of the newly elected Constituent Assembly, unless Mujib agreed to negotiate on his six points before the session. He declared: 'We can't go there only to endorse the Constitution already prepared by a party and return humiliated.' He made it clear that he was willing to accept a 'two-subject centre'.[6] His main objection was against the separate currency demand, but he hoped that some arrangement could be arrived at the points about taxation and foreign trade.

The currency issue could have been solved to satisfy the Bengalis, who had seen transfer of capital from their province to West Pakistan for 24 years, by shifting the State Bank of Pakistan's head office to Dacca. Mujib had asked for two parallel reserve banks. To save the federation the transfer of the Pakistan State Bank, which serves as the reserve bank, and appointing a Bengali governor, was not a high cost. In any case, the capital of Pakistan should have been Dacca as majority of the population lived there. With maximum autonomy, as it was promised during the Pakistan movement, the need to travel to the federal capital would have been less. But Jinnah wanted his own hometown to be the capital and was supported by his party because it was dominated by the Mohajir and Punjabi elite.

***

A perfidious West Pakistani establishment ruled East Pakistan as a colony for 24 years (1947–71). Historians and political analysts have dug out reams of data, which show how East Pakistan was exploited by West Pakistani establishment. Let us take a cursory look at a few disparities:

> The total government expenditure in 20 years 1950–70 in Pakistan was US $30.95 billion, out of which West Pakistan extracted the lion's share of US $21.49 billion meaning over 69 per cent, while East Pakistan, despite having 55 per cent population, was doled out only US $9.45 billion, which was just 30.45 per cent of the total.

The Punjabi establishment did not accept the appropriation of government revenue in proportion to the population ratio as long as East Pakistan remained in the country. But once that half of the county was lost and in the remaining Pakistan the Punjab constituted 56 per cent of the population, its establishment was reminded that distribution on population was the best criterion.

This distribution of resources was in sharp contrast to the income generated by East and West Pakistan. All through the 24 years, East Pakistan had enjoyed foreign trade surplus. In a paper 'Why Bangladesh', a group of scholars in Vienna collected data from the government of Pakistan's official papers showing how East Pakistan was exploited by West Pakistan. Taking stock of the foreign trade they pointed out: 'In foreign trade East Pakistan exports constituted 59 per cent of the total but imports only 30 per cent of the total imports .... During the same period West Pakistan earned 41 per cent of the total foreign exchange and was allowed 70 per cent of the foreign exchange earnings.'[7]

While the surplus generated by East Pakistan was invested in the infrastructure and industry of West Pakistan, it was a secured market for the West Pakistani goods. For instance, between 1964 and 1969, West Pakistan exported goods worth Rs 5.29 billion to East Pakistan, while it imported goods worth Rs 3.17 billion. Of the total foreign assistance almost 80 per cent was consumed by West Pakistan. On the whole, again according to the Vienna Group, 77 per cent of the funds allocated for development went to West Pakistan in the first 20 years.

It was because of these policies that East Pakistan's population was disillusioned with the rule of the Punjab-dominated establishment. The net outflow of financial resources from East to West Pakistan led to the inclusion of a rather impractical demand of two separate but exchangeable currencies in the six points of the Awami League in March 1966. As the business classes of Pakistan had little say in the ruling elite, which comprised the feudal class and military-civil bureaucracy, an important economic factor was completely undermined. Not only all the major investments in the jute and paper industry in East Pakistan were owned by the big business houses of West Pakistan, East Pakistan was their undisputed market of over 50 million people. It was because of the loss of this colony that Pakistan had to devalue its currency by 135 per cent in 1972, and as a result its textile and consumer industry had a great fall.

***

The East Bengal middle classes were also bitter because of their meagre share in government services. For example, by 1971 the share of 54 per cent of East Pakistan's Bengalis in the central civil services was 16 per cent; in foreign services, 15 per cent; in the army, out of total 17 generals, there was only one Bengali. And in Pakistan International Airlines (PIA), the state-owned airline, only 280 employees were from East Pakistan as against 7,000 from West Pakistan.

That was then. Today after 'the cruel birth of Bangladesh', 42 years ago, it seems the pain of economic and political exploitation of East Pakistan by the West Pakistan establishment is now a sad history. The wounds inflicted by a ten-month military operation in 1971 have healed, leaving some scars on the memory of the older generation. But all said and done, even today in the background interviews done by me, most of the Bengali intellectuals and businessmen were of the view that East Pakistan would not have separated had power been given to Awami League. They also believed that Mujib was willing to give concessions on some of the six points, but in the Constituent Assembly and not outside, as opposed to what Bhutto wanted, because he (Mujib) was afraid of the wrath of his followers and compatriots.

Way back in 1956, Professor Hans J. Morgenthau of Chicago University wrote: 'Pakistan is not a nation and hardly a state. It has no justification in history, ethnic origin, language, civilization or the consciousness of those who make up its population. They have no interest in common save: fear of Hindu domination …. West Pakistan belongs essentially to Middle East and has more in common with Iran or Iraq than that with East Bengal. East Bengal, in turn, with a population which is one third Hindu is hardly distinguishable from West Bengal which belongs to India.'[8]

***

Why not join India? Though much of this observation is true even today, the question remains, why did the people of East Pakistan not join West Bengal of India after liberation in 1971? The supporters of the 'two-nation theory' use this as proof that Muslims of the subcontinent are a separate nation. This question had always bothered me, so I decided to put it to the businessmen and journalists I met during my visit to Bangladesh in 2010. The editor of *The News Today*, Reazuddin Ahmed explained that the people in East Pakistan were not willing to move from the subjugation of West Pakistan to that of India and West Bengal was not interested in separating from India. So there was not a possibility of having an independent state comprising East and West Bengal.

My take is that 'the Hindu fear' still lives on. A strong dislike for India's big brother attitude also explains why Bangladesh did not join India, although its liberation war was supported militarily by the then prime minister, Indira Gandhi. On the other hand, she made no effort to annex Bangladesh. The extraneous reason for India not taking over Bangladesh was that it would have provoked international reaction, and both the Americans and the Soviets wanted India to do its job of helping the Bangladeshis and then get out of the new country. The internal reason was very important, but often underplayed by the Pakistani establishment to keep the 'India fear' alive, claiming that it was not in the interest of the Indian establishment to have the solid Muslim pockets within its fold. As it is at present, Muslims of India constitute around 15 per cent of the country's population, and it is often difficult to manage them.

What started as a protest against the postponement of the Constituent Assembly's first session on 3 March 1971, in which women members were to be elected, soon became the liberation struggle. The Bengali writers and the Mukti Bahini museum claim that over 250,000 people were killed by the Pakistan Army during the military operation, to defend the strong Centre proposition. Many Pakistanis place the number of killings as much lower. I probed General (retd.) Tikka Khan, when he was the secretary general of PPP during Bhutto's trial. To my observation that they shouldn't be talking about democracy because they had killed over 200,000 Bengalis in East Pakistan, his simplistic answer was: 'You people in the media always exaggerate such figures, only 35,000 Bengalis were killed during the military operations.' The generals of course are not trained to value human life whether it is 250,000 or 35,000, which is not a small figure either. The real figure of Bengalis killed by the Pakistan Army and Al-Badr and Al-Shams, the JI militant arms, may be somewhere between the two claims. This does not include the killings of the Biharis and West Pakistani civilians by the Mukti Bahini.

In spite of these killings the demand for liberation could not be suppressed. Many years ago Major (retd.) Arif Mehr narrated an incident with tears rolling down his cheeks. He said that he was one of the first platoon commanders who were sent out to quash the general strike against the postponement of the Assembly elections: 'Our commander told us that these bloody Bengalis are Indian agents and cannot fight. Go out and kill a few if they defy the writ of the government on the streets, and the protest will die down. When we went out on patrol the whole city was echoing with only one slogan "Joy Bangla". We fired and a couple of guys fell in one of the by-lanes, but the echo of the slogan did not die. At this point my junior non-commissioned officer from the back seat of our jeep, said in Punjabi "Sir-*ji, assi banday toh mar lawan gay per iss awaz noo kaun maray ga*?" [Sir, we can kill the people but who will kill this voice?].' Arif said: 'I told him to shut up, but now on hindsight I realized he was right.' Major Arif was one of the 90,000 Pakistanis who surrendered and was made a prisoner of war.

The mindset of the West Pakistani Punjabis and Mohajirs, particularly after the East Pakistan movement turned into a liberation war, was that anybody supporting them was either an Indian or a Russian agent. A local intelligence officer, Muhammad Tathir, opened files on a few of us as anti-state elements and many of our friends were arrested. But two years after the separation of East Pakistan, he met me and apologized saying: 'Son, you guys were right, we were losing the country and we thought you were foreign agents.' Alas, the realization was too late. A Punjabi poet Ahmad Salim wrote a powerful poem: '*Bootaan vaali Sarkaar*' (the government of the army boots), condemning the military operation and a communist leader Dr M. R. Hassan published it in his magazine *Awami Awaz* (people's voice). Both were arrested and tried before a summary military court. Both accepted bravely the full consequences of their views. They were jailed for one year.

During the military operation in 1971, there was a systematic killing of Hindus, which scared away many to India. Then again in 1992, the Islamic parties went on the rampage against the Hindus of Bangladesh, in reaction to the Babri Masjid demolition by the Hindu fundamentalists in India. (This sordid episode is recorded by Taslima Nasrin in her novel *Lajja*. She was hounded away by the fundamentalists from Bangladesh on frivolous charges of blasphemy. The actual fact, according to a senior Bangladeshi journalist, was that the Bhartiya Janata Party [BJP] in India tried to capitalize on her book and distributed its free copies in India. This rattled the government of Bangladesh also and it corroborated with the Islamists in victimizing Nasrin.)

As a result of all this, the Hindu population of Bangladesh has declined from 30 per cent in the Fifties to 10 per cent in 2001. Under pressure from the fundamentalists, Bangladesh changed the secular character of its Constitution in 1978 by making Islam the state religion. But in a historic decision, the Supreme Court of Bangladesh restored the secular character of its Constitution in 2010, and banned the making of political parties for exploiting religion. However, the country continues to be called the Islamic Republic of Bangladesh, but it is Islamic in name only.

***

Now, let's have a look into the Bangladeshi internal politics from the perspective of a Pakistani democrat. When we were one country it was generally believed that East Pakistani democrats were in the vanguard of the democratic movement in Pakistan. When East Pakistani leaders were pushed to the wall where they could only fight for liberation, most of the democratic leaders of West Pakistan were pleading that power should be transferred to the Awami League to save the country. The only major exception was Zulfikar Ali Bhutto's PPP, which was doing the politics of the establishment. Most of us, who eventually supported the Bangladesh liberation after the military operation started, believed that Bangladesh politics would at least be free of military interference after the independence. Sadly, we were wrong!

Mujib, who was forced by the circumstances engineered by General Yahya Khan and Bhutto to declare independence, was murdered with most of his family on 15 August 1975 by a rebel faction of the Bangladeshi Army. Another leader, General Ziaur Rahman, took over in April 1977 from Khondaker Moshtaque Ahmed's government, which came in after Mujib's death. Zia was also killed by the people from his own forces in May 1981. Army intervention in politics, like Pakistan, has been frequent in Bangladesh. The justification was also the same – restoring peace in the country and weeding out corruption. The story continued and ran parallel – Benazir Bhutto and Nawaz Sharif were allowed to return to politics by the junta here, Sheikh Hasina and Khaleda Zia were permitted to enter politics there. PPP returned to power here (but unfortunately Benazir was assassinated). Awami League is back in power there, led by Sheikh Mujib's daughter Sheikh Hasina. (She was saved at the time of the coup because she was out of the country with her sister.)

On the economic and human development count, Bangladesh is doing much better than Pakistan and India, although its per capita income on purchasing power parity basis is less than both the countries mentioned here.[9] While Pakistan's economic growth has dropped to 3.7 per cent in 2011–12, Bangladesh's has grown by 5.9 per cent. They are aiming at over 6 per cent growth during the current year, as against our 3 per cent. They have managed to contain inflation to around 5 to 6 per cent in a sharp contrast to 10 to 15 per cent. However, Bangladesh's per capita income on purchasing power parity basis is $ 1,909, in contrast to Pakistan's $ 2,786. At the time of independence East Pakistan's per capita income was about 40 per cent less than West Pakistan, although its exports income was much higher.

But the good thing is that unlike Pakistan, Bangladesh is spending only 1.5 per cent of its GDP on defence as against the 3 per cent of Pakistan. Its total armed forces strength including the reservists is 200,000 as against Pakistan's 634,000. Remarkably, Bangladesh has managed to control its population growth successfully. At the time of Bangladesh liberation in 1971 total population of Pakistan was 135 million of which East Pakistan was 72.5 million i.e., almost 57 per cent. In 2012 Bangladesh grew into a nation of 150 million, while Pakistan, failing to control its population, had a whopping 177 million. The important point here is that though the population of both countries is Muslim, Bangladesh has traditionally been more secular, hence the control of mullah is less. It is the mullah who has been one of the major opponents of not only family planning but also child immunization programmes in Pakistan. Bangladesh still has 32 per cent of the population living below poverty line. For these poor people, whose wages are very low, not much has changed because of independence as they were the poor cousins of West Pakistan. The new government says that it will concentrate on poverty alleviation. At present the fruits of faster economic growth are not flowing down to the poor as their economic managers are also enamoured by the 'trickle-down theory'.

Most businessmen and intellectuals had pinned lots of hope on Sheikh Hasina's government. But her shine wore off in the last four years of her rule as it appears she has not learnt from her past mistakes and has failed to keep a distance from the corrupt and rogue elements of the Awami League. Unfortunately, the history of most developing countries has shown that in a democracy the process of cleansing the politics of fraudulent elements is very long and is contrary to the impatient people's aspiration. Her success has been on signing a peace accord with the tribal people who were up in arms against the government for many years. And an ever bigger success has been normalizing relations with India and signing an agreement to allow transit facility to Indian goods through Bangladesh. Internally, uneven development and concentration of business in and around Dacca, pulls the rural unemployed to this city in large numbers. That is the reason why a tourist is struck by the poverty and chaotic traffic jams. All cities which face massive inflow of immigrants in the developing countries have crumbling infrastructure. Dacca is no exception.

Notes and References

1. Y. V. Gankovsky and L. R. Gordon-Polonskaya, *A History of Pakistan*, People's Publishing House, Lahore, 1974, p. 27.
2. Quoted in Tariq Rehman *Language and Politics of Pakistan*, Oxford University Press, New York, 1997.
3. Ibid., p. 87.
4. Mehrunnisa Ali, *Politics of Federalism in Pakistan*, Royal Book Company, Karachi, 1966, p. 71.
5. Shaikh Maqsood Ali, *From East Bengal to Bangladesh: Dynamics and Perspective*, the University Press, Dhaka, 2009, p. 9. See also, K. B. Sayed, *Political System of Pakistan*, Houghton Mifflin, Boston, 1967.
6. *Dawn*, 16 February 1971.
7. *Why Bangladesh: Bangladesh Papers* (compiled by scholars from Vienna), Vanguard Books, Lahore, 1971.
8. Ibid., p. 4.
9. *The Economist*, 3 November 2012.

Chapter 7

BALOCHISTAN – INSURGENCY FOR INDEPENDENCE

Mujhe jang-e-azaadi ka maza maloom hai,
Balochon per zulm ki intheha maloom hai,
Mujhe zindgi bhar Pakistan mein jeenay ki dua na do,
Mujhe Pakistan mein saath saal jeenay ki saza maloom hai.

— Habib Jalib

These lines roughly translated:

I know the taste of independence
I know the heights of oppression inflicted on the Balochs
Don't pray that I should live my entire life in Pakistan
I've known the punishment of living in Pakistan for sixty years.

Many years ago I called on Nawab Akbar Shahbaz Khan Bugti, leader of the Awami Jamhoori Party (AJP), at his Quetta residence. He was a bitter man, although his son Salim was a senior minister in the Balochistan government. During the discussion on harnessing the Balochistan oil and gas resources, he said that no fresh exploration should be allowed in the province.

Knowing the reasons of his reaction, I suggested that the Balochistan government or the people living on each concession should establish their respective holding companies, which should partner with the prospective exploration companies. 'For instance,' I explained 'you can have, say, 15 to 20 per cent equity in the company, so that when oil and gas is discovered you can share the profit.' Nawab Bugti laughed at my suggestion cynically and said: 'Babar, you are naïve, the government [federal] is not willing to give us control over our resources, so how can we negotiate with others?' He was right because the Constitution of Pakistan did not give the native people any right over their oil and gas reserves.

He was not the only one in Balochistan who felt that the natural resources should not be developed till the province got control over them. 'Let them be under the ground as this is the asset of our people, we don't want to lose them like the Sui [a sub-district of Dera Bugti in the south of Balochistan] natural gas reserves.' This has been the common stand of most Balochs and that of other nationalists in Sindh and the NWFP.

But as explained further down, the 18th Amendment and the 7th National Finance Commission (NFC) Award have now given equal control to the federation and the respective provinces over their oil and gas resources. Minerals and coal were already in provincial control. But this only happened in 2010 when the federation and the provinces made a leap forward to granting provincial, political and financial autonomy. Not every government in Islamabad in the past believed that natural resources were provincial assets and not those of the federation. It was this unresolved provincial autonomy issue which has, among other things, haunted Pakistan since its inception. Provinces were denied their right to control their economic resources, and half the country was lost because of this stupidity of the establishment in this regard.

Balochistan has been going through its limited-level insurgency for independence for the fourth time since the killing of Nawab Bugti by the army in 2006. Since then a medium-level insurgency led by mainly four Baloch militant groups has kept the independence demand alive. Every day, reports about either the killing of some Baloch nationalist allegedly by the intelligence agencies, or the killing of security forces and Punjabi settlers by one of the four major Baloch liberation militants are published or telecast as a matter of routine. It is one of the worst examples of Centre-province relationship in what remains as Pakistan.

Here I would like to briefly scan through the Balochistan and Pakistani establishment relations.

'Baluch* [sic] political unity,' according to historian Selig Harrison, 'came in the 18th century when several successive rulers of the Baluch principality of Kalat succeeded in expanding their domain to bring the Baluch areas under one political umbrella. Mir Nasir Khan, who ruled Kalat for 44 years beginning in 1749, set up a loose bureaucratic structure embracing most of Baluchistan for the first time and got principal Baluch tribes to adopt an agreed system of organization and recruitment.'[1]

Academician Adeel Khan's contention is, that 'Baloch nationalism emerged in a tribal set-up well before partition of India, and was opposed to Balochistan's accession to Pakistan. After partition, however, the Pakistani state's treatment of the region turned Baloch nationalism into a potent force, which attracted international attention...'[2] First the understanding was reached between the Khan of Kalat and the British Empire representatives on 4 August 1947, that Kalat would be independent on 15 August 1947, enjoying the same status as it originally held in 1863, having friendly relations with its neighbours. Another agreement was signed with Pakistan on the same date which said that: 'The government of Pakistan agrees that Kalat is an independent state, being quite different in status from other states of India, and commits to its relations with the British Government as manifested in several agreements.'

It was agreed that in the meantime 'a standstill agreement will be made between Pakistan and Kalat by which Pakistan shall stand committed to all responsibilities and agreements signed by Kalat and the British government from 1839 to 1947 and by this Pakistan shall be a legal, constitutional and political successor of the British.' (The British had only control over Quetta and some other areas.) A few weeks later, Kharan and Lasbela states and Marri–Bugti tribal areas were returned to the Kalat fold. The Kalat government made a formal independence declaration on 15 August 1947 and a delegation came down to Karachi to discuss the future relationship with Pakistan.

While the Khan of Kalat seemed inclined to merge his state with Pakistan, the Baloch sardars of his jirga** were not interested in doing anything in haste without settling the provincial autonomy issues. The Khan was under considerable influence of Muhammad Ali Jinnah

---

* Baluch and Baluchistan were previously spelt with a 'u' but later this was officially substituted with an 'o'.
**Jirga is a tribal assembly of elders, which takes decisions by consensus.

and had promised to work out the merger details in three months, but as Jinnah was unwell, the issue was handed over to his cabinet. They mishandled the whole issue and used the usual British tactics to pit the Baloch against each other by carving out three states of Kalat – Kharan, Lasbella and Makran. This resulted in the first uprising against Pakistan in 1948. The unilateral decision to break the Kalat state by Pakistan was contrary to the earlier understanding that in case the relations of Kalat with any government got strained, Kalat would exercise its right of self-determination.

That was the beginning of the Baloch revolt against the Centre. They have been to the hills many times since then, the on-going armed revolt by some groups started in 2004 but it gathered momentum after Nawab Bugti was killed by the army in August 2006. Earlier too, in 1973, Baloch had waged armed struggle for independence when their elected government dissolved by Zulfikar Ali Bhutto. It was just a few days after the signing of the Constitution. The prominent leader Nawab Khair Bakhsh Marri and young Dr Abdul Hai Baloch refused to sign it as it did not recognize the rights of the provinces over their economic resources.

Although gas was found in Sui in 1952, the province was not given any share from its profits. The province's right over 12.5 per cent royalty on oil and gas was accepted as late as in 1995. And what Balochistan used to get on the gas produced by it, which meets almost 21 per cent energy needs of the country, was pittance. This royalty goes into the provincial kitty but not much trickles down to the people of the area, who actually own this precious natural resource. The provincial governments in Pakistan have also been denying them the local governments and people their due economic rights. Imagine how rich the Bugtis would have been if they were in the US, where people became billionaires when oil was found on their land. The government always tried to pacify Nawab Bugti by giving him some money through Pakistan Petroleum Limited (PPL), a federal government-owned company, which controls and produces from the Sui natural gas fields. But in all fairness, what he got and what the province got were peanuts.

True, Nawab Bugti was a brutal tribal sardar (chief), who had a stake in maintaining the status quo which is socially, politically and economically primitive – all in the name of Baloch traditions. But he was not much different in this from a number of other tribal chiefs who side with the governments. All governments had worked towards preserving this system, even though sometimes they talked about breaking the 'sardari' system. Social systems are not changed through decrees that are not worth the paper they are written on. This change can only be brought in by changing the economic relations in that society. Not selectively only in the areas of the hostile tribes, but across the board. What is needed is to empower the people of the area and not the 'sardars'.

I had suggested in an article published in *Business Recorder* in September 2006: 'This objective can be achieved by giving a substantial percentage of the earnings from natural resources to the local governments in that area. As a matter of fact they should be allowed to collect it directly from the exploration and production companies. They should decide what development projects they want and it should not come from above. The issue of areas which are not blessed with natural resources can be dealt with through federal and provincial grants. The federal and provincial governments then should ensure that the information about the funds collected is widely publicized. The rest would be done by the people themselves.'

The prosperity and high-income level of the people living in resource-rich areas would encourage others to seek investment in their areas. They would also benefit from a rise in consumption in rich districts and would find something to sell to their rich cousins. If the Bugtis were given their due share from Sui earnings, the Marris would not have stalled the exploration in their areas. They would have rather competed to get the investors to explore what lies in their land.

In the interest of the country the Constitution has to be amended, accepting that provinces have a right over their economic resources. The federal government, can browbeat the people who stand for this right, but cannot win. Remember what well-known Urdu poet Habib Jalib said when General Yahya launched a military operation in the then East Pakistan:

Mohabbat golion sey bo rahey ho
Watan ka chehra khoon sey dho rahe ho
Gumaan tumko ke rasta kat raha hey
Yaqeen mujhko ke manzil kho rahe ho.

These lines roughly translated:
You are sowing love with bullets
And smearing the face of the country with blood
You are presuming that you are on track
But I am sure you are losing your destination.

Even though as stated above, the NFC Award and the 18th Amendment have met the Baloch nationalists demands halfway, the killing of Baloch youth has not stopped, for which even the moderate leaders blame the intelligence agencies. 'They [intelligence agencies]', a leading Baloch senator told me in a background interview, 'have changed the tactics; instead of facing the cases in the courts for the missing Baloch activists, they kill them and throw their bodies after interrogation.' Baloch leader and poet Habib Jalib, who was assassinated, wrote in a lament before his death:

Mujhe jang-e-azaadi ka maza maloom hai,
Balochon per zulm ki intheha maloom hai,
Mujhe zindgi bhar Pakistan mein jeenay ki dua na do,
Mujhe Pakistan mein saath saal jeenay ki saza maloom hai.

These lines roughly translated:
I know the taste of independence
I know the heights of oppression inflicted on the Balochs
Don't pray that I should live my entire life in Pakistan
I've known the punishment of living in Pakistan for sixty years.

The trouble with Balochistan is that the establishment has fragmented the society by fuelling inter-tribal and intra-tribal feuds. When it comes to armed struggle there are four major groups and many splinters, as it happens in all such movements. Only one group, which is led by Marri fighters, has allegiance of people from other tribes. The one led by Brahamdagh Khan Bugti has most fighters from his own tribe. Though there are a number of small splinter groups that have formed their own political parties, only the Baloch National Party-Mengal (BNP-Mengal) and National Party are the two major contenders among the nationalist parties of Balochistan. A Karachi-based Baloch leader, Yousuf Mustikhan, believes that the independence movement would get stronger if moderate leaders like Jalib were eliminated and the management of the province was not transferred to the civilian government by the establishment.

For over six decades Balochistan has been exploited. This has now convinced many Baloch leaders that nothing short of independence would solve their problems. But political analysts hope that the 7th NFC Award should strengthen the hands of the Baloch leaders who want to follow politics through democratic means within the structure of Pakistan. Although all democrats support the right of self-determination of nationalities, as Pakistan supports this for Indian Kashmiris, apprehensions are that if Balochistan's militant groups' independence dream is ever realized, it would slip into an internal war between various groups and tribes just as it did in Afghanistan and many other such tribal societies. Over the years each major tribe has been divided into pro-independence and pro-Pakistan establishment groups. This fragmentation of tribes on sub-tribe basis is a source of strength for the establishment as they follow the policy of divide and rule.

Notes and References

1. Selig S. Harrison, 'Ethnicity and the Political Stalemate in Pakistan' in S. Akbar Zaidi (editor), *Regional Imbalances and the National Question in Pakistan*, Vanguard, Lahore, 1992, p. 231.
2. Adeel Khan, *Politics of Identity: Ethnic Nationalism and the State in Pakistan*, Sage Publications, New Delhi, 2005, p. 109.

Chapter 8

SINDH – A MAJOR LOSER

...[the] creation of Pakistan in the name of religion was a mistake. But now that this country has survived for 42 years since 1971 in the present shape, its undoing would be a greater mistake and bloody too, as much water has flowed under the bridge and many common interests have evolved between the different ethno-linguist communities of Pakistan. With more respect, equity and recognition to the different nationalities living here, Pakistan is a viable country. As far as the various studies that propose Balkanization of Pakistan, Afghanistan and Iran are concerned, these are actually exercises in scenario building by analysts of a different creed.

Sindh was the first province in undivided India which supported the Pakistan resolution moved by the Jeay Sindh Movement pioneer Ghulam Murtaza Shah Syed on 3 March 1943. By this time all the big feudal lords had joined the Muslim League. Further on, in December 1943, Syed welcomed the 'well-to-do Muslims of Hind [to] please direct your activities in the field of trade and commerce to this land, so that it may in future become economically independent and self-supporting .... If the people from Gujarat and Bombay could go out to the Frontier to establish Hindu dominance there, could we too not repose some hope in your friends? ... The inhabitants of this land mostly belonged to the agriculture profession, and are very backward in trade and industry. Your money and experience could remove this drawback.'[1]

Syed and his colleagues had little idea that the investment from Indian Gujarat and Bombay would not come alone when the idea of Pakistan was realized. Syed and other landlords had supported Pakistan, as stated earlier, because the members of the Muslim elite were afraid of the land reform programme of Congress. They did not want to be put under a strong Hindu-controlled Centre as they had bitter memories of the merger of Sindh with the Bombay Presidency. This was because the professional and civil services were dominated by the Hindu middle classes and also because the change in the land laws made by the British allowed Hindu money-lenders to take away their mortgaged lands. Though miniscule, the Sindhi Muslim middle classes were looking forward to fill the positions vacated by the Hindus if they migrated or by way of getting some preference in a country ruled by the Muslims.

But as early as 1945, Syed fell out with the Muslim League over the distribution of seats for the forthcoming 1946 elections. The Provincial Parliamentary Board was suspended by Jinnah and the Central Parliamentary Board gave only three seats to Syed's nominees out of the ten he wanted. The critics of Syed, however, pointed out that he was biased in favour of the Syeds* of Sindh. The intervention of the central Muslim League pushed Syed to become the major ideologue and leader of the Sindhi nationalist movement and an ardent anti-Jinnah politician.

Sindhi nationalism had its roots in history, because it was a country even when the Arab invaded it. Sindh was the last province which was taken by the British in 1843 and was ruled by the Talpurs. It was different from other provinces of North-West India because Sindhi had had official-language status since the mid-1880s. All the Sindhis were looking for, by supporting the cause of Pakistan was autonomy, the right to rule their province. But soon after Pakistan was made, they were in for a rude shock. The Muslim League leadership, which was dominated by the Punjabi- and- Urdu-speaking elite, as stated earlier, did not accept the fact that Pakistan is a multi-ethnic country and each ethno-linguistic nationality had its own reasons for joining the federation. In the first Muslim League national council meeting after independence,

*Syed is title for the decedents from the family of Prophet Muhammad who migrated to undivided India.

160 delegates out of 300 members were of Mohajir origin. The slogan of one Muslim nation denied the multi-ethnicity of Pakistan. So, their right to have autonomy was also curbed.

The first shock to the Sindhis was that they lost their most important city, Karachi, as it was made the capital and a federally administrated city in 1948 'despite the vehement opposition by the Sindhi Chief Minister Muhammad Ayub Khurho. G. M. Syed later described the decision in the most vivid terms: "Mr Jinnah dismembered Sindh by cutting off Karachi, its leading city, from it and handed it over to Liaquat Ali Khan as its head, for the colonization of the city by Mohajirs".[2]

The Sindh Assembly building, from which the members passed the resolution to support Pakistan, was taken over by the Central Government and the provincial government was pushed to operate from Hyderabad. The seed of an urban-rural divide was sown. Next, the Sindhis saw that under the emergency declared by the federal government, along with a handful of Muslim investors came hundreds of thousands of immigrants from the Muslim-minority provinces of India.

***

Within a few years the demography of Karachi changed. Interesting statistics have been included by architect and town planner Arif Hasan and academician Masooma Mohib in a study conducted in the 1990s[3]: In 1941 when Karachi's population was around 400,000, Sindhi-speaking people were 61 per cent, but after the partition the number was reduced drastically to only 8.6 per cent. Reason: As a result of the advent of immigrants from India, the population of Karachi swelled to over 1.13 million, which led to the Urdu-speaking population grow to 50 per cent in 1951 from a mere 6.3 per cent in 1941. The major influx of immigrants, over 1 million, came to Karachi between 1947 and 1952; thereafter the flow slowed down.

It was in 1952 that the government stopped accepting migrants from India officially. Many considered this a blow to the 'two-nation theory', which expounded the idea that the Muslims of India were a separate nation. Immigration continued till the late Fifties. Karachi also attracted an inflow of streams of people of all nationalities from within the country, because it was the federal capital till 1962 and is the commercial and financial hub of Pakistan at present. The inflow was much higher till the mid-1980s. After that it slowed down, and to my knowledge, there is no study on this subject. The main reason for the drop in immigrants' inflow was that Karachi's industrial growth slowed down in the last two decades, mainly because of the ethnic riots between the locals and the immigrants from up-country. This discouraged people to come down to the city.

In spite of these factors, according to a 1998 survey, demographic linguistic break-up by language is as follows: Urdu 48.52 per cent; Punjabi 13.64 per cent; Pashto 11.96 per cent; Sindhi 7.34 per cent; Balochi 4.34 per cent; Saraiki 2.11 per cent and the rest 12.09 per cent. The rest includes Gujarati and other languages.

The next census was constitutionally due in 2008, but the work on it started in 2011 and it is already a disputed census in Sindh between the Urdu-speaking and Sindhi-speaking Sindhis, and till the writing of this chapter only house numeration work has been completed in the province. The city, according to international figures, has a total population of 15.7 million people and ranks as the thirteenth largest city of the world. However, if one extrapolates its 1998 population as reported by the census and on the basis of the official 3.5 per cent growth rate, it should be 14.3 million. But the Muttahida Qaumi Movement (MQM) maintains that the city population is much larger. How they calculate a higher figure is not known. By and large, the urban population's growth rate has two components: natural growth, which is close to 1.9 per cent, as it is usually below the national average in urban centres; and by way of immigration, which in Karachi's case is estimated to be 1.5 per cent. So, the rate of growth based on 1998 looks quite realistic.

Even in 2011, the city is dominated by the Mohajirs. The MQM's definition of Mohajir as given to me by its slain leader, Azeem Tariq, in 1986 was 'those immigrants from India to Pakistan who originally do not belong to any province which became part of Pakistan'. MQM changed its name from Mohajir Qaumi Movement to Mutahida Qaumi Movement (United National Movement) and has been bending over backwards to get a foothold in other provinces but it has not been able to attract many from other ethnic groups. In Sindh they have managed to gain support from most of the Urdu-speaking people and has a simmering tussle for more power with the Sindhis. But it is also in a violent tussle over the division of power in the city with the Pakhtuns, who have migrated for economic reasons from Khyber-Pakhtunkhwa or KP (formerly known as the NWFP) and Federally Administered Tribal Areas (FATA).

Although the Sindh provincial government is Sindhi-dominated now, it has little control over the megapolis of Karachi. The MQM jealously guard their power over Karachi and Hyderabad, the second-largest city of the province, to the extent of using violence when required. The Sindhis are by-standers and their elected President of Pakistan Asif Ali Zardari remains helpless as he has to compromise with the MQM to keep relative peace in the city.

Second, the biggest shock for the Sindhis was that while Karachi was annexed by the federal government and was made the capital of the country, their share in government jobs remained nugatory. According to the Constituent Assembly and Legislature Debates Volume 1, No. 5, April 1952, out of the 91 central secretariat secretaries, joint and deputy secretaries, 40 were Punjabis, 33 Mohajirs, 5 Bengalis, 3 Pathans, only one deputy secretary was Sindhi and there was no Baloch. A similar situation existed for lower jobs.

The third shock was that the bulk of evacuee properties in Sindh were allotted to the Mohajirs. As Dr Tanvir Ahmad Tahir has documented in his book *Political Dynamics of Sindh*, though most of the Mohajirs were not agriculturist they got themselves allotted 417,585 acres of agriculture land in Sindh, out of which 114,096 acres were self-cultivated. Similarly, most of the Mohajirs filed claims for evacuee properties and acquired houses in the cities of Sindh. I have witnessed it happening as a kid, living in Sukkur, a city in upper Sindh. My mother, Zohra Khalida, was an office bearer of the Pakistan Mohajir Board as we had migrated from Bombay at the time of the partition. Every morning hordes of Mohajirs, who were mostly living in thatched huts, used to flock our home and ask my mother to help them get the land and houses, claiming that they had left huge properties behind. Interestingly, as soon as one went out the other would say: 'I am from the same town and this fellow who just left had only a small shanty hut and was not a landlord, contrary to what he claims.' My mother used to say humorously that if all the claims of the Mohajirs who came to Pakistan were to be calculated as filed by them, then perhaps the total would be bigger than the whole land of India. Our neighbour, Kaim Din Jatoi, was one of the best criminal lawyers of the province and had bought a bungalow from a Hindu landlord when he was leaving Pakistan, but his house was declared an evacuee property and allotted to a Mohajir shopkeeper of Urdu Bazaar in Karachi. Our house was also allotted to somebody in Karachi who had never been to Sukkur. Both my father and our neighbours had to buy the claims from these bogus allottees to continue living in these houses. My father had not filed the claim to get a house against his upper-storey house in Bombay because he believed it was unjust. I remember bitter arguments between him and my mother, who was in favour of filing a claim.

Such allotment to the Mohajirs and their overwhelming share in the government jobs established their hegemony over Sindhis. The strong resentment against the federal government, which engineered Punjabi-Mohajir domination of Pakistan, was not limited to Sindh; it also emerged in Bengal, NWFP and Balochistan in the early years of Pakistan.

The fourth shock to the Sindhis and other nationalities living in Pakistan was the creation of 'One Unit' by the Punjabi–Mohajir establishment, by merging all the western provinces and federally controlled Balochistan in one province – West Pakistan – in 1955. The creation of One Unit was, again, a manifestation of two hang-ups of the Punjabi–Mohajir ruling establishment: First, since they ran away from the rule of majority in India and claimed to be a separate nation, they were not willing to accept East Bengal's majority; and second, they were obsessed with the idea that Muslims were one nation because they a had a common religion. Hence, the division into provinces was on an administrative basis only. One Unit was thus created to disenfranchise the Bengalis, who formed 54 per cent of the country's population. Even the majority of their Muslim brethrens of Bengal was not acceptable to the champions of the one-Muslim nation.

The merger of all the West Pakistan provinces and Balochistan in One Unit with its capital in Lahore was unjust and created problems for the people of the smaller provinces and Balochistan as they had to commute to Lahore for all official work. It also concentrated the power in the hands of the Punjabi ruling elite and bureaucracy. The idea of creating One Unit was old. 'As early as November 1947, Sir Archibald Rowlands, M. A. Jinnah's adviser on economic matters, recommended the unification of the western wing, but "although the father of the nation approved the proposal in principle, he considered it premature and postponed the scheme." The advocates of unifications [sic] alleged that M. A. Jinnah intended to carry out the plan in 1948. Barely eight months after the partition, daily *Nawa-i-Waqt*, Lahore, a representative of the Punjabi interests, pleaded for the integration of the provinces in West Pakistan in the supreme interest of Pakistan.'[4] Once again this proved that the basic objective of autonomy for the Muslim majority provinces, as advocated by Jinnah and his Muslim League, was either a trap for these provinces or got lost in the slogan that Muslims are one nation.

The fifth shock to the people of Sindh came in 1958, when General Muhammad Ayub Khan stopped the teaching of Sindhi in schools. Sindhi was not taught in Karachi, but was taught as a compulsory subject in the interior of Sindh. Even though I studied in a convent in Sukkur, I remember Sindhi was taught to us till 1958. As a result, I can read Sindhi newspapers and understand it. Nobody in our class, which had a non-Sindhi-speaking majority, resented the idea of learning or speaking Sindhi when given a chance. However, according to leading Sindhi intellectual and academician Dr Feroz Ahmed, the action of discontinuing Sindhi 'coincided with his [Ayub Khan] decision to allot the newly-irrigated lands in Sindh to non-Sindhi retired military officers and bureaucrats.' The action was to favour the children of the new migrants at the cost of the Sindhis. The decision did not affect the Sindhi elite. as much as it did the lower classes of Sindh, because elite children were either studying in convents in the major cities of the province or were sent to Lahore's elitist schools. This decision hampered the growth of the Sindhi middle classes as most of the lower middle class, and even some landlords' children, used to go to the Sindhi schools for the first five years before coming to other schools where the medium of teaching was English or Urdu.

***

The paradigm shift for the Sindhis came in 1972, when power was handed over to Zulfikar Ali Bhutto, the person who had never opposed One Unit. General Yahya Khan had earlier abolished the One Unit in response to the major movement for democracy in 1968–69. As no democracy is complete unless the federating units have democratic relations among them, the demand for breaking One Unit and restoring the provinces was strong. Bhutto, who played a major role in the anti-Ayub Khan movement, was shy of supporting the demand of undoing the One Unit because he wanted to carry Punjabi leaders with him.

I remember he wanted to enter the mainstream Sindh politics by addressing the Sindh University students, as it was the bastion of the Sindhi nationalist movement. The student leaders led by Jam Saqi, a dedicated communist, opposed Bhutto's entry on the grounds that he did not support breaking of One Unit, and that he opposed the Tashkent Agreement between Pakistan and India that followed the 1965 war and once said, 'we will fight for a thousand years with India'. Finally, with the intervention of Rasool Bakhsh Talpur, a respected leader from Hyderabad (Pakistan), it was agreed that he would not speak on either of the topics and, instead, would only keep his speech restricted to the issue of restoration of democracy. After the speech, Bhutto specially thanked Jam Saqi for agreeing to invite him to speak to the university students. Incidentally, Saqi was the first political person to be arrested under Bhutto's government from Sukkur, under the cooked-up charges, which were framed during the military operation in East Pakistan.

The military operation was vehemently opposed by the Communist Party of Pakistan and Sindhi nationalists. Interestingly, the Sindhi nationalist poet Shaikh Ayaz – who was also an office bearer of the Awami League – had shooed us away when, led by labour leader Aizaz Nazir and poet with Leftist leanings Hasan Hameedi, we invited him to speak at a public meeting to condemn the military operation. He considered it foolish to speak against the military at that juncture. But this couldn't save Shaikh Ayaz from arrest as he was targeted by the biased Mohajir intelligence.

In the 1970 elections, Bhutto's PPP was two seats short of majority in the Sindh Assembly. But as history would have it he became the greatest benefactor of the Sindhis.

Two major developments happened in 1972 that changed the face of Sindh politics. First, for the first time after the creation of Pakistan, the Sindh government got Karachi back, as the capital was shifted to Islamabad in 1960. This brought in Sindhi landlords and middle classes to Karachi and increased their share in government jobs gradually. Second, Bhutto, who had won the majority of national and provincial seats in the Punjab, managed to attract two independent Provincial Assembly members in Sindh to cobble a majority. This gave Sindhis, a chance for the first time after the creation of Pakistan, to head a government at the Centre. Consequently, the gateway of Islamabad was opened for the Sindhi elite and middle classes. At the same time it affected the popularity of the umpteen Sindhi nationalist parties. Even after the assassination of Benazir Bhutto and PPP leadership being hijacked by her husband Asif Ali Zardari, the Sindhi voters would rather vote for PPP if they want a say and influence in the provincial and federal governments. Most voters all over the world have opportunistic tendency, as they want to vote for a winning party. In developing economies this factor is stronger, because more than systems, it is important to have people in government who can help the voters in their day-to-day affairs.

***

To further discuss the consequences of the political formulation that Muslims of India are one nation, and the dynamics of Pakistan's politics in general and of Sindh in particular, the role of Mohajirs has to be discussed.

The Mohajirs migrated from the Muslim-minority provinces of India mainly for three reasons: economic opportunities, personal security, which was endangered by the communal riots, and under the delusion that Muslims of India are one nation.

At the time of partition over 70 per cent migrants were from East Punjab because Punjab was one of the two provinces of India, which was divided on communal basis, the other being Bengal. As the migrants from East Punjab belonged to the same ethnicity and spoke the same language most of them settled in West Punjab and have easily assimilated with the local Punjabis. The rest of the migrants were from Muslim-minority areas such as Uttar Pradesh, Bihar, Central Provinces, Delhi, Hyderabad (Andhra Pradesh), Gujarat and Bombay, etc. It is this lot which migrated to Sindh: one, because for some strange reason Jinnah's government dictated that Sindh would take 200,000 refugees from the first influx, while Punjab was given 100,000, other provinces quota was much smaller; and two, Karachi was made the capital of the country; and three, it was a business hub with an international sea port and airport.

Hence, most of the middle-class immigrant came to this city in search of better economic opportunities. Some who came by crossing the Sindh border with India settled in Hyderabad and Mirpur Khas. By mid-Fifties over a million Mohajirs had settled in Karachi, completely changing its demography. They formed over 60 per cent of the population, while Sindhi ratio dropped to some 7 per cent.

For the first 11 years the Mohajirs had it too good as they held many more jobs in the government than their ratio in the country's population and advanced their businesses. They were happy to be the junior partner of the Punjabi ruling elite although they formed only 3.3 per cent of the country's population. In 1951 of the 95 senior civil services jobs 33 were held by the Mohajirs and 40 by the Punjabis. In 1959 out of 48 top-military elite positions 11 were held by Mohajirs i.e., 23 per cent of the total. In the same year, of the total top (Class 1) Bureaucracy 3,532 positions, the Mohajirs' share was 1,070, that is 30 per cent of the total.[5] This was the time they supported the Muslim League, which was the ruling party for most of this period.

General Ayub Khan ousted the elected government and imposed martial law, initially they continued to enjoy privileged positions particularly in the civil bureaucracy. However, the Mohajirs' share in power started declining by early Sixties. Ayub's first constituency was obviously the army, which had 20 per cent Pakhtuns. And for the first time Mohajirs were replaced by the Pakhtuns as the junior partner in the ruling power set up.

The Muslim League was divided into pro-government and opposition factions. But the leadership of the disgruntled Mohajirs started rallying around the religious parties. They were the first generation of immigrants and needed the moral reason to be at Bunder Road of Karachi, instead of being at Chandni Chowk of Delhi. And what could be a more honourable reason than the cause of religion. Nobody wanted to say that they came to Pakistan in search of better economic opportunities because this sounds too materialistic in a society that had feudal social values. Their association with religious parties was more for opposing Ayub Khan, who had changed the power equation and was a secular man, and less for the love of religion.

The first flash point of ethnic violence in the city between the Mohajirs and Pakhtuns was on the celebration of 1965 elections' victory by Gohar Ayub Khan in Karachi. Mohajir leadership had opposed Ayub and sided with Fatima Jinnah. Several people were killed in these clashes. The Mohajirs have since then resented the influx of the Pakhtun immigrants from KP and FATA to Sindh, although Pakhtun workers are mainly associated with the transport and construction industry – the job Mohajirs were not interested in.

Once the military-blessed democratic government of PPP came in 1972, in what is today's Pakistan, the power equation changed again and the Sindhi's got the first opportunity to be the junior partner of the Punjabi ruling classes. As Sindh is the second largest province of Pakistan, after Punjab, with 23 per cent population this equation is likely to remain unchanged in any democratic dispensation. This again irritated the Mohajir leadership who instead of joining hands with the mainstream political parties like PPP opposed the government from the religious parties' platform. On the other hand for the first time after 25 years of independence the Sindh government got back the secretariat and Assembly building, which belonged to them before the partition.

An anecdote here may explain the level of resentment of Mohajirs on this change of the power equation. As I was going through the corridors of Sindh Assembly, where I had gone to meet a friend, I met two Mohajir leaders of Sukkur Muslim League, Syed Hasan Mian and Ashfaq Ahmed pointing out towards some Sindhis who were passing by dressed in their 'shalwar kameez' and Sindhi caps. Hasan Mian lamented: 'Isn't it sad such people who don't know how to dress-up have now flocked in droves to the Assembly?' I pointed out respectfully, because he was a friend's father: 'Uncle, isn't this a fact that the province belonged to Sindhis who gave shelter to the Mohajirs when they came from India? So why should they not be here?' His immediate response was: 'You have never been on the side of the *Qaum* [Mohajir nation] even as a student, so you will not understand.' Note the use of term 'Qaum' as early as 1972.

During Ayub Khan's military dictatorship we witnessed the civil administration dividing the people of Sindh by creating Mohajir students and political organizations to weaken the movement for the restoration of democracy. In Sukkur, our Students' Action Committee against Ayub Khan was divided, following the same policy, by the deputy commissioner. And in Hyderabad a Karachi–Hyderabad–Mohajir–Punjabi–Pakhtun Mahaz (front) was established by the commissioner through an information department official, Ishtiaq Azhar, who later joined the Mohajir Rabita Council in the 1980s and supported MQM.

Another major upsetting development for the Mohajirs was that Mumtaz Bhutto, who was the first chief minister under Zulfikar Ali Bhutto's government, restored the status of Sindhi as an official language and ensured that it was taught in schools. Fanning hatred,

Urdu newspaper, *Jang* wrote in black border on the first page *'Urdu ka janaza hey, zara dhoom say niklay'*. (Let the funeral of Urdu be carried out fervidly!) This unleashed the wide-scale Mohair-Sindhi language riots in Sindh for the first time. Both Mohajirs and Sindhis attacked each other. Many were injured and properties burnt.

The Sindhi leaders protested in the early Fifties when Karachi University was established with the option to choose Urdu or English as a medium of instruction. The Sindh University was packed off to Hyderabad because Karachi was made the capital. Hari (peasant) leader Hyder Bakhsh Jatoi had pointed out that this decision will be disadvantageous for the Sindhi students living in Karachi. But Jinnah and his colleagues erroneously believed that making Urdu as one national language was the corollary of the Muslim League's theorem One Religion One Nation. This policy denied equal status to other major languages of the provinces and hence slowed down their growth to become official and commercial languages. The formation of the Sindh government and PPP's government in the Centre finally opened doors for the Sindhi-speaking middle class. They started getting more jobs in the government and public sector particularly, which had head offices in Karachi. Mohajir bureaucracy and leaders were not willing to accept that their share in the jobs and economic opportunities in future would be in proportion to their demographic position, which was more or less the position by 1989 in the federal government. The Mohajirs played an important role in the 1977 movement against Bhutto's government and were happy when he was removed in a military coup by General Muhammad Zia-ul-Haq in July 1977.

Once again the Mohajirs were faced with the same position which they thought they had left behind in the Muslim-minority areas of India, and for which they had supported Muslim League's politics under the British. Remember Sir Syed had asked for 50 per cent quota in jobs for the Muslims, although they formed 13 per cent of the population in Uttar Pradesh? This was the main reason that Muslims of the Muslim-minority provinces played a leading role in the Muslim League's movement although eventually it evolved into the demand for Pakistan comprising Muslim-majority provinces. This movement, as convincingly explained by Hamza Alavi, was driven by the 'salariats … that class of people who receive a formal education to qualify for jobs in the colonial state apparatus' and the professionals. According to him the

Muslims in Uttar Pradesh constituted 13 per cent of the population in 1857 but held 64 per cent of the jobs. However, after the British takeover by 1913, their 'share of jobs fell to 35 per cent'.[6]

Once the demand for Pakistan was accepted, a large number of migrants had come to Pakistan scouting for better opportunities. Once settled they invited their kith and kin. Though they got a major share of the evacuee properties in Sindh, they were again not willing to accept the shrinking share of jobs and other economic opportunities after the restoration of Sindh as a province. However, there was reverse discrimination against the Mohajirs as the power started shifting in the hands of Sindhis. In the good old times when the Punjabis and Mohajirs had the second largest share in the establishment the discrimination was against the Sindhis. Still there are more Mohajirs in the government jobs, if public sector is included, as against the 7.5 per cent share in the population.

Bushra Zaidi's killing in a bus accident in 1985 unleashed violence against the Pakhtuns, who controlled Karachi's transport sector thanks to Ayub-era favouritism. There was pent-up anger at the transporters because of the rough behaviour of the drivers and frequent accidents due to rash driving of the buses and mini-buses. Inadequate public transport was and is a constant irritant for the Karachiites. The Mohajirs who form a bulk of the commuters, started burning buses, the Pakhtuns attacked some Mohajir settlements in retaliation. And soon what started as a spontaneous reaction to an accident turned into an ugly ethnic conflict, which killed many people.

Meanwhile, the Mohajir youth, who are equal sons of the soil of Sindh as they were born and bred in this province, started feeling the pinch of unemployment and lack of educational institutions. Bhutto had nationalized all the educational institutions in 1972 after which not a single new college was added in Karachi. At an average, by the late 1970s and mid-1980s, some 20,000 students who got lower grades in matriculation examinations could not get admissions to any college or technical institute every year. It was this crowd of unemployed Mohajir youth, standing idle at the corners of the streets, which was given a voice by Altaf Hussain and Azeem Tariq by launching the All Pakistan Mohajir Students Organization (APMSO). Tariq was assassinated in October 2003, after he parted ways with his comrade Altaf Hussain.

Later, Hussain said in an interview that when he went to the University of Karachi to join BSc pharmacy class, he was shocked to see welcome banners of various ethnic student organizations and forced to think about his own identity. The Mohajir students till that time used to rally on the basis of ideology behind the Leftist groups of National Students Federation (NSF) or the Rightist student wing of JI called Islami Jamiat-e-Talaba (IJT). The creation of a Mohajir organization delighted perfidious Zia's intelligence, who considered it as an antidote to the rising Sindhi nationalism after Bhutto's hanging by the military government on 4 April 1979 at the age of 51.

The division of students on ethnic basis did raise a question in the minds of the founders of APMSO about their identity. They were told by the older generation that all Pakistanis belonged to one Muslim nation. The second generation of the Mohajirs soon realized that they did not need religious reasons to be in Pakistan. The rise of ethnic politics around them made them think that there was no such thing as a Muslim nation. Instead, the strong ethnicity-based politics was the order of the day. Addressing the APMSO rally at the University of Karachi on 15 December 1980, Hussain maintained that Mohajirs should be accepted as the fifth nationality of Pakistan. He thus moved away from the thinking of the older Mohajir generation, which by and large (leaving aside some Leftists) always strongly proclaimed that Pakistan had one Muslim nation and those who claimed that the nation had four nationalities were traitors or agents of Jews and Hindus. However, the MQM later dropped the fifth nationality slogan officially and declared that Mohajirs were Urdu-speaking Sindhis. This position was reiterated by Hussain in his marathon press conference on 10 September 2011. That is what the Sindhi nationalists had advised them in the early 1980s. But, in spite of this official declaration, the MQM is still privately stuck to its earlier political formulation that Mohajirs were a separate 'Qaum', to keep their vote bank intact. The politics of constituency is not allowing MQM to expand.

As a matter of fact, MQM literature shows that both Altaf Hussain and Azim Tariq dismissed the theory that Muslims were one nation on the basis of common religion. They asked that if religion made one Muslim nation, then why were the Muslims divided on national basis in many countries. APMSO Secretary General Azim Tariq maintained in a speech in December 1980: 'Soon after the creation of Pakistan the ideology of Pakistan or ideology of Islam was negated because Muslims from the Indian Muslim minority areas who were going through the phase of migration were stopped at the borders of Pakistan in 1954 and returned back [*sic*].[7]

MQM leaders courageously exposed the hypocrisy of the Pakistan movement's basic argument. They said that if Muslims were one nation there was no reason why the Muslims from anywhere in the world and particularly from India should be denied entry into Pakistan at any time. They were courageous enough to refer to the analogy of Israel where the Jews from anywhere in the world can go and acquire Israeli nationality. It was courageous because any comparison of Pakistan with Israel is deplored by the majority of the people in Pakistan. It was on the basis of this thinking that Altaf Hussain 'has on several occasions said that the creation of Pakistan was a mistake.'[8] The Mohajirs' younger leadership led by Hussain takes the sensible course to declare that they do not want the division of the province – the position they continue to hold even today. They also support Sindh's major demands at the NFC Award and on the waters' distribution issue. While they have been rightly supporting Sindh's stance against the domination of Punjab, within the province MQM has been asking for control over the big cities – Karachi and Hyderabad. In a foreword to Altaf Hussain's recent book *My Life's Journey*, Professor Matthew A. Cook rightly pointed out: 'The principle of negation also appears to drive tension between Mohajirs and Sindhis from one historical crisis to another. Nonetheless, while these crises are anti-Sindhi, Mohajir politics not only illustrates how negation produces alterity but – by opening socio-political conversation – the possibility of mimesis.'

The alliance of PPP and MQM in Sindh suffers from this mimesis and alterity between the parties, which represent the Sindhi and Urdu-speaking Sindhis. It is unfortunate that in spite of officially announcing a few years earlier that 'M' in MQM stood for 'Mutahida' and not for Mohajir, the leadership vacillates between the two incompatible positions. Unfortunately, Hussain's many statements are not reassuring that MQM would change its strategy. Such statements are torpedoing MQM's desire to emerge as a multi-ethnic middle class party. However, realizing that the MQM was getting isolated politically, MQM leader shrewdly did not reply directly to the former PPP government's Home Minister of Sindh Zulfiqar Mirza's allegation made in 2012 that Hussain had confided in Mirza that the US wanted to Balkanize Pakistan and that MQM was going to support it. On the contrary, MQM's supreme leader, Altaf Hussain, spent more time in reassuring the Pakistani establishment of his party's full support in foiling such a conspiracy to break Pakistan. Referring to old books and a series of articles by the American analysts, he joined the Right-wing club, which has been harping that the Americans want to break Pakistan.

Though the MQM leader Mustafa Kamal vehemently denies that his party has a militant wing, the public perception is otherwise. Only MQM voters believe in what the Nine Zero (MQM head office address popularly referred by its number) says. If this perception has to be proven wrong, it would not happen by lengthy speeches and eloquence but by a change in the future strategy. The MQM has a sound middle and lower-middle class Mohajir base in Karachi, Hyderabad, Sukkur and Mirpur Khas city centres but not in the suburbs. This is enough power to show and bargain with other parties for the rights of its vote bank through non-violent democratic means. It doesn't need to rely on any militant wing particularly if it wants to attract the middle and lower-middle classes of the other ethno-linguistic communities of Pakistan. Consistent non-violence politics in spite of provocations from other parties alone would help the MQM to change the existing perception about it.

The MQM says that this negative perception about them was created by the political parties and nationalities that represent the ruling elite of Pakistan, but being a party with arguably the highest literacy rate among its supporters it has to realize that perceptions are stronger than reality. And they are not completely baseless either.

Altaf Hussain lectured his followers in 2003 on the philosophy of 'Realism and Practicalism': 'An act of doing things, making or taking decisions, adopting means and ways in accordance with the actual spirit and essence of reality (realities) and realism is called Practicalism.' And that is precisely what the MQM is not doing.

The MQM maintains that the city population is much larger. How they calculate a higher figure is not known. By and large the urban population's growth rate has two components: natural growth, which is close to 1.9 per cent as it is usually below the national average in urban centers; and by way of immigration, which in Karachi's case is estimated to be 1.5 per cent. So the rate of growth based on the 1998 study looks quite realistic. Now take a look at the 1998 survey's demographic linguistic break-up: Urdu 48.52 per cent; Punjabi 13.64 per cent; Pashto 11.96 per cent; Sindhi just 7.34 per cent; Balochi 4.34 per cent; Seriaki 2.11 per cent and the rest 12.09 per cent; the rest includes Gujarati and other languages. The Pakhtuns, however, claim that their number is higher now. But a large number of Pakhtun workers live alone in the city and are not registered as Karachi voters. Similarly, the MQM can also claim that Gujaratis are part of the Mohajirs as their younger generation is Urdu-speaking.

In the last 13 years there has been a big inflow of Sindhis and Pakhtuns to the province, so they do claim that in the next elections they should have more seats from Karachi. Ideally the big cities should be a melting pot and voting should be done on non-ethnic basis, but the reality is that except for the PPP, JI and Pakistan Muslim League (PML) all other parties are voted on ethnic basis in Karachi. Given the reality that Urdu-speaking people are not more than 50 per cent of the city considering the MQM's claim, the other ethnic groups feel they are under-represented because most of the constituencies are carved to suit MQM. Awami National Party (ANP) claims that the Pakhtun population is over 20 per cent in Karachi.

That is the reality and 'practicalism' would be to step back and change the present strategy thinking for a better and long-term future of the country in general and Karachiites in particular. If this doesn't happen, the Mohajir youth will lose more than anybody else in Karachi for they have nowhere to go for education and jobs. The leaders of MQM have been fighting Sindhis and Pakhtuns over the Karachi and Hyderabad election turf, although it is in their prime interest to maintain the peace in the city. The city law and order situation has scared the private sector away to Punjab and to the Gulf countries. The Mohajir leaders have failed to understand that in these times where governments are shrinking the employment for the Mohajir youth is in the private sector. That is where no quota works (which MQM resents) and merit matters. The Mohajir youth have not been shown the path of excelling in merit but are being fed on lectures that they are being deprived by other communities and are being armed. The result of this Mohajir policy is that the merit-quality of Mohajir youth has been consistently declining in proportion to the increase in their reliance on the barrel of the gun. The MQM leaders deny vehemently that they encourage violence and at the same time admit that their youth picks up the guns in self-defence against onslaught of other ethnic and political forces.

Altaf Hussain, as mentioned before, said that creation of Pakistan in the name of religion was a mistake. But now that this country has survived for 42 years since 1971 in the present shape, its undoing would be a greater mistake and bloody too, as much water has flowed under the bridge and many common interests have evolved between the different ethno-linguist communities of Pakistan. With more respect, equity and recognition to the different nationalities living here, Pakistan is a viable country. As far as the various studies that propose Balkanization of Pakistan, Afghanistan and Iran are concerned, these are actually exercises in scenario building by analysts of a different creed. On the other hand, one should also refer to the number of analysis which warn of such an eventuality destablizing the region, including India – the region which has the damned nuclear arsenal also.

Notes and References

1. Quoted by Tanvir Ahmed in his dissertation 'Political Dynamics of Sindh', Pakistan Study Centre, Karachi, p. 124, from Sharifuddin Pirzada, *Foundation of Pakistan*, Vol. II, National Publishing House, 1970.
2. Owen Bennett Jones, *Pakistan: Eye of the Storm*, Penguin Books, New Delhi, 2005, p. 118.
3. http://www.ucl.ac.uk/dpu-rojects/Global_Report/pdfs/Karachi_bw.pdf
4. Tanvir Ahmed, *Political Dynamics of Sindh*, Pakistan Studies Centre, Karachi, 2010, p. 318.
5. Tariq Rahman, *Language and Politics in Pakistan*, Oxford University Press, New York, 1977, p. 121.
6. 'Pakistan and Islam: Ethnicity and Ideology' in Hamza Alavi and Fred Halliday (editors), *State and Ideology in the Middle East and Pakistan*, Monthly Review Press, New York, 1988.
7. MQM booklet published in 'Mohajir Qaumi Movement: Tashkil aur Jedojehad' (edited by Ahmed Salim).
8. Stephen Philip Cohen, *The Idea of Pakistan*, Vanguard Books, Lahore, 2005, p. 216.

Chapter 9

KHYBER PAKHTUNKHWA –
FINALLY GETS ITS IDENTITY

Was Jinnah intellectually dishonest in betraying Pakistan's objective? His critics do believe it. But they fail to realize that he, like many other Muslim leaders of pre-partition days, became victim to his own propaganda, which was used to get mass support: That being Muslim the people of Pakistan were one homogenous nation and that any talk about the rights of the various nationalities in Pakistan or more provincial autonomy was an intrigue against the existence of the country.

The people of the NWFP were deeply divided on the eve of Pakistan's independence. In the 1937 election the Congress, supported by the social movement of Khudai Khidmatgar (servants of God) of Khan Abdul Ghaffar Khan, won 17 of the 50 seats in the provincial elections and 'it was more impressive with 15 out of 36 reserved Muslim seats in comparison with Muslim League which could not win a single seat.'[1] In the election just a year before partition (1946), in spite of official support to the Muslim League, Congress and Khudai Khidmatgar alliance 'defeated the Muslim League and emerged as the majority party, with 30 out of 50 seats.'[2]

A devout Muslim, Ghaffar Khan, was popularly known as 'Bacha Khan'. Some called him 'Sarhadi Gandhi' (Frontier Gandhi) as he was a staunch Pakhtun nationalist and was impressed by Mohandas

Karamchand Gandhi (commonly known as Mahatma Gandhi) and the anti-colonialist movement of the Congress. He apprehended from the very beginning that the Muslim League was supported by the British to divide the people of India and their anti-colonialist movement. At the same time he was also apprehensive that in the proposed Pakistan, NWFP would be dominated by the Punjab. The fear of Punjab domination perhaps also stemmed from history since the Punjabi Sikhs had ruled over southern parts of Pakhtun areas. The Ranjit Singh rule ended when the British defeated the Sikhs in 1845.

That fear was not unfounded as in Pakistan for the first few years Punjabi–Mohajir elite ruled all other nationalities. But during General Ayub Khan's ten years of military rule the Pakhtuns prospered as junior partners of the Punjab. However, as the NWFP was merged in 'one unit', the nationalist leadership vigorously campaigned for provincial autonomy and for dismantling the 'one unit'.

In the 1970s the power equation changed and the Sindhi landed elite replaced the Pakhtun elite. That a Sindhi Bhutto was the prime minister till 1977 should not be taken as the Sindhis having an upper hand, as Bhutto had swept the Punjab but he knew it well that to rule Pakistan he had to give the Punjab's interest precedence over that of other provinces. This was evident in the distribution of financial resources and water during his tenure.

The British named the southern Pakhtun belt as the North-West Frontier Province since the area had strategic importance for them. The tribal areas bordering Afghanistan, which had not been under the control of the Sikh rulers, were kept under a loose arrangement called tribal agencies. Pakistan Constitution declared these agencies as the Federally Administered Tribal Areas, which had its own law and only served as a buffer between the British-managed territories of India and Afghanistan and Afghanistan's ally, Russia. The British thus divided the Pakhtuns between 'settled areas' and 'tribal areas'. This division of areas, which exist even today, has created a wide gulf between the two areas in terms of social, economic and infrastructure development. It is a subject I will be discussing in a later chapter regarding the impact of the Afghan War on Pakistan, and Pakistan's policies on Afghanistan.

The Congress government which took over after the 1946 elections in NWFP was headed by Ghaffar Khan's elder brother, Khan Abdul Jabbar Khan, popularly known as Dr Khan Sahib. According to Adeel

Khan, the success of the Congress and the Khan Brothers was, in spite of the British government's intrigues, to divide the people on the basis of religion. 'A Cunningham policy note of 23 September reads: "Continuously preach the danger to Muslims of connivance with the revolutionary Hindu body. Most tribesmen seem to respond to this." In another paper about 1939–43 Cunningham wrote: "Our propaganda since the beginning of the war had been most successful. It had played throughout on the Islamic theme".[3] The same tool of exploiting the religiosity of the Pakhtuns was used during the ten-year war against Afghanistan by the Pakistan Army and the US administration. But now it is being exploited by the Taliban and the Al Qaeda against their former mentors.

However, this spadework of whipping up religious fervour was used by the Muslim League to gain support for the referendum in NWFP, which was held on the demand of the Congress. Ghaffar Khan and Dr Khan Sahib first resisted the referendum on the grounds that the 1946 elections gave a clear mandate to the Congress and Khudai Khidmatgar. But the Muslim League insisted on the referendum, to which the Congress finally agreed. The option given to the NWFP people was whether they would like to join India or Pakistan. Ghaffar Khan wanted that a third option should be added asking whether they wanted an independent Pakhtunistan. This demand was rejected and the Khudai Khidmatgar decided to boycott the referendum. Dr Khan Sahib's government reforms, and Khudai Khidmatgar's support to smaller khans (landlords) and peasants had alienated the big khans. Their secular policies had also alienated the British-paid mullahs and pirs. This element rallied with Muslim League. NWFP was not the only province where Jinnah relied on the big landlords, Sindh and Punjab had the same story. After losing the 1937 elections badly, Jinnah was of the view that once the big landlords were convinced in all Muslim-majority provinces that the Muslim League's demands for more autonomy would be accepted, the 'corruption advantage of the big landlords' would bring them to support his agenda.

Just a few months before independence, in June 1947, the Khudai Khidmatgar gave a call for an independent Pakhtunistan. This call was also supported by Afghanistan, which was to be the only country to oppose Pakistan's membership of the United Nations. The Afghanistan government has never accepted the Durand Line, not even to this day. The line was drawn by the British under an agreement with the Afghan

King Amir Abdur Rahman Khan on 12 November 1893 defining the border between the British dominion and Afghanistan. The call for independent Pakhtunistan created distrust for the Khan Brothers' nationalist politics in Muslim League. Thus the first arbitrary action of Jinnah as governor-general was to dismiss the majority government of Dr Khan Sahib, although he had agreed to be part of Pakistan. But it can be said in defence of Jinnah that Dr Khan Sahib had told General Sir R. M. Lockhart in a meeting on 7 July 1947 that he could never participate in a ministry which stood for Pakistan. '[He] said that he would not rule out the possibility of some colleagues being willing to take their place in temporary inevitable i.e. they would perhaps accept portfolios until the General Elections are held .... He did clearly however say that, should there be a clear vote in favour of Pakistan, he himself would certainly resign and that his ministers would too ....'4

Ghaffar Khan, who was a nationalist inspired by the Afghan King Amanullah Khan's teachings, also accepted the fait accompli given to them by the British in the form of Pakistan. He however insisted that the province should have autonomy and the Centre should only hold foreign policy, communications, defence and currency – same as Jinnah had outlined in a meeting with General Lockhart. But that was when Jinnah and his party had to lure the provinces to the idea of Pakistan; once Pakistan was established and he took over as the powerful governor-general, to renege on his earlier policy statements was easy.

Was Jinnah intellectually dishonest in betraying Pakistan's objective? His critics do believe it. But they fail to realize that he, like many other Muslim leaders of pre-partition days, became victim to his own propaganda, which was used to get mass support: That being Muslim the people of Pakistan were one homogenous nation and that any talk about the rights of the various nationalities in Pakistan or more provincial autonomy was an intrigue against the existence of the country.

It was because of this thinking that most Muslim League leaders always considered Ghaffar Khan and later his son Khan Abdul Wali Khan as traitors and agents of Afghanistan and India. They were incarcerated for many years and their loyalty to Pakistan was always considered doubtful, as the ruling establishment did not differentiate between their self-interest and that of the state.

The demand that NWFP, which was just a strategic name given by the British, be changed to Pakhtunistan or Pakhtunkhwa was a red-herring to the establishment that felt that it would be a step towards secession. It took 63 years for the Pakhtuns to get a name which gives them an identity accepted through the mega 18th Amendment. The ANP, which is led by Wali Khan's son, Asfandyar Wali Khan, bargained hard with the Punjab leadership in the parliamentary committee, which drafted and built consensus on the 18th Amendment. It was a matter of give and take. The Punjab leaders reluctantly gave consent after taking a media bashing, but not without getting the prefix of 'Khyber' added to the name Pakhtunkhwa. By adding 'Khyber' the Punjab leadership wanted to differentiate the Pakhtuns of Pakistan from the Pakhtuns across the Khyber Pass in Afghanistan.

Any efforts by the Pashto intelligentsia to promote their language were considered a threat to the solidarity of Pakistan, because the establishment believed, and they still insist, that Urdu alone should be the national language of the country. As Pashto is also a language of around 40 per cent of Afghans, the NWFP intellectuals were in constant touch with their counterparts in Afghanistan. These connections were suspected and intelligence always hounded the promoters of the native language of the Pakhtuns till a few years back. 'Indeed, at the height of the Pakhtunistan issue in the fifties and the sixties, the government was almost paranoid about Pashto, which it took to be the major symbol of Pakhtun ethno-nationalism.'[5] This policy is, ironically, diagonally opposite to the national security policy of Pakistan, which considers Pakhtuns of Afghanistan as their allies in that country.

The National Awami Party (NAP) government had declared Urdu as the official language in 1972, because Pashto was only taught at lower levels in some schools and it has remained subjugated by Urdu, which has stunted its growth. The policy to promote Urdu and English as the languages of government, trade and the economy has hampered the growth of major nationalities' languages. This language policy is favourably inclined in maintaining the class status quo in the country. The middle classes thrive on Urdu and the upper-middle classes on English, excluding the lower-middle class and peasantry from the process of economic prosperity and social mobility. It is a universal truth that children learn faster in their mother tongue but medium of instruction in Pakistan is biased in favour of the Urdu- and- English-speaking classes. This is the reason that Punjabi middle classes have adopted Urdu as the first language instead of their own Punjabi. It had become a status symbol in the Punjabi middle class to speak Urdu in their homes.

However, the Pakhtuns never abandoned their language. There are Pashto newspapers written in Persian script, and now Pashto TV and radio channels have also become popular. But the English-speaking elite have no idea that various local language TV channels have wider viewership in their respective provinces. This lack of understanding among the advertiser is, in turn, not favourable for the local language media of all provinces. The Pashto media is no exception.

While the Afghanistan government had tacitly supported the Pakhtunistan movement, it increased its support when the NAP government was dismissed in Balochistan in 1973 by Zulfikar Ali Bhutto, and the NAP government in KP resigned in solidarity. After the attack on a NAP rally held at Liaquat Bagh in Rawalpindi on 23 March 1973 by Bhutto's Federal Security Force in which seven NAP workers were killed, some of the leaders led by the leading Pashto poet Ajmal Khattak migrated to Afghanistan. They were given shelter by the Parcham Party leaders (a faction of the Afghan Communist Party headed by Babrak Karmal), who had supported Mohammed Daoud Khan's coup against the last king of Afghanistan, Mohammed Zahir Shah.

Daoud's support to Balochistan and Pakhtunistan increased, but it always remained measured as he did not want a major conflict with Pakistan. Bhutto's answer to this was providing shelter and training to Engineer Gulbuddin Hekmatyar's Islamic militants. Wali Khan and Baloch leaders were put in jail and a conspiracy trial was started against them in Hyderabad prison.

Interestingly, the same army that was used by Bhutto to quash the Baloch resistance, which started after their elected government was dismissed, released the NAP leaders after deposing Bhutto's government. The army announced a general amnesty for all the Baloch and Pakhtun leaders who had fought against them and had used Afghanistan as their hinterland. This action was taken by the army after killing thousands of Balochs and destroying many villages in the period between 1973 and 1977. Earlier, behind the scene attempts by Bhutto to patch up with the jailed NAP leaders were foiled by the army intelligence agencies.

However, Pakhtun nationalism started getting mellow with the development of Pakistan. The Pakhtuns' share in government services improved and some of them got posted at high positions, their share in the army rose to 20 per cent as against their share in Pakistan's population, which stood at around 13 per cent. The Pakhtun businessmen started investing in Karachi and looking southward for their growth. As a major part of Pakhtunkhwa is infertile and rugged, the push factor has always been strong in KP and FATA regions. This has resulted in the migration of many Pakhtuns to Karachi and some other major cities of Punjab and Sindh. (But most Pakhtun male members migrate in search of jobs without their families, which is a sore point for the Karachi Mohajir population, because they transfer what they earn out of the province and being alone have little stake in the city's peace-keeping.)

Today in 2013, Pakhtun lobbies claim that Karachi has more Pakhtuns than Peshawar. This statement can be disputed on the basis of the extrapolation of the 1988 Census demographic profile of Karachi. However, for the first time in the 2008 elections, the Pakhtuns living in Karachi captured two Provincial Assembly seats under the banner of the ANP. In the coming local government and general elections they are looking for more seats from Karachi and have tasked their people to register their votes in the city. This is not acceptable to the MQM, which does not want to give in on even a single seat. The tussle to secure constituencies before the completion of the new census and delimitation of constituencies has turned violent, as each day many people are murdered in ethnic and target killings from both sides. In the first nine months of 2012 over 1,820 persons were killed in Karachi.

Another factor that is dangerously gaining strength in Pakhtunkhwa is the rise of the filthy-rich drug smugglers, gun-running mafia, smugglers of electronic and other consumer goods who take advantage of the Afghan transit trade, and money traders who run Hawala (sending money abroad through unofficial channels) and Hundi (receiving money from abroad through unofficial channels) businesses. This class has sidelined the people who do legitimate business, and is gaining political influence. The state of Pakistan and the provincial government of Pakhtunkhwa appear to be helpless before this set of mafias, who now contest elections and even manage to capture a couple of seats.

All these factors have changed the politics of Pakhtunkhwa. Their present problem is not getting their due share from the federal government, which has accepted their major demands in the 7th NFC Award, but the rise of Talibanization and terrorist attacks is the number one problem of the province for which they blame the Pakistani establishment and its support to the militant Islamic ideology in the past and its Afghan policy. In the mid-1980s when Pakistan was deeply involved in supporting the so-called Islamic insurgency against Afghanistan, I recall having asked Wali Khan at a press conference at the Karachi Press Club, that, given the large influx of Afghan refugees and the unbridled proliferation of arms sold by the 'Islamic Mujahidin', did he smell Beirut? Wali Khan spoke for half an hour and predicted that Zia's policies would first burn Wali Khan's province and then the Pakhtuns. And that is what history is witnessing today.

However, reassessing from hindsight, the Pakhtun nationalists must be happy that they joined Pakistan, because their earlier desire to join their Pakhtun brethren in Afghanistan could have brought them destruction and not integration with the more socially and economically developed Pakistan. But to get here they had to go through many testing times as the Centre was not willing to accept their identity and economic rights. And while going forward, they are likely to suffer more bloodshed due to the illusory so-called National Security Policy of Pakistan, which wanted Afghanistan as a client state providing the strategic depth to its defence forces. But forced by the international circumstances the establishment is gradually reconciling with the idea that at best they can hope to have a friendly government in Afghanistan. That is possible only if they play an important role of bringing Afghan Taliban leaders to the negotiating table.

Notes and References

1. Adeel Khan, *Politics of Identity: Ethnic Nationalism and the State in Pakistan*, Sage Publishers, New Delhi, 2005, p. 94.
2. Ibid., p. 95.
3. Khalid B. Sayeed, *Politics in Pakistan: The Nature and Direction of Change*, Praeger Publisher, New York, 1980, p. 20.
4. *The Transfer of Power*, Vol. XII (Sir R. M. Lockhart's Communication to Mountbatten), HMSO (Her Majesty's Stationery Office), London, 1983.
5. Tariq Rahman, *Language and Politics in Pakistan*, Oxford University Press, New York, 1977, p. 145.

Chapter 10

Punjab – The Major Beneficiary

Jinnah's good intentions of having a state where minorities could feel equal and comfortable were in contradiction to the whole Pakistan movement's communal objectives and dynamics. Eventually, after a few months, both Punjab and Bengal were partitioned on communal basis. Sikhs were forced to leave West Punjab, as were the Muslims of East Punjab after one of history's bloodiest communal cleansing, undertaken by the Muslim and Sikhs in the areas which they dominated. And what Jinnah got as Pakistan was in his own words 'a truncated or mutilated and moth-eaten Pakistan.'

The West Punjab that became the ultimate beneficiary from the creation of Pakistan had suffered most when the province was divided by a line drawn by Sir Cyril Radcliffe. It saw one of the worst massacres of Punjabi Muslims, Sikhs and Hindus – more than any other province of India. Historians maintain that the number of Punjabi migrants from East Punjab to West Punjab rose to 70 to 80 per cent of the total migrants from India. Muslim, Sikh and Hindu immigrants of Punjab suffered most from the communal killings at the time of partition of India. But the good thing is that after 66 years the wounds of massacre have healed most people on both sides of the border. They regret and are ashamed about this painful chapter of history, just as the

Germans are about the Jews pogrom. Irrespective of the debate about who had started the pogrom, the birth of the Punjab in Pakistan was bloody and painful.

Unfortunately, Jinnah and his mediocre team had not foreseen the division of Punjab and Bengal as a part of the partition. The Muslim League leaders would neither forecast the immigration of over 10 million people, nor the communal massacre on both sides of the divide they created. Statements issued by Jinnah, on the partition of Punjab and Bengal, as late as 30 April 1947, show that he had not envisaged the partition of these two provinces. A reading of the statements also shows he had not thought about emigration of the Muslim and Hindus from the provinces in which they were in minority, but it seems he was thinking about more orderly emigration after the partition. In his statement Jinnah said: 'I find from the press reports that the Congress has started emphasizing that in the event of Pakistan and Hindustan being established, the Punjab will be partitioned, while the Hindu Maha Sabha has started a vigorous propaganda that Bengal should be partitioned....'[1]

He considered it as a conspiracy, '[To] unnerve the Muslims by repeatedly emphasizing that the Muslims will get a truncated or mutilated and moth-eaten Pakistan .... Merely because a portion of the minorities in the Pakistan provinces have taken up this attitude, the British government should not countenance it, because the result will be logically [sic] that all other provinces will have to be cut in the similar way, which will be dangerous to embark on this line and lead to the breaking up of the various provinces, and create a far dangerous situation in the future. If such a process were to be adopted, it would strike at the root of the administrative, economic and political life of the provinces, which have for nearly a century been developed and built up on that basis and have grown and are functioning at present ... as autonomous provinces.'[2] Regarding the emigration of the Hindus after the partition he said, 'subsequently the respective Governments in Pakistan and Hindustan can effectively carry out the exchange of population wherever it may be necessary and feasible.'[3] For the Sikhs he had a different message: 'The Sikh do not stand to gain from the partition of the Punjab but will be split into two halves. More than half of their population will have to remain in Pakistan, even if the partition of the Punjab takes place according to their conception, whereas in

Pakistan, as proposed by the Muslim League, they will play, as one solid minority a very big part.'⁴

The partition of the Punjab and Bengal had to happen, by the very logic of Muslim League communal politics, in the undivided subcontinent. That the Congress and Hindu Maha Sabha did play a role by provoking communal riots in these provinces further hastened the process. Jinnah's good intentions of having a state where minorities could feel equal and comfortable were in contradiction to the whole Pakistan movement's communal objectives and dynamics. Eventually, after a few months, both the provinces were partitioned on communal basis and Sikhs were forced to leave West Punjab, as were the Muslims of East Punjab after one of history's bloodiest communal cleansing, undertaken by the Muslim and Sikhs in the areas which they dominated. And what Jinnah got as Pakistan was in his own words 'a truncated or mutilated and moth-eaten Pakistan.'

Historian Ayesha Jalal has pointed out that Jinnah had not expected the massive immigration and massacre. He was heart-broken on seeing so much bloodshed. Jinnah had expected to get the whole of Punjab and Bengal, thus having a sizeable Hindu and Sikh population in Pakistan. His view was that the safety of the Muslims in the Muslim-minority provinces would be ensured because it would be linked with the security of Hindus and Sikhs in Pakistan – the bulk of which was in undivided Punjab and Bengal. But the partition line drawn by the British was mischievous. That is the reason why Jinnah admitted that he was getting 'a truncated Pakistan'.

Another setback to the Punjab was that almost all the refugees who migrated from East Punjab had to be settled in various cities of West Punjab. Some of the Urdu-speaking immigrants who had small business and agricultural background settled in Multan and Bahawalpur. According to the *Census of Pakistan 1951* (Vol. 1), the total number of refugees who came from India till that year were over 7.22 million out of which 5.28 million settled in Punjab, about 699,000 in East Bengal, 616,000 in Karachi, and 550,000 in the rest of Sindh. Only a few thousand settled in the NWFP and Balochistan. In the case of Punjab, as most of the immigrants came from East Punjab, their language and cultural affinity helped them to assimilate with the local population without much difficulty. But for the new province it was indeed a huge strain on their resources although the migration of Sikhs and Hindus from West

Punjab was around 3.80 million out of the total outward migration of 5.08 million to India.[5] This created space for the newcomers.

***

The Punjab had no problem in accepting the supremacy of Urdu because they resigned from the promotion of their language long ago and adopted Urdu to reap economic benefits all over Pakistan. Interestingly, although at present only 3 per cent of Indians claim that Punjabi is their mother tongue it has been given the status of official language there, on the other hand, over 50 per cent have Punjabi as their mother tongue in Pakistan but it is not even taught in schools. This is perhaps one of the unique cases where a person can do his Masters in Punjabi, but is not taught the same in schools.

Besides, the Punjab managed to get in the driving seat of Pakistan soon after the creation of the country. One of the main reasons for Punjab's power was its strong presence in the civil and military bureaucracy. Out of the 95 federal government senior bureaucrats in 1951, 40 were from Punjab although its share in the undivided Pakistan population was just 27.7 per cent. The share of Bengalis, who constituted 55.5 per cent of the population, was only 3 per cent. The Mohajirs (who were just 3 per cent of the population) held 33 senior positions among the top federal officials. The situation did not improve and by 1959, according to statistics quoted by linguist and academician Dr Tariq Rahman, almost 49 per cent of the top bureaucracy positions were held by Punjabis, 30 per cent by Mohajirs and the Bengalis had around 10 per cent. Similarly, in the top military elite positions, Punjabis had 35 per cent, Pakhtuns almost 40 per cent, while the Bengalis a solitary 1 position, which came to 2 per cent of the total 48 such positions.

'A few years after submitting his report [Hamoodur Rahman Commission Report] on the loss of East Pakistan, Chief Justice Rahman touched upon the issue of the Punjabi dominance in Pakistan in a lead article in the [Pakistan Army] *Journal*. Justice Rahman reminded his readers that the main culprits in the corruption that led to the disintegration of the old Pakistan were invariably Punjabis, and that "this gave rise to the feelings of Punjabi domination which in turn propelled into prominence regionalistic and parochial aspirations".'[6]

***

A more important factor contributing to Punjab's rule over Pakistan was that almost 75 per cent of the country's army is recruited from the northern districts of this province. Among the officers their ratio is even higher. As the army in Pakistan has acquired the role of the biggest and most organized political player, it continues to dominate policy-making overtly when it is in power directly and covertly when a controlled democracy is permitted by them. This indirectly benefits the political and economic interests of the Punjab. According to the 2011–12 budget allocations, Pakistan spends almost 30 per cent of its total revenue income on defence. The hidden expenses are in the shape of pensions of retired army personnel in the civil government budget and the millions of dollars spent on non-budgeted nuclear and missile programme. Most of the cantonments are also in the Punjab. The maximum benefit of the war economy is thus going to this province. This is besides the lion's share they get from the federal revenue pool where a major criterion is population of the provinces. However, for the first time, other factors such as inverse poverty and revenue generation have been given a little weightage in the revenue divisible pool distribution in the 7th NFC Award.

***

Over the years industrial and financial investment has flowed towards Punjab. By 1972 before the nationalization of industries and financial institutions by Zulfikar Ali Bhutto, a list compiled by a research scholar H. Papanek revealed that out of the 16 top business houses, seven had Punjabi origin. The rest were mainly Gujarati-speaking immigrants from India, barring a lone Pakhtun family. If a similar list of top 16 business houses is compiled today, the Punjabi businessmen's share would be far larger since many Gujarati-speaking families either left Pakistan or failed to keep the growth pace with their well-heeled Punjabi competitors.

The Punjab was also the major beneficiary of the irrigated land distribution in Pakistan, much to the resentment of the Sindhis. The allotment of 24,903 acres of land to 244 Punjabi civil officers in the land irrigated by Guddu Barrage, and 273 acres of Sukkur Barrage land instead of its distribution to the landless peasants of Sindh became a hot topic in the Sixties. However, 10 Sindhi officers were also allotted 1,460 acres in Guddu Barrage area and 23 officers received 2,618 acres in Sukkur Barrage. The Mohajir officers were also not behind in this loot, as 15 officers were allotted 2,240 acres and 4 officers got 1,769 acres in Guddu and Sukkur Barrage areas, respectively. But as expected the army officer got the chunk of the Sindh land booty. The grant to the army officers mainly belonging to Punjab was 78,300 acres by 1969. To give land to his fellow army officers, Ayub Khan ejected poor peasants of the area. The retired Punjabi and Mohajir officers also poached another 38,000 acres of Sindh irrigated land. The Sindhi feudal lords, who otherwise are known for exploiting their 'Haris' (share-croppers) and landless peasants, were able to rally support of the people on a nationalist plank that the Sindhis' land was being allotted to the Punjabis and Mohajirs.[7]

***

Another advantage taken by the Punjabi ruling elite is that it has managed to get a larger share of the river water and the issue remains unresolved till this day. The differences between the Punjab and Sindh and to a certain extent Balochistan on the water issue are outstanding, in spite of the fact that General Pervez Musharraf's military government held several meetings to resolve this issue. The last water accord is now 20 years old, and since then the ground situation has changed a lot, particularly because of the weather conditions. The canals, which were drawn from the Indus in the Punjab to take the flood water, have now been used as perennial irrigation canals. The 1991 Water Accord was knocked together by Nawaz Sharif's government quite secretively and was never discussed in the Provincial Assemblies. Sindh water experts were of the view that their chief minister, Jam Sadiq Ali, succumbed to the pressure and accepted the terms, which in fact reduced the provinces' share. The Punjab managed to get the ad-hoc water withdrawals, which it had been drawing since 1971 under an understanding that it was a provisional arrangement and without prejudice to the claims of other provinces. This issue remains unresolved between the provinces and takes an emotive turn whenever the water in the rivers is less than average. As it is Sindh has suffered from the unjust water distribution because it is not getting the required 10 MAF (Million Acre Feet) water down the Kotri Barrage to stop the sea from intruding in the delta area. Many villages of the delta area have been wiped out because of the salty sea water intrusion. Fish production has declined, forcing many people from these fishing villages to migrate to other areas of

Sindh, as fishing is the sole means of livelihood of the people living along the Indus delta.

***

However, the growth of Punjab cannot be attributed entirely to the patronage from the Punjabi civil-military bureaucracy and politicians who ruled the country. The people of Punjab are extremely hard working and have strong entrepreneurship qualities. They are willing to move out easily from their home towns in search of economic opportunities because the small family agriculture landholdings cannot sustain big families. The population growth rate of the Punjab is obstinately stuck at 2 per cent per annum. As a result of these factors a number of industrial cities have emerged in Punjab and are growing very fast, specializing in different sectors.

The destablization of Karachi since the rise of Mohajir ethnicity has also contributed to the shifting of large and medium businesses to Punjab. Though Karachi is the financial hub and the State Bank of Pakistan is also situated in the city, two large private sector banks – Muslim Commercial Bank (MCB) and Allied Bank – owned by Punjabi industrialists Mian Muhammad Mansha and Mohammad Naeem Mukhtar, respectively, have moved their head offices to Lahore. Even some of the Gujarati and other Memon business houses have moved portions of their businesses to Lahore, mainly because of the poor law and order situation in Karachi.

Rapid industrialization of the Punjab, particularly during the military rule of General Zia-ul-Haq, has also changed the class equilibrium of the provincial politics. Punjab is now led by industrialist-politicians and not by the scions of feudal lords, who were created by the British Raj to win their loyalties. At the same time as some of the businesses have grown quite big and want to enter the Indian market, the hostility against India in Punjab has dampened in the last two decades. On the contrary, Lahore Chamber of Commerce and Industry has been quite vocal about opening trade and investment avenues with India.

***

To sum up, the Punjab is the only province of Pakistan which has nothing to regret for jumping on to the Pakistan bandwagon by their leaders, though reluctantly. But much of the growth and prosperity of its elite has been at the expense of other provinces and through their undermining of the basic objective for which Pakistan was made. To achieve this end, its leaders have continued to exploit the religious emotions of the people of Punjab and other provinces. They are the ones who lead the symphony that the army is not only the guardian of our frontiers but of Pakistan's ideology also, because they serve as tools to suppress smaller nationalities and the working classes of Pakistan.

Notes and References

1. Amarjit Singh (editor), *Jinnah and Punjab: Shamsul Hasan Collection and Other Documents 1944-47*, Kanishka Publishers, New Delhi, 2007.
2. Ibid.
3. Ibid.
4. Ibid.
5. Quoted by Waseem Ahmed in *Politics and the State in Pakistan*, Government of Pakistan, Karachi, 1948, from *Pakistan: The First Year* (publication details not available).
6. Stephen Philip Cohen, *The Idea of Pakistan*, Vanguard Books, Lahore, 2005, p. 223. Justice (retd.) Rahman quoted by him from an article: 'Ideology of Pakistan: The Raison d'être of Our Country', *Pakistan Army Journal*, June 1978.
7. Land distribution source in Sindh Assembly Debates, Vol. IV, 22 December 1972 quoted by Tanvir Ahmed in *Political Dynamics of Sindh*, Pakistan Studies Centre, Karachi, p. 518.

Chapter 11

Journey to the Promised Autonomy

... a Parliamentary Committee for Constitutional Reforms (PCCR) was formed with the representation of all those political parties that have presence in the two houses of the parliament ... it did the historic job of introducing 102 amendments in the Constitution of Pakistan, all rolled up in the jumbo 18th Amendment. The political dimension of this momentous event is that a consensus document was approved unanimously by the National Assembly, amply proving that democracy can work in Pakistan. It also shows that in a country where extremists have resorted to terrorism, the majority of the people is moderate and believes in accommodating each other's views in the democratic spirit.

It took 66 painful and bloody years for Pakistan to reach the threshold of the promised provincial autonomy. The main objective of the Pakistan movement looks attainable now. At least major constitutional hurdles have been removed by the mega Constitution (18th Amendment) Act, 2010.

Pakistan's 1973 Constitution was amended to give provinces their rights and to remove many of the distortions inserted in it by military dictators – General Zia-ul-Haq and General Pervez Musharraf. But it is just the beginning, as the implementation of the new amendments may take time. Pakistan has a Constitution but had only short interludes of constitutionalism. For almost half of its life, Pakistan has been ruled by the military dictators, who either abrogated the Constitution or held it in 'abeyance' or 'suspension'. And when it was restored to legitimize their rule, the military rulers mutilated the 1973 Constitution.

***

A brief recap of the chequered constitutional history of Pakistan is important in order to understand how the 'two-nation theory' played a retrogressive role in the constitutional development of the country, and consequently, in the uneven economic development of the constituent provinces. The first Constituent Assembly took seven years and when it had nearly completed the draft Constitution, the governor-general dissolved the Assembly because all powers rested with him. Finally after nine years of its inception, Pakistan's second Constituent Assembly passed a Constitution in March 1956, adopting the parliamentary system. These nine years the country was ruled on the basis of Government of India Act 1935, and the consensus could not be reached mainly because the Centre was unwilling to give the political powers and economic resources to the provinces.

Before adopting the 1956 Constitution, the provincial rights were trampled by the government in 1955, when it merged four provinces of West Pakistan and Balochistan into 'one unit'. The devious motive was to claim parity with East Pakistan, which had 55 per cent of Pakistan's population. But this Constitution was abrogated by General Ayub Khan, who declared martial law in the country in October 1958. When he needed to lift the martial law, he brought in his own Constitution in 1962 embodying the presidential form of government inspired by the American system. He was replaced by General Yahya Khan in March 1969, who promised to hold the elections and conceded to the major demands of the people's movement by promising a parliamentary democracy and restoration of the four provinces of West Pakistan.

After the elections, the National Assembly was supposed to give a new Constitution within a year. But the reluctance of the Pakistani establishment and Zulfikar Ali Bhutto to accept the six points of Awami League leader, Sheikh Mujibur Rahman, unleashed a liberation movement in East Pakistan. Awami League was demanding more provincial autonomy. After the liberation of Bangladesh, Bhutto took over the remaining Pakistan and managed to give a consensual Constitution in 1973. But he took no time in violating the spirit of his own Constitution and dissolved the ANP's provincial government in Balochistan. The ANP-led government in KP resigned in protest.

Bhutto was removed by General Zia-ul-Haq in 1977, and once again martial law was imposed. All fundamental rights given in the Constitution were held in 'abeyance.' When he restored the Constitution in 1985, the 8th Amendment was introduced to validate his rule. This transferred most of the prime minister's powers to the president. For future military interventions, without resorting to martial law, he opened a burglar's window in the Constitution by inserting Article 58(2) and 2(B). This gave constitutional powers to General Zia to dissolve the National Assembly and oust the government at his discretion. This became the most controversial clause of the Constitution. It was first used by General Zia for dismissing the government of Muhammad Khan Junejo in 1988. It was invoked by the establishment to sack Benazir Bhutto and Nawaz Sharif governments twice in the 1990s. In the last stint Nawaz Sharif had come to power with a 'heavy mandate' and removed this clause from the Constitution through an amendment. So, when Musharraf led a coup against Nawaz Sharif in October 1999, he had to come in directly as the 'so-called safety valve of Article 58(2) and 2(B)' (as the establishment likes to call it) was not available for ambushing an elected government. To legitimate his rule, Musharraf further mutilated the Constitution by bringing in the Legal Framework Order 2002 and the 17th Amendment 2003. This amendment increased the powers of the president and validated all the actions of Musharraf, since his take over in 1999. However, the 17th Amendment had some positive features also, like increase in the reserved seats for women in National and Provincial Assemblies and in local councils; lowering the voting age to 18 years; abolition of separate electorates system for the minorities; and an increase in National and Provincial Assembly seats.

**

It was in this political setting that Benazir Bhutto and Nawaz Sharif, each having been bitten twice by the military establishment, met in London in May 2005 and decided to bury their hatchets. They signed a Charter of Democracy (CoD), underlining 'that the military dictatorship and the nation cannot co-exist – as military involvement adversely affects the economy and the democratic institutions as well as the defence capabilities, and the integrity of the country – the nation needs a new direction, different from a militaristic and regimental approach of the Bonapartist regimes.'

Both the leaders reaffirmed in the CoD their commitment to undiluted democracy, decentralization and devolution of power, maximum provincial autonomy, empowerment of the people at the grass-roots level, a free and independent media, an independent judiciary and settlement of disputes with the neighbours, through peaceful means. They pledged cleansing the 1973 Constitution from the amendments made by the military rulers, particularly repealing of the 17th Amendment of Musharraf.

Once the PPP-led coalition came into power, Nawaz Sharif's Pakistan Muslim League (PML-N) started pressing for the implementation of the CoD. Their contention was that the 17th Amendment should be repealed right away. But the PPP-led coalition wisely linked deletion of disputed clauses of the 17th Amendment with the issue of provincial autonomy and the demand of the NWFP government that their province should be renamed Pakhtunkhwa.

As in most of the democracies in the world, the regional ethnic leadership has emerged much stronger in Pakistan in the last two decades. The political future of the region is that no national party would be able to form a government without the support of the regional parties. This trend has strengthened the centrifugal forces in Pakistan also, who demand more autonomy for the federating units. These regional parties insisted that the 18th Amendment should deal with the provincial autonomy issue also because it was more important to them.

To achieve these objectives, a Parliamentary Committee for Constitutional Reforms was formed with the representation of all those political parties that have presence in the two houses of the parliament. This committee was criticized for taking too long, but it did the historic job of introducing 102 amendments in the Constitution of Pakistan, all rolled up in the jumbo 18th Amendment. The political dimension of this momentous event is that a consensus document was approved unanimously by the National Assembly, amply proving that democracy can work in Pakistan. It also shows that in a country where extremists have resorted to terrorism, a majority of the people is moderate and believes in accommodating each other's views in the democratic spirit.

This historic amendment has restored the parliamentary system, which was distorted into a quasi-president system, by the military dictators, through the 8th and 17th Amendments. At the very outset the 18th Amendment first repealed the Legal Framework Order 2002 and 17th Amendment 2003, instead of accepting them as part of the Constitution. In the past the amendments introduced by the dictators were accepted as a part of the Constitution by the democratic government and only some controversial articles and clauses were deleted or changed. The most important gain of the proposed amendments is that the Centre has ceded more autonomy to the provinces. This would strengthen the federation, as its units would be more satisfied with the new division of powers. Undoubtedly there will still be grumblings from the nationalist forces in smaller provinces, but these amendments coupled with the NFC Award would help in assuaging the nationalists to a certain extent.

An upsurge in Balochistan has pushed all political parties to take the autonomy issue seriously. Whether the powers, which would now be transferred to the provinces, will actually flow to them remains to be seen. The positive role played by PML-N leaders in agreeing first to the changes in the criteria for distribution of fiscal resources in the NFC, and then to the expansion of provincial autonomy in the 18th Amendment has to be noted. It shows that Punjab's bourgeois leadership has resisted the pressure of the Centrist establishment against devolution of powers to the provinces. The development of capitalist relations in the country has also created interdependent economic relations among the major ethnic communities of the country.

The transfer of the subjects listed in the concurrent list of the Constitution to the provinces was a long-pending demand of the smaller provinces. The 18th Amendment fulfills this demand. Some of the important subjects have been transferred from the Federal Legislative List Part 1 to List 2, which is a good omen. This would include the provinces in decision-making on the subjects which were earlier decided unilaterally by the Centre because they were in List 1. But a close look at the concurrent list subjects shows that the provinces would not be enriched by this change. Most of the 47 subjects mentioned in this list would bring no financial gain to the provinces. However, the transfer of the concurrent list subjects to the provinces would add to their responsibilities and financial liabilities. The provinces have been also allowed to make their own penal laws and marriage and divorce laws.

The provinces wanted control over their natural resources and fiscal authority on such taxes as have buoyancy and elasticity. The 7th NFC Award dealt with some of these issues. But the most important victory of the provinces was that their demand to have control over their natural resources, including oil and gas, was met halfway in the 18th Amendment. The provinces finally managed to get an equal share, and control over these natural resources and the territorial waters adjacent to them, 'jointly' with the Centre.

The agreement to rename NWFP also settled an old demand of the 73 per cent people living there. It gives great psychological comfort to these people and would cement their bond with the rest of Pakistan even further.

***

In any federation the provinces seek autonomy to have political powers, but the most crucial demand is that they should be given powers over their economic resources. This has not been an easy task in Pakistan, where the federal government has been resisting parting with economic power. The federating units' demand for the redistribution of resources was linked to the decentralization of the constitutional functions and powers of the federal government. The history of NFC Awards in Pakistan shows how successive federal governments deprived East Pakistan and other smaller provinces in order to protect the Punjab-dominated establishment's interest.

Under the Government of India Act 1935, the Centre was made responsible exclusively for the conduct of foreign affairs, defence, communications and currency control. Concurrently it was dealing with maintaining law and order, agriculture and social sector services like health and education. The point to be noted here is that this was the time when the British Raj wanted to keep a tight control of the Central Government.

This division of power became the basis of the Niemeyer Award 1937. The provinces were awarded 50 per cent of the income tax collected in their region and 62 per cent of the export duties on jute. This tax structure was adopted by Pakistan after independence, but it was amended in 1948 on the pretext of the influx of refugees and defence needs. Sales tax, which was a provincial subject, was temporarily undertaken by the Centre and was subject to allocation of 50 per cent proceeds to the provinces. Two major demands of the smaller provinces were based on the historical fact that even in the colonial period the Centre took only 50 per cent of the income tax collected in the region and that sales tax was a provincial tax.

Again, in Raisman Award 1951, Sir Jeremy Raisman awarded net proceeds of the income, excluding corporate tax and federal taxes, to the provinces. And 50 per cent of the net collection of the sales from their respective provinces was shared with them. Even if this formula was adopted, Sindh would have been better off as it was generating a bulk of personal income tax and sales tax. The net loser would have been Pakhtunkhwa and Balochistan.

Then, after a gap of ten years, a commission was appointed in 1961, which gave its recommendations in 1962 setting the provinces' share on the following basis: Taxes on income including corporate tax 50 per cent; sales tax plus other taxes 70 per cent; exports duty on jute and cotton 100 per cent; estate and succession duties 100 per cent; and capital value tax on immoveable property 100 per cent.

To provide more for the development of provinces, NFC was appointed in 1964, which gave its award in 1965. The provinces managed to push the Centre to raise their share from 50 per cent to 65 per cent. The commission also recommended that agricultural income should be taxed. But in spite of such a recommendation by the urban population and sometimes by the Centre, elusive agricultural income, which remains a provincial tax, has been taxed nominally by all the provinces. This is mainly because the representation of the agriculturist in the assemblies is in a majority as almost 60 per cent population live in rural areas.

A new commission was set up in 1970, which gave its award in 1971, before the liberation of Bangladesh. Provinces got the major boost, as their share in the divisible pool was raised to 80 per cent from 65 per cent. However, the provinces were allowed to retain 30 per cent of sales tax from their region and 70 per cent was divided on population basis. Even this arrangement had some incentive for the provinces to raise the payment of sales tax.

The 1st NFC Award that came after the 1973 Constitution was promulgated in 1975. This was based on the new strategy under which 80 per cent of the divisible pool was distributed on population basis. Ironically, Zulfikar Ali Bhutto's (who was Sindhi) government dished out the NFC Award that was tilted heavily in favour of the Punjab. The previous arrangement regarding sales tax was retained. It created a feeling of deprivation among the smaller provinces.

The martial law government of General Zia appointed the 2nd NFC Award under the 1973 Constitution in 1979. In spite of the fact that all the provinces had military administrators, the provinces could not come to a consensus. While Punjab wanted to maintain a status quo, Sindh was against the distribution on the basis of population alone.

In 1985, the 3rd NFC Award was established, in which eminent economist Dr Mahbub ul Haq suggested giving more taxes to the provinces and that the Centre should only retain income tax, corporate tax and customs duty. This commission died without an off-spring. The military government failed to give an NFC Award during its 11-year tenure, although it is mandatory in the Constitution to constitute the NFC Award every five years and review the distribution of financial resources. The major reason of Zia's failure was that the conflicting interests of the provinces could not be reconciled, and the provincial autonomy issue remained a ticklish one that they did not want to touch. The civil servants who represented their respective governments did not budge, in spite of the pressure from the Centre. The resource distribution from the divisible pool thus remained the same, as awarded in 1974, up to 1990.

Prime Minister Nawaz Sharif's government, constituted the 4th NFC Award in 1990. This NFC was headed by Finance Minister Sartaj Aziz, who declared the award successfully after a break of almost 16 years. The most significant development under this award was the expansion of the divisible pool. The excise duties on sugar and tobacco, which came under the non-divisible pool, became a part of it. However, this commission too failed to reach a consensus on changing the population-based formula for the distribution of resources.

It was interesting to note that, contrary to the smaller provinces' fears that the Punjabi prime minister-led government would not increase the share of provinces, the 1990 award did raise the provincial shares by around 18 per cent as compared to the 1974 award. This increase was due to the inclusion of excise duty on sugar and tobacco in the divisible pool.

The major contribution of this award was acceptance of the financial autonomy demand of the provinces. In addition to this, for the first time the provinces' right to net hydel profit, development surcharge (on gas) and excise duty on crude oil was accepted and amounts relocated in the shape of straight transfers to the provinces. However, the proportion of horizontal distribution remained the same, because population was still the sole criterion for resource distribution and there had been no census since 1981.

The 5th NFC Award was constituted in December 1996. But the commission announced the award in February 1997 during Nawaz Sharif's second term. All taxes/duties were included in the divisible pool. It comprised: (a) income tax (b) wealth tax (c) capital value tax (d) sales tax (e) export duties (f) custom duties (g) excise duties (excluding excise duty on gas, charged at wellhead), and (h) any other tax collected by the federal government. In addition to that, royalties on crude oil and net development surcharges on natural gas were also given to the provinces. An incentive of matching grant was introduced, although up to a certain limit, to the provincial governments, meaning that if they exceeded their revenue growth target of 14.2 per cent, they would be provided matching grants.

An important aspect of the 1996 NFC Award was that it bifurcated the public expenditures into priority and non-priority expenditures. The priority expenditures were described as expenses on defence, debt servicing, social sector and development expenditures, while those on general administration, community services and law and order were termed non-priority expenditures. This, according to a Pakistan Institute of Development Economics report, was done to solve the emerging financial challenges, issues and accordingly to prioritize the path of development.

However, while on one hand the federal government included more taxes in the divisible pool that slightly increased the provincial share, on the other hand the share to the federal government in the divisible pool was pushed up to 62.5 per cent from just 20 per cent in the past; and that of the provinces was slashed to 37.5 per cent from 80 per cent.

The 6th NFC Award was constituted in July 2000 under the chairmanship of Shaukat Aziz, the federal finance minister. It held 11 meetings but could not finalize its recommendations due to the lack of consensus among its members. In an interview with me for *Pakistan Business Update,* which was telecast by Pakistan Television (PTV), Aziz was optimistic that he would be bringing the divergent views of the provinces to an agreement.

The 7th NFC Award was constituted in July 2005, but it met with the same fate and could not come up with an award. As a result, the provincial chief ministers vested the authority to the president to announce a just award. The president, under Article 160(6) of the Constitution, announced an award through an ordinance. Under this award, the provincial share was revised and it was decided to be 45 per cent (share in total divisible pool plus grants) for the first financial year, reaching 50 per cent with subsequent increase of 1 per cent per annum.

However, once again while military governments had failed to build the consensus, the democratic government managed to bring all the stakeholders on a meeting point. Consensus on the 7th NFC Award was no small feat. Critics who hold maximalist positions may still cry for more, but they do not realize that it was a step forward qualitatively and quantitatively. Democracy is the system of evolution and not revolution.

In an atmosphere of gloom and doom the flexibility shown by the Central Government and by the four provincial governments was indicative of their maturity. It also shows that politicians have the capacity and political will to resolve the issues. Those qualities the military dictatorship lacked because it was not willing to dilute the Islamabad powers. The award was indeed a good omen for the country where many provincial autonomy issues remain to be solved.

All the NFC members, wisely, addressed the Balochistan issue first as it was the most exploited province of Pakistan. For over six decades, Balochistan was exploited, which has now convinced many Baloch leaders that nothing short of independence would solve their problems. While President Asif Ali Zardari's government tried to appease the people of Balochistan with a special package, the 7th NFC Award tried to reach out to the angry Baloch. Dr Gulfaraz Ahmad, who was Balochistan's member in the NFC, while talking to me hoped that the award would go a long way in satisfying even those voices in Balochistan who are very critical of the federation. He pointed out that Balochistan would not have to look towards the Centre for their due share in the form of grants and subventions. That the other three provinces and federal government realized that it was vital to correct the historical injustice to Balochistan is evident from the fact that as against a population ratio of 5.11 per cent in Pakistan, the share from the divisible pool from 2010 to 2011 was 9.09 per cent. In addition to this, Balochistan's demand for Rs 4 billion as Gas Development Surcharge (GDS) was also accepted. To compensate for the GDS loss of the province from 2002 to 2009 the government agreed to give them another Rs 10 billion. And additionally for the period (1954–90) when no royalty on gas was given to the province, the federal government agreed to pay Balochistan Rs 120 billion in ten equal installments. Together with the collection of provincial taxes, Balochistan would have sufficient funds to work for the development of the province.

The problem however is that the angry Baloch nationalists and their progressive supporters who are used to criticizing the federal government do not build pressure on their provincial government for efficient management of the available resources. The corrupt officials of the provincial government are not held accountable for what resources they have; instead, they are allowed to hide behind the slogans that others are exploiting them. This does not mean that the importance of the struggle for more provincial autonomy and control over their natural resources should be undermined.

The 7th NFC Award was a big feather in the cap of the PPP-led coalition government. Why? The basic reason is that the credit goes to the Central Government, which for the first time has shown commitment to give more provincial autonomy to the provinces. The federal government thus agreed to slash its share in the revenue from 52.5 per cent to 44 per cent in 2010–11 and 43 per cent thereafter. That is a substantial cut, considering that transfer of sales tax on services to the provinces would raise their actual share to over 60 per cent. This is what they had been demanding in the past.

The major beneficiaries of the transfer of sales tax on services would be Sindh and Punjab, in that order. In a background interview, Kaiser Bengali, who was a member of NFC from Sindh, said that Sindh would get additional Rs 40 billion from this transfer of tax in 2010–11 and it could go up in future. Sales tax on the services is applicable to banks, telecommunications, courier services, etc. The provinces would have the right to impose sales tax on other services, also, keeping in mind that it is not harmful to the investment climate of their province.

Another major success of the 7th NFC Award was an agreement on the horizontal distribution of taxes. Dr Gulfaraz Ahmad aptly called it a 'horizontal equalizer', as it is a first step to remove uneven development of the provinces. The old formula of distributing taxes on the basis of population was always a sore point for the three smaller provinces.

Now it has been agreed that 10 per cent weightage would be given to backwardness and poverty. Eminent economist Kaiser Bengali explained that poverty level would be worked out on the basis of an average drawn from three studies: 1999 poverty estimates; 2003 UN Human Development Index; and 2008 Federal Bureau of Statistics survey. It had been a long-pending demand of Balochistan and Pakhtunkhwa. But all the provinces claim that they have high poverty regions.

Though Sindh had demanded greater weightage to revenue collection in the horizontal distribution of resources, claiming that it was collecting the bulk of revenue, the 7th Award gives it 5 per cent weightage only. It is a good beginning as the basis of calculation would be revenue generation. Withholding income tax on electricity would be used as a 'proxy' yardstick to measure the revenue generation of the provinces. This formula has yet to be fine-tuned.

One of the major demands of the smaller provinces was that inverse population density should be included in the multiple distribution formula. It has been accepted with a weightage of 2.7 per cent. This would most benefit Balochistan.

The PPP-led democratic government was also credited for resolving some of the issues, which were technically outside the preview of the NFC. It worked out a long-standing hydel royalty issue to the satisfaction of Pakhtunkhwa. And all the political leaders of the provinces in tandem with the federal government acknowledged the devastation caused by terrorism in that province. Rising above their technical mandate, they promised to give 1 per cent of their share to Pakhtunkhwa for meeting this challenge, which has ravaged the whole country.

Chapter 12

DEMARCATION OF PROVINCES

'What is certain is that language policies are so intimately related with politics that, if they change, the political map of Pakistan will also change. Whether such a change occurs with or without violence, or whether the status quo continues, with the present low level violence is for the decision-makers to decide.'

The question of demarcation of provinces on language-based ethno-nationalism has woken up after years of coma. The first step in shock treatment was the renaming of NWFP. Some Saraiki-belt members of the PCCR had demanded a separate province. They have reportedly written what was euphemistically called a 'note of reiteration' on the PCCR report. But the Hindko-speaking members instead opposed the renaming of the NWFP within their respective political parties and did not raise the issue of a separate province.

The movement for a separate province at best can lay claims on Hindko-speaking districts – Abbottabad 92 per cent and Mansehra 47 per cent. The Hindko-speaking population in Peshawar is 7 per cent and Kohat 10 per cent only; hence no claim can be made on these districts. According to the 1998 Population Census of NWFP, the following is the language-wise break up: Pashto 73.9 per cent; Urdu 0.78 per cent; Punjabi 0.97 per cent; Sindhi 0.4 per cent; Saraiki 5.46 per cent; and others 20 per cent. Surprisingly and quite unjustifiably, Hindko was lumped with other languages, although other studies show that 18 per cent people in NWFP speak Hindko.[1] So when a separate province is being demanded by them is it a voice of 18 per cent people of the province?

Whether they should have a separate province or can they be assuaged within KP would depend on the sagacity and statesmanship of the Pakhtun leaders. Increase in the KP income from Tarbela Dam has also tempted the Hindko leaders to demand a separate province. The protagonists of the Hindko province have been claiming their right to this income. Their just demands KP could meet half way by allocating at least 25–30 per cent of the income from Tarbela to the local governments of Hindko-speaking Abbottabad and Mansehra. Devolution of maximum powers to the local councils is the answer to satisfy smaller communities within a province. In his well-researched and most objective book *Language and Politics in Pakistan*, Dr Tariq Rahman has dealt with the Hindko ethnic issue succinctly. He has pointed out: 'The alleged discrimination by the NWFP government led to the formation of the Hindko Qaumi Mahaz [HQM] in 1987.'[2] But HQM did not win a single election and most Hindko-speaking Hazaras traditionally voted for PML-N. That is why Nawaz Sharif was reluctant to accept the renaming of the province. Once it was renamed, Pakistan Muslim League Quaid (PML-Q) leaders opportunistically fanned the issue of Hazara province to win over PML constituency. The PML-Q, which has lost central Punjab to Nawaz Sharif, did not stop here but has also started supporting the possibility of carving out a province comprising the Saraiki-speaking region. This new province can build its economy on income from cotton production. Taj Muhammad Khan Langah, the leader of the Saraiki province movement, says that the Chaudhrys of Gujarat had managed to win 14 seats from the Saraiki belt in the last election, and that is the reason they have now changed their previous stance against the division of the Punjab. On the other hand, the former information minister, Muhammad Ali Durrani has been showing his new-found love for Bahawalpur province. Reports are that when and if Musharraf league jumped into politics, the popular slogan of changing demarcation of the provinces would be one of his main springboards. Progressive forces have been demanding demarcation of provinces on linguistic lines since the Sixties. Demarcation of provinces on an ethnic basis started getting support in 2011 by a section of the establishment, which opposed the same demands of the progressives in the 1960s and 1970s as an agenda of the communists to break the country. Should the progressive forces withdraw from this demand as a reaction? No, as it would be foolish.

So let's address the issue of demarcation of provinces on ethnic basis. There is nothing wrong in re-examining the demarcation of provinces whether it's done in the name of 'linguistic and ethnic rationalization' or right-sizing by taking a slice from the Punjab. Uttar Pradesh was sliced for precisely the same reason. The main objective should be that this demarcation should bring better management and give people easier access to their provincial government.

Learning from the Indian experience is not out of place. Both India and Pakistan inherited the distorted division of the country, which was done purely to suit the British Raj. Both are blessed by the diversity of various nationalities with their own languages and cultures. Both have built their Constitution on the foundation of the Government of India Act 1935 and moved to adopt a federal parliamentary system. India has created 15 new states (provinces) since 1950. The following nine states were created dividing the existing states in the last 60 years: Andhra Pradesh from Madras; Maharashtra and Gujarat from the state of Bombay; Kerala after reorganizing Travancore and Cochin; Mysore was renamed Karnataka; Nagaland was carved out from Assam; Haryana from Punjab; Chhattisgarh from Madhya Pradesh; Uttarakhand from Uttar Pradesh; and Jharkhand from Bihar. Besides, seven union territories were given the status of a state: Himachal Pradesh; Meghalaya; Manipur; Tripura; Sikkim; Mizoram; and Goa. The latest attempt to create Telangana from Andhra Pradesh was foiled by a strong reaction from the Opposition in the Andhra Pradesh Legislature.

The procedure followed for demarcation in India is:

- A Bill giving effect to any or all the changes stated above can be introduced in either house of the Parliament, only on the recommendation of the president.
- If such a Bill affects the boundary or name of the state, then the president, before introducing it in the Parliament, shall refer the Bill to the State Legislature concerned for its opinion, fixing a time limit within which an opinion may be expressed by the State Legislature.

- If the State Legislature fails to express an opinion within the stipulated time limit then it is deemed that it has expressed its views. If it submits its views within the period so specified or extended, the Parliament is not bound to accept or act upon the views of the State Legislature. Further, it is not necessary to make fresh reference to the State Legislature every time an amendment to the Bill is proposed and accepted.
- The Bill is passed with simple majority.
- However, in the case of union territories, it is not necessary to obtain the views of legislatures of union territories before a Bill affecting their boundaries or names is introduced.

In Pakistan correction of provincial boundaries and rationalization on ethno-lingual basis of the existing provinces is long overdue. It would keep on emerging and would not go away, particularly when some less-developed ethnic groups continue to feel deprived. The issue is that a rising middle class in any ethnic group wants more shares in jobs and direct control over their development plans. The elite of these ethnic groups jump on to the bandwagon as they feel that creation of a new unit would give them control over their respective provincial governments.

The present surge in the demand for Hindko and Saraiki provinces is also primarily led by economic interests. The talk about promotion of language and culture is secondary and of emotive flavour. For the time being, the middle class and elite of these ethnic groups teach their children English and Urdu, which is the language of economic opportunities in Pakistan.

The whole issue has been better summed up by Dr Tariq Rahman: 'What is certain is that language policies are so intimately related with politics that, if they change, the political map of Pakistan will also change. Whether such a change occurs with or without violence, or whether the status quo continues, with the present low level violence is for the decision-makers to decide.'

***

The fact that Pakistan and many other countries are moving towards greater autonomy is not because the dominant ruling elite have become charitable. The times have changed. In the last 66 years economic development coupled with information explosion have imploded the strong Centre system. Each region has developed and in that course thrown up their local middle classes, bourgeois and political leadership.

If we look at the election results of Pakistan since 1970, signs of centrifugal forces getting stronger are written on the wall. Even the national parties know that no government can be made without alliances with the regional parties. The coalition governments thus created are noisy, weak and slow-moving but the positive side of this is that the centralist ruling classes are getting weaker. The regional leadership in almost all the democratic countries is now bargaining for a better deal in the federation or a union, whatever they are called. Pakistan is not typical in this regard; even developed countries are giving more autonomy to the regions and their major parties are constrained to sit in coalition with their arch rivals.

The struggle for greater autonomy in Pakistan has also disrupted the struggle between the haves and have-nots. The nationalist leaders who generally come from the regional elite and middle classes seek collaboration with the exploited local working classes by using the ethnic slogan. Resolution of exploitation of the smaller nationalities is thus important to move on to the next phase of struggle for equity and social justice. What short-sighted politicians cannot see and adjust to easily, dialectics of human development teaches them by force. The pain of evolution of democracy is, however, unavoidable.

Notes and References

1. 1981 Population Census.
2. Tariq Rehman, *Language and Politics in Pakistan,* Oxford University Press, New York, 1996

PART - III

Chapter 13

EXPLOITING ISLAM

In the modern age, nations are founded on homelands;
nations are not founded on the basis of race or religion. The
dwellers of England are recognized as one nation, whereas
they have Jews and Christians as their citizens, and such is
the case with America, Japan and France.

– Maulana Husayn Ahmed Madani

What had initially started as a struggle for power between the Muslim salariats and feudal classes on one side and the Hindu rising bourgeoisie, on the other, within the framework of India, eventually evolved into the division of India on communal basis. The ruling Muslim elite of India had used the emotive religious propaganda as a 'means' to achieve an 'end' to secure their right to rule in Muslim-majority areas. In the province where the Muslims were in minority they wanted reserved quotas in jobs and legislature. A similar pattern can be seen emerging in Pakistan. Throughout the post-independence history of Pakistan there has been a constant conflict between the Islamist parties who want to exploit the Islamic propaganda to establish religious laws and rule and the Muslims who want to see Pakistan as a modern democracy. Since the 1980s, because of a number of factors that are discussed further on, the conflict has turned violent. The 'means' are thus consuming Pakistan slowly and painfully.

The trouble with the contemporary discourse is that it is mostly within the framework of the 'two-nation theory', Islamic ideology and at best within the parameters set by its founding leader – Muhammad Ali Jinnah – and his colleagues. Many liberals are in search of 'Jinnah's Pakistan', heavily relying on his speech of 11 August 1947 and his interviews to the foreign media in which he said that Pakistan would not be a theocratic state or that the state had nothing to do with one's religion. According to Indologist and author Stanley Wolpert: '[R]eligion never played an important role in Jinnah's life – except for its political significance – he left the Aga [Agha] Khan's "sevener" Khoja at this stage of maturation, opting instead to join the less hierarchally structured Isna Asheri sect of "twelver" Khojas who acknowledged no leader.' What is interesting was Jinnah's personal secular lifestyle. Quoting from renowned Indian jurist M. C. Chagla's autobiography *Roses in December,* Wolpert has narrated that Jinnah declined his wife, who had brought 'lovely ham sandwiches' because as a leader of Muslims he did not want to be seen having ham in public. But when he moved to Cornaglia restaurant with Chagla 'Jinnah ordered two cups of coffee, a plate of pastry and a plate of pork sausages...'[1]

Reformer, writer and activist Asghar Ali Engineer has also alluded to this lifestyle: 'Jinnah was a thoroughly Westernized person right from his younger days. He never had religious training. He did not observe Islamic taboos like ban on liquor and pork. He never observed religious rituals.'[2] Here an anecdote narrated to me by late S. M. Jamil, who was the first secretary of the Muslim Chamber of Commerce, would be in place as it substantiates Engineer's observation. According to Jamil, he had gone to see Jinnah in Delhi for some work in the month of Ramadan. Jinnah came out of the meeting where many people were waiting for him. He was smoking a cigar. A bearded man walked up to him and said, 'Quaid, you are a leader of the Muslims of India, you should not smoke a cigar publically in Ramadan.' Jamil said, 'Jinnah took a deep puff and said, "What nonsense," then he walked away telling me "Come, we will talk in the car"'.

As stated in the previous chapters Islam and Sharia were not the main issue even when the Government of India Act 1935 was promulgated. It was only after the dismal defeat in the 1937 Punjab elections that Jinnah changed his tactics and started identifying himself with Muslim symbolism. It was in October 1937 that he wore the sherwani and karakuli cap to identify himself with conservative Muslims, instead of his usual Savile Row suits. And the Muslim League turned to solicit the support of the ulema and the pirs.

Author David Gilmartin has documented (in the *Journal of Asian Studiesm*, 'Partition, Pakistan and South Asian History: In Search of a Narrative', 1998) the important role that some leading pirs in Punjab played, in popularizing the idea of Pakistan. However, the fundamentalist dimension in the Pakistan movement developed more strongly only when the Sunni ulema and pirs were mobilized to prove that the Muslim masses wanted a Muslim/Islamic state. While the central leadership at Deoband led by Maulana Husayn Ahmed Madani indeed allied itself to Congress, some prominent dissidents from Deoband such as Maulana Ashraf Ali Thanvi and Allama Shabbir Ahmad Usmani and their factions rallied around the Muslim League. Also, the fact that the central Deoband leadership was allied to the Congress meant that the Muslim League was rendered attractive to their much bigger and more influential rivals, the Barelvis, who entertained their own ambitions of establishing an Islamic state. The tables were turned when the Barelvi ulema and pirs of Punjab, NWFP and Sindh joined the Muslim League.

According to Sayyid A. S. Pirzada: 'Disappointed by this [pro-Congress] attitude of the JUH stalwarts, Maulana Ashraf Ali Thanvi (1863–1943), a renowned "alim" and a mystic, issued a "fatwa" which stated that supporting the AIML (All India Muslim League) and joining its ranks was the only course in accordance with the dictates of *"Sharia"*.' This 'fatwa' was issued in response to the JUH leader Maulana Husayn Ahmed Madani's stand: 'In the modern age, nations are founded on homelands; nations are not founded on the basis of race or religion. The dwellers of England are recognized as one nation, whereas they have Jews and Christians as their citizens, and such is the case with America, Japan and France.'[3]

The JUH stand that Hindu and Muslims were a composite nation was rejected by many Muslim ulema. That added a religious flavour to the secular demand of having more autonomy. Maulana Zafar Ahmad Thanvi, Allama Shabbir Ahmad Usmani, Maulana Khair Muhammad Jalandhari all issued 'fatwas' against the concept of the composite nationalism of JUH. According to Pirzada, the 'masterstroke however was the scholarly fatwa by Mufti Muhammed [Muhammad] Shafi, the grand Mufti of Deoband, in which he ruled that demand of the All India Muslim League (AIML) was the only Islamic course open to the Muslims in the light of the Quran and Sunnah.'[4]

To get the support of the ulema and to counter the move by JUH to collect all the pro-Congress Muslim ulema, a four-day conference was called on 26 October 1945. This was attended by the AIML Bengal leaders including Khawaja Nazimuddin and Huseyn Shaheed Suhrawardy. Leading ulema were invited and a message from Allama Usmani was read out. In his message, according to Pirzada, 'Usmani argued that according to Islam, there are only two nations – one comprising the Muslims, and the other consisting of non-Muslims.... They [Muslims] needed a centre where they could live according to the principles of Islam.' When some people criticized, saying that AIML has the support of the communists, Shias and Ahmadis, and that the educational syllabi would be secular in Pakistan, Usmani said that majority of the AIML were Sunnis. A group of Deobandi influential ulema did support Pakistan and they were the ones who mobilized the support of the masses and all the pirs and *gaddi nashins* (those who now sit on the seat of the Sufi saints).

Pirzada has noted in his introduction that 'Maulana Zafar Ahmed [Ahmad] Thanvi and Allama Usmani met the Quaid in Bombay on 11 June 1947, when he assured them that Pakistan would have an Islamic Constitution, that it would be an Islamic state and the pattern of secular Turkey would not be adopted. A similar account has been given by the Pir of Manki Sharif from NWFP.'[5]

After the announcement of the 3 June 1947 plan, Ain Saz Majlisul Ulema Pakistan, the Constitution-making body of ulema, was established by Maulana Shafiq Ahmad Siddiqui to frame an Islamic Constitution of Pakistan. This shows that right from the very beginning the religious lobby was active and was given assurances by the opportunistic leaders of AIML that the Constitution would be Islamic. Against this backdrop, Jinnah's speech of 11 August 1947, which is so often invoked by the Pakistani intellectuals, was in conflict with the assurances given by him and by the AIML to the religious lobby to seek the support of the masses.

Prime Minister Liaquat Ali Khan in his speech in 1951 further elaborated the Islamist agenda: 'The underlying idea of the movement for the achievement of Pakistan was not just to add one more country to the conglomeration of countries in the world, or to add one more patch of colour to the multi-coloured global map. Pakistan came into being as a result of an urge felt by the Muslims of this subcontinent to secure territory, however limited, *where the Islamic ideology and way of life could be practised and demonstrated to the world. A cardinal feature of this ideology is to make Muslim brotherhood a living reality.'*[6] (Author's emphasis.)

It was therefore, part of the Pakistan mission to do everything in its power to promote Islamic ideology and fellowship with other Muslim countries. The spirit of this resolve to 'make Muslim brotherhood a living reality' still lives in a section of the ruling establishment and their middle-class camp followers, showing the extent of influence gained by the Islamists in Pakistan. They derived strength from the major follies of Pakistani leaders to exploit religion for their objective to secure a separate country for the Muslim elite. 'The significance of an Islamic state in Pakistan's political culture is so dominating that even parties committed to socialist way of life mention an Islamic system of government in their manifestos.'[7] This reference is directed to the country's largest political party i.e., PPP, which had a confused agenda of 'Islamic Socialism'.

The AIML was launched in 1906 and had the patronage of 'wealthy landlords and Muslim professionals', who were secular in character and had not raised the demand for a separate land to establish Islamic 'Sharia'. They were entrusted to protect the rights of the Muslim elite by assuring the British that they would remain their loyal subjects.

Perhaps they were not aware of the fact that it would not be easy to go back to a secular rationale after inciting people in the name of Islam. It was clear evidence of their short-sightedness or lack of understanding of the political and social processes and dialectics in society. The 11 August 1947 speech and some interviews to the foreign media cannot turn the tide of other statements that Jinnah made in favour of an Islamic system. Pirzada has collected a number of Jinnah's statements such as 'we will march to the renaissance of Islamic culture'; 'Our aim should be "to secure liberty, fraternity and equality as enjoined upon in Islam"'; Pakistan was aimed at a 'free play of Islamic social justice'; 'if we take our inspiration and guidance from the Holy Quran, the final victory would be ours'; 'Pakistan's Constitution will be of democratic type, embodying the essential principles of Islam.'

In a translation of the speech delivered by Jinnah on the life of Prophet Muhammad (Peace be upon him or PBUH) perhaps in 1934, and published by a monthly Islamabad magazine *Nazria* (ideology), Jinnah said that the teachings of the Prophet have set a foundation of such a political religion, which has brought in a positive revolution in all walks of life from Delhi to Granada. 'Even today', he observed, 'the teachings of the Prophet are calling to us'. The magazine has taken this speech from an old undated pamphlet published by Syed Sarwar Shah of the Organization of Mosques, Misri Shah, Lahore. As a policy, articles published in this magazine project the Islamic ideology of Pakistan and portray Jinnah as a religious man.

Dr Niaz Murtaza, a Berkeley researcher, pointed out in an article that in a radio address to the Americans in February 1948, Jinnah stated: 'I do not know what the ultimate shape of this Constitution is going to be, but I am sure that it will be of a democratic type, embodying the essential principles of Islam.' Addressing the Sindh Bar Association in Karachi on 25 January 1948, Jinnah clarified: 'There are people who want to create mischief and make the propaganda that we will scrap the Shariat Law. Islamic principles have no parallel.' Eminent scholar Dr Murtaza poses a relevant question: 'What should one surmise from these seemingly contradictory speeches? I am a proud liberal secularist. However, being one means analyzing reality objectively. In doing so, I find more in his speeches to warm a conservative heart than to delight a liberal mind, though the scales are not decisively tilted towards conservatism.'[8]

The discussion ensuing since this speech and continuing today has revolved on the question: What are the 'essential principles of Islam?' Whether the Parliament will decide Islamic principles and laws or the ulema by forming a supra-parliament body à la' 'Velayat-e Faqih' in Iran?

It was because of this confusion that Sadakat Kadri pointed out that the 'practical significance of that commitment [to Islamic law] remained unclear for the next thirty years.'[9] Power oscillated between secular politicians and army officers, and theologians made their mark only by stirring up unrest during crises. One reason for their lack of influence, which now seems almost quaint, was that the most vocal religious movements, including Deobandis and JI had positively opposed the creation of Pakistan. The JI founder, Maulana Abul Ala

Maududi, had asserted before 1947 that 'Islamic nationalism' was 'as contradictory a term as a "chaste prostitute".[10] Conceptually Maulana Maududi was right, as nation state is a secular term, while Islam preaches that all Muslims are part of 'one ummah'. But in reality the Muslim states guard their national sovereignty and have never even talked about merging into one grand Muslim ummah. Therefore, any rationalization by the liberals and some Left groups that Pakistan was envisaged as a modern Islamic state leads us into the trap laid by the Right-wing ideologues.

Much earlier Allama Muhammad Iqbal had laid down what is considered, by the Pakistan movement supporters, his dream, at the Allahabad Conference in 1930. In his presidential address at the annual session of the AIML in Allahabad on 29 December he said: 'I lead no party; I follow no leader.' While denigrating the German professor of theology Martin Luther and the Genevan philosopher Jean-Jacques Rousseau, Iqbal said: 'The conclusion to which Europe is consequently driven is, that religion is the private affair of the individual and has nothing to do with what is called man's temporal life. Islam docs (do) not bifurcate the unity of man into an irreconcilable duality of spirit and matter. In Islam God and the Universe, spirit and matter, church and state, are organic to each other .... The Muslim demand for the creation of a "Muslim India" within India is, therefore perfectly justified.'[11]

He continued: 'I would like to see the Punjab, NWFP, Sind [Sindh] and Baluchistan, amalgamated into a single state. Self-government within the British Empire or without the British Empire, the formation of a consolidated North West Indian Muslim State appears to me, to be, the final destiny of the Muslims at least of North-West India.' Note that he did not include East Bengal in his proposed holy land for Muslims of India. And more importantly, also note that he clearly said: '*Islam does (do) not bifurcate the unity of man into an irreconcilable duality of spirit and matter. In Islam God and the Universe, spirit and matter, church and state, are organic to each other.*' (Author's emphasis.) Since the inception of Pakistan the Islamists draw their strength from this philosophy. Iqbal's thinking had influenced Punjab's educated youth and even today it is imbibed through various lessons in the curricular books.

Unless the democratic values of pluralism are promoted, the people who are indoctrinated from an early age that Pakistan is an Islamic Republic and was made for the implementation of Sharia; any secular democratic reform is difficult. From their childhood Pakistanis are told about Allama Iqbal's dream about an Islamic nation, which is supposed to strengthen the Islamic ummah. Iqbal was against separation of religion and state. He said:

> Juda ho deen sayasat say
> to reh jati hai changezi

These lines roughly translated:
 If religion is separated from politics
 only Genghis's barbarianism remains.

The Muslim League's religious messages were enough to reassure the ulema that Pakistan would have Islamic laws, so their Ain-saaz Majlis demanded that the Constitution should be based on Islamic principles and suggested: a) That government and sovereignty belong to Almighty Allah; b) That the sovereignty that Allah has bestowed upon this state (mumlikat) through the medium of the masses (jamhur) would be utilized within the precincts prescribed by Him; c) Muslims would practice Islam through their individual and collective actions; d) No ordinance, bill, or law would be adopted contrary to Islamic teachings; e) The Constitution would protect the predetermined rights of the minorities; however, they would enjoy full freedom of creed.

In the early years it was part of Pakistan's mission to do everything in its power to fulfill, that it seeks to promote closer fellowship and cooperation between Muslim countries. Emphasis placed on the Islamic ideology and fellowship on the basis of religion in Pakistan's foreign and national security policies has led it to where it is today. The natural corollary of this policy was giving more space and a free hand to the religious elements in the country's politics. It was because of this bent of mind that Liaquat Ali Khan was soft on the religious demand to include the so-called objective resolution in the Constitution. Some of the Muslim League intellectuals had opposed this move and pointed out that he was giving too much space to the religious leaders and prophetically warned about the negative outfall of this policy of appeasement. For instance, the Dawn's editor Altaf Husain wrote a powerful editorial against this policy of pandering to the mullahs: 'The ulema have suggested that five of them attached to the Supreme Court should decide whether a law is Islamic or un-Islamic! It is therefore deplorable that the ulema should have put forward a proposal of such a reactionary and anti-democratic nature. The proposal can be seriously considered at the peril of converting Pakistan into a theocratic state where democratic institutions will be reduced to a mockery and chosen representatives of the people will be no more than helpless puppet.'[12]

However, the ulema remained steadfast. While moving the Objectives Resolution the Muslim League leaders, in spite of their statements that Pakistan would not be a theocracy, were forced to accept it as the guiding principle of the Constitution on 12 March 1949. No sooner was this resolution adopted, in spite of opposition by some of the members of the Constitution Assembly, than the ulema decided to set up a board of Talimat-i-Islamiyah led by Allama Sayyid Suleman Nadwi. They wanted it to be the supra-constitutional body, which would guide the law-makers from outside on legislation, if in conflict to Islam.

Even today an Islamic Ideology Council (IIC) is supposed to do this work, but at present it is quite toothless. The recommendations made by it are at times challenged in the Supreme Court, which keeps them pending. The most important recommendation in this regard is abolishing interest from the banking system of Pakistan. As this recommendation cannot be accepted without completely upsetting the capitalist economic system of the country and as it is impractical in the modern world, the Supreme Court has wisely buried its file under the thousands of pending cases in its cellar.

The troubles of Pakistan thus started compounding because of the theocratic strand of politics and the confused position taken by its leaders regarding the future of the country. The compromises with the ulema were a natural outcome of the promises made during the Pakistan movement that the new country would be governed by Islamic principles. To be fair to the ulema, they were right in demanding the Islamic Constitution because that was the deal sold to them by the AIML leadership to get the support of the Muslim masses of India. The pure secular objective of having maximum autonomy within the framework of India got lost in the campaign propaganda. This objective of more autonomy would have been followed through on non-communal basis by joining hands with the leaders of the principalities who were also demanding the same thing in spite of the fact that their subjects were sympathetic to the Congress.

The historian Amarjit Singh has objectively maintained that his British counterparts, Penderel Moon and C. H. Philips, 'considered Indian leaders responsible for the partition of India ....' They 'simply absolved the British from the responsibility of [dividing] India whereas, I [Singh] am of the opinion that it was only with the help of the British that All-India Muslim League under the leadership of Muhammad Ali Jinnah consolidated its demand of Pakistan which subsequently led to the partition. The tactical errors of the Congress also proved beneficial to the success of the Muslim League.'[13] I think Amarjit Singh has been charitable to the Congress leaders, who had decided at one point to get rid of the Muslim-majority provinces. Otherwise, Nehru would not have reneged on the Cabinet Mission Plan arrangement.

Judaism, Christianity and Islam are semitic doctrines and could have been sects of the same religion had the Jewish people of Jerusalem and Medina accepted the new reformers as prophets. Both Jesus and Muhammad relied heavily on the Torah. In the same way, had the Congress, which represented Hindu majority and a large number of Muslims, also accepted to share power with the ruling classes of Muslim-majority areas, perhaps the geography of the subcontinent wouldn't have been scarred with silly borders drawn in ten weeks by a dysentery patient – Sir Cyril Radcliffe.

The founders of Pakistan were confused and thought that 'the ends justify the means'. As columnist Irfan Husain says: 'One central truth most of us are unwilling to face is that much of the increasing extremism we see around us is deeply embedded in Pakistan's DNA. When a country is created in the name of faith, then inevitably that faith will come to dominate modes of thought and behaviour.'[14] This was demonstrated by the various incidences and Islamic laws introduced in Pakistan conflicting with the accepted twenty-first century version of fundamental human rights.

The fact that religion was exploited by the founders of the country to achieve a 'temporal end' – a separate homeland for the Muslim-majority ruling elite – has given enough space to the religious leaders in this country. They want to dictate because their strength comes from the dangerous political formulation, forwarded by the rulers during the Pakistan movement and thereafter till today.

Notes and References

1. Stanley Wolpert, *Jinnah of Pakistan*, Oxford University Press, New York, 1999, p. 86.
2. Asghar Ali Engineer, *Secularism, Democracy, and Experience of Muslims of India*, Centre for Study of Society and Secularism, Mumbai, 2010.
3. Sayyid A. S. Pirzada, *The Politics of Jamiat Ulema-i-Islam Pakistan*, Oxford University Press, New York, 2000.
4. Ibid.
5. Ibid.
6. Liaquat Ali Khan's speech 1951, reported by *Pakistan News* and cited by Mohammed Ahsan Chaudhry in his paper 'Foundation of Pakistan foreign Policy' (publication details not available).
7. Sayyid A. S. Pirzada, *The Politics of Jamiat Ulema-i-Islam Pakistan*, Oxford University Press, New York, 2000.
8. Niaz Murtaza (a research associate on political economy issues at the University of California, Berkeley), *Jinnah: Secular or Islamist?* Link to the article: http://criticalppp.com/archives/57909. Source for both quotes of M. A. Jinnah: *Speeches by Quaid-i-Azam Mohamed Ali Jinnah*, Governor-General of Pakistan, Government of Pakistan, 1948.
9. Sadakat Kadri, *Heaven on Earth: Journey through Sharia Laws*, The Bodley Head, London, 2012.
10. Ibid.
11. Allama Muhammad Iqbal's Allahabad address, 1930.
12. *Dawn*, 9 March 1952.
13. Amarjit Singh (editor), *Jinnah and Punjab: Shamsul Hasan Collection and Other Documents 1944-47*, Kanishka Publishers, New Delhi, 2007.
14. Irfan Husain's column in *Dawn*, 1 January 2011.

Chapter 14

A Journey to a Dangerous 'End'

The questions now being asked by the younger generation in Pakistan are: Why does one Muslim sect consider the other Muslim sects apostate and thus liable to death? Why has any sect the right to decide who is Muslim and who is not? Why has human life lost its value? Why are Pakistanis shy of facing the reality that many people sitting in Parliament and judiciary are bigots? Why are so many people willing to blow themselves up?

Right from the inception of Pakistan, the Islamists have pushed for laws that are contrary to the democratic norms. First, they pushed the weak Liaquat Ali Khan government in accepting the Objectives Resolution. Then they unleashed attacks on the Ahmadiyya community in 1953. The demand was to declare Ahmadiyya (both sects, the Qadianis and Lahoris) non-Muslims.[1] Soon after the All-Pakistan Muslim Convention in Dacca (now Dhaka) in 1953, the demand to declare Ahmadiyya followers non-Muslim gathered support, particularly in the Punjab. The other two demands were the removal of Sir Zafarullah Khan, who was foreign minister, and of other Ahmadis who were in important government positions. According to military officials, who imposed martial law in Lahore, 11 persons were killed and 49 injured caused in quelling the disturbances in Lahore alone.[2] This movement which was jointly spearheaded by Majlis-e-Ahrar and Jamaat–e-Islami was led by Maulana Abul Ala Maududi.

145

The government, however, did not give in and imposed martial law in Lahore and the leaders of this hate movement were arrested. A court of inquiry was established in 1954 under Justice M. Munir as president and Justice M. R. Kayani as member. The inquiry report noted that both the anti-Ahmadi ulema and Ahmadiyya Jamaat quoted extensively from the Holy Quran and hadith in support of their respective claims. It also noted that as the demand was to declare Ahmadis non-Muslims, the pertinent questions were: 'What is Islam and who is a Momin or Muslim?' The inquiry report noted: '[W]e cannot refrain from saying here that it was a matter of infinite regret to us that the ulema, whose first duty should be to have settled views on this subject hopelessly disagreed among themselves ... keeping in view the several definitions given by the ulema, need we make any comment except that no two learned divines are agreed on this fundamental.' Even today there are over 72 sects of Islam in Pakistan, each having their own interpretations of the scripture, hadith and Sharia. What started in 1953 against one sect of Islam, (Ahmadi declare themselves a sect so respecting their freedom of expression nobody has the right to label them otherwise), has now spread to violence against other sects. Sunni-Shia sectarian killings have acquired the dangerous dimension.

The report rightly pointed out: 'When it is alleged that the demands were unanimous and religious in their character, what is meant is that according to all sects in Islam they [sic] are clear deductions from some theological assumptions or doctrines. Almost all the ulema who we questioned on the subject have stated that the demands are a corollary from the Objectives Resolution .... And from the religio-political system which they call Islam. It has been most vehemently urged that Pakistan was claimed and was brought into existence so that the future political set-up of the new state may be based on Qur'an and the Sunnah ... that demand had created in the minds of the ulema and the citizens of Pakistan, the belief that any demand that would be established on religious grounds would not only be conceded but warmly welcomed by the people on the helm of affairs of the State who had during the last several years been crying themselves hoarse over their intention to establish Pakistan as an Islamic State with a set-up of political, social and ethical institutions of Islamic pattern.'[3]

This substantiates my point that the use of Islam by the leaders created space for the Islamists and the leadership had to live up to its propaganda. The clash between the modern value system and the pull by the ulema to a sectarian and medieval agenda continued. Even Zulfikar Ali Bhutto, who, like Jinnah, was known for his secular lifestyle, proved to be an opportunist on this issue. Following skirmishes between a group of Multan students and the local people at Rabwah (a town in Punjab, with headquarters of the Ahmadis), Bhutto jumped in to get the Ahmadis declared non-Muslims by the Parliament in 1974, through a Second Amendment to the 1973 Constitution. Even the secular NAP abstained instead of opposing it in the Assembly. But Left parties opposed this law. However, religious parties backed his undemocratic move with fervour. Clause (3) was added to Article 260, which gives definitions. The sub-section 3(b) was added which says: 'non-Muslims' means a person who is not a Muslim and includes a person belonging to the Christian, Hindu, Sikh, Buddhist or Parsi community, a person of Qadiani group or the Lahore Group (who call themselves 'Ahmadis' or by any other name), or Baha'i, and a person belonging to the scheduled caste.

Bhutto had constructed his part in the mid-1960s by appealing to different sections of the society with different slogans. He cashed in fully on the anti-Ayub Khan movement in the country and sentiment built by the 1968 student movement around the world. To the Punjabi middle class, who were disillusioned by the Tashkent Agreement of Ayub because they had been fed on the lies that the war was started by the Indians deviously, he talked about a 1,000-year war against India and rejected the peace agreement. Before the workers, he bemoaned the accumulation of industrial and financial assets in the hands of the 22 families. To the peasants, he talked against the big feudal and of land reforms. For the Islamists, he proclaimed that Islam was the main guiding force and came out with the oxymoron 'Islamic Socialism'. This political mixture worked and brought support from the anti-Indian Punjabis and pro-China Left, who were also anti-Indian. This explanation is necessary here to explain Bhutto's political opportunism.

Bhutto dismissed the elected NAP government in Balochistan. The NAP government, which was in the government of KP resigned in protest. Bhutto also launched a military operation in Balochistan in the name of Pakistan's solidarity, which resulted in the political alliances in the country. Ghaus Bakhsh Bizenjo, who was the most visionary democratic leader of Pakistan I have ever met, had predicted in early 1972 at the NAP National Council meeting in Peshawar, where I was present, that the break-up of PPP-NAP alliance would force a Left-inclined secular NAP to sit with JI and push Bhutto into the lap of the army. 'And after that there are so many martial laws as far as I can see,' he lamented.

By 1977 every bit of Bizenjo's prophecy had come true. Bhutto not only resurrected the demoralized Pakistan army, he gave them an inlet to meddle in politics by launching a military operation in Balochistan and by opening a political wing in Inter-Services Intelligence (ISI). NAP and other democratic parties formed the Pakistan National Alliance (PNA) with the religious parties like JI, JUP and JUI. Even the underground Communist Party supported this alliance and worked under the umbrella of NAP.

To begin with, it was a democratic alliance but was hijacked by the religious parties only when Bhutto's government rigged the 1977 elections on around 36 seats. This resulted in a mass movement throughout the country, which initially was only for re-election and sanctity of vote, but the religious parties whipped up the slogan of Nizam-e-Mustafa (Muhammad's system). Bhutto had also turned to appease the religious vote. After dumping, and in some cases incarcerating his old socialist comrades, Bhutto changed the socialism slogan to 'Musawat-e-Muhammadi' (Muhammad's egalitarian system). In contrast to his 1970 Nishtar Park rally in Karachi where the red backdrop on the stage said 'East is Red', his 1976 rally had a green backdrop with an Islamic slogan. Once the PNA movement was started after the 1977 elections, instead of agreeing to re-election on selected seats, he tried to please the Islamists, among other things, by imposing a ban on liquor and announcing Friday (Islamic holy day) as a weekly holiday.

By late April 1977, it started becoming evident that Bhutto's resurrected military was planning to oust him. Two incidents personally witnessed by me signalled that the military was preparing ground. In Lahore senior military officers refused to follow orders regarding quelling protest rallies, while in Karachi I saw army officers pull back their soldiers and order Bhutto's notorious Federal Security Force (FSF) men to fire at the protesting people near Sindh Assembly. In another development a communist leader, Dr M. R. Hassan, organized a meeting of all trade union leaders in Karachi where it was decided to take the initiative and give an indefinite country-wide strike call to the workers. The objectives were that the working classes should steer the movement to get working classes' rights and dilute the religious parties domineering influence on the democratic movement. It was decided that one of the labour leaders would inform Nawabzada Nasrullah Khan, who was then leading the PNA movement. The politically sharp Nawabzada retorted by asking the caller where they wanted to take the movement. He immediately pre-empted the workers' initiative by giving a three-day strike call. Some of the PNA leaders had developed secret relations with the army and were interested in his ouster rather than getting re-elections on the disputed 36 seats. Bhutto agreed to this demand only a few hours before General Muhammad Zia-ul-Haq-led military coup. It was in this political situation where the ground was prepared by the religious parties' Nizam-e-Mustafa slogan, that an Islamist General, Zia, had an opportunity to oust the country's most popular leader and then hang him. It was widely dubbed as a mistrial. The charge against Bhutto was that he conspired to murder Ahmad Raza Khan Kasuri. (While Kasuri was saved in an attack by FSF men, his father was killed). This is also underlined by Professor John L. Esposito: 'Appeals to Islam reached their zenith in March 1977 General elections .... Although member parties spanned the political spectrum, the PNA's symbols and slogans were stated in an Islamic framework, e.g., "Islam is in danger" and "Nizam-e-Mustafa" [the system of the Prophet]. The vast network of ulema and mosques and their associated Madrassahs [advanced schools for Islamic learning] were employed as centres for PNA political organization and communications.'[4]

In this prepared field, Zia stretched Bhutto's anti-Ahmadi law to a ridiculous level along with the blasphemy law. The Ordinance promulgated by the USA's closest ally, General Zia, in 1984 amended the law 'to prohibit the Qadiani group, Lahori group and Ahmadis from indulging in anti-Islamic activities':

'Whereas it is expedient', it stated, 'to amend the law to prohibit the Qadiani group, Lahori group and Ahmadis from indulging in anti-Islamic activities; and whereas the President is satisfied that circumstances exist which render it necessary to take immediate action: now, therefore, in pursuance of the Proclamation of the fifth day of July, 1977, and in exercise of all powers enabling him in that behalf, the President is pleased to make and promulgate the following Ordinance':

1. Short title and commencement.

    (i) This Ordinance may be called the Anti-Islamic Activities of the Qadiani Group, Lahori Group and Ahmadis (Prohibition and Punishment) Ordinance 1984.

    (ii) It shall come into force at once.

2. Ordinance to override orders or decisions of courts. The provisions of this Ordinance shall have effect notwithstanding any order or decision of any court.

The Pakistan Penal Code (ACT XLV of 1860) was also amended by the Islamist military dictator:

3. Addition of new sections 298B and 298C, Act XLV of 1860.

    In the Pakistan Penal Code (Act XLV of 1860), in Chapter XV, after section 298 (A), the following new sections shall be added, namely:

    298 (B). Misuse of epithets, descriptions and titles, etc., reserved for certain holy personages or places.

    (i) Any person of the Qadiani group or the Lahori group (who call themselves 'Ahmadis' or by any other name) who by words, either spoken or written, or by visible representation:

    > (a) refers to, or addresses, any person, other than a Caliph or companion of the Holy Prophet Muhammad (PBUH), as 'Ameerul Mumineen', 'Khalifa-tul-Mumineen', 'Khalifa-tul-Muslimeen', 'Sahaabi' or 'Razi Allah Anho';

    > (b) refers to, or addresses, any person, other than a wife of the Holy Prophet Muhammad (PBUH) as 'Ummul-Mumineen';

    > (c) refers to, or addresses, any person, other than a member of the family (Ahle-bait) of the Holy Prophet Muhammad (PBUH), as 'Ahle-bait'; or

(d) refers to, or names, or calls, his place of worship as *'Masjid'*; shall be punished with imprisonment of either description for a term, which may extend to three years and shall also be liable to fine.

(ii) Any person of the Qadiani group or Lahori group (who call themselves Ahmadis or by any other name) who by words, either spoken or written, or by visible representation, refers to the mode or form of call to prayers followed by his faith as 'azan' or recites azan as used by the Muslims, shall be punished with imprisonment of either description for a term, which may extend to three years and shall also be liable to fine.

298 (C). Person of Qadiani group, etc., calling himself a Muslim or preaching or propagating his faith.

Any person of the Qadiani group or the Lahori group (who call themselves 'Ahmadis' or by any other name), who, directly or indirectly, poses himself as Muslim, or calls, or refers to, his faith as Islam, or preaches or propagates his faith, or invites others to accept his faith, by words, either spoken or written, or by visible representations, or in any manner whatsoever outrages the religious feelings of Muslims, shall be punished with imprisonment of either description for a term which may extend to three years and shall also be liable to fine.[5]

Now compare these laws to the twentieth- and twenty-first-century global democratic value system. It will emerge as one of the most discriminatory laws against a targeted community. It reminds us of the anti-Jew measures taken by Hitler's fascist regime. It is based on the presumption that Ahmadis are anti-Islam and is in direct conflict with the principle laid down in the 1973 Constitution. Article 20 of the Constitution guarantees 'Freedom to profess religion and to manage religious institutions.' But anti-Ahmadi laws are in sharp contradiction of the human rights-related clauses of the Constitution and that of the UN Human Rights Charter. The opposition from religious extremists to any amendment regarding inhuman Ahmadi laws is so strong that the framer of the mega 18th Amendment did not dare to touch it. Even in the 2013 elections nomination form all Muslim candidates have to declare on oath that they do not belong to Ahmadi or Lahori group.

The Ahmadis who claim that they are Muslims boycotted all elections because they do not want to contest on minorities seats.

The fascist laws are also in conflict to the UN UDHR to which Pakistan is also a signatory as a member state. On the other hand Article 19 of the declaration says: 'Everyone has the right to freedom of opinion and expression; this right includes freedom to hold opinions without interference and to seek, receive and impart information and ideas through any media and regardless of frontiers.' And Article 20 maintains: 'Everyone has the right to freedom of thought, conscience and religion; this right includes freedom to change his [her] religion or belief, and freedom, either alone or in community with others and in public or private, to manifest his religion or belief in teaching, practice, worship and observance.'

There are many other clauses in the Constitution of Pakistan, which are in contradiction to the UN UDHR. This reflects the inner conflict of the society, which is torn between adopting modern democratic values while also leaning to a religion-biased value system. The state's discriminatory laws against the Ahmadis have resulted in encouraging the anti-Ahmadiyya sects of Islam who have killed hundreds of followers of this community in target killings. The irony is that when one of their mosques was attacked in May 2010, killing 90 Ahmadis at the Friday prayers, the television channels were afraid to call it a 'mosque' and kept on referring to it as a 'place of worship'. The Punjab Chief Minister Shahbaz Sharif was scared even to call on the Ahmadi leaders for offering condolence. His elder brother, former prime minister and the leader of the PML-N, Nawaz Sharif, however expressed sympathy with his 'Ahmadi brethren'. The religious leaders were quick to demand that he should withdraw his words, since Ahmadis could not be regarded as 'brethren' of the Muslims, warning him that if he did not, his marriage would stand annulled.

The International Khatam-e-Nabuwat Conference (finality of Prophet Muhammad PBUH) was held on 8 September 2011 in Chiniot. The conference alleged that the Qadianis were agents of Christians and Zionists. They incited the people against the Qadianis, but the government did not take any action. As a matter of fact all leading Urdu newspapers gave extensive coverage to the event. The Assembly itself was unlawful because nobody is allowed under the law to incite the people against any other religion or sect.

A large section of media reports the statements of the hate-mongers with impunity. Of late, some blogs have been targeting the Ahmadis for hatching conspiracies against Pakistan. Posters and hoardings are openly displayed against Ahmadis by different organizations with their addresses and telephone numbers, but no action is taken against them. Even some TV anchors of religious programmes declare Ahmadis non-Muslims and condemn them for blasphemy. After one such programme on the popular Geo TV, two Ahmadis were killed in Sindh. The channel did not ban the 'Aalim' Aamir Liaquat Hussain nor did Pakistan Electronic Media Regulatory Authority (PEMRA), which was supposed to take notice of such things, take any action. Each month there are target killings of Ahmadis and Shias in the country.

**

The anti-Ahmadi laws were inserted into Pakistan's Constitution by Zulfikar Ali Bhutto and further expanded by General Zia by amending the Penal Code. Zia's hand-picked Parliament amended the Criminal Procedure Act of 1886 by introducing Criminal Law (Amendment) Act 1986 under which the expanse of the blasphemy laws was broadened. Article 295 of the Criminal Procedure Act of 1886 related to 'Injuring or defiling places of worship, with intent to insult the religion of any class.' Clause 295 (A) is about 'Deliberate and malicious acts intended to outrage religious feelings of any class by insulting its religion or religious beliefs.' While maximum punishment for offence under clause 295 was two years and fine or both, the punishment under 295 (A) was ten years and fine or both.

There are standard blasphemy laws in many countries and are basically secular in nature. But the 1986 Amendment 295 (C), which was inserted into the Constitution, says: 'Use of derogatory remarks, etc., in respect of the Holy Prophet. Whosoever by words, either spoken or written, or by visible representation, or by any imputation, innuendo, or insinuation, directly or indirectly, defiles the sacred name of the Holy Prophet Muhammad (peace be upon him) shall be punished with death, or imprisonment for life, and shall also be liable to fine.'

At the same time Pakistan Penal Code or PPC 298 (A) says that 'Use of derogatory remarks etc., in respect of holy personages are punishable by 3 years and fine;' 298 (B) is about: 'Misuse of epithets, descriptions and titles etc., reserved for certain holy personages or places, by

Ahmadis;' and 298 (C) relates to: 'An Ahmadi, calling himself a Muslim, or preaching or propagating his faith, or outraging the religious feelings of Muslims, or posing himself as a Muslim' can be punished by three years and fine or both.

These additions to the century-old blasphemy laws, which were secular in nature have allowed the bigots to victimize and murder many people, mostly of Ahmadi and Christian descent. Personal scores are also settled by implicating people in false blasphemy cases. Human Rights Commission of Pakistan's (HRCP) observation on this issue is pertinent: 'Incidents of this nature [killings in the name of punishing blasphemer] are not unknown in the sub-continent except that earlier, they were rare and when they occurred they shook up the society and the administration. Now, religious intolerance has been sharply on the increase. It finds acquiescence, if not an active encouragement, in the recent government voluble invocations of Islam. Intolerance is becoming holy. Crimes are feared without fear of official retribution or social disapproval and in the knowledge that any voices of isolated protest will not in the given atmosphere get far.'[6]

As most of the blasphemy allegations are made by the people who want to settle some personal agenda, Council of Islamic Ideology (CII) proposed, that to stop misuse of blasphemy law, the death penalty for anybody misusing this law should be abolished. 'The wrongful complainant and witness should be handed similar punishment as a guilty person.'[7] This recommendation has been pending before the Parliament for the past four years.

According to a study done by researcher Mansoor Raza, 'Between 1988 and 2005, Pakistani authorities charged 647 people with offences under the blasphemy laws. Fifty per cent of the people charged were non-Muslims. More than 20 people have been murdered for alleged blasphemy. Two third of all the cases are in the Punjab province of Pakistan, which is home to 81 per cent Christians. A little more than half of Pakistani Christians live in six districts – Lahore, Faisalabad, Kasur, Sheikhupura, Sialkot and Gujranwala. The seven districts that have contributed most to the blasphemy cases are Lahore, Faisalabad, Sialkot, Kasur, Sheikhupura, Gujranwala and Toba Tek Singh. The total population of these districts is 25 million, of which five per cent are Christian; 50 per cent of the total Christian population of Pakistan of 2.0 million, lives in these seven districts.

An analysis of the 361 cases of blasphemy offences registered by the police between 1986 and 2007 shows that as many as 49 per cent cases were registered against non-Muslims. The cases against non-Muslims should be contrasted with the population of religious minorities, which is not more than four per cent of Pakistan's population. Moreover, 26 per cent cases against Ahmadis and 21 per cent cases against Christians are not commensurate with their ratio in the total population, which is 0.22 and 1.58 per cent of the total population respectively. The number of persons nominated in 361 cases was 761, which suggests that the average number of the accused per case is two.'[8]

***

The most high-profile cases in this regard are the killings of the Punjab Governor Salman Taseer and the Federal Minorities Minister Shahbaz Bhatti. Neither of them had committed blasphemy even if the all-pervasive blasphemy laws were invoked. They merely criticized the man-made laws and declared them as bad laws because of their misuse. The case in point was that of a Christian farm labourer Aasiya Bibi, who was implicated by other women after some altercations. Both the local police officials and the lower court were obliging to the complainants either because of their Islamic views or because of the fear of the religious bigots, who push such cases. Aasiya was sentenced to death and her appeal was also turned down.

In the case of Salman Taseer, the police guard Mumtaz Qadri assigned to protect him, in front of his other colleagues who gave him tacit support, shot Salman many times till he was sure that he was dead. He confessed that he had managed to get himself assigned to this duty with a plan to kill the governor because he (Taseer) was against Aasiya's conviction. Qadri got a hero's reception by the Islamist lawyers and public. He was sentenced to death by the Anti-Terrorism Court (ATC) but the judge was harassed to the extent that he had to flee from the country with his family. The government helped him to go into exile as they could not assure his safety from the fanatics. He returned after a few months, once the religious fiery-mood cooled down.

Taseer and many other victims of religious intolerance have been assassinated and buried. But the fundamental question that cannot be buried with them is: Why is religious intolerance on the rise in Pakistan? This question has been haunting the bloodied people of the country since its inception. We will deal with the rise of intolerance question in the concluding chapter.

What Pakistan is facing today is the logical outcome of the dangerous policies of the past. Salman Taseer's murder has shown that even discussion about the blasphemy laws is dubbed as 'blasphemy' by the religious parties. Instead of the murderer, the victim is blamed by these bigots. It is because of the space provided to the religious leaders that some newspapers were not shy of publishing the statements of some extremists who offered head money for killing Salman Taseer and Aasiya Bibi. No case was registered against the mullahs and their extremist supporters who offer money for murders, and the media that amplifies these messages also goes scot-free. The Islamic Republic of Pakistan, which has the policy of appeasing the religious parties, did not gather courage to take action against these instigators who influenced people like Mumtaz Qadri.

According to Qadri's testimony, he was motivated to kill Taseer after listening to a fiery speech at a religious congregation of Qari Haneef in his neighbourhood on 31 December 2010. Nuclear physicist and proponent of secularism Dr Pervez Hoodbhoy in his article has observed that Qadri participated in this meeting and 'recited the *"naat"* in praise of the Holy Prophet [PBUH], with his official gun slung around his shoulder. Four days later he fulfilled his goal.'[9]

Qadri also influenced his colleagues who were on duty that afternoon as they agreed with him (Qadri) that they would not kill him. And sure enough, they arrested him quite easily because Qadri gave himself up, to become another 'Ghazi Ilm-ud-din Shaheed'.[10] A trader offered Rs 50 million to Taseer's family as *diyat* (blood money) for forgiving Qadri. All these persons who supported or instigated Qadri before the assassination and those who projected him as a hero after the murder should have been tried for abetting and promoting violence in the country. But the PPP-led coalition government was too weak even to contemplate any such action. Taseer's own party – PPP – was afraid of the religious extremists and did not stick its neck out.

A Lahore lawyer, Saroop Ijaz, aptly raised this issue in a column: 'Whereas the religious rightist component of the lawyer's movement is almost obscenely visible, there has been curious reluctance by the liberal elite leadership to comment on the murder of Salman Taseer .... It is only appropriate that one of the top guns now stands up to the occasion and publically volunteer to represent the complainant and assist the prosecution.'[11]

Qadri confessed in the ATC that he killed Taseer and maintained that anybody who opposed the killing of a person who had committed 'blasphemy' should also be killed. The rot has spread even to the highest level of the judiciary in Pakistan; a former chief Justice of Lahore High Court filed an appeal against Qadri's conviction in the Islamabad High Court, on pro bono basis. And the suo motu-happy judges of the superior courts did not take notice of any statements that incite murder by announcing handsome rewards. Neither did the otherwise active superior judiciary take the media to task for abetting by publishing such statements. The government is also too scared of the religious militants and does not check the hate speeches made by extremists in mosques and madrassahs because the state is defined as an Islamic state. The whole tragic affair brings us to the same fundamental issue that was highlighted by a leading Pakistani analyst and human rights activist I. A. Rehman who observed: 'the [Objectives] Resolution gave rise to a concept of two sovereignties and a Muslim's right to defy/violate the man-made laws by invoking the superior commandment of Allah.'[12]

It was General Zia who amended the blasphemy law. He converted the prevailing political Islam into militant Islam. Subsequently, religious intolerance increased when it received a boost from General Zia's so-called 'Islamic jihad' against Afghanistan. The extremists were not only trained but armed to the teeth by Zia and his American and Saudi allies. Little did they realize that the means they were using to bring down a modernist progressive government of Afghanistan would ultimately be dangerous for Pakistan and the world. Both the Pakistani establishment and American leaders stupidly led this region to the present explosive situation.

The questions now being asked by the younger generation in Pakistan are: Why does one Muslim sect consider the other Muslim sects apostate and thus liable to death? Why has any sect the right to decide who is Muslim and who is not? Why has human life lost its value? Why are Pakistanis shy of facing the reality that many people sitting in Parliament and judiciary are bigots? Why are so many people willing to blow themselves up?

There is broad consensus among the intelligentsia that for years the establishment has supported and nourished the extremists. Saudization of our otherwise tolerant Islam in Pakistan has nourished intolerance in the country. They agree that all sects have a right to believe in their own interpretation of Islam, but nobody should have the right to preach hatred against another sect. It is easy to say but difficult to implement unless there is broad consensus among all the institutions of the state.

The religious extremist leaders take advantage of these laws and the so-called Pakistan ideology to the extent that they do not even spare their Right-wing leaders. Nawaz Sharif was taken to task by them for his speech on Independence Day, 2011, in which he expressed his goodwill for some Sikh guests from Amritsar in the audience. He said he shared with them many attributes of culture, including places of origin, food and dress, and a common provider (Rab or God). A leading political analyst and human rights activist noted that 'there was nothing in this speech that Mr Nawaz Sharif had not said earlier or to which anyone could in fairness take exception.' (But Nawaz became the target of a heavy barrage of friendly fire.) Of all the people, the JI chief poured scorn on him for deviating from the 'two-nation theory'. A leading Urdu daily editorially wondered about 'the state of his mind in which he did not realize how much he had lost in terms of his future politics by being extremely lyrical in praise of Bharat, the eternally deceitful enemy.' He was viciously censured for referring to shared cultural norms and for asking Pakistan and India to give up their traditional stand on Kashmir. Finally, he was told to apologize to the people and seek God's forgiveness for his speech if he wanted to stay in politics. The redoubtable Mian was visibly rattled by this 'criticism in the harshest possible words' as he wrote in a personal letter to the editor concerned. He pleaded that his remarks had been torn out of context. He explained that 'while telling the Sikhs that he worshipped the same Rab that they worshipped he was following the Quran that defines Allah as Rab-ul-Aalameen [Provider for the entire world]. He did not say that he worshipped the Bharat gods.'[13]

A cursory view of the whole debate about the blasphemy law shows that there are many saner and intellectually sound Muslims who do not support the existing draconian blasphemy law. Except for a small extremist coterie of bigots, politicians are all for removing Section 295 (B) and (C). To my pleasant surprise, even Punjab Home minister, Rana Sanaullah, who is generally considered to be a fundamentalist, agreed to the change in law in Nasim Zehra's talk show on TV channel Dunya. The gutsy Member of the National Assembly (MNA) Sherry Rehman (now ambassador to the USA) had moved a bill in the Assembly suggesting some changes in the blasphemy law. Her approach was pragmatic as she was of the view that the bill demanding abolition of law would not be possible at this juncture. Several sections of Pakistan's criminal code comprise blasphemy laws.

The issue is that according to Islamic history and tradition some people were killed for speaking against the Prophet. But such punishments came into Islamic jurisprudence much later. While the Hanafites took a milder view, the Malikites introduced tough punishments leaving little room for forgiveness. The case of the Sufi Mansur al-Hallaj is a good example. But the bigots, who had section 295 (C) inserted, feel justified fighting for it. These additions were made in Section 295 by General Zia without any parliamentary sanctions and thus should be deleted. Sherry's proposed change was too soft because the courts are too intimidated by the Islamic extremists to give the verdict against the accused on technical grounds, as it did in the Aasiya Bibi case.

Islamic teachings clearly say that the Muslims should respect other people's religions and should not hurt their feelings. But some extremist take license to break idols from the Islamic tradition when idols kept in Kaaba were destroyed. This principle is precisely enunciated in 295 (A), so the matter should rest there. (But unfortunately all those Muslim invaders who destroyed temples and churches are revered in our Islamic history.) The problem is more deep-rooted than the laws alone; there are psychological, historical, social and political reasons for the Muslims to be over-sensitive about the blasphemy issue. And in this society where freedom of expression is limited, any intellectual discourse about these factors is risky.

The laws allow a person to change his/her religion. But the militant Islamists believe that the change of religion or renouncing it by a Muslim invokes the death punishment. A person can quietly renounce religion but cannot do so publically. An atheist in Pakistan cannot declare it publically that he doesn't believe in God or any religion except to his/her close people. The law requires a person not only to declare that he/she is a Muslim but also that he/she considers Ahmadis as non-Muslims.

Notes and References:

1. Note: A brief note on the Ahmadiyya controversy: According to the Munir Commission Report, the 'Ahmadiyya movement' was founded by Mirza Ghulam Ahmad. He was born in his ancestral village Qadian in district Gurdaspur, now in India. Ahmadis are thus also called 'Qadianis' and 'Mirzais.' He claimed in late nineteenth century that he gets *Ilham* (revelations) and started taking homage from his followers. He also claimed to be the 'promised Mehdi' – 'a reasoning Mehdi who would vanquish his opponent by argument.' This claim started controversy and many Muslim ulema declared that he is a kafir (apostate). Most Muslims do not accept the followers of Ghulam Ahmad's teachings as part of Islam as they believe that Mohammed was the last Prophet and the divine revelations were completed with him. The Ahmadis claim to be a sect of Islam but the Muslims in many countries challenge their basic right to label themselves as Muslims as they believe in the finality of the Prophet Mohammed.

2. *Munir Inquiry Report*, Nia Zamana Publications, p. 9.

3. *Munir Inquiry Report*, Nia Zamana Publications, p. 277.

4. 'Islam: Ideology and Politics' in Pakistan by John L. Esposito in Ali Banuazizi and Myron Weiner (editors), *The State, Religion, and Ethnic Politics: Pakistan, Iran and Afghanistan*, Syracuse University Press, 1986.

5. The Gazette of Pakistan, *Extraordinary*, Authority Islamabad, April 26 1984.

6. The Blasphemy Episodes, Human Rights Commission of Pakistan Inquiry.

7. *Express Tribune*, 13 January 2011.

8. Blasphemy fact sheet prepared by Mansoor Raza (a researcher affiliated to an international NGO).

9. Pervez Hoodbhoy, 'Remembering Salman Taseer', *Express Tribune*, 2 January 2012.

10. Note: Ilm-ud-din killed Mahashay Rajpal for publishing a defamatory book 'Rangeela Rasool' in 1929 in Lahore. Interestingly, secular Jinnah defended him as a lawyer in the court.

11. Saroop Ijaz, *Express Tribune*, 16 October 2011.

12. I. A. Rehman, The News, 16 October 2011

13. I. A. Rehman, 'The Nawaz Dilemma', *Dawn*, 25 August 2011.

Chapter 15

ZIA'S CONTROVERSIAL ISLAMIC LAWS

Who would decide what the Islamic injunctions are? One sect believes that going to a saint's mazar (tomb) is sacrilegious; to the other, it is Islamic. One believes that Ali was deprived of the right to caliphate by Umar and Usman, while the other sect thinks that Shias are distorting Muslim history and can be killed for that. If one goes with Saudized Islam then former Prime Minister Yousuf Raza Gilani and many other parliamentarians should be disqualified because they are heirs of the saints of South Punjab or Sindh or are Shias.

Most of the existing Islamic laws were promulgated by General Zia-ul-Haq, particularly during 1979–86. General Zia-ul-Haq, who considered himself a kind of religious guardian of the country, added some disputable clauses to Article 62 of the 1973 Constitution of Pakistan. These clauses of Article 62 say, 'A person shall not be qualified to be elected or chosen as a member of Majlis-e-Shoora [Parliament] unless:

62 (D) he is of good character and is not commonly known as one who violates Islamic injunctions;

62 (E) he has adequate knowledge of Islamic teachings and practices obligatory duties prescribed by Islam as well as abstains from major sins;

62 (F) he is sagacious, righteous and non-profligate and honest and ameen; and

161

62 (G) he has not, after the establishment of Pakistan worked against the integrity of the country or opposed the ideology of Pakistan.' (Author's emphasis.)

Until the National Reconciliation Ordinance (NRO) 2007 struck down by the Supreme Court of Pakistan in December 2009, these clauses of the Constitution had remained dormant. Nobody had sought disqualification of any member of the Parliament, or the president and the prime minister by invoking these clauses. If these clauses are invoked will the superior judiciary acquire the role of 'religious guardian' à la Iran? Who else would make the decision on subjective issues such as whether a member of Parliament or for that matter president who 'does not violate Islamic injunctions, has adequate knowledge of Islamic teachings, abstains from major sins and is honest and ameen?'

Who would decide what the Islamic injunctions are? One sect believes that going to a saint's mazar (tomb) is sacrilegious; to the other, it is Islamic. One believes that Ali was deprived of the right to caliphate by Umar and Usman, while the other sect thinks that Shias are distorting Muslim history and can be killed for that. If one goes with Saudized Islam then former Prime Minister Yousuf Raza Gilani and many other parliamentarians should have been disqualified because they are heirs of the saints of South Punjab or Sindh or are Shias. Who would decide then, but the worthy judges, what adequate knowledge of Islamic teachings is, what a major and a minor sin is, and which parliamentarian is honest or dishonest? Who would decide what the 'ideology of Pakistan' is, as it is not defined in the Constitution?

By invoking such dormant clauses a window has been opened for 'inspired litigants like Maulvi Iqbal Haider to challenge the qualification of more than half, if not more members of the Parliament. Would our judges then be qualified to take decisions on such wide-ranging religion-loaded issues? Perhaps the court would not like to be put in a tight spot. The superior judiciary should not be blamed for referring to what is in the Constitution. They are there to interpret the Constitution and not to make it. I asked Senator Raza Rabbani, chairman of the Constitution Amendment Committee, before the 18th Amendment was passed by the Parliament unanimously, whether deletion clauses of Article 62 were on the agenda. He said: 'We have bigger issues to discuss and nobody is interested in including these clauses.' The point is that the court has heavily relied on Islamic clauses and the leading parties are in no mood to reform the Constitution. While the PML-N is Right of the Centre, the PPP has always tried to appease the mullah but unsuccessfully. Only the ANP and MQM, who are in the Parliament, are clear on the issue of separating religion from politics. The whole issue is ultimately attached to taking the Objectives Resolution and other religious clauses out of the Constitution but the political parties are afraid that the religious parties together with their militant wings would launch a movement against any such move.

Zia's Islamic laws create a parallel legal system. He incorporated the disputed Objectives Resolution as a substantive provision of the Constitution by inserting Article 2A. The principles and provisions set out in the Objectives Resolution were reproduced in the annexure of the Constitution. He also established the Federal Shariat Court (FSC) through an order in 1980. According to the FSC's website it is a 'unique institution with no parallel in the entire Muslim world. It is backed by the powerful provisions of the Constitution .... The preamble of the Constitution explicitly affirms that sovereignty over the entire universe belongs to almighty Allah alone and the authority to be exercised by the people of Pakistan within limits prescribed by Him is a sacred trust.' But in spite of the supra-Constitution powers given to the FSC it has not been able to establish its power over the Supreme Court of Pakistan, which has unequivocal powers to interpret the laws made by the chosen representatives of the people.

Let's take only some of Zia's Islamic laws, which remain controversial: The offence of Zina (Enforcement of Hudood) 1979. This deals with both consensual sex and rape; and the Qanun-e-Shahadat 1984, which deals with witness and evidence.

In the case of Zina (consensual sex) Section 5 (2 and 2A) of the 1979 law says: 'Whoever is guilty of Zina liable to "hadd"* shall be subject to the provisions of this Ordinance: (a) if he or she is a "muhsan"** be stoned to death at a public place; or (b) if he or she is not a "muhsan" be punished at a public place, with whipping numbering one hundred stripes.'

*Hadd means limit or restriction. It is often used in Islamic literature for the bounds of acceptable behaviour and the punishments for serious crimes.
**Muhsan means an adult male or female who has consensual sex with a married man/woman.

Mode of execution of punishment, of stoning to death – the punishment of stoning to death awarded under Section 5 (B) executed in the following manner, namely: 'Such of the witness who deposed against the convict as may be available shall start stoning and while stoning is being carried on, he [sentenced person] may be shot dead whereupon stoning and shooting shall be stopped.'[1]

No court has given the above mentioned punishment because the conditions laid down for the witness are very tough. The law requires that there should be 'at least four adult witnesses about whom the court is satisfied having regard of "tazkiyah-al-shahood" that they are truthful persons, abstain from major sins and give evidence as eye-witness of the act of penetration during intercourse necessary to the offence.' That's why the leading lawyer Khalid Ishaq, who was well-versed in Islamic jurisprudence, once said that it seemed the punishment was not for having sex but for exhibitionism. Over the period, fortunately, the courts have acted prudently and have not pronounced any stoning-to-death punishment but this has not stopped private 'iirgas' (unofficial courts of the elders of a tribe or tribes) from awarding this sentence quite often and implementing it brutally.

Those who don't stone to death, kill using other means in the name of honour. This shows that such primitive laws are incorporated in Pakistan's legal system because it promised the people Islamic laws. While judges have avoided giving this punishment, the people living in tribal and feudal structures in Pakistan take law in their hand in the name of custom and Islam. Many couples have been stoned to death, particularly in the northern tribal areas, where people claim that they follow true Islamic laws. In other rural areas of Pakistan, honour killing is common and most of the culprits manage to avoid the maximum punishment prescribed for a murder in the Pakistan laws. The mullah who influences their minds is usually supportive of such medieval punishment and the state just turns a blind eye.

**

The laws for Zina-bil-Jabr

Section 6 of the Hudood Ordinance says: A person is said to commit Zina-bil-Jabr, if he or she has sexual intercourse with a woman or man, as the case may be, to whom he or she is not married, in any of the following circumstances, namely:

1. Against the will of the victim;
2. Without the consent of the victim;
3. With the consent of the victim, when the consent has been obtained by putting the victim in fear of death or of hurt; or
4. With the consent of the victim, when the offender knows, that the offender is not validly married to the victim and that the consent is given because the victim believes that the offender is another person to whom the victim is or believes herself or himself to be validly married.

In the case of rape the perpetrator is 'stoned to death' if the victim or the offender is married and the punishment is 'whipping' if the offender is not married. The law does not qualify if rape occurs between the married couple, which is an offence in many democratic societies. However, contrary to the general belief about the Zina-bil-Jabr laws among some ill-informed critics, the victim's own complaint is enough to file a First Information Report (FIR) with the police. And a medical test confirms the validity of the victims claim. The need for four male witnesses is only required in the cases of Zina-bil-Razaa (consensual sex). Human Rights activists and all humanists are basically against the primitive sentences of stoning to death and public whipping.

National Commission on the Status of Women's Report on Hudood Ordinance 1979 was of the view that 'After the introduction of these ordinances, in particular the ordinance relating to the offence of Zina and Qazf, coupled with the subsequent enforcement of Qisas and Diyat Ordinance, it was found that instead of remedying social ills, these ordinances led to an increase in injustice against women and, in fact, became an instrument of oppression against women. There were hundreds of incidents where a woman subjected to rape, or even gang rape, was eventually accused of Zina, and thereby subjected to wrong and unjust persecution and great ordeal. In this connection, the lacunae in the law were greatly exploited by unscrupulous elements, to perpetrate great cruelty on women and children, particularly minor females. The strict requirements regarding witnesses and sustained pressure from women's rights groups in civil society, no women were subjected to the punishment of flogging [lashes], or for that matter "Rajam", but nevertheless, the threat remained and in itself cause great distress to the women who even otherwise remain the most exploited individuals in our society.'

Some ulema's view is that the punishment of 'Rajam' (stoning to death) is un-Islamic because it is not mentioned in the Quran, but others claim it *was* pronounced in the Prophet's time. The same report continues: 'Various women's NGOs and human rights organizations repeatedly protested against the injustice and ill effects of the enforcement of these Ordinances but the protests were in vain. More and more women were subjected to torment because of these laws and the incidents of rape increased as time went by and the jails began to be filled with women on trial under the Zina Ordinance. Even though the Qazf Ordinance was meant to eliminate incidents of false accusations against women, it brought no relief to the women, because often their tormentors were powerful individuals and any attempt by the victim to seek redress under this law resulted in further misery for them.'[2]

The fact remains that no modern and civilized polity can have laws like stoning to death and whipping in this day and age. On an individual basis, most educated Pakistanis are shocked when somebody is stoned to death, because a modern value system abhors such treatment. They respect people's personal freedom and right to make their own decisions in their personal lives as long as they do not become a nuisance for others. But when the same people are told that what they abhor is an Islamic punishment most find it difficult to swallow. Such is the inner conflict a Muslim of the twenty-first century experiences when a choice has to be made between the present and archaic value systems. The trouble is the state has given too much space to the obscurantist as that's what suits the ruling establishment to exploit religion in their own interest.

***

Qanun-e-Shahadat (Law of witness)

Section 17 of this law says: 'Competence and number of witnesses:

1. The competence of person to testify, and the number of witnesses required in any case shall be determined in accordance with the injunctions of Islam as laid down in the Holy Quran and Sunnah.
2. Unless otherwise provided in any law relating to the enforcement of Hudood or any other special law;

(a) The matter pertaining to financial or future obligations, if reduced to writing, the instrument shall be attested by two men, or one man *and two women, so that one may remind the other, if necessary,* and evidence shall be led accordingly; and (Author's emphasis.)

(b) In all matter of the Court may accept, or act on the testimony of one man or one woman or such other evidence as the circumstances of the case warrant."[3]

The demand that in cases of financial or future obligation two women witnesses are required is quite ridiculous in this century when women are heading banks and other corporations and are signing and witnessing a number of documents.

The law perceives that women are inferior to men. Women rights activists have been protesting against this law ever since it was promulgated. But given the fact that the law has been sanctified by the proclamation that this is how it has been ordained in the holy scripture and Sunnah these activists are outwitted. In a Geo TV religious programme 'Alif', there was a debate a few years ago on this issue. Women rights activist Anis Haroon, assisted by a Leftist journalist Ahfazur Rehman, said that it was an unfair law. The religious scholar Asad Thanvi said that it was an Islamic law. Anis retorted that keeping in view that women were now in all fields and were even heading banks, the ulema should do 'Ijtehad'. Asad quickly brought in the Quran and said that Ijtehad was only done where there was some ambiguity, not when the holy book was categorical and unambiguous. He also rejected the argument with a fundamentalist position that the Quran was a book sent by God, who knows all and also what the future world is to be. Both Anis and Ahfaz looked dumbfounded.

Reason: In the Islamic Republic of Pakistan the state has a religion and expects all to adhere to it, so any rational discussion outside the strict realm of Islam is forbidden or may attract charges of apostasy.

Nevertheless, in practice the pragmatic ulema, who consider themselves custodians of Islam, did not object to the single signature of a woman Prime Minister Benazir Bhutto on papers of much greater 'financial and future obligations'. Or, for that matter, to the former governor of the State Bank of Pakistan, Shamshad Akhtar, signing and issuing Pakistani currency notes guaranteeing their value.

The Constitution is also deliberately vague on the issue of whether a woman can be the president of Pakistan. Article 41 (2) of the Constitution says: 'A person shall be not qualified for election as President unless *he is a Muslim* of not less than forty-five years of age and is qualified to be elected as a member of the National Assembly.' (Author's emphasis.) This clause started with the drafters of the Constitution using the word 'person', which is gender neutral, but moving forward it says 'unless he is a Muslim.' Does that mean no women can ever be a president of Pakistan? It is also discriminatory against the non-Muslims who are otherwise supposed to be equal citizens.

This is an important point because there was a debate in the mid-Sixties whether a woman could be the head of state when Fatima Jinnah was pitched against Ayub Khan in the presidential elections. The ulema, who disliked Ayub's secular government, and the democrats, who were against the military rule, jointly supported Fatima. The clever clergy accepted to have a woman head of the state as a lesser evil, while some felt it was un-Islamic. Maulana Abul Ala Maududi invoked the injunction that in case of 'Iztirar' (necessity), one was allowed to eat pork.

There are a number of laws, Quranic verses and Sharia laws that contradict the claims of religious parties that Islam gives equal rights to women. It is true that in the primitive tribal society of Hijaz, Prophet Muhammad's preaching did provide some rights, which were previously not given to women. Perhaps that was a revolutionary cultural step then, but with the passage of 1,400 years those Islamic rights needed to expand. The trouble is that aggressive Muslim scholars who support the status quo have not let the Islamic jurisprudence grow after the twelfth century.

***

Islamic inheritance

In Muslim history, at no time were women given equal rights. One of the greatest injustices to women is in the Pakistani law of inheritance. Under the Islamic laws a daughter gets half of the inheritance that a son gets. Similarly, the wife gets one-eighth share in the assets left by her husband. To top it, a Muslim cannot write a will declaring how much share he/she is leaving for the people. So the only way to distribute your inheritance in an Islamic republic is to gift it during your life time. Even in the case of blood money women get half the amount. The religious instructions coming from the scriptures and traditions called Sharia obstruct the organic growth of laws, which are required by changing world realities and human progress. It is because of this that a very small percentage of women in most Muslim countries have the title of properties in their name.

Similarly while men are allowed to even strike their wives to reprimand them, women cannot strike their husbands. Men are allowed polygamy because it existed at the time of the Prophet but women are not allowed polyandry. Muslim men can marry an 'Ahle Kitab', meaning a Jew or a Christian woman because Islam recognizes that these monotheist religions were bestowed with the holy books from God. Women, however, cannot marry a non-Muslim. So how can it be claimed that they have equal rights? It is futile for the women rights activist to invoke religion and ask for the rights, which a twenty-first-century woman has in advanced democracies. They should ask for their rights without invoking Islam and let the clergy or religious parties oppose this proposition.

Nilofar Bakhtiar, a woman minister in General Pervez Musharraf's regime, not only had the courage to go for paragliding (in France to raise funds for a good cause) but also to stand up to the Islamist vigilantes of the Lal Masjid. The self-styled vigilantes were quick to issue a fatwa (edict) against her just because she hugged another veteran paraglider after landing safely. She decided to challenge the mullah's right to issue a fatwa against her in the court and not a single colleague came forward to second her. What she did was her personal choice and did not hurt anybody. No law in the country says that she cannot hug anybody.

In yet another case an Islamic fanatic, who was let loose, in spite of two murders on his hands, shot a Punjab government lady minister because according to him women should not be working with men. The problem with religious extremists is that they want to enforce their social and moral values on others and use violent means.

***

Qisas and Diyat laws

In line with the Objectives Resolution mandate, all laws would be in accordance with the Quran and Sunnah, and no law would be made repugnant of these holy principles. Accordingly, they introduced the Offences against Human Body (Enforcement of Qisas and Diyat) Ordinance, 1984. The law was re-promulgated by an interim government in 1990, after Benazir Bhutto's government was ousted by President Ghulam Ishaq Khan. This changed the basis of the criminal laws related to murder as given in the PPC. It provides for an agreement between the murderer and heirs of the victim, whereby the heirs can either seek compensation or forgive the murderer.

The Judicial Commission of Pakistan in its report on Qisas and Diyat law had raised two questions and then discussed the issue in detail. Briefly, it said: 'Before commenting on the intrinsic merits or demerits of the "Offences Against Human Body (Enforcement of Qisas and Diyat) Ordinance, 1984" two main questions requiring consideration are:

1. Whether it was necessary to have an absolutely new Statute for the purposes of enforcement of Injunctions of Islam, as laid down in the Holy Quran and Sunnah, in accordance with the administration of Criminal Justice in the Country or the present Penal Code could, by suitable amendments, be brought in conformity with the injunctions of Islam, and
2. Whether the draft Ordinance, in its present form, is enforceable, or it suffers from any serious lacunae, contradictions or other defects which make it difficult, if not impossible, to enforce in the country.'

As regards the first question, it may be mentioned that the two previous Law Commissions, one of 1958–59 and the other of 1967–70 headed by late S. A. Rahman and late Hamoodur Rahman, chief justices, respectively, did not advocate the substitution of existing penal laws by new Statutes. The latter Commission was particularly of the view that the laws in force in the country were not, by and large, against the tenets of Islam and that these laws could be modified and brought in consonance with the injunctions of the Quran and Sunnah by means of carefully drafted amendments. The Federal Shariat Court also, in its judgment dated 23 December 1980, delivered in nine connected Shariat petitions (General Gul Hassan Khan, etc., *vs* The State), expressed the view that 'the provisions of the Pakistan Penal Code relating to harm to human body could be brought in line with the injunctions of the Quran and Sunnah with suitable amendments.'

Qisas and Diyat law is against the basic principle that killing or injuring any person is a crime against state and society. This principle is important, because any leverage given to the offender, in the form of buying out the heirs of victims or pressuring them to make a compromise, is detrimental to the law and order in a society. The National Commission for Women's Rights had maintained in its report that most of the offenders in the cases of so-called 'honour killing' had managed to get off scot-free. The high-profile case of Saima Sarwar, who was killed in the office of the human rights' activist and lawyer Hina Jilani, by a hired killer, is the glaring example of the flagrant use of this law. The mother and uncle of Saima had orchestrated this killing, because the girl had eloped to marry a person of her choice. The father, who is a prominent businessman in Peshawar, invoked his right to forgive under the Qisas and Diyat law. And all the offenders were released. This is a common practice.

After the notorious Raymond Allen Davis case in 2011, even the American media started understanding the Qisas and Diyat law. Davis belonged to a security agency in the US and reportedly was a Central Intelligence Agency (CIA) contractor in Pakistan. He killed two young men who were riding a motorbike. Davis said he killed them in self-defence as they were following him. Pakistani authorities did not accept the US embassy's plea that Davis enjoyed diplomatic immunity and said diplomats were not supposed to carry weapons. Another US Consulate vehicle, which was coming to rescue Davis, killed a pedestrian. After a few days of national frenzy, the hypocrite American administration used the Qisas and Diyat law, which they had always said was medieval and 'barbarous'. Somebody paid US $2.3 million to the families of the victims as 'Diyat' and Davis flew off to the US. Unfortunately, the wife of one victim allegedly committed suicide and the wife of the other victim was killed by his family over the disputed blood-money distribution.

Columnist Shahid Saeed has rightly observed: 'While murder is still treated as an offence against the public and the state initiates prosecution against alleged culprits, Islamic criminal law has been understood to treat murder as a civil offence where the aggrieved party (legal heirs of the deceased) alone can bring forward the case or forgive on their own without bringing it in front of a judge, as is the case in Saudi Arabia and was in the Mughal era. The social contract that has evolved in Pakistan requires the state to treat murder not as a private wrong but a criminal offence against the public.'[4]

In support of his argument, Shahid says, 'Based on research in 10 districts in Punjab regarding the Multan Bench of the Lahore High Court [LHC], Federal Shariat Court and Supreme Court [SC], between 1981 and 2000, the murder rate rose at an average of 6.5 per 100,000 per annum. It has increased since the Qisas and Diyat laws were introduced, contrary to the claims of its supporters. The percentage of cases cancelled by the police on their own, without sending a challan to the court, has doubled and stood at 11 per cent in 2000. Conviction rates at the trial stage have steadily decreased and stood at an abysmal 12 per cent in 2000, while compromise rates increased to 29 per cent. This means, that one out of every three murderers walks free after striking a deal. The total conviction rate in the Multan Bench of the LHC fell from 51 per cent in the 1980s to 33 per cent in the next decade. At the same time, the acquittal rate in the SC increased from 28 per cent to 67 per cent while the conviction rate dropped from 79 per cent in 1984 to 35 per cent in 2000. No person has ever been convicted of murder under Qisas.'[5] Such are the ramifications of mixing religion with the affairs of the state.

Heightened religiosity and the support given to it by the state and Arab donors have sharpened the conflict in the minds of the people. They are torn between the desire to have a modern democracy and an Islamic ideological state. Khaled Ahmed maintains, 'Ideology doesn't sit well with democracy. Since Pakistan is trying the two together, it has an intense unspoken longing for the "perfect" state that Iran, for instance has become. The slogan of going back to Sharia actually hides the desire to do away with democracy and its insistence on the rights of an individual citizen.'[6]

Notes and References:

1. M. Farani, Islamic Laws (Hudood Laws), Nadeem Law House, Lahore, 2012.
2. http://www.hrcp-web.org/showdocument.asp?id=12
3. (Bare Act) The Qanun-e-Shahadat (order 10 of 1984) published by Nadeem Law Book House, Lahore.
4. Shahid Saeed, 'Effect of Qisas and Diyat Laws on Criminal Justice', *Daily Times*, 18 September 2010.
5. Ibid.
6. Khaled Ahmed, *Religious Developments in Pakistan 1999-2008*, Vanguard Books, Lahore, 2010, p. 28.

Chapter 16

UNBRIDLED GROWTH OF MOSQUES, MADRASSAHS AND JIHADI GROUPS

... there are 12,448 madrassahs with 1.6 million male students in the country (2010 data). As these madrassahs are not merely teaching institutions, the education and training given there are of a vocational nature, with religious overtones, of course. The students who graduate from there are trained to be pesh imams, khateebs and madrassah teachers. According to a conservative estimate, even if 50 per cent madrassahs graduates adopt the above-mentioned profession, and the rest go back to join their parents' farms or businesses, the system is producing one mullah for every 225 Pakistanis every year. It is in sharp contrast to one nurse for over 3,600 persons, and one doctor for some 3,400 persons.

Are modern democracy and Islamic ideology compatible? Many ulema have taken a reformist position that there is no clash between Islam and democracy. In doing so, they want to meet the people's desire to have democracy, because it gives them a say in the running of the government, and at the same time introduce the Islamic laws. They ignore the fact that in democracy power to make laws and government rests with the people and not with the divine Sharia. Among the Muslim states only a few have some form of democracy, though it may not be 'an ideal democracy' where all the people, irrespective of their religion, sect, gender, caste and creed are treated as equal. Turkey, which has a secular democracy, has an Islamist party in power but it has not tried to roll back the secular basis of the Constitution. Bangladesh has recently tried to go back to secular democracy, thanks to their Supreme Court verdict, which has also banned the forming of religious political parties. But the power of global Islamic revivalism is such that Prime Minister Sheikh Hasina's government has not dared to drop the word 'Islamic' from the country's official name although the first Constitution named it as the Socialist Republic of Bangladesh.

A democratic dispensation has to adopt the UN Human Rights Charter, which has many clauses that are not followed in Muslim states including Pakistan. Women and non-Muslims do not have equal democratic rights in a country that does not separate religion from state.

**

The propaganda that Pakistan was needed by the Muslims of India to live according to the Islamic values was just exploitation of religion for political gains. By implication, it suggests that before partition the Muslims of India were living with non-Islamic values. Or for that matter, the Muslims who are living in countries where they do not rule are less Islamic than those of Pakistan. Once Pakistan was carved out of the Indian subcontinent, it succumbed to the propaganda that had been whipped up for a limited purpose. The religious parties and clergy have since then exploited religion to get maximum mileage.

To begin with, the state lost control and the number of mosques continued to increase exponentially every year. No democrat would have an issue with the increase in the number of places of worship for any religious community, provided their construction remains within the legal framework and is not at the cost of other people's rights. For example, in USA the number of mosques have increased in the post 9/11 period, although much is said about the apprehensions of the Americans against the growing Islamic fundamentalism. At the same time, all democratic societies respect freedom of expression, hence the right to preach any religion or school of thought. But the issue in Pakistan is that, emboldened by state patronage and sometimes dithering, many mosques have been built on encroached land. If the state or the individual on whose land an illegal mosque is erected tries to demolish it, the clergy declare that 'Islam is in danger'. Though there are laws in the penal code, which declare making hate speeches, publishing hate material or use of any other means to incite people against any religion, sect, ethno-linguistic group unlawful and punishable, no government dare implement these laws.

The Lal Masjid incident is one glaring example of this. The madrassah attached to the children's library there was occupied by female students led by Maulana Abdul Aziz's wife. This was in spite of the fact that Lal Masjid is supposed to be government-funded and Maulana Aziz was a government-appointed 'khateeb' (prayer leader and preacher). His wife and female students of the madrassah arrogated to themselves the role of Islamic vigilantes, arresting a Shia woman and some Chinese women on charges of running prostitution dens. In a stand-off with the General Pervez Musharraf government, they collected a huge cache of weapons, gave refuge to the jihadi volunteers who roamed openly and were visible to the people on TV screens. They went out and burnt a government building and killed a member of a law enforcement agency. Local police officials claimed that they had arrested Maulana Aziz for transporting a large quantity of unlicensed arms in his car. But he was released on the intervention of the Minister of Religious Affairs Muhammad Ijaz-ul-Haq. That till they got out of hand they had the state's patronage was also evident from the fact that Lal Masjid is a walking distance from the so-called omnipotent ISI headquarters.

The government tried to take over the Lal Masjid from the control of a khateeb, who claimed that he had seen the Prophet Muhammad telling him in a dream that an Islamic revolution would rise from his blood spilled on the floor of the mosque. Armed resistance was put in by the jihadi volunteers. In the process ten soldiers, including an officer, and 70 persons who were resisting were killed.

Majority of the Pakistani media, particularly TV anchors, supported the armed resistance by blaming the government for using excessive force against the Lal Masjid self-proclaimed Islamic revolutionary and his accomplices. The public opinion was turned against the government by the media so much so that two judges of the Supreme Court ordered in favour of Maulana Aziz and instructed the government to give him free land and building to expand his madrassah for women. Such is the power of aggressive clergy. The prosecution, either because of fear of the suicide force Maulana Aziz claimed he has, or because of their faith that he was waging jihad, has not presented all the evidence to the court. The government wants to appease the religious militants and has no interest to get him convicted for harbouring armed jihadis on a government property. Most of the judges, who are religious, have also preferred to forget the electronic evidence, which had shown firing coming from within the masjid. The state was blackmailed by the Lal Masjid's khateeb and his supporters and has been instructed to build a new madrassah for them in Islamabad.

No official census of mosques in Pakistan is available. As most of the mosques have been built without government's permission and on encroached lands it is difficult to find an authentic figure. Dr Pervez Hoodbhoy once estimated there were 250,000 mosques in the country. This figure is apparently on the lower side. Pakistan's male population over 14 years of age is around 61.7 million and the estimated number of mosques is 250,000, which means the country has one mosque per 246 male population. I have not deducted 3 per cent Pakistanis of other religions.

Do we really need that many mosques? If not, why is the unrestricted proliferation of mosques happening in the country? Some of the major reasons are: one, there are too many sects in the country, so they all need a separate mosque in each locality; two, a mosque is a source of income for the maulana designated to be in charge of it along with at least one assistant; three, in many cases a mosque provides living quarters to these clergymen; and four mosques provide jobs to at least 50 per cent of madrassahs graduates or even non-graduates.

Even if the most conservative figure of 2010 is taken as standard, there are 12,448 madrassahs with 1.6 million male students in the country. As these madrassahs are not only teaching institutions, the education and training given there is of a vocational nature, with religious overtones, of course. The students who graduate from there are trained to be pesh imams, khateebs and madrassah teachers. According to a conservative estimate, even if 50 per cent madrassah graduates adopt the above-mentioned profession, and the rest go back to join their parents' farms or businesses, the system is producing one mullah for every 225 Pakistanis every year. It is in sharp contrast to one nurse for over 3,600 persons, and one doctor for some 3,400 persons.

So, either these madrassah-educated youth will make new mosques, join the existing ones, or, quite often, fight over a mosque on the pretext of sectarian differences. Alternatively, they teach at the growing number of madrassahs – the unofficial estimate is that there are 20,000. The madrassah-dense areas are Islamabad and Ahmedpur, in southern Punjab. Those who do not get a job in a mosque and are lured by the Islamic revolutionary romanticism join any of the many jihadi outfits. Reportedly, once a person trains in a three-month Islamic ideology course and three-month guerilla fighting, he gets almost double the amount of the government-fixed minimum wages, which is Rs 8,000 or US $ 84 (2012 figure).

We have already discussed the proliferation of mosques and madrassahs in the country. But let us see their ratio to other educational institutions. Of the total 256,088 educational institutions in the country there are only 12,448 madrassahs (if we go by the official figures), 4.8 per cent of the total, and the number of students enrolled in the madrassahs is only 4.27 per cent of the total 37.46 million students.[1] The madrassah students mainly study the religious courses and have little freedom of expression as no questions can be asked relating to divine revelation or on the settled issues of tradition. There are six federations of madrassahs, each teaching the children their respective sectarian courses. They are indoctrinated with Islamic ideology. For young students, anyone who follows the militant groups to bring an Islamic revolution is a hero. It is because of this romance and persuasion by some of their teachers who want to establish a theocratic state that the madrassah students are more likely to join the jihadi groups. Another important factor is that as most of these madrassahs are boarding schools – the only boarding schools for the rural and urban poor – their entire surrounding and Spartan living makes them physically and psychologically good Mujahid material. According to leading journalist and author Amir Rana's study, 60 per cent of madrassah students and teachers are from the rural poor background. The cultural differences and economic inequity these students see in the urban localities when they are moved to urban madrassahs is shocking for them. They are also under full-time control of their ideological mentors and have only small breaks with the families who could give them any other view of life. All this prepares their minds for an Islamic revolution, which their teachers tell them will not only bring an egalitarian system but also God's blessings. With the setback to the socialist ideology in contemporary history, the Islamic revolution slogan is attractive to those who want a change. They fail to realize that no Muslim country has the promised egalitarian system. There was none ever.

The madrassah students are the main source of strength for the religious parties and are often brought out for street protests. Saleem Ali, in his researched book *Islam and Education: Conflict and Conformity in Pakistan's Madrassahs* has emphasized this: 'In one particular publication of the religious parties of Pakistan, called Al-Muslim, the writer Ali bin Mawiya stated, if 1.8 million students of the religious schools come out on the streets today for the implementation of the rule of Shariat in the country, no power on earth can stop them, not even the 0.6 million strong army of Pakistan.'[2] Ali further observed: '[T]he metaphor of fortress is a potent symbol in this regard – as one madrassah leader, Maulana Sharif (who is also the imam at a government mosque), when interviewed by a journalist commented: "it is we Madrassahs [*sic*] who are keeping the Islamic values and traditions intact for hundreds of years. If the religious schools had not been there, Islam and the so-called Muslim would have faced irreparable losses at the hands of liberal and Western agents".'[3] Maulana Sharif claims that of most of the religious parties, imams, mosques and madrassahs have thousands of domestic and Arab world donors. As the state is committed to supporting promotion of the Quran and Sunnah it contributes large amounts to finance and subsidize these institutions. The Arab funding has strengthened the Deobandi and Ahle-Hadith sects in Pakistan and promoted Saudization of Islamic culture and thought. Similarly, after the Iranian Revolution was hijacked by the Shia clergy, several Shia outfits in Pakistan are supported by Iran.

Nevertheless much of the funding to mosques and madrassahs comes from the local people, mainly the agriculturists and trading class. Saleem Ali has explained there is a strong tradition of charity among Muslims. They contribute for such causes. Clergymen fully exploit the people by telling them how each donation takes the donor a step nearer to heaven, to which all religious persons aspire. Sometimes in their sermons the imam gives mathematical equations as to which good deed would earn them how many brownie-points from God. Interestingly, many, if not most, of the people who donate generously are not necessarily ethical or pious in their practical lives. In some cases the bigger a tax evader, smuggler or gangster the more he donates, believing that such donations would wash away his sins like a good washing powder.

Many in successive Pakistani governments have said that the madrassahs are playing a positive role as they are housing and providing education to around 1 to 2 million students. They do not realize that the whole culture of madrassahs is pernicious and needs to be changed. The country needs doctors, nurses, scientists, mathematicians, engineers, architects, electricians, plumbers, masons, welders, engineering and industry workers, IT experts and professionals. And youths with good English reading, writing and speaking abilities as that is the language of business whether we like it or not. It does not need thousands of clerics, which the madrassahs are capable of producing. One option for Pakistan is to convert the madrassahs into technical and vocational schools, with religion as a subject along with ethics. If this course is not adopted the country will continue to have a bumper crop of extremists every year, slowing down the pace of progress and contributing nothing to the economy.

A cursory look at the reproduction of *Dars-e-Nizami*, the curriculum of madrassahs, included in Saleem Ali's book, shows that the prescribed books were written between 61 and 1190 al Hijrah (AH). Apparently for the ulema who adopted this curriculum do not see the need to update it to meet the twenty-first century requirement. Compare this with the situation when the Catholic Church was ruling and resisted scientific thought and advancement, the Muslim scholars were benefiting from the knowledge of Greek and Indian philosophers and were contributing to new thinking. Christianity gradually compromised after the mid-fifteenth century Renaissance with the idea that with the change in time and place the values and mindset have to change. Interestingly, as pointed out by US-based academician Nader Hashemi, 'the Muslim societies are going through same pains and turbulence after about 14 centuries of the advent of Islam that the Christians had faced before them.'[4]

Muslim narcissists are living on past glory rejecting and resisting inevitable modernization, which they call Westernization. Societies evolve with the progress in economic growth; they can neither be rolled back to medieval period, nor stopped from moving with time. Afghanistan is one failed example of rolling back the society to medieval cultural and social relations by the Taliban. It would be stupid to blame the American intervention only, an issue we shall deal with in another chapter. In spite of their love of Islam, the people of Pakistan rejected the attempt by the Taliban to enforce Islamic values in Swat and other tribal areas. They stood behind the army operation, the conservative Muslim League included.

But this does not mean that madrassahs, which have come into the limelight because they have multiplied since the early 1980s and produced militant Islamic forces, are the only source of recruitment. Even the students who go to government schools are taught distorted pre- and- post-Pakistan Independence history. Some surveys have shown that anti-Indian and anti-Hinduism are promoted particularly by most of the Islamiat and Urdu teachers. But background interviews with some leading educationists reveal that all attempts to change the syllabi by previous governments were sabotaged by the bigots sitting in important official positions. They believe that to justify Pakistan's existence a separate Islamic identity has to be kept alive. A syllogism of this argument is that because we are Muslims and live in Pakistan, we are one nation. But the flip side of this argument, which the students are faced with when they start understanding the politics and economic realities, is that this syllogism is a way to negate the fact that Pakistan is a multi-national state. This state of denial has already led to the liberation of Bangladesh, and Balochistan is slowly drifting away.

Dr Mubarak Ali has explained this dilemma: 'In Pakistan, historiography has developed under the framework of "Pakistan Ideology", which is based on the idea of a separate Muslim nationhood and justifies partition of India. The Pakistani historians are told from the very beginning to construct their history within this framework. It is well understood that whenever history is written under the influence of an ideology, its objectivity is sacrificed. Facts are manipulated in order to justify the political acts of leadership.'[5]

The trouble is that these militants have gone beyond the stage of return; they want to capture power by force. It is difficult to have an argument with religious fundamentalists, no matter which religion they belong to. Their position is that what is pronounced divine by them and cannot be argued or discussed. Hence, they show all the intolerance whether it is regarding issues of interpretation of religion or the values, which they think are ordained by the divine power and are sacred.

The impunity with which the Islamic terrorists operate and kill people in Pakistan is alarming for all enlightened people. Dr Pervez Hoodbhoy warns: 'Surely, it is time to reflect on what makes so many Pakistanis disposed towards celebrating murder, lawlessness and intolerance. To understand the kind of psychological conditioning that has turned us into nasty brutes, cruel both to ourselves and to others, I suggest that the readers sample some of the Friday Khutbas [sermons] delivered across the country's estimated 250,000 mosques ... often using abusive language, by the mullah.'[6] Many educated Muslims who go to mosques for prayers are found criticizing the Friday khutbahs, both for their reactionary content and hate campaigning against other sects. In the collective prayer in most of the mosques for the last 66 years the mullah prays: 'Oh God, destroy the enemies of Islam, the Hindus and the Jews.' Quite often it is the prayer for the destruction of Israel, India and America. Mateen Ahmed, who was my colleague in the *Dawn* newspaper in the 1980s once asked me after attending a Friday prayer why God was not answering our prayers as, instead of destroying the Jews, Hindus and Americans He was letting them prosper. Over 250,000 pulpits in these mosques are equipped with powerful microphones and captive audiences. This opportunity is usually misused to incite the people against a person or a sect if the mosque imam or his financier has a vested interest.

There are many cases in which after listening to anti-Christian and anti-Ahmadiyya hate speeches, the incited people have attacked and killed the person or burnt the houses of the targeted communities. Where do they draw this licence to incite violence from, if not the state? The state in Pakistan has not only followed the policy of appeasing the religious extremists, as they are self-styled custodians of the ideology of Pakistan, but has armed them for short-term tactical gains endangering the future of the society.

Most prayer leaders at the mosques also have played a negative role against the family planning programme. Children, they say, are God's gift and any attempt to stop child-birth while having sex with your wife is fornication. As a result, in spite of a huge family planning programme run by the government since the 1960s, the population growth in Pakistan is still hovering around 1.9 to 2.1 per cent, depending on which figures one accepts. The economic growth of Pakistan is directly linked to the economic prosperity of the country. In about 13 years, Pakistan's population has almost doubled to touch 180 million. A number of less-educated mullahs have been telling people that getting their children inoculated to prevent them from various diseases like polio was intervention in God's will. Any attempt to book these mullahs is considered a threat to Islam. However, in spite of their power, the KP government has passed a law that anybody who hinders the polio campaign can be arrested. Although mullahs are more powerful in KP than in any other province of the country, the KP government has shown that when the state wants it can draw the line. That is when the mullah-led militants challenge the writ of the government. If they stay clear of challenging the establishment power and if they misuse the religious freedom to spread misgivings against other sects and religions, the state of Pakistan is not bothered. What divides people always suits the rulers.

The religious parties, which wants more say and space in the country's affairs as the country was made in the name of Islam, insist that Islamic ideology is Pakistan's ideology. But when it comes to vote – the only way people can express on whose side they are – the Islamic religious parties have not received more than 10 to 11 per cent votes, that too with the help from the hidden hands of the establishment. Although there are '246 religious organizations operating in Pakistan; 25 are politically active and participate in elections; 145 have a sectarian base; and 12 do not believe in democracy and want to establish Islamic caliphate.'[7] It is the last two who are particularly dangerous for the country's democratic and economic growth, especially when they are aided by a hundred odd militant groups. Both the political and the militant Islamic organizations usually cooperate to operate in the name of the Islamic ideology of Pakistan.

Khaled Ahmed has referred to the MQM leader Altaf Hussain's questions to the intellectuals, historians and religious scholars in order 'to correctly define for him the ideology of Pakistan: Did the Quaid ever use the word ideology during the Pakistan Movement? Did he refer to it in his famous 11 August 1947 address? Does the Constitution reflect it? Are the courts run in accordance to it?' He has then pointed out that '[b]eing a politician, he [Altaf] knows that a liberal Muslim will reject the first two questions. The clergy and its followers will say no to the last two questions. If the Constitution could speak it would say, either liberal or make me ideological.'[8]

This cleavage between moderate Muslims, who keep religion as a private affair and are secular in their daily life and outlook, and the rising number of staunch believers, who want to introduce Sharia in every facet of life, is a common dilemma of all the Muslim societies. As a matter of fact, Osama bin Laden has sharpened this contradiction in Muslim societies to a dangerous level. The Al Qaeda philosophy, which has its franchisees across all the Muslims states, preaches that

Islamic revolution is inevitable and predestined. To make it possible 'true Muslims' should first take over their own country from the rulers who are Westernized. Once the Islamic caliphate is established, bringing together the Muslims of the world and the countries ruled by the infidels would be conquered. The militant Islamists are working on that agenda; one of their leaders even preached that if all the major leaders who supported Western democracy were assassinated, the Islamists would have the opportunity to capture power.

Simplistic solutions for dealing with the militant Islamic forces, which have challenged the writ of the government, are presented by some popular talk-show hosts and their guests. An easy and populist line is just to blame the government for towing the American 'war on terror'. One cannot walk away by just blaming the US and its allies for dividing Pakistani society into those who believe in militant Islam and and those who believe in moderate Islam. This is a clash of ideologies within Muslim societies.

On one side is 'Islamic fundamentalism' and on the other, moderate Islam. Fundamentalism has its foundation in the radical Islamic movement. It is well-explained by Professor Peter van der Veer of University of Amsterdam in his paper published by South Asian Policy Analysis: 'Fundamentalism is a social phenomenon that occurs during rapid social change, is marked by a profound experience in crises by revitalization of religion and a search for authenticity. Fundamentalism is a global phenomenon in so far as it is a response to global transformation.'

The trouble is that Pakistani media anchors and politicians talk without having any historical and ideological perspective. Islamic fundamentalism and the Islamic militant movement in Pakistan and globally should not be studied in isolation as a theological issue only. It has to be studied in the light of social, political and economic environment of Pakistan's society and its geostrategic conditions. Unless we understand this phenomenon on a domestic and international perspective, the issue cannot be resolved. Most politicians who appear on television channels are looking at this issue as a reaction to General Pervez Musharraf's policy on 'war against terrorism' and US wrong-doings going back to the Afghan War 1979–89.

The secular narrative gets limited space in Urdu print and electronic media. The Left of the Centre parties have access to a couple of Urdu magazines but their circulation is limited to their sympathizers. Only a couple of liberal analysts have their programmes on the mainstream TV channels. In popular Urdu newspapers only a few liberal columnists are accommodated. Mostly progressive analysts columns are declined space because the owners or the page editors are mostly sympathizers of the Islamists.

Because of their ideological bias most journalists are not telling the people that jihadi groups want to work against the UN resolutions. International law says no country should harbour terrorists and allow its land to be used as sanctuary for an armed interference in a neighbouring country. Journalists who are apologists of jihadis do not give the full perspective and agenda of these groups. Some of their demands as reported in the media from time to time are:

1. Pakistan should not support the Western policy in Afghanistan.
2. Pakistan should not stop the Taliban from using it as a hinterland for their war against the Afghanistan government and its Western supporters.
3. Pakistan should not stop its people from joining jihadi groups, getting trained and participating in the jihad declared by the Al Qaeda and its associates against all such governments which fall in the category of Jahiliyya. (See Sayyid Qutb's *Maalim fi al-Tariq* or *Signposts on the Road* and Zawahiri's speeches.)
4. Pakistan should support all Muslim militant groups, LeT and Jaish-e-Mohammadi (now operating freely under different names) who fight in India.
5. Pakistan should let the local Taliban enforce their version of Salafist Islam in the country. Pakistan's Taliban leader Baitullah Mahsud who was killed in a drone attack, is on record that his goal was to impose his brand of Sharia in the country. His successor Hakeemullah Mehsud has the same agenda.

Jihadi apologists conveniently ignore the fact that the militant Islamists have a strong hold on the madrassahs, where young minds are influenced and prepared for suicide bombing. There is sufficient research material published by local writers that can help in understanding the gravity of the challenge, for example, *A-Z of Jihadi Organisations in Pakistan* written by Amir Rana in 2004 and Khaled Ahmed's paper published by South Asia Policy Network, let alone scores of Western writers.

There is no doubt that many innocent people are dying in the terrorist attacks. But television talk-show hosts avoid, perhaps deliberately, asking tough questions, such as: Why were terrorist training camps allowed in Afghanistan and Pakistan? Why was the Al Qaeda given an open licence to create havoc in Nairobi, Saudi Arabia, Spain, London and New York? Why are the Taliban not joining the democratic process and contesting elections in their respective countries to remove governments they consider un-Islamic? Why do the Taliban support sectarian organizations like Lashkar-e-Jhangvi (LJ), which is killing Shias with impunity in Pakistan? Why have the local Taliban killed over 150 Maliks and elders of the tribal areas and 500 local leaders of the ANP in KP, who differed with them?

The Taliban, as stated above in the five points, have their own world view and the future role of Islam. This view is influenced by the Al Qaeda's thinking that time has come to fight the world's infidels led by the West, particularly by the US, everywhere. And in Muslim countries power should be grabbed from the 'infidel' lackeys of the West. They believe that the promised time has come when Islam shall rule the world. Anybody who stands in the way is an infidel and needs to be annihilated. Knowing their agenda and willingness to fight for it, various countries intelligence services have infiltrated these organization to achieve their short-term agendas in the region. The Saudi-Iranian proxy war in the region through these militant organizations is one such example.

***

Liberals and progressives have lost the propaganda war in Pakistan. And same is true of the West, because there is no communications strategy to support the alternate narrative. The media has to build public opinion to isolate the jihadi forces and the Taliban against interference in Afghanistan politics. The choice is limited; if a non-interference policy is not adopted honestly and transparently then Pakistan is in for trouble from the Americans, from the Indians and even from the Afghan government. Pakistan cannot hoodwink them by declaring that they are not interfering and at the same time covertly encouraging selected local jihadi and Afghan Taliban.

Nurtured on the Islamic nationalist education fed by the Pakistani state, overzealous media celebrities do not realize that such retrogressive forces cannot be idealized as great nationalists fighting an anti-imperialist war. At the end of the day, the Taliban's philosophy of life will hurt the poor people of Pakistan and Afghanistan; inflict social oppression and political suppression. Pakistani journalists have to choose between religious fascism of the Taliban and democracy.

In a polity which has a quasi-democracy, strong autocratic tendencies and violent religious and ethnic intolerance, freedom of expression has been made subject to restrictions imposed by laws, whims of the fascist parties and militant groups. All thanks to the exploitation of religion by the founding fathers of Pakistan.

Undoubtedly Pakistani society is up against protecting its liberal and tolerant values, in spite of many in the media who subscribe to the conservative and medieval school of thought. A civilized debate on these issues has to be carried on a rational basis. But the jihadi groups prefer resorting to violence and suppressing the other side in the name of absolute divinity, which allows no questions. Period.

Notes and References:

1. Pakistan Education Statistics 2008, Academy of Educational Planning and Management.
2. Saleem H. Ali, *Islam and Education: Conflict and Conformity in Madrassahs*, Oxford University Press, 2009, p. 84. Ali has taken the quotation from Maqsood Ansari's article 'The Crackdown Begins', *Newsline*, May 2012.
3. Ibid.
4. Nader Hashemi, *Islam, Secularism, and Liberal Democracy*, Oxford University Press, New York, 2009.
5. Mubarak Ali, *Pakistan in Search of Identity*, Pakistan Study Centre, Karachi, 2009, p. 62.
6. Pervez Hoodbhoy, *Express Tribune*, 2 January 2012 (Khutbas can be read from www.mashalbooks.org).
7. Muhammad Amir Rana, 'Financial Resources of Pakistani Militants and Religious Organisations', Conflict and Peace Studies.
8. Khaled Ahmed, *Religious Developments in Pakistan 1999-2008*, Vanguard Books, Lahore, 2010, p. 5

Chapter 17

ISLAMIC IDEOLOGY'S INFLUENCE ON POPULAR MEDIA

Pakistani media is also under grave threat from the Tehrik-e-Taliban Pakistan (TTP), militant ethnic groups and the intelligence agencies. The country has been declared the most dangerous place for the journalists as over 40 journalists have been killed in the last ten years.

Most of the Muslim-owned media in India supported the Pakistan movement, barring a few examples that were under the influence of Congress and the Deoband school of thought. This was particularly true about the Urdu media. Though Urdu was written and spoken by many Hindus and Sikhs in India, during the Pakistan movement, it was presented as the language of Muslims' identity. Perhaps the main reason was its Persian script, which was the language of the court during Mussalmans' rule in India.

The Urdu daily *Nawa-e-Waqt*, launched in 1940, campaigned for Pakistan as an Islamic state, which came into being in August 1947. As stated earlier, Muslim League appealed to the Muslims' religious sentiments vigorously after it badly lost the elections in the Punjab, where a secular local alliance Unionist Party formed the government. The Muslim League used every trick in its bag to break this alliance. It was in the Punjab that the slogan *Pakistan ka matlab kya – La Illaha Ilallah* (What is the meaning of Pakistan? There is no god but God).

189

In Sindh the *Jang* became the most popular newspaper because of the migration of Urdu-speaking Muslims from India. Majority of these migrants settled in Karachi, followed by Hyderabad and Sukkur. The target readers' plea was that they had migrated to Pakistan for the love of Islam, and nobody wanted to talk about the real motivation i.e., the factors of the economic opportunity pull and communal riots push.

This market demand and some genuine beliefs set the Islamic overtone of the Urdu media. Even leading Sindh newspapers catered to the same policy in Pakistan's early years. To top it, the Pakistani establishment wanted to keep the communal fire alight among the Muslims, fearing that the Indians might try to conquer Pakistan or damage it. It was because of this fear psychosis, that the ruling establishment clung to the so-called Islamic ideology of Pakistan and promoted it through the media. The *Jang* became the largest Urdu daily of Pakistan and a major trendsetter in Urdu journalism. This newspaper had migrated from Delhi and has remained tilted to the Right. To begin with the domineering trend in Urdu media was to support a conservative Islamic politics; the same trend has been kept alive to this day. This made it easy for the Right-wing journalists to find jobs.

The English media was led by the *Dawn*, the official Pakistan movement newspaper, which also migrated from Delhi to Karachi. It followed Muhammad Ali Jinnah's vision of a democratic Pakistan where all citizens irrespective of their religion and sect would be equal citizens. According to Pakistan's media historian, Zamir Niazi, when some of the bureaucrats who did not like Jinnah's 11 August 1947 speech, in which he stated this principle of equality between the Muslims and minorities of other religions, tried to censor his speech, it was the *Dawn* editor Altaf Husain, who reacted strongly and threatened that he would talk to Jinnah directly. The officials and some leaders who had instigated this move backed off.

In Lahore the Leftist businessman Mian Iftikharuddin had established the Progressive Press Trust, which published the *Pakistan Times* and an Urdu daily, the *Imroz*, the famous Left-wing poet Faiz Ahmed Faiz was its chief editor. The newspaper continued to present a progressive point of view till the military government took over these newspapers for supporting the cause of progressive and democratic Pakistan and used them as spokesmen of the government. These two papers and the Left movement nurtured a number of progressive and liberal democrat journalists. The policy of supporting liberal democratic causes continues in English media even today.

During the Fifties and Sixties, the Left movement was strong, in spite of the government clampdown on it in 1954, to humour the anti-communist USA; still, there were many leading Left-inclined journalists both in Urdu and English media. However, the popular Urdu media moved further to Right-wing policies. Amir Rana sheds light on the religious parties' propaganda strategies: 'First, they would attempt to penetrate mainstream media by "planting" like-minded individuals in media houses in order to deliver their ideological, intellectual and political messages to the public. The Jamaat-e-Islami, a leading religious political party, followed this strategy during 1960s and 1970s. Second, they would try to develop an alternative media platform of their own, parallel to the mainstream. However, both strategies have one common goal; influence the public opinion and also the mainstream media.'[1]

The Pakistan print media scene started changing in the mid-Eighties, when Prime Minister Muhammad Khan Junejo's government relaxed the rules for granting 'declarations' (permission licences) to new publications. This rule was further relaxed in the 1990s spell of democratic governments. Working journalists' fierce struggle, particularly in the worst of days, during General Zia-ul-Haq's regime, was successful and the media claimed back press freedom. This opened a floodgate and a number of newspapers and periodicals started coming out. The majority of them were in Urdu and Sindhi. The English media did not expand as much as its vernacular press did.

Two things happened as a result of this boom: one, most of the new small publications could not survive without government advertisements, so they towed the official line; and two, there was acute shortage of trained journalists in the fast-expanding market. This vacuum was filled by young men coming from low-quality state schools, where they are influenced by the history dipped in the Islamic ideology of Pakistan. They work in the media with zeal to promote Islam and ultra-nationalism.

In view of the advent of the private sector electronic media, the mushrooming of the print media and extreme shortage of experienced professional journalists' editorial judgment about what is printable or fit for telecast is scarcely exercised. Almost everything is telecast and printed without considering its consequences. In the absence of an effective agency to monitor the watchdog, a label the media likes to use for itself, it's free-style wrestling in the arena of journalism. Both mainstream and small local Urdu publications lose balance when it comes to religious and so-called national security issues. The electronic media has at least eight religious channels and the mainstream 24 news channels also have religious programmes. Similarly, Urdu newspapers have a religious weekly supplement. Nobody can have an issue with the right of these media outfits to have religious programming. The issue is that most of the so-called ulema who write and appear on television have irrational and unscientific approach towards real-life issue. Some very learned Islamic scholars such as Javed Ahmad Ghamidi were threatened by extremists and their programmes were cut. The media is also in race to get the advertisements for which their editorial policies are dictated by the owner-editors and marketing departments.

When the Ahmadis were massacred in their two mosques in May 2010 most of the media followed the official policy and called these 'mosques' as 'Ahmadis' places of worship'. Only the Express TV anchor Mubashir Luqman had the courage to allow the leader of the Ahmadis to explain his community's position on a number of issues. Though the participants of his programme were ideologically against Ahmadis, they at least condemned the killings. However, when an Ahmadi leader, Mirza said that the governor of the Punjab was the only one who visited them, Luqman's comment that one didn't know about Governor Salman Taseer's religion was unbecoming. It did not gel with the theme of the programme, which was about tolerance for another's faith.

The state has given a free hand to the militant Islamic groups to take out their own publications. According to a Pakistan Institute for Peace Studies (PIPS) study: '[a]round 100 militant monthlies and 12 weeklies were being published in the 1990s. These publications were published in Peshawar, Quetta and Islamabad.'[2] These publications belonged to various jihadi groups; in some cases like Jamaat-e-Daw'ah/LeT, they have several publications targeted to different sets of readers. These magazines are mainly in Urdu, and one each in Sindhi and English.

Even when some jihadi groups were banned along with their publications, they reappeared after a short break with new names. To play it safe, publishers of most of the militant's publications are individuals, so that their publications are not banned if the government decides to ban their respective jihadi organization. There is sufficient hate material and call for jihad and glorifications of their 'martyrs' in these publications, which can prove that they are supporting violence in the country and in some cases globally. Pakistani media is also under grave threat from the Tehrik-e-Taliban Pakistan (TTP), militant ethnic groups and the intelligence agencies. The country has been declared the most dangerous place for the journalists as over 40 journalists have been killed in the last ten years.

Pakistan's National Security Policy is schizophrenic – one part of the strategy is to fight the militant Islamic groups who challenge the writ of the establishment, the other is to support the friendly jihadis who can be used against other countries when needed. Most of the TV anchors and columnists in the media, instead of condemning terrorism, follow the official line and are apologists of terrorists in the name of anti-Americanism and an imaginary war and conspiracy against Islam.

The media in today's world has evolved as the biggest vehicle of opinion-making. The electronic media has taken a lead by initiating the debate on sizzling issues. But the selection of the guests for the programmes is such that at any given time, Right-wing participants out-number secular or even moderate thinking people. Add to this the weight of TV talk-show hosts, who are usually heavily tilted towards the lobby, which has been dismissing the 'war against terrorism' as an 'American war', and are proud to be ultra-nationalists. The result of this imbalanced choice of people used by TV channels and Urdu media is that the public is being misled and the various jihadi groups are being glorified as anti-imperialist warriors. All this suits the establishment and the major media groups who have vested interests to support the establishment's agenda. For them media is like any other money-making industry. The additional benefit of being in this industry is that it gives them power to seek favours from the government, which do not appear on their media houses balance sheets.

Notes and References:

1. Understanding the Militants' Media in Pakistan: Outreach and Impact, Pakistan Institute for Peace Studies, Islamabad, 2010.
2. Ibid.

PART - IV

PART IV

Chapter 18

Pakistan Army Has a Nation

Douglass C. North points out that 'Path dependence means that history matters. We cannot understand today's choices ... without tracing the incremental evolution of institutions' and that 'once a development path is set on a particular course ... the historically derived subjective modelling of the issues reinforce the course.' The argument alerts us to the importance of understanding the historical role and subsequent growth of the military as the most powerful institution in Pakistan.

– Mazhar Aziz

The demand for Pakistan on the basis of the 'two-nation theory' and exploitation of religion by its leaders established the country as an antithesis to the concept of one Indian nation. To achieve its goal the Muslim League maintained during the course of Pakistan movement quite frequently that the 'Muslim India' cannot live with 'Hindu India'. On the other side Indian Congress gave in to the idea of independent Pakistan, but was of the view that the new Muslim state would not survive for long. In pre-partition India, Islam was used in the twentieth century as a divisive force to get maximum autonomy for the Muslim-majority areas, as explained in Part I. In Pakistan, Islam was used as a cohesive force to suppress the sub-nationalities that aspired for maximum autonomy.

As the raison d'être for Pakistan was based on a communal slogan, the ruling establishment has always kept the Indian threat spectre alive. To achieve this end they continue relying on exploiting the religious sentiments of the people. Pakistan, most objective writers agree, has been positioned as a security state and not as a welfare state. And to draw strength, the rulers exploit religion – it is often propagated that the armed forces are also defenders of the Islamic ideology of Pakistan; or, that they are defenders of the 'Fortress of Islam'. Consequently, the security forces – military – have acquired domineering power in the polity of the country.

Former Pakistan ambassador to the United States, who is much-maligned by hawks within the country, Husain Haqqani's major fault was that he wrote *Pakistan: Between Mosque and Military*. This book has indeed exposed the axis of power that has delayed the political and economic growth of the country. It reads like a critique of the establishment's political history and exploitation of Islamic ideology.

Author Shuja Nawaz, director of the South Asia Center of the Atlantic Council of the United States, has aptly underlined the religious tenor of Pakistan army right from the beginning: '786: these three numbers represent the numerological equivalent of the opening sentence of Quran, *Bismillah ir-Rehman ir-Rahim* [In the name of Allah, the Merciful and beneficent], the words that all Muslims intone before the start of anything worthwhile in their lives. 786 became the identification number for the GHQ [general headquarters] of the new Pakistan army when it took over operations and office of the British North Command in India in Rawalpindi after independence. The numerical number was emblazoned on all gates, posts and vehicles as a reminder that this was the army of a Muslim country.' However, he has hastened to add: 'But the Islamic identity was only in name at that stage. The senior echelons were still British officers who had opted to stay on, and they were in turn succeeded by their native clones, men who saw army as a unique institution, separate and apart from the rest of civil society and authority.'[1]

This observation of Shuja pointed out to genetic composition of the Pakistan army. It has brought to face the 'war within' the institution and has put the army in constant tussle for maintaining its supremacy over the civil society. Writer Mazhar Aziz explains that 'the military has come to identify itself with the state, rather than see itself as just one of the key components of a constitutional state. This analysis then reveals how a powerful military has incrementally penetrated and exercised control over political developments. The constitutional, political and economic dimensions of this control show that the institution perceives, and arrogates to itself, the task of nation-building as part of the military discourse. The evidence presented illustrates the almost universal mistrust that the senior military commanders have of the political leadership in Pakistan.'[2]

The gulf between senior officials and the non-commissioned officers and soldiers coming from lower middle class and working classes has been broadening, in spite of the fact now many generals come from the junior non-commission soldiers' families. The Muslim identity given to Pakistan army logically opened gates for the Islamist President General Zia-ul-Haq to set the process of converting it to an Islamic army – from just 786 it was led to adopt the slogans of *Iman, Taqwa* and *Jihad fi sabillillah* (Faith, Abstinence, and War in the name of God).

Former national security adviser to the prime minister of Pakistan, who also served as Pakistan's ambassador to the United States, Major-General (retd.) Mahmud Ali Durrani is of the view that Pakistan has been using the Islamic jihad spirit from the very beginning. 'In 1948 the Jihad was used for the first time by Pakistani military and a "Lashkar" [legion] was orchestrated to seize Kashmir. Troops were given lectures on Jihad. Thus, consciously it was ingrained in the national psyche.' Durrani, who served directly under Zia for three years, says: 'General Zia believed in Afghan Jihad and that Islam should be the guiding force for Pakistan.' He also pointed out that the Islamic indoctrination of army cannot be looked in isolation as it cannot be 'hermitically sealed out from the rising Islamization of the society'.

This is true as the Pakistani society is going through a metamorphosis – and is torn between the conservative Islamist society values and the modern globalized liberal society demands. The army cantonment boundaries cannot be raised high enough to keep the Islamists influence out. Given the fact that officially declared 'enemy India' is much stronger than Pakistani army in terms of manpower and equipment, the Pakistan army has relied heavily on giving its soldiers a religious morale booster. This is done by giving the operations and army commands Islamic names. Most of the missiles are also named after Muslim conquerors. The common example given in Pakistan is that of the battle of Badar in which it is said Prophet Muhammad defeated 1,000 Meccans, who attacked Medina with the force of 313 fighters.

Brigadier (retd.) Waqar Durrani, observes that Pakistani army is motivated by inspiring the spirit of jihad at the time of operation; otherwise army is not indoctrinated during the course of training and on day-to-day basis. It is imbibed more with the Pakistani nationalism, which indeed is based on the theory that the Muslims of the subcontinent are one nation by virtue of their religion. He also maintains that the role of a khateeb (preacher) who is employed by the army for leading prayers at the official mosque is limited. 'The commanding officer [CO] approves the khutabas [Friday sermons] and that keeps the check on keeping extremism and sectarianism out of the army's rank and file,' Brigadier Durrani explained. He also pointed out that army rank and file belonging to different sects of Islam offer prayers in the same mosque without any hesitation. 'However, a CO would only know as to how many Shias he has under his command when special permission is asked for the use of trucks and buses by the subordinates for going to Imambargah (Shias prayer place) during the month of Muharram*.'

Well-known scholar on South Asian armies, Stephen P. Cohen, was hosted by the Pakistan army in 1980 and given access to meet army officials and visit various corps. Although the army tries to keep Pakistani scholars and journalists at an arm's length, Cohen was allowed by General Zia, as at that stage he was courting the US for getting involved intensely in the insurgency against Afghanistan. Writing on 'Islam and the Officer Corps', Cohen maintained: 'Several widely held images of the Pakistan army have tended to blur our understanding between Islam and military. These images verge on stereotypes: that Pakistan soldier goes into battle dreaming death and heaven or that he pursues an "Islamic" strategy in conjunction with Muslim brethren in other states. Neither statements are wholly true, although there have been occasions when the cry of Islam has been given by the military. The argument that the Pakistani soldier is an Islamic fanatic is not entirely without basis, but neither is it an accurate characterization.'[3]

*Muharram is the first month of the Islamic calendar; Prophet Muhammad's grandson, Imam Husain and his companions were killed at Karbala on the 10th of Muharram by a Muslim caliph Yazid 1 of Umayyad dynasty in A.D. 680.

In a guarded assessment Cohen says that Islam is a factor in the Pakistani army but it is not an overwhelming factor. This assessment was made by him after a few years of General Zia's take over and his bid to further Islamization of the army. It is also pre-dated to the army's deep involvement in the so-called Islamic jihad in Afghanistan both, before 1989 Soviet forces withdrawal and till this date when Afghan Taliban's jihad is being covertly supported by the Pakistan army. General Zia, Cohen has said in the same book, had raised the status of the unit's maulvis (religious teacher) 'and required them to go into battle with the troops'. Close association with the Afghan Mujahideen in the 1980s, with Afghan and Pakistani Taliban and Pakistani and Kashmiri jihadis in the 1990s, and again with Afghan Taliban after 9/11 has led to deeper penetration of Islamic extremism in the army. The Islamic jihad slogan and propaganda used to motivate these non-state religious guerillas has naturally also influenced many officers and soldiers in the Pakistani military, who are ingrained already with the religious teachings at every level.

However, in his more recent lead paper 'Pakistan: Arrival and Departure' among the 'Six Warning Signs', Stephen enumerated 'Further Appeasement of Islamists' as the last sign: 'Pakistan is becoming polarized, with liberal elements on the defensive. The global dialogue on reforming Islam has Pakistan dimension, but much ground has been conceded to doctrinaire Islamist, who receive considerable state patronage. That has already changed Pakistan markedly, and the problem is not just the strength of intolerant and narrow Islamists but also the weakness of the tiny Westernized elite. Pakistan is becoming one of the centers of global Jihad.'[4] Cohen has stressed on the importance of sequencing the factor that will probably impact the future of Pakistan in the same paper. But it seems he disregarded his own advice while sequencing the 'six warning signs'. In my opinion this last 'sign' should be first and the fifth sign, which is regarding 'Fresh Crises with India', should be second. Here another important factor that has to be noted is that the Pakistan army appeases and uses the most dangerous non-state actors – militant Islamists.

Like Cohen, Carey Schofield, an Oxford research fellow, too was given almost unrestrained access by General Pervez Musharraf to embed with the army officials at the headquarters and at the frontline where army is fighting the terrorists. Her research period interestingly coincides with the need to convince the outside world that Pakistan army is not that 'Islamic' as the West perceives. She disagrees with the notion that the Pakistan army has been 'riddled with extremism' and explains: 'Pakistan society is becoming more pious, and the army necessarily reflects the country. The army prays more and drinks less than it did a generation ago. It is not, however riddled with violent extremists. There have been publically documented cases of soldiers and officers being radicalized, and others that have not been revealed, but there is no real evidence that this is widespread. The army goes to a great deal of trouble to ensure that soldiers and officers are given sound Islamic teachings. It is highly unlikely that significant numbers of army personnel are actively involved in terrorism.'[5]

It is not the duty of the state to take 'great deal of trouble to ensure that soldiers and officers are given sound Islamic teachings' as this is supposed to be a personal affair of the people, whether they are soldiers or civilians. These teachings may not have created 'significant numbers of the army personnel … actively involved in terrorism' as noted by Schofield, but these teachings do create sympathizers for the jihadis, who follow the same teachings as an inspiration for their Islamic revolution.

Senior retired army officials maintain that General Zia paid particular attention to proselytizing the army rank and file and also allowed access to Tablighi Jamaat (TJ), instigating groups to preach Islamic doctrines in the army ranks. TJ apparently keeps a non-political stance but it prepares peoples mind, which are further cultivated by the jihadi organizations. Many retired general and ISI chiefs, junior officials and soldiers join the TJ after retirement. Many young captains and majors took early retirement to join the jihadi groups and Afghan Taliban in post 9/11 period when US forces attacked Afghanistan.

During General Zia's command, senior army and civil officials wanted to bring pointedly to his attention that they offered prayers regularly. In one incident witnessed by me, Karachi Port Trust (KPT) Chairman Admiral M. I. Arshad was visiting a socialist bloc cargo ship, named after a Czechoslovak communist journalist Julius Fučik, which called on the Karachi port. As it was the biggest cargo ship that came to Karachi a group of journalists were also invited. The admiral sent his public relations officers to fetch the press photographer who could photograph him offering his evening prayer at a socialist bloc container ship. Zia used the Islamic jihad fervour when he launched the insurgency in

Afghanistan after the Left parties' take over in April 1978, much before the Soviet Union was invited by the Afghan government to intervene in their support.

During the ten years that followed the close interaction of Pakistani officials, particularly belonging to ISI, resulted in creating support for jihad by non-state religiously motivated Mujahideen in the agency. There was widespread corruption in doling out arms, ammunition, money and other supplies. Most journalists, who covered the Afghan War, were of the view that almost 50 to 70 per cent arms and ammunition given to the Mujahideens were sold by them to the Pakistani people. Many ISI dealing officials started taking their share from these sales. According to a conservative estimate at least $1 billion arms proliferated in the Pakistani society in the 1980s. In the early 1990s US secretary of state told the Congress that in ten years of Afghan War $3 billion arms were given. Generally it was accepted by foreign correspondents that 70 per cent of arms given to the 'Mujahideens' were sold by them to Pakistanis. To be on the conservative side, if we take that only 33 per cent were sold to Pakistan we come to the stunning figure stated above.

The legacy of this dangerous war was that Pakistan became a highly weaponized country, where a Kalashnikov could be bought in the 1980s for a few hundred dollars, and many jihadi groups equipped themselves heavily. Afghanistan and Pakistan became granaries for training these jihadis, who were dubbed as terrorists only after the heat got to New York. In the early 1980s at a press conference at the Karachi Press Club, referring to this weaponization of the Pakistani society, I had asked Pakthun leader Wali Khan, 'Do you smell Beirut?' He spoke for over half-an-hour on this subject and predicted burning and bleeding of the Pakhtun society because of Zia's dangerous policies. Sadly, he predicted right.

As it was a lucrative business and less dangerous for the army, the jihadi groups, who had perfected the art of guerilla fighting in Afghanistan, were redirected towards Kashmir in India. It is lucrative because no auditable accounts are kept for the secret slush funds provided to the agencies-sponsored jihadi groups. Non-state Islamic militant groups have always been a not-so-secret arm of the Pakistani establishment against India and Afghanistan.

Pakistan's good fortune is that after General Zia was killed no extremely religious person has risen to the position of the army chief. But this does not mean that the idea of bringing a true Islamic revolution could be kept out of the cantonments. In 1995, Major-General Zahirul Islam Abbasi, along with his 35 officers, 'was arrested on 26 September, having failed to carry through a plan to kill all those at the Corps Commanders Conference (chaired by the army chief) and then eradicate the cabinet.'[6] He was involved with extremist Islamic groups and wanted to bring a coup against un-Islamic government of Benazir Bhutto. In two attempts to assassinate General Pervez Musharraf some armed forces were found involved along with the joint-jihadi outfit Brigade 313. The attack on the GHQ was also led by one of the army deserters. And more recently, in May 2011 the army arrested Brigadier Ali Khan along with four other military officers for links with the UK-based banned organization Hizb ut-Tahrir (HT). He was sentenced in a court martial for five years. His comrades Major Inayat Aziz, Major Iftikhar, Major Sohail Akbar and Major Jawad Baseer were also convicted, though for lesser terms. They believed in establishing 'Islamic Khaliphate' for all Muslim countries through a revolution.

Hizb ut-Tahrir mostly, attracts educated, professional anti-US Islamists around the world. According to Associated Press (AP), the world's largest news gathering organization, Brigadier Ali Khan issued a six-page manifesto from prison a year after his arrest calling the 'army to sever its anti-terror alliance with United States, which contends forcing Pakistan to fight against its own people.'[7] HT activists are usually seen distributing literature against the Army Chief General Ashfaq Parvez Kayani. Their slogan is 'The people want a new Khalifah.' Amir Rana is of the view that: '[t]he ability of radical elements to infiltrate government departments and security agencies is emerging as a critical threat that can undermine the state's response to militant extremism. Accounts of links of a retired army major, Osaid Zahidi, with militants indicate the seriousness of the issue. Major Zahidi served in the Military Intelligence for almost nine years and had gone missing in 2010. His family claimed that he had been picked up by intelligence agencies. With the caveat that due process and other human rights must not be abandoned in the name of fighting terrorism, the danger that radicalization poses across all sections of society deserves the attention of the authorities.'[8]

Earlier, a brave Pakistani journalist Saleem Shahzad was tortured and killed allegedly by the intelligence agencies. He reported in May 2011 that the attacks on Pakistan Naval Station Mehran (PNS Mehran) and two naval buses were in retaliation to the arrest of the ten naval officials by the intelligence agency of navy. They were suspected of having relations with a banned jihadi group. Terrorists who attacked the PNS Mehran on 22 May knew the 'security blind spot'. At least that's what Interior Minister Rehman Malik told the media soon after the operation. Further follow up reports confirmed his observation. Pakistani media asked how the terrorist knew about this 'blind spot?'

The obvious conclusion was that the terrorists had some sympathizers inside the forces. This suspicion was further collaborated by the fact that the routes and timings of the naval buses were compromised by some insiders. The attackers on GHQ also had insiders with them, as was also the case in the assassination attempts on Musharraf.

A 35-feet blind spot (the PNS Mehran outer wall, which was not covered by security cameras) at the PNS Mehran can be covered to stop further physical intrusion of the terrorists, But the intrusion of the ideology of jihad and establishing 'Islamic Emirates of Pakistan' or an 'Islamic Khilafat' in Pakistan cannot be stopped by any operational security measures. The model for this Islamic 'Emirates' or a 'Khilfat' is that of Taliban's rule in Afghanistan.

What is not recognized at the civil–military policy-making level in Pakistan is that while the military is selectively fighting the terrorist organizations and thousands of security personnel have been martyred, they have not challenged the ideology of jihad. Thousands of mosques, madrassahs and religious organizations are preaching jihad against the West and its allied governments in the Muslim countries. Aren't Pakistani leaders blind to this glaring fact?

Except for the PPP, the ANP and the MQM others don't even have the courage to stand up to condemn the jihadi ideology, which is fuelling the killing of thousands of Pakistanis. If one was to look back at the 2 May incident, only PPP and ANP had the courage to say that Osama bin Laden was the enemy of the people of Pakistan and that the Al Qaeda has damaged the Muslims' image around the world. The military establishment and Right-wing politicians instead turned the debate to the violation of Pakistan sovereignty by the American choppers. Then the media started beating the 'effect' – US intrusion – and completely underplayed 'the cause' – bin Laden had also violated the sovereignty of Pakistan. Terrorist organizations influenced by the Al Qaeda ideology have caused more damage to Pakistan, than any other foreign power. The literate journalists, religious parties, a section of lawyers offered prayers for bin Laden, honoured the murderer of Salman Taseer, organized dharnas (sit-ins) against drone attacks, but these blind people did not see the killings of the 95 Frontier Constabulary (FC) young recruits in Peshawar, the 12 soldiers and technicians who laid their life at the PNS Mehran.

The fact is that the Pakistan military is finding it difficult to use religion at its will, like the Pakistan movement leaders did, and to insulate the army from the Islamic jihadi propaganda at the same time. They are caught in their own web. It may be a great tactical move to build the religious fervour, but strategically the country is suffering from this expediency since its inception. At times, looking at Pakistan army's adventures, one wonders why the line between military tactics and multi-dimensional strategy looks blurred from the GHQ. Let us briefly look at some of the Pakistan army's adventures, which prove the point made above.

Notes and References:

1.   Shah Shuja, *Cross Swords: Pakistan Its Army, and the Wars Within*, Oxford University Press, Karachi, 2008, pp. xxx–xxxi.
2.   Mazhar Aziz, *Military Control in Pakistan: The Parallel State*, Routledge, London, 2007.
3.   Stephen Philip Cohen, *The Pakistan Army*, Oxford University Press, London, 1984, p. 86.
4.   Stephen P. Cohen, *The Future of Pakistan*, Oxford University Press, London, 2011, p. 59.
5.   Carey Schofield, *Inside the Pakistan Army*, Biteback Publishing London, 2011, p. 208.
6.   Brian Cloughley, *The History Pakistan Army: Wars and Insurrections*, Oxford University Press, London, 2000, p. 355.
7.   *Dawn*, 14 May 2012.
8.   Muhammad Amir Rana, 'Jihadi Inspiration', *Dawn*, 26 February 2012.

Chapter 19

The Jihads

The legacy of General Zia-ul-Haq today haunts Pakistan more viciously than it did when he was alive. He was the man who played a leading role in converting political Islam into militant Islam more than anybody else with the support of US. He weaponized Pakistani society and contributed in dividing the people on sectarian lines by patronizing less tolerant sects.

First Jihad: Liberation of Kashmir – 1948

After the partition of the subcontinent in 1947 when Pakistan came into being, the nation was keen on building its armed forces as it had acquired only a rag-tag army. The Muslim officers and soldiers in the Indian army did opt for Pakistan, but Pakistan did not get its due share, which was agreed upon at the time of partition. The need for a better-equipped army was also strongly felt by the Pakistani leadership as it was wary of the intentions of the Maharaja of Kashmir Hari Singh. A two-month delay by the maharaja in taking the decision whether to join Pakistan or India panicked the Pakistani leadership and it made the first mistake, which no civilized country should. The mistake was of violating the standstill agreement with the maharaja, and sending in private lashkars in Kashmir on 22 October 1947. But the orders for sending the private army of Pasthun tribes and for arming Kashmiris to capture the state came from the civilian leadership led by Prime Minister Liaquat Ali Khan. Major-General Muhammad Akbar Khan was given the task of preparing the plan. Pakistan, according to him 'had assumed that Kashmir would naturally join Pakistan. In fact, the very concept of Pakistan had included it as an integral part, the letter K in the name Pakistan standing for Kashmir.' Even the Quaid-e-Azam, Muhammad Ali Jinnah had assured the Kashmiri delegation, which called on him expressing doubt about the maharaja's intentions, particularly when he was pushed towards India by popular nationalist Kashmiri leader Sheikh Abdullah, that he felt confident 'that the opinion of two persons alone could not distort the future of the whole state. Firstly, he explained, the idea of Pakistan had swept over Kashmir as it had over rest of India and thus in spite of Sheikh Abdullah, the Kashmiri Muslims had geographically no choice but to join us.'[1]

On hindsight it can be said that the Pakistani leaders were too presumptuous to include the letter 'K' in the name of a country without any legal authority at the time of the partition. The presumption was theoretically right as almost 75 per cent population of 4 million Kashmiris was Muslim, and the understanding with the British was that Muslim-majority areas would be part of the new nation of Pakistan. And Kashmir was economically and geographically connected to Pakistan. However, the fact which was not given its due weightage was that the rulers of the princedoms were given the right to join any one of the two dominions – Pakistan or India. By getting impatient and sending in a private army of tribal people and arming local Kashmiris through a clandestine operation, Pakistan gave Maharaja Hari Singh an opportunity to seek Indian help.[2] The Indian government obliged him quickly. According to Major-General Muhammad Akbar Khan while the tribal Lashkar fought well, the 4,000 rifles channeled to the Kashmiris through police secretly were switched with shoddy local rifles. 'I hurriedly contacted people to check if the necessary men, for whom rifles had been issued, were in their proper places. I discovered that they were not. The thousand men on the Kathua road were not there because their country-made rifles meant for Srinagar had not been given by Khurshid Anwar to the people concerned.'[3]

Pakistan thought that intrusion of private Lashkars and armed Kashmiri groups would not be taken as a violation of the standstill arrangement with the maharaja of Kashmir. The justification for this adventure being that the trap was laid by the British and Indian governments and Pakistan walked into it. 'The trap was baited by awarding Gurdaspur, a Muslim-majority area, to India. Without this award India would have had no land access, and no temptation to get involved in Kashmir. For Pakistan the trap was Junagadh, a Hindu-majority state with Muslim ruler. Junagadh acceded to Pakistan in August 1947 at the instance of Dewan Sir Shah Nawaz Bhutto. The accession of Junagadh to Pakistan provided the necessary precedent for the Hindu ruler of Muslim majority Kashmir to accede to India.'[4]

Two points come out of this narration. First, the Pakistani civil-military leadership was not capable to see the long-term repercussions of what they did. Bad decisions and underestimating the Indian response was evident. However, it can be said that while Kashmir issue still remained unresolved both from the stand point of Pakistani establishment and the people of Kashmir, the only gain of the adventure was that Pakistan managed to retain a small portion of Kashmir. Second, it was on the initiative of the Indian government conveyed to General Douglas David Gracey, the then commander-in-chief of the Pakistan army through Brigadier C. S. J. Manekshaw, who was later to became a field marshall in India, that ceasefire was agreed upon on 30 December 1948. So, like Punjab, people of Kashmir were also divided but it has helped Pakistan to keep the Kashmir issue alive. The main concern of Pakistani leadership, notwithstanding their lip service to the right of self-determination of the people of Kashmir, was revanchist. Naked reality is that Pakistan's policy-makers' primary concern is that India's control over Kashmir gives it the control key to three main rivers – Indus, Jhelum and Sutlej – which are the lifeline of Pakistan. In spite of the World Bank-initiated Indus Waters Treaty signed in September 1960 between Pakistan and India, which has withstood the pressure of three wars fought by the two countries, the level of distrust of India in Pakistani ruling establishment is so high that Kashmir remains an inflammable issue that needs to be resolved. It is also a source of strength for the military and the water issue is exploited when needed.

Pakistan military historian Major-General (retd.) Shaukat Riza admitted that the 'military power in the subcontinent had little to spare for influencing the events in the Indian Ocean. For Pakistan there was no alternative, i.e., a liberation war fought by the Muslims of the state [Kashmir]. Pakistan had neither the political, military, nor social caste to sponsor such a war.'[5] But no lesson was learnt from this experience by the Pakistani military establishment.

After the setback of 1948 Kashmir war, Pakistan has tried many a times to organize and sponsor a liberation war fought by the Kashmiri and Pakistani state and non-state actors. Major-General Akbar promoted the idea of building a peoples' army to take over Kashmir, but was arrested on charges for conspiracy to hatch a military coup in tandem with communist leaders. There was intense pressure on the Liaquat government to call for an all-out jihad against India. Fearing that there can be an attack from Pakistan, Indian forces were moved to the bordering areas in early 1950s. Pakistani intelligence alarmed the government about this 'aggressive movement of Indian troops'. In turn, the government, which had no intention to hear the nettlesome calls for jihad, was perturbed by the intelligence report. But the good thing was that Liaquat–Nehru communication channel was working and both the countries clarified their respective positions.

***

Second Jihad: Operation Gibraltar – 1965

The next major adventure to keep the Kashmir issue alive was the 'Operation Gibraltar' in 1965. President General Muhammad Ayub Khan and his generals had started this covert war by sending the army-official led Mujahideen across the Line of Control (LOC) to Indian part of Kashmir in August 1964. Foolish presumptions were that they could hoodwink the world by pretending it to be Mujahideen's war; Kashmiris will join the militant struggle; and India would be defeated through an undeclared war. But the unassuming Indian Prime Minister Lal Bahadur Shastri roared that if he has to fight he will choose his own battle grounds, and consequently attacked from Lahore and Sialkot borders. Within two weeks Pakistan's stamina and arsenal ran off and its establishment was yearning for international intervention to stop the war.

Even 48 years after 1965 war, children in schools across Pakistan are taught that the unreliable India attacked Pakistan in the middle of the night on 6 September 1965. Though military historians agree that Pakistan did not win the war, which in the first place they did not anticipate, the entire propaganda machinery misinformed the people that war had been won and how the Hindu army cannot fight the Muslim army. Pakistan had to lobby hard with the international community to intervene for a ceasefire. Though the Pakistani soldiers and officers fought valiantly, so did the other side. India did not open the East Pakistan front in a big way; they just bombed Dacca and Chittagong a couple of times. Either they wanted to concentrate on West Pakistan, or they just wanted to teach a lesson that no covert war would be tolerated. Shaukat Riza underlined: 'As early as 1950 Indian Prime Minister Nehru had warned Pakistan that an attack on Kashmir would mean a general war, and if a war is imposed on India it would be fought, as far as possible, on Pakistan soil.'[6] India had moved its forces towards Jammu and Kashmir in 1951, when there was a lot of irresponsible talk about 'jihad' against India as mentioned by Nehru, in his letter written to Prime Minister Liaquat Ali Khan. Though Riza has discussed the perspective of the 1965 war and accepted the involvement of Mujahideen, he has not mentioned 'Operation Gibraltar'. Instead, he has talked about 'Operation Grand Slam', which he says 'was a gamble in which the other side did not play according to our rules. To Indian troops in Chhamb area the trajectories of shell landing on their position was immaterial. In attacking across the ceasefire line we convinced ourselves that the other side would limit the fighting to Kashmir.'

Riza puts the blame of this war harshly on the then foreign minister, Zulfikar Ali Bhutto, for convincing Ayub that the war would remain restricted to Kashmir. And mildly blames Ayub for his naiveté to believe in the advisers, who failed to envision the Indian reaction. More criticism of Bhutto's hawkish policies as foreign minister, which resulted in the 1965 war, can be found in other recorded history of this futile Pakistani adventure. He (Bhutto) also tried to woo the US-led Central Treaty Organization (CENTO) countries to help Pakistan, although it was clear that the only purpose of this alliance was to counter communism in this region. America had already warned Pakistan on using its equipment in the Rann of Kutch battle a year earlier.

Quoting Air Marshal Asghar Khan, Pakistan's retired chief of air staff, former foreign minister, Abdul Sattar has recorded: 'The operation name Gibraltar, prepared by Major General Akhtar Hussain Malik, was approved. Calling for incursions by Kashmiri volunteers into India-held Kashmir, it was based on three assumptions – people of Kashmir would rise to support guerillas, a large-scale Indian offensive against Azad Kashmir was unlikely, and the possibility of attack across international border could be ruled out – all of which turned out to be wrong.'[7] Sattar has also disclosed that 'neither the air force nor the navy was informed about Operation Gibraltar and the fact that the army did not prepare for the contingency of war is further evidence of his [Ayub] anti-war intentions.'[8]

Finally, the then Soviet Union prime minister, Alexei Kosygin, who had good influence on the Indian government, brokered the Tashkent Agreement. Ayub Khan signed it but his Foreign Minister Zulfikar Ali Bhutto, who had assured him of Chinese help before starting the Operation Gibraltar, opposed this peace treaty. Sensing that he might be sacked for the 1965 debacle, Bhutto left Ayub and cashed on the anti-Indian sentiment of the people in Punjab. The Punjabis were also under the spell of the propaganda that the war was started by India, as they knew nothing about Pakistan's covert operation. Although now the consensus among various writers on this subject is that there was a stalemate at the end of this seventeen-day war, Pakistanis are still fooled that they were winning the war when Ayub agreed to the ceasefire. Islamic fervour and Pakistani nationalism was exploited to the hilt during and after this war.

***

Third Jihad: Conquering the Bengalis – 1971

The case of Bangladesh liberation has already been discussed in Part II (chapter 6). What is important here is the linkage between the decision to launch a military operation against the Bengalis who wanted autonomy and the theory that all Pakistanis are one Muslim nation. The Islamist dubbed East Bengalis as half Hindus because their women wore sari and at times a 'bindiya' (a red vermillion dot worn on the forehead). They were also suspicious of the Hindu minority in East Bengal, who Pakistanis were told were not loyal to the country. This time India took full advantage of the internal turmoil and liberation movement started by the East Bengal people and the spill-over of millions of refugees to West Bengal in India. India not only supported the Bengali liberation fighters Mukti Bahini but made 94,000 Pakistani army soldiers surrender and captured over 5,000 square miles of land. The ultra-nationalists and Islamists blamed the humiliating defeat, once again as often in the past, on the Indian invasion and heavy drinking and womanizing of President General Yahya Khan. No one wanted to accept that Pakistan's policies were wrong and that people of East Bengal could not be exploited anymore in the name of one Muslim nation. Two myths were broken by the 1971 war: One, that religion can be the basis of creating one nation, as ethno-linguistic ties proved to be stronger than the religious binds. Two, that wars can be won by religious fervour alone. Even in 1971 Pakistan was no match to India's economic strength. As a university student my favourite argument was that India has 13 steel mills and many sea ports, while Pakistan had no steel mill and only one sea port, which could be made un-operational by the Indians through naval blockade. It was also clear that an army of predominantly Punjabis and some Pakhtuns cannot win a war 1,000 miles away from their homeland while living in hostile population. All through the military operation in Bangladesh and the consequent war after the intervention of India, Pakistani people were kept in dark by muzzling the media. War hysteria was built. Even till the last moment the military government was not willing to tell the truth. According to Brigadier (retd.) A. R. Siddiqui, who was head of Interservice Public Relations, at times hours were wasted on trivial issues by senior most generals to discuss how the phrase 'gloomy' situation' should be diluted and finally it was decided that it should be replaced with 'grim situation'.

Religious parties like JI were used as private armies by the Pakistan army, their fundamentalist goons were used to kill many leading Bengali intellectuals. Jamaat-e-Islami leaders are being tried for war crimes in Bangladesh by the Awami League government. Some of them have been sentenced in spite of the strong movement launched against such a move by the Bangladesh Islamists and in spite of international criticism that trials were not fair. This does not mean that Mukti Bahini forces were any less ruthless with non-Bengali-speaking Biharis and West Pakistanis, who were supporting the military operation. The liberation of Bangladesh amply proved three political facts: One, that ethno-linguistic solidarity is stronger than religious solidarity. Two, that India does not want to capture or undo Pakistan and that it has accepted it as a separate country, otherwise 1971 gave her the opportunity to separate Sindh and Balochistan, which opposed the military operation in Bangladesh. Three, that in multi-national federation equity among the federating units should not be undermined. The Pakistani politicians have learnt these lessons but the army generals resist accepting them, as it is against their doctrine. For them religion is still the main binding force and can be used recklessly, which they do by supporting their loved jihadi assets.

***

Fourth Jihad: Afghan Insurgency – 1978–89

The support for Afghan insurgency was a joint-venture with the United States, which has now been fighting the same school of thought that was supported by them for ten years. As a matter of fact till the Al Qaeda turned against the US, the religious political and militants were the US darlings. Once a senior US diplomat visiting Karachi asked me why the religious Right was so strongly anti-US? I told him 'They are complaining because Islamists are your [US] divorced wives.' The US had always supported religious parties of various shades during the period of Cold War. Islamic parties were even funded for instance, by buying huge quantities of Maulana Abul Ala Maududi's books. The student leaders of the Islamic Jamiat-ul-Tulba (Islamic students party) were given scholarships to study in the US once they graduated from Pakistan universities.

Then in the 1980s ISI and CIA had a joint venture against the Afghan government, which was supported by the Soviet Union. It was evident soon after the Khalq and Parcham parties of Afghanistan captured power after over-throwing Prime Minister Mohammad Daoud Khan's government in 1978 that Pakistan and Iran wanted to destabilize the new government of Nur Muhammad Taraki. It was their internal matter. But Pakistan supported Gulbuddin Hekmatyar's Hezb-e-Islami insurgents against the new government. Other leaders of the Afghan Islamic groups, who were always against the Kabul pro-Soviet governments, started pouring in to Peshawar and Quetta. In the beginning, the Pakistani army fully supported them to form their own militant groups but after the Soviet intervention, the US and Saudi Arabia jumped in the world's longest and biggest covert operation. The Saudis got in particularly after the Iranian movement against Mohammad Reza Shah Pahlavi, the Shah of Iran, was hijacked by the Shia clergy led by Ayatollah Khomeini. Fahd bin Abdulaziz Al Saud, the then Saudi King, belonging to the Wahabi sect that is bitterly against the Shias, was worried about the new Shia state led by the clergy. This could inspire people in other Muslim kingdoms to rebel and take over power. To get their foothold in Afghanistan and Pakistan, predominantly Sunni-majority states started pouring in their petro-dollars in the Afghan War directly and in financing the extremist anti-Shia sects in Pakistan. The Iranians were not far behind in financing their Shia sect in Pakistan. As a result there is an on-going proxy sectarian war in Pakistan for the last three decades.

General Zia-ul-Haq's dream to offer victory prayer in Kabul did not materialize because the major attack planned on Jalalabad by the Mujahideen with the support of ISI failed, although the Soviets were retreating under an agreement. Zia was killed in a mysterious air crash at Bahawalpur, a city 532 kilometre south of Islamabad, after witnessing the performance of American M1 Abrams tanks, which Pakistan wanted to buy. Although US Ambassador to Pakistan Arnold Raphel and a visiting US General Herbert M. Wassom died in the same crash, Pakistan government's inquiry did mention that traces of some chemical, which is used in small bombs, were found from the aircraft and concluded that it was sabotage. Zia's son Ijaz-ul-Haq blamed General Mirza Aslam Beg, who was soon appointed army chief, for the conspiracy. The US administration covered it as an accident. The circumstantial evidence however created an impression that it was an inside job. Zia was isolated by 1988 and he was careful not to travel much for fear of an assassination attempt.

On hindsight, some of the incidences when recollected makes one suspect that Zia was killed in a bloody coup in August 1988. First sign of dissent in Zia's constituency was when the hand-picked Prime Minister Muhammad Khan Junejo allowed Benazir Bhutto to return to Pakistan from self-exile in 1986 against Zia's wish. Second, both Junejo and Benazir wanted Lieutenant General Shamsur Rahman Kallu to be appointed vice chief of staff in place of Lieutenant General K. M. Arif's, who was due for retirement. Zia managed to blackmail Prime Minister Junejo into withdrawing Kallu's nomination by planting a reference against him (Junejo) in the National Assembly. Third, Junejo took a bold step to participate in the peace talks on Afghanistan in Geneva, very much against the wishes of General Zia. But clever Junejo had gathered support from major political parties. I asked his Minister of State for Foreign Affairs Zain Noorani: 'Is the prime minister drawing his strength against the wishes of the President General Zia from some other set of generals?' First, he tried to evade the question. When pestered, he confided: 'Why do you want me to say what you already know.' I sensed General Zia's displeasure regarding the Geneva talks when my editor at *Dawn*, Ahmad Ali Khan wanted to play down Noorani's talks in Geneva. Ahmad Ali Khan was a professional editor, who couldn't have suggested playing down what was the most important story. Later I found out that the owner of *Dawn*, Mahmoud Haroon, who was General Zia's trusted Interior minister had requested Ahmad Ali Khan that Noorani's Geneva talks should not be projected. Fourth, during a breakfast meeting the then Indian High Commissioner K. D. Sharma asked if I saw any change in the government, to which my immediate reply was: 'No way because the army is solidly behind General Zia.' Sharma, who spoke flawless Urdu, told me: 'Like any other diplomat we have to keep our eyes and ears open. Your army, Babar Sahib, is not as monolithic as you think.' On my way back I thought that it could be a good 'intro' to a news story, which I could obviously not file in the days of censorship. Fifth, the Ojhri Camp where arms received from the US for distribution to the Afghan Mujahideen blew up one fine morning in April 1988, just when the Afghan War was coming to an end. There was a rain of bombs and rockets on the twin-cities of Rawalpindi and Islamabad killing about 1,000 people. An inquiry was conducted by one Lieutenant General Imran Ullah Khan but was not made public in spite of Prime Minister Junejo's promise to the nation. But at least one political leader, former Federal Minister Begum Kulsoom Saifullah came on record to have alleged that it was General Zia who ordered the blast so as to hide the pilferage of Stinger missiles, which were sold to Iran. Sixth, three days before Zia's airplane crashed on 14 August 1988, former army chief and the PPP General Secretary General (retd.) Tikka Khan, during a Movement for Restoration of Democracy (MRD) rally at the historic Liaquat Bagh, Rawalpindi, warned Zia that the huge turn-out in a city from which most of the officers and soldiers are recruited is a clear indication that 'your constituency [army] is not with you.' Finally, the seventh circumstantial evidence: Immediately after Zia's death, vice chief of staff, General Aslam Beg, who had taken off from the Bahawalpur airport in a separate airplane did not stay on or come back to check whether there were any survivors. He flew back to Islamabad and called the army's trusted man Ghulam Ishaq Khan, who was the senate chairman, to GHQ and asked him to take over as president in accordance to the Constitution. Ishaq Khan took over and announced general elections in three months. It was neat. There was no panic and all the balls fell in the right slot.

Zia's remaining body parts were buried at the Faisal Mosque. He was given sentimental burial by his supporters, mainly the Afghan Mujahideen leader Gulbuddin Hekmatyar. The legacy of General Zia-ul-Haq today haunts Pakistan more viciously than it did when he was alive. He was the man who played a leading role in converting political Islam into militant Islam more than anybody else with the support of the US. He weaponized Pakistani society and contributed in dividing the people on sectarian lines by patronizing less tolerant sects. He allowed the heroine trade to finance the Afghan jihad and in the process, Pakistan has over 2 million heroin addicts today. He showed a way to the ISI that they can make the neighbours bleed by using jihadi groups, which they did in Kashmir. He made these jihadi groups Pakistan's assets, which today have become the nation's biggest liability. Though no Islamist general was promoted to chief of army staff (COAS) position after him, the legacy however, lives with the Pakistan army tacticians.

***

Fifth Jihad: Kashmir Insurgency – 1990 to …

The fifth adventure, which has not been called off, is the support and encouragement being given to a number of jihadi groups who operate primarily in the Indian Kashmir. The insurgents include both the Kashmiris and Pakistani fighters. This time around Pakistan's army and intelligence agencies were confident that insurgency would not turn into full-fledged war like 1965, because it was no secret, internationally, that Pakistan had acquired the nuclear bomb by late 1980s. The nuclear bomb project, which was launched by Zulfikar Ali Bhutto in response to the first Indian nuclear explosion in 1974, and the humiliation suffered by Pakistan in 1971 war, was completed by General Zia. The US government, which was otherwise dead against nuclear proliferation, preferred to turn a blind eye because Pakistan was serving their cause against the Soviet Union in Afghanistan. Pakistani and Indian establishments know that a full-scale war can turn into a nuclear war, which would be frightening for the world. A senior army intelligence official told a group of parliamentarians in a briefing that Pakistan is a smaller conventional military power compared to India, that's why we want the world to have the perception that if pushed to a wall, we are mad enough to use the nuclear option. Thus, it is safe to conclude that the nuclear bomb only makes irresponsible countries confident to indulge in dangerous proxy wars through non-state brigades as a mean to achieve their strategic end.

Second factor that emboldened Pakistani agencies was that they had successfully managed the world's longest and biggest insurgency in Afghanistan for ten years. The expertise in running a covert operation, availability of trained and motivated jihadi human resource and arms that are required for such operations gave the agencies a new mission in Kashmir. During these ten years the Pakistan establishment tried to keep its eastern border quiet. But once the Soviet forces were withdrawn, the army decided to use its expertise and started training and arming various jihadi militant groups for supporting the Kashmiris movement against the Indian government. Army had the money, arms and trained Mujahideen from the Afghan War, so what could be a better use of these 'assets' than to turn their guns to the Pakistan's official enemy India and Pakistan's primary cause – Kashmir.

Third factor was that unlike 1965, this time mass movement in Kashmir against Indian control provided a window of opportunity to Pakistan. India has mishandled Kashmir ever since it acquired control over it in 1947. Though the accession of Kashmir to India by the maharaja was contrary to the fact it was a Muslim-majority state, India was able to get sizeable public support because the revered independence movement secular leader Sheikh Abdullah had supported joining India. However, his government was dismissed by Delhi and he was arrested in August 1953. Prime Minister Jawaharlal Nehru and his colleagues started feeling that Abdullah was vying for a semi-independent status, which was beyond the scope of promised autonomy at the time of accession and enshrined in the Article 370 of the Indian Constitution. This struggle for more autonomy gradually turned into a movement of independence by 1990. The support of the pro-Pakistani Kashmiri parties had started declining particularly after a 1958 martial law. Sheikh Abdullah's son Farooq Abdullah swept the 1983 elections dashing all the hopes of the Indian Prime Minister Indira Gandhi to have a Congress Party government in Kashmir. His government too was removed in 1984. Congress Party's obsession for a strong Centre had resulted in the creation of Pakistan in 1947, the same myopic view led to the dismissal of Farooq's government. Prime Minister Indira Gandhi was upset that Farooq was instigating other states of the union to demand greater autonomy. Soon, Indira Gandhi was assassinated by her security guards, who were enraged by her ordering the army to enter the Sikhs' highest place of worship, the Golden Temple in Amritsar, Punjab, to flush out militants under Operation Blue Star. Her son Rajiv Gandhi entered into a pact with Farooq Abdullah in Kashmir in 1986, which was known as National Conference–Congress Alliance, which swept the elections amidst charges of massive rigging. This disappointed the Kashmiri youth who felt deprived of their democratic rights and agitated on the brutal power used by the Indian forces got attracted by the militants. This was an ideal situation for the Pakistan army to launch its jihadi groups to make India bleed in Kashmir, and its forces bogged down with the insurgency in a land, which was always considered by them (Pakistan army) suitable for guerilla warfare instead of conventional war. First to be used was JI's militant group Hizbul Mujahideen. 'The official Hizbul Mujahideen objective was reunification with Pakistan. The Harkat ul-Ansar was not yet part of mainstream militancy. Smaller groups believed to favour Pakistan were Hizbullah, Al-Umar Muhjaheddin [Mujaheddin], Laskar-i-Toiba [*sic*], Ikhwan-ul-Mujaheddin, Hizb-ul-Momneen, Tehrik-ul-Mujaheddin, as well as other splinter groups.'[9] However, LeT was a smaller group in early 1990s, but now in 2013 it is considered to be the largest and the most well-organized group. Banned by the United Nations for its terrorist activities it has renamed itself as Jamaat-ud-Dawa. Harkat ul-Ansar splinted group Jaish-e-Mohammed (JeM) is now quite powerful and is based in southern Punjab, in Pakistan. It is led by Maulana Masood Azhar, who was arrested in Kashmir for kidnapping a British tourist and later swapped by the Indian government when an Indian Airlines' aircraft IC 814 was hijacked from Kathmandu on 24 December 1999 and taken to Kandahar in Afghanistan, after stopovers in Amritsar in India, Lahore in Pakistan, and Dubai. Maulana Azhar came back to Pakistan, made his own militant party and today roams about with impunity. The majority of these two groups' recruits are from the Punjab.

Though Pakistan has restrained the jihadi groups from crossing the border and the number of insurgencies, according to the Indian government, has also gone down, some stray terrorist attacks in Kashmir do take place. At the same time the Kashmiri independence movement has slowed down. There is a growing realization that an independent Kashmir would be landlocked and would have to survive as a client state of India, which would remain the big power of the subcontinent. Another important factor is that over the last 66 years Kashmiri businessmen and middle classes have developed economic interest in the Indian business and employment market. Pro-Pakistani parties in Indian Kashmir have also weakened as Pakistan is no shining temptation considering the fact that it is perpetually living in a state of instability. Therefore, the strand that supports maximum autonomy within India, as envisaged by the National Conference in early 1950s, is offering practical solution to the Kashmiris and the Indian government

The sponsors of militant insurgency accept, once again, that they did not expect Indian government to face the insurgency and domestic Kashmiri movement for so long and that too with full resources. Once again, the only gain they can claim is to have kept the Kashmir issue alive in the international media, which the big powers remained concerned about. The Indian government's atrocities were condemned by the international and domestic human rights groups. It also nudged India to discuss softening of border between Indian Kashmir and Azad Kashmir.

The flip side of insurgency was that the Kashmiri movement for autonomy and independence was turned into a communal movement by the holy insurgents – jihadi groups. Moved by the perception that India was settling Hindus in Kashmir to change its demography and undermine the Muslim majority of the valley, the insurgents started killing the Kashmiri pundits. 'In a mass exodus, at the beginning of March [1990], about 140,000 Hindus left the valley for refugee camps outside Jammu. The more affluent took up residence in their second home in Delhi, but the vast majority was housed in squalid tents in over 50 camps on the outskirt of both Jammu and Delhi.'[10] There is growing realization among the Pakistan policy-makers that Jammu and Ladakh, which have predominantly Hindu and Buddhist populations respectively, have no interest in separating from India. Similarly, the people of Gilgit-Baltistan want to remain as a part of Pakistan. They do not consider themselves Kashmiris and had fought to free the region from Maharaja Hari Singh in 1948 to join Pakistan. This issue, as Victoria Schofield (a well-known military historian) said during a session at the Karachi Literature Festival on 17 February 2013, is only about the valley of Srinagar because of which India is suffering due to excessive use of force by the Indian government against the local population.

Islam in Kashmir had spread through Sufis and hence it adopted to the local culture and the Muslim practice a tolerant Barelvi version. On the other hand most of the Punjabi and Pakhtun jihadis belong to the rigid Deobandi and Salafist school of thought. This contradiction spurred sectarianism, which was abhorred by some leading Kashmiri leaders like Mirwaiz Farooq.

***

Sixth Jihad: Kargil – 1999

The shallowness of military leader strategic understanding could be seen when the so-called 'Stars of this War Course' (an army course, which the officers have to pass) General Pervez Musharraf, who was army chief, and Major-General Javed Hassan, who was head of commander of the Force Command Northern Area (FCNA), planned and executed the dangerous Kargil adventure. I had heard interesting stories about this adventure in 1999 from some federal ministers, but Major-General Durrani, who was present at the occasion, confirmed that Kargil option was presented by Musharraf to Prime Minister Benazir Bhutto during her second term in office (1993–96). She shot it down saying that it was not doable diplomatically and that Indian reaction had not been fully accounted for in the planning. But when the same plan was presented to Prime Minister Nawaz Sharif in 1999 telling him that it would open the door to the resolution of Kashmir issue he allowed it without taking into account the serious ramifications of such a move.

Today, a school of thought blames it on the perception that Nawaz Sharif was naïve. However, it cannot be that simple. One reason for giving in to the Musharraf dream tactical plan could be that when presented to Nawaz Sharif, Musharraf was the army chief and not just one of the many generals. At the same time by inviting Indian Prime Minister Atal Bihari Vajpayee and moving towards peace process, Nawaz Sharif had sensed military annoyance. Hence, to appease them and show that he was equally committed to the Kashmir cause he prayed for the success of the Kargil plan. It can today best be described as a poor tactical move by the so-called war strategists. It is clear that no one had assessed how strong would the Indian reaction be? What would be the reaction of other countries? Whether or not the cock-and-bull story about the

Kashmiri Mujahideen taking over Kargil vantage points was sellable? The intelligence of the world, and of the Pakistanis, was insulted by telling a lie that Kargil heights were taken over by Mujahideen, while the fact is that the Northern Light Infantry (NLI) soldiers were sent up in guerilla outfits. Above all, no one estimated as to what would be the political, economic and diplomatic outfall. To the generals it was a great tactical move and a tit-for-tat to the take over of Siachen Glacier by the Indian forces in 1984. As a matter of fact, Pakistan's military strategists were thinking that by taking over Kargil clandestinely they would cut the supply route to Siachen and then walk in when the Indian soldiers would die of hunger and cold. They had also believed foolishly that India will not use their Air Force. In 1999, two days after the Pakistan army embarked on its Kargil misadventure, Lieutenant General Mahmud Ahmed gave a 'crisp and to the point' briefing to a group of senior Army and Air Force officers. Air Commodore Kaiser Tufail, who attended the meeting, later wrote that they were told that it was nothing more than a defensive manoeuvre and the Indian Air Force will not get involved at any stage. 'Come October, we shall walk into Siachen – to mop up the dead bodies of hundreds of Indians left hungry, out in the cold,' General Mahmud told the meeting. Mohammed Hanif, author of *A Case of Exploding Mangoes*, wrote in one of his articles on Zia-ul-Haq: 'Perhaps it was the incredulousness of the whole thing that led Air Commodore Abid Rao to famously quip, "After this operation, it's going to be either a Court Martial or Martial Law"'.

Kargil is also a classic example of failure of strategic planning even from the military angle by the 'smart generals'. According to the background interviews nobody at the top knew about this clandestine Musharraf adventure except for four three-star generals who were directly concerned. Even the air and naval chiefs were not trusted fearing that they might oppose the venture. A retired brigadier ,who doesn't want to be named, then working in the ISI says that even they were not taken into confidence. As a result, the ISI India desk was not activated till the conflict came to light, so Musharraf did not even ask for the intelligence assessment from the other side of the border, perhaps because he did not trust Nawaz Sharif's appointed Director General ISI Lieutenant General Ziauddin Butt. These facts are further supported by Lieutenant General Shahid Aziz in his book and articles. He was head of ISI analysis wing when Kargil operation was launched. He says that even he did not know that Musharraf had launched the operation. Now, on hindsight, Aziz once a close buddy of Musharraf, says the Kargil operations 'derailed the peace process with India'. He has also criticized Nawaz Sharif for not sacking Musharraf as his 'army chief had betrayed him ... or PM should have resigned'. In an article Aziz said: 'I was then heading the Analysis Wing of Inter Services Intelligence and it was my job to know. Our clearly expressed intent was to cut the supply line to Siachen and force the Indians to pull out. This was not a small result we sought, and cannot be classified as a tactical manoeuvre, where no one other than the local commander needed to be aware. General Musharraf himself writes, "800 sq kms of area was captured ... and it created strategic effects". To say that occupying empty spaces along the Line of Control was not a violation of any agreement and came under the purview of the local commander is astounding. This area was with the Indians as a result of Simla Agreement, and there had been no major violation of the Line of Control since 1971.'[11]

However, after the failure of Kargil adventure a report was prepared about it by the ISI but was removed the day Butt was arrested after a couple of hours' of glory as the army chief. Aziz says that inquiry report on Kargil was removed from the prime minister's house when Sharif was removed and arrested in a coup on 12 October 1999.

The Musharraf team, which was responsible for getting so many Pakistan's brave soldiers killed unsung, unwept, because officially they were civilians not military or para-military soldiers, was never taken to task for such a grave mistake. Not only did the Kargil adventure show the world that Pakistan is an irresponsible nation but also that the Pakistan military top brass has not learnt anything from the history of 1965 'Operation Gibraltar' debacle. They had under-estimated the power of Indian counter-offensive. Once again Pakistan had to run to the US President Bill Clinton on 4 July – American Independence day – seeking his help to stop the war that was started by our 'strategy-savvy generals'. And what happened to them? Nothing. All got promoted. Major-General Durrani told me: 'Instead Prime Minister Nawaz Sharif, who helped in saving the country's face, was booted out by General Musharraf.' However, a question that has not been asked so far is: 'Was the ISI report on Kargil one of the many reasons that Nawaz Sharif was deposed and General Ziauddin Butt, who was the ISI chief then, arrested?'

Notes and References:

1. Muhammad Akbar Khan, Major General (retd.), *Raiders in Kashmir*, Jang Publishers, Lahore, 1992, p. 14.
2. See Maharaja Hari Singh's letter to Lord Mountbatten and his reply reproduced by A. G. Noorani in *Article 370: A Constitutional History of Jammu and Kashmir*, Oxford University Press, New Delhi, 2011.
3. Muhammad Akbar Khan, Major General (retd.), *Raiders in Kashmir*, Jang Publishers, Lahore, 1975, p. 28.
4. Shaukat Riza, Major General (retd.), *The Pakistan Army 1947-1949*, Army Education Press, Rawalpindi, 1989, p. 264.
5. Ibid., p. 297.
6. Shaukat Riza, Major General (retd.), *The Pakistan Army War 1965*, Services Book Club, Lahore, 1984, p. 110.
7. Air Marshal Asghar Khan's statement quoted by Abdul Sattar in *Pakistan's Foreign Policy: 1947–2009*, Oxford University Press, Karachi, 2010, p. 105.
8. Abdul Sattar, *Pakistan's Foreign Policy: 1947–2009*, Oxford University Press, Karachi, 2010, p. 114.
9. Victoria Schofield, *Kashmir in Conflict: India, Pakistan and the Unending War*, I. B. Tauris, London, p. 145.
10. Ibid., p. 150.
11. *The Nation*, 7 January 2013.

Chapter 20

THE CONQUESTS OF PAKISTAN

During its direct and indirect rule the military in Pakistan has not only acquired political power, but amassed immense wealth as an institution .... But a large portion of the armed forces (army, navy and air force) business is related to real estate, farming, stud and livestock farming, poultry farming and other businesses like travel agencies and security companies, etc. According to one estimate if everything is taken into account the Military Inc. owns 10 per cent of the business assets of the country.

Though their adventures in India failed and Pakistani army could not win a single war, it captured Pakistan four times in its short history. Over the years it has successfully propagated the 'India threat' and the importance of acquiring Kashmir to protect the sources of the three rivers demarcated to Pakistan under the 1960 Indus Waters Treaty. The icing on this security state cake is that of Islam. As a logical corollary of these political formulations it is maintained by the military and its co-evolutionists that Pakistan needs a large well-equipped army. In any democratic welfare state the three pillars of the tripod on which this edifice stands are: executive, parliament and judiciary. Over a period with the expanding outreach and opinion-making power the media is often the fourth pillar of democracy. But in Pakistan military acquired the role of the most organized, disciplined and a lavishly funded political party.

First Conquest

Taking advantage of the political squabbling, which is natural in a newborn state, the Pakistan army first conquered the country in a coup d'état led by General Ayub Khan in October 1958, who later self-appointed himself as a field marshal. He was already enjoying complete control over the defence policies of the country and consequently over the foreign policy issues relating to India and the US – the former being the declared enemy, while the latter being the major donor to Pakistan army. As stated above, he pushed the country in to the 1965 war and managed to get a ceasefire when Pakistan was on the verge of losing it. Without any justification he abrogated the 1956 Constitution and imposed martial law. He ruled the country for ten years and gave the nation his own Constitution, introducing the presidential system in a country that was conceived as a parliamentary democracy. The concentration of power in the hands of a military dictator derailed the evolution of democracy and federalism. By 1965 people were fed up and launched a movement against him in 1967. He was ousted by General Agha Mohammad Yahya Khan in 25 March 1969.

Second Conquest

Ayub Khan's colleagues in the army could see that he was extremely unpopular and was bringing a bad name to the institution. In a quiet coup on 25 March 1969 General Yahya Khan removed President Ayub Khan. It was a quiet coup. General Ayub was told to resign and go home by Yahya Khan and his colleagues. Though it was a coup against Ayub – one military man removed by his own army colleagues – it is usually not recorded as a 'coup' in Pakistan. This also proves that military at times brings a coup against its own men. Yahya Khan stepped in promising direct elections and restoring the provinces in West Pakistan, which were merged in one unit usurping their rights in a bid to undermine the East Pakistan majority. However, Yayha Khan lost the 1971 war to India along with losing half the country – East Pakistan, giving birth to a new nation Bangladesh. Under him the army killed thousands of East Pakistanis in a military operation. He was removed by General Gul Hassan Khan, in yet another quiet coup in December 1971, who

226

took over as COAS, asked Yayha Khan to resign and hand over power to Zulfikar Ali Bhutto.

Third Conquest

It was led by General Muhammad Zia-ul-Haq in July 1977 in which he ousted popular leader Zulfikar Ali Bhutto and imposed martial law. He later appointed himself as president in August 1978. Deceived by Zia's over-obedient demeanour, Bhutto had promoted him as COAS, superseding seven generals. After Yahya Khan, it was Zia who proved too dangerous a leader for the country. He sponsored violent insurgency against the Afghan government and consequently made Pakistan a highly weaponized society. The militant Islamic terrorists from all over the world gathered in Pakistan and became a force that is still haunting the country. As explained above, his support to the Saudization of Islam resulted in spreading extremism and sectarianism in a society, which was tolerant and modern.

Fourth Conquest

General Pervez Musharraf, was hand-picked by Prime Minister Nawaz Sharif as the COAS but in a coup, ousted his benefactor in 1999. Nawaz was arrested on charges of hijacking the aircraft in which Musharraf was coming from Sri Lanka. Musharraf alleged that Nawaz Sharif had not allowed the PIA flight, carrying him from Colombo to Karachi, to land so that he could install General Ziauddin Butt as COAS. Nawaz Sharif was removed because he had announced the dismissal of Musharraf earlier in the evening. General Musharraf got his god-sent opportunity to prolong his rule when the Al Qaeda suicide squads blew up the World Trade Center in New York and Pentagon in Washington. As a COAS he had on his record planning, executing and losing the Kargil War. He was eased out honourably by the army and the PPP-led coalition at the heel of restoration of judges movement and assassination of Benazir Bhutto – the country's most popular political leader.

***

Even when the army was not directly in power in the 1990s, it exercised full control over the political governments on all major policy issues.

And when it felt that these leaders – Benazir Bhutto or Nawaz Sharif – were moving out of the parameters given to them, the generals intrigued and got the elected governments removed. Not once but 4 times in 10 years.

During its direct and indirect rule the military in Pakistan has not only acquired political power, but amassed immense wealth as an institution. According to military analyst and political commentator Ayesha Siddiqa, 3.6 per cent of the listed companies' assets are owned by the Military Inc. This includes only the stock market listed companies of the Army Welfare Trust (AWT) and Fauji Foundation. But a large portion of the armed forces (army, navy and air force) business is related to real estate, farming, stud and livestock farming, poultry farming and other businesses such as travel agencies and security companies, etc. According to one estimate if everything is taken into account the Military Inc. owns 10 per cent of the business assets of Pakistan. The Fauji Foundation, which is the richest of all armed forces organizations has 12 business enterprises: three sugar mills – Tando Mohammad Khan, Khoski and Sangla Hill; Fauji experimental seed farm; Fauji Cereals; Fauji Corn Complex; Fauji Polypropylene Products; Foundation Gas; Fauji Security Services; Fauji Foundation Institute of Management and Computer Sciences; National Logistic Cell (NLC); and Foundation Medical College. However, Fauji Foundation's mainstay is the fertilizer industry that holds 60 per cent of the market. The NLC controls the major chunk of the transportation sector of Pakistan and has also cornered Pakistan railway's goods transportation business. Its younger cousin, the AWT, has 23 organizations ranging from a bank, leasing company, travel agencies, stud farms and real estate projects. Frontier Works Organization (FWO) has almost taken over the major highways construction business of the country. While the Shaheen Foundation of the air force and Bahria Foundation of the Pakistan navy are in the real estate, education and IT business.[1]

This does not include the huge amount allocated for defence expenditure in the budget and the hidden amount in the civilian budget, which is basically taken by this Leviathan. A close look at the last 12-year figures (financial years 2001–02 to 2012–13) shows that the declared budget for defence has been Rs 3.6889 trillion and the 12-year average defence spending has been 20.31 per cent of the total revenue collected by the government. When calculated against the tax revenue alone the defence budget allocation is over 28 per cent in 2012–13 budget. This does not include the three heads of defence spending: One, the pension for the defence personnel, which was parked in the civilian budget by the Musharraf regime in the middle of the last decade. At that time it was Rs 27 billion, it must be twice the amount now. Second, the expenditure on the nuclear and missile development; and finally, the debt servicing related to the defence equipments purchased on loans.

Armed forces are the biggest land developers and marketers after the civil government. Individually the military senior officials are given so much property that even the average major generals are worth a few millions dollars. At the senior level the living style is ostentatious. Pakistan public felt angry to see on the national television that the country's Chief of Naval Staff Admiral Noman Bashir, arrived in a sparkling BMW 7 Series, soon after the Mehran Base was attacked in Karachi on 23 May 2011 in which many naval officials and firemen had lost their lives fighting the terrorists who had destroyed two $ 70 million worth naval reconnaissance aircrafts. On the other hand, the Indian naval chief drives around in a car equivalent to Pakistani Suzuki Liana displaying his four stars. The fact is, the vested interest of the army in maintaining the war economy with the help of its civilian co-evolutionists is bleeding Pakistan. They need an enemy and a threat to Pakistan's integrity to continue the exploitation of the people of Pakistan. The latest mantra being that the Americans are trying to break the country, so let's befriend India for the time being.

Notes and References:

1. Ayesha Siddiqa, *Military Inc.: Inside Pakistan's Military Economy*, Oxford University Press, Karachi, 2007

Chapter 21

Military's Private Jihadis

No civilized country breeds and nurtures militant groups within its own boundaries. Pakistan has been doing it as an extension of its national security policy. Once non-state militant groups are allowed to grow and used against any other country in the name of religion, these private armies are bound to dictate the policies of the state. In Pakistan the jihadi organizations have created hurdles in the way of normalization of relations with India and other foreign policy objectives .... As they are armed and trained to fight, the state has to either fight them or appease them. Both ways the country has to suffer destabilization.

Pakistan-supported jihadi insurgency continued with full vigour in Kashmir from 1990 to 2005 and the Kargil advent sure was part of this great game. Its operations deep inside India, such as the attacks on the Parliament in Delhi on 13 December 2001 and the 26 November 2008 attacks in Mumbai brought the two countries close to a war-like situation. The common motivating factor in all these terrorist activities was the religious slogan of jihad. Religion was fully exploited by the Pakistani establishment to counter the perceived Indian threat. From 1948 to this day 'holy warriors' of various jihadi groups were used without giving any serious consideration to the ramification of such a dangerous policy.

Today, the worried common people of Pakistan ask each other why is militancy on the rise? Why the government has failed to check these terrorist organizations? Who are these so-called jihadi organizations? How serious is the militant Islamist threat to Pakistan? The world is worried whether Pakistan would be able to fight the terror Hydra or be consumed by it.

Not only the educated elite of the country but many TV anchors, newspaper columnists and arm-chair analysts (thanks to TV they are dime a dozen in Pakistan these days) seem to be clueless about the actual gravity of the situation. The government and the judiciary are squabbling on issues of much less importance. The media plays to the tune of the day and takes full advantage of the judicial and government power-wrestling match to catch attention of its target publics. The army is fighting with the selected TTP and other jihadi organizations that adhere to the Al Qaeda ideology and challenge the writ of the government. But it is cautious enough not to take the conflict theatre to Punjab where most of the Al Qaeda-inspired jihadi organizations are based. Leading journalist and writer Khaled Ahmed has explained this double game at the very outset of his foreword of Mujahid Hussain's book: 'The state has used terrorists in the past through "non-state actors" in foreign policy of covert "proxy war" in Afghanistan and India. It has not abandoned its intent to do so even after these elements have aligned themselves with Al-Qaeda [sic] and the Taliban. The use of fully armed non-state actors in deniable wars has tended to create multiple centres of power in Pakistan, meaning that the state has abdicated a large portion of its claim on the "monopoly of violence" in the Weberian sense. Parts of the state handling these clerical headed non-state organizations have suffered a split from the decision-making apparatus of the state, in this case the military and the intelligence agencies.'[1]

Braving many odds political commentator and director of PIPS, Muhammad Amir Rana has collected basic data about all the major jihadi organizations and their leadership. The data according to Rana is based on 'visits to one hundred and twenty-five madrassahs and offices in forty-seven cities in Pakistan and Azad Kashmir and one hundred and sixty interviews of leaders and workers of religious, sectarian and Jehadi [sic] organizations.'[2] According to Rana there are 236 religious organizations in Pakistan (basis: 2002 research), of which 104 are jihadi,

24 political, 82 sectarian and 26 Tableeghi. Besides giving who's who of the jihadi organizations, Rana has given details of party structures, teaching and training methodology and background of the leaders. He also gives sect-wise breakdown of these organizations, the numbers of offices, martyrs and basic ideology. He points out that the total number of madrassahs in the country till 1980 were only 700 and were growing at the rate of 3 per cent. But 'by the end of 1986 that increased by 136 per cent.' Today, if we take the official figures, this number has increased to over 12,000. (Unofficial estimates put the figure at 20,000 madrassahs.)

Rana has also quoted extensively from the literature of leading jihadi organizations like LeT, JeM, Harkat-ul-Jihad-al-Islami (HuJI) and narrated how these organizations multiplied and what has been their relationship with the local and US intelligence agencies. The TTP leaders have interestingly named these jihadis on their ethnic origin – Punjabi Taliban. It shows that ethnic bondage is stronger than religious bonds. Thus all the talk about one Muslim ummah is trivial. Those who express doubts about the role of LeT can find enough material in Rana's book to clear their mind as he quoted extensively from the defunct LeT magazine *Dawa*, wherein he has proudly narrated how its 'brothers' attacked Delhi Red Fort and Srinagar Airport. But most revealing is an excerpt from an invitation to 1998 ijtema (congregation): 'Along with thousands of Pakistanis, mujahedeen [sic] from Kashmir, Bosnia, Chechnya, Philippines, Eriteria, Somalia, Africa, America, Arab and European states we are forming an impenetrable wall at every front in the world receiving their training from Muaskar Taiba in Afghanistan .... You can go to any Jehadi [sic] front in the world and you will find Markazul Dawa Wal Irshad mujahedeen's [sic] crushing the infidels and destroying the fortresses of the devil, God willing.'[3]

Amir Mir, a Lahore-based journalist who specializes on the jihadi organizations in Pakistan, gives us a startling and thought-provoking picture that forces readers to think about the danger to the internal security of Pakistan from the jihadi organizations in his books *Fluttering Flag of Jehad* and *The True Face of Jehadis*. With the help of a number of international research reports, personal interviews and off-the-record information, Mir has thrown light on the killing of Benazir Bhutto, journalist Daniel Pearl and assassination attempts on Pervez Musharraf. Highlighting the danger posed by the Islamic militants after 9/11, Mir says: 'Terror attacks can be well-gauged from the fact that it is now spreading from the border areas to the settled areas like Peshawar and might eventually reach into the heart of Pakistan.'[4] His forecast was not wrong as Karachi, Islamabad and Lahore are frequently hit by these jihadi groups and the end is not in sight.

Pakistani middle-class apologists who defend the Taliban under Islamist or Leftist pretext are oblivious of the fact that these groups are not fighting without a cause – to take the jihad to almost all the countries of the world. Amir Mir has quoted from the TTP's Amir Baitullah Mehsud's interview to Al Jazeera: 'Our main aim is to finish Britain and United States and to crush the pride of non-Muslims. We pray to God to give us the ability to destroy White House, New York and London …. Very soon we will be witnessing Jehad's [sic] miracles.'[5] Mir also explains how some jihadi organizations are divided when they become too strong for their handlers in the intelligence agencies. But he laments that the major problem is that the Pakistani establishment believes these jihadi organizations are their first line of defence against any foreign aggression and how they are being used for operations in India and Afghanistan.

Discussing Islamic revivalism and extremism a veteran journalist Khaled Ahmed in his paper on 'Islamic Rejectionism and Terrorism' takes a close look on the role of madrassah education, taking case studies of institutions like Banuri Mosque Madrassah, which produced some of the most prominent leaders of the Taliban and jihadi movement and their link to extremist organizations. He discusses the issue with an insight of a scholar concluding: 'In conclusion, one can assert that the extremist Muslims have the same world view. It is based on the belief in the unchangeability of the sources of Islamic Shariah [sic]. This trend has negated the efforts of the 19th century Muslim reformists who thought that [S]hariah [sic] could be reshaped in accordance with modern times what the founding Thinker of Pakistan Allama Iqbal called reconstruction.'[6] He also points out the crux of the present predicament of the Muslims: 'If these are times of trouble for Muslims they do not register them as such: there is no self-doubt in the minds of those who see the Muslims suffering in many parts of the world. Normally self-doubt produces the instinct for self-correction through notification of fundamental beliefs. On the contrary, extremist Muslims use the device of denial to avoid registering the fact about their situation.'[7]

In his next article 'Islamic extremism in Pakistan' Khaled Ahmed has particularly touched the rise of Salafist Islam in Pakistan. The resistance to change is rather most vehemently defended by the Salafists who believe that Sharia as practiced in the first 38 years of Islam should be copied and implemented. Any deviation from what they preach should not be tolerated.

Pakistan army is connected with several of the 104 jihadi organizations, which still comply with the norms set by it. Ahmed Rashid, who specializes in Taliban and jihadi organizations linkages and operations, has pointed out in his writings how closely Pakistan is linked with the Taliban's resistance movement in Afghanistan; how its government has been double crossing the US and North Atlantic Treaty Organization (NATO) forces by covertly supporting the Taliban; what are backward linkages of Afghan Taliban with the local jihadi organizations of Pakistan; how the whole region is affected by the destabilization of Afghanistan and by 'Descent into Chaos.'[8]

Pakistan had supported the Taliban to take over Afghanistan giving it covert military, material and moral support. In a discussion on the prospects of Turkmenistan–Afghanistan–Pakistan gas pipeline in 1994, the Minister for Interior General (retd.) Naseerullah Babar boasted that the Taliban 'are my children'. He debunked my observation that this pipeline would remain a dream for at least two decades as Afghanistan is not going to settle down. Pakistan used Taliban to remove the progressive government of Dr Mohammad Najibullah in Afghanistan, who had managed to survive for four years after the withdrawal of the Soviet forces. By the time the Taliban, who were largely Pakhtuns, took over Kabul the resentment against Pakistan in non-Pakhtun population and liberal Pakhtun population of Afghanistan had completely eroded. It is this section of the population, which was garnered by the Indians. The very purpose of supporting the Taliban by the Pakistani military establishment was its perennial desire to counter the Indian influence in Afghanistan. The objective failed because of its conspicuous manoeuvres to install a government of its choice in Afghanistan – something which is resented by the Afghans. ISI has been deeply involved in the Afghan game of misery. It was the then ISI DG Naseem Rana, who advised Nawaz Sharif to recognize the Taliban government in 1997 'against the advice of then army chief Jehangir Karamat.'[9]

The fact that is apparently undermined by the army policy-makers is that while they are fighting TTP and have lost many lives, they are treating them as completely independent of the Afghan Taliban. TTP on the other hand openly accepts Mullah Mohammed Omar as their amir. 'The Pakistan Taliban's main strength lies in their ideological bond with Al-Qaeda [sic] and their connection with the Islamization discourse in Pakistan. They gain political and moral support by associating themselves with the Afghan Taliban. Their tribal and ethnic ties provide social space and acceptance among a segment of society.'[10] They have declared Waziristan as 'Islamic Emirates of Waziristan' and run a parallel government on the basis of their brand of Sharia. On the other hand the policy-makers covertly support the bands of the Afghan Taliban for balancing northern Afghanistan pro-Indian forces in the government across the border. But it was evident that even the Pakistan supplanted Taliban government was not equipped to listen to its request. The delegation led by the then Interior Minister Moinuddin Haider was shunned away by Mullah Omar when he was asked not to blow up the Buddha statues in Bamiyan. Attempt by the delegation to convince the Mullah, who had declared himself as Amirul Momineen, were rebuffed. At another occasion he refused to give Osama bin Laden to the Saudi intelligence, although the Saudis were one of the three countries that recognized Afghanistan.

After 9/11 again the Mullah who was supported to set up an Islamic Emirate of Afghanistan refused to give bin Laden so much so for Pakistan's investment in installing 'a pro-Pakistan Afghan government'. For years senior ISI officials used Islamic indoctrination to charge the Afghan Mujahideen in the 1980s and the Taliban in the 1990s for the jihad. In the process these officials were also radicalized. The then ISI DG Mahmud Ahmed, was assigned to convince Mullah Omar after 9/11 to either hand over bin Laden or ask him to leave Afghanistan. 'But Ahmed was in quandary. He says he "didn't try to persuade Mullah Omar to do anything against his beliefs." "I am a Muslim," stated Ahmed in his interview with the author. "Why would I go against another Muslim?"'[11] This is the critical thematic problem of Pakistan. The fact that it has declared itself as an ideological state, it cannot tell its officials to go beyond the limit of this ideology whether it is detrimental to the country or not.

No civilized country breeds and nurtures militant groups within its own boundaries. Pakistan has been doing it as an extension of its national security policy. Once non-state militant groups are allowed to grow and used against any other country in the name of religion, these private armies are bound to dictate the policies of the state. In Pakistan the jihadi organizations have created hurdles in the way of normalization of relations with India and other foreign policy objectives. At the same time the Islamic ideology that is used to motivate them for operating across the border also gives them space to fight for the Sharia implementation in Pakistan. As they are armed and trained to fight, the state has to either fight them or appease them. Both ways the country has to suffer destabilization. There is no dearth of apologists for the Taliban/jihadi organizations in Pakistan. These apologists are led by the religious parties and other persons, including more recently the Oxford-educated cricketer Imran Khan, who is proud of his Right-wing politics. Imran Khan too has joined the Taliban apologists' camp.

Notes and References:

1. Mujahid Hussain, *Punjabi Taliban: Driving Extremism in Pakistan,* Pentagon Security International, New Delhi, 2012, p. viii. Hussain is a free lance journalist based in Brussels.
2. Muhammad Amir Rana, *A to Z of Jehadi Organisations in Pakistan,* Urdu edition: 2002; English edition, translated by Saba Ansari, Mashal Books, Lahore, 2007.
3. Ibid.
4. Amir Mir, *The Fluttering Flag of Jehad,* Mashal Books, Lahore, 2008, p. 2.
5. Ibid.
6. *Religious Revivalism in South Asia* (a collection of research papers), South Asian Policy Analysis Network (SAPANA), 2006.
7. Ibid.
8. Ahmed Rashid, *Descent into Chaos,* Penguin Group, London, 2009.
9. Shuja Nawaz, *Cross Swords: Pakistan, Its Army and the War Within* by, Oxford University Press, Karachi, pp. 242–43.
10. Muhammad Amir Rana, 'Why Pakistan Taliban Matter', *Dawn,* 1 July 2012.
11. Shuja Nawaz, *Cross Swords: Pakistan, Its Army and the War Within* by, Oxford University Press, Karachi, p. 243.

Chapter 22

THE JIHADIS APOLOGISTS

Apologists of the Taliban in Pakistan do not realize that no matter who is ruling, it's high time that these terrorists be dealt with. That is the agenda of the people of Pakistan. It is what Pakistan needs .... There are no two options. Of course talks with the local and Afghan Taliban are possible if they renounce violence and join the democratic process in their respective countries.

To give apologists of the Taliban and jihadi groups among the politicians and journalists the benefit of doubt let's presume that either they are politically naïve or they are suffering from Alzheimer's. Their usual refrain is that the Taliban's terrorism would go away if the government stops taking foreign dictation. Statements of Punjab Chief Minister Shahbaz Sharif, senior conservative and public figure of the PML, Saad Rafique, Imran Khan and many Pakistani journalists reflect this mindset. One is amazed how they tend to forget the historical and ideological background of the rise of militant Islam in Pakistan. Blaming the government in this regard is just political point scoring; though sadly on a wrong issue.

Nobody can deny their assertion that interference in the national security policy should not be allowed. But for a moment let's assume Pakistan has no US interference in deciding its policy regarding the local and Afghan Taliban, and there is no pressure to wind up the India-specific terrorist network. In that case what should be Pakistan's policy to deal with the Taliban groups? Pakistani establishment has no other option but to analyze what are the objectives of the people of Pakistan as against the objectives of the Afghan Taliban and the local jihadi organizations? Then see whether these objectives are reconcilable with the interest of the majority of Pakistanis. This analysis has to be dispassionate and realistic, once burdened with the power to rule. The government's ultimate responsibility is to protect the democratic rights of the people and work towards raising their standards of living. Taliban apologists in Pakistan do not realize that in a country where almost every third person lives below the poverty line, it cannot afford to fight the world in the name of promoting an Islamic caliphate.

What do the major actors of this sad saga want:

1. **People of Pakistan**: End of Talibanization, sectarianism and religious extremism in the country; stop interference in Afghanistan; protect Pakistan's legitimate interests in Afghanistan; good relations with the Afghan government and US; and normalization of relations with India.

2. **Local Taliban and jihadi organizations**: Control over the tribal areas to begin with and enforcement of their version of Sharia by force; support the Afghan Taliban's war against US and Afghan government; fight with Pakistani forces if they try to stop militants from joining the Afghan war and entering India for terrorist attacks; continue support to the Al Qaeda; bring down Afghanistan government; oust US and NATO forces from Afghanistan; and liberate Kashmir through an armed struggle.

3. **Afghan Taliban**: Take over Afghanistan by force and establish a government with its brand of Sharia; and resist any move by Pakistan to stop it from using its territory as a hinterland.

4. **Al Qaeda**: Help Taliban in restoring its government in Afghanistan; continue using Afghanistan as its headquarters to export Islamic revolution through the barrel of the gun to the world; and bring down Pakistani government, which does not support the Al Qaeda's ideals.

These demands of the various shades of Islamic militants are in direct conflict with the interest of the people of Pakistan. It is clear that whether Pakistani government listens to the Americans or it develops a home-grown policy, no compromise can be made with the Taliban and jihadis. First, the people of Pakistan are Muslims but they do not approve extremism. They support democracy, which in essence is pluralistic and means tolerance of dissent. Second, it does not suit Pakistan to help the Afghan Taliban, who wants to enforce religious fascism in Afghanistan and annoy the West. Third, Pakistan has to stop its interference in Afghanistan. There can be no two views about it. The UN Resolution 1373 says: 'Decides also that all States shall: Refrain from providing any form of support, active or passive, to entities or persons involved in terrorist acts, including by suppressing recruitment of members of terrorist groups and eliminating the supply of weapons to terrorists.' True, Pakistan should neither support the Taliban nor the US and NATO forces. But this would only be possible if the Taliban stop using Pakistan as their base and join the Afghan democratic process. Fourth, Pakistan's legitimate interest can only be protected in Afghanistan if there is a stable government in Kabul. A prerequisite of achieving this objective is to find a regional solution instead of Pakistan-India proxy war in Afghanistan. Fifth, Pakistan has to have good relations with the Afghan government. Those who suggest that we should stop supporting the Hamid Karzai government tend to forget it is recognized by the entire world and the United Nations. Sixth, Pakistan cannot afford to have adversarial relations with the US and other Western countries. There is no reason that it should be fighting with them. Almost the entire economy of Pakistan is dependent on these countries. Over 50 per cent exports go to these countries, leave alone the investment and loans that Pakistan gets from them. Any conflict with them would lead to sanctions that would mean closure of industries and immense damage to economy – directly hurting the poor. And lastly, no country is supporting the Al Qaeda agenda because it is not in sync with the 21st century political, social and economic values. Also their terrorist means and Salafist ideology is unacceptable to the overwhelming Muslims of the world.

Apologists of the Taliban in Pakistan do not realize that no matter who is ruling, it's high time that these terrorists be dealt with. That is the agenda of the people of Pakistan. It is what Pakistan needs. Just because Americans are saying the same thing does not mean Pakistan should foolishly tell the Taliban that we are on their side. There are no two options. Of course talks with the local and Afghan Taliban are possible if they renounce violence and join the democratic process in their respective countries.

Then there are some liberal and Leftist groups who believe that Taliban's guerilla war in Afghanistan is a 'national liberation war'. It is indeed their democratic right to say what they think is right. But the issue is most opinion-makers use political terminology without going into dispassionate objective analysis, which sends wrong messages to the people. At the face of it, this is quite a populist statement used by Pakistani journalists and some analysts. They claim that the Taliban are actually fighting to get the foreign forces of International Security Assistance Force (ISAF) out of their country, hence it is a national liberation war. Anything which is anti-American sounds good and erroneously considered anti-imperialist. They glamorize the Taliban's war in Afghanistan, without going into the depth of the issue and forgetting a major point that these forces are there to help stabilize an elected government. If the Taliban join the democratic process and Afghanistan is stabilized, then any presence of ISAF/NATO forces would have no justification to be there. Any attempt of colonizing Afghanistan should be opposed at that stage.

Any political scientist would first refresh his memory about the circumstances in which such a war started. Second, ask a question where this so-called 'national liberation war' would lead the country? Third, what does it promise to the people of the country, particularly the poor people? Fourth, who are these 'liberators' fighting? Fifth, how are they fighting? Sixth, are the majority of the people in the country supporting this war? And seventh, will 'Taliban-led national liberation lead the people to peace, progress and prosperity' or to the medieval society's political and social system? There can be a number of other minor questions, which we should not deal with here.

***

Here it is worth a look into the recent history of Afghanistan. The 1978 April Revolution was led by the communist parties of Afghanistan. Some of the early reforms they introduced were things like compulsory male and female education; abolition of 'walwar' which is a tradition of buying a bride; reformation of oppressive private money lending system; women's rights, etc. There was nothing un-Islamic in these reforms. But Pakistan decided to interfere in their internal affairs and created batches

242

of so-called Islamic Mujahideen led by Gulbuddin Hekmatyar – a long-time ISI client. Then General Zia-ul-Haq sucked in the US and Saudi governments and increased incursions in Afghanistan. The Afghan government made a mistake and invited the Soviet Union to defend them, who being wary of the US-led insurgency in their backyard were tempted to send in their forces. They paid a heavy price for this mistake. The communists also lost their ground because of infighting.

Once the Pakistan-US-Saudi-sponsored counter-revolution was successful and the Soviet forces pulled back, the inevitable happened. There was all-out war between various Mujahideen groups, and Afghanistan was divided among various war lords, with Pakistani intelligence seeking to establish its proxy government in Kabul. Who suffered most in this game? The poor people of Afghanistan. It is important to remember this phase of Afghanistan history, because once the ISAF are out without preparing the Afghan government to take effective control, the country would again drift into a civil war among tribal war lords.

Then came the Pakistan-sponsored Taliban, who managed to conquer almost 80 per cent of the country and establish its brand of Deobandi-Salafist Sharia. No doubt it brought peace to the area they controlled, but in bargain established a government based on religious and ethnic fascism. Intolerance to other sects and religions was rampant. Should it be forgotten that when the whole world was pleading they were destroying Buddha statues? They gave sanctuary to extremist anti-Shia groups such as Sipah-e-Sahaba, who went on a rampage against the Shias in Pakistan and Afghanistan. This style of government gave Islam a bad name across the world. Men were forced to keep beards, women were wrapped from head to toe, their education was stopped, and economy was managed in the most primitive manner, which further made life difficult for the people. Above all they agreed to provide shelter to the Al Qaeda for training the jihadis for a global Islamic revolution. The list is long and does not given credentials of national liberation front to the Taliban.

The foreign forces, which are now in Afghanistan, did not come to colonize the country, they were sucked into the region thanks to the Taliban's foolish policies. Pakistan and the world did give them enough time to move away from exporting terrorists to the world. The 'Great Terrorist University' created by the Taliban and its worthy friends, the Al

Qaeda, played havoc not only in Western countries (who they consider infidel) but in Muslim countries too.

The present Afghan government cannot be brushed aside, like some analysts do, as an American stooge. We have to again recall that in a highly volatile and fragmented atmosphere there were elections in Afghanistan in which people from all the ethnic communities and areas participated. Many women were also elected, who were previously not allowed to even go out of their homes. The Afghans elected the present government. These elections were indeed far from what one would like them to have been. The same goes for the government that has been elected. But the fact is that the process of democratization has started no matter how ugly it looks at present and is definitely better than the dictatorship of Mullah Omar. The Taliban, if it has any love for the people and respect for democracy, should participate in the coming election. That is the only civilized politics in today's world. Once Afghanistan were to stabilize and develop its own forces for maintaining law and order, the whole world would support withdrawal of foreign forces.

Second question: Who are they fighting for? An important factor, which is often overlooked by many political commentators is the demographic composition of Afghanistan, which is as following: Pakhtun 42 per cent, Tajik 27 per cent, Hazara 9 per cent, Uzbek 9 per cent, Aimak 4 per cent, Turkmen 3 per cent, Baloch 2 per cent and others 4 per cent. Thus, 58 per cent of the population is not Pasthun and even they are divided between Pashto- and- Dari-speaking populations. The bulk of the Taliban forces come from the Pashto-speaking Afghans. Hence, it is factually incorrect to claim that the Taliban represent the aspirations of the majority of the Afghans. President Karzai comes from an important Pakhtun tribe called Popalzai. His father was killed in Quetta by the Taliban, which according to Karzai had ISI backing. There are other Pakhtun tribes, which are against the Taliban. It should also be kept in mind that the situation is not that bad in much of Afghanistan, because the Taliban support is mostly in southern Afghanistan. Many other cities up in the north and the west have little support from the Taliban.

Third question: One has to see what the Taliban is offering to the people if its so-called 'national liberation war' is successful. The answer is no progress for uplifting Afghanistan from its abysmal position, but retrogression for sure. If one has the interest of the common Afghan people in mind a reactionary movement cannot be glorified. Our minds should not be clouded by our dislike and aversion for the US government's mistakes.

The answer to the Afghan problem is that the elected government has to be stabilized and it cannot do it alone. It needs international support. True, US-led forces' presence in Afghanistan is not a good idea. Perhaps they should be replaced with the Muslim countries' force under the UN umbrella. This umbrella is there already, and has brought in ISAF. Initially some Muslim countries were invited but they shied away. All said and done, stability in Afghanistan is not only important for the country but also for the world. The Taliban-cum-Al Qaeda terrorist university has to be closed. Period. Pakistanis have been the worst sufferers of terrorism, after Afghanistan, as the Taliban's war has spilled over into this country. Pakistani establishment has nourished these people, dreaming that one day they will help get the Kashmir issue resolved and be successful in installing a proxy government in Kabul.

The time is up for this old policy. The parliament did declare that Pakistan would not allow anybody to use its land for 'interference in our neighbour's affairs'. At the same time, its resolution said that Pakistan would not tolerate their crossing the border at free will. Policy of traditional soft borders with Afghanistan has to be changed so that nobody can blame us for providing safe havens to the Taliban and there are no more incursions into Pakistan from the Afghan side. But the parliamentary resolution does not mean anything in Pakistan because the real policy regarding Afghanistan is crafted at the army headquarters in Rawalpindi, which still believes that it should have a say in the final settlement of Afghanistan and hence is harbouring the Taliban and Haqqani group. However, by supporting the Afghan Taliban, Pakistan has gained importance in the final settlement in Afghanistan. As the US forces' withdrawal by end 2014 comes near, the US administration's reliance on Pakistan for delivering Taliban on negotiating table is increasing.

Similarly, all jihadi organizations, which are still operating openly in the country, should be convinced and pressurized to close shop. They cannot be used as a pressure lobby in dealing with India any more. The geopolitical situation has changed. Pakistan has to bury its old tools. This realization is finally sinking in at the senior level of army leadership. Pakistan COAS General Ashfaq Parvez Kayani has started talking about the paradigm shift in the national security policy, which was India centric. He has declared that the number one threat to Pakistan is from terrorists within its border. But this does not mean that he has undisputed support from the entire rank and file of the armed forces. There are still many hawks that cannot stomach the idea of being friends with India and stop considering it as their enemy number one. Such hawks are on both sides of the Pakistan–India border, making the policy shift difficult. Pressed by the elders of tribal areas TTP leaders made a non-starter conditional peace offer in December 2012. The key conditions were that Pakistan should stop supporting the US in Afghanistan; rewrite the present Constitution; and impose one in accordance to Quran and Sunnah. They appointed Abdur Rauf, an absconder terrorist, to negotiate on their behalf and wanted PML-N and JI as the guarantor of the agreement. Awami National Party, which is ruling KP, organized an all parties conference to consider the peace offer. All the major parties attended it except JI. In a joint declaration they offered to talk but within the framework of present Constitution and on the condition that TTP lays down arms. It was clear that both sides were just playing to the galleries as they often say that TTP and government should negotiate peace to stop unabated terrorism in the country. The TTP offer doesn't leave any other choice but to launch a military operation against its stronghold in North Waziristan. But before the 2013 elections and induction of new government the chances of military operation could not be taken by the armed forces.

PART - V

PART IV

Chapter 23

FOREIGN POLICY TAILORED TO FIT THE NATIONAL SECURITY FEARS

A security state is bound to have large armed forces and huge defence expenditure, which in turn creates the war economy that breeds its co-evolutionists among politicians, civil society and media. Pakistan has large segment of military co-evolutionists who survive on the war economy. They are vociferous supporters of the so-called 'national interest', 'national security' and 'chest-thumping champions of sovereignty'.

'The most fundamental task in devising a grand strategy is to determine a nation's national interests. Once they are identified, they drive a nation's foreign policy and military strategy; they determine the basic direction that it takes, the types and amounts of resources that it needs, and the manner in which the state must employ them to succeed. Because of the critical role that national interests play, they must be carefully justified, not merely assumed.'[1] This is what, a neo-realist professor of international relations and a fellow of Massachusetts Institute of Technology (MIT) Center for International Studies, Robert J. Art says, should be the basis of the formulation of a foreign policy.

But then the first question that needs to be asked is who would decide 'the national interest' in a state. In Pakistan the 'national interest' is defined by its security establishment; hence the 'national security' has been the main driver of the foreign policy. This succinctly answers the primary question, which any student of international relations is trained to ask i.e., why a country (in this case Pakistan) behaves the way it does in conducting its foreign policy?

To understand why and how national security was determined as the prime and over-riding national interest by Pakistani civil and military leaders, the objective conditions in which this new state was born has to be briefly revisited. Pakistan was born out of the womb of India in a caesarian operation by the withdrawing British colonial power, thus it suffered from the trauma. It was born in a hostile environment as the national Indian leadership was against its birth. The Indian National Congress had resisted giving maximum autonomy to the Muslim-majority provinces; thus giving away independence to these provinces was strongly resented. This resentment was shown by the Indian leadership by delaying transfer of the agreed share of assets to Pakistan and in the statements of its hawkish leaders – Congress President Acharya J. B. Kripalani and its first Home Minister Sardar Vallabhbhai Patel – who said 'sooner than later, we shall again be united in common allegiance to our country.'[2]

In spite of this hostile attitude, Jinnah, who was once the advocate of Hindu-Muslim unity, wished in an interview to a German newspaper: 'Personally I have no doubt in mind that our paramount interests demand that the Dominion of Pakistan and the Dominion of India should coordinate for the purpose of playing their part in the international affairs and the developments that take place, and it is of vital importance to Pakistan and India, as independent sovereign states, to collaborate in a friendly way jointly to defend their frontiers both on land and sea against any aggression.'[3]

Jinnah was not alone in suggesting joint defence. According to Congress leader and former diplomat Mani Shankar Aiyar, who is one of the foremost champions of friendly relations between India and Pakistan: 'Mahatma Gandhi made the suggestion (in August 1947) that India and Pakistan should have a common army that would protect both from outside aggression for otherwise there was the danger that the two armed forces would only be ranged against each other.' This suggestion, Aiyar said, was criticized by *Pakistan Times* editor Mazhar Ali Khan in an editorial published on 10 August 1947: 'The Mahatma was wrong in thinking that after Independence the two countries would be locked in armed confrontation because the only quarrel between the two countries was whether or not there should be Partition, and now that Pakistan was being constituted as a separate sovereign nation, there would be no further differences between the two countries, who would happily co-exist as good neigbours.'[4]

Later a similar offer was made by President General Ayub Khan, in which he suggested an India and Pakistan joint defence. A condescending Nehru retorted argumentatively 'defence against whom?' Indeed Jinnah's, and later Ayub's, offers were with the caveat that it 'depends entirely on whether Pakistan and India can resolve their differences and grave domestic issues in the first instance.'[5] In a speech Jinnah reiterated the 'jointly defend the frontiers' offer but also maintained stance that all small nations take: 'The Indian government should shed their superiority complex and deal with Pakistan on equal footing and fully appreciate the realities.'[6] This offer of having a joint defence was also echoed by some other leaders in mid-1950s but India failed to seize the opportunity when it was extended by Jinnah. India declined this offer as it did not want to give away Kashmir, which was a pre-condition in Pakistan's offer. The offer was also ignored as by that time Pakistan had joined a US-led anti-communist alliance, and India was playing a non-aligned balancing act between the USSR and the USA.

At the same time, much against the expectations of Pakistan's complacent leadership, the raja of Kashmir decided to join India, although majority of his subjects were Muslims. Pakistan did not see this move as a mere annexation of the Muslim-majority area by India, but more importantly, though less emphasized, its concern was, and is, that India has assumed control over her 'jugular artery' – Kashmir rivers that flow in this country. Pakistan had made a last-minute effort to conquer Kashmir by using the tribal Lashkar. But this attempt only gave Pakistan control over a small portion of Kashmir and internationalized the issue. This adventure has already been discussed in detail in Part IV.

Propaganda whipped up during the Pakistan movement was on the communal proposition that the Muslims of India would never be given equal rights in an overwhelming Hindu India. This gave fuel to the Hindu–Muslim and Sikh–Muslim riots throughout India in which millions and the world's biggest immigration of people followed. Brutal killings by Hindus, Sikhs and Muslims of one another also killed rational thinking on both sides. The generation, which saw the riots and killings, was deeply affected by this pogrom. It impaired any objective view of the situation. With these atrocities fresh on their minds the majority of leadership on both sides of the divide lost the balance. Pakistan being a smaller and weaker country was affected more by this trauma, which had not been foreseen by its leadership including the ailing Jinnah.

On the other side of the divide were the leaders who accepted the division of India reluctantly as their dream of 'Akhund Bharat' (One Bharat) was shattered. They were bitter about the division and most of them believed that the new state would not survive long. Their apprehensions were proved right partly when half the country – East Pakistan – seceded. A helping hand was indeed given by the Indian government to what had become a liberation movement in what is now Bangladesh after a military operation was launched by West Pakistan army.

The Kashmir issue and fear of India have thus remained the driving factors in formulating the foreign policy of Pakistan. How this policy led to two wars and two battles, which had the potential of spreading in all-out wars has been dealt with in Part IV. Feeling threatened by the bigger powers of India in the east, the USSR in the north-west, and China in the north-east the Pakistani leadership, like most states in this frame of mind, looked for alliances with the USA and support from the Muslim countries. Dr Aneesa L. Kimball explained this mindset of leaders, which drives them to join the 'minimum winning coalitions'. The less '[d]efence burden the state has to shoulder; more resources can be directed to domestic demand like the demands of the welfare state. Political leaders may determine they can more efficiently produce national security this way and provide greater domestic security and protect their own chances of remaining in power. The contracting explanation claims states form alliances to increase the efficiency of their security policy allocations and, more specifically, so that the security resources freed through alignment can be allocated to domestic demands for social security policy expenditures.'[7]

But, in the case of Pakistan the main emphasis remained on national security and not on creating a welfare state. The Western states welcomed Pakistan into an alliance because even before the independence of the country they were conscious of the geostrategic role it could play in the region. 'If the British Commonwealth and the United States of America are to be in position to defend their vital interests in the Middle East, then the best possible stable area from which to conduct this defence is from Pakistan territory ... Pakistan [is] the keystone of the strategic arch of the wide and vulnerable waters of the Indian Ocean.'[8]

Pakistan's foreign policy is thus reactive to its 'India threat perception'. It unrealistically assumed that alliances with the USA would guarantee its defence against India. The ruling elite vision that Pakistan has been made to ultimately strengthen the 'Muslim Ummah' hence it would lead to rally support of other Muslim countries was based on putting too much faith in the common faith bonds. It was with this objective that soon after the creation of the Muslim-majority state of Pakistan it started working for the revival of the Motamar Al-Alam Al-Islami (The World Muslim Congress). This congress held its first conference in Saudi Arabia at the invitation of King Abdulaziz in 1926 and after five years it was organized under the Grand Mufti of Palestine in 1931 in Jerusalem.

Even before Pakistan was created the Indian Muslim League had remained vocal on issues that touched Muslim sensibilities, for example the Muslims of India reacted strongly against the British in support of maintaining Muslim caliphate in Turkey and always provided support to the Palestinian cause. The fact that Pakistan was created with the slogan of establishing a country where Islamic ideals would be adopted, led its leadership to seek alliance with Muslim countries. This, the founding leaders thought, could be best achieved with the revival of Pan-Islamism. Pakistan hosted an international Islamic Economic Conference in Karachi, the then capital, during February 1951 avowedly with a view to developing a programme of economic and social justice among the societies of Muslim states. Ghulam Muhammad in his presidential address maintained: 'We cannot put implicit faith in the western democratic system nor can we subscribe to communism, although there are some aspects of this vast and comprehensive experiment which we must appreciate .... Islamic society has never been subjected to stress and strains of class war and morbid hatred of the rich has never been one of its characteristics .... Islam is the golden mean between these two extremes; it is non-violent method of rectifying unsocial and detrimental inequalities.'[9] Sayed Abdul Muneem Pasha has noted that this statement 'reflected in what it does in name of Islamic Resurgence in the contemporary Muslim world.'[10]

This was followed by a bigger conference of the Motamar-e-Islami (Motamar Al-Alam Al-Islami) held in Karachi in February 1951.[11] However, the Muslim countries' support crumbled in the beginning by the rise of Pan-Arabism and Pakistan's fast-changing position on the Suez Canal conflict. The idea that the 'Islamic Ummah' should stand united and support each other has not worked beyond the creation of Organization of Islamic Countries (OIC) and its subsidiaries like Islamic Development Bank and Islamic Chambers of Commerce. But in times of conflict between states, the OIC has not played any important role because each nation has its own vested interest and cannot agree on a joint policy. Their ineffectiveness has given the abbreviation a cynical name 'Oh! I see' and that's all. As a matter of fact some of its members are working against each other's interests overtly and covertly. In Pakistan the proxy war between Saudi and Iranian intelligence agencies has manifested itself in their support to the sectarian Sunni and Shia militant groups, since the Iranian revolution was hijacked by the clergy. In the Pakistan-India conflict most of these countries prefer to stay neutral. Thus Pakistan's desire to be a part of Islamic alliances and seek strength from them has not been productive. *The Economist* in its issue published on 3 December 1949 commented on the conference sagaciously: 'Whether Pakistan will be able to assume the leadership of the widely flung people who, however much they may have in common, have hitherto been more noted for their "agreement to disagree" than for any effective cooperation. Pakistan undoubtedly has ambition of this sort.'[12]

As a matter of fact, the first country which opposed its entry in the United Nations was a Muslim country – Afghanistan. Once again ethnic solidarity proved stronger than the religious solidarity as Afghanistan supported the cause of independent Pakhtunistan.

This means, as discussed above, that the national interest as primarily defined by the ruling establishment, is guarding Pakistan against the perceived Indian threat. And this guides national security policy or fancifully called foreign policy of the country. Consequently, Pakistan's security establishment has taken over the function of crafting foreign policy sidelining the civilian leadership of the country. A logical outcome of this policy is that the country has to maintain the armed forces beyond its means. As a result, the military finds it difficult to differentiate between its own vested interest and the interest of the people of Pakistan. Their myopic viewpoint has led the country to two wars and two battles with its 'prime enemy India'. In this situation any analyst would search for a 'national security policy' or policies because every country is supposed to keep readjusting its foreign and national policies to meet the changing global, political and economic situations.

So what is the national security policy of Pakistan? To the best of my knowledge there is none. If there is any such policy, which may have evolved with the changing geostrategic situation of Pakistan, the nation doesn't know anything about it. Even some of the people who are supposed to know about such a policy have stated in background interviews, that they have not seen or discussed any document or documents laying down the national security policy. Major-General Durrani said in a background interview that there was no such entity as 'national security policy'. Mind you, he was the national security adviser to the PPP-led coalition government. Some other serving senior army generals admitted that to the best of their knowledge there was no hard or soft copy of any national security policy. This may be difficult to believe. But it is true. One can presume that the national security policy has remained an unwritten document like the United Kingdom's Constitution.

Such a state of affairs also leaves analysts and writers guessing at what the policy is. It is thus surmised on the basis of GHQ's statements and actions taken by the army and its intelligence agencies. An unwritten national security policy leaves the space open for ad hocism, for the security establishment's whims and caprices. The irony is that the nation, which is supposed to be protected by this security policy, doesn't know what the policy is. The people have no hand in the making of this policy because it is left to the army generals. This situation gives a free hand to the army and its intelligence agencies to stretch and expand on national security and use it as a synonym for 'national interest'. The line between the 'armed forces' interest', 'national security' and 'foreign policy' was washed away long ago. Any questioning of this unwritten gospel by the civilian intelligentsia and politicians is considered against the national interest.

However, there is an unofficial document prepared in 2011 by a military-run National Defence University (NDU). It was shared with the security and civilian establishment and has an indemnifying statement that the views expressed are those of the researchers and 'do not imply necessarily the policy of the NDU'. And that's all.

The NDU researchers' document too highlights the absence of the 'National Security Management System'. As the national security policy-making domain was jealously guarded by the GHQ in the past, no civilian-led national security institution could be developed. In any case, out of the 66 years of its existence, for about 34 years the military ruled Pakistan directly. Judging by the previous performance of the military it is evident that one-line and single-dimensional national security policy has focused singularly on meeting the 'Indian threat' militarily. This fact was also acknowledged by the NDU research paper: 'However, until recent past, our primary focus has been on kinetic threats, whereas, awareness about non-kinetic challenges impinging on our national security is slowly being realized. It goes without saying that with the strong standing armed forces and credible nuclear deterrence, Pakistan possesses a formidable response to kinetic domain. But we also need to bring non-kinetic dimension of the threat under sharper focus. This will help us evolve prudent policies and workable strategies to formulate befitting response against multitude complex external as well as internal challenges, which confront us today.'[13] Though the NDU paper has been categorized as not an official document but the establishment, it indicates, is shifting policies recognizing 'slowly' the non-kinetic 'challenges': 'In the face of growing global acceptance of India as the regional leader, Indo-US and Indo-Israel nexus and growing asymmetry between India and Pakistan, strategic reappraisal of our security calculus particularly in the non-kinetic domain is extremely important ....'[14]

To counter the kinetic threats (India threat) the cornerstone of Pakistan's foreign policy has been the same as the one set by Jinnah, namely that the country is geostrategically placed to serve the security interests of the USA, if it guarantees our security against India. All relations with other countries were and are in correlations with the above formulation. This is where Pakistan, blinded by myopia, has gone wrong. Ahmad Faruqui points out in his book *Rethinking the National Security of Pakistan: The Price of Strategic Myopia*: 'National Security does not reside solely in military's combat effectiveness, but in a complementary set of five dimensions that include four non-military dimensions and one military dimension. The non-military dimensions are political leadership, social cohesion, economic vitality, and a strong foreign policy.'[15]

But in Pakistan, which is an ideological security state, this policy has been standing upside down. The GHQ has not allowed any civilian government to interfere in the making of the crucial foreign policy decisions since early 1950s. History has shown that when institutions and individuals grow too strong or dominant they consciously or unconsciously fail to distinguish and separate their own vested interest from that of an institution or the country. The terms 'country' and 'nation' are often used not representing the interest of the people of that nation or country. For the ruling elite the country is just a geographical entity and 'one nation' and 'one national interest' slogan serves to further their own interests. This propaganda of the ruling elite, which is not challenged in everyday life, has successfully negated the existence of the various ethno-linguistic nationalities and economic classes in a country. It is also a fact that the military together with the war economy co-evolutionists consider themselves as a guardian of the nation and its security. It has always denied that their interests are mostly in conflict with the interests of the people they rule. The media both consciously and inadvertently promotes the ruling establishment's political formulations. A security state is bound to have large armed forces and huge defence expenditure, which in turn creates the war economy that breeds its co-evolutionists among politicians, civil society and media. Pakistan has large segment of military co-evolutionists who survive on the war economy. They are vociferous supporters of the so-called 'national interest', 'national security' and 'chest-thumping champions of sovereignty'.

But the changing global realities and repositioning of relations between USA and India, USA and China, and India and China are forcing the Pakistani army to do some hard rethinking about its long-standing India-centric national security and foreign policies. Some senior retired army and foreign service officials have been suggesting changes in the course of these policies for quite some time. Saner politicians and intellectuals have been opposing the India-centric policies for many years but their voices are muzzled by the military co-evolutionists in the media, religious political and militants groups and intelligence agencies.

However, there is a non-conventional narrative also. In a paper presented by Major-General Durrani at the Pakistan National Forum on 6 February 2012, he admitted that his 'treatment of National Security is going to be somewhat different from the one crafted by the GHQ, or ISI or the Foreign Office.' He emphasized the following:

- Today the primary threat to our National Security is internal and not external. A weak economy, poor governance, poor law and order and injustice in our society are the main problems.
- Yes, we are an Islamic state but we seem to be unsure of what it means: Do we follow the Turkish model, the Iranian model, the Afghan model or expand on what the Quaid-e-Azam wanted? My fear is that a well-organized minority may take the silent majority where it does not want to go.
- Our present economic state is unsustainable. To be put simply, our government spends more than it earns. We seem to be sustained by uncontrolled borrowing.
- India will continue to be our adversary in the coming years and *we need to defuse this threat.* (Author's emphasis.)
- Afghanistan, with or without foreign presence will continue to be unstable for the foreseeable future and be the cause of instability in Pakistan. The US failed miserably in Afghanistan and will try to make us the fall guy.

The issue is: Do these various departments, discussed above, have different national security policy or perception? The weakness of an unwritten national security policy has been that it was always formulated and adjusted from military's geostrategic perspective in Pakistan. The geopolitical and geoeconomic perspective has been missing. Consequently, the military-strategy tunnel vision has resulted in the doubling of Pakistan's armed forces strength from over 324,000 in 1971 to over 612,000 in 2000, although the size of the country was halved with the separation of East Pakistan. Thus we have one armed force personnel per 294 Pakistanis. This means an increased expenditure on defence, which has remained between 30 to 40 per cent of the revenue income of the country. It does not include the expenditure on nuclear bomb and missile-making programmes. According to one estimate Pakistan has spent close to US $10 billion (Ahmad Faruqui, 2003) building its nuclear arsenal and the programme continues as recurring expenses pile up. Debt servicing of the loans borrowed for buying armed forces equipments and the forces personnel pensions are hidden in the civilian budget.

Realizing that there was weakness in the higher direction of war and composite strategic thinking, Lieutenant General Sahibzada Yaqub founded the National Defence College in 1971, which was upgraded as a university in 2007. 'After going through this war course, which includes a kind of short course of social sciences, the officers started feeling that they had learnt a lot about national aims, national objectives. Very few got a better understanding but most learnt the buzz-words and strategic phraseology,' a senior army officer confessed. The president of NDU, Lieutenant General Farooq Agha, said in an interview for this book that the NDU has prepared a paper 'National Strategy Paper: Non-kinetic Challenges to the State of Pakistan.' Mark yet another buzz-phrase 'Non-kinetic Challenges'. What the document has recommended is the need for a multi-dimensional approach – as suggested by Fauruqi in his book – to analyze the geostrategic and geoeconomic situation objectively.

After assuming power, the PPP-led coalition government appointed Major-General Durrani as its national security adviser but his views did not match those of GHQ and ISI, and consequently compelled the prime minister to remove him. It was a signal from the army that the task of framing national security thinking and decision-making should be left to it. But forced, particularly, by the 2 May 2011 US attack to get Osama bin Laden and the circumstances surrounding the 23 May 2011, PNS Mehran attack, the army has finally conceded that tactically it needs the civilian cover. Though an institution to manage the national security, as suggested by the NDU paper, has not been established, pushed by public humiliation in May 2011, the army conceded to take 'guidance' from parliament. It is also a tactical move to ease the US administration pressure on the military leadership. Both the bipartisan Parliamentary Committee on National Security (PCNS) and the cabinet committee have been activated as suggested in the NDU paper, which has an annexure model of the national security management system of five countries. The two most relevant are those of the USA and India, although some generals would still prefer the military-dominated Turkish model. 'In the US, the National Security Council [NSC] advises the president and comprises only civilian members .... The chairman of the Joint Chiefs of Staff is the only uniformed in NSC and acts as an adviser on military affairs. This body limits the role and input of the military and asserts on the primacy of the civil.'[16]

'In India the military has no representation in NSC, which functions under the prime minister. The services chiefs sit in the second tier committee [Strategic Planning Group] with union [federal] secretaries, chaired by the Cabinet Secretary.'[17] This is unthinkable in Pakistan, where the army chief usually deals on such matters directly with the president and prime minister. All army chiefs after General Ayub Khan have held the charge of defence ministry also, and have usually undermined the constitutional position of a defence minister as a ceremonial post. Attempts to make the NSC in Pakistan by the military have always suggested heavy armed forces strength.

This prologue was necessary before analyzing the last (2012) tactical move by the military establishment to engage the elected parliament in making a policy regarding the US and its allies in Afghanistan War. With background approval the PPP-led coalition government assigned the PCNS to revisit the terms of engagement with the USA and the NATO in the war in Afghanistan. The committee produced a five-page document 'Guidelines for Revised Terms of Engagement with USA/NATO/ISAF and General Foreign Policy.' It was a significant step forward, because it is a first on three counts in the history of national security policy-making in Pakistan: One, that this was the first parliament-approved written document on the issue; two, it was the first time that a committee of parliament was asked to prepare the policy guidelines and put it before the elected representatives of the people for approval; and three, for the first time the military establishment had to lean on the people's representatives (though forced by circumstances and to seek cover) to deliberate and give the guidelines after listening to all relevant ministries and representatives of the political parties present in the parliament. This was indeed a positive development contrary to what the democracy-bashers say about it.

Now, let's first see under what circumstances, the military establishment opened the window of this sacred zone for the politicians? Some of the major reasons, as stated above are: The army needed the people's support in countering the Taliban, who challenge its writ in Pakistan and are responsible for attacks on the military and civilians – it cannot have a hostile civilian government and fight the Taliban at the same time; that on 2 May 2011 the intrusion of US forces and killing of Osama bin Laden lowered the image of Pakistan army as it was proof of intelligence and security failure; the PNS Mehran attack made many think how our security was woefully weak as the terrorists took out the specific target they had come for. The attack also proved that the Islamic militants groups had their sympathizers in the armed forces; the country is bursting at the seams because of the independence movement in Balochistan and rising Sindhi nationalism, which is encouraged by a section of the powerful US lobbies; that there has been cross-border infiltration by the US forces and some Taliban groups, who the establishment feels had the backing of the US; and that the attack by the US forces on Salala checkpost in which 24 army soldiers were killed, jolted Pakistanis. (Surprisingly the slaughter of 25 soldiers by the Taliban in the tribal areas did not upset Pakistani ultra-nationalists.) It is the Salala incident that was shocking for the boys in the garrison and the people on the streets. The anti-American feelings were further fuelled by the politicians and the media. In this backdrop the PCNS began working. Its report says: 'It may be recalled that NATO/ISAF forces attacked Salala checkpost in Mohmand Agency on 25-26 November 2011. The prime minister of Pakistan taking serious note of the incident called a meeting of the Defence Committee of the Cabinet [DCC] on 26 November 2011 wherein the issue was discussed at length and it was, inter alia, decided that the matter be sent to the Parliamentary Committee on National Security to debate and advise on the future course of action ....'[18]

These developments show that the whole process was undertaken not because, in a democratic polity, PCNS and an elected government should be making the country's national security policy, of course with the input of the security establishment, but because it was a reaction to the hostile action taken by the American troops. The scope of the PCNS was limited to 'revise terms of engagement with USA/NATO/ISAF,' which actually boils down to revising terms of engagement with our major ally and donor – the USA.

Credit should be given to the 16-member PCNS, which expanded its scope by touching the issues other than the terms of engagement. They were right to take a broader view because Pakistan's relations with the US and 47 other members of the NATO/ISAF cannot be guided unless the whole ambit of national security is revised. In line with the recommendations made by the NDU researchers' paper, the report includes Pakistan's relations with China, Russia and defusing tension with India. It has a number of clauses, which suggest that actually Pakistan is asking for a better price for its services. The report implicitly concedes that Pakistan is with the US, NATO and ISAF, who are in Afghanistan with the UN's blessing, for the sake of money; because it is clear that Pakistan does not share the US agenda in Afghanistan. This puts the policy-makers in a difficult position. On the one hand they want to pander to the 48-nation alliance forces in Afghanistan and on the other hand they want to carve a place of their choice for the Taliban in the future set up and counter the growing Indian influence.

But to put things in the right perspective such a report should not have been presented without a preamble outlining – the overall geopolitical, geoeconomic and geostrategic situation. No national security policy can be made in this day and age without deliberating on the whole spectrum. The NDU and Ahmad Faruqui have underlined this fact as stated above. It was only after considering these factors that the committee could have arrived at any pragmatic and achievable objectives. At the same time this rationale and analysis of the overall situation could have explained the thrust of the policy guidelines to the parliamentarians and the media. It could have explained that while individual chivalry and unrealistic nationalist chants are understandable as a part of the rhetoric, the state has to act with responsibility and dispassionately in the interest of the people.

Though the bipartisan PCNS approved it unanimously, once the report was presented in the parliament, the PML-N, which is the major Opposition party, did not honour the document signed by its party representatives. As this report came in 2012, close to the scheduled elections in 2013, the PML-N hawks used the opportunity for playing to central Punjab and KP anti-American wave, keeping an eye on their major election rival Imran Khan's ultra-nationalist stance. As it was for the first time that the parliament was given a chance to frame this policy, majority of the parliamentarians did not take it seriously and in turn followed the GHQ line.

The PCNS emphasized three recommendations: the US or NATO should apologize for the attack on Salala checkpost as this was needed to dampen the anger in the garrisons; drone attacks in the tribal areas should cease, as it was a clear violation of Pakistan's sovereignty under international law; and a better price should be paid for allowing transit facility for NATO goods.

All Pakistan got after a few months of tough talking was a polite 'sorry' from the Secretary of State Hillary Clinton for the Salala attack. Neither the drone attacks stopped nor could Pakistan extract better financial deal for allowing ground supplies transit through its land. Apparently, these were the three sticking points on which Pakistan and US relations have changed from that of an ally to an adversary. But there are many more points of difference that are usually not discussed openly. Let us follow the stream of Pak-US relations, which have been important not only in pulling this region out of the present morass, but have also affected the domestic political, economic and social narrative of Pakistan.

Notes and References:

1. Alan G. Stolberg, *Crafting National Interests in the 21st Century* in J. Boone Bartholomees, Jr. (editor), *The U.S. Army War College Guide to National Security Issues*, Vol. II, 4th edition, July 2010.
2. *Amrita Bazar Patrika*, 18 August 1947, as quoted by General Muhammad Ayub Khan in his political autobiography *Friends Not Masters*, Oxford University Press, Karachi, 1967.
3. *Dawn*, 12 March 1948.
4. Ibid.
5. Ibid.
6. *Jinnah Speeches* as quoted in Abdul Sattar, *Pakistan Foreign Policy: 1947–2009*, Oxford University Press, Karachi, 2010, p. 45.
7. Anessa L. Kimball, *Explaining the Relationship between Foreign Policy Substitution and the Distributional Dilemma*, Département de science politique, Université Laval, Quebec, Canada, 2010.
8. Unsigned memorandum dated 19 May 1948, entitled 'The Strategic and Political Importance of Pakistan in the Event of War with the USSR', Mountbatten papers, Hartley Library, Southampton, UK.
9. Note: Quoted by S.A. M. Pasha in *Islam in Pakistan's Foreign Policy*, Global Media Publications, New Delhi, 2005 (33)
10. Ibid., p. 57.
11. http://www.motamaralalamalislami.org/history.html
12. Quoted by S. A. M. Pasha in *Islam in Pakistan's Foreign Policy*, Global Media Publications, New Delhi, 2005, p. 33.
13. National Strategy Paper – A Division of Non Kinetic Challenges to the State of Pakistan; National Security and War Course 2011/12; National Defence University, Islamabad.
14. Ibid.
15. Ahmad Faruqui, *Rethinking the National Security of Pakistan: The Price of Strategic Myopia*, Ashgate Publishing Company, Hampshire, 2003.

16. 'National Security Paper: Non-kinetic Challenges to the State of Pakistan, National Security and War Course', 2011–12, National Defence University, Islamabad.
17. Ibid.
18. Report of the Parliamentary Committee of National Security on Guidelines for Revised Terms of Engagement with USA/NATO/ISAG, 2012.

Chapter 24

POLICING FOR THE US

It must be highlighted here that it was General Zia and the US administration who created a number of Islamic jihadi groups of Afghans and Pakistanis during 1979-89. The second generation of 'techno-guerillas' created by the US and Pakistani establishment have now turned their guns towards their creators. The country is reaping the bloody harvest of this dangerous policy.

All armies are raised to counter external threats. Pakistani armed forces have kept the Indian threat perception alive not only within the institution, but have also cast all propaganda in an Islamic idiom, something which most people believe in. This threat perception justifies huge military expenditure. Indian forces have also played on their perceived threat from Pakistan and China. Being economically and geographically a smaller state, the India paranoia has converted Pakistan into a security state, instead of a welfare state. To galvanize the nation it was in the interest of the armed forces to use religion and establish it as a self-styled guardian of the 'ideology of Pakistan'. The perceived fear of 'Hindu imperialism' also pushed Pakistan to seek American assistance and offer the country's services as an ally against the communist Soviet Union.

Without historical context and conceptual clarity about what is in the interest of the people of Pakistan, discussion about the present Pakistan–US relations would be superfluous. The prevalent emotionally charged narrative does not clear the fundamental litmus test, which every policy should pass through. The test is that whatever domestic or foreign policy decisions are taken by the government and the establishment, they should contribute towards improving the lives of the common man of Pakistan.

Let us briefly run through Pakistan–US relations history, which has seen some ups and downs. Muhammad Ali Jinnah positioned Pakistan as an ideological state that would partner the West against the spread of atheistic communist surge. 'On 1 May 1947 Mohammed [Muhammad] Ali Jinnah, leader of the Muslim League, received two American visitors at his Bombay residence. They were Raymond A. Hare, head of South Asian Affairs, Department of State and Thomas E. Weil, second secretary of the US Embassy in India. Jinnah asserted that under no circumstances would he accept the concept of Indian Union since the Muslim League was determined to establish Pakistan. *He sought to impress on his visitors that the emergence of independent, sovereign Pakistan would be in consonance with American interests. Pakistan would be a Muslim country. Muslim countries would stand together against Russian aggression. In that endeavour they would look to the United States for assistance, he added. Jinnah coupled the danger of "Russian aggression" with another menace that Muslim nation might confront. That was "Hindu imperialism." The establishment of Pakistan was essential to prevent Hindu imperialism into the Middle East, he emphasized.*'[1] (Author's emphasis.)

Thus the role was cast for Pakistan as an ally of the US in the regional politics by its founder, Muhammad Ali Jinnah. History has shown that subsequent governments and the military establishment have played this role with only slight variations. Pakistan started making demands on the United States for arming its armed forces as early as two months after its inception and not for development, which clearly indicated that it was set on the path of becoming a security state. It asked for five years military assistance for buying weapons. The request included $170 million for the Army, $75 million for the Air Force and $60 million for the Navy.[2] That was big money then, even from the American standard.

The leaders of the newly created Pakistan lived under fear of Indian aggression and to strengthen its rag-tag army they needed American support, and as quid pro quo they offered their services to counter the socialist threat to the region. Jinnah's vision was actively followed by his Prime Minister Liaquat Ali Khan and Finance Minister Ghulam

Muhammad. They begged the Americans for aid and assured their support against Russia. In return the Americans offered the first tranche secretly in May 1950 as a gesture when Liaquat Ali Khan was on a visit to the US. However, the secret was exposed when the shipment exploded in an accident at a small New Jersey port. However, the Americans warned that the arms given to Pakistan would not be used for aggression against any other country, implicitly meaning India.

A beginning had been made and Pakistan, driven by the perceived Indian threat and pandering to its military leadership, kept on forging closer relations with the US. First they signed a Mutual Defence Pact, which had a clause to combat any communist insurgency. To please the Americans the Communist Party of Pakistan (CPP) and Left-leaning organizations such as Democratic Students Federation (DSF) and Progressive Writers Associations were also banned. Pakistan then joined the Baghdad Pact/CENTO and South East Asia Treaty Organization (SEATO). Prime Minister Khawaja Nazimuddin, who resisted joining an alliance, was booted out by Governor-General Ghulam Muhammad, Prime Minister Mohammad Mossadegh's government was toppled in Iran in a coup engineered by the CIA. The path for US military alliances was cleared, as was desired by the US Secretary of State John Foster Dulles.

However, in spite of signing the Mutual Defence Pact with the US, Pakistan military's great expectations were not met by the US. This is evident from the de-classified letter written by General Muhammad Ayub Khan to the US Chairman Joint Chiefs of Staff Admiral Arthur Radford on 27 September 1955: In a 'meeting in Washington in October 54 Pakistan was told that "America would be prepared to complete 11/2 Division of our Armour and four divisions of Infantry, as we are expanding the maximum we could on the armed forces, apart from weapons etc., required our additional internal expense would also be covered for these formations. The programme was to take three years to complete …. Unfortunately I failed to obtain the American cooperation on this, with the result that when our staff presented our requirements list it was objected … that our Divisional strength was in excess of theirs [US], which could not be supported. In any case no more than 40,000 additional men could be catered for. Our figure was 56,000 men." Pakistan army readjusted to this US suggestion …. then came the bomb-shell in the form of the message from the head of the USMAAG [US Military Assistance Advisory Group] … shorn of verbiage it reads that as far as the army is concerned, the ceiling of military aid is 75 million dollars and all the talk about 5 ½ Divisions is revoked.'

After explaining at length how Pakistan had been cutting down its military assistance wish list in accordance with the suggestions of the US to curtail the size of a military division, the frustrated General Ayub then moved to create the fear of Pakistan's public opinion against the US: 'Forgive me for being frank, but I would be failing in my duty if I do not tell you that our people are completely frustrated .... They are in a mood not to accept an American word however solemnly given .... What the political repercussions be [sic] when this news gets known, and after all you cannot conceal facts indefinitely in a Democracy.'[3] Now if the dates are changed General Ashfaq Parvez Kayani's unwritten letter to his counterpart has the same tenor in June 2012. This time Pakistan told America that they are not doing enough and public opinion is against them. Democracy, thus, comes to help the military agenda.

US military assistance kept on pouring in, and training to senior officials continued till 1965 when it was stopped because Pakistan had launched a covert 'Operation Gibraltar' across the LOC. As military assistance given to Pakistan was with the caveat that it would not be used for offensive purpose, US stopped military equipment supplies to both India and Pakistan. In Pakistan that was the first time the government propaganda machine built feelings against the US. The common refrain was that the 'US was not a reliable friend'. Military and civilian assistance was revived in 1975, but only to be discontinued under the Symington Amendment in 1979, which expressed concern over Pakistan's nuclear programme. But all exhortations against nuclear proliferation were forgotten by the US once the Soviet Union forces entered Afghanistan (in December 1979) on the invitation of the government in Kabul to curb Pakistan-sponsored insurgency. The US assistance was then restored and Pakistan was offered over $332 million. General Zia-ul-Haq, the architect of insurgency, turned down this US assistance describing it as 'peanuts'. The US administration was lured by Zia through a pretty socialite lobbyist Joanne Herring, who was made Honorary Consul General of Pakistan in Houston. Thanks to Congressman Charlie Wilson, the US was convinced that they could avenge Vietnam defeat in Afghanistan by supporting the Islamic jihad against the Left-leaning Afghan government and its supporter, the Soviet Union.

It must be highlighted here that it was General Zia and the US administration who created a number of Islamic jihadi groups of Afghans and Pakistanis during 1979–89. The second generation of 'techno-guerillas' created by the US and Pakistani establishment have now turned their guns towards their creators. The country is reaping the bloody harvest of this dangerous policy.

True, the Americans left Pakistan and Afghanistan high and dry to deal with these Islamic warriors and the 'Islamic techno-guerillas', once the Soviet forces were withdrawn, but the fact remains Pakistan was equally responsible for creating these militants and continued to use some for insurrections in India. It was evident when these militant groups would be told to pack up, their corrupt leaders who were on the payroll of intelligence agencies might oblige, but the motivated rank and file would consider Pakistani establishment as renegades of Islamic jihad. Some of them have already taken up arms against Pakistani establishment.

Once again after the Soviet forces withdrawal in 1989, the US remembered Pakistan's nuclear programme, and all military and economic assistance were stopped under the Pressler Amendment. Senator John Glenn in his testimony maintained that the US had given US $4 billion assistance to Pakistan during 1982–90. This was on assurances that Pakistan was not following the nuclear bomb programme, but the evidence was that on the contrary Zia never stopped the nuclear programme. In fact in the mid-1980s at a stone-throw distance from the US Consulate in Karachi, the general announced, at a reception given by the Karachi Chamber of Commerce and Industry, the good news that Pakistan had acquired the technology, which only a handful of countries have. He didn't use the word 'nuclear'. I was reporting for *Dawn*, when I filed the story with this obvious disclosure, the news editor told me that the government press advice is that no reference was to be made to this disclosure, though frustrated, I had to rewrite the story around midnight; the only satisfaction was that even President General Zia was censored. Thus, the flow of military and financial assistance from the US to Pakistan dried up between 1991 and 2001. After the 1998 nuclear explosion by Pakistan and the military coups against the elected Nawaz Sharif government in 1999, the sanctions on Pakistan became harsher. But, once the World Trade Towers were blown up by the Al Qaeda militants, the US gave no option to Pakistan but to join the war against terrorism. While all earlier engagements with the US were ostensibly those between consenting adults and solicited by Pakistan, post-9/11 marriage was a forced one. The American president made it clear: 'You're either with us or against us.' Pakistan decided to join the war against the Al Qaeda, which had emerged as a threat to the rulers of all Muslim countries. But it was not ready to go against the Taliban government, which was installed in Kabul after significant investment by Pakistani intelligence agencies. Hence, Pakistan decided to play the deception game by giving the Taliban a safe haven and support while supporting the US against the Al Qaeda. The US started providing financial and military assistance once again and from 2002 to 2012 it pumped in around US $23.6 billion into Pakistan. Out of this $15.82 billion was military assistance and $7.77 billion economic assistance. Pakistan economic affairs ministry's sources say that $8.8 billion out of $15.82 billion military aid was not assistance, as it came under the Coalition Support Fund (CSF)* so it should be deducted from $23.6 billion grand total. This leaves the real assistance to $14.8 billion. At the same time not all the money has been disbursed, according to the US Congress report.

It was only under the Kerry-Lugar Bill that the US announced $1.5 billion each for military and economic assistance per annum for five years. The Pakistan army detested the clause in the bill, which said that the US secretary of state would have to testify that the civilian government had supremacy over its military establishment. The Pakistan Constitution also guarantees that. Even if the US Congress figures are accepted Pakistan has received over $30 billion from the US since 1948, out of which over $23 billion was allocated in the last ten years, when the US foolishly unleashed a direct war in Afghanistan. The 'US assistance to Pakistan has fluctuated considerably over the past 60 years. In the wake of 9/11, however, aid to Pakistan has increased steadily as the Bush and Obama administrations both characterized Pakistan as a crucial US partner in efforts to combat terrorism and to promote stability in both Afghanistan and South Asia .... Many observers question the gains accrued to date, viewing a lack of accountability and reform by the Pakistani government as major obstacles. Moreover, any goodwill

---

*Coalition Support Fund is the reimbursement of the money spent by Pakistan in support of the US war on terror.

generated by US aid is offset by widespread anti-American sentiment among the Pakistani people.'[4]

According to a US report, 81 per cent people have 'unfavourable' views about their country. Most Pakistanis are confused as to whose war they are fighting? There is a strong propaganda that Pakistan should not have embroiled itself in the 'war against terror'. At the same time these people ask for higher price to fight this war. If it is not a just war and not in the interest of Pakistan, why do Pakistanis blame that the Americans are not paying the right price? Does that mean Pakistan is willing to fight an unjust war just for a few billion dollars? Most Pakistanis hate such introspection and accept that resistance to Talibanization is their war, perhaps more than the Americans. The US may walk away but these Islamists will continue to reduce the space for the Pakistani way of life. But after haggling for an apology and new terms of engagement for seven months, Pakistan had to open the Ground Line of Communications (GLOC) in July 2012. This was much to the dislike of the Islamist parties and their grand alliance Defence of Pakistan Council. Here it is important to discuss why the government was forced to open the GLOC.

As stated earlier the basic litmus test, which a government action or a policy should pass is simple: its outcome should be in the interest of the teeming millions of the country. This broad test is universal and applied by pro-people journalists and politicians across the world. Unfortunately, in Pakistan it is applied sparsely. Let us have a litmus test of the belated government (read the establishment) decision to reopen the ISAF/NATO forces supply route from Pakistan. As expected there was an uproar on this decision from the TRP-seeking media and Right-wing politicians. An important question arises in this context: What outcome do we want for the people of Pakistan – ego-massaging of the people or economic relief for them?

The proponents of high national values and pride of the country talk about national sovereignty, blood of Salala checkpost martyrs, Pakistan not selling itself cheap and ban on drone attacks. Those who are the real decision-makers have the stark realities in front of them:

1. Pakistan cannot afford to be completely isolated from the world's most powerful 48 countries that form the NATO/ISAF

271

alliance. Why? Almost 42 per cent of Pakistan's exports go to these countries;

2. Most of the foreign assistance and investment comes from these countries;

3. Pakistan's air force, navy and army are heavily dependent on the US and other Western countries for armaments and their spares;

4. These countries have the power to get Pakistan slapped with worst sanctions for harbouring terrorist groups such as Afghan Taliban, including the Haqqani group, LeT and other franchisees of the Al Qaeda;

5. As Pakistan moves away from or rather takes a hostile posture towards the US and its allies, the Indian influence with them increases in geometrical proportion;

6. The stalemate with the US and its allies was sidelining Pakistan from the Afghanistan solution table; and

7. It has to be realized that Pakistan can be defeated economically without firing a single bullet, if the West and India collude.

The net impact of all these factors will affect the poor man the most, not the SUV-riding mullahs, who preach a highly nationalistic line.

It is indeed easy to sit in the opposition and talk-shows, where no single question can be discussed in depth, and brag about national pride and sovereignty. Some politicians give the examples of Iran and Turkey saying that they have managed to withstand the pressure of US and its allies. Let us first talk about Iran in detail. Iran has oil and gas dollars, which it is earning in spite of sanctions. It is the major supplier of oil to India, China, some European countries and Africa. This helps it keep domestic prices suppressed, but at the same time as the money is getting concentrated in the hands of the rentier classes, poverty is increasing. It is smuggling oil to all its neighbours like Pakistan and Afghanistan, which according to a former Pakistani diplomat is even used by the US army. As for Turkey it is conveniently forgotten that while Turkey had taken a stand not to support the invasion of its neighbour Iraq, it also did not give sanctuary and arms to the Sunni militants who were resisting the US forces. Unlike Pakistan, Turkey had not used armed jihadi groups against any of its neighbours as a tool to further its foreign policy. It has a strong economy and is almost part of Europe. It is not fortunately placed next to turbulent Afghanistan. In spite of an Islamic party's rule

Turkey maintains diplomatic relations with Israel. And, the major point missed by our zealots is that Turkey is part of the NATO forces that are fighting along with the US in Afghanistan and not covertly supporting the Taliban like Pakistan.

Take a look at the other myth that people of Pakistan are against opening of the NATO line and are anti-US. The polls by the US agencies cannot be accepted as gospel. In the first place their sample size is too small to know what people think and secondly, it is how the question is framed that leads to a desired answer. Before moving forward and taking you on a quick trip of Pakistan let me make it clear, I am not saying that Pakistanis like the US, but that they want normal relations and not an antagonistic relationship with it. They don't want to suffer economic hardship as a consequence of upping the false pride ante. Sweeping statements regarding the so-called public opinion of 180 million of Pakistan are heard ad nauseam. The fact is that Pakistani public opinion has never been monolithic because it is a multi-ethnic and multi-structural society. Just analyze how different people think in Pakistan: Baloch and Pakhtun population of Balochistan are not anti-American unlike what as we are told. The Baloch are more anti-Pakistani, and seek the American help to get them their rights, if not the independence; and Balochistan Pakhtuns, mostly led by Mahmood Khan Achakzai, believe that Pakistani agencies' support to the Afghan Taliban should be stopped to restore peace in their area.

Travel down to Sindh. The Sindhi-majority votes for the PPP, which is not an anti-American party and the nationalists again want the US help to get independence of Sindh. The Urdu-speaking Sindhis of this province vote for MQM, which is a secular pro-West political party. The businessmen of Karachi back them fully. Further to the north in the Saraiki belt the people are ambivalent on such issues as foreign policy. The majority votes for the PPP. Yes, there is a strong militant Islamist strand in some pockets of Saraiki areas, which are, in fact, closely tied up with TTP and the Al Qaeda. They are powerful because they have guns and trained militants, but in numbers they do not represent the public mood. The real anti-US sentiment is in central and northern Punjab that too in the middle- and- lower-middle classes, who are directly affected by the jingoism and propaganda by the religious parties and media.

Even in central Punjab a sizeable number of businessmen know which side of their bread is buttered. However, the mood of this area also depends on the political stance of three parties – PML-N, PPP, PTI (Pakistan Tehrik-e-Insaf) and the mother of all parties – the army. Up in the north, close to the war theatre, the lines are drawn more clearly with the ANP and PPP having the majority. Therefore, it can be said that they represent the popular mood and are not anti-US. On the contrary ANP is in war with the Taliban. Over 700 of its office bearers have been killed by the TTP. In the last elections, in spite of the anti-West hype, the majority voted for the parties, which were anti-Talibanization and pro-West. The religious parties, which are in the forefront of Difa-e-Pakistan Council (DPC), secured only a handful of seats. Given this ethnic and political landscape, the media needs to be careful in making sweeping statements and should take the sample surveys of various perception research outfits with a pinch, if not with a bottle of salt.

The problem with Pakistan's establishment is that right from its inception it has fallen victim to the propaganda it continues to generate. After the 2 May 2011 Abbottabad humiliating fiasco, which rubbished Pakistani intelligence agencies and security forces' preparedness, the media, political parties abetted with the establishment in deflecting the people's anger against the US to cover up their failure. Whether the DPC was cobbled by the establishment or it appeared logically, is immaterial. What is important is that their viewpoint was projected and amplified to save the skins of those who failed the nation. Finally, forced by the domestic weakness and international pressure right decisions had to be taken. Just a polite 'sorry' over the telephone by Hillary Clinton was accepted from the US to come back to the business as usual. However, this reconciliation has not warded off Pakistani security forces.

In spite of all the talk about being allies of the US, Pakistan's security establishment has come at the crossroads. The establishment's objective in building security alliances with the US was to counter the Indian threat. The US objective was to use Pakistan against the Soviet Union – a job Pakistani establishment did well by creating and supporting the Afghan Mujahideen against a Left-leaning government of Afghanistan and the Soviet forces.

But 9/11 was the game changer. The US administration wanted Pakistan to fight the Islamic militant forces, something which was never discussed in the terms of engagement. It was difficult for the establishment to fight against the jihadi groups created by it after the Afghan War with the purpose of using them against India. While the Pakistani establishment was playing with fire and was happy that it could bleed the Indians without a formal war, India emerged as a more important strategic partner of the West. It is now one of the G-20 countries and is becoming important for the US-led bloc to counter China in the region. On the other hand, the Pakistani establishment wants to support China in this tussle, without annoying the US. In the 1980s Pakistan was afraid that the Russians would come over to gain access to Balochistan's warm water. Now there is a strong apprehension in the security establishment that the US wants to capture the warm water to choke the energy route of China. Hence, before the US gets to Balochistan directly or by supporting the on-going independence movement, there is a strong lobby in the GHQ, which wants to bring in the Chinese in a big way – by contracting out Gwadar Port and the mineral mines to them.

As Pakistan's foreign policy has remained hostage to its India-centric national security policy it is important to deal here briefly with Pakistan–India relations and the shifting paradigm.

Notes and References:

1. The US chargé d'affaires in New Delhi (George R. Merral) to the secretary of state (George C. Marshall) 2 May 1947. Quoted from M. S. Venkataramani, *The American Role in Pakistan: 1947–1958*, Radiant Publishers, New Delhi, 1982.
2. Ibid., p. 3.
3. General Muhammad Ayub Khan's 'secret' letter to Admiral Radford, D.O.No. 7/36/C-in-C declassified NND 959417.
4. US Congress report, 'Pakistan: U.S. Financial Assistance', Congressional Research Service, April 2012.

Chapter 25

LIVING UNDER INDIAN FEAR

Pakistan has to remember Niccolò Machiavelli's advice to smaller nations: 'Small states should ensure that their friends are nearby and their enemies are as far away as possible.' And India has to remember former British Prime Minister William Ewart Gladstone's advise: 'It is one of the uniform and unfailing rules that guide human judgment, if not at the moment yet of history, that when a long relation has existed between a Nation of superior strength and one of inferior strength and when that relation has gone wrong, the responsibility and guilt rests in the main upon the stronger rather than upon the weak.'

The Mumbai based International Centre for Peace Initiatives (ICPI) has observed: 'At the deepest level, this [India–Pakistan rivalry] confrontation can be traced to the identity crisis. India traces its origin to a civilization 4,000-5,000 years ago. Pakistan traces its nationhood either to the Lahore Resolution of 1940 or to the conquest of Sindh by Mohammed [Muhammad] bin Qasim in the 712 A.D. [*sic*]. If Lahore Resolution is the basis of Pakistan's identity, the state of Pakistan is a protest against Indian dominance of the region. If Mohammed [Muhammad] bin Qasim's conquest is the basis, the state of Pakistan is representation of foreign conquest.'[1]

This summation is not far from the truth. Both countries have allowed the crucial relations to remain hostage to the history of the Muslims and

Hindus of the subcontinent. Pakistani rulers have inculcated anti-Indian mindset in the country because it justifies the religious nationalism, which was the basis of the 'two-nation theory'. The Indian rulers have always looked down on Pakistan as the younger brother who strayed out and broke away from a joint family system. Pakistan being a smaller and weaker country has depended on foreign alliances as already explained, and has always relied on the non-state actors – jihadi groups – to make up for its military and economic resources deficiencies. These jihadi groups are considered the front line of Pakistan defence by some Pakistani security officials. Hatred against India and Hindus is part of syllabus in schools across Pakistan. Some states in India too have a similar approach to education.

As a result of this tension-ridden relation between the two countries both Islamic fervour and large army have been fed by Pakistan at the cost of economic development, leading to a high-cost of opportunity loss. Result is that Pakistan has not been able to stimulate domestic investment to its full potential; there is constant flight of capital because of instability and uncertainty in the country; and foreign investment has dropped drastically because Pakistan is considered a high-risk country. On the political side the consequence of this tension-ridden relation with India has resulted in a dominating role for the military establishment – whether when it was in power directly for over three decades or when it micro-managed the political governments.

The acrimonious relations between the two countries have created at least three border issues: Sir Creek, Siachen and Kashmir. The latter two are connected. Then there are other issues, which have remained a stumbling block in relationship building. The issue of Kashmir is undoubtedly the core issue as defined by the Pakistan side, with the Indian government insisting it to be its internal issue. The claim of Pakistan on Kashmir is on the ground that being a Muslim-majority state it should have been acceded to Pakistan and that India has occupied it using force under the pretext that the Hindu raja had appealed to India and Lord Mountbatten to help repel the tribal Lashkar attack engineered by Pakistan army. Pakistan has always pleaded that the people of Kashmir should be given their right of determination, while at home the ruling establishment has denied this right to the people of Balochistan, although the state of Kalat was annexed through a military take over.

The Kashmir issue has become more complex over the last 66 years. Majority of Kashmiris, unlike their predecessors do not want to join Pakistan. If at all, they want independence from India and Pakistan, preferring to be a land-locked independent country like Nepal. The unstable and terrorism-infested Pakistan is no more an attractive option for anybody in the region. Kashmiris are also realizing that Pakistan's interest in their valley is not for the people's right but in reality for taking control over the rivers that flow from Kashmir and irrigate Pakistan. Some Kashmiri leaders have even blamed Pakistan for getting Kashmiri youth killed in the struggle in Kashmir for the sake of securing its river sources. Thus, the perception is that the real issue is gaining control over the rivers that are the lifeline of Pakistan. It is because of this that on a number of occasions in Track II (unofficial talks held secretly and parallel to official talks) talks Pakistan had proposed making Chenab as the dividing line. Pakistan 'advocated using the Chenab River as the border. The special envoy of Pakistani Prime Minister, made this proposal to his Indian interlocutor on March 29, 1999 [sic] in Delhi.'[2]

This fear of India has earned for the hawkish army generals and their jihadi assets much support in the people of Pakistan, who are afraid of India choking water flow to Pakistan and making it a desert. No less than the head of the major India-specific jihadi group Prof. Hafiz Saeed stressed while addressing a Faisalabad traders convention in 2003: 'Pakistan is rightly perturbed about depleting water resources of the country, and it is most important it realizes that all the deposits of water are in the Indian Kashmir. The only way by which economic prosperity of Pakistan can be guaranteed and its farms can be prevented from getting barren is to increase its efforts in wresting control of India-occupied Kashmir. Only if Kashmir is freed from India control, can Pakistan's economic interests be safeguarded.'[3]

One factor that is often overlooked in this discourse is that the Kashmiri leadership on the Indian side is bitter about the Indus Waters Treaty of 1960 between Pakistan and India. Their contention is that Kashmiris who 'own the rivers' were never consulted when this treaty was signed. A former Chief Secretary Ashok Jaitley of Indian–Kashmir once told me that the state government had asked for billions of rupees from the Union Government in Delhi as compensation to giving away their right over rivers to Pakistan. Hence, even if the much-aspired demand of Kashmir independence ever materializes, Pakistan will have to face another water conflict and this time with its 'Kashmiri Muslim brethren'. They have stated that they want to use the Kashmir rivers first for their own irrigation and production of electricity. In negotiations with Pakistan on Baglihar Dam with India, a former Water and Power Federal Secretary Ashfaq Mahmood, who was part of the Pakistani delegation in the mid-1990s, told me that India always includes Muslim Kashmiris in its delegation, who would present the importance of the dam for electrifying the power-deficit Kashmir.

Although the Pakistan–India water dispute was decided after cumbersome negotiations, which culminated in Indus Waters Treaty 1960, Pakistan's fear about India using the water weapon has not come to rest. It was signed by Indian Prime Minister Jawaharlal Nehru and Pakistan President General Ayub Khan in September 1960 in Karachi and has withstood the two wars and the Kargil battle. But as water is becoming scarce both because of climate changes and faster growth of population, the per capita availability has dropped drastically, a fact which has not been explained to the people. They are incited to believe that India is diverting or will divert water from the three rivers allocated to Pakistan in the treaty – Indus, Chenab and Jhelum. These fears further fuel anti-Indianism when there are reports about the dispute over the number of dams being made by it on the rivers allocated to Pakistan. India's contention is that it is allowed to build run-of-the-river dams for producing electricity – meaning the dams would not be used for irrigation purposes. Reportedly, India has started work on constructing nine dams on these rivers, and the Pakistani establishment and farmers are worried about the future of their needs when these dams get completed and filled. Though there is a provision that India would have to compensate Pakistan for the water loss as result of the filling of dams, these issues would have to be sorted out to satisfy the water stakeholders in Pakistan for building confidence between the two countries. The prevailing lack of trust between the two countries on such issues is fully exploited by jingoist politicians and media on both sides; this does not make the normalization process easy in Pakistan.

Here it needs to be mentioned that water issues are not seen in the right perspective. It is not a typical issue of Pakistan and India. The construction of Tipaimukh Dam on the River Barak in Manipur by India has agitated Bangladesh politicians across the political divide. The dispute over Mekong river water is between China and Vietnam. Even within the country, the Sindh–Punjab dispute over share of Indus river water has not been fully resolved. At times Balochistan blames Sindh for not giving its due share of water. In California the upper and lower riparian have dispute over water share. In India there is a water dispute between Karnataka and Tamil Nadu.

As water scarcity is deepening and population of Pakistan and India is rising, both the countries should change their traditional crop watering methods. Per capita water availability has dropped from 5,000 cubic metres at the time of partition to 1,200 cubic metres in Pakistan and 1,800 cubic metres in India. Almost 70–80 per cent water is used for agriculture and in both countries farmers are used to over-watering the crops, plant crops that guzzle water and irrigation water is highly subsidized and supplied at a nominal rate. This is particular to the canal-irrigated arable land. Investment of resources and human energies should be focused on efficient water-conserving ways rather than on building arsenals of expensive war machines and nuclear arms in the name of protecting water rights.

***

Siachen is an issue related to Kashmir and is subject of most irrational positions taken by both sides. After the avalanche in which around 130 Pakistani soldiers lost their lives at Siachen in 2012, the Pakistan army chief, General Kayani openly called for both countries to get down from Siachen as it served no purpose. But talks between the two countries are stalemated by military strategic semantics. According to Pakistan's former ambassador Maliha Lodhi: 'No progress was made in the thirteenth round of talks on the 28-year-old dispute. Negotiations mimicked the May 2011 round in which Pakistan believed India hardened its position. The main sticking point remained India's insistence that before demilitarization Pakistan should agree on authentication of present troop positions and demarcation of the Actual Ground Position Line [AGPL]. Pakistan's call for a settlement on principles agreed by the two countries in 1989 and its offer to evolve a withdrawal schedule identifying "present" and "future" positions was rejected. Pakistan's effort to discuss a non-contentious aspect of Siachen, environmental degradation, was also spurned by the Indians on the grounds that military activity had caused no such impact.'[4] Both countries are spending huge amounts collectively on this military standoff at the Siachen Glacier. According to a rough estimate Pakistan has spent over Rs 153 billion and India Rs 357 billion on this foolish venture in 28 years. It is the world's first and perhaps last military standoff on such a high altitude. More soldiers die or fall seriously ill in this military adventure by frost bites and lack of oxygen, than are killed by each other.

Sir Creek, a marshy land at the tip of the Indus river delta is another unresolved issue because of irrational positions taken by the negotiators. These issues can only be resolved if there is strong political leadership with a will to move forward. At present and in the foreseeable future, both countries are expected to have weak coalition governments and strong oppositions. To draw consensus with the Opposition on issues, which have been made emotive by the establishments over the years is not an easy task. In the case of Pakistan, the military establishment has to give the political government its clearance, and in the case of India, the BJP-led Opposition must agree to give the government a hand in resolving these sensitive issues between the two countries.

However, there are a number of indicators which suggest that Pakistan had started moving away from its internationally stated position that Jammu and Kashmir should be part of Pakistan. Pakistan's official is now flexible on its stated position that a plebiscite on Kashmir, as laid down in the 21 April 1948 UN Resolution should be held. But in the Simla Agreement, Pakistan moved from this position and agreed to bilateral negotiations, and the UN declared 'ceasefire line' in Kashmir was mentioned as the 'line of control'. Further on in the 1990s emphasis on the solution, which is acceptable to Kashmiris increased, and in back-door diplomacy during General Pervez Musharraf's regime the talks advanced on making the LOC irrelevant. It was under this arrangement that a bus service was started between the two Kashmirs, special visa arrangements were made to allow the divided Kashmiri families meet and Kashmir–Kashmir trade was allowed through trucks. This trade flourished. A leading commodities trader, Raees Ashraf Tar Mohammed, told me in an interview that Kashmir–Kashmir trade of spices has increased rapidly reducing the quantum of trade of these commodities through other official channels. Kashmir–Kashmir trade has been given tariff advantage over the Pakistan–India trade regime. But Kashmiris on both sides complain of undue delays in issuing visit permits to them for visits because of the bureaucratic mindset of mistrust and interference of intelligence agencies on both sides.

However, the feel-good factors are few and far between for Pakistanis. This despite the fact that there is a growing realization that normalization of relations with India or 'diffused', as the cautious army think tank officials would like to put it, is crucial for the peace and prosperity of the subcontinent. Indeed, more for Pakistan politically, economically and strategically, than for India. This approach has started reflecting in the initiative Pakistan has taken to normalize relations with India. The NDU paper concedes: 'Adroit employment of non-kinetic tools by the Indians, [the] US, Afghanistan, supranational entities and Non-State Actors [NSA] has helped them exploit our internal fault lines and capitalize on international concerns. Resultantly, our high moral ground with respect to Kashmir freedom struggle has been compromised due to persistent Indian narrative linking LeT and other jihadi outfits with terrorism.' This realization is slowly sinking in as far as the ruling establishment is concerned, but instead of booking these jihadi groups as a liability, which is what the above NDU observation says, they are still considered as an asset and have been only put on a pause. Some retired generals believe that the only way to get Kashmir is to repeat 1947–48 and send the Taliban Lashkars for its liberation of India. They are supported by the extremist religious parties, who have organized in a loose alliance – the DPC. On the other hand, the evidence of the warming up of relations with India – one time enemy number 1 – started appearing in the second half of 2011. The cabinet decision was to finally grant most-favoured nation (MFN) status to India by the end of 2012, which actually means having non-discriminatory trade relations was not possible without the blessing of the military establishment. But this deadline was missed by Pakistan creating doubts about its intentions. The government says it will honour its commitment but was under pressure from farmers who are concerned about the cheaper flow of agricultural commodities into Pakistan from India. This protectionist attitude of Pakistani farmers is not particular in nature, as it is typical of even the farmers of the rich G-8 countries. The relaxation of visa regime agreement between the two countries in September 2012 was another positive move. This process has been derailed because of the killings of Pakistani and Indian soldiers on the LOC in January 2013. But there are fair chances of the revival of confidence-building measures in spite of such hiccups and efforts by the hawks to stall the peace process. *Pakistan Army Green Book*, which contains policy articles has also underlined that Pakistan's immediate issue is internal threat from terrorist groups. Army Chief Kayani has also offered the olive branch to India by saying that it is high time Siachen issue is resolved. However, as Pakistan is expected to have general elections in May 2013, not much progress is expected in the intervening period. Any major peace break-through would only be possible once Pakistan stabilizes after the elections.

What has led to the change of decades' old anti-India policy? Among many reasons two are prominent. First and foremost, background interviews reveal that the establishment is getting apprehensive about the US 'game' in the post-2014 scenario. One probable scenario on the drawing board of the security establishment was that by 2020 the US would try to establish control over the energy supply routes of China. 'But it seems that our fears have come true now,' a senior official explained to me. As China has become the world's second-largest economy, much before the expected time frame, many reports indicate that the scramble for securing the South China Sea and Strait of Hormuz has already started. The security establishment does not want to be caught in this tug of war because of Pakistan's energy corridor strategic position. At the same time they are not sure about the future of Afghanistan, where they believe Pakistan should have a say in the final settlement. This desire to interfere in Afghanistan's internal affairs is very old and has resultantly antagonized the majority of Afghans and power players. The driving argument given by Pakistan in favour of this stance is that it does not want to have a pro-India government in Afghanistan.

Pakistani security establishment is now more worried about the north-western borders, where NATO forces intend to stay for long. Their apprehensions are that the US would give support to Balochistan's separatists to control Gawadar and use it as base against Iran and control the Central Asian energy supply line to China. Thus, the establishment has changed its tactics not because normalization of relations is the long over-due need of Pakistan, the apprehensions about the future policies of the US has forced them to at least 'diffuse' the tension with India. In an interview a senior security official, who does not want to be named, told me that while Chinese officials do not dictate Pakistan, they usually give their own example about how their approach helped them in moving ahead in their relations with India. 'In the case of relations with

India they have advised us to follow their example. The Chinese have normalized business relations with India although they have a number of outstanding border disputes with them. Pakistani establishment has taken this hint or advice,' this official confided.

A question is raised by the sceptics as to why DPC was encouraged to spread hatred against India and the US? They are against the decision to normalize economic relations with India. This question is raised on the presumption that the DPC and religious parties are puppets of the military establishment. This may be true partially, but it should be kept in mind that the establishment of any country, including Pakistan, is not monolithic. For the top brass DPC is only serving as a pressure tool against the US administration. The Pakistani establishment has been cleverly using the negative propaganda that Islamic extremists are very strong in Pakistan because it scares the US and its allies. They want to scare the world that it's better to deal with the moderate Pakistani establishment or else the Taliban would take over a nuclear country. But at the same time the rank and file of DPC genuinely believes in anti-Indianism and anti-Americanism.

Also, since the 1990s a paradigm shift has been seen in the position taken by the Pakistani business community vis-à-vis economic relations with India. The same class used to be against opening up trade in the past, fearing that it would not be able to compete in the open market. What brought this change of heart? One, Pakistan's business, which grew under protectionist policies, has finally come of age to acquire a level of confidence where it is willing to compete with its Indian counterpart. As the Indian rupee is still stronger and cost of production rising since the turn of the century, Pakistani businessmen are eyeing the Indian market of over one billion people. Most importantly, fears that they would not be able to compete with India were washed away, once they braved the avalanche of cheap Chinese products coming into Pakistan. The inflow of Chinese consumer products became possible because the previous government lowered the import duty tariff and there was no World Trade Organization (WTO) caveat to restrain imports from our 'best friend'. This ended the era of protectionism, which was at the cost of the consumers – the common man. Take for example import of knocked-down Chinese motorbikes, which pushed down the Japanese bikes prices overnight by 20 per cent. This did not close the market leaders Atlas Honda. On the contrary, its Chairman

Yusuf Shirazi admitted to me that they were still making more bikes and selling at premium claiming that they have better quality. Similarly, the number of Chinese motorbike assemblers and electronic goods industry mushroomed in Pakistan, employing thousands of people directly and indirectly. This debunked the claim of the industry, which sought protection all in the name of creating local jobs. Cheaper consumer goods expand the market and the businesses are forced to sharpen their competing skills.

The establishment was lobbied by the Pakistan Business Council or PBC (Pakistan's big business lobbying organization) and Federation of Pakistan Chambers of Commerce and Industry (FPCCI) to allow opening up the trade barriers with India. From the Indian side the Confederation of Indian Industries (CII) has also played a major role in softening the Indian establishment for the normalization of trade relations between the two countries. A leading businessman of Pakistan, Mian Muhammad Mansha told me that there is a huge market for Pakistani textiles in India. 'We are thinking of appointing our franchisees in India for our textile products.' He is not alone. There are many others who, though hesitant about the reaction of Pakistani intelligence and some Indian non-tariff trade barriers, are quite hopeful to enter the market where the size of the middle class is as big as the European population.

Similarly, Pakistani cement industry, which has almost 40 per cent excess capacity, is eagerly waiting for the development of better infrastructure facilities for expanding its exports to India by road and rail. As India does not have limestone availability from Wagha to Delhi, cement is brought from considerable distance in the fast-growing Indian states of Punjab and Haryana. This could be a dollar-churning opportunity for Pakistani cement industry, which is at present groaning under heavy debts of banks. The utilization of capacity will also increase their loan repayment capacity, which will be helpful for the banks. Cement exports to India can shoot up if hurdles in the way of the exports of cement to India are removed. Information technology is another area of great potential. Though India has a booming IT industry fetching around $50 billion in exports, the cost of human resource in India has been rising consistently, giving Pakistan an edge. The Indian IT industry leaders, who visited Pakistan under the 'Aman ki Asha' initiative run by two large media groups of Pakistan and India, feel that they can subcontract large volume of IT business to Pakistan if the trade relations normalize and they are allowed to set up joint ventures.[5]

One of the major impediments to expanding trade between the two countries has been the nonexistence of branches of each others banks. The decision by the central banks of both the countries to allow their banks to open branches has been made and applications of the banks were in the process of approval in September 2012. Modalities of removing other non-tariff barriers signing of a customs cooperation agreement, mutual recognition agreement and redressal of grievances agreement are also being worked out. Though official figures stand at $ 2 billion, estimates are that the unofficial trade between the two countries is over $5 billion, excluding the smuggling of goods. The balance of trade with India is expected to remain tilted against Pakistan – a point which anti-peace lobby never tires of making. This imbalance may not go away but Pakistani businessmen told me in background interviews, under restricted trade regime much of the trade between the two counties is being done through third countries. UAE is one of the major routes. But as Pakistan has agreed to grant MFN status to India (effective from 2013), Pakistani businessmen feel that direct trade will increase in the coming years.

In fact, India has gone a step ahead in normalization of business relations – something it had always demanded in the Confidence Building Measures (CBM) talks with Pakistan. It has allowed Pakistanis to invest in India. Pakistan would indeed benefit by reciprocating this measure. Given the fact that both countries share many business communities like Sindhi Hindus, Parsis, Gujaratis, Punjabis and Bohras, there is wider scope for investment in each other's countries. A leading Pakistan hotelier Byram Avari says: 'Peace between the two countries would be strengthened if the businessmen have long-term investments in each other's countries. The expansion of the economic relations would create a strong foundation for a lasting peace, only if our establishment allows debundling it, from other complex historical disputes. India and China have done that and today China is the biggest trade partner of India.'[6]

To keep the normailzation process going 'uninterrupted and uninterruptable', to borrow Mani Shankar Aiyar's term, both the countries have to allow unrestricted people-to-people contacts as the perception of the people who visit India or Pakistan changes dramatically. It is the goodwill bank of peoples' relations that needs to be built as it cannot be robbed by any terrorist outfit.

Though political leaderships of both countries have apparently moved towards making peace, the intelligence agencies on both sides need to be reined in. The tendency of the intelligence agencies in almost all the security states is to run 'invisible governments' of their own. British political analyst Jonathan Paris has rightly pointed out that since in India, Research and Analysis Wing (R&AW) is controlled by the civilian government, it 'should be easier for India' to control it. In Pakistan the civilian government has failed so far to bring ISI under its control. These intelligence services have been fighting tit-for-tat wars 'through the use of proxies.'[7]

In conclusion, Pakistan has to remember Niccolò Machiavelli's advice to smaller nations: 'Small states should ensure that their friends are nearby and their enemies are as far away as possible.' And India has to remember former British Prime Minister William Ewart Gladstone's advise: 'It is one of the uniform and unfailing rules that guide human judgment, if not at the moment yet of history, that when a long relation has existed between a Nation of superior strength and one of inferior strength and when that relation has gone wrong, the responsibility and guilt rests in the main upon the stronger rather than upon the weak.'

Notes and References:

1. Sundeep Waslekar, *The Final Settlement: Restructuring India Pakistan Relations*, International Centre for Peace Initiatives, Strategic Foresight Group, Mumbai, 2008.
2. Ibid.
3. *Daily Millat*, Faisalabad.
4. Maliha Lodhi, 'Mixed Scorecard', *The News*, 23 August 2012.
5. 'Aman Ki Asha' (Hope for Peace) is the peace initiative of the Jang Group of Pakistan and *The Times of India* Group.
6. Byram Avari's speech at the South Asia Free Media Association's Karachi–Mumbai Exchange Seminar in 2007.
7. Jonathan Paris, 'Prospects for Pakistan', Legatum Institute, London, 2010.

Chapter 26

PAKISTAN–CHINA ENDURING RELATIONS

Pakistan moved closer to China particularly when the latter's relations started deteriorating with the Soviet Union. The China–Soviet differences had strong ideological overtone as the former rubbished the economic reforms carried out by the Soviet and dubbed them as 'capitalist roaders'.

As discussed at the very outset of this chapter Pakistan, a weak and small state compared to its declared adversary, needed support to balance its standing with India. It was conscious from the very beginning of being surrounded by two huge nations – India and China. It was also afraid of the Soviet Union's lengthening shadow particularly when Afghanistan was the only nation that opposed the membership of Pakistan in the United Nations. Against this backdrop it moved to develop close relations with China. It is Pakistan's most stable relationship: one, because the Chinese have always been patient with Pakistan; two, they do not interfere in the tumultuous domestic politics of the country; and three, they see Pakistan as a counter-balancing force to India.

The Pakistan–China relations were best explained recently by an authentic NDU report: 'Pakistan-China relationship is unique and enduring. Both countries have different belief systems yet the friendship is bound by a high level of trust. It has matured into a comprehensive partnership at multiple levels, especially in the political and security domains. Whilst it is recognized to be of crucial importance for the

National Security of Pakistan, it is of equal importance in the regional security considerations of Beijing. '*The defining moments in the Pakistan China [sic] relationship can be traced back to 1956, the year of first high level visits and 1963 Trans Karakoram Tract Treaty.*'[1] (Author's emphasis.) What the cautious NDU paper has for obvious reasons not mentioned is that in an earlier real defining moment Pakistan refused to support India during China–India War in 1962 in spite of the US pressure. And it had settled its own border issues with China in 1962. This was the changed position of Pakistan as earlier it had ambivalent policy regarding China's entry in the UN. Though Pakistan had recognized China as early as 1950, it used to abstain on the issue of granting membership to China under pressure from the US. It had also criticized China on the Tibet issue, though it did not succumb to the US dictates and was the first country to start a flight to China. On the other hand former Foreign Secretary Abdul Sattar has paid 'tribute' for the relations between the two countries 'to the wisdom and foresight of Chinese leaders that Beijing continued to show extraordinary forbearance, overlooking Pakistan's aberrations.'[2]

The Chinese support during the Pakistan–India War in 1965 was the real turning point, although China had advised not to start the war. As the Pakistani establishment was pretty disappointed with the US, which had stopped military supplies on the grounds that Pakistan had violated its undertaking that arms given to it would not be used against India. Eminent writer Anwar H. Syed highlights this point: 'Of the Pakistan allies Iran and Turkey supported her vigorously, as did Jordan, Syria, Saudi Arabia and Indonesia. But of all the Pakistan supporters, China spoke the loudest. It gave Pakistan unqualified moral support and at the same time, threatened India with grave 'consequences' for allegedly violating Chinese territory along the Sikkim border. But after the Chinese sent an ultimatum to India, the American and British ambassadors advised him (Ayub Khan) that the Chinese action might lead to a general, and possibly nuclear, war. Unwilling to risk relations with the United States, and unnerved by the thought of large war, Ayub Khan now appealed to the Chinese to withdraw the ultimatum.'[3] Syed says that Prime Minister Zulfikar Ali Bhutto and senior Pakistani diplomats told him that the 'Chinese had not been consulted before the government of Pakistan had made the decision to send "freedom-fighters" to the Indian side of Kashmir. In fact hardly any of Ayub Khan's or other officials – beyond Mr Bhutto, General Akhtar Malik [who trained the "freedom-fighters" and apparently not so well], and a few other generals – knew the plan.'[4] But Pakistan was encouraged when the visiting Chinese Premier Zhou Enlai supported its stance on Kashmir in a joint communiqué saying that the dispute should be solved according to the understanding between Pakistan and India, and the wishes of the Kashmiri people.

Pakistan moved closer to China particularly when the latter's relations started deteriorating with the Soviet Union. The China–Soviet differences had strong ideological overtone as the former rubbished the economic reforms carried out by the Soviet and dubbed them as 'capitalist roaders'. Those who were against Mao Zedong's 'great leap forward' and 'cultural revolution' in China were packed to the reformatory cells in the oblivion. This also divided the communist parties in most of the countries. Pakistan was no exception. The pro-Chinese communist were thus, the new supporters of their government's closer relations with China.

Not only did China create pressure on India during the 1965 War, it also moved in to give substantial military assistance to Pakistan, which was badly needed in view of the embargo imposed by the US. General Ayub Khan used to give such great importance to the Chinese card that he made a clandestine visit to 'Beijing on the night of 19/20 September [1965] .... Neither Ayub nor Bhutto, who accompanied him, was prepared however to accept an offer of unconditional support from Zhou Enlai dependent on Pakistanis preparedness to fight a long guerilla-type war in "which cities like Lahore might be lost" but the 'Indian forces would be sucked into a quagmire of popular resistance.'[5] It was undoubtedly the Chinese leader's attempt to get the common enemy drawn at the cost of Pakistan. Somehow sanity prevailed and Ayub Khan accepted the ceasefire, as he could see that Pakistan had not much to fight India. Although Pakistan did not follow the Chinese advice, China has always sided with Pakistan and has, at times, used its veto power in Pakistan's favour. It has also extended financial aid to Pakistan and helped it to build heavy industries – Kamra Aeronautical Complex, Karakoram Highway, and more recently the Gwadar Port in Balochistan.

During the 1971 Pakistan–India War, China again supported Pakistan. It blamed India for having interfered in the domestic affairs of Pakistan and 'continued to supply military equipment under existing agreements and extended political support to the Pakistan position in the

United Nation.'[6] It was only when Pakistan was internationally isolated as it had launched military action against the people of East Pakistan (now Bangladesh) and realizing that it would not be able to squash the independence movement in East Pakistan, China's support turned more rhetorical than substance. According to Ian Talbot, director of the Centre for South Asian Studies, Coventry University, London campus: 'The delivery of military aircrafts, which it promised only arrived after the fighting had ceased.'[7]

Strong military-to-military links between China and Pakistan have always been comforting for the security establishment of the latter state. The Pakistani security forces closely watched India's desire to acquire nuclear weapons. In 1958 Indian nuclear scientist Dr Homi Bhabha 'felt confident enough to publically proclaim that India could produce a nuclear explosive devise within eighteen months of the political decision to do so.'[8] But first nuclear explosion was made by China in 1964, six years before India did. This also gave Pakistan assurance of balance of power in the region and motivated it to get closer to China. Over the years China has assisted Pakistan in its nuclear and missile programme, which is one of the most important developments for Pakistan. The Pakistani security establishment's estimate was that the time to choose between the US and China would come around 2020. The establishment's probable scenario was that China would be able to compete with the US economically and militarily by 2020. But according to an updated assessment, 2020 has arrived now and the scramble for covering the energy routes, they feel would become acute by 2014, once the US forces pull out from Afghanistan.

The spectre haunting the custodians of Pakistan's national security is of Americans trying to get control of Balochistan's warm water in the post-Afghanistan scenario. They reason that the Americans are planning to keep control over the energy routes of China. Remember, the great American plan to have a Bamboo-curtain around China in the East, and to control the Persian/Arabian Gulf? In this game Balochistan's waters and natural resources are important.

Pakistan has given Gwadar Port in Balochistan (February 2013) for operation and investment in the infrastructure around the port. Chinese company bought over the rights from the Singaporean Company. Pakistan government has also approved Iran–Pakistan Gas pipeline project, much to the dislike of the US.

Notes and References:

1. National Strategic Paper – 'Pakistan China Strategic Relationship Issues, Challenges and Opportunities' 2011-12.
2. Abdul Sattar, *Pakistan's Foreign Policy 1947-2009*, Oxford University Press, Karachi, p. 78.
3. Anwar Hussain Syed, *China and Pakistan Diplomacy of an Entente Cordiale*, University of Massachusetts Press, Amherst and Oxford University Press, London, p. 109.
4. Ibid., p. 116.
5. Ian Talbot, *Pakistan: A Modern History*, Hurst & Company, London, 2005, p. 178. Note: Talbot has quoted this incident from Altaf Gauhur *Ayub Khan: Pakistan's First Military Ruler*, Oxford University Press, New York, 1996.
6. Abdul Sattar, *Pakistan's Foreign Policy: A Concise History 1947-2009* by, Oxford University Press, Karachi, 2010, p. 132.
7. Ian Talbot, Pakistan: A Modern History, Hurst & Company, London, p. 212.
8. Naeem Salik, *The Genesis of South Asian Nuclear Deterrence: Pakistan Perspective*, Oxford University Press, Karachi, 2009, p. 15.

Chapter 27

PAKISTAN–SAUDI ARABIA – A SOURCE OF RISING RELIGIOSITY

The Pakistani extremist groups ... are a direct challenge to national security but because of the close relations of Pakistani establishment with the ruling family of Saudi Arabia, Pakistan has never protested to the Saudi government or urged that the support to various Islamist groups should be stopped or at least the finances should be routed through the official channels only.

Saudi Arabia monarchs draw their strength from two major sources: One, the US government's assurance to protect the government of the House of Saud; two, from the custodianship of Makkah and Medina – the two most-revered holy places for the Muslims of the world. The latter source has led successive Saudi Arabian governments to develop strong bond with the Sunni Muslim states and the Muslim diaspora around the world. It was this importance to the Muslim audience, which resulted in the support of Pakistan movement because it was created in the name of Islam.

Pakistani leaders in the early years had the delusion that the newly born populous Muslim country, which was made in the name of Islam, would ultimately play a major role in the Muslim 'Ummah'. This was short-lived delusion, as pan-Arabism was a stronger bond than Pan-Islamism. Even within the Arab countries, each nation is more wedded to the secular idea of being a separate nation than pan-religions nationalism. The days of dying caliphate, in which temporal and divine power were ostensibly combined, came to an end in the early twentieth century with the removal of the Ottoman Caliph of Turkey. But the real warming up of relations with Saudi Arabia started during Zulfikar Ali Bhutto's government, when the Gulf countries gained control over their oil assets in 1972 and came into big money. They started many mega development projects in their countries and Pakistan was their first stop for hiring construction workers and some middle-rank officers. Although Saudi Arabia has now diversified its labour requirement by tapping other sources like Bangladesh and Indian Muslims, Pakistan still gets over $600 million remittances from the workers placed there.

Saudi Arabia supported Pakistan on the most important issues like Kashmir and during the wars with India in return for being provided with military support to the ruling family in times of crisis and for defending them against internal threat. Pakistan was quick to send troops to defend Saudi Arabia in the 1990–91 Gulf War in spite of the fact that some military generals wanted to support Iraq, which had moved into Kuwait. Pakistan stationed about 15,000 of its troops in Saudi Arabia to defend it. Pakistan's Air Force pilots flew Saudi aircrafts when it attacked Yemen. Unconfirmed reports are that Saudi Arabia was the only country, which was consulted by Pakistan when it decided to go for the nuclear explosion in May 1998, as also that Pakistan passed on some missiles to this trusted friend. In return, Saudi Arabia agreed to give oil on deferred payment. This $500 million oil loan was later converted into a grant by Saudi Arabia. This came as a great relief for the Nawaz Sharif government, which was slapped with sanctions by the US government to punish it for going ahead with the nuclear weapon declaration.

The Pakistan military has close relations with Saudi Arabia. Under the 1982 Defence Agreement it was agreed to place a sizeable contingent of Pakistan forces in Saudi Arabia on deputation. These relations were further expanded when the Pervez Musharraf government and Saudi monarchs decided to support war against terrorism. An interesting aspect of the 2006 Defence Agreement was that it talked about sharing technology.[1] Everyone knows that there is not much technology available in Saudi Arabia, hence it was interpreted as transfer of technology from Pakistan. And what Pakistan has is nuclear and missile technology that the Saudis cannot buy off the shelf from their close ally – the US. However, the flip side is the involvement of Saudi Arabia in the 1980s

US–Pakistan led jihad against the Afghanistan government and its Soviet allies. Saudi Arabia, according to US congressional reports, matched every dollar which the US spent on financing the 'Islamic jihad' against the infidel Soviets. It was not the support to the Afghan Mujahideen only; it was also heavy Saudi investment in support of the hard line Sunni Islamists in Pakistan. The number of Deobandi madrassahs proliferated rapidly to 64 per cent of the total madrassahs in Pakistan, though majority of Pakistanis do not subscribe to this sect.[2] The Saudi monarchy was equally worried about the overthrow of Shah of Iran by a people's movement, which was hijacked by the Shia clergy. But their real protégé in Pakistan are the Ahle-Hadith, the Wahabis preferred to be called with his name in Pakistan. Prof. Saleem H. Ali has noted that the 'Saudi Arabian organization Harmain Islamic Foundation is said to have helped the Ahle-Hadith and made them powerful. Indeed the Lashkar-e-Tayyaba [sic], an organization which has been active in Kashmir, belongs to Ahle-Hadith.'[3] This organization is the major anti-Indian jihadi outfit and allegedly master-minded the Mumbai carnage to sabotage the peace overtures made by the Pakistan politicians.

However, the arrest of Abu Jundal, a Lashkar terrorist and his handing over to India is interpreted by some security analysts as a change in Saudi policy towards India. India has become one of the major buyers of Saudi oil and has trade partnership with it touching $25 billion. Saudi investment in Pakistan is far less than the latter looks forward to. The relations with Pakistan since the induction of the PPP-led government have cooled down comparatively to what they were with the previous government. The Saudis want to bet on Nawaz Sharif, a conservative Sunni Muslim, instead of Shia Zardari who is keen on implementing the Iran–Pakistan Gas Pipeline Project. But the Saudi government meetings with Pakistan in the fall of 2012 suggest that the importance of Pakistan–Saudi relations will not diminish in view of the rise in 'Riyadh-Tehran tensions and increasing sectarian uncertainty in Eastern Saudi Arabia and Bahrain, which is why Prince Bandar bin Sultan bin Abdulaziz met with President Zardari in Islamabad in March 2011. The Shia–Sunni conflict is becoming more intense in the Middle East. Journalist and writer Lesley Hazleton has underlined '[i]n the Middle East heartland of Islam, Shia are closer to 50 per cent, wherever oil reserves are richest – Iran, Iraq and the Persian Gulf coast, including eastern Saudi Arabia – they are in the majority ... Shia Iran and Sunni Saudi Arabia today vie with each other for influence and political leadership of the Islamic world, a power struggle demonstrated most painfully in the cities of Iraq and in the mountains of Afghanistan and Pakistan.'[4]

The financing of Sunni extremists by Saudi Arabia and Shia groups by Iran has unleashed a proxy sectarian war in Pakistan. The Saudization of Islam and culture with Saudi government support is affecting the otherwise-tolerant Islamic values of Pakistan, which have a strong Sufi influence. The Saudi support to the Islamic organizations comes from the government and non-government sources. The Rabbat-e-Aalam-e-Islami based in Makkah is one such major source. But what is dangerous for the countries like Pakistan is that Wahabi ideology is also exported with the funding, which 'has certainly helped in promoting a Jihadist vision though often with the acquiescence of the Western government.'[5] The Afghan jihad of the 1980s against the progressive Afghanistan government and its Soviet supporters was one such example. Even at present Saudi government maintains close relations with the major jihadi groups of Pakistan and Afghan Taliban. The Pakistani extremist groups are involved in sectarian killings of Shias and Sunnis as well. These groups are a direct challenge to national security but because of the close relations of Pakistani establishment with the ruling family of Saudi, Pakistan has never protested to the Saudi government or urged that the support to various Islamist groups should be stopped or at least the finances should be routed through the official channels only.

Notes and References:

1. *Foreign Affairs Pakistan*, Issue IV, Vol. xxx, May-June 2003.
2. Muhammad Amir Rana, *A to Z of Jehadi Organizations in Pakistan*, Mashal Books, Lahore, 2007.
3. Saleem H. Ali, *Islam and Education: Conflict and Conformity in Pakistan's Madrassahs*, Oxford University Press, Karachi, 2009, p. 37.
4. Lesley Hazleton, *After the Prophet: The Epic Story of the Shia-Sunni Split*, Anchor Books, London, 2009, pp. 209–210.
5. Ibid., p. 100.

Chapter 28

PAKISTAN–IRAN RELATIONS – A BALANCING ACT

In the changing regional geopolitics Iran and Pakistan are getting closer to China, which is expected to gradually drift Pakistan away from the US, particularly in post-2014 withdrawal of US/NATO forces from Afghanistan. This changing geopolitical situation has also hardened the views of the Pakistani establishment.

Pakistan was recognized by Iran in May 1948, which encouraged Prime Minister Liaquat Ali Khan to visit it in March 1949. The Shah of Iran, Mohammad Reza Pahlavi, was the first foreign head of state to visit Pakistan in May 1950 and subsequently both the countries entered into a Friendship Treaty, the first ever to be signed by Pakistan.

Pakistan's relations with its Western neighbour have not remained steady as it has to balance it vis-à-vis the US and Saudi interests in the region. During the days of the Shah, Pakistan had excellent relation with Iran, as both the countries were members of CENTO, which was a US-sponsored anti-Soviet alliance. Iran supported Pakistan during the 1965 War with India and even allowed Pakistan Air Force to park its fighter at its bases – giving strategic depth, which Pakistan needed. Pakistan supported Iran during the eight-year Iran–Iraq War despite Saudi Arabia's displeasure, which backed Iraq. 'Pakistan's transfer of nuclear technology to Iran can be regarded as a product of their long nourished relationship. Pakistan-Iran nuclear cooperation began in the

1980s during Zia-ul-Haq's rule. The transfer of technology to Iran was continued even under the civilian governments of Benazir Bhutto and Nawaz Sharif.'[1]

This relationship was further expanded after the liberation of Bangladesh in 1971, which created fears that the remaining Pakistan might also prove fragile in view of discontent in the smaller province. Both countries have almost similar policy towards the simmering independence movement in Pakistan and Iranian Balochistan. Even today there is agreement that the Greater Balochistan movement on both sides of the border has to be quashed by force.

Both Pakistan and Iran played an important role against the Left-wing government of Afghanistan, which came in power in April 1978 and its Soviet supporters. The Islamist military government in Pakistan and the monarchy in Iran were apprehensive of the Left wing in their countries and feared that the Soviets might move in to Pakistani Balochistan to get access to the warm waters. They supported the Mujahideen's insurgency in Afghanistan with the support of the US exploiting the religious feelings of the Afghan tribes. But there was one difference, which cast a shadow on Pakistan–Iran relations and Afghan politics – the Iranian theocracy, which came into power in early 1979, supported the Shia militants of Herat, Hazara tribes and northern Afghanistan militant groups, while Pakistan backed Sunni Deobandi and Wahabi insurgents as it was funded by Saudi Arabia. This sectarian divide created many Sunni and Shia armed groups in Pakistan as stated above. Sectarian killing claim more lives today than does any other form of terrorism and is considered to be a Saudi–Iranian proxy war. The state in Pakistan has not been able to contain Shia killings. According to a blog 'Let us build Pakistan', 19,000 Shias have been killed by the Sunni extremist groups between 2001 and 2012.

Conflict of interest in Afghanistan, where Iran supports the Shia ethnic groups and the Northern Alliance parties while Pakistan is backing hardliner Sunni Taliban, Iran's growing relations with India and rising Shia killings in Pakistan will continue to remain sensitive points in their relations. Both countries have a problem that they rely on religion as once a country declares that it is a religious country it cannot escape the question – which sect of the religion?

The PPP-led government is resisting the US pressure, which is evident from the meeting between President Asif Ali Zardari and

President Mahmoud Ahmadinejad in Baku, Azerbaijan, in February 2012. At the side-line of the 12th Economic Cooperation Organisation (ECO) meeting 'Asif Zardari and President Ahmadinejad called for expediting work on projects like the Iran-Pakistan gas pipeline, the 1,000MW [megawatt] Taftan-Quetta power transmission line, 100MW Gwadar power supply project, construction of Nushki-Dalbandin section of Quetta-Taftan highway and upgradation of Quetta-Taftan railway track.'[2] This is in defiance of the US and Saudi pressure. The US has managed to get sanctions imposed on trade with Iran by the UN and has been putting pressure on Pakistan not to pursue the Iran–Pakistan Gas Pipeline Project. Iran has already completed laying of pipeline on its side, but because of US pressure Pakistan is finding it difficult to finance the multi-billion dollar project. But brushing aside US pressure the Zardari government has signed agreement with Iran for financing the gas pipeline in Pakistan in February 2013. For the energy-starved Pakistan, supply of gas and electricity from Iran is crucial for its economy, but the American administration has been insisting that Pakistan should concentrate on the Turkmenistan–Afghanistan–Pakistan (TAP) gas pipeline project. Afghanistan is not expected to stabilize in the medium term, which means there can be no safe passage for the gas pipeline through it. In 1995, at The Economist Conference, roundtable with the Government of Pakistan, I had maintained that this project was not possible because Afghanistan would not settle down for the next 15 years at least. The then Minister of State Sardar Aseff Ahmed Ali contradicted me because he had great hopes in the Taliban takeover of Afghanistan, who were described by the Interior minister as 'our boys'. It seems I had underestimated the timeframe in which Afghanistan would stabilize.

In the changing regional geopolitics Iran and Pakistan are getting closer to China, which is expected to gradually drift Pakistan away from the US, particularly in post-2014 withdrawal of US/NATO forces from Afghanistan. This changing geopolitical situation has also hardened the views of the Pakistani establishment. As stated earlier, it fears that the US is supporting the Balochistan independence movement against Pakistan and Iran to counter Chinese influence in the Strait of Hormuz. Almost 20 per cent of the world's oil is transported through this route. Gwadar, which is situated just outside the Strait of Hormuz tip, has thus acquired immense importance in this energy route-control politics.

This has great implications for the politics of Balochistan, a province which is 44 per cent of Pakistan's territory and just 4.5 per cent of the country's population. The new relations with Iran will have to be based upon mutual interests, independent of Saudi and US relations. Similarly, the Balochistan issue will have to be resolved by Pakistan by giving maximum autonomy and winding up the undeclared military operation, if it wants to secure this province from the forthcoming struggle. The Islamic fraternity and nation card has worn out. It would not work. Only neutral, democratic and secular policies would be able to withstand international pressures that are gathering momentum.

Notes and References:

1. Shah Alam, 'Iran–Pakistan Relations: Political and Strategic Dimensions', *Strategic Analysis*, Vol. 28, The Institute of Defence Studies and Analysis, New Delhi, 2004.
2. *Dawn*, 17 October 2012.

Chapter 29

PAKISTAN–AFGHANISTAN – RELATIONS OF MISTRUST

For the next decade, Pakistan aided by the US, Saudi Arabia
and China trained, armed and provided safe haven to all the
Islamic militants of the world. This was the biggest mistake
of the military establishment as it did not foresee how hugely
it would compromise the national security of the country.

The short-sighted policy of Pakistan's national security managers that it should have a client Afghan government, which could provide strategic depth to Pakistan against any threat from India, has boomeranged. Afghanistan today is the bottomless quagmire for Pakistan and extricating from it is becoming difficult. Pakistan is paying huge human, economic and political cost for its dangerous policies in Afghanistan. Over 50,000 Pakistanis have been killed in terrorist attacks, over 3,500 soldiers have lost their lives in combats with the Al Qaeda-franchised jihadi organizations, and Pakistan's economy has suffered a loss of over $70 billion in the last ten years because of political instability and economic insecurity caused by the terrorists. Terrorists attacks on the military and other security forces, assassinations of political and religious leaders and bombing of public places even mosques and shrines have created a sense of insecurity among the people. The country is facing brain drain, particularly of the educated youth who are precious to Pakistan's human resource power.

The world powers have hyphenated Pakistan's fate with Afghanistan. It is a reality much disliked by Pakistan's ruling establishment. All the existential threats to Pakistan are unfortunately real and there is no light on the other side of the tunnel, at least not in medium-term future. Why Pakistan has landed itself in this quagmire is often blamed by the Right-wing parties and intellectuals on the U-turn taken by the Musharraf regime after the 9/11 terrorist attacks in the US. They dub the Pakistan 'war against terrorism' as a US-imposed one disregarding the history of Pakistan–Afghanistan difficult relations. Let's review some of the sticking points of this relationship, which have led us into the present bloody impasse.

Pakistan got a rude shock when, instead of welcoming the creation of an 'Islamic State', Afghanistan, which has an overwhelmingly staunch Muslim population, was the only country that opposed its membership to the United Nations on 30 September 1947. Afghanistan's stance was a clear manifestation of the political fact that 'ethnic solidarity' is usually stronger than 'religious solidarity'. The Afghan government was in favour of independence of 'Pakhtunistan'. Historically, the 'Pakhtunistan' issue took birth when Sir Mortimer Durand drew a line to define the frontiers of Amir Abdur Rahman Khan's dominion and the British rule in the NWFP in 1883. The Afghan rulers were not happy about this demarcation. The 1919 Anglo-Afghan War launched by King Amanullah Khan, who was a great reformer, to liberate his nation from British influence. British defeated Amanullah with their superior war machinery, bombed Kabul and Jalalabad, and his government was forced to sign a treaty in Rawalpindi conceding the Durand Line. The issue was revived when the British were leaving India as the nationalist Pakhtun leader Khan Abdul Ghaffar Khan demanded independence. The Afghan government supported his demand that a third option should be given to the people in the referendum asking whether or not they wanted to have an independent Pakhtunistan. But the British who had worked to raise Islamic forces in NWFP to support the Muslim League gave only two options: whether the people of NWFP wanted to join India or Pakistan. Zahir Shah's government in Afghanistan thus never had warm relations with Pakistan and was closer to India. Another strong reason was that Afghanistan was friendly with the super power next door – the Soviet Union, while Pakistan had aligned itself in an anti-communist alliance with the US.

Pakistan was always wary of the Indian influence in Afghanistan and felt itself encircled by the 'enemy no. 1' – India. In July 1973 Mohammad Daoud Khan ousted King Zahir Shah in a coup supported by the Leftist parties of Afghanistan. As he was known-supporter of Pakhtunistan, the relations between Pakistan and Afghanistan deteriorated even further. About the same time Prime Minister Zulfikar Ali Bhutto dismissed the NAP government in Balochistan and launched a military operation against its supporters who had taken to the mountains for armed resistance. NAP-led government in NWFP resigned in protest. The NAP's Pakhtun leaders had close relations with the Daoud government, its leader. This helped leading Pakhtun leader and poet Ajmal Khattak, as stated in Part II, to take refuge in Afghanistan after their rally was attacked by Bhutto's FSF in Rawalpindi. To get even with Daoud's government, Bhutto armed and supported the Islamist insurgency in Afghanistan led by Gulbuddin Hekmatyar. The game of using non-state jihadi actors to further the national security was revived. Under pressure from the Shah of Iran and Pakistan, Daoud 'agreed to a three-cornered deal involving him, Bhutto and the Shah of Iran. It was agreed that in return for Daoud's approval of Durand Line as permanent frontier, Bhutto would release the Pashtun leaders of National Awami Party, while the Shah would provide up to 3 billion dollars aid.'[1]

The Durand Line issue still hangs over the relations of the two countries. But as Pakistan support is needed by the US for withdrawing from Afghanistan the US reiterated its stand in October 2012, when US Special Envoy for Afghanistan and Pakistan Marc Grossman told an Afghan TV channel that 'our policy is that border [2,640 kms border between Afghanistan and Pakistan] is the international border.' The State Department later reasserted the position taken by Grossman that 'we see this as the internationally accepted border.'[2] However, in a rejoinder the Afghan Foreign Ministry said 'it rejects and considers irrelevant any statement by anyone about the legal status of this line.'[3] This shows that in spite of its existing trouble and the help needed by the Kabul government, it still maintains the 1947 stand on the Durand Line that the agreement with the British was obtained under duress.

When Daoud decided to move against the People's Democratic Party of Afghanistan (PDPA), which had strong support in the military, the PDPA removed him in April 1978, established its control, and announced many progressive reforms. But once again General Zia-ul-Haq's regime in Pakistan organized Islamist insurgency using Afghan refugees, who had fled the Left government reforms. Hekmatyar once again came handy in this game. PDPA was described as a communist party by intelligence agent Anthony Arnold.[4] Take over of power by PDPA thus attracted CIA, which started supporting the Afghan Mujahideen cautiously. 'The CIA time-honoured practice was to introduce into a conflict area weapons that cannot be traced back to the United States. Hence, the spy agency's first shipment to scattered Afghan rebels – enough small arms and ammunition to equip a thousand men – consisted of weapons made by the Soviets themselves that had been stockpiled by the CIA for just such a moment.'[5] This support started multiplying once Congressman, from Texas, Charlie Wilson started taking interest in this insurgency started by General Zia-ul-Haq. Dandy Wilson was lobbied by Zia's favourite lobbyist and socialite Joanne Herring. She was appointed Honorary Consul General of Pakistan to legalize payments to her. Charlie Wilson, who was a member of the Defence Appropriation Subcommittee 'knew enough about the eccentric working of the subcommittee to know when a member can act alone to fund a programme. "How much are we giving the Afghans," he asked van Wagenen. "Five million" said the staffer. There was a moment's silence. "Double it," said the Texan.'[6]

But as Professor Hassan Gardezi said in a recent article: 'The mastermind behind all these manoeuvres was Zbigniew Brzezinski, a virulent anti-communist and National Security Adviser to President Jimmy Carter. Brzezinski, in fact, admits that it was the covert operation organized by him, which drew Soviet Union into the "Afghan trap", and gave the "USSR its Vietnam war". It was by no means an easy scheme to put into effect without enlisting the immediate support of two Muslim countries, namely Pakistan, the next-door neighbour of Afghanistan with its brand new military dictator, and Saudi Arabia the authoritative seat of Salafi Islam … '[7] In fact as stated above Pakistan had taken the initiative of launching insurgency in Afghanistan before the Soviet forces entered the country. The chronology of the events proves this amply. The PDPA-led revolution came in April 1978. According to Selig Harrison's *Washington Post* article: 'The Shah, not the Kremlin touched off the Afghan coup' because Daoud under the influence of Shah had cracked down on the Leftists. The USSR forces entered Afghanistan on December 1979 – a good 18 months after the 'Saur (April) Revolution'. In between, there was factional fighting between Khalq and Parcham;

killing of US Ambassador Adolph Dubs by an extremist group in February 1979, when Afghan forces tried to rescue him; and 'in March, the guerillas killed about 40 Soviet citizens in Herat including advisers, women and children.'[8] The Soviet Union sent the forces on the invitation of the Afghan government under the 1978 Friendship Treaty with Afghanistan and invoking Article 51 of the UN Charter, which says: 'Nothing in the present charter shall impair the inherent right of individual or collective self-defence if an armed attack occurs against a member of the United Nations.'

For the next decade, Pakistan aided by the US, Saudi Arabia and China trained, armed and provided safe haven to all the Islamic militants of the world. This was the biggest mistake of the military establishment as it did not foresee how hugely it would compromise the national security of the country. Once this war was over in 1989, it used the same groups to train another batch for insurgency in India. Pakistan tried to establish the government of its choice in Afghanistan but only created ill-will against this intervention in their internal affairs to this day. After 9/11 Pakistan has continued to support the Afghan Taliban and the Haqqani group, while hunting for the Al Qaeda and 'bad Taliban' sponsored by it. All this, as stated in Part IV, has increased terrorist activities, which are existential threat to Pakistan

That Afghanistan is Pakistan's neighbour has been a blessing for the military dictators, smugglers, drug mafias and gun-runners. For the people of Pakistan the ramifications of these 'blessings' have been prolonged dictatorships; increasing terrorism; rising extremism; large number of drug addicts; weaponization of the society to the teeth; above political instability and colossal economic loss; and there are no sign in the change of policy regarding change in the existing policy that contributes to the destabilization of Afghanistan even in the post-2014 withdrawal, if it happens.

Notes and References:

1. Tariq Ali, *Can Pakistan Survive?* Pelican Books, London, 1983, p. 167.
2. *Dawn*, 26 October 2012.
3. Ibid.
4. Anthony Arnold, *Afghanistan's Two-Parties Communism: Parcham and Khalq*, Hoover Institution, Stanford University, Stanford, 1983.

5. George Crile, *Charlie Wilson's War: The Extraordinary Story of the Largest Covert Operation in History*, Vanguard Books, Lahore, 2003, p. 15.
6. Ibid., p. 20.
7. Hassan Gardezi, *US Occupation: Root cause of Terrorism?* Viewpoint Online, Issue 123, 19 October 2012.

PART - VI

PART VI

Chapter 30

A CASE FOR SECULAR PAKISTAN

'While the ISI encourages the media to give space to madcap theories by former war-mongering generals (and defence analysts), critical and thoughtful journalists and intellectuals are constantly harassed, tortured or just ostracized.'

– Ahmed Rashid

The basic argument of the book so far has been that what is purported as the ideology of Pakistan – establishing an Islamic state – was not its objective. The basic objective, as laid down in Part I, was securing the economic and political interests of the Muslim-ruling elite and the 'Salariats' to borrow Hamza Alavi's term for the Muslim salaried class. To mobilize the mass support religion was used as a propaganda tool. Even after acquiring a separate homeland, religion was exploited to rule the country, which in turn made Pakistan a perilous security state.

The large majority of people during the Pakistan movement lived in the rural areas and had no obstruction or pressure from the Hindu majority to follow the basic tenets of Islam – namaz (prayers), fasting, Haj (pilgrimage of Kaaba in Makkah), zakat (giving alms/wealth tax) and kalma (declaration that there is no god but God and Muhammad is His prophet).They were free to go to their places of worship. The masses were equally suppressed by the Muslim and Hindu ruling classes. The Muslim masses could not have been mobilized with a non-emotive secular slogan on the issue of division of power between the Congress-dominated federal government and Muslim elite-led provinces of the north-west and East Bengal. The Muslim Salariats could not have acquired control of the civil-military bureaucracy in the undivided India without constructing a religious nationalism narrative to attract the rural poor support for a separate homeland.

In Part II, I have traced the history of centralization of power by the ruling elite by raising the slogan of 'one Islamic nation'. Denial of a stark reality that Pakistan is a multi-ethnic country was deliberate in order to keep a strong Centre. This led eventually to the break-up of the country in 1971 and it is still a source of armed insurgency in Balochistan.

In Part III, I have discussed how Islam was exploited during the British Raj to drive a wedge between the masses of India on communal basis to serve the interest of the Muslim elite and middle class. That is why the religious leadership continues to insist that 'Ideology of Pakistan' was to implement Islamic laws and Sharia.

At the same time majority of the people want a modern democratic state. Although Pakistan turned 65 on 14 August 2012, it is still not sure of its identity. The good thing is that the debate about its identity continues, though both the people and its leaders are confused as to whether Pakistan is an 'Islamic state', or it should be a 'democratic state'. But democracy has to be secular if it is democratic in the true sense. There is a third equally strong strand, which tries to synthesize the irreconcilable two: Islamic state with Islamic laws and a modern democratic state with the laws and values of the twenty-first century polity. This predicament is being faced by most of the Muslim-majority countries whose societies are being pulled in two different directions. It is not the clash of civilizations, contrary to what was suggested by US writer Samuel Huntington, it is the clash within the Muslim societies, who being at different stages of economic development are finding it difficult to withstand the strong wind of globalization. There are multiple streams of thought and aspirations in Muslim societies that are at variance with each other.

Trouble with contemporary discourse is that it is mostly within the framework of the 'two-nation theory', 'Islamic ideology' and at best within the parameters set by the Quaid-e-Azam, Muhammad Ali Jinnah and his colleagues' political speeches. Many liberals in search of 'Jinnah's Pakistan' are heavily relying on his speech of 11 August 1947 and his interviews to the foreign media in which he had said that Pakistan would not be a theocratic state or that the state had nothing to do with religion. But at times Jinnah gave out different and contradictory messages to different audiences. To the foreign press he said in no uncertain terms that Pakistan would not be a 'theocratic state', which implicitly meant not based on religious tradition. To the ulema he assured that Pakistan would be a country where Islam and Sharia laws will apply. His 11 August speech does talk about equal rights for citizens of Pakistan irrespective of their religion, which is essential to establish a secular democracy. A reference to the British history of sectarianism alludes to the secular solution. Indeed this speech was delivered from the position of power and from an important platform only three days before Pakistan's independence and was meant to change the course of Pakistan from 'an Islamic state' to a secular democratic state. He did not need the support of the pirs or ulema at that stage, as their role to provide people's support had ended with the achievement of the 'end' that was Pakistan. This was contrary to Allama Iqbal's philosophy that when politics and Islam (Din) are separated, barbarity rules.

On hindsight it can be said that the 'Quaid-e-Azam of Pakistan' had not considered the fact, that it was not easy to go back to secular rationale after inciting people in the name of Islam. It was a clear evidence of the lack of understanding of the dialectics of political and social processes working in a society. What the secularists overlook is that one speech of Jinnah on 11 August 1947 cannot turn off the religious fervour created in ten years 1937–47 by the statements in favour of an Islamic system. The ensuing discussion since this speech has been as to what were the 'essential principles of Islam', which Jinnah had talked about in his address at many other forums? Who will decide principles of Islam – the parliament, the ulema, the religious parties? Or is it the prerogative of the Supreme Court to define the Islamic laws incorporated in the Constitution, mainly by a military regime of former President General Zia-ul-Haq? In the final analysis the Supreme Court of Pakistan is using the Islamic clauses and interpreting them in its judgments.

In Parts IV and V, I have explained that emphasis on religion was used to justify the creation of the huge war machinery, which needs an aggressive and adventurous foreign and national security policy of Pakistan. The natural corollary of this policy was giving more space and a free hand to religious extremists in the country's politics and promotion of jihad as a tool for the extension of the national security policy crafted by the armed forces. The same so-called 'assets' of the security establishment are now the biggest liability of Pakistan threatening its future. The people of Pakistan have been suffering nerve-racking uncertainty for decades because of these perilous policies. With each turn of event in the country and in the region or as far off as the US, they have been asking the same question again and again: What will happen now? Will the country survive? Will it further drift into chaos and civil war? Will democracy survive? Will the US attack or try to take over our nuclear assets? So on and so forth. It seems that all faces are now just question marks dancing around in public debate and in private gatherings.

Many writers and scholars have attempted to deal with these questions and forecast the probable future of Pakistan – the country that is described as the 'world's most dangerous.' Let us first briefly review what these pundits are forecasting.

***

Stephen P. Cohen, as stated in Part IV, has highlighted 'Six Warning Signs,' which he says 'point to the immediate and urgent issues, although none alone are sufficient to ensure normalization of Pakistan.' I list these warning signs but change the sequence on the basis of my understanding of the situation in Pakistan and prioritizing them to provide a logical flow. The six warning signs are: Further appeasement of Islamists; Fresh crisis with India; Unwillingness to deal quickly with economic issues; [Dependence on] the begging bowl; Absence of governance at the top; and Unwillingness/inability to rebuild state institutions.[1] To these six, I would add two more warnings: As mentioned in Part V, one is the fear of US–China scramble to secure the Gulf waters and their conflicting interests in the coastal belt of Balochistan. Second, widening economic inequality between the haves and have nots.

Cohen – and many other writers – concur that Pakistani society is becoming increasingly polarized between the Islamists 'who receive considerable state patronage' and the liberal democrats who are on the defensive. The rise of Islamists' militant movement to become the vanguard of Islamic jihad in the world has plunged the country in a near civil war situation. This has destabilized the country so much that both domestic and foreign investments have slowed down, economic growth has dropped; the informal sector has bourgeoned to 91 per cent of the GDP[2]; and it is difficult for the inefficient government to raise its revenue from many parts of the country to bring informal sector under the tax net. This in turn has made Pakistan an addict used to carrying a 'begging bowl'.

However, faced with the immediate threat to the country from within and fearing the post-2014 probable geostrategic scenario, there has been some realization in a section of the security establishment that tension with India has to be eased. Majority of the big business has also been pushing for normalization of relations with India, as they see huge business potential between the two countries. Pakistan's most-trusted friend China has also advised to diffuse the relations with India, keeping border dispute in the cold storage as they have done. Is this a temporary tactical move as many Indians suspect, or a conscious strategy shift? The answer to this, I feel, would be clear once the US forces withdraw from Afghanistan, where both Pakistan and India are competing with each other for creating an influence over the future government in Kabul. Finding a right equilibrium is not going to be without a tough tussle, notwithstanding the interest of the peoples of Afghanistan. Underlining the importance of this issue, professor and journalist Anatol Lieven has suggested: 'The US needs to continue to limit Indian involvement in Afghanistan if it is to have any hope of long-term cooperative relationship with Pakistan. The West also needs to seek peaceful solution of the Kashmir dispute, despite the immense obstacles in both Pakistan and India.'[3] He has quoted similar views of the former US Ambassador to Pakistan Anne Patterson. His book *Pakistan: A Hard Country* was well-received in Pakistan as many Pakistanis felt that unlike some foreign writers he has presented Pakistan as they would like to see it.

On the other hand there is a danger of jihadi forces derailing the process of building bridges with India. It cannot be ruled out. They have grouped together in the DPC and have been openly threatening that once the Afghan jihad is over, they will divert their brigades to fight a decisive battle for the independence of Kashmir. Some Al Qaeda groups go even further as they believe in an unconfirmed hadith[*] that conquest of India by Islam would lead to the establishment of the promised

---

[*]This Hadith is related to Hazrat Abu Hurairah (R.A.). He says that my intimate friend Hadhrat Muhammad (Sall-Allaho-'Alayhe-Wasallam) told me that: 'In this Ummah, the troops would be headed towards Sindh & Hind' "Hazrat Abu Hurairah (R.A.) says that if 'I could find a chance to participate in any of such movement & (while participating in it) I be got martyred, then well & good; if came back as a survived warrior, then I would be a free Abu Hurairah, to whom Allah Almighty would have given freedom from the Hell.'" Link: http://www.ghazwa-e-hind.com/english-hadith1.htm

Islamic empire over the world once again. It would be at that juncture that the maturity of both Pakistan and Indian governments would be tested. Establishments on both sides of the divide will have to be alert and prevent these adventurers from hijacking the peace process between the two countries. Pakistanis worries about the future of their country are also fuelled by the retired military conspiracy theorists like General Mirza Aslam Beg and General Hamid Gul who see American and Indian intelligence agencies behind any and all the terror attacks in Pakistan. Ahmed Rashid has pointed out that 'while the ISI encourages the media to give space to such madcap theories by former generals [and defence analysts], critical and thoughtful journalists and intellectuals are constantly harassed, tortured or just ostracized. Under such circumstances, it is not surprising that Pakistanis are worried about their future. Where will the ideas and hopes for Pakistan's future come from if the intellectual landscape is dominated by the likes of Beg, Gul, and the Mullah.'[4]

Rashid has not lost all hope unlike what the title of his last book of the trilogy suggests – *Pakistan on the Brink: The Future of Pakistan, Afghanistan and the West*. He has also shown the path back from this precipice: 'The bitter public disappointment with Asif Ali Zardari and Yousaf Raza Gilani [prime minister of Pakistan March 2008-June 2012] must not become public rejection of democracy; extremist ideology must not replace democratic aspiration. Elections must be held in 2013 without interference from extremists and the military, and a new government must take office and be allowed to govern, one hopes with better results.'[5]

Notes and References:

1. 'Pakistan: Arrival and Departure', in Stephen Philip Cohen, *The Future of Pakistan*, 2011.
2. *The News*, 16 November 2012: Pakistan Institute of Development Economics' report on informal economy based on 2007-08 data. The report was presented by M. Ali Kemal at the PIDE 28th AGM and Conference 13-15 November 2012.
3. Anatol Lieven, *Pakistan: A Hard Country*, Allen Lane, London, 2011, p. 480.
4. Ahmed Rashid, *Pakistan on the Brink*, Allen Lane, London, 2011, p. 185.
5. Ibid., p. 212.

Chapter 31

DIMENSIONS OF RELIGIOUS EXTREMISM

A question often asked is: When there are extremist strands in all religions why are Muslims extremists profiled as terrorists? One of the major reasons is that Muslim terrorists are more in number, they are spread all over the world, are more organized, more violent and above all, the Al Qaeda has given them a global agenda. Unlike others who have local issues, the Muslim extremists have the Al Qaeda manifesto to establish Islamic supremacy over the world.

An overwhelming majority of Pakistanis are against religious extremists. On 10 October 2012 TTP terrorists targeted 14-year-old Malala Yousafzai in Swat, as she had become a symbol of resistance against the Taliban's views that girls should not be educated. Though she was wounded along with her other school friends Shazia and Hina, all survived. As I write these lines (April 2013) Malala has recovered and joined a school in the UK. There was a nationwide reaction against the attack on Malala. Two daughters of Swat have galvanized the resolve of the Pakistanis to fight against religious extremism. Earlier, in 2009, a girl was publicly whipped in Swat by Taliban's moral force to which the nation reacted sharply. The government, which had earlier acquiesced to Taliban demands and agreed to implement a parallel Shariat system in Swat, had to stand up. A successful military operation was launched forcing Mullah Fazlullah and his bunch of zealots to run away across the border, which certainly encouraged the government and the military that the people will back any action taken against ruthless religious extremists. But the worrying point is that there is little debate in Pakistan on why religious extremism is violent. Some of the questions that should be debated and explored by social scientists are:

1. Is religious extremism a new phenomenon or was it embedded in the Pakistan movement in the undivided India?
2. Is religious extremism spreading and strengthening in Pakistan?
3. Does it (religious extremism) appear to be expanding because religious extremists are using terrorist tactics to achieve their ideological goals?
4. What external and internal factors have sharpened the contradiction between the religious extremists and modernists?
5. And is religious extremism and modernity contradiction specific to the Muslim societies, or are other major religions also inflicted with this malaise?

Let's briefly discuss the questions as they are on the top of Pakistanis' mind:

First, religious extremism was embedded in the propaganda of the Pakistan movement, as it was based on religious nationalism seeking emancipation from the Hindu majority that was to rule India in the post-colonial set up. This propaganda gave the extremists enough space after independence to demand for an 'Islamic State' and Sharia-based public and private laws. Israel is another state that was set up as a Jew homeland. It is also facing religious extremism because the religious extremists want the law in accordance with 'halakha' (Judaism equivalent to Sharia). Islam like Judaism maintains that it offers the complete code of life. Hence, there is constant struggle between the extremists who want all laws in accordance to the true letter and spirit of the religion, while the modernists believe in the evolution of laws and regard to social conditions. But the dialectics of religious nationalism gives more leeway to the extremists or, in the case of Pakistan you can say the Islamists, instead of modernists.

Second, is religious extremism spreading and strengthening? No. People may appear more religious but they are not attracted to extremism. The Nobel Laureate Amartya Sen has rightly pointed out in his book *Identity and Violence* that 'Islamic terrorism is a muddled vocabulary of contemporary global politics.'[1] He has observed: 'to focus just on the grand religious classification is not only to miss other significant concerns and ideas that move people; it also has the effect of generally magnifying the idea voice of religious authority. The Muslim clerics, for example, are then treated as ex-officio spokesman for the so-called Islamic world, even though great many people who happen to be Muslim by religion have profound differences with what is proposed by one mullah or another.'[2]

Closer to home good indicators are: the people have always condemned acts of terrorism by the extremists. The way of life which these extremist want to impose on the people is impractical in our society hence, while people may not contest the extremists stance in public, in action they do; there are more girls going for education and work now than they were when the extremists started forcing their agenda on the people; there are more liberal television channel dramas offering programmes opposing extremist values (religious channels are an exception); Bollywood movies are more popular today and are easily accessible than when the extremists started burning DVD shops and attacking singers; there are more fashion shows now than there were when the extremists started calling women's fashion un-Islamic; there is a bigger interest-based economy today than it was when the extremists' godfather General Zia-ul-Haq tried to Islamize the economy; and the very fact that religious extremists are using terrorist activities to gain media space for their fascist objectives shows that their argument is weak and losing. It is only the losers who try to push their cause through violent means.

Third, yes, religious extremists have become more prominent because they are using terrorist activities to attract attention, and terrorism gets more space in the media, creating uncertainty and fear among the people. But this does not mean that more people are becoming supporters of the extremists' narrative. The religious extremists know that the majority of Pakistanis are not going to vote them to power. Religious parties, which participated in the election process, did their best in the 2002 polls but bagged only 49 out of 342 seats in the National Assembly. The reason was that all religious parties formed an alliance called the Muttahida Majlis-e-Amal (MMA) and thought that they were riding high on the huge anti-American and pro-Afghan Taliban wave benefiting from the fact that Nawaz Sharif and Benazir Bhutto had been exiled. Most of the seats were in KP and Balochistan. However, in 2008 this tally dropped drastically to just four seats. But '[t]he Islamic parties ... might operate within current political order, their ultimate aim is to replace it with one that is based on narrow, discriminatory interpretation of Islam. They have also taken equivocal positions on militant jihad: on the one hand, they insist on their distinction from militant outfits by virtue of working within the democratic system; on the other hand, they admit to sharing the ideological goal of enforcing Sharia, while maintaining sizeable madrassa [sic] and mosque networks that are breeding grounds for many extremists groups.'[3] That is why the Islamist militants want to establish their cherished 'Islamic Khilafat' through jihad against the government, which is 'siding with the infidel Americans'. They draw their inspiration from the teachings of Ibn Taymiyyah, Mohammad Farraj and Sayyid Qutb that ulema have failed to rise and call for jihad against the government, declaring the rulers as infidel lackeys of the West.

Fourth, the US-led war in Afghanistan, Iraq and unabashed support to the Israeli government has turned many Muslims (not most) against the US and its allies. There is a perception of US domination of the world and perceived rejection of 'Islamic culture' by the West. These perceptions touch the imagination of the Muslim youth, but this support is for getting the US and NATO forces out of the region, it is not for the militant religious groups which are involved in terrorist activities in Pakistan.

Fifth, as stated in Parts IV and V, internally the establishment adopted the dangerous policy of nurturing these Islamic militants on extremist religious doctrine. The military establishment believes that it would be an asset in its conflict with Afghanistan and India. These people were armed and trained to fight across the border. But when the establishment wants them to stop or postpone the jihad, the militants believe that their former masters are renegades of the Islamic revolution. At the same time Pakistani society has become deeply weaponized because the so-called Afghan Mujahideen sold a bulk of the arms and ammunition to the people in Pakistan. Each jihadi group, big landlord and tribal chief, has its or his own private army. The militants' ability to destabilize the evolution of the normal democratic process sends jitters to the rest of world. Particularly some American analysts have an exaggerated fear that the 'fall of Pakistan to radical Islamic forces would be calamitous for rest of the world. The possibility of nuclear war on the Asian subcontinent would be dramatically increased.'[4] But sitting in Pakistan most analysts would dub this theory of the extremists taking over the government and control over nuclear assets an extremely remote probability. Pakistan is a multi-ethnic and multi-sectarian country, where taking over the power by one sect's radical Islamic militants doesn't seem to be probable. At the same time Pakistan is no Afghanistan, where a Taliban could take over Kabul. They could do it with massive support from the Pakistan government and the West turning a blind eye. There are more odds against the radical Islamic militants than in their favour. Nevertheless, Pakistan has to be clear about its policy towards these militant groups, as there are no good and bad Taliban.

It is wrong to think that religious extremism is a peculiar problem of only Muslims. Israel is going through one of the worst phases of extremism, where the extremists resist the policy of withdrawal of Israeli forces to the pre-1967 position and want to force women to wear long-sleeved shirts and long skirts. In Christianity there are some small violent groups in Assam and the US. A Christian extremist killed 151 people in Norway. Ireland suffered a long sectarian war. In Hinduism the extremists are working under the banner of Hindutva and Rashtriya Swayamsevak Sangh (RSS), which takes part in anti-Muslim and anti-Christian riots. Among the Buddhists we have violent extremists who killed many Rohingya in Myanmar.

One of the major reasons for the revival of religious extremism is that in each religion there are puritans who want to keep cultural and religious status quo and resist any change, particularly when it appears to be foreign. Many scholars have used the term 'Islamists' for the extremists. 'Islamists are defined as those among Muslim revivalists who focus on taking over the state – they certainly seem to take the state, both as an idea and as a material object, very seriously.'[5] They are asking for 'more' Islamic laws and a lifestance in accordance to the Islamic code as practised in the seventh century. Religious extremism in all religions is the natural outcome of the fact that 'religion claims absolute truth about ultimate reality. It knows the route one must follow to live one's life in accordance with that which is ultimately right and ultimately just .... The search for stricter or harsher interpretation of the law is consistent with the desire to assure one self and others that one is indeed living in accordance with what one is commanded to do rather than simply in accordance with what one would like to do.'[6] That explains why the Islamists are afraid of change and are fighting the proverbial 'windmill' like *Don Quixote*. The world, as famous journalist and writer Thomas Friedman stated, is now flat because of the information flow, thanks to digital technology and optic fibre. In each country foreign ideas, culture and political debates are beamed in the sitting rooms of the people. Internet has broken all barriers. Knowledge is being democratized. All this is scary for the retrogressive conservative forces. They are fighting back, declaring that globalization of culture is a threat to religion and religious tradition. Even some of the Leftists and liberal activists in Pakistan are resisting the change and, instead of moving on with the changing times, they want to remain attached to the antiquated theories and systems. French scholar Olivier Roy explained that Muslim neo-fundamentalism 'looks at globalization as a good opportunity to rebuild the Muslim ummah on a purely religious basis, not in the sense that religion is separated from culture and politics, but to the extent religion discards and even ignores other fields of symbolic practices. Neo-fundamentalism promotes the decontextualization of religious practices.'[7] In Pakistan we have seen that along with the petro-dollars of Saudi Arabia, the cultural and religious influences are also coming to the country, decontextualizing the local culture. Saudi-funded Mullahs and even some educated people are influenced by the Wahabi thinking and denigrate local cultural practices because they are not practices in Arabia.

A question often asked is: When there are extremist strands in all religions why are Muslims extremists profiled as terrorists? One of the major reasons is that Muslim terrorists are more in number, they are spread all over the world, are more organized, more violent and above all, the Al Qaeda has given them a global agenda. Unlike others who have local issues, the Muslim extremists have the Al Qaeda manifesto to establish Islamic supremacy over the world. There is a debate among the Muslims as to whether the Salafi explanation about the permanent jihad by the individual is correct or jihad has to be a collective action declared by an Islamic state. Roy maintains that '[w]hatever the complexity of the debate among scholars since the time of the Prophet, two points are clear: jihad is not one of the five pillars of Islam [profession of faith, prayer, fasting, alm-giving (zakat) and pilgrimage (Haj)] and it is therefore a collective duty [fard kifaya] under given circumstances. But the radicals, since Sayyid Qutb and Mohammad Farrag [Farraj], explicitly consider jihad a permanent and individual duty [fard ayn].'[8]

The Pakistani military establishment, as stated in Part IV, made the historic blunder to launch an Islamic jihad in 1978 against the Left government. It not only trained and armed the Afghan jihadis, but allowed the Islamic militants from all over the world to join the jihad. This made Pakistan 'world's biggest terrorist training university' and haven. Once that jihad was over, these professional jihadis, who believed in the extremist Salafi version of Islam, took upon themselves the duty of launching a global jihad. Though they were successful in Afghanistan because of massive support from the US, Saudi Arabia, Pakistan and China (and the change of policy in the former Soviet Union), they came to believe that they had defeated a super power only because of their religious fervour. This delusion of grandeur has given them a belief that they can take on the world to establish 'Islamic Khilafat.'

In a tribal part of Pakistan they have declared the 'Islamic Emirates of Waziristan'. As the jihadi groups are fully armed and speak through the barrel of the gun, they do not tolerate dissent. They have also joined hands with militant Sunni sectarian organizations. In a highly weaponized society small dispute can become bloody and the power of the gun kills tolerance for any alternative narrative. The Afghanistan adventure of Pakistan has changed the nature of all conflicts and the crime world in Pakistan. There has been a technological revolution whereas sticks and daggers were used in the yesteryears' sectarian and ethnic conflicts; now all the parties are equipped with the most sophisticated weapons.

This brings us to the crucial question asked frequently in Pakistan: For how long will terrorism continue? Pakistan has been bleeding from terrorists' attacks for almost 32 years now. The French Scholar Maxime Rodinson was of the view: 'Islamic fundamentalism is temporary, transitory movement, but could last another 30 or 50 years – I don't know how long. Where fundamentalism isn't power it will be an ideal, as long as the basic frustration and discontent persists that leads people to take extreme position. You need long experience with clericalism to finally get fed up with it – look how much time it took in Europe!'[9] Pakistan has already experienced clericalism in the shape of Taliban's fascism in Afghanistan, Swat which has spread now from the KP province to all the provinces of the country; General Zia-ul-Haq's Islamist regime; and religious parties' government in the KP province during 2002–08. These experiences are fresh in mind. The most likely scenario is that terrorism in Pakistan would not subside in the medium-term future. Much will also depend on how soon Afghanistan would stabilize after the NATO forces' withdrawal. The fate of both wretched countries has been made interdependent because of the myopic policies of Pakistan and India's urge to increase its influence in Kabul. But Pakistan would be in a better situation to manage this chaotic situation if elections are held in the spring of 2013, as it seems likely, and if power transfer is smooth in a democratic spirit.

Notes and References:

1.   Amartya Sen, *Identity and Violence*, Allen Lane, New Delhi, 2006, p. 12.
2.   Ibid., pp. 12–13.
3.   'Islamic Parties in Pakistan', *Asia Report* No. 216, 12 December 2011.
4.   John R. Schmidt, 'The Unraveling of Pakistan', *Survival*, London, Vol. 51, Issue 3, 2009.
5.   Humeira Iqtidar, 'Secularism Beyond the State: The "State" and the "Market" in Islamist Imagination', *Modern Asian Studies*, Cambridge University Press, Vol. 45, Issue 3, 2011, pp. 491–99.
6.   Charles S. Liebman, 'Extremism as a Religious Norm', *Journal for the Scientific Study of Religion*, Vol. 22, Issue 1, 1983, pp. 75–86.
7.   Olivier Roy, *Globalised Islam: The Search for a New Ummah*, Hurst & Company, London, 2004, p. 258.
8.   Ibid., p. 41.
9.   Maxime Rodinson on Islamic fundamentalism, as quoted by Nader Hashemi in *Islam: Secularism and Liberal Democracy*, Oxford University Press, Karachi, 2009, p. 23.

Chapter 32

HAS DEMOCRACY DELIVERED
IN PAKISTAN?

The real issues of the common man in Pakistan are terrorism, religious extremism, sectarian and ethnic killings, continuing deterioration of law and order and poor governance in government institutions. These issues have not cropped up because of democracy but got accumulated because democracy was not allowed to function. It was democratic consensus that gave strength to the armed forces to fight the terrorists. It is the consensus developed by all leading political parties, which is challenging religious extremism and cutting across the sectarian divide.

In spite of the Islamists militancy to change Pakistan into an autocratic theocracy, the redeeming factor is that an overwhelming majority of the people are in favour of democracy. This is evident from the support to mainstream parties, which are committed to advance their political programmes remaining within the constitutional framework. The process of rebuilding the state institutions and absence of governance at the top are co-related issues. Stephen P. Cohen is right that at present there is no coherence in the state policies, mainly because the political process was killed in its infancy by the omnipotent military establishment. The Zardari government is the only political government that ever completed its term. And he is the only political leader who, in spite of his alleged corruption tales and bad governance, has managed to keep a political coalition of four parties together for a full term of five years. At the same time Mian Nawaz Sharif, the leader of the second biggest political party in the parliament, has also shown signs of political maturity. Unlike past practice, where the party in Opposition would conspire with the military establishment to oust the elected government of its rivals, they have not played in the hands of military establishment.

As stated in Part V on national security, there is a suggestion of setting up a NSC, but not much progress has been made in this direction. However, other positive signs of institution-building are: the PCNS has been given some elbow room by the military establishment as explained earlier because of the setbacks to its image from incidents like the US unilateral action to invade Pakistan and kill Osama bin Laden, attack on GHQ and the Mehran Airbase in Karachi in May 2012; the superior judiciary is exercising its powers independently and zealously – it disqualified one prime minister, got a letter written by the government to the Swiss Court to continue with the corruption case against its own President Zardari; for the first time many retired army generals are being tried for corruption; in a unanimously adopted 18th Amendment and 7th NFC Award, after 66 years, the process of devolving power and resources to the provinces started (see Part II). Thus, on the political front all is not lost, and for the first time it appears that the democratic evolutionary process is moving forward, though slowly, and at times disappointingly.

As for the often raised question whether 'Pakistan is fit for democracy or has democracy delivered in Pakistan?' the quick and pithy answer is 'Yes'. It may not satisfy many critics who see historical evolutionary process only through their personal likes and dislikes of a party or a person. In Pakistan where such complex issues are seen in 'black' and 'white' this answer is not satisfactory. Most of the people who generally raise this question in a disgusting tone have no stamina for indulging in serious discourse.

A point to be noted here is that any particular government should not be confused with democracy. Democracy is a system, which provides for electing the government and the Opposition. And if they do not deliver they can be removed as prescribed in the Constitution, which is supposed to be the consensus bible guiding the system in any society. As stated earlier, first it has to be understood that economically and socially Pakistani society is multi-structural and multi-ethno linguistic. Its structure has a direct bearing on the level of democracy or even dictatorship in any country. While most critics of democracy in Pakistan undermine this hard fact, there are many who argue that given the low literacy rate, tribal and quasi-feudal structure of the society, democracy is not suitable for Pakistan. This is urban middle-class intellectual snobbery and insult to the 60 per cent rural population of the country. History, of even partially fair elections, has shown that people have given votes to those parties and their local leaders who they felt would be useful for them.

Second, there are those who want to see revolutionary changes ignoring the fact that democracy evolves. It does not give overnight solutions. One has seen many premature revolutions eventually fail more because of their internal weaknesses and untimely birth, and less because of external interference. Pakistan has to go through the evolutionary process of democracy, which was interrupted and mauled many times – directly and indirectly – by the military. Former Federal Secretary Roedad Khan, who remained close to power for decades, admitted in an interview to Geo TV that 'real sovereignty in Pakistan has always lain with the GHQ.'[1]

Third, in the absence of a democratic dispensation the institutions of the state did not get enough time to find the right equilibrium, hence the present scramble for more space in the power structure. This tussle for more power between the normal institutions of the state power i.e., executive, judiciary and parliament is not letting the system, which is in its infancy, to stabilize. Unlike many other countries, where democracy has evolved, in Pakistan military has been a dominant power and has refused to accept the supremacy of any elected civilian government. This factor has played an obstructive role in the development of democracy and has created distortions.

Fourth, compared to the developed capitalist society institutions like military and civil bureaucracy and judiciary, the quasi-feudal political parties are handicapped when it comes to claiming rightful space in the policy-making and political power. Attention can be drawn to the fact that there are strong urban-based businessmen and middle-class led parties in Pakistan like PML-N, PTI of Imran Khan and MQM of Altaf Hussain. Yes, but the mindset and power structures of the leaders of these parties are still quasi-feudal. There is little democracy in almost all the parties, their leaders are supreme. John R. Schmidt, who served in Pakistan US Embassy as political counselor (1998–2001), observed in a paper: 'Pakistan is run by two groups of political actors, a civilian aristocracy consisting of wealthy agricultural landowners and their industrial counterparts and the Army. The civilian elite has arrayed themselves into political parties built around prominent families, individuals or institutions .... These parties function predominately as patronage networks, using political power to distribute favours and resources to members of the network. This is a manifestation at the political level of an underlying feudal culture centred on agricultural landowners that has dominated the region for generations.'[2]

Fifth, Pakistan has always concentrated on its geostrategic position from a military perspective and India phobia. This embroiled the country in regional disputes with devastating social, economic and political consequences. People of Pakistan and the region could have benefitted much more had its rulers exploited the geostrategic position of the country for economic growth. Pakistan could have become a peaceful neutral hub of business, connecting East to the West and prospered by leaps and bounds.

Sixth, the global and historical perspective is important for assessing the success and failure of democracy. In India many governments changed in the 1990s because the coalitions fell apart. Nobody questioned the efficacy of democracy and the constitutional process was followed. Coalition partners in all democracies play hard ball with the majority party and take their pound of flesh. Nobody blames democracy for all the noises and bargaining in the parliament. Even the old Westminster-style democracy is going through these pangs. The United Kingdom is faced with the question of separation of Scotland. It has offered to hold a referendum as the Canadians did on the Quebec issue. Nobody said that they would send the British troops for protecting the national integrity and the military has not toppled the government. This is the civilized and democratic way of settling disputes and difference of opinion, in sharp contrast to what our establishment is doing in Balochistan. Left to the politicians Balochistan issue can be resolved amicably with the Baloch dissidents.

***

Now, for a change, let's look at what democracy has delivered in Pakistan. It helped the bloodless ouster of a military general by the politicians.

Arbitrary presidential powers to oust an elected government and dissolve the assemblies were taken away. Press freedom, which some people use to show their disappointment with democracy, is an integral part of the same. The Opposition, which is a part of any democratic dispensation, is playing a positive role in the parliament and outside. The political parties have matured and stand united against any unconstitutional intervention, a great proof of democracy at work. Only fools, who don't know about the responsible role an Opposition is supposed to play, taunt the PML-N as friendly Opposition.

Critics of democracy have a valid point when they ask how these constitutional changes and new formula of division of resources between the Centre and provinces is going to help the common man. Teething pains of devolution of power and poor handling of the transfer of ministries and resources, both by federal and provincial governments are raising such questions. Undoubtedly inefficiency has to be criticized. But gradually these problems would be solved as it is in the interest of the provincial governments. This would help in bringing power closer to the people and development decisions would be made at the provincial level. It would be easier for the people to hold their leaders accountable at the provincial level, instead of running to Islamabad for everything. However, the biggest failure of all the provincial governments is that the power and resources have not been devolved by them to the local governments. This issue gets little coverage in Pakistani media, although it is more crucial for the people than the much-talked about corruption.

As stated above, on the governance side the real issues of the common man in Pakistan are terrorism, religious extremism, sectarian and ethnic killings, continuing deterioration of law and order and poor governance in government institutions. These issues have not cropped up because of democracy but got accumulated because democracy was not allowed to function. It was democratic consensus that gave strength to the armed forces to fight the terrorists. It is the consensus developed by all leading political parties, which is challenging religious extremism and cutting across the sectarian divide.

Failure to control law and order and poor governance are not the failure of democracy in Pakistan. Many countries face such problems but it is the government that is blamed for its poor management, instead of questioning whether the country should have democracy or not. The solution lies in democracy, which allows voters to push their elected representatives to perform. And if they fail to do that, voters are free not to elect them again. In contrast in a dictatorship neither can you push the bureaucrats, nor can you dislodge them through vote. Major failures for which the PPP-led coalition government is criticized are: corruption, energy shortage, rising inequality, increased unemployment, high inflation, low tax revenue collection, the public sector's haemorrhaging impact on economy; depreciation of the rupee against dollar; falling foreign direct investment; and low GDP growth. The issue of rising inequality is directly linked with the classical economic system, in which emphasis is just on growth assuming that the benefits will trickle down automatically.

In a country where poverty is high, inequality is on the rise and the growth rate is depressed, the accumulated anger of the dispossessed erupts on the smallest pretext. That is why no matter whether people are protesting against energy shortage in the country, or against the anti-Prophet cartoons and films, cars, motorbikes and public property is burnt and destroyed. Interestingly most critics of democracy and its defenders only talk about its political aspect. Nobody talks about economic democracy. Some Left parties with their outdated theories talk about economic disparity but they promise a distant dream of a socialist revolution.

Is this a failure of democracy? No. It is the failure of the coalition government, though partially. Its acts of omissions and commissions have played a large part than the objective economic constraints. The PPP-led coalition has not only failed in checking corruption, the public perception is that it has broken all previous records of corruption and cronyism.

The energy crisis of Pakistan is not a recent creation. It was clear as early as late 2004 that by 2010 Pakistan will have a 5,000 MW shortage during peak hours. The then Musharraf government started on a mission to attract foreign investors. But the approval process was slow and the bureaucracy too afraid to approve projects as the private sector was asking for eight to nine cents a unit, which only helped in delaying investment in power sector. Today, the Zardari government can be blamed for inefficient management of this crisis and for its failure to check rampant corruption in the energy economy of Pakistan. Many drawing-room critics blame democracy for not harnessing the indigenous coal. The fact is otherwise. Benazir Bhutto had brought in investors during her first term of government (1989–90), but as she was dismissed in about 18 months, those investors were chased away. It was during General Pervez Musharraf's era that one witnessed the babus of the Federal Ministry of Water and Power sabotaging the Thar coal project because they were not willing to give away power to the province to exploit its coal reserves and produce power. The issue of control over these resources has been sorted out in the 18th Amendment with the Opposition's consensus. As a result, progress has been made on the coal-power projects. It is under a democratic dispensation that consensus on Diamer-Bhasha Dam[3] emerged and work started. But after lobbying by India which considers Gilgit-Baltistan as part of Kashmir, the international donor agencies are hesitating in financing this project. The military government led by General Musharraf wanted to impose highly controversial Kalabagh Dam[4], but it was resisted by the people of Sindh and KP. Sindh fears that Kalabagh Dam would be used for irrigation of Punjab, which would reduce the flow of water to the lower riparian. Pakhtunkhwa has environmental concerns as Kalabagh Dam is likely to submerge some of its towns because of rise in water table and also cause displacement of people.

Another issue is the shortage of natural gas, and there are only three options to meet this shortage: import through a pipeline, which is a long-term solution; import of liquefied natural gas (LNG) to ease some pressure in a shorter time frame; and raise the gas price to attract more investment in the exploration and production of oil and gas resources of Pakistan. As a matter of fact, these are not and/or options. All these measures will have to be taken simultaneously. The stand taken by the government to import gas from Iran was quite daring: The Zardari government has signed an agreement with Iran in February 2013 for gas pipeline project, in spite the US pressure that Pakistan should abide by the UN sanctions against Iran. The energy-starved Pakistanis hope that the government would not buckle under the US pressure and move away from it. A democratic government can withstand this pressure better than a dictatorial one. People are angry about the energy shortage, which leads to frequent 'electricity and gas riots': They want gas and electricity at subsidized rates. No country around the world would be able to subsidize energy in future, unless it is a huge producer of oil and gas – like Saudi Arabia, Qatar and UAE.

Unemployment is increasing and the population growth rate is still unsustainable. This is Pakistan's chronic problem. The mean age is 21. This population dividend of having over 60 per cent people in the working age group can only be cashed in if more employment is generated. Pakistan needs to create at least 3 million jobs every year.

The fragmentation of agricultural land by natural course of inheritance and mechanization of farming are pushing the rural surplus labour to the cities where, because of the security situation and constant efforts to destabilize the democratic system, investment in new projects has slowed down. Hence, not enough jobs are being created. At the same time the impact of prolonged recession in the West, depreciation of the euro and the appreciation of dollar have hit the rupee badly, exports growth has slowed down while the import bill has been rising and creating a yawning current account deficit. This coupled with mismanagement of economy has created a large fiscal deficit resulting in high inflation rate, particularly upsetting the urban population.

This is hurting the urban poor more, but the answer is not demanding lower commodity prices, which would hurt the agriculture producers who employ 42 per cent of the workforce. Keeping to the policy introduced by Zulfikar Ali Bhutto, all PPP governments had tried to make policies that led to transfer of money from urban to the rural areas. The policy has paid in terms of higher cash crops production. The Zardari government has done the same as a result purchasing power in rural areas has increased. The middle class professionals who shed tears on rural poverty should instead be happy.

The landless peasants and wage workers are still being exploited – an issue that has not been addressed by many writers on Pakistan. The growing inequality and non-implementation of labour laws for the agriculture workers too are important issues. Similarly, while focus of the Left organizations and trade unions is on the rights of the organized labour in industry and utility companies and financial sector, there is support for the labour working in the Pakistan's massive informal sector. Unfortunately the democracy-busters do not address the inequality and exploitation issues.

Notes and References:

1. Roedad Khan's interview to Saleem Safi, Geo TV, 11 November 2012.
2. John R. Schmidt, 'The Unraveling of Pakistan', *Survival*, London, Vol. 51, Issue 3, 2009.
3. Diamer-Bhasha Dam is an under-construction roller compacted concrete (RCC) dam on the River Indus in Gilgit-Baltistan, Pakistan. Its foundation stone was laid by Prime Minister Yousuf Raza Gilani on 18 October 2011. Upon completion, it would be the highest RCC dam in the world. The dam site is situated near a place called 'Bhasha' in Gilgit-Baltistan's Diamer district, hence the name. (Source: Wikipedia)
4. The Kalabagh Dam is a proposed hydroelectric dam on the Indus River at Kalabagh in Mianwali District of the Punjab province in Pakistan.

Chapter 33

IS PAKISTAN A FAILED COUNTRY?

Pakistan is not early twentieth-century Turkey, where a Kemal Atatürk could rise to abolish the 'caliphate', which was a symbol of temporal and divine world. But it can take a break from its stated religious national narrative and move towards secularization of the society based on reason and scientific life stance – the process that has been started by Bangladesh.

In spite of the perilous policies of the successive establishments, which have led the country 'to the brink', Pakistan as it stands in the spring of 2013 cannot be called a failed state. But this claim has to be hastened with a proviso that Pakistan did fail in 1971 when it was just 24. Uncertainty about its future and fear of failure is embedded in its history.

Let us analyze Pakistan's probability of failure on the basis of the Legatum Prosperity Index, which includes the following areas:

1. Governance;
2. Rule of Law;
3. Economic growth;
4. Democracy;
5. State security;
6. Military;
7. National cohesion;
8. Health;

9. Population control;
10. Personal freedom;
11. National resources management; and
12. Smart power (positive projection of the country).

In most of the above areas Pakistan can score 'average' ranking. Exception can be made for number 6: 'Military', which because of its organizational discipline and availability of substantial funds can perhaps score 'good'. Yet, in spite of such a strong military, Pakistan's internal security and national cohesion would score 'weak'. Average ranking in most of the criteria means that Pakistan is a 'borderline' case and not a 'failed' state. I would place its economic growth better than average as almost 91 per cent of the economy is in the informal sector, and therefore growth rates are underestimated as is the case with many other developing economies. Similarly, as stated earlier the continuation of the democratic process is on the right trajectory, in spite of the wrangling for power between institutions of the state – executive, parliament, military and judiciary. The process is long and painful, but it has already started showing some positive signs.

***

To put back the country on the prosperity trajectory in the field of diplomacy, the Pakistani establishment would have to change its policies from the narrow geostrategic perspective to a multi-dimensional political and economic prosperity perspective. This is only possible if Pakistan moves away from the basic formulation that it is an Islamic ideological state poised against India and, may be, the West in the future. It has to have peace with all the neighbours, putting aside the historical revanchist policies and relaunch itself as a non-aligned country, keeping equal relations with all the super powers and the super powers in the making.

Economically, Pakistan has to learn to live within its means, reducing dependence on foreign funding and heavy domestic borrowing. Accepting a loan for development is not bad if it is not for non-productive expenditure. Whole economic growth depends on it. However, it has to be directly correlated with input and output. The output has to be more for building national savings and paying back the loans. Since decades Pakistan has been borrowing internally and internationally to meet its huge non-development expenditures. The time to sell its militarily important geostrategic position is running out at a fast-forward pace. The huge informal sector has to be brought under the tax net, shunning all pressures from the political parties, which patronize the tax evaders of the bazaar. The country has to utilize its youth bulge for productive purposes by investing heavily in human resource development and not in tanks, bombs or missiles.

Politically, the armed forces have to hand over real power to the elected government. Pakistan has maturing political parties, independent judiciary and vibrant media, which are the perquisites for democratic evolution and provides necessary checks and balances. Let the elected government decide its foreign and economic policies. Pakistan's troubles have been compounding because it is still stuck with the religious nationalism slogan, which Jinnah wanted to depart from on 11 August 1947. The purely secular objective of having maximum autonomy within the framework of India got lost in the campaign under religious propaganda. This objective has to be revived and all nationalities living in this state have to be given full control over their resources and politics.

Religion and politics have to be separated to check the sectarian strife and stop the state patronage to the Islamists. The jihadi organizations have to be wound up with a programme for the rehabilitation of their foot soldiers. Mosques and madrassahs have to be closely monitored to stop them from spreading hatred against other sects and other countries. Madrassahs have to be converted to technical schools and other institutions imparting modern education on humanistic lines. Such reforms mean moving away from the religious nationalism narrative to build a secular society. Pakistan is not early twentieth-century Turkey, where a Kemal Atatürk could rise to abolish the 'caliphate', which was a symbol of temporal and divine world. But it can take a break from its stated religious national and move towards secularization of the society based on reason and scientific life stance – the process which has been started by Bangladesh.

The dos and don'ts list is long but what has been suggested above is most urgent. Otherwise Pakistan would not be able to pull itself out of the quagmire in which it is sinking inch by inch, day by day.

Chapter 34

2013 AND BEYOND

Just when this book was going to the press Pakistan held its 10th elections braving terrorist attacks. Once again, the country proved that it was far from being a failed state. The general elections were held on 11 May 2013 and the country moved ahead on the democracy trajectory. A democratically elected Parliament completed its term for the first time in the history of Pakistan. The ruling coalition government stepped down and handed over the power to the interim federal and provincial governments with the consensus of the Opposition without any military intervention.

But the moments of rejoicing are few and far between in Pakistan. The spectre of political formulation that Pakistan is a state wedded to Islamic ideology continued to loom over the 2013 elections' process and left strong imprints on the politics of the country. While the democrats were rejoicing that for the first time a smooth transfer of power is in sight through free and fair elections, their spirits were dampened by the 'holy warriors' of the country.

In the 2013 elections, unlike the ones held in 1990, no General Hamid Gul, General Aslam Beg or General Mahmud Durrani were needed to engineer the defeat of the Left of the Centre political parties by supporting formation of Islami Jamhoori Ittehad. The TTP threatened PPP, ANP and MQM that their candidates and election rallies would be attacked. These were not empty threats – bomb attacks continued on the election offices and in the rallies of the target political parties.

Just two days before the elections Punjab Provincial Assembly candidate Haider Gilani, who is the son of former PPP Prime Minister Yousuf Raza Gilani was kidnapped by the extremists from his constituency in Multan. This dampened the election campaign of the Gilani family candidates and resulted in their defeat from their traditional constituencies. While these three comparatively secular parties had to cut down on their election campaign, Right of the Centre political parties like PTI, various factions of PML, JI and other religious parties were free to hold large rallies. This gave an advantage to the Centre–Right parties that appease Taliban and their associate militants groups. But the religious parties could only bag 5 per cent of the total seats in the National Assembly. This is keeping in line with the trend of most of the previous election results in Pakistan. The fact that people have never voted the religious parties to rule Pakistan, in spite of the propaganda of indoctrination of children in schools, reflects peoples' belief in democracy and a liberal government.

The kind of religious questions asked to the candidates by some returning officers (RO) at the time of filing up the nomination papers shows that the Taliban mindset was not limited to the militant groups only. However, responding to the appeals by some candidates and the public's reaction, the Punjab High Court instructed the ROs not to ask irrelevant questions. Election commission's RO had rejected papers of some of the candidates for their lack of knowledge about Quranic verses or Islamic history. The most prominent case of rejection of nomination papers was that of journalist and politician Ayaz Amir. He was told that from his columns it appears that he doesn't believe in the Islamic ideology of Pakistan. And he does not qualify as a good Muslim because of his 'habits' and so, he cannot contest elections. However, this decision was turned down by the Punjab High Court. But the RO's decision and the support given to him by the Islamist journalists scared Amir's party – PML-N – which did not give him a ticket.

From where does the RO draw this power? It is from the perfidious clause of Article 62 and 63 of the Constitution. As discussed in Part III of the book, these clauses were there ever since they were inserted by General Zia-ul-Haq but were not invoked in full force, to purge the candidates, in this election.

As discussed earlier, Islamic ideology's proponents base their case on the 1949 Objectives Resolution, which was made a substantive part of the Constitution through a Presidential Order No. 14 of 1985, and is now referred to as Article 2 (A) of the Constitution. This was done by General Zia-ul-Haq, the man who damaged Pakistan more than anybody else. The relevant part of the Objective Resolution says:

'Wherein the State shall exercise its powers and authority through the chosen representatives of the people; Wherein the principles of democracy, freedom, equality, tolerance and social justice as enunciated by Islam shall be fully observed; *Wherein the Muslims shall be enabled to order their lives in the individual and collective spheres in accordance with the teachings and requirements of Islam as set out in the Holy Quran and the Sunnah.*' (Author's emphasis.) What is missed deliberately is that the word used here is 'enabled' not 'enforced'.

The Islamists argue in support of their argument that Article 31, Clause 2 (A) of the Constitution, which was inserted by Zulfikar Bhutto (in the early 1970s) to appease the religious parties.. This Article says that the 'state shall endeavour – as respects [*sic*] the Muslims of Pakistan – "to make the teaching of the Holy Quran and Islamiat compulsory to encourage and facilitate the learning of Arabic language ..."'

Article 31 says that teaching of Quran should be compulsory hence some suras are included in the school curriculum of Islamiat. However Arabic teaching is nots mandatory for a Muslim.. It shouldn't be as the religion and its learning are a private matter of a citizen and nobody has the right to impose them on anybody Any compulsion in this regard would be in conflict with a fundamental right of the people, a right universally accepted by all civilized nations. Also, such compulsion would be at odds with the spirit of all major religions, which are against forced learning of their respective teachings.

As a consequence of the thesis that Pakistan is an Islamic ideological state the nomination requires a candidate to solemnly affirm his/her belief in this ideology and that he/she does not belong to the Ahmadiyya community. The parliamentarians should not be forced to file a declaration along with the nomination papers that they believe in the Islamic ideology of Pakistan. The new parliament should be free to debate, and separate state and religion in doing so. This is crucial for Pakistan if it has to survive and put the jihadist genie back in the bottle; or else Pakistan would be consumed by hyper-religiosity. Even Israel, which was created by the British imperialists as a Jewish state, has left the highly controversial subject of the relationship between religion and state in abeyance.

The discourse on the 'Islamic ideology of Pakistan' once again took prominence in the country in the run-up to the 2013 elections. The TTP's contention was that Pakistan was made for Islam and deviation from this would deprive the country its basic rationale and hence its ability to survive. They rejected democratic system and Pakistan's Constitution as un-Islamic and called for setting up an Islamic caliphate. Thus, the fundamental question that needs to be discussed in Pakistan, without fear at the intellectual level would be: Is an ideology, whether spiritual or philosophical necessary for a country to exist on the world map?

The Islamists' assumption is that Islamic ideology is the basis of one nation and the glue that keeps the country together. This argument is based on the basic lack of knowledge about what makes a nation. Religion is just one of the many factors (but not a necessary one), which are required for the making of a nation. There are other stronger binding factors like geographical continuity, common ethnicity, common culture, common language, civilization, history and above all common economic interests. If religion would have been the over-riding factor that makes one nation, then why are the Arab Muslim countries – which have a common language, similarities in culture, common history of Muslim empire and geographic continuity – not one? If Islamic ideology is the adhesive for keeping the country together, then why was Bangladesh separated from West Pakistan's subjugation? If Islamic ideology was the binding factor, then why are Muslims killing each other on sectarian basis? Why do Balochistan and Sindh have strong nationalist movements? Why could the communist ideology not keep Soviet Union and Yugoslavia together? Why has capitalism not led to a merger of all nations? Why could the Christian and Muslim Empires not hold themselves together and why did nation states emerge on the globe? Most countries in the world have no state ideology and they have prospered better. Perhaps because the ideological overhang saps the creative energy of the people.

Next argument is that the Islamic ideology of Pakistan gives Pakistan a separate identity? It is a delusion Pakistan suffers from and hence has so many problems. The people of Pakistan feel more strongly about their ethnic identity. If Islamic ideology would give a separate identity then why do Muslim countries like Afghanistan and Iran proudly hang on to their respective identities and have not merged with Pakistan? Why do the Muslims living in India prefer to be identified as Indians, if religion is the basis of a nation? Why can't they migrate to Pakistan and get a citizenship automatically? Why does Saudi Arabia not allow immigration of Muslims to their country and be an equal citizen? From the logic given by the advocates of one Islamic ideology (one nation), all Muslim countries have the same religious identity, thus they should be the citizens of one nation!

The Centre–Right parties' 2013 election campaign led the Chief of Army Staff General Parvez Kayani to give two significant statements before the election week. These statements came under discussion, inviting criticism from ideologically opposed politicians and journalists. First speaking at the graduation of the 127th Long Course of the Pakistan Military Academy at Kakul on 20 April 2013, General Kayani said: 'Let me remind you that Pakistan was created in the name of Islam and Islam can never ever be taken out of Pakistan. However, Islam should always remain a unifying force.'

Then on 30 April 2013 at the Martyrs' Day function, he made a significant statement: 'However, despite all this bloodshed, certain quarters still want to remain embroiled in the debate concerning the causes of this war and who imposed it on us. While this may be important in itself but the fact of the matter is, that today it is Pakistan and its valiant people who are a target of this war and are suffering tremendously.' He posed the question to those who claim that Pakistan is fighting USA's war: 'I would like to ask all those who raise such questions that if a small faction wants to enforce its distorted ideology over the entire [n]ation by taking up arms and for this purpose defies the Constitution of Pakistan and the democratic process and considers all forms of bloodshed justified, then, does the fight against this enemy of the state constitute someone else's war?' And then contended: 'Even in the history of the best evolved democratic states, treason or seditious uprisings against the state have never been tolerated and in such struggles their armed forces have had unflinching support of the masses; questions about the ownership of such wars have never been raised. We cannot afford to confuse our soldiers and weaken their resolve with such misgivings. Every drop of blood, shed in the national cause, is sacred and no one can better understand its value than the families who are present here today; because their dear ones have already made the ultimate sacrifice. We must not hurt the sentiments of these saviours of the [n]ation through our words and deeds.'

The first statement was criticized by the political Left and liberals since they believed that the emphasis on the Islamic ideology by the army chief would support the Rightist political parties. But General

Kayani, who was standing at the crossroad of Pakistan's history, I believe, was addressing his officials and not the politicians, as the army has indoctrinated its rank and file for the last 66 years that they are the soldiers of Islam hence also the guardians of ideological borders. The terrorists they are fighting gallantly claim that they are the real soldiers of Islam as they want to establish real Sharia in the country, they believe that democracy, the Constitution of Pakistan and the army are anti-Islam and agents of the West. Now it is a battle between the moderate Islam of Kayani, majority of Pakistanis and the extremist Salafi/Wahabi Islam of the Al Qaeda franchisees and their Islamist supporters.

PTI which has emerged as the third largest party in the National Assembly and first largest party in KP in the 2013 elections, believes that terrorism in the country is because Pakistan is fighting USA's war on terror. Instead of owning war against TTP, PTI view is that the conflict could be resolved through negotiation. What these supporters of Taliban forget is that Pakistan has been supporting the Afghan Taliban covertly against the US, without the army's support they wouldn't have been able to continue their war. It is not the issue of USA's presence in Afghanistan; it is the Al Qaeda agenda to seize power in Muslim-majority countries as the first step towards Islam's domination over the world. They also ignore the fact that Talibanization of Pakistan tribal belt started in late 1990s, when there was Taliban government in Afghanistan. And weaponization of militant Islamic groups was done in 1980s when General Zia launched insurgency in Afghanistan.

Political leaders and some journalists are of the view that TTP and other Al Qaeda franchisees are those 'who had rebelled against the fallout of the US imposed strategy'. Anybody who argues against this dangerous proposition that lends support to the terrorists is labelled as a 'liberal fascist' by the people who cannot argue rationally. The oxymoronic term 'liberal fascist' can only be coined by people who are either naïve enough to not understand the contradictory meaning of the two political terms or want to hide the fascist designs of the religious extremists and terrorists. The liberals do not want to impose their views on others by force and respect the rights of Islamists, even if they disagree with them.

On the other hand the militants qualify to be labelled as 'fascist' because they do not tolerate dissent and kill for their cause. The TTP and its affiliate terrorist groups do not believe in democracy – in which the

Islamists are free to contest elections and JI leader Syed Munawar Hasan maintains that the liberals should register themselves in the minorities' voting list. The TTP and other Islamic militant groups are against freedom of expression; this is fascism and not the liberal democracy that gives you a right to write freely. The TTP is against television but uses this medium for their messages and its supporters are keen to appear on TV to proselytize. They also forget that terrorism existed before the US forces came to Afghanistan because Pakistan launched the world's biggest covert operation with the US, launching a number of jihadi groups. Even sectarian killings increased when Taliban government allowed LJ's Riaz Basra to open his office in Kandahar.

Coming back to the COAS's statements, what the army does not realize is that exploiting religion for statecraft and making it a basis of national security doctrine is a dangerous political formulation. The means used in politics, which in this case is exploitation of Islam, have their own dynamics, leading the country to a chaotic end. The use of religion in politics has given a wide space to political and militant Islamic forces in Pakistan and has thrown the country at the mercy of these elements. The threat to all the political parties, which are clear that the war against terrorists is 'Pakistan's own war', is directly proportionate to the staunch belief in the so-called ideology of Pakistan.

The military establishment should realize that the policies followed in the last 66 years have brought us to the brink. Armies of most of the countries are not mobilized on the basis of religion of the majority in their respective countries. They are motivated to protect their country, not on ideology but because of their belief in their nationhood. Using ideology for motivating the army is dangerous, as any other group or country can claim that they are the followers of the more puritan version. Iranian religious government wants to support the Shia groups in other countries on ideological grounds. Saudi Arabia wants to further its puritan Wahabizm on the Muslim countries.

The COAS's statement at Pakistan Military Academy in Kakul was actually to reassure the army officials that the army still believes in Islamic ideology. This statement was to address the confusion in the military rank and file created by different messaging in the media and mosques. Many armed forces personnel, like an average Pakistani is bound to think whether TTP's or HT's Islamic movement is right, or the one which they are asked to fight for? The statement that urged political parties not to add confusion by saying 'fighting terrorism is not our war, but it is America's war', cannot remove the inherent doctrinal confusion in the army's ideological foundation. Political messages and ideologies discussed in the society cannot be stopped from entering the garrisons' doors. So when an army, which is groomed as an 'Islamic Army', is called to fight the 'Islamic militants', who are waging jihad to set up the caliphate, it becomes too difficult and confusing for the soldiers to combat. The only solution is to, once and for all, separate religion from politics and educate the army personnel that it is their national duty to defend the country, and that they are not soldiers of Islam to start a jihad against the infidel countries.

The 2013 elections, thus, left a strong imprint on the Islamic militant groups as the political parties, which believed war against terrorism is our war, were defeated and Centre–Right PML-N emerged as the largest political party in the Centre and in Punjab. PML-N had tacit support of some of the militant groups. The most dangerous TTP had proposed PML-N's name as one of the guarantors of peace agreement when they made the offer a few months before the elections.

Both PML-N leader Nawaz Sharif and PTI Chairman Imran Khan were advocating that Pakistan should ask the US to stop drone attacks and negotiate peace with the TTP and its allies. As Sharif is expected to form a government at the Centre and Punjab, and Imran Khan is likely to form the government in terror-torn KP, the burden to prove that this issue can be resolved on the negotiating table would be on them. The big question is: Can Pakistan accept the unconstitutional demands of TTP and its allies? Indeed no elected government would think of doing so. The chances are that the present policy of first establishing the writ of the government and humbling TTP would continue till the terrorist groups accept the terms offered by the government. The military establishment is clear about this strategy and to change this, Sharif's government's major challenge would be to correct the power imbalance in civil–military relations, which has traditionally, for many decades, remained heavily tilted in favour of the latter. Sharif has stated more than once that he wants to be the real boss, not the military. But it is easier said than done.

Now that he has been elected to be the prime minister of Pakistan (for the third time) he wants to resurrect the peace process from where he had started, with the former Indian Prime Minister Atal Bihari Vajpayee in 1999, before General Musharraf's Kargil operation sabotaged it. This might suit the military for the time being as it has been looking for ways and means to diffuse tension with India and concentrate on the internal terrorist threats. But the jihadi groups and their Islamist supporters have already started opposing Nawaz Sharif's peace policy with India. They are bound to sabotage such efforts by stepping up terrorist activities in India. In both countries the peace process is held hostage by these extremist elements who survive on a war economy. The leadership and the peace-loving media have to realize not to get provoked and derail the entire peace process.

Decision of the last government to sign Iran–Pakistan gas pipeline agreement and signing off control of Gwadar to China are also hot potatoes thrown in to Nawaz Sharif's lap. The pipeline project is liked by Sharif's Saudi patrons and the US. The Gwadar decision is disliked by the US, India and UAE. Nawaz Sharif will have to walk a tight rope here in balancing these relations, while honouring Zardari's decisions on these two crucial issues. As the projects are in the interest of the country, the nationalist Nawaz Sharif will find it difficult to back out. However, the clever bureaucracy may advise him just to go slow on the projects, if the foreign pressure gets too hard to bear.

The PPP-led coalition government has left behind a heavy baggage packed with multiple problems – the major one being, besides terrorism and bleeding Balochistan, shattered official economy that includes serious energy crunch. While in Opposition PML-N leaders have made the people believe that they can solve these problems. The challenge for the new government would thus be to take bold measures in the first year of their rule, before the shine wears off and opposition to reforms by vested interest gets stronger. These reforms are going to be painful for various sections of the society particularly the rentier class, which evades taxes and lives on subsidies. Whether Mian Nawaz Sharif, who has the support of this rentier class, would have the courage to bring the economic reforms, irrespective of the fact that whoever gets hurts, will be the test of his parties earnestness?

List of Abbreviations

AGPL	:	Actual Ground Position Line
AIML	:	All India Muslim League
AJP	:	Awami Jamhoori Party
AJP	:	Awami Jamhoori Party
AL	:	Awami League
ANP	:	Awami National Party
APC	:	All Parties Conference
APMSO	:	All Pakistan Muhajir Students Organization
ATC	:	Anti-Terrorism Court
AWT	:	Army Welfare Trust
BJP	:	Bhartiya Janata Party
BNP-Mengal	:	Balochistan National Party-Mengal
CARs	:	Central Asian Republics
CBM	:	Confidence Building Measures
CENTO	:	Central Treaty Organization
CIA	:	Central Intelligence Agency
CII	:	Confederation of India Industries
COAS	:	Chief of Army Staff
CoD	:	Charter of Democracy
CPP	:	Communist Party of Pakistan
CSF	:	Coalition Support Fund
DCC	:	Defence Committee of the Cabinet
DPC	:	Difa-e-Pakistan Council
DSF	:	Democratic Students Federation
ECO	:	Economic Cooperation Organisation

FATA	:	Federally Administered Tribal Areas
FC	:	Frontier Constabulary
FCNA	:	Force Command Northern Area
FIR	:	First Information Report
FPCCI	:	Federation of Pakistan Chambers of Commerce and Industry
FSC	:	Federal Shariat Court
FSF	:	Federal Security Force
FWO	:	Frontier Works Organization
GDS	:	Gas Development Surcharge
GHQ	:	General Headquarters
GLOC	:	Ground Line of Communications
HQM	:	Hindko Qaumi Mahaz
HRCP	:	Human Rights Commission of Pakistan
HT	:	Hizb ut-Tahrir
HuJI	:	Harkat-ul-Jihad-al-Islami
ICPI	:	International Centre for Peace Initiatives
IIC	:	Islamic Ideology Council
IJT	:	Islami Jamiat-e-Talaba
ISAF	:	International Security Assistance Force
ISI	:	Inter-Services Intelligence
JeM	:	Jaish-e-Mohammmed
JI	:	Jamaat-e-Islami
JUH	:	Jamiat-e-Ulama-e-Hind
JUI	:	Jamiat-e-Ulama-e-Islam
JUP	:	Jamiat-e-Ulama-e-Pakistan
KP	:	Khyber Pakhtunkhwa
KPT	:	Karachi Port Trust
LeT	:	Lashkar-e-Taiba
LHC	:	Lahore High Court
LJ	:	Lashkar-e-Jhangvi
LNG	:	Liquefied Natural Gas
LOC	:	Line of Control

MAF	:	Million Acre Feet
MAO	:	Mohammedan Anglo-Oriental College
MCB	:	Muslim Commercial Bank
MFN	:	Most-Favoured Nation
MIT	:	Massachusetts Institute of Technology
MMA	:	Muttahida Majlis-e-Amal
MNA	:	Member of the National Assembly
MRD	:	Movement for Restoration of Democracy
MQM	:	Muttahida Qaumi Movement
NAP	:	National Awami Party
NATO	:	North Atlantic Treaty Organization
NDU	:	National Defence University
NFC Award	:	National Finance Commission Award
NFC	:	National Finance Commission Award
NLC	:	National Logistic Cell
NLI	:	Northern Light Infantry
NRO	:	National Reconciliation Ordinance
NSA	:	Non-State Actors
NSC	:	National Security Council
NSF	:	National Students Federation
OIC	:	Organization of Islamic Countries
PBC	:	Pakistan Business Council
PCCR	:	Parliamentary Committee for Constitutional Reforms
PCNS	:	Parliamentary Committee on National Security
PDPA	:	People's Democratic Party of Afghanistan
PEMRA	:	Pakistan Electronic Media Regulatory Authority
PIA	:	Pakistan International Airlines
PIPS	:	Pakistan Institute for Peace Studies
PML	:	Pakistan Muslim League
PML-N	:	Pakistan Muslim League Nawaz
PML-Q	:	Pakistan Muslim League Quaid
PNA	:	Pakistan National Alliance
PNS Mehran	:	Pakistan Naval Station Mehran

PPC	:	Pakistan Penal Code
PPL	:	Pakistan Petroleum Limited
PPP	:	Pakistan's People's Party
PTI	:	Pakistan Tehrik-e-Insaf
PTV	:	Pakistan Television
R&AW	:	Research and Analysis Wing
RO	:	Returning Officer
RSS	:	Rashtriya Swayamsevak Sangh
SEATO	:	South East Asia Treaty Organization
TAP	:	Turkmenistan-Afghanistan-Pakistan
TIP	:	Tehrik-e-Istiqlal Pakistan
TJ	:	Tablighi Jamaat
TTP	:	Tehreek-e-Taliban Pakistan
UDHR	:	Universal Declaration of Human Rights
UP	:	United Provinces
USMAAG	:	US Military Assistance Advisory Group
WTO	:	World Trade Organization

INDEX